MARKETING STRATEGY: RELATIONSHIPS, OFFERINGS, TIMING & RESOURCE ALLOCATION

D. SUDHARSHAN

Department of Business Administration
University of Illinois, Urbana-Champaign

 Prentice Hall, Englewood Cliffs, New Jersey 07632

Library of Congress Cataloging-in-Publication Data

Sudharshan, Devanathan.
   Marketing strategy : relationships, offerings, timing, and
resource allocation / D. Sudharshan.
     p.   cm.
   Includes index.
   ISBN 0–02–418264–8
    1. Marketing—Management.   2. Strategic planning.   3. Competition.
  I. Title.
HF5415. 13.S895   1995
658.8—dc20
                                                              94–39777
                                                               CIP

Editorial/Production Supervision: Tele-Composition
Acquisitions Editor: David Borkowsky
Cover Designer: Jerry Votta
Cover Art: Philadelphia Museum of Art: A. E. Gallatin Collection, *The Table* by Juan Gris
Buyer: Marie McNamara

© 1995 by Prentice-Hall, Inc.
A Simon & Schuster Company
Englewood Cliffs, New Jersey 07632

Printed in the United States of America
10 9 8 7 6 5 4 3 2 1

ISBN 0-02-418264-8

PRENTICE-HALL INTERNATIONAL (UK) LIMITED, LONDON
PRENTICE-HALL OF AUSTRALIA PTY. LIMITED, SYDNEY
PRENTICE-HALL CANADA, INC., TORONTO
PRENTICE-HALL HISPANOAMERICANA, S.A., MEXICO
PRENTICE-HALL OF INDIA PRIVATE LIMITED, NEW DELHI
PRENTICE-HALL OF JAPAN, INC., TOKYO
SIMON & SHUSTER ASIA PTE. LTD., SINGAPORE
EDITORA PRENTICE-HALL DO BRASIL, LTDA., RIO DE JANERIO

Contents

Part 1   Competitive Context

CHAPTER 2:   ANALOGICAL AND ANALYTICAL LENSES ON COMPETITION   *21*

Contents

Preface

THE INTENDED AUDIENCE

This book is for those interested in understanding the basis of marketing strategy with a view to its development and implementation. The reader is presumed to have had exposure (either formal or informal) to the discipline of marketing management.

An instructor of an advanced course in marketing or marketing strategy will find it useful as a supplement to marketing strategy cases. It may also be used in a firm's internal development courses to help in analyzing its marketing strategy.

The concepts presented enable a marketing manager to take a fresh look at existing marketing strategy and its development and implementation systems.

CONTENTS

The book's primary thrust is to provide a solid foundation in the principal issues underlying marketing strategy. These issues relate to the coherence among a firm's smarketing pathways, organizational processes, and resources that determines whether a firm has a relative advantage in the context in which it competes. In keeping with contemporary marketing, it suggests that its relationships, offerings, timing, and resource allocation (ROTR) decisions constitute a firm's marketing strategy. Thus the book provides substantial discussions on the context of marketing strategy decisions, relationships (in particular, customers and channel members), offerings, timing, and resource allocation.

The book is divided into four parts. The first provides conceptual frameworks from other fields to help the reader understand the context and the dynamics of competition. It also describes the core domain (product-market) within which marketing competition takes place.

The second part establishes frameworks for analyzing and establishing strong relationships with customers, channel members, and competitors—the three key publics (stakeholders) for marketing strategy.

The third part describes and discusses the various analytical tools and models available for the financial analysis and evaluation of strategic opportunities, resource allocation, and the development of norms.

The final part details the alternatives available to a firm in offerings, timing, and distribution channels. It also discusses the firm's changing environment and implications for implementation.

The material presented overlaps material presented in texts on marketing management and on strategic management. This is done deliberately to provide continuity, reinforce essential concepts, and to present a complete view of marketing strategy—one which includes its implementation by marketing managers. This overlap also strengthens the thorough discussion of the principles of marketing strategy—the primary aim of this book.

SPECIAL FEATURES

This book is goal-directed and stresses that the process of strategy development is as much based on *intuition* as on *formal analysis*. It suggests that a process of intuition accompanies the process of formal analysis.

Generic competitive strategies and competitive dynamics from other fields are discussed. It discusses *formal game theory* in sufficient depth so that this concept can become the basis for discussion and decision making.

It provides a new model of customer satisfaction based on *relationships* and *customer values.*

The use of marketing *norms* and processes for obtaining such norms, i.e., *Benchmarking* and the *PIMS* project, is discussed.

A discussion of *financial models* and accounting systems, including *activity-based costing,* provides *integration* with other functional business areas.

Chapter 11 on timing provides new material on the issues of entry-timing, signaling, and defensive strategies.

Chapter 14 on marketing strategy implementation systems takes a novel approach—that of integrating work on strategic planning systems, marketing implementation, fast decision making, and changes that are occurring in the social, technology, and human resources subsystems that constitute the environment of an organization.

ACKNOWLEDGMENTS

This book has its origin in a class on Marketing Strategy that I taught at the University of Illinois, Urbana-Champaign, and in a draft prepared by Professor Robin Wensley

(Warwick Business School) and Barton Weitz (J.C. Penney Eminent Scholar and Professor of Marketing, University of Florida). They invited me to join them as a co-author. Unfortunately, other commitments did not permit them to continue participation in the book. I considerably reshaped it based on my own research and views on marketing strategy developed through corporate contacts. They kindly allowed me to use their writing, some of which is included in this book. Chapter 5 is almost as originally written by them. The balance of the book is either completely new or significantly amended. They have my gratitude; I consider them co-authors.

I would be remiss if I did not thank Dave Borkowsky and his staff at Prentice Hall who helped shape the book. To Tom Colaiezzi, thanks for a superb copy-editing job; and to Phyllis Robertson, thanks for your professional approach to composition.

My intellectual debt is to three institutions: The Indian Institute of Technology at Madras, which made me humble and yet gave me analytical confidence; The Graduate School of Business at the University of Pittsburgh, which provided the opportunity to learn marketing and management; and the University of Illinois which has provided a fertile environment in which to grow professionally.

I am also indebted to Allan Shocker and Gerry Zaltman for having introduced me to research.

Ravi Kumar (now at the University of Southern California) and Tom Gruca (now at the University of Iowa) have collaborated with me on several projects over the years. Discussions with them have sharpened my insights and views on strategy for which I thank them. I am also indebted to my students in various marketing courses at the University of Illinois as well as to the many participants in executive seminars. Through discussions and questions they have also shaped my views on marketing strategy.

I offer my deep gratitude to Carol Halliday and Hope Cook of the Word Processing Center at the University of Illinois, who managed to read my scrawl and convert it into a readable manuscript.

I should like also to express my sincere appreciation to Kjell Gronhaug, who read the entire first draft and made several critical observations and suggestions. Others to whom I owe thanks for their suggestions are Dick Hill, Chuck Linke, Bruce Newman, Kash Rangan, Roy Howell, Greg Winter, and Joe Mahoney. My thanks to these reviewers who helped me "walk in their shoes:" James Wolter, Grand Valley State University; Michael Minor, University of Texas-Pan American; Joseph Sirgy, Virginia Polytechnic University; Robert Woodruff, University of Texas-Knoxville; Alan G. Swayer, University of Florida; Murray Young, University of Denver; Dr. Ken Rowe, Arizona State University; Dr. Sanjit Sengupta, University of Maryland; Roy Howell, Texas Tech University; Charles Patton, University of Texas-Brownsville; Mike Messina, Gannon University; Bill Ross, Wharton School, University of Pennsylvania; Ralph Unnava, Ohio State University; Jan Sajkiewicz, Duquesne University.

Thanks to my parents for their support. Special thanks to my father for his help in checking the proofs.

Finally, and most importantly, to my wife, Nalini, and to our children Venkat (thanks for your typing help), Amit, and Sangita, who have put up with my long hours of reading, writing and "not now," and "don't disturb me" with considerable patience. Thank you. I love you.

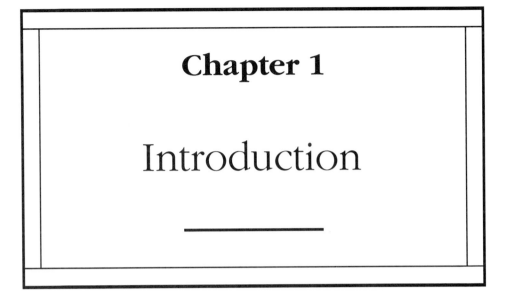

Chapter 1

Introduction

Marketing strategy creates pathways to a desirable future. Marketing management is travel through these pathways to achieve the desirable future. For example, International Flavors and Fragrances, Inc.,[1] made a mark for itself creating some of 1989's most successful perfumes, like Calvin Klein's *Eternity* and Giorgio's *Beverly Hills' Red,* and is now developing flavoring systems for low-fat and sugar-free food products. This is choosing a pathway to the future. Developing the specific systems and gaining acceptance for them in the marketplace are achieved through marketing management decisions and actions.

How do companies choose one set of pathways as compared with another? This question is at the heart of marketing strategy analysis. Royal Dutch-Shell, headquartered both in London and in Rotterdam, selects strategic pathways by considering, among other factors[2]:

Oil demand by market class and at different rates of growth.

The possible reactions of consumer governments to higher oil prices.

Interfuel competition and the impact of higher oil prices.

It builds and analyzes possible scenarios for the future concerning these factors to evaluate alternatives.

The output from such marketing strategy analysis and choice (or strategic marketing decision) is a marketing strategy statement.

---

[1]Roman, M. "Beef–Fat Flavor May Not Sound Glamorous, But…," *Business Week,* March 11, 1991, p. 70.

[2]Wack, P., "Scenarios: Unchartered Waters Ahead," *Harvard Business Review,* September–October, 1985, pp. 73–89.

In this text, our goal is to provide frameworks to enable you to formulate, evaluate, and implement marketing strategies. This first chapter presents a framework for understanding marketing strategy analysis and decision-making.

MARKETING STRATEGY: A POSITIVE FRAMEWORK

Kim Woo-Chong, Chairman of Daewoo, Korea's fourth ranking conglomerate (chaebol) is embarking on a major strategic change to save his nearly bankrupt company.[3] Traditionally, Daewoo designed, manufactured, and marketed a wide variety of sophisticated products to major world corporations such as General Motors, Boeing, and Caterpillar. These corporations often then resold the products under their own brand names. Daewoo is changing its strategy carefully to move into marketing some products directly to end consumers under the Daewoo name. The first of these is likely to be a Daewoo PC to be sold in Europe. This is a marketing strategy decision to achieve intended objectives. Our framework provides a way to capture the essence of such strategies (Exhibit 1–1).

EXHIBIT 1-1   A Positive Framework

A MODEL FOR UNDERSTANDING AND BUILDING MARKET STRATEGY

GOAL
|
COMPETITIVE ADVANTAGE
IMPLEMENTATION
MARKETING   CONTEXT
STRATEGY

Outcome	=	f (Competitive Advantage)
Competitive Advantage	=	g (Marketing Strategy, Implementation, Context)
Marketing Strategy	=	Marketing Relationships × Marketing Offerings × Timing × Resources Allocation
Implementation	=	Communications, Inducements, Infrastructure, Timing, Information, Opportunism, Leadership, Diligence, and so forth
Resources	=	Hardware, Software, Intelligentware, Money, Information, Human Resources
Context	=	Suppliers, Buyers, Substitutes, Potential Entrants, Industry Competitors, Other Publics, Chance Events
Relationships	=	Publics × Contracts
Offerings	=	Benefit Bundles Products × Prices × Services
Timing	=	(Starting time, Ending time) w.r.t. Competitors, Customers, Distributors, Other Publics

---

[3]Sakarmi, L., "At Daewoo, A 'Revolution' At The Top," *Business Week,* February 18, 1991, pp. 68–69

Outcomes

Outcomes such as the firm's financial performance arise from the relative competitive advantage that a company has. From a marketing standpoint, outcomes usually are defined as sales, share, or profits. For example, at a more detailed level in developing an advertising strategy, outcomes may be stated as awareness, or trial-induced or "likability."

These outcomes generally span a period of time, called a planning horizon or planning period. We are concerned not just with sales, market share, and profits at a point in time, but rather with their trajectory over time.

This trajectory may be market share, sales, or profit growth. For example, consider market share. Does a company have a special relationship with a distributor manufacturing private label brands for a grocery store chain? Does this provide an advantage for new product development in private and brand name products that will allow it to gain overall market share? Does a company have a high brand recognition and loyalty, for example, Coke? Is this translatable into either higher margins or more efficient new product introductions? These examples provide a link between competitive advantage and outcome trajectories. A company can build sustained competitive advantages to attain its desired outcome trajectory.

Outcomes arise from the relative competitive advantage that a company possesses in the eyes of its consumers, its intermediaries, and other publics that together make up the market. The presence of such a competitive advantage over time is called a *sustained competitive advantage,* and outcome over time arises through sustained competitive advantage.

Competitive advantage is realized based on three factors: (1) the company's marketing strategy, (2) its implementation of this strategy, and (3) the context in which competition unfolds. Let us consider these factors.

Marketing Strategy {R,O,T,R}

Relationships.   Daewoo's chairman, Kim Woo-Chung, in shifting his strategy is deciding *who* his company shall have relationships with and also the *kind* of relationships. Should he continue his relationships with the General Motors, Boeings, and Caterpillars of the world by providing them with products for their labels? Should Daewoo establish direct relationships with its end consumers? Should it set up joint ventures (as it did in France for distribution)? Should Daewoo take over some previous buyers of its products? A myriad of questions about who to have relationships with and about the nature of each such relationship need to be answered. Thus, relationships form a key component of marketing strategy. Each relationship is defined by the identity of the partner public and the contract with it (i.e., the nature or mode of the relationship).

Two major publics are the focus of building marketing relationships: *customers* and *channel members.* By customers we mean both existing and potential customers. What should be the nature of a company's relationship with them? Should it contract just to sell them equipment (e.g., IBM PCs or SONY VCRs), or to provide them with bundled systems (e.g., IBM mainframes, early Macintosh PCs), or also to provide them with the possibility of building systems with a multiplicity of our offerings? Clearly the strategic questions are which customer groups should be targeted (segments) and what is the relationship with them? Typically, reaching customers requires linkages. These linkages are called *channels.* Goods or services, financial instruments (cash, checks, credit, etc.), and information travel through these channels. The marketing offerings provided relate to all these flow elements. The channel publics with whom relationships must be developed should be those who will provide these flows. Examples are distributors to handle grocery products, credit agencies to provide credit for the purchase of automobiles, advertising agencies to handle communications, and marketing research organizations to provide information from the market. The customer segments and channel publics chosen to have relationships with and the nature of contracts to be established with them also form an essential part of marketing strategy.

Offerings. What products should Daewoo offer to Caterpillar? What products should Daewoo sell directly to end consumers? These questions address the next component of marketing strategy: offerings. To each of the publics (or partners) with whom a company has a relationship it provides a benefit bundle. The benefit bundle to provide to each marketing partner is part of the development of marketing strategy. Leon Gorman, President of the L.L. Bean Company, the mail-order firm, made a painful strategic decision to charge for delivery.[4] To end consumers with personal computing needs, Daewoo must decide on the type of products, prices, service, service availability, convenience of purchasing, credit terms, and so forth. The elements of offerings constitute the usual and important substance of marketing.

Timing. When should a relationship start? When should Daewoo's joint venture in France go into effect? When should certain relationships end? In the U.S., Kim Woo-Chung plans to acquire small allies in textiles, electronics, and auto parts to market Daewoo's products. He has given this set of relationships three years in which to bear fruit. If that does not occur, he plans a broader direct marketing of Daewoo products.

Resources. For a company's choice of relationship, offering, and timing combinations to become a reality requires resources. Choosing the appropriate resources and allocating them across various relationship × offering × timing combinations, is an inherent part of a marketing strategy decision. These resources consist of hardware, software, intelligentware, information, financial resources, and human resources.

Often idiosyncratic assets are required to build a sustainable competitive advantage. The asset may either be company, relationship, or timing related and may not be usable elsewhere. For example, in developing personal computers "for the rest of us," Apple invested in developing an operating system designed to offer specific benefits—ease of use and exceptional graphics. This idiosyncratic asset may not have been redeployable to other publics if the intended consumers had rejected this offering. The decision to commit its resources in this way in order to create this idiosyn-

[4]Montgomery, M.R., "Reality Arrives C.O.D.," *Chicago Tribune,* Thursday, March 14, 1991, Section 2, p. 9.

cratic asset (operating system) was risky. Making such decisions to develop the right blend of relationships, offerings, and timing is the essence of marketing strategy development.

Marketing strategy is developed to provide a competitive advantage over a period of time by building relationships, offerings, timing, and resources {R,O,T,R}.

Implementation.   The other elements that lead to a competitive advantage are implementation and context. Proper implementation makes the bud that is strategy bloom into a flower. Context allows this flower to look beautiful compared with its surroundings, by providing sustained nourishment for it, and by providing the bees that pollinate this flower to ensure the development of succeeding generations.

Detail is the stuff of implementation. Without strategy, implementation is possible; but there is no sense of direction and the outcome occurs simply by chance. On the other hand, strategy without implementation, is hollow. It is an unread masterpiece, an unseen van Gogh. Strategy and implementation are complementary, one aiding the other, one preceding the other: today's strategy guides tomorrow's implementation which guides the day after's strategy. A wonderful symbiosis of strategy and implementation creates a sustained achievement of desired outcomes.

Context.   Outcomes arise out of a complex interplay between a company's strategy, its implementation, and the context in which competition takes place. A powerful approach to visualizing rivalry in an industry was provided by Michael Porter (Exhibit 1–2).[5] To his portrayal of context we have added elements of chance. The rules of competition and the players define rivalry. Some of the rules of the game arise through chance events. For example, discovery of the carcinogenic properties of a component of a company's product, discovery of an alternate and major use for a company's product, discovery of a major source of supply of a critical material, and so on. By definition, chance elements are not predictable. For example, emerging markets in Eastern Europe (which were not predictable as late as the early 1990s) could open up opportunities for scents for medium-priced cosmetics—an opportunity that International Flavors and Fragrances might capitalize on. At the same time, buyers of designer perfumes in the U.S. are debt-laden. Thus, International Flowers and Fragrances can no longer grow only by providing fine scents for designer perfumes. Context has had an important role in defining the competitive advantage and outcome trajectory for this company.

Transition.   Having set the stage by developing a positive framework linking marketing strategy, a trajectory of outcomes, and by spelling out its general components, we now turn to the development of marketing strategy. First, we describe marketing strategy as a decision-making process. Then we discuss how strategic decisions are coordinated, and finally we present a heuristic approach to developing a marketing strategy.

[5]Porter, M. E., *Competitive Strategy: Techniques for Analyzing Industries and Competitors,* New York, The Free Press, 1980.

EXHIBIT 1–2   Forces Deriving Industry Competition in Porter (1980)

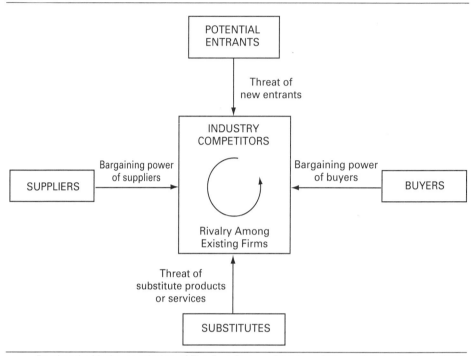

Reprinted with the permission of The Free Press, a Division of Simon & Schuster from COM-
PETITIVE STRATEGY: Techniques for Analyzing Industries and Competitors by Michael E. Porter.
Copyright © 1980 by The Free Press.

Decision-Making Process

Strategic decisions are more concerned with sustainable competitive advantage implications, therefore the process for making strategic decisions differs from the process
for making tactical decisions. These differences are described by dimensions five
through eleven in Exhibit 1–3. Strategic marketing decisions are made infrequently
but are continuously reexamined. The business must continuously monitor events
such as the development of new technologies and changes in customer and channel
values and needs. When this monitoring process uncovers new opportunities or
threats, an intense planning activity is triggered. The impact of these events on the
present strategy is considered, and appropriate changes in strategy are made. While
strategic decisions are made infrequently, the tactical implementation decisions are
usually made periodically within a predetermined time schedule. For example, the
advertising and promotion program may be developed and reviewed each quarter.
  Strategic decisions are typically unstructured and unique, so it is difficult to use
simple models to arrive at marketing strategy statements. Considerable creativity is
required to synthesize the large amount of external and internal information to arrive at
a concise statement outlining the future direction of a business. The intensively cre-

EXHIBIT 1–3   Dimensions for Contrasting Types of Decisions

Dimension	Strategic Decisions	Tactical Decisions
1. Importance to firm	High	Low
2. Personnel involved	Top management	Middle management
3. Viewpoint	Corporate	Functional area
4. Time horizon	Long-term	Short-term
5. Regularity	Continuous process, irregular decision	Regular process and decisions
6. Range of alternatives	Wide	Narrow
7. Uncertainty	High	Low
8. Subjectivity of input information	High	Low
9. Nature of problem	Unstructured	Structured
10. Detail	Less	More
11. Ease of evaluation	Difficult	Easier

ative nature of strategy is "the essential nature of strategy" described in Exhibit 1–4. Tactical decisions concerning advertising budgets and sales territory evaluations are made more frequently. The problems are more structured and so are more amenable to the use of models and decision support systems.

Since the context is continually changing, the marketing strategy must also change. Strategies are dynamic. Strategy decisions are made to alter the course of marketing activities and to maintain an outcome trajectory. New paths must be chosen to the future.

EXHIBIT 1–4   The Essential Nature of Strategy

The kernel of a strategic plan is the rule that it breaks, the orthodoxy that firm is choosing to challenge. Without a clear definition of the myth that drives the competitors and the truth that is the future touchstone of the firm's own future operating principle, the plan cannot be called STRATEGIC. It's just another of those boring documents that we've all seen (and probably written) full of pious platitudes signifying nothing. As Philip Larkin said of the modern novel recently: "A beginning, a muddle and an end."

The other defining property of a strategic plan is that the analytical section is devoted to dispelling the myth by which the competitors live; it cannot, by definition, lead to the truth by which the firm itself is choosing to live. This has to be a jump of the imagination. A plan that doesn't make such a jump is a fraud. In other words a strategy cannot be fully rationalized. It has to be an act of faith. This is the central message of the modern philosophy of science. No general statement, not even the simplest iterative generalization, can be derived from raw data without some imaginative effort on the part of the mind. Einstein suggested that, "a theory can be proved by experiment; but no path leads from experiment to the birth of a theory."

From Jules Goddard, "The Essential Nature of Strategy," *London Business School Journal,* Vol. 10, No. 1, Autumn, 1985, pp. 31–32.

COORDINATION OF STRATEGIC DECISIONS

Level of Decision Making

Strategic decisions can be made at all levels in the firm from the CEO to the individual salesperson. They can also be made in each functional area and in each business unit. While strategic decisions can be made throughout the corporation, normally, where should these decisions be made? Should they be made solely by people at the top levels of the corporation or should this responsibility be given to personnel at lower levels? When attempting to answer this question, one is faced with a classical trade-off between developing a globally optimal strategy based on limited information versus a set of locally optimal strategies based on more complete information.

The CEO and corporate planners are in a position to consider all the synergies between business activities directed toward product-markets in which the firm participates. From this global perspective, these people are in a position to develop an "optimal" strategy that exploits these synergies. However, the information available to corporate planners is limited by the planners' knowledge and the homogenized nature of the information flowing up from lower levels in the organization. Whereas people at lower levels have more detailed information, they are largely unaware of the relationship between their activities and other activities within the firm. While these people are able to make more informed decisions, their decisions will be "optimal" only for their limited domain.

Historical Trends in Strategic Decision Making

Recently, the rate of change in politics, economics, and technology has increased dramatically. This rapidly changing environment spawned books like *Future Shock* and *Power Shift* as well as growing interest in strategic considerations. Business people needed to develop strategies for coping with the growing uncertainties they face— new technology in communication, bioengineering, and electronics, and new production methods, changing government policies, and increased domestic and foreign competition.

In addition to enormous changes in the business environment, the increased complexity of the business organization itself fostered a need for explicit strategy statements. Between 1949 and 1970, most *Fortune 500* companies shifted from single product, functional organizations to multi-divisional, multiple industry, and even multi-national corporations. Prior to this change, strategic direction could be provided by a key idea in the head of the entrepreneur. Modern businesses now require explicit strategic statements to coordinate the activities of complex organizations facing rapidly evolving environments.

During the 60s, strategic direction was determined at the highest level of the corporation. Professional planners dominated their companies, and the influence of operating managers on the strategic direction of their businesses declined dramatically.

However, the role of the corporate planner is now changing. Responsibility for strategic decision making is now shifting from a corporate staff function to the line business unit managers.   Many firms feel that strategic top-level insights are limited because of a lack of intimate knowledge of the dynamics in the strategic plan.   For example, corporate planners at General Electric recognized major environmental trends that would impact GE's home appliance business.   They foresaw the internationalization of markets and the potential entry of Japanese manufacturers, the rising oil prices and the emphasis on energy efficiency, and the shrinking size of both houses and families.   However, the corporate planners arrived at some incorrect implications for product-market strategies based on these observations.   They predicted an overall decline in the refrigerator business and a need to develop smaller, better insulated refrigerators.   Because the planners were not in contact with the marketplace or technology, they did not realize that whereas homes were getting smaller, the sizes of kitchens were not shrinking.   In addition, families with working women, a growing market segment, wanted larger refrigerators so that they could shop less frequently.   Finally, technology suggested that the greatest gains in efficiency could be realized by improving compressors, not insulation.

Relationship Between Corporate and Marketing Strategy

The "approach" level for strategic decision making is a function of the number of product-markets in which the firm operates and the degree to which activities between product-markets are interrelated.   At one extreme, strategic decision making can be restricted to the highest levels, when a firm operates in a few, highly interrelated product-markets.   In this situation, there is substantial overlap between corporate and marketing strategy.   In fact, the only difference is that marketing strategy (as we define it) focuses on a limited set of competitive advantages—advantages based on the performance of the marketing function and relationships under the control of the marketing function (customers and channels)—while corporate strategy must consider a wider set of business activities and relationships.   There is a natural dilemma between top-down and bottom-up approaches to strategic decision making.   Mr. Maljers, Chairman of Unilever, put this nicely in perspective:

> If a global company is to function successfully, strategies at different levels of the business need to inter-relate.   The strategy at the corporate level must build upon strategies at lower levels in the hierarchy (the bottom-up element of strategy).   At the same time, however, all parts of the business have to work to accommodate the over-riding corporate goals (the top-down approach).
>
> Because these two forces work in opposite directions they can present a dilemma to the person who has to oversee strategy formulation.   The requirement is to find the right equilibrium for the particular circumstances.   Excessive instruction from the top stifles management creativity.   Yet, at the same time there must be sufficient direction to allow for the interest of all the corporation's stockholders (p. 63).
>
> The balance "between top-bottom and bottom-up" is often determined by the culture and philosophy of the company involved.   Unilever's basic approach to the organization is decentralization (p. 64).[6]

[6] Maljers, F. A., "Strategic Planning and Intuition in Unilever," *Long-Range Planning,* Vol. 23, No. 2, 1990, pp. 63–68.

Thus marketing strategy has to fit with corporate strategy and with other functional strategies to provide coherence.

A Heuristic Process for Marketing Strategy Development

As mentioned earlier, the essence of strategy is creativity in understanding the pathways to a desired outcome trajectory. The process is an amalgam of intuition and analysis that leads to a choice of the right pathways.

Marketing strategies are almost never arrived at in a vacuum. In an entrepreneurial start up, the founder may have obtained a patent for a new technology that satisfies a specific market need. Therefore, a part of the offering is already fixed. For example, an acoustic coupled device for radars was conceived of first and a business was then set up to commercialize it. The relationship between the founder and certain potential clients may further limit relationship possibilities. Or, in an ongoing business, several years of operations usually have already evolved into constraints on marketing strategy development. This strategy, however, may need to be changed in light of changes in context. For example, the early success of Walt Disney Productions was, in part, because of the fact that the 6 to 13-year-old segment of the population from 15% in 1950 increased to 18.2% of the population in 1960. But this segment is beginning to decline. Realizing this change, Walt Disney Productions, facing a declining product-market, altered its product-market focus toward the growing segment of 21 to 35-year-old adults. To implement this new approach, Disney has made changes in its marketing mix. "PG" rated movies, such as *Splash,* are replacing traditional "G" rated movies; thrill rides like Space Mountain were added to theme parks, and entertainment offerings are being directed toward new markets— Japanese and European theme parks and U.S. adults (Epcot Center).

In developing a marketing strategy, the past provides the basis on which to build the future. The core strategy questions are the choice of the right combinations of relationships, offerings, timing, and resources. The necessary systematic analysis consists of four steps (Exhibit 1–5). The first is the careful monitoring of changes in the context. The second is assessing competitive advantages that arise with alternative strategy sets in the emerging context. The third step provides an explicit forecast of the outcome trajectory based on the competitive advantages that arise from the interplay between a particular strategy set and the emerging context. (Sometimes, steps two and three are combined in a decision support system.) The last step, before the process starts again, is formally choosing of a strategy and communicating it as a Marketing Strategy Statement. This statement identifies the relationships to be created through specific offerings with specified timing and the resources to be committed to do so.

EXHIBIT 1–5   Four Analytical Steps in Strategy Development

* Monitoring Changes in Context
* Determining Competitive Advantage Link (Context + Strategy)
* Competitive Advantage → Outcome Trajectory Link
* Marketing Strategy Statement

EXHIBIT 1-6   Three Intuitive Steps in Strategy Development

* Making Sense of Context Changes
* Challenging Emerging Context Constancy or Changes
* Challenging Status Quo or Conventional Strategy Sets

In parallel with these analytical steps are three creative steps or steps of intuition (Exhibit 1–6). Analysis can reveal (1) much growth is not expected in the designer perfume markets, and (2) that a growing demand for low-calorie food exists. Eugene P. Gerisanti, Chairman of International Flavors and Fragrances, did just that and was able to identify the second as a major business opportunity—a most insightful conclusion. This is an example of the first step that we call making sense of context changes.

The second intuitive step is that of challenging an assessment of the nature of the emerging context. Consider, for example, the sneaker market in Europe.[7] Using any traditional measure, it is maturing. However, while Americans spend $10 per capita on Nike products, Europeans spend only $3 per capita on them. Nike has challenged the forecast that the European sneaker market is a mature one and, by inference, one of less importance. It has, along with Reebok, interpreted the data to mean that there is much room for its growth in this market.

The third step explores new relationships, offerings, timing, and resource requirements. Drugs such as insulin (large molecule drugs) must be injected and not taken orally to avoid being metabolized in the digestive tract. Clinical Technologies Association, Inc. has licensed a new technology to Upjohn and to Genetics Institute that permits the manufacture of an oral form of the drug.[8] This is an example of changing a part of the benefit bundle, thereby changing the strategy set.

Why should not a company and its joint venture operation compete? This is not a traditional relationship, but Merck & Co. and its joint venture with DuPont Co., DuPont Merck Pharmaceutical Co., may do exactly that.[9] They might sell the same product, albeit under different names, in the same markets.

What we are emphasizing through our four A plus three I process is a combination of analysis and intuition that leads to sustained competitive advantage. Clearly this requires analytical ability, judgment, intuition, and a decisive attitude. Further, it portrays the process of strategy development as one of setting up "what if" questions and then seeking answers. To systematize our four A plus three I process, we suggest that the marketing strategy process be viewed as a large simulation. While not every possible combination of context, strategy, and competitive advantage is ever going to be simulated, parts of these are changed and the consequences, both as regards what might happen as well as what paths are being closed, are often asked or need to be considered. The balance of the book is built around this notion of providing input to a strategist who is in the process of developing a marketing strategy.

[7]Reichlin, I., D. J. Young, K. H. Hammondy, "Where Nike and Reebok Have Plenty of Running Room," *Business Week,* March 11, 1991, pp. 56–60.

[8]Freundlich, N., "From Chemical Soup, Drugs That Go Down the Hatch," *Business Week,* March 4, 1991, p. 57.

[9]Weber, J., "Think of It As A 3,600 Person Startup," *Business Week,* March 18, 1991, p. 103.

OVERVIEW

This book is divided into four parts. These are to be viewed in light of the 4A+3I process that was discussed earlier and shown in Exhibits 1–5 and 1–6. The four parts are:

Competitive context.

Framework managing relationships in the three key publics of customers, channels, and competitors.

Analytical tools for evaluating strategies, and resource allocation and redirection.

The scope of alternatives and systems for the choice and implementation of the {R,O,T,R} set of marketing strategy.

Part 1: Competitive Context

This first part is made up of three chapters, excluding this introductory one. These chapters provide both conceptual and analytical discussions of marketing competition. Chapter 2 provides general perspectives on competition and its context. The nature of competition and alternative trajectories of the competing participants are described. Competition among species for existence and growth, nations (or militaries), and sports teams are discussed to provide a broader view of the dynamics of competition. In a sense, these are presented as analogs to marketing competition. Like any analogy, they must be critically examined in interpreting the particular competitive context that a marketing strategist faces. They are intended to provide analogs that may be used to obtain a better sense of the competitive marketing context faced, to create new alternatives, or simply to use metaphorically in communicating to others the particular sense of the competitive context that has been arrived at. To bring the matter closer to marketing, an understanding of competition based on the literature in industrial organization economics is provided. This discussion focuses on mobility barriers to competition and a critical examination of what are termed *generic strategies* in this literature.

While these analogical "lenses" provide descriptions of competition, and some prescriptions (e.g., generic strategies), the key analytical mechanism for both describing and prescribing strategies is provided in the literature on formal game theory. This is a rich field in mathematics and has become increasingly more the engine of analysis in both industrial organization economics and in marketing. An in-depth treatment of this field is clearly beyond the scope of this book. However, we provide some of the key conceptual ideas and analytical tools that may be useful in thinking through the development of and implementation of marketing strategy. One of these key ideas is that of strategic moves—those moves that are intended to manage the change in behavior of relevant publics (in the case of marketing, this is mainly channels, competitors, and customers) in favorable ways. Central to achieving cooperation in such competitive games (both sequential and simultaneous) is the establishment of commitment and credibility. These are also central to the development of fruitful and strategic relationships and are discussed in depth in Part 2.

Chapter 3 is on forecasting the competitive environment. The reader who is either familiar with forecasting techniques or is eager to get into "marketing" more quickly may wish to skip most of this chapter or come back to it later. It is suggested, however, that the section on the use of scenarios be read. This analytical tool can provide a way of describing the key elements of the context that might emerge and for which strategies have to be developed. This chapter provides an overview of various forecasting techniques and summarizes when each is most applicable. The use of scenarios is suggested as an important method for arriving at alternative contextual possibilities that require strategic action for a firm or business to achieve its goals. We again emphasize that while the outcome itself is important, the process that the management team uses in understanding their markets for developing such scenarios is at least as important. The knowledge gained through this "learning" becomes an important resource as the assumptions made get really tested in competition.

Chapter 4 is on the core domain of marketing context, namely, the product-market. While the environment in general influences marketing strategy, the major (or first-order) publics who are the centers for attention for marketing strategy are customers, competitors, and channels. Therefore the starting point of marketing strategy is the choice of the product-market(s) to participate in, or the identification of those in which a business is already participating. The definition of a product-market is also important for another reason: that is the determination of whether a particular strategy is anti-competitive and therefore in violation of existing laws. To determine if a particular strategy is anti-competitive requires an appropriate definition of the boundaries of competition or the product-market.

This chapter has two parts. The first provides a discussion of the legal viewpoint and the second, a viewpoint which focuses more on the process of choice making (both judgment and behavior) by customers. The latter provides a basis for identifying and choosing alternatives, and the former a basis for setting some constraints on such choices.

Part 2: Relationships with Key Publics

This part focuses on relationships with channels, customers, and competitors. Chapter 5 discusses the reasons for the emergence of various forms of distribution channels. It also discusses the economic basis, largely based on transaction cost economics, of how strong channel relationships are developed.

Chapter 6 deals with relationships with customers. Hal Rosenbluth, President and CEO of Rosenbluth Travel, in a first person report[10] in the *Harvard Business Review* says, "In fact, building mutually beneficial relationships—with our clients, suppliers, and, most importantly, with our associates—has been the key to our success in everything we've done" (p. 36).

Randy Myer, a Vice President of Booz, Allen & Hamilton, also writing in the *Harvard Business Review*[11] says, "Wal-Mart, The Limited, Toys "R" Us, and others

---

[10]Rosenbluth, H. Hal, "Tales from a Nonconformist Company," *Harvard Business Review,* July–August, 1991, pp. 26-36.

[11]Myer, R., "Suppliers—Manage Your Customers," *Harvard Business Review,* 1989, pp. 160-168.

like them have unilaterally redefined relationships with their suppliers. By all accounts, they are not particularly interested in preferred supplier arrangements or supply-chain concepts. Instead, by extracting concessions and dictating terms, they determine how their suppliers will service them" (p. 161).

Patricia Sellers in a *Fortune* article[12] says, "Giant General Motors, tiny Techsonic, and countless other smart companies are keeping customers loyal by listening to them" (p. 39).

All three obviously reiterate the maxim, *Put the Customer First.* More than this, they refer to profound trends and attitudes toward customers. They direct attention, first, to a redefinition of the customer: a change from the old thinking in consumer markets that Jane and John Doe in Dubuque, Iowa are the only "customers" and that the channel intermediaries are a means to the end, to a new thinking that both the intermediaries and the Does need to be treated as customers. Second, to the building of relationships-partnerships with customers, expressed through words like loyalty and warmth. Although neither of these thoughts is new, the way in which they are emerging in today's corporations is. Technology and competition are dismantling barriers to entry and access for customers. Today, a customer can easily order merchandise from around the world using a telephone. Today, a manager can reach a customer anywhere on the globe within a few seconds with a fax, electronic mail or, of course, telephone. Buyers and end-users are increasingly separated by considerable distance, both geographically and by larger number of intermediaries (and therefore personnel), from key marketing decision makers. Buyers and users also may be reached in many more ways (both physical product-service delivery and communications) than ever before. The three forces of rapidly growing transportation and communication technology, increasing competitive intensity, and growing separation between key decision makers and buyers/ consumers are making marketing managers contend with an institutionalization of "humanism" in designing market interactions. Clearly this humanism has an economic component. Therefore, we expose marketing strategists to knowledge in the area of relationships which will aid them in developing and evaluating market strategies.

Toward this end, a relationships-based model of exchange is provided in which customer satisfaction is shown as depending on not only the product or service that is acquired, but also on the nature of the relationship of the exchange. The discussion in this chapter provides a sociopsychological view of relationships. Since these relationships are often associated with brands (or store names) by customers, and since considerable marketing expenditures are devoted to building brand recognition, the last part of this chapter focuses on branding.

Chapter 7 is on competitive analysis. The key elements of competitive analysis are (a) identifying competitors and (b) anticipating their moves. Since Chapter 4, on product-market definition, identifies specific product competitors to a business's offerings, this chapter focuses on the second element. Competitive actions are influ-

---

[12]Sellers, P., "Getting Customers to Love You," *Fortune,* March 13, 1989, pp. 38–49.

enced by the competitive environment and the specific nature of individual competitors. Both of these are discussed here.

Seven environmental factors influencing rivalry are also described.

To understand the competitiveness of individual competitors (or businesses) several frameworks are described. The frameworks (for a broad understanding) include: a taxonomy of dominant cultures, identification of strategic intent, competitive advantage analysis, the value chain, and synergy. To obtain a more detailed view of the cost-based advantage a business may have, two traditional frameworks of strategic management accounting systems and also a more contemporary approach called activity-based costing systems are discussed.

Finally, the *Strength-Weakness Opportunity-Threat* (SWOT) analysis framework, or actually its extended form is described as an integrating and forward-looking framework for analyzing competitors. Note that the same discussion provided in this chapter is also intended for self-analysis. Strategic moves that consider the motivations and resources of all the publics are likely to succeed.

Part 3: Analytical Tools

Chapter 8 discusses financial models, Chapter 9, resource allocation models, and Chapter 10, benchmarking and the *Profit Impact of Market Strategies* (PIMS).

Chapter 8 summarizes various models that are useful for a marketing strategist. These include models for capital budgeting or investment decisions and those of capital structure. Knowledge of the former enables the evaluation of the financial worthiness of a proposed investment. The latter allows for an understanding of whether a project or investment is feasible.

Whereas Chapter 8 focuses largely on models of individual investment decisions, Chapter 9 discusses frameworks for the allocation of resources to the various strategic opportunities that form the strategist's opportunity portfolio. Two major frameworks, the Boston Consulting Group matrix and the General Electric framework, are examined in detail. The chapter ends with a discussion of STRATPORT, which is an optimization model for making resource allocation decisions. Incidental to the discussion on STRATPORT, we also discuss the mixing of objective and judgmental data via decision–calculus and the use of response functions in marketing strategy.

The last chapter in this part, Chapter 10, is about norms. The first part of the chapter describes the benchmarking process of identifying and understanding the best available processes for satisfying customers. The second focuses on the PIMS project of the Strategic Planning Institute. The use of information from this database allows a business to obtain (a) knowledge of the range of investment values (e.g., advertising intensity), (b) the relationship between various market conditions and investment decisions on performance, and (c) how other businesses that look like the one under consideration perform on average. Together these give a comprehensive picture of the possibilities for all the competitors in a market.

Part 4: Alternatives and Implementation

This final part consists of four chapters which discuss timing, channels, offerings, and implementation.

Chapter 11, on timing, discusses three key issues: order-of-entry, signalling, and defensive strategies. Besides describing a wide range of alternatives, these three keys are also intended to provide information on the advantages and disadvantages of being a first-mover or a late-mover; on when a new product (or other action) should be announced to the world, and on the appropriateness of various defensive strategies based on the stage of a competitor's new product decision phase.

Chapter 12 assesses obtaining the maximum leverage from channel relationships. The chapter first describes the major changes occurring in distribution channels. These changes are being driven by customer requirements, which, in turn, are being changed by the emergence of new technologies and changing materials management and product design paradigms. The second part focuses on frameworks for the choice of appropriate channels for a given product.

Chapter 13, on offerings, describes what a business provides to its customers: the function, form, and price of a product, and transaction facilitators. Each of the elements of function, form, and price has several dimensions. These are discussed and provide alternatives for consideration. The key decisions are discussed regarding the scope of each element and its relative positioning with respect to competition. The exchange or transaction facilitators, information, customer service, and financing service are also discussed. A panoramic framework on competitive positioning summarizes the discussion in this chapter.

Chapter 14, the final chapter of the book can also be read as the first chapter. It focuses on implementation systems. The first part of the chapter describes the evolution of strategic planning systems. It also provides guidelines for designing systems to be used in strategic planning for complex and surprise-laden environments.

Since implementation, as well as the development, of a strategy occurs within the context of the particular combination of social, technology, and human subsystems, a marketing strategist should be aware of changes in these subsystems as well as develop a mind set to manage them and to work within them. Social subsystems refer to the formal and informal group and reporting that are used. Changes, like the development of horizontal organizations, alliances, the concept of an inquiry center, transnational corporations, and the consequence of such changes are described and discussed.

Only marketing strategy-related technology subsystems are described and discussed. Information technology has a major impact on marketing activities. Various types of information technologies that affect relationships, offerings, and timing (and, of course, resources) are described and discussed.

The last section discusses the human resource subsystem. The discussion focuses on if there is a difference between strategists and implements, requirements for decision making in complex and fast changing environments and guidelines on how to blend strategic thinking with opportunistic behavior. The chapter ends with a summary of the cross-impact of organizational subsystems and the strategy variables: relationships, offerings, timing, and resources (ROTR).

Concept Questions

1. What is a marketing strategy set?
2. What is the relationship between corporate strategy and marketing strategy?
3. Describe a heuristic process for marketing strategy development.
4. What are the key factors influencing competition in an industry?

Discussion Questions

1. Why can marketing strategy development only be defined as a heuristic process rather than as a formula?
2. Must a strategy always be directed at achieving certain objectives?
3. What is the role of intuition in marketing strategy development?
4. How do the concepts described in this chapter relate to the concepts of segmentation, product, price, promotion, place, and people?

Part 1

COMPETITIVE CONTEXT

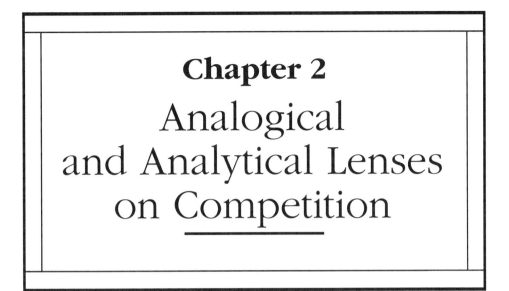

Chapter 2
Analogical and Analytical Lenses on Competition

Each individual and each field develop unique ways of looking at areas of interest. Strategies for the survival and growth of biological species are studied by evolutionary ecologists; strategies for winning sports games, by coaches and sports specialists; competitive behavior among firms, by industrial organization (IO) economists, and strategies for winning wars, by military strategists. Strategic thinking and observed strategies from these fields often provide templates or analogies for building strategic options for marketing action. Formal game theory provides analytical mechanisms with which these strategies may be evaluated. It provides a formal approach to prescribing the best strategy for a given context which is often highly stylized, and for studying changes in the context as the various competitors carry out their competitive or cooperative activities. This chapter first provides descriptions of "generic" strategies suggested by these fields and then provides an introduction to formal game theory as applied to marketing.

INTRODUCTION

In 1985 Helmut Schmidt, the former chancellor of the Federal Republic of Germany, delivered a series of lectures at Yale University. In the book in which these lectures were published, he says,

> What do I mean by the word "strategy?" Nowadays, almost everyone claims to have a strategy. For the advertising managers of the soft drink industry it is a marketing or sales strategy, for football coaches a game strategy, or in America a "game plan." Professors of economics preach economic strategies to their governments, the World Bank offers a full set of development strategies, and of course the military in every country have mili-

tary strategies, as they have had for three thousand years since the word strategy was first coined.[1]

Given this abundance of thoughts on strategy in many fields, it is pertinent to see what we can learn about strategic possibilities from other fields so that we might apply them to marketing. We wish to point out, however, that many of the possibilities in other fields have at best metaphorical usefulness to marketing strategy. This is still of considerable value, for as Professor Mintzberg put it so metaphorically, strategy development is itself a crafting process.[2] Such a process of skillful performance, according to Polanyi, is "achieved by the observance of a set of rules which are not known as such to the person following them."[3] Perhaps a way of seeking to learn marketing strategy is to use metaphors which by definition, intent, and origin are "closer to experience and consequently more vivid and memorable."[4] For example, speaking of the way Donald J. Tyson of Tyson Food Inc. views prospective acquisition candidates, his chief financial officer Gerald Johnson says, "Don equates looking for companies with fishing. He puts the bait on the line, and then he reels the catch in."[5] We should not, however, interpret thinking in these fields as "recipes" for success (or generic success strategies) via sustainable advantage in market. In drawing an analogy one must assume that all relevant information is recorded and that unrecorded information (that might be personal experiential-judgmental knowledge) does not provide insights. This is particularly true if one considers writing in the field of military strategy. For example, Napoleon Bonaparte, who was considered a great strategist, did not complement this greatness with the written word. Consequently, we are left only with the interpretations of his strategic thinking written by two others: General Antoine Henri Jomini (1779–1869) and General Karl Maria von Clausewitz (1780–1831).[6] What has been left out we cannot even guess. What has been added we do not know. Thus, we "know" Napolean's great strategies but the true context in which they were great is less well known. We must also keep in mind, as pointed out in Chapter 1, that competitive advantage arises out of interaction between strategy and context. So, we emphasize that a strategist needs to think about the principles by which a strategy may be developed for a context, rather than simply to "borrow" a strategy. A study of such strategy–context pairs from the past is likely to be of value. However, strategy development cannot be codified into a recipe book. Much like the systematic study of chemistry brings the alchemist's dream closer, a systematic study of strategy gives a strategist confidence and discipline in approaching this complex task.

[1]Schmidt, Helmut, *A Grand Strategy for the West,* New Haven, Yale University Press, 1985.

[2]Mintzberg, H., "Crafting Strategy," *Harvard Business Review,* July–August, 1962, pp. 66–75.

[3]Polanyi, M., "Personal Knowledge, Towards a Post-Critical Philosophy," Chicago, Chicago University Press, 1962.

[4]Ortony, A., "Why Metaphors are Necessary and Not Just Nice," *Educational Theory,* 25, 1975, pp. 45–53.

[5]Forest, S. A., "Tyson Is Winging Its Way to the Top," *Business Week,* February 25, 1991, pp. 57–58.

[6]Collins, John M., *Grand Strategy: Practices and Principles, Annapolis,* Naval Institute Press, 1973, p. xxi.

There are four endeavors from which strategists have sought analogies and guidance: military strategy studies; sports games; a study of evolutionary ecology; and industrial organization economics. Studying these, it is clear that sustainable competitive advantage arises out of a fit between strategy and context.[7] What follows is a summary of the salient elements from each of these fields that might help us develop a marketing strategy–context understanding.

MILITARY STRATEGIES

"LOCKHEED VS. NORTHROP: A $75 Billion Battle" beckons a banner on the front cover of April 8, 1991's *Business Week.* "It was just another day in a five-year battle between Lockheed and Northrop Corp. over the last huge weapons contract of this century. The prize is $75 to $100 billion in orders over the next 20 years for the Advanced Tactical Fighter, the successor to the Air Force's F–15 long-range fighter." (Lockheed was awarded this contract on April 22, 1991, p. 64.)

Another issue of the same magazine (February 25, 1991) talks about "TOBACCO'S NEW WAR: Cigarette makers are fighting antismokers on a new front: Asia."

The dedication to a popular book by Ries and Trout, *Marketing Warfare,* reads, "Dedicated to one of the greatest marketing strategists the world has ever known: Karl von Clausewitz." Given this considerable interest in military strategies by marketing strategists we examine what we can learn about marketing strategies by studying writings on and by war strategists.

In our discussion we focus on understanding (a) what military strategy means and what are its objectives, (b) generic strategic options, (c) context differences and changes, and (d) outcome and competitive advantage.

What is Military Strategy?

von Clausewitz defines it as "the theory of the use of combats for the objective of war." And he further says that, "By the strategic plan is settled when, where, and with what forces a battle is to be delivered—and to carry that into execution the march is the only means."[8] "The object of war is to "compel opponents to fulfill our will.""[9] To attain this objective of bending the will of an opponent to one's own will, von Clausewitz says that it is necessary to completely disarm or overthrow the enemy or to credibly threaten such an action. The objective of war for von Clausewitz is the total domination of the enemy by the use of arms and military marches. For von Clausewitz, strategy is about the conduct of war.

---

[7]Collins, *op. cit.,* makes this point tellingly, when he says, "In the final analysis free lessons to be learned from the plethora of historical strategic advice are clean cut. The mission is to understand what transpired before and to appreciate the context, so that experience can be applied to the future with perspicacity."

[8]von Clausewitz, K. M., *A Short Guide to Clausewitz on War,* in Roger Ashley Leonard, (ed.), New York, G. P. Putnam, 1967.

[9] von Clausewitz, K. M., *op. cit.,* p. 41.

More recently, the British strategist, Liddell-Hart, has suggested that a more appropriate objective is a "better state of peace." This state is realized by achieving a position (an advantage) which is so secure than an enemy would not consider an attack. In his words, "the true aim is not so much to seek battle as to seek a strategic situation so advantageous that if it does not of itself produce the decision, its continuation by a battle is sure to achieve this."[10]

Thus, we understand von Clausewitz's strategy as a theory of combat to achieve certain ends, whereas Liddell-Hart's strategy is about a theory of all possible endeavors to achieve, specifically, a better state of peace. Liddell-Hart's approach is called a "Grand" strategy.

Collins refers to three different types of strategy that are pertinent to the management of a nation. The first he calls National strategy. This "fuses all the powers of a nation, during peace as well as war to attain national objectives."[11] This in turn is comprised of political, economic, national, military and other strategies. The second, Grand strategy, is "the art and science of employing national power under all circumstances to exert desired degrees and types of control over the opposition through threats, force, indirect pressures, diplomacy, subterfuge, and other imaginative means, thereby satisfying national security interests and objectives." The third, Military strategy, "is predicated on physical violence or the threat of violence. It seeks victory through force of arms." A successful Grand strategy makes war unnecessary and "controls" military strategy.

In drawing on these definitions for parallels to the business world, it appears that (a) Military strategy is analogous to functional strategies such as marketing, finance, human resources, technology, and so forth, (b) National strategy is analogous to corporate strategy, and (c) Grand strategy is analogous to business unit or product-market strategy. These comparisons suggest that marketing strategy is predicated on action in the marketplace (aiming to achieve market share, sales and profit objectives).

Corporate strategy is greater than just the combination of finance, marketing, human resources strategy, and so forth. Rather it harnesses all the energies of the entire corporation to achieve a purpose, namely, the satisfaction of all or some of its stakeholders.

Grand strategy maps onto business unit strategy. It focuses attention on a narrow scope of security goals. We translate this as ensuring an outcome trajectory (survival and growth) for the business unit. It is thus a compilation of various functional strategies that have to fit together to achieve the business unit's outcome trajectory. One could view the creation of excess capacity to prevent others from entering or blocking access to distribution channels through contractual agreements, and the like. However, a snag in this analogy is that marketing and other functional strategies are always to be implemented, whereas a truly successful Grand strategy obviates implementation of a Military one.

---

[10]Liddell–Hart, B. H., *Strategy,* New York, Praeger, 2nd ed. 1967, p. 339.

[11]Collins, John M., *op. cit.,* p. 14.

Generic Strategy Options

The generic approaches that are presented by Collins are for Grand strategy. These approaches also apply to some extent to marketing strategy. This adds to the confusion of mapping ideas and concepts in the broader field of strategy to marketing strategy. He suggests that approaches to strategy consist of four pairs, four schools of thought and strategic options. Exhibit 2–1 provides an overview of these approaches.

The four basic sets of strategies are (1) sequential and cumulative, (2) direct and indirect, (3) deterrent and combative, and (4) counterforce and countervalue.

Sequential and Cumulative Strategies

Sequential strategies, as the name suggests, are step-by-step and are temporally apart. Cumulative strategies, are simultaneous (or nearly so) and have a joint effect. For example, introducing a succession of new products would be a sequential strategy. Introducing several products simultaneously would be a cumulative strategy in Collin's language.

EXHIBIT 2–1   Strategic Approaches

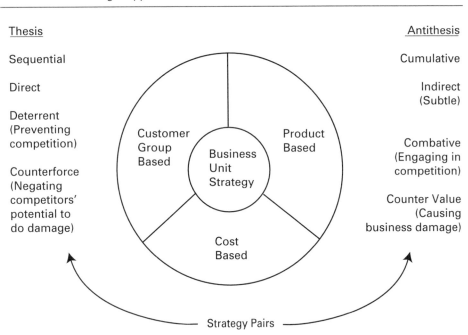

Adapted from J. M. Collins, *Grand Strategy: Practices and Principles,* Annapolis, The Naval Institute Press, 1975, p. 15.

Direct and Indirect Strategies

Is brute force used or are subtleties brought to bear against competition? Consider the potential competition between two Cupertiono, California-based companies, Apple Computer, Inc. and Nutek Computers, Inc. The latter is a start-up company gearing up to deliver the raw technology necessary to produce clones of Macintosh computers.[12] A direct approach by Apple may be the outright acquisition of Nutek. An indirect approach may be to aid Nutek in the hope that the overall market for Macs will grow because of the availability of increased ancillary (e.g., software, peripherals, etc.) suppliers.

Deterrent and Combative Strategies

Deterrence prevents wars and combat prosecutes wars once they start. A choice is called for at the business unit level regarding whether a deterrent or a combative strategy is to be pursued. The choice of an appropriate marketing strategy then follows. In deciding between the two, it is necessary to determine what functional strategies might fit each approach and then to simulate or think about their consequences. The same marketing action is applicable to both deterrence and combat. However, pre-combat marketing is different from that for combat. The marketing strategy for combat specifies change in market offerings, or relationships, or resource allocations to be deployed at different times.

Counterforce and Countervalue Strategies

A counterforce strategy calls for the disabling of a competitor's weapons, or resources that can cause damage. In marketing strategy, this implies control of a competitor's ability to modify marketing offerings and relationships that could potentially cause damage. A countervalue strategy calls for delivering as much damage to the competitor as has been caused. In other words, a tit-for-tat strategy. These have obvious implications for marketing strategy.

Besides these four strategy pairs, Collins summarizes four schools of military thought (1) the Continental, (2) the Maritime, (3) the Aerospace, and (4) the Revolutionary. In our opinion, these schools appear to correspond to Porter's three, so-called generic strategies of focus, differentiation and cost leadership.

The military schools of thought concentrate on the medium (land, air, or water) of combat which determines the outcome of a battle. A set of strategies is based on this choice. In business, Porter's strategies of overall cost leadership, differentiation, and focus also possess similar meaning. That is, a differentiation strategy is predicated on the basis that a superior product-based strategy is effective (Exhibit 2–2), a focus strategy is based on customer groups as targets, and cost leadership is what its name implies. There is a parallel between the military schools of thought and Porter's generic strategies.

[12]Buell, Barbara, "Mac vs. Mac: How Apple Plans to Cure its High-End Headache," *Business Week,* April 29, 1991, pp. 30–31.

EXHIBIT 2–2   Michael Porter's Three Generic Strategies

Overall Cost Leadership

The first strategy, an increasingly common one in the 1970's because of popularization of the experience survey concept, is to achieve overall cost leadership in an industry through a set of functional policies aimed at this basic objective.   Cost leadership requires aggressive construction of efficient-scale facilities, vigorous pursuit of cost reductions from experience, tight cost and overhead control, avoidance of marginal customer accounts, and cost minimization in areas like R&D, service, sales force, advertising, and so on.

Differentiation

The second generation strategy is one of differentiating the product or service offering of the firm, creating something that is perceived *industry-wide* as being unique.
Approaches to differentiating can take many forms: design or brand image, technology, features, customer service, dealer network, or other dimensions.   Ideally the firm differentiates itself along several dimensions.   It should be stressed that the differentiation strategy does not allow the firm to ignore costs, but rather they are not the primary strategic target.

Focus

The final generic strategy is focusing on a particular buyer group, segment of the product line, or geographic market: as with differentiation, focus may take many forms.
Although the low cost and differentiation strategies area aimed at achieving their objective industry-wide, the entire focus strategy is built around serving a particular target very well, and each functional policy is developed with this in mind.   The strategy rests on the premise that the firm is thus able to serve its narrow strategic target more effectively or efficiently than competitors who are competing more broadly.

However, it is the last *focus,* generic strategy, which has proved more difficult to sustain.   In his more recent book, Porter distinguishes two "generic approaches" within the "focus" strategy.

The focus strategy has two variants.   In *cost focus* a firm seeks a cost advantage in its target segment, while in *differentiation focus* a firm seeks differentiation in its target segment.   Cost focus exploits differences in cost behavior in some segments while differentiation focus exploits the special needs of buyers in certain segments.

From Michael Porter, *Competitive Strategy*, New York, Free Press, 1980.

In military parlance, however, strategic options are generic to the schools of thought and are derived from the four strategy pairs. Some of these options are shown in Exhibit 2–3.   From these options the attack and defense strategies in marketing,

EXHIBIT 2–3   Strategic Options

Within the matrix of interests, objectives, theories, concepts, and schools of thought, countless strategic combinations are conceivable.   A few sample strategic options, paired to emphasize contrast, are listed below:

Offensive War or Defensive War	Armed Strife or Subversion
Preemptive War or Second Strike	Passive Resistance or Active Response
Massive Retaliation or Flexible Response	Isolationism or Collective Security
Forces in Being or Rapid Mobilization	Counterforce or Countervalue
Regional War or Global War	Controlled Escalation or Insensate Attack
Blitzkrieg or Attrition	Spheres of Influence or Universal Confrontation

popularized by Kotler and Singh, are deducible. Their options are shown in Exhibit 2–4. This exhibit shows that a limited number of basic categories of military response can be clearly related to competitive strategy.

Limitations of the Military Analogy

Territorial Versus Communication Control Perspective. Classical military (like von Clausewitz) strategy (like American football) emphasizes territorial advantage. Military strategy is implemented in a terrain that is clearly defined and known to the participants and does not change over time. The valleys remain valleys

EXHIBIT 2–4 Strategies Based on the Military Analogy

ATTACK OFFENSE STRATEGIES

1. *Frontal attack.* An aggressor is said to launch a frontal (or "head-on") attack when it masses its forces right up against those of its opponent. It attacks the opponent's strengths rather than its weaknesses. The outcome depends on who has the greater strength and endurance. In a pure frontal attack, the attacker matches product for product, advertising for advertising, price for price, and so on.
2. *Flanking attack.* An army on a battlefield is deployed to be strongest where it expects to attack or be attacked. It is necessarily less secure in its flanks and rear. Its weak spots (blind sides), therefore, are natural points of attack for the enemy. A flanking attack can be directed against a competitor along two strategic dimensions—geographical and segmental.
3. *Encirclement.* The pure flanking maneuver is defined as pivoting on a gap in the existing market coverage of the enemy. The encirclement maneuver, on the other hand, is seen as an attempt to disperse this coverage so that the enemy's segment differentiation (and therefore brand loyalty) is diluted and a more fluid front is created that can be pierced at a number of points and enveloped into new segments.
4. *Bypass attack.* The bypass is the most indirect of assault strategies and eschews the belligerent move directed against the enemy's existing segment span.
5. *Guerrilla warfare.* Guerilla warfare consists of making small, intermittent attacks on different territories of the opponent, with the aim of harassing and demoralizing the opponent and eventually securing concessions.

DEFENSE STRATEGIES

1. *Position defense.* The traditional concept of defense is closely tied to a psychology of "fortification." Static, fortlike defense, like frontal attack, is apparently one of the riskiest strategies in the military theater.
2. *Mobile defense.* Far superior to position defense, mobile defense is the firm's attempt to stretch its domain over new territories that can serve as future centers for defense or counterattack.
3. *Preemptive defense.* Offense as a form of preemptive defense assumes that prevention is better than cure—that war and not peace is the natural state of the business. Preemptive defense includes all the attack strategies considered earlier.
4. *"Flank–positioning" defense.* The flanking "position" is established by a defender as a hedge against some probable but uncertain eventuality, or as a defensive corner overlooking a real front.
5. *"Hedgehog" defense (strategic withdrawal).* Strategic withdrawal is a move to consolidate one's competitive strength in the market and concentrate mass at pivotal positions for counterattack.

Adapted from Phillip Kotler and Ravi Singh, "Marketing Warfare in the 1980's," *Journal of Business Strategy,* Winter 1981, pp. 30–41.

and high ground remains high ground. However, the marketing "battlefield" is constantly changing. In addition to external forces of change such as technology and customer values, businesses are continually changing the relationship-offering space as they attempt to erode advantages established by competitors. In addition, the competitive "terrain" in the business context is not as well defined as the physical contours on a map. Various competitors might have quite different views of the offerings space and where the "hills and valleys" are located.

However, modern military strategy (like Liddell-Hart) has been forced to contend with the type of situations confronting marketers. The progressive evolution of rapidly deployed long-range and accurately targeted methods of delivery for offensive weapons has dramatically reduced the relevance of geographic boundaries. The crucial strategic imperative has become both the maintenance of one's own *Communication, Command,* and *Control Intelligence* system (C3I) and the disruption of the enemy's (a form of counterforce strategy). Perhaps, the future of market information systems will be equally important in marketing and corporate strategy. Modern military strategy, therefore, has advanced into an area in which simple maps are no longer of value because they do not provide a good indication of relative position.

The concept of guerilla warfare arose, in part, as a reaction to the reliance on a sophisticated C3I structure to deal with the complex logistics and communication needs of high technology warfare. By adopting a different organizing strategy, the military can be less susceptible to a highly disruptive attack on its C3I system. Specifically, a "cell" command structure in guerilla warfare relies on relatively autonomous small units and a much more limited logistical supply infrastructure because local units depend on local supplies (markets). Of course, this decentralized autonomous organization needs something to hold it together: an ideology, a sense of commitment and coherence that does not require complex systems. Thus, marketers and military strategists have shown a great interest in integrating and coordinating mechanism which do not involve complex C3I systems.[13]

Internal Versus External Focus. In general, military strategy is developed based on the premise that critical resources must be supplied internally. When Patton was driving his tank corps across Europe, he could not rely on buying gasoline at local outlets. However, businesses (and guerilla warfare units) often use intermediary markets to provide raw materials, assembled components, financial resources, and distribution services. In addition, firms can form strategic alliances with other firms to provide a competitive offering. For example, the IBM PC represents the integration of a microprocessor supplied by Intel, an operating system provided by Microsoft, distribution production performed by retail computer stores, and standard components available from a number of suppliers. However, the reliance on external sources for critical elements made the IBM PC vulnerable to

[13]See W. D. Henderson, *Why the Vietcong Fought: A Study in Motivation and Control in a Modern Army in Combat,* Westport, CO, Greenwood Press, 1979; and J. R. C. Wensley, "PIMS and BCG: New Horizons or False Dawn?" *Strategic Management Journal,* 3, 1982, pp. 147–158.

competitive attack by clone makers who easily assembled these same elements from external sources.[14]

Zero-Sum Game.   Any gains in a military context are made only at the enemy's expense.   However, Day[15] indicates that "An effective business strategy is not a zero-sum game, where customers of distributors gain or lose at the expense or benefit of the business." That is, we perhaps overemphasize the nonzero-sum game nature of business competition.   At least in terms of opportunity lost, most competitive actions are taken with an expectation that they represent a cost to one's competitors even if they do not recognize it at that time and even when sometimes the expectation turns out to be wrong.

Summary

Drawing upon the military analogy, Kotler and Singh[16] provide some generic strategies (Exhibit 2–4).   However, these strategies often represent the classical emphasis on physical terrain—an emphasis that is inconsistent with the competitive business arena. Modern military strategy recognizes a context which is analogous to the business environment and provides some interesting insights into the importance of communications and control, the objective of a strategy, and the context of marketing strategy and corporate strategy.   It stresses the development of strategies as varying combinations of timing, nature of engagement sought, and choice of distribution of the points of engagement.

SPORTS GAME

"Business organizations and their problems are often defined using analogies to sports teams."[17]   The sports game analogy is a common basis from which to discuss competitive activities.   These analogies appear to capture the essence of competition compared with the economic approaches we have considered previously.
    Consider the following hypothetical comment made by a CEO:

> It's taken my staff and me a sizable chunk of time, but we now have a solid game plan for the XYZ job. Jack, I want you to quarterback this thing all the way into the end zone. Of course, a lot of it will be making the proper assignments—getting the right people to run interference and the right ones to run with the ball. But my main concern is that we avoid mistakes. No fumbles, no interceptions, no sacks, no penalties. I don't want us to have to play catch-up; no two-minute drills at the end. I want the game plan executed exactly the way it's drawn. When we're done we want to look back with pride at a win and not have to Monday-morning-quarterback a loss.

[14]"The PC Wars: IBM vs. The Clones," *Business Week,* July 28, 1986, pp. 62–68.

[15]Day, George, *Strategic Markets Planning,* St. Paul, MN, West Publishing, 1984, p. 118.

[16]Kotler, Phillip and Ravi Singh Achol, "Marketing Warfare in the 1980's," *Journal of Business Strategy,* Winter, 1981, pp. 30–41.

[17]Kadel, Robert W., "A New Game for Managers to Play: Football's Out, Basketball's In," *The New York Times,* December 8, 1985, F3.

Sports games have many similarities to business competition. In sports, the nature of competition is evident, the sequence of decisions both within and between games is clear, and the problems of coordinating the activities of a number of individuals are obvious.

Offense and Defense

In many team sports, distinction is made between offense and defense, between scoring and preventing a competitor from scoring. In American football, baseball, and cricket there are well-defined periods of time in which players engage in either offense or defense. Because of the particular skill of players at a point in time, a sports team may be characterized as emphasizing its offense or defense. Throughout this book we emphasize the importance of these generic strategies—offense and defense. It is not enough to use "offense" to gain market share, a firm must also defend any gain against competitive retaliation.

Whereas American football, baseball, and cricket treat offense and defense as distinct strategies, sports with an international appeal which have continuity, such as soccer and basketball, consider offense and defense to be simultaneous. For this reason, Kierstead[18] suggests that international sports provide a better analogy to economic competition (Exhibit 2–5).

However, the complexity of sports games and competition over time means that sports analogies are more powerful than just these simple distinctions between offense and defense. In sports, rules change which means that new ways of exploiting potential strengths emerge. Thus, one strategy is to control the rules of a game. For example, several changes in rules governing field hockey favored the European countries to the detriment of traditional powerhouses like Pakistan and India. The new rules gave advantage to those with superior power as opposed to those who use finesse. In addition, the fortuitous discovery of new plays, or the availability of different types of player talent, means that opportunities exist for change. The changes themselves, however, take place in a public arena. If these new developments are successful, they are open to direct imitation and they can influence the market price of the "resources" involved, that is, the specific types of players needed to exploit these opportunities.

Limitations

While sports games provide an interesting source of analogies concerning competitive strategies, the unique form of some games produces metaphors that may not result in appropriate business strategies. For example, American football has these unique characteristics:

- A crucial concern with territorial advantage. Except in extreme cases, going "backward," even for a short time, is a competitive failure.

[18]Kierstead, B. S., "Decision Taking and the Theory of Games," *In* C. F. Carter and J. L. Ford (eds.), *Uncertainty and Expectation in Economics: Essays in Honor of G. L. Shackle*, Oxford, Blackwell, 1972.

- A disjointed pattern of play, which results in the development of complex and complete game plans for each play.
- The existence of various specialized "teams": offense, defense, and special teams for punting, field goals, short yardage situations, and kickoffs.
- A hierarchial relationship among the head coach, other coaches, and the individual players.

EXHIBIT 2–5 Kierstead on Games Analogies

It seems to me that the theory of games applies only to discontinuous games, i.e. games like checkers or chess wherein each move may be planned in the light of revealed counter-strategies. This may also be true of American field games such as baseball and American football. Baseball is a game in which the strategy of every play may be calculated by the coach both of the team at bat and the team in the field. There is ample time for such calculations between each pitch. We have even seen the pitcher walk out of the box to consult with the catcher, the team captain or the team coach. And on every base the batting side has "base coaches" who indicate to the base runners the decisions of the team coach. It is so, also, in American football. Anyone who has watched or studied this game will remember that on every single play a round table conference is held by both the attacking and the defending teams. There they are, all in two concentric circles, their big and padded bottoms facing, shall we say, into the television cameras. They talk it over; they take their time; the coach sends in a substitute with new orders and a fresh strategy . . . The American football coach could, I should think, use a computer with advantage. He would have lots of time, while the commercial was inserted, to choose his strategy. It is not without significance that American economists should think of strategies in games in discontinuous terms. Sociologists might give thought to the fact that the great American games, baseball and football, are played solely in the United States. Games are a cultural expression and American games have never "caught on."

By contrast, ice hockey, originally a Canadian game, soccer and rugger, which in origin were British, are international games. They are played everywhere and nowhere with more vim and vehemence than in the United States. Americans, tied as they are by a kind of mystique to their own games, which are so terribly dull and serious, still do like to play games for fun . . . We shall look at these three international games, and when we do so we observe that they have one thing in common. There is a play-maker—the center in hockey, the center-forward in soccer, the stand-off in rugger—and he adapts himself, to a continuous flow. On the move the playmaker continuously adjusts himself, and takes decisions, as the play flows on. We submit that this is not just a practical matter of the much greater speed at which the international games are played: it is surely a question of the type of mathematics applicable to the analysis of these games. On the one hand we have the discontinuous analysis of the theory of games and difference equations, on the other hand we have the mathematics of continuous flow, the differential calculus, and we have the continuous adjustment of strategies to counter-strategies as the play, the experiment, develops. Anyone who has watched the play of the Hon. L. Kelly can see how consistently he is thinking, how persistently he follows through his pattern, how rapidly he adjusts when things "go wrong." He is the very picture—on the ice and on the television screen—of the decision maker, a symbol of the flow of consciousness and the intelligent conscious control of the flow of consciousness.

Reprinted with permission by Basil Blackwell, Carter, C. F. and Ford, J. L. *Uncertainty and Expectation in Economics,* pp. 172–173, 1972.

Therefore, while some requirements in a football team, such as the development of "team spirit," are generic to most team games, many others are not. In particular, the whole nature of the game encourages a focus on competitive strategy which is (to put it in business terms)

- Biased toward clear and quantitative measures of intermediate performance.
- Focused on detailed monitoring and control of performance.
- Concerned with the use of tightly defined specialist personnel rather than generalists.
- Related to the role of the CEO (head coach).
- Provides a clear distinction between planning and implementation.

Therefore, it is not surprising that football analogies encourage a top-down notion of strategy development as well as an emphasis on having the right person for the right strategy, whereas analogies with other sports games encourage continual coordination between plan implementation and a set of generalists who all touch "the ball" and develop and implement strategies.

Sports games analogies are highly constrained by the rules of the game. There is little option within the game to change the rules. Yet a number of business writers emphasize the importance of competitive strategies which implicitly or explicitly "change the rules."

Changing the Rules of the Game

The idea of "changing the rules" is actually not as simple as it appears. In practice, it is a matter of degree. None of the business strategists who recommend changing the rules actually proposes sabotaging or burning a competitor's factories. Nor, in most cases, do they recommend encouraging legislation to ban crucial ingredients in a competitor's products. In fact, what they recommend is often no more than an explicit attempt to examine assumptions about the norms in the marketplace—the rules that have governed competitive behavior on the basis of shared learning and commonly held beliefs.

For instance, shared experience within an industry can act as an important source of analogies, influence competitive strategy, and restrict the options that are considered.

> Until 1970, for example, members of the airline industry assumed that they were a growing industry fed by growing demand. Until 1974, they took regulation as an established fact of life. In the automobile industry of the 1950's (LINGERING INTO THE 1980'S), meta-strategic assumptions included shared beliefs about American desires for luxury, speed and size.[19]

[19]Huff, A. S., "Industry Influences on Strategy Reformulation," *Strategic Management Journal,* 3, 1982, pp. 119–131. Also see J. C. Spender, "Strategy-Making in Business," unpublished doctoral dissertation, England, Manchester University, 1980.

Thus, the prescription to "break the rules" is to challenge the conventional wisdom.

The domain of military strategy provides a more useful analogy to apply to competitive strategy. In military strategy the option of challenging conventional wisdom is clearly open, and yet, as in business, there remain certain conventions, the most obvious being the Geneva Convention, which are generally accepted and not challenged.

ECOLOGICAL ANALOGIES

r and k Strategies

Evolutionary ecology has also emerged as a popular analogy for understanding the types of strategies pursued by companies. These analogies have been used to describe both the nature of the competitive process itself[20] as well as the notion of "niche"[21] strategy. Organizational theorists and sociologists[22] have adopted an ecological mode that describes the growth of a species in an environment. Ecologically, there is an upper limit on the population of a species in a resource environment. This upper limit, K_1, is referred to as the *carrying capacity* of the environment. The growth rate of a species is the following function of the natural rate of growth, r, and the carrying capacity.

$$\frac{dx}{dt} = \frac{rx\,(k-x)}{k} \,,$$

when x is the population at one point in time. When the population of a species is small, the effects of the carrying capacity are minimal and growth is an exponential function of the natural growth rate. The carrying capacity only becomes important when the population size is large, relative to the carrying capacity. The parameters of this growth model have been used to describe two alternative strategies—r–strategies and k–strategies. r–strategists are those that enter a new resource space (offerings–relationship space) at an easy stage when few other organizations are present, whereas k–strategists join later when there are a larger number of organizations in the environment. Once a particular type of organization has established itself in an environment, it resists change because of the development of vested interest within the organization. The number of

[20]Henderson, B. D., "The Anatomy of Competition," *Journal of Marketing,* 2, 1983, pp. 7–11.

[21]Hofer, C. W., and D. Schendel, *Strategy Formulation: Analytical Concepts,* St. Paul, MN: West Publishing, 1977.

[22]Aldrich, H. E., *Organizations and Environments,* Englewood Cliffs, NJ, Prentice–Hall, 1979; J. W. Brittain and J. H. Freeman, "Organizational Proliferation and Density Dependent Selection," *In* J. R. Kimberly, R. H. Miles and associates, *The Organizational Life-Cycle: Issues in the Creation, Transformation and Decline of Organizations,* San Francisco, Jossey-Bass, 1980; J. Freeman and W. Boeker, "The Ecological Analysis of Business Strategy," *California Management Review,* 26, Spring 1984, pp. 73–86; M. T. Hannan and J. Freeman, "The Population Ecology of Organizations," *American Journal of Sociology,* 5 1977, p. 82.

firms in an environment at one point in time, referred to as the population density, is a proxy for the intensity of competition.

Based on this perspective, the initial entrants into an environment are usually r–strategists—small, new firms that are quick to move and not constrained by the inherent inertia confronting firms with established traditions in other environments. Whereas r–r–strategists are flexible, they are also inefficient because of their inexperience. After several r–strategists have entered a new environment, established organizations, k–strategists, overcome their inertia, enter the environment, and exploit their advantage of greater efficiency based on extensive experience. The characteristics of the environment determine if these successive entrants can coexist.

Generalist Versus Specialist Strategies

A *niche* is the specific combination of resources needed to support a species or type of organization. Niche width indicates whether this combination of resource is available over a broad range of the resource space or whether it is only available in a narrow range. A generalist is able to operate in a broad range whereas a specialist is restricted to a narrow range. The nature of the environment favors either generalist or specialist companies.

Environments are described by two dimensions: variability and frequency of environmental change. In a highly variable environment, changes are dramatic, and fundamentally different strategic responses are required for survival. In contrast, strategic alterations are not required to cope with low variability. A specialist in which high performance occurs in a narrow portion of the environment is appropriate when environmental changes are dramatic and frequent. Under these conditions, it is unlikely that a generalist has sufficient flexibility to cope with the wide-range environmental conditions it would face. A generalist strategist is most appropriate in an environment characterized by infrequent, minor changes because this environment allows the generalist to exploit large scale efficiencies.

Generic Strategies

The population density and nature of the environment suggest the following generic strategies based on the ecological analogy

1. *r–specialists:* Small organizations which focus on exploiting first mover advantages, rather than on efficiency.

2. *r–generalists:* Larger and established organizations that can exploit the new opportunity simply by minor expansion and modification of their existing activities.

3. *k–specialists:* Small and probably new organizations that trade on the basis of greater efficiency in exploiting a stable, narrow area. They can often survive because the area of their focus is seen as marginal by other competitors or they are protected by captive demand.

4. *k–generalists:* Large established organizations, with the advantage of experience in closely related areas, which can compete efficiently on a large scale.

Niche

Frequently, business people link the concept of a niche to a competitive exclusion principle that no two species (identical organisms or companies) can occupy the same niche (compete in the same manner). Ecologists are quite critical of this concept of a niche.

> A niche, then, in either meaning is a description of the ecology of the species and there is absolutely no justification for supposing that each area has a number of pigeon-holes into which species can be fitted until the community is full. The most unfortunate result of using the term niche is to predispose the minds of readers into thinking that species occupy exclusive compartments in communities and, therefore, competition leads to displacement because there is no room for two species in one niche. We have already seen that competition does not lead to displacement in a number of representative samples.[23]

There are an infinite number of niches (offerings–relationships markets) or specific source combinations in a resource environment (offerings–relationships) space.

INDUSTRIAL ORGANIZATION (IO) ECONOMICS

Industrial organization (IO) economics examines the nature of competitive behavior when assumptions about homogeneous firms and customer are relaxed. This branch of economics recognizes that all firms are not alike and that customers are not the same. The dominant IO paradigm is the structure–conduct–performance (SCP) linkage.

This paradigm suggests that a firm's performance results from competitive interactions (conduct in the marketplace) and that conduct is determined by the structure of the industry in which the firm competes. Within IO, performance is defined as providing benefits to society (social welfare). Some aspects of social performance are allocating resources efficiently across firms, minimizing costs, and providing innovations. Conduct is the decision made by individual firms such as prices, building capacity, advertising, and investing in research and development (R&D). Structure is measured by properties of the industry (the set of firms using similar technologies), such as number and size of firms (concentration), advertising intensity, capital intensity, concentration of suppliers and customers, the degree to which products are differentiated (demand is inelastic), and barriers to entry. Thus, the IO paradigm identifies a set of industry conditions (or context) which ultimately affects the competitive behavior and performance of firms.

> ***Relevance of IO Paradigm to Competitive Evolution.*** Whereas a substantial body of research has been undertaken concerning the SCP paradigm, this research has had only a limited impact on marketing strategy issues because of differences in the unit of analysis of IO and the unit of concern of marketing strategists.[24]

[23]Pontin, A. J., *Competition and Coexistence,* London, Pitman, Longman, 1982.

[24]See Michael E. Porter, "The Contribution of Industrial Organization to Strategic Management," *Academy of Management Review,* 6, 1981, pp. 609–620.

Objective Profit Versus Social Welfare.   Managers are interested in improving their firm's profits, while most IO research focuses on improving social welfare by reducing firm profits to a fair, competitive level. The SCP paradigm can make a contribution to either perspective. Whereas public policy makers wish to alter industry structure (reduce entry barriers and concentration) to minimize excess profit, managers are interested in altering structure (increasing entry barriers and concentration) to realize greater profit. Until recently the SCP paradigm has not been translated to provide insights into the manager's problems.

Unit of Analysis—Firm Versus Industry.   While managers are keenly interested in the problems facing an individual firm, IO research generally adopts the industry as the unit of analysis. IO theory implicitly assumes that all firms within an industry are identical except for differences in size. Rather than consider the impact of industry structure on firm conduct and performance, IO research has been concerned with industry profits. The focus of IO research on interindustry rather than intraindustry performance is consistent with its objective of enacting public policy at an industry level to maximize social welfare.

Static Versus Dynamic Perspective.   IO research takes a static perspective by focusing on the relationship of industrial structure and performance, ignoring the dynamic competitive process (the conduct) that resulted in these relationships. But managers are interested in the dynamic marketplace. They want to alter the existing situation—raise entry barriers, gain market share, develop a sustainable competitive advantage. IO research takes industry structure, an exogenous, beyond the control of managers; however, managers actively attempt to alter structure. For example, gaining market share can increase industry concentration.

Strategic Groups and Mobility Barriers

During the last 15 years, IO economists, especially Richard Caves and Michael Porter,[25] have redirected the development of IO to their strategic management issues. The concepts of strategic groups and mobility barriers are key elements in this new IO perspective. As Richard Caves indicates

> . . . the concepts of strategic groups and mobility barriers do not add up to a tight formal model. Rather, they serve to organize predictions that come from tight models and assist in confronting them with empirical evidence—a dynamised add-on to the traditional structure—conduct–performance paradigm.[26]

[25]Caves, Richard E., "Industrial Organization, Corporate Strategy and Structure," *Journal of Economic Literature,* 43 March, 1980, pp. 64–92; Michael E. Porter, *Competitive Strategy,* New York, Free Press: 1980; Michael E. Porter, *Competitive Advantage,* New York, Free Press: 1985.

[26]Caves, Richard E., "Economic Analysis and The Quest for Competitive Advantage," *American Economic Association Papers and Proceedings,* May 1984, p. 130.

Strategic Groups.   The concept of strategic groups was first articulated by Hunt,[27] based on his study of the U.S. major household appliance industry. Hunt observed that producers in this industry differed in the range of products offered, the degree to which their efforts focused on offering premium features or minimizing costs and price, and the type of distribution channel used (private label for mass merchants, specialty retailers, builders of residential homes and apartments), or broad-based distribution through retailers.   Based on these observations, Hunt suggests that all firms within an industry do not compete vigorously against each other.   The most vigorous competition occurs between firms in a "strategic" group which use similar approaches to attract customers—similar product line breadth, the product benefits offered, and distribution channels.   A strategic group is the set of competitors who operate within a common offering-relationship space.

Porter generalized Hunt's observation to other industries and concluded that:

> Common observation suggests that the firms in an industry often differ from one another in their degree of vertical integration or diversification, the extent to which they advertise and brand their product, whether or not they use captive or exclusive distribution channels, whether they are full-line or narrow-line sellers, whether they are operated in a national market or regionally, whether they are multinational in operation, and so forth. That is, strategies differ among firms in an industry.   An industry thus may consist of groups of firms, each group composed of firms that have similar strategies.   We define such groups as strategic groups.[28]

Mobility Barriers.   Entry barriers are the potential costs incurred by a new entrant into an industry.   The concept of "mobility barriers" generalized the notion of entry barriers to include strategic groups.[29]   Mobility barriers are the potential costs incurred by a firm in one strategic group that wishes to reposition itself into another strategic group.   Thus, mobility barriers provide a deterrence to firms attempting to shift their strategic position within an industry.   These mobility barriers also characterize the competitive advantage of firms within a strategic group over firms outside the group.   The existence of strategic groups might offer an explanation for differing levels of firm performance (independent of size) within an industry. The evidence is, however, weak at best.

The concept of strategic groups and mobility barriers is illustrated by the com-

---

[27]Hunt, M. S., "Competition in the Major Home Appliance Industry, 1960–1970. "Unpublished doctoral dissertation, Harvard University, 1972. See also H. H. Newman, "Strategic Groups and the Structure Performance Relationship: A Study with Respect to the Chemical Process Industries." Unpublished doctoral dissertation, Harvard University, 1973.

[28]Porter, Michael E., "The Structure Within Industries and Companies' Performance," *Review of Economics and Statistics,* 61, May 1979, pp. 214–227.

[29]Caves Richard E. and Michael E. Porter, "From Entry Barriers to Mobility Barriers: Conjectural Decisions and Contrived Deterrence to New Competition," *Quarterly Journal of Economics,* 91, May 1977, pp. 241–262.

petitive structure of the U.S. Chain Saw Industry in 1976 (Exhibit 2–6).[30]   In this industry there were three strategic groups.   Stihl, Jonsereds, Solo, Husqvarna, and Skil compete against each other in the professional group selling chain saws to professionals who cut trees and work with wood.   The strategies of the five firms in this group emphasize a high quality brand image and sales through dealers.   The branded mass market group, consisting of Homelite, McCulloch, and Skil, sell branded products with a modest quality image, but lower price through mass merchants, to woodworking hobbyists.   The final group includes firms whose strategy is to manufacture private label, low cost chain saws for people with an occasional need for them.   Note that only Skil attempts to compete in more than one strategic group.

To identify the mobility barriers within an offering relationship space (as we said earlier, much of the existing work in this area ignores timing issues, and represents resource allocation by size, often measured as sales) one has to look at industry dynamics.   The movement (and potential movement) of the various competitors has to be studied to discover the dimensions on which movement did occur and those on which it did not.   While a dimension on which shifts take place cannot be identified

EXHIBIT 2–6 Illustration of Strategic Groups—U.S. Chain Saw Industry (1976)

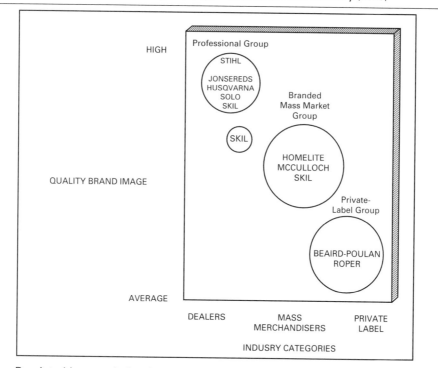

[30]Porter, Michael, *op. cit.,* 1980.

as a mobility barrier, an unambiguous interpretation cannot be made for the others: movement may not occur because there is no change in the status quo. For example, Stihl may not have thought of adding an offering of high quality, but private label, through upscale department stores like Nordstrom. Seeing no change makes us ask, "Why did they not move?," to determine if the cause is inertia or if that dimension is indeed a mobility barrier. Easy movement on a strategic dimension implies that this dimension is unlikely to be a mobility barrier.

Generic Strategies. Based on observations of the nature of strategic groups in many industries, Porter concluded that two types of strategic groups exist in most industries. One group (the D–group) contains firms that emphasize marketing to develop highly differentiated products (types of offering) and the second group of firms provides undifferentiated product (U–group), often forsaking marketing and providing private labels for other firms (different forms of relationships), and emphasizes manufacturing to minimize costs. For sustainable competitive advantages, the firms in the D–group emphasize a customer loyalty advantages whereas firms in the U–group emphasize a cost advantage. Porter expanded these two basic orientations to the four generic strategies (described in Exhibit 2–7 and illustrated in Exhibit 2–8), by considering a second dimension—breadth of focus. This second dimension separates firms with differentiation costs or cost leadership strategies targeted at broad markets as opposed to the use of their strategies to focus on narrow segments.

Porter also emphasizes that competition and the changing environment are attempting to break down the protective mobility barriers around each type of strategic group. The competitive advantage possessed by firms pursuing each of the generic strategies and the potential threats to these advantages are summarized in Exhibit 2–7.

EXHIBIT 2–7 Competitive Advantages and Threats for Each Generic Strategy

Generic Strategy	Basis of Advantage	Competitive Threats
Cost Leadership	High market share; Sustained capital investment	Innovation makes capital investments obsolete
	Process engineering skills needs because of cost focus	Inattention to changing market
	Low-cost distribution	Narrowing of price differential with a differentiated product
Differentiation	Strong marketing	Excessive differential with a cost-oriented product
	Product engineering	Need for differentiations benefit disappears
	Channel cooperation Creativity	Imitation by competitors
Focus	See above Specialized expertise	Cost differential with broad scope cost-leader widens
	Relationships	Submarkets within focus market arise

EXHIBIT 2–8 Porter's Four Generic Strategies

	Strategic Orientation	
Broad	Differentiation	Cost Leadership
Narrow	Focus Differentiation	Focus Cost Leadership

Focus (row label spanning Broad/Narrow)

Criticism of Porter's Generic Strategies. The concepts of strategic groups, mobility barriers, and generic strategies redirected the focus of IO theory from an industry level to a firm level (or at least a strategic group level). This "new look" in IO research has also added a dynamism by indicating generic methods that firms use to construct mobility barriers around their position. Through their conduct in constructing these mobility barriers, they change the nature of industry structure, defend their position against competition, and improve their performance.

While Porter's observations and conclusions concerning strategies describe the strategies pursued in various industries, they may be of limited use in prescribing how a firm should develop an advantage over its competition. The development of D–groups and U–groups within an industry reflects the outcome of a competitive process in which each firm has made a sequence of decisions directed toward establishing a competitive advantage and maximizing return to shareholders. It is unlikely that each of these decisions concerning R&D projects, marketing programs, and production capabilities can be characterized simply as differentiation–oriented or cost–oriented. As Day indicates

> In reality, the presumed choice between reducing cost versus building in more value to customers is seldom so clear-cut as the generic competitive strategies would suggest. Indeed most strategies are a balanced mix of the generic alternatives.[31]

In the Appendix an empirical study that bears on this issue is described.[32] This study suggests that low cost and high product quality (differentiation) are not mutually exclusive strategic directions. These approaches are, in fact, interrelated. High quality can actually reduce costs.

Rumelt has emphasized that dichotomizing generic strategies into cost leadership and product differentiation may mask the variety of options available to firms as they seek a competitive advantage

> In Caves' and Porter's view, industries can be broken into groups of firms that exhibit distinct characteristics. Mobility barriers both define these groups and are reinforced by

---

[31]Day, George, *Strategic Markets Planning,* St. Paul, MN, West Publishing, 1984, p. 118.

[32]Phillips, Lynn, D. R. Chang, and Robert D. Buzzell, "Product Quality, Cost Position, and Business Performance: A Test of Some Key Hypotheses," *Journal of Marketing,* 47, Spring, 1983.

the strategic activities of group members. The group concept is frequently all that is needed, but there is no theoretical reason to limit mobility barriers to groups of firms. I shall, therefore, use the term isolating phenomena which limit the ex post equilibration of rents among firms.[33]

The concept of isolating mechanisms emphasizes each individual firm's, not just each strategic groups', attempts to isolate itself from competition using a variety of potentially competitive advantages. Whereas some groups of firms using similar bases of competitive advantages may arise at a point in time, each firm within the group is continually attempting to isolate itself from other members of its group using all mechanisms at its disposal.

FORMAL GAME THEORY

The ability to sustain a particular advantage with a strategy depends not only on how the market itself develops but also on how competitors respond to these market changes. Thus, both models of the evolution of competition action and strategy development are needed to assess the nature of sustainable advantages. Formal game theory (which often underlies much of the analysis also found in Industrial Organization economics) offers a formal, analytical set of models of competitive behavior.

THE INTERACTION BETWEEN MARKET EVOLUTION AND COMPETITIVE ACTION

As we have suggested, any assessment of sustainable competitive advantage must consider the impact of market changes and competitor responses. However, this simple principle has been largely ignored by many writers in marketing and management strategy.

In marketing there has been a tendency either to ignore or at least to underestimate the nature of possible competitor reactions.[34] For instance, it might have been appropriate for the railroads to have recognized that they were in the "transportation" business and to consider investing in the newly emerging airlines.

Recent writers in the strategy and business policy area, particularly some economists, have made the error of assuming very naive models of market evolution against which to judge various competitor strategies.[35]

---

[33]Rumelt, R. P., "Evaluation of Strategy: Theory and Models," *In* D. E. Schendel and C. W. Hofer, *Strategic Management: A New View of Business Policy and Planning,* Boston, Little Brown 1979, p. 18. See also R. P. Rumelt, "Towards a Strategic Theory of the Firm," *Proceedings of Conference on 'Non-Traditional' Approaches to Policy Research,"* Graduate School of Business, University of Southern California, November 1981, pp. 12–13.

[34]Levitt, Theodore, "Marketing Myopia," *Harvard Business Review,* 38, July–August, 1960, pp. 26–34.

[35]For example, Michael Porter, *Competitive Strategy,* New York, Free Press, 1980. In a more recent book, *Competitive Advantage,* New York, Free Press, 1985, Porter recognizes this uncertainty in market evolution when discussing forecasting approaches as scenario development. He does not, however, consider the extent to which the increased degree of uncertainty about market evolution might question the appropriateness of the basic economic analysis he presented earlier in the book.

One can criticize approaches that focus only on market evolution or competitive strategy development as being overly simplistic. However, this focus on only one aspect of market dynamics is almost inevitable because market evolution and competitive response are highly interactive and occur simultaneously. Because of this simultaneity and interactivity, we confront a "chicken and egg" problem when attempting to assign causality.

Market evolution, marketing strategy, and competitive response are complex. To understand and communicate these issues, one must attempt to develop simplified models. As long as the simplified models focus on the essential issues, the models can provide valuable insights.

This chapter considers the nature of potential competition strategies within an evolving market domain. In so doing, there is a potential problem in underestimating the effects of interaction. Competitor actions often may be an essential precursor to certain forms of market evolution. Both market and technology evolution in the broad sense are probably better seen as external events which both shape and prescribe the competitive arena. The notion of technology-led innovation, although often inevitably linked to the actions of research and development groups within individual competitor firms, does not focus our attention directly on the essence of competitive behavior. Such behavior relates both to the nature of competition and the arena in which it takes place.

MODELING COMPETITIVE BEHAVIOR

Any investigation of the nature of competitive strategies requires four basic definitions:

1. The nature of the area in which the competitive activity takes place. From our perspective, this arena is the offerings-relationship space (or the product-market space).

2. The rules which govern the behavior of the participants.

3. The competitive behavior options available. (When these consist of a sequence of actions through time, or over a number of "plays," in game theory they are often referred to as strategies.)

4. The payoffs or outcomes that accrue to the competitors as a function of their competitive interaction.

There are two basic approaches to understanding the evolution of competitive behavior: (1) examining complex cases, and (2) developing simple, constrained models of competitive interactions. Many marketing writers begin with complex case studies to develop an understanding of the strategy development process in actual firms. This approach enables one to "borrow experience"[36] from firms that have encountered similar situations. However, by drawing an analogy from a specific situation, one must assume that all relevant information is correctly recorded and that unrecorded information does not provide important insights.

---

[36]Huff, A. S., "Industry Influences on Strategy Reformulation," *Strategic Management Journal,* 3, 1982, pp. 119–131.

The second approach begins by thoroughly specifying a simple model and gradually increasing the complexity of this model. In this chapter we have adopted the second approach. Each model or analogy has been used to uncover key insights, but we have also considered the limitations of various analogies used by business people to simplify the complex nature of strategic decision making.

Before we proceed, we need to discuss two basic issues remaining from the simplest methods to the most complex analogies: the notion of *rational competition* and the distinction between *understanding the competitive situation* and *prescribing specific action* for a particular competitor.

Rational Competition

Rationality plays an important role, particularly in game-theory models of competitive behavior. Rationality implies a link between actions and intentions but not common intentions among competitors. To misquote a former British Prime Minister: "One man's irrationality is another man's rationality."

Models describing competitive activity are designed to allow us to understand the behavior of "free" economic agents. Therefore, these models start with an assumption of "weak" rationality—the agents will take actions which are consistent with their long-term objectives. The models also assume a more extreme form of rationality—the intentions of the agents can be expressed in a number of economic measures of outcome states such as profit, sales, growth, or market share objectives.

Rational Expectations.[37]
The strongest assumption of rationality involves the concept of "rational expectations." This concept simply means that competitors are assumed to be as smart as the firm developing a marketing strategy. Thus, if competitors have access to the same information as the firm developing a strategy, *ceteris paribus* (all things being equal), they would make the same strategic decisions, on average. This concept of "rational expectations" has some interesting implications concerning the ability of a firm to develop a sustainable competitive advantage and the usefulness of strategic principles.

In the extreme, rational expectations along with identical competitors in all other aspects means that sustainable advantages cannot be achieved. This is because all the competitors will respond similarly and so no one competitor will have a relative advantage over the others. Failure by a competitor to make the appropriate move often implies that the competitor is not wise enough to select among the alternative strategies available—a contradiction of the rational expectations.

Rational expectations also suggests that principles of strategic decision-making espoused in books and articles have only limited usefulness in providing a competitive advantage. Since these principles are available to all competitors, they offer no opportunity for one competitor to develop an advantage. For example, when a well-known

---

[37]The concept of rational expectations was introduced by J. F. Muth, "Rational Expectations and the Theory of Price Movements," *Econometrica,* July 29, 1961, pp. 315–353 and reviewed by H. A. Simon, "Rational Decision Making in Business Organizations," *American Economic Review,* September, 1979.

strategist writes a book emphasizing that high market share and subsequent low relative cost is the key to profitability, this information will be appropriately acted on by all firms. No one firm will be able to exploit this insight if one assumes rational expectations. However, by not using such an insight (i.e., not being in accordance with the principle of rational expectations), one could hand advantage over to a competitor.

Validity of Rationality Assumptions.   In the assumption of "weak" rationality, it is reasonable to assume that firms attempt to achieve long-term objectives. In a competitive environment, firms that do not undertake actions consistent with long-term objectives eventually will be driven from the market. For example, executives who make decisions based on their own self-interest rather than the stockholders' are susceptible to corporate raiders and hostile takeovers.[38]

The stronger assumption of rationality embodied in the rational expectations principle indicates that attempts to develop a sustainable competitive advantage are futile. However, the rational expectations principle emphasizes that when competitors have access to *the same information*, they will reach the same decisions, *on average*. In most situations, there are only a few competitors that deal with highly complex situations. It is unlikely that individuals in different organizations will attend to the same information and process it in the same manner. In other words, it is very unusual for the *ceteris paribus* situation to occur. Consequently, individual opportunities to achieve a competitive advantage will exist; however, as these opportunities are successfully exploited, they become more evident to competitors who react to reduce the long-term effect of the advantage.[39]

Prescription Versus Description

For some of the models discussed in this chapter, there is potential confusion over the extent to which descriptions of competitive behavior can be used to provide normative statements about how firms should act in competitive markets.[40] By observing competitive activity at one point in time, one is not aware of the prior sequence of actions that resulted in the present condition. Thus, using strategies that are effective in present conditions may not be effective at a different stage of the competitive process.[41]

---

[38]This issue is referred to as a principal-agent problem in the economics literature. See M. C. Jensen and W. H. Meckling, "The Theory of the Firm: Managerial Behavior, Agency Costs and Ownership Structure," *Journal of Financial Economics,* October 1976, pp. 305–60.

[39]Moorthy, K. S., "Using Game Theory to Model Competition," *Journal of Marketing Research,* 22, August, 1985, pp. 262–82.

[40]Kadane, Joseph B. and Patrick D. Larkey, "Subjective Probability and the Theory of Games," *Management Science,* 28, February 1982, pp. 113–20; "Reply to Professor Harsany," *Management Science,* 28, February 1982, p. 124; "The Confusion of Is and Ought in Games Theoretic Contexts," *Management Science,* 29, December, 1983, pp. 1365–79, J. C. Harsany, "Subjective Probability and the Theory of Games: Comments on Kadane and Larkey's Paper," *Management Science,* 28, February, 1982, pp. 124–125; "Rejoinder to Professor Kadane and Larkey," *Management Science,* 28, February, 1982, pp. 124–124; Martin Shubik, "Comment on 'The Confusion of Is and Ought in Game Theoretic Contexts,'" *Management Science,* 29, December, 1983, pp. 1380–1383.

[41]Kadane and Larkey, *ibid.*

Context thus plays a key role in whether a particular strategy results in a competitive advantage.

GAME THEORY MODELS OF COMPETITION

Macroeconomic theory is based on an assumption of perfectly competitive markets—markets in which a large number of small firms having complete information sell homogeneous products so that the actions of an individual firm have no effect on the market or the actions of other firms in the market.   In contrast, oligopoly theory posits a competitive situation with markets composed of interdependent firms in which the actions of each firm affect the actions of other firms in the market. Strategically, this interdependency is the essence of competition.   Noncooperative game theory is the dominant paradigm used by economists to study competitive behavior in oligopolistic markets.

Structure of Game Theory Models

A game is characterized by a set of rules[42] which describe (1) the number of firms competing against each other, (2) the set of actions that each firm can take at each point in time, (3) the profits that each firm realizes for each set of competitive actions—do these actions occur simultaneously or does one firm move first?—and (4) the nature of information about competitive activity—who knows what, when?
The following game illustrates the nature of these rules:

Two airlines, United Airlines and Air France, are the only competitors on the Paris-to-Chicago route.   Each airline has two actions concerning price—charge $600 or $900 per round trip ticket.   If both airlines charge $600, say they will both make an annual profit of $40,000.   If they both charge $900, they will both realize an annual profit of $50,000. However, if one firm charges $600 and the other charges $900, the lower-priced firm will earn $65,000 and the higher-priced firm will earn only $20,000 (see Exhibit 2–9). Both United and Air France have full information about the potential actions and payoffs of their competitor.   Finally, at the beginning of each month, both airlines establish a price simultaneously (without knowing each other's price) and maintain that price for the entire month.

Equilibrium Conditions

Given the competitive situation described in Exhibit 2–9, what price will United and Air France charge for the Paris-to-Chicago route? From a noncooperative game theory perspective, the Nash equilibrium indicates how rational firms will compete in such conditions.   This equilibrium is defined as the strategy (sequences of moves) for each firm that will result in neither firm being willing to change its strategy *unilaterally*.

[42]Dolan, Robert J., "Models of Competition: A Review of Theory and Empirical Findings," *Review of Marketing, In* B. M. Enis and K. J. Roering, (eds.), Chicago: American Marketing Association, 1981, pp. 224–34

EXHIBIT 2–9   Paris–Chicago Airline Price Game

Price		$600	$900
Air France	$600	◨ $40K, $40K	○ $65K, $20K
United	$900	▢ $20K, $65K	$50K, $50K

K → × 1000.
First entry in each cell refers to Air France's payoff; the second entry, United's payoff.

Nash Equilibrium.   In the airline example, clearly both firms are better off if they both establish a fare of $900. But if United thinks that Air France will charge $600, United will make more profits by pricing at $600 also. The $900 price level for each firm is not a Nash equilibrium because, at $900, each firm has an incentive to *unilaterally* lower its price to $600. However, the $600 price level is a Nash equilibrium because neither would want to unilaterally raise its price to $900.

A simple approach to finding a Nash equilibrium solution for such a two-player game is:

1. Construct a payoff table as in Exhibit 2–9.
2. Take Air France's point of view first. Find the price (strategy) that Air France should choose if it knew that United would choose a price of $600. Mark the cell of this choice by a circle.
3. Repeat step 2 for an assumed United price of $900. Again mark the cell of this choice by a circle.
4. Now take United's point of view. Find the price that United should choose assuming that Air France would choose $600. Mark the cell of this choice with a square.
5. Repeat step 4, for an assumed Air France price of $900. Again mark the cell of this choice by a square.
6. To find a Nash equilibrium solution, look for the cell with both a circle and a square marking it.

You may ask, why do not United and Air France each assume that their competitor is smart enough to know that cut–throat prices will hurt both of them, and each set a price of $900 and both make more money? (This example is a form of the classical prisoner's dilemma—both stand to benefit through cooperation, but each has an incentive to deviate from this strategy if unsure of the other, and if the other follows a different strategy.) Without a binding agreement (collusion), how can Air France trust United not to act in its own self-interest and drop its price to $600 for a month?

The notion of cooperating could be incorporated in the game by restricting the pricing options to $900 (as the result of a binding agreement which may be illegal) or adjusting the payoffs to reflect "good judgment." However, the model of this competitive situation does not incorporate these elements.

Multiple Equilibria. In some models of competitive situations there are multiple equilibria. Consider the following hypothetical example:

Michelin has the only automobile tire manufacturing facility in Zambia. Because of its monopolistic position, say the NPV (net present value) of Michelin's Zambia operation is 160 million francs. Pirelli is considering building a plant and entering the market. If Pirelli enters the Zambian market, Michelin can either "acquiesce" and share the market or "fight" for market share by reducing prices and increasing advertising. If Michelin acquiesces, Michelin will realize a NPV of 108 million francs and Pirelli will realize a NPV of 72 million francs. However, if Michelin fights, the anticipated NPV for Michelin is 72 million francs and Pirelli will have a 0 NPV. If Pirelli does not build the plant in Zambia, it will make a capital investment in an Italian factory that will result in an NPV of 36 million francs.

This market entry[43] situation is illustrated in Exhibit 2–10. In this competitive

EXHIBIT 2–10   Michelin Versus Pirelli Example

[43]For an in-depth treatment, please see: A. Dixit, "The Role of Investment in Entry Deterrence," _Economic Journal,_ 90, 1981, pp. 95–106; B. Eaton and R. Lipsey, "Exit Barriers Are Entry Barriers: The Durability of Capital as a Barrier to Entry," _The Bell Journal of Economics,_ 11, 1980, pp. 721–729; "Capital, Commitment and Entry Equilibrium," _The Bell Journal of Economics,_ 12, 1981, pp. 593–604.

model, the parties make sequential moves. First, Pirelli decides to enter or not. Then, Michelin decides to fight or acquiesce. The payoffs indicate that Pirelli should enter, if it is assured that Michelin will not respond vigorously; however, if Michelin's response is to fight, then Pirelli should not enter the Zambia market. From Michelin's perspective, it would be best if Pirelli did not enter; however, if Pirelli enters, Michelin would make more profit if it acquiesced rather than responded vigorously.

This game has the following two equilibria:

Equilibrium	Pirelli Strategy	Michelin Strategy
1	Do not enter	Fight, if entry undertaken
2	Enter	Acquiesce, if entry made

How will this competitive situation evolve?   Clearly, the concept of equilibrium does not provide an answer because there are two possibilities.   Each equilibrium favors one of the competitors.   However, the second equilibrium seems to be more reasonable.   The first equilibrium is supported by a potentially spurious threat—Michelin threatens to fight but actually will be motivated to acquiesce if Pirelli enters the Zambia market.   Even though game theorists have devoted considerable effort to evaluating multiple equilibria, the issue of determining a unique solution has not been resolved.[44]

SOME GENERALIZATIONS

Please note that the treatment of game theory presented here is *rudimentary.*   We have provided some generalizations from this field, but these are very limited, compared to offerings in this field.[45]   We have provided game theory as a way to stimulate thinking about it and because it is helpful in making a choice among alternatives.   For example, the analysis of optimal defensive strategies (discussed in Chapter 11, Timing) in marketing has used game theory as its analytical core.   It has also been used for competitive product positioning (discussed in Chapter 13, Strategic Assessment of Offerings), and also in analyzing the types of channel arrangements that are optimal (discussed in Chapter 5, Relationships with Channels of Distribution).

Examples of two different types of games, simultaneous and sequential, were discussed earlier.   The United–Air France game is an example of a simultaneous game, that between Michelin and Pirelli of a sequential one.   In sequential games, the decisions of the various players (for simplicity we refer to two–person examples) are

[44]The interested reader is referred to several excellent books in this area. For example: T. Schelling, *The Strategy of Conflict,* Cambridge, MA, Harvard University Press, 1960; and M. Shubik, *Game Theory in the Social Sciences,* Cambridge, MA, MIT Press, 1982. For a more applied and a nonmathematical exposition to A. K. Dixit and B. J. Nalebuff, *Thinking Strategically,* New York, W. W. Norton, 1991.

[45]For more details please see R. Axelrod, *The Evolution of Cooperation,* New York, Basic Books, 1984.

made temporally apart. The first mover does so without knowing what the other player has done (though such moves should be anticipated), whereas the second player knows the first one's moves. In simultaneous games, both act at the same time without knowledge of the other's actions. However, they do know that others are playing and that the others know that others are playing and so on. First, we present some general rules regarding simultaneous games, then about sequential games, and then about sequential games that are repeated.

Simultaneous Games

The first step in analyzing a simultaneous game is to set up a payoff table (Exhibit 2–9). This implies knowledge of the available alternatives (or strategies) and their interactive payoffs to all parties. Then, if any player has a dominant strategy, this will be that player's best choice. A dominant strategy for a player is the alternative which is best for that player no matter which alternative is chosen by the other players.

If such a strategy exists, then the choice is obvious. If not, the solution process starts at the other end—with dominated strategies. A dominated strategy is one that is worse than another for at least one alternative of the other player, and not better for all the other alternatives. Such dominated strategies should be eliminated from consideration. Again the payoff table should be checked to see if there is a dominant strategy. If one exists, then it is the one of choice.

If even after all the dominated strategies (for all players) have been eliminated, then it means that the game is one of, "it depends on . . ." quality. The solution now is to find an equilibrium for the game. The equilibrium solution is not necessarily the one that is best for all parties. But, it does capture the logic that once in that solution there is no other solution that will remain stable. A Nash equilibrium solution was described in the United–Air France example.

In some instances, there can be more than one equilibrium or multiple equilibria. If these equilibria lead to outcomes to which a player is completely indifferent, then it does not matter what that player chooses—and the player may be assumed (or advised) to choose randomly from among these alternatives, using a probability distribution so as to make the others indifferent about their alternatives' respective outcomes.

Sequential Games

The first step in analyzing a sequential game is to draw a decision tree (Exhibit 2–10). Obviously, this requires knowledge of all the players' options (or strategies) and the conditional payoffs of all the strategy combinations for all time periods of the game. The principle underlying the solution of this game is to start from the outcomes and reason backward to the best set of moves.

It has been established in the literature that for any game with a finite number of moves a best strategy (or solution) always exists, though finding it is sometimes not easy. Further, for the backward-reasoning solution procedure to work, all the earlier moves must be observable to the competitors and these moves should be irreversible.

Repeated Simultaneous Games

When a simultaneous game is repeated, it provides an opportunity for players to signal via actions or statements what their responses and intentions are in following periods to actions in a particular period by the other players.   The signals and actions that are used to "alter the beliefs and actions of others" so as to benefit a player are that player's *strategy moves*.   Such a move is preemptive and signals a commitment to a course of action.   These moves could be to specify a response rule.   That is, a rule that states what response will follow the other players' particular actions.   This, if stated before the other players' move, is preemptive and thus also a strategic move, just as much as a preemptive action would be.   (However, note that following an equilibrium strategy is what would be expected by the others, and thus it possesses no extra information and is therefore not termed a strategic move.)

Preemptive action can be used to turn simultaneous games into sequential games. Of course, this move must be observable to all the other players and be irreversible.   In the United–Air France game, one of them could decide on a price of $900 before the other and make this decision widely known.   This is a nonequilibrium strategy and would be a strategic move.   It would convert the game into a sequential game as opposed to a simultaneous, prisoners' dilemma game.   Therefore, the solution would be different.

How should strategic moves be chosen in order to get the other players to cooperate (in a sense) so that the desired result is obtained for the "first-mover" for strategic move maker?   This is a key question of considerable relevance to marketing, in getting, for example,   competitors to stop promotions if they are harmful.   A strategy that has been found to be successful in computer tournaments is called the *tit-for-tat* rule.   It calls for the choice of "cooperative" solutions as the first move and then mimics the other players' actions, thus punishing them for not cooperating if they do not do so.   However, as pointed out by Dixit and Nalebuff,[46] even slight mistakes and miscalculations "echo" through this rule and it is said to be a flawed strategy.

An alternative to *tit-for-tat* is:

1. Start by cooperating.
2. Continue to cooperate.
3. Track defections (from the cooperative solution) by the others while you have cooperated.
4. If this rule fails the test for acceptable defection, then go back to tit-for-tat.

The rules for acceptability of the percentage of defections is made based on the other players' actions on the first round; and short-, medium-, and long-term.   They are:

First round:	A defection in this round is not acceptable.
Short-term: (3 moves)	If out of three moves, two are defections, then it is not acceptable.
Medium-term: (20 moves)	More than three defections out of 20 moves is not acceptable.

[46]This rule is from Dixit and Nalebuff, *op. cit,* pp. 113–114.

Long-term: Five out of 100 defections is not acceptable.
(100 moves)

A first cooperative move (for a stated intention to do so), while deviating from an equilibrium solution may still not result in cooperation. One of the reasons for this is perhaps disbelief that the first mover intends to continue to cooperate (the irreversibility criterion). Sometimes, strategic moves are in the form of stated contingent threats or promises or *response rules*. Again, to be effective these must be credible.

How can credibility be achieved? Again, from Dixit and Nalebuff (see Footnote 46), we provide eight "devices" for attaining credibility.

1. Building a reputation and using it.
2. Entering into contracts.
3. Cutting off communication.
4. Burning bridges.
5. Leaving the outcome to chance.
6. Moving in small steps.
7. Using teamwork.
8. Employing third-party negotiators.

Using one or several of these may be useful in building commitment. As is discussed later, commitment or trust are key in building marketing relationships, and as such, these devices are useful. In particular, reputation building (for obvious reasons), burning bridges (e.g. with former customers to serve a new set of customers), using teamwork (e.g., by forming distributor joint-ventures), and employing third-party negotiators (for conflict resolution) are of interest in marketing strategy.

Normative and Descriptive Implications of Game Theory Models

Do the results of game theory models show how firms should act in competitive situations? Do the models describe the evolution of competitive interactions in the real world? These questions have spawned a lively debate among management scientists concerning the usefulness of game theory models (see Footnote 40). Kadane and Larkey (see Footnote 41) suggest that game theory models are conditionally normative and conditionally descriptive. The results of these models indicate how firms should behave given a set of assumptions about the alternatives, the payoffs, and the properties of an "optimal" solution (the equilibrium). Similarly, game theory results only describe the evolution of competitive strategy, given a specific set of assumptions.

The seemingly unrealistic and simplistic nature of the competitive reactions incorporated in game theory models and the nature of the equilibrium concept have led some marketing strategists to question the managerial relevance of these models (see Footnote 42). However, all models involve simplifying assumptions. The issue is whether these models provide some insight into the competitive process.

Consider the two examples presented. The airline pricing model describes competitive behavior in the airline industry as well as in other industries. Airlines offer discounts, automobile manufacturers offer reduced interest rates, and consumer packaged goods companies offer promotions to consumers and to retailers even though these financial incentives are matched by competitors. By offering these incentives, the profit of all competitors is reduced. However, if one did not follow the others, its profit might be even more reduced.

The market entry model emphasizes that entry can only be deterred by changing the payoffs. Specifically, the incumbent (Michelin) must reconstruct its payoffs so it has an incentive to fight if Pirelli enters. Michelin must make some defensive moves such as making an investment in "excess capacity," creating an exit barrier, or offering proliferation of products to establish a credible, rather than the spurious threat that it will be forced to "fight" if Pirelli enters (see Footnote 43).

While game-theory models are highly structured, including a set of simplifying assumptions, these models underpin any attempt to apply economic analysis to issues of competition among a limited number of firms. To use these models the following critical questions must be answered.

1. What specific strategies can be undertaken?
2. What will be the outcome relative to the different sets of strategies?
3. What information do the parties possess about each other?
4. What will be the sequence of competitive actions and reactions?

These questions have been studied by experts in Industrial Organization Economics to which we turn for guidance in marketing strategy.

CONCLUSION

Each of the analogies presented can be examined from: (1) the particular key elements of the competitive situation highlighted, (2) the types of generic competitive strategy that can be derived from it, and (3) the key limitations of the particular approach.

Key Elements

The strategic groups and mobility barriers in the Industrial Organization Economics' approach recognizes the critical asymmetries among competing firms. It identifies three methods by which firms can isolate themselves from competition: (1) differentiation, (2) cost efficiency, and (3) collusion (although this issue has generally been ignored). The developments within the IO paradigm have focused on the nature and significance of various mechanisms for isolating the firm from its competition.

The sports game approach focuses on the relationship between any prior planning and the action in the game itself (including the degree of coordination among individual players), the interaction between competitive response within different time periods (play, game, season), the multiple routes to success, but the general evidence that it is necessary to compete on more than one dimension, and that success rapidly encourages imitation. Finally, we recognize within the sports game analogy the key role of "rules," and particularly changes in rules, as a means of influencing competitive strategies.

The military analogies raise the related issue of what happens in competitive situations when the rules themselves are neither well codified nor necessarily fully accepted, and there is no analogy to the referee in the sports game context. Perhaps most useful in competitive strategy is the focus on the balance between clarity and confusion in one's intentions and the general notion of signalling. It is important to avoid becoming overcommitted to a particular approach because one's intentions can be read unambiguously by the enemy; however, a sense of direction is required to maintain internal cohesion and morale. The military perspective also reinforces the multiple time periods of the sports game competitive analogy. In most military conflicts it is assumed that the problems can be overcome given enough resources and effort, but this degree of commitment could prove too much from a wider perspective; hence the old adage of winning the battle but losing the war.

The evolutionary ecology analogy focuses on scope with the distinction between specialists and generalists. The ecological approach also raises interesting questions about the form, level, and type of "organization" being considered. In particular, we need to recognize most markets as firms of organization in their own right, as those who have argued the "markets as networks" approach have done, and question how far we can justify an exclusive focus on the firm as the key organizations unit. Finally, the analogy directly raises the concern about the interaction between different units (species) and their evolving habitat. The marketplace, like the habitat, can become relatively unstable so it can both affect and be affected by the strategies of the individual firms.

Generic Competitor Strategies

Exhibit 2–11 summarizes not only the key elements that can be derived from each analogy, but also the related generic competitor strategies and key limitations of the particular analogy. In this exhibit we summarize the elements that correspond to our strategy framework of Exhibit 1–1 (p. 2) for each analogy. As we have suggested earlier, each of the analogies introduces a different dimension into our analysis of competitive behavior and each is also constrained by the actual limitations of the analogy or by the way in which it is commonly used. Various considerations and marketing strategy variables are summarized in Exhibit 2–12.

It is useful to identify the underlying choices in forms of competitive behavior that are not revealed in these various groups of generic strategies. One way of doing this is to recognize that we are merely attempting to answer the *where?* and *how?* of competitive response, and not the *why? when?* and *who?*

EXHIBIT 2-11   The Various Competitive Strategic Analogies

STRATEGY	KEY ELEMENTS	GENERIC STRATEGIES	KEY LIMITATIONS
Organizational Economics	Competition versus Collusion Isolating Mechanisms	Cost Competition Product Differentiation Strategic Group Competition (Inter- versus Intra-Group)	Interaction between Cost and Quality Nature of "Mixed" Strategies Stability of Groups
Sports Games	Planning and Coordination Importance of Time Impact of Rule Change	Offensive Defensive Imitative Innovative	Territorial Logic of the game Fixed Rules Degree of Control
Military	The Role of Signalling Direction vs. Surprise Multiple Time Periods	Direct Confrontation Flanking Guerrilla Avoidance	Focus on Conflict Importance of Terrain Focus on External Factors and Logistics
Evolutionary Ecology	Scope of Competition Forms of Organization Interaction between Firms and their Markets	Generalist Specialist Niche	Nature of Competition Level and Unit of Analysis Every Species had a "Niche"

In the set of generic strategies, competitors can choose the *where* and *how* of their response in terms of the scope of competition (generalist, specialist, niche), the nature of the competitive set (intra- or intergroup), the direction in which they act (cost competition or product differentiation), and the type of response (from confrontation/offensive-avoidance/defensive).

We have not left out the *why, when,* and *who* because they are unimportant, but because, to a considerable extent, the initial simplistic notion of generic competitor strategies does not cope with such questions. The *why* is the very problem of the purposeful nature of strategies that we have considered throughout. Indeed, one of the practical problems of an excessive use of generic strategies as a way of modeling competitive behavior is that there is little point in considering the detailed impact of various potential competitor moves if there is little or no reason in a particular situation to believe that they will actually take place.

The final questions of *when* and *who* are also outside the domain of a concept of generic strategies, but are present in some of the analogies that we have used. In both military practice and sports games, the nature and impact of opportunism has to be recognized: having the right person in position at the right time is clearly crucial.

Key Limitations

As we have suggested, each analogy is far from perfect. The limitations are as critical as the issues that are raised because they give us some sense of the bounds within which the analogy itself is likely to be useful. Extending it outside these bounds is likely to be counterproductive and misleading.

EXHIBIT 2-12   Analogies and Analysis With Respect to Marketing Strategy

	MILITARY	SPORTS	EVOLUTIONARY ECOLOGY	GAME THEORY
Outcomes	Victory. Reductions in enemy's strengths capabilities, collateral, damage	Victory/championship different levels Awards Honors	Survival of species Growth	Payoff/utility
Competitive Advantage	Superior weapons Superior training Superior terrain Superior size Information/ Intelligence Coordination Content	Superior equipment Superior training Superior coaching Trajectory	Superior adaptability	Information + Generic/unspecified advantage
Relationships	Enemies Allies Neutral countries	Competitors Spectators Organizers Sponsors Media	Flora/Fauna Predators/Preys/ Sycophants	Competitors
Offerings	Weapons of war Psychology aid	Type of plays (play assortment styles)	Camouflage	Generic
Timing	Surprise Preemptive (start to stop) Attack (start) Defense (respond) When to stop sequential	Practice Respond/react Preempt Surprise	Seasonal Tide into the tides of time	Simultaneous Sequential One period Multiperiod
Resource Allocation	Among weapons Across theaters Across services	Between offense and defense Among players and other staff Across equipment	Across different parts of the body	N/A
Context	Local threat/ Global threat Nuclear threat/ Conventional weapons Conventional threat/ Guerilla threat Availability of supplies Number of competitors/skills	At home/Away Regular season/ postseason Championships Regional/National/ International Rules	Weather Predators Nourishment Isolation/Density Immigration Rules	Competition Cooperation Leader-Follower Full Information Imperfect Information Rules

In practice the Organization Economics approach tends to neglect the interaction between cost and offering sophistication. We have already suggested that whereas the notion of "focus" within this analogy is an attempt to recognize this problem, it is only partially successful because it transfers a characteristic of any successful competitive strategy to one particular type only. We must further consider the extent to which we can reliably distinguish among the various forms of mixed strategies over time and the extent to which the strategic groups themselves remain stable.

Sports game analogies, or at least the ones most common currently, also have a number of key limitations. They focus on a simple territorial logic and a well-defined and unchanging set of rules. They also presume a high degree of control over the activities of individual players.

Military analogies inevitably focus on conflict, and, in their most popular manifestations, direct and immediate conflict. The physical terrain often occupies a critical role in the analysis of competitive dispositions and there is a focus on the nature of external factors, as opposed to internal organization and control, and supply logistics.

Finally, the limitations of analogies from evolutionary ecology are more concerning the questions that are not answered than those in which the answers are misleading. The nature of "competition" is both unclear and complex; there is confusion as to the level and appropriate unit of analysis, and the notion of "niche," which has become so current in much strategy writing, overlooks the fact that by definition every species has one.

To bring this chapter to a close, we quote this apt poem by Rupert Sargent Holland:

THE SECRETS OF OUR GARDEN*

You think it is only a garden,
With roses along the wall;
I will tell you the truth about it—
It isn't a garden at all!

It's really Robin Hood's forest,
And over by that big tree
Is that very place where fat Friar Tuck
Fought with Milley of Dee.

And back of the barn is the Cave
Where Rob Roy really hid;
On the other side is the treasure chest
That belonged to Captain Kidd.

That isn't the pond you see there;
It's an ocean deep and wide,

Where six-masted ships are waiting
To sail, on the rising tide.

Of course it looks like a garden,
It's all so sunny and clear
You'd be surprised if you really knew
The things that have happened here.

*R. S. Holland, "The Secrets of Our Garden." In Elizabeth Hough Sechrist, (ed.), Philadelphia, Macrae-Smith, 1946, p. 68.

Concept Questions

1. What are some alternative definitions of strategy?
2. (a.) What are some of the fields from which marketing strategy has and can draw knowledge?
   (b.) For each such field, what are the primary objectives of a strategy?
3. (a.) What is meant by generic strategies?
   (b.) For each field identified in response to 2a., what are the generic strategies?
4. What are the contributions to marketing strategy knowledge for each of the fields identified in response 2a?

Discussion Questions

1. What are the relative strengths and weaknesses of using analogies in developing a marketing strategy?
2. Combining ideas from formal game theory and generic military strategies, discuss when each of the various generic military strategies may be more relevant.
3. When should (a) niche strategy and (b) generalist strategy be pursued? What are their respective advantages and disadvantages?
4. What is the usefulness of mobility barriers in marketing strategy thinking?
5. What are the limitations of formal game theory in marketing strategy development and implementation?
6. Discuss the statement: marketing strategy is the choice of an option of actions and signals that "alter the beliefs and actions of others so as to benefit the strategist."

APPENDIX. EMPIRICAL STUDY OF COST, QUALITY, AND BUSINESS PERFORMANCE

The objective of strategic marketing decisions is to build a sustainable competitive advantage. By achieving such an advantage, the business unit earns a supernormal rate of return. Porter suggests that two approaches for achieving a sustainable competitive advantage are through:

> Cost leadership, and
> Product differentiation.

The cost leadership approach involves realizing higher margins relative to competition.

Product differentiation is based on reducing the level of competition by having customers perceive your product as unique. Under these circumstances, competitive activity is reduced because of high customer loyalty. Whereas there are many ways of differentiating a product, superior product quality is typically the basis used for product differentiation.

Many strategists feel that these two approaches are incompatible. A business must decide between these approaches and pursue one approach at the expense of the other. If a business adopts the quality (product differentiation) approach, it will use expensive components and customized production procedures, thus sacrificing product cost to increase quality. The cost leadership approach focuses on minimizing costs and perhaps sacrificing quality.

Phillips, Chang, and Buzzell (see Footnote 32) used the Profit Impact of Market Strategy (PIMS) database to make a detailed analysis of issues related to product quality. To examine these uses, they investigated the following viewpoints about quality, cost, and performance:

- Product quality has a direct impact on Return on Investment (ROI). The mechanism suggested for this direct effect is that product quality reduces competitive pressures enabling the business unit to maintain relatively high prices. By maintaining a differentiated position the unit will not be able to dominate a market, but this low relative share will not affect ROI.
- Product quality does not directly impact ROI. The effects of product quality are indirect. It attracts customers and thus increases market share. These increases in market share result in greater ROI through cost economics and their mechanisms.

In their model (a simplified model is shown in Exhibit 2–13), relative product quality affects relative direct costs (B_2), market share (B_3) and prices (B_4), and has a

Exhibit 2–13   A Simplified Version of the Phillips, Chang, and Buzzel Model

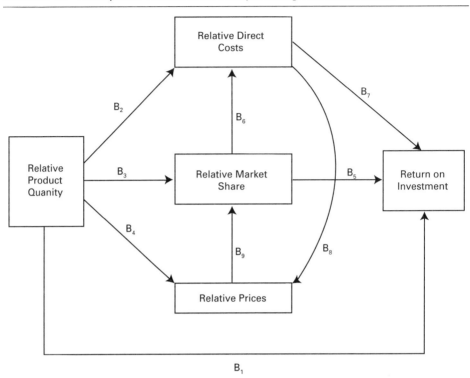

direct effect on return on investment (B_1).   Relative market share affects costs (B_6) and, because of experience curves, return on investment (B_5).   Costs affect ROI (B_7) and prices (B_8).   Finally, prices affect market share (B_9).

Based on the first viewpoint described, there will be a strong direct relationship between product quality and ROI.   Thus B_1 will be positive and statistically insignificant.   In addition, B_4 will be positive and significant because higher product quality leads to higher prices, but the higher prices may result in lower market share, so B_9 will be negative and significant.

The second viewpoint suggests a strong relationship between product quality and market share; thus B_3 will be positive and significant.   The improvement in market position will result in a direct positive effect on ROI, B_5, and an indirect effect through lowering costs, B_6.

Chapter 3
Forecasting Contextual Possibilities

INTRODUCTION

This chapter is an overview of forecasting methods as they apply to marketing strategy formulation, development and analysis. Strategy development without a forecast is like traveling without a map. The better the map, the greater the chance of getting to a desired destination. Even more important than the map, is the process of making it. This map-making process is essential to learning about the possibilities and how they might be realized. Much of forecasting deals in assumptions and knowledge of these assumptions is key to the development and to the implementation of a marketing strategy.

We discuss methods used to develop such a map of the future. We are confronted with two major problems as we begin to prepare the map. First, we do not have a "time machine". Second, we do not know all the possible directions of travel. In particular, for products at the cutting edge, for example, products made with high temperature superconducting materials, forecasting is extremely difficult. In marketing strategy development, it is critical in forecasting to be able to provide clues to the possible, that is, the directions on the map, and not just to focus on the probable. As Aristotle stated, "It is part of the probable that the improbable will happen." The forecaster (as the technical expert) should be able to provide the strategist(s) with a vivid learning experience of the possibilities. It is then up to the strategist to map out a plan for an organization from these possibilities, building it to exploit the right opportunities.

We assume there is either a forecasting expert available to perform the necessary specific technical tasks, or that the strategist has both the time and knowledge to perform them. This chapter is more about learning the possibilities and their attendant probabilities using forecasting tools and techniques than about forecasting.

WHAT NEEDS TO BE FORECAST?

Digital Electric Corporation (DEC), the second largest computer company in the world, announced a shift in an element of its marketing strategy.[1] It developed a new $20 million campaign called "Open Advantage." It planned to provide software and services that linked computers of any manufacturer. This strategy was expected to win it new customers and to compensate for the slowing of VAX (one of its major products) sales. Before choosing this direction, DEC clearly had to think about the consequences of the decision.

Fundamentally, the direct result of this decision would be from sales of this software package and from increased sales of new DEC hardware because of the availability of this software. This, in turn, would depend on the size of the market and on the share of this market that DEC would be able to obtain. The size of the market affects the number of competitors who would be attracted to it and the project margins that would be available. The size of the market, therefore, is affected by changes in the context (the environment) of the served market. So, in order to forecast the size of the opportunity, context needs to be forecast. A strategy's goal attainment is a function of its context (Chapter 1). If the key factors which determine a change in the context of a company's marketing strategy are identical, then change in this context may be easier to forecast, and a better understanding of opportunities for goal attainment obtained.

More concretely the questions may be: What is the size of the overall market? What level of sales can be obtained? What cash flow can be expected? What investments are necessary?, and so forth. To answer these questions the impact of competition, customers, and other relevant publics need to be explored.

Let us consider a simple example. Assume that the size (S) of a market has to be forecast. Also assume that this market has grown at a rate of $r\%$ a year, every year. To forecast the size of this market, a simple calculation, based on compound growth, may suffice. This calculation is valid under the assumption that this market's environment is constant (not necessarily static, but that any change occurs at the same rate as before).

The constant growth rate in the market may be a result of a constant rate of growth in the demand for computing. But this may not remain so. For example, a technological innovation may change computing needs. This change may lead to (a) gradual acceleration, or (b) gradual deceleration, or (c) a tremendous increase in both the size and nature of computing requirements, or (d) a tremendous decrease in the size of the market caused by the fundamentally different approach to computing.

Factors leading to (a) or (b) act gradually and in the absence of other factors, it is their balance that determines the net size or growth rate (as examples of the measure that is being forecast) of a market. Factors leading to (c) or (d) are metamorphical

[1]For more details please refer to McWilliams, "Open Systems' May Be DEC's 'Open Sesame,' " *Business Week,* June 24, 1991, pp. 101–103.

forces—those that cause major disruptions in prevailing market relationships, including perhaps a redefinition of the market. Exhibit 3–1 shows, schematically, these four types of forces.

Together the first two types of forces have a direct impact on the magnitude to be forecast. They are perhaps gradual in their impact. Thus, extrapolation methods may be more useful for them.

The other two types of forces impact indirectly, but possibly with greater effect. These forces deal with changing the nature of market relationships. For example, the invention of the transistor had a significant effect on the sales of vacuum tube electronic devices. This effect was caused not just by a gradual saturation of the market, or lengthened life of these devices, but because of a fundamental change in the status of these devices in daily life. The semiconductor revolution caused a profound change in customer behavior. There may be forces that favor such a metamorphosis in customer behavior and forces that oppose it. For example, the purchase of nuclear reactors to generate electricity by electric utility companies (power generating corporations) is helped by some factors and opposed by others. Yet, it was a fundamental shift in society's attitudes that changed utility company's buying behavior regarding gas-fired, coal-fired and hydroelectric generating equipment.

To forecast metamorphoses and their impact is not easy. Nor is it likely that methods that extrapolate statistically from the past will be helpful. More subjective methods that involve considerable deliberation and expertise are more useful.

Forecasting for marketing strategy formulation typically refers to prognostications on those environmental variables that are assumed to be outside of or not

EXHIBIT 3–1   Fundamental Forces in Forecasting

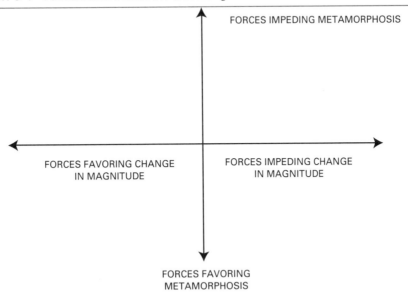

impacted to any major extent by a firm's own actions. However, good forecasts of such variables should be followed by a careful assessment of what it means in the local competitive arena. For example, DEC's "Open Advantage" campaign may make it attractive for more computer hardware manufacturers to enter the market, thereby increasing DEC's overall size. A technical forecast is like a newly-mined diamond. It takes careful cutting and polishing by an experienced diamond expert (strategist) to make it brilliant and increase its value.

Besides forecasting environmental variables, managers need to anticipate competitors' actions and their consequences. These are discussed in later chapters.

We now discuss the use of different methods of forecasting.

SPECIFIC TECHNIQUES

There are many techniques available for forecasting in this context and we review those available. Exhibit 3–2 is a selection guide to many of these techniques.

Before we discuss the specific techniques please note these caveats. First, we will not look in detail at techniques to design or forecast brand, or even new product performance, against a relatively stable, or static total market. This is itself an important area of development and application, but our concern is with forecasting changes in the environment, not brand or product variables per se.

Second, this review will be cursory: those who have taken courses in statistical analysis will have covered many of the techniques in much greater detail, as will many who have studied market research. This chapter merely assesses the application of various techniques in strategic marketing.

Third, in considering issues of environmental change, the techniques used involve either qualitative approaches and considerable expert judgment, or both. Often the phenomenon that we are attempting to forecast will not have frequent repetition and therefore any statistical approach has only limited application.

We start with naive and trend analysis, the methods that are best suited to the factors that have gradual and well-structured changes.

THE NAIVE METHODS

In using a naive method, the value of a variable in time period t is obtainable from that of period $t-1$. For example, the number of potential customers in period t (C_t) is exactly equal to that in period $t-1$ (C_{t-1}), or $C_t = C_{t-1}$. Perhaps the intent is to forecast the size of a market which is, for example, a multiple of the number of potential customers. Another naive formulation is to assume that $C_t = C_{t-1} + \alpha (C_{t-1} - C_{t-2})$, where α is an assumed constant.

If such a method is used, and its forecasting error is low, then it means that the planning horizon is short, otherwise these methods are not used, or there is little or no change in the factor being forecast. Variables such as these are rarely useful for strategic analysis. However, there might be an opportunity, if this relatively low change is true, to consider how such a process may be disturbed with advantage.

EXHIBIT 3–2   A Guide to Selecting an Appropriate Forecasting Method

Forecasting Method	Amount of Historical Data	Data Pattern	Forecast Horizon	Preparation Time	Personnel Background
Naive	1 or 2 observations	Best when data are stationary	Very short	Very short	Little sophistication
Regression Trend Models	10 to 20 minimum for seasonality	Trend and seasonality	Short	Short	Moderate sophistication
Simple Exponential Smoothing	5 to 10 observations to set weight	Data should be stationary	Short	Short	Little sophistication
Holt's Exponential Smoothing	10 to 15 observations to set both weights	Trend but no seasonality	Short	Short	Slight sophistication
Winters' Exponential Smoothing	At least 4 or 5 observations per season	Trend and seasonality	Short	Short	Moderate sophistication
Time-Series Decomposition	Enough to see 2 peaks and troughs	Can handle cyclical and seasonal patterns and may identify turning points	Short to medium	Short to moderate	Little sophistication
Box-Jenkins	Great deal—50 observations suggested	Must be stationary or transformed to stationary	Short, medium, or long	Long	High sophistication
Sales Force Composite	Little	No restriction	Short to medium	Short once sales force estimates are in	Little sophistication
Causal Regression Models	10 observations per independent variable	Can handle complex patterns	Short, medium, or long	Long development time, then shorter for implementation	Considerable sophistication
Customer Surveys	None	Not applicable	Medium to long	Long	Knowledge of survey methods
Jury of Executive Opinion	Little	No restriction	Short, medium, or long	Short	Little sophistication
Delphi Method	Little	No restriction	Long	Long	Little sophistication

From #10-266-801 Business Forecasting by Wilson & Keating, 1990, p. 359. Reprinted with permission from Richard D. Irwin, Inc.

When the relationship between a variable being forecast and its values in the past is more complicated than discussed, then more advanced trend analysis, for example, regression, simple exponential smoothing, Holt's exponential smoothing, Winters' exponential smoothing, time-series decomposition, or Box–Jenkins analysis, may be more suitable.

TREND ANALYSIS

The basic idea in trend analysis is to derive the underlying trend in a chronological sequence of numbers and to extend the trend into the future to generate a forecast.

Simple Univariate Trends

In the simple univariate trend, we consider merely a chronological sequence of numbers. In the simplest case, we can consider the possibility that the underlying trend is itself "monotonic," that is, always either increasing or decreasing. In such circumstances, we are estimating a straight line trend and the ruler is probably still the most common method! More complex approaches do exist, and the most commonly used is simple linear regression.

In univariate linear regression we generally assume that the relationship is captured by a "best fit" estimated trend line: in most cases the lowest sum of the squares of the deviations of the actual data points from the estimated ones. Although convenient, the impact of this definition has been widely discussed, both in the general statistical literature as well as in that relating specifically to marketing.[2] In particular, perhaps the most important issue is that of the potential bias towards "outliers": the use of a "squares" statistic means that an individual outlier may exert a significant effect on the estimation of the overall trend line, as opposed to the impact of using, say, an absolute deviation measure (Exhibit 3–3). Significant outliers could signal either opportunities or threats. Looking at only the regression results without viewing a plot of the data can hide these outliers and thus suppress potentially significant strategic information.

Sometimes the series of observations may not be linear and thus a linear regression is not appropriate. However, a transformation of the series may lead to a linear relationship. A major reason to attempt to develop a linear relationship is that whereas a linear relationship itself may be difficult to build, a nonlinear one is far more complex.

The most common form of variable transformation is to use natural logarithms. We use this approach in Chapter 6 to estimate cost–experience curves. In this situation we expect the relationship between unit cost and cumulative experience to be curvilinear, but by taking natural logarithms of the variables we convert this into a linear relationship.

The potential problem with the application of transformations, particularly logarithmic ones, is not that they do not often improve out trend estimate, but that they can

[2]A. S. Ehrenberg, Data Reduction, Chichester, England, Wiley, 1975.

EXHIBIT 3–3   Differential Impact of Outliers in Estimating Trend Lines (Ehrenberg)

With an exceptionally high or low value in a set of readings, how sensitive are

(i) the mean, median, and mode?
(ii) the mean deviation, standard deviation, variance, and range?

Discussion.

Consider two simple sets of 1,000 readings A and B:

A: 100 3's, 800 4's, 100 5's,

B: 100 3's, 799 4's, 100 5's, 1 1,000.

The "outlier" at 1,000 in B might be a measurement or recording error. These are often very dramatic and are important to spot and to eliminate from the main analysis.

The mean, median and mode of the two sets of data are

	A	B
Mean	4	5
Median	4	4
Mode	4	4

Only the mean is at all sensitive to the outlier. The single reading of 1,000 in Set B increased it by 25%, but even here the effect is not dramatic. Unless the means of other such data are generally very close to 4, one would probably not react to the value of 5 as implying an aberrant value.

The mean deviation, standard deviation, variance and range of the two sets are approximately

	A	B
Mean Deviation:	0.2	2
Standard Deviation:	0.4	3
Variance:	0.2	10
Range:	2	997

In terms of absolute increase, the standard deviation is a little more sensitive than the mean deviation. The variance is even more sensitive because the odd outlying value is *squared* before averaging, and thus becomes more dominant. The range is clearly too sensitive to act as a measure of "average" or typical scatter at all, but it is highly efficient for actually spotting outliers.

From: A.S. Ehrenberg, *Data Reduction*. Chichester, England, Wiley, 1975.

work too well. Logarithmic transformations have a lower bound at the unit value of the relevant variable. Mathematically, they can represent any situation in which a particular approach asymptotically to a particular value. However, in doing so, they also "undervalue" the impact of significant scale divergences from this asymptotic value and can appear to generate linear relationship solely because significant nonlinearities are "hidden" by the transformed values. Hence the statistical adage that just about any bivariate relation can be linear if we take natural logarithms of both variables!

Many applications of such trend analysis are based on short-time period data, but examples also exist in the application of such approaches to trend extrapolation in the case of technology or functional capability. A number of examples are given in Exhibit 3–4. These extrapolations or regression models could form part of a larger environmental forecast.

EXHIBIT 3–4   Examples of Trend Extrapolation

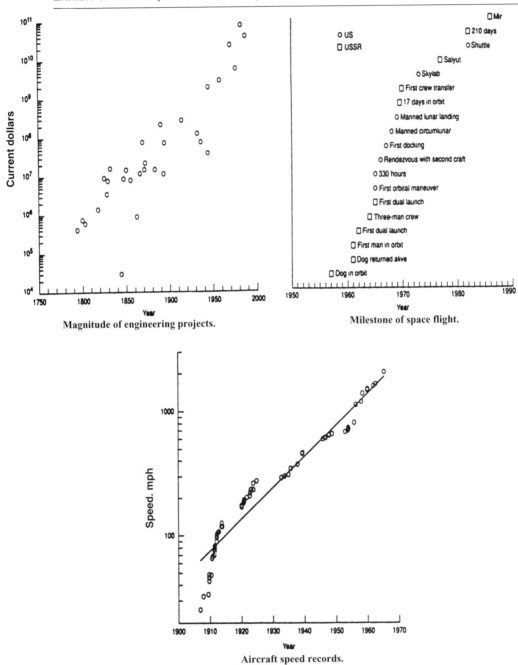

Magnitude of engineering projects.

Milestone of space flight.

Aircraft speed records.

From: Martino, J. P., *Technological Forecasting for Decision Making,* 3rd ed., New York, North Holland, 1993, pp. 80, 90, 91. Reproduced with permission of McGraw-Hill, Inc.

Smoothing Methods

Sometimes the data series has many short-term fluctuations, but a long-term trend. When such a data series represents the variable or factor being forecast, then these short-term fluctuations are smoothed out in order to develop a forecasting model. The key assumption is that these fluctuations are mere random variations from an otherwise smooth series. Once these fluctuations are smoothed out or suppressed, then an extrapolation of the modified series produces reasonable forecasts.

One problem with these methods is that they often fail to predict accurately peaks and valleys for short-term use. In strategic planning, they may hide the variable nature of this factor and prevent a possible advantage. For example, a just-in-time inventory system in an environment with considerable fluctuation would need to be monitored much more closely than one in which less fluctuation occurs. More random fluctuations, in general, suggest the development of more contingency planning than otherwise.

Choice of the appropriate smoothing method depends on the presence or absence of a trend or seasonality in the data series. A simple exponential smoothing method requires less data; however, it does not adjust for either trend or seasonality. Holt's and Winters' methods incorporate more sophisticated methods for such adjustments. Holt's method is best suited when there is a linear trend, but when seasonality is either absent or mildly present. Winters' method is the choice when both trend and seasonality are present.

A business or economic data series over time often consists, in varying degrees, of four time-varying components: long-term trend, seasonal variations, cycles, and short-term random fluctuations. Besides these, trends may themselves change or "turn." Forecasting is often improved by first identifying and modeling these components individually and then by combining them to generate the forecast. Time-series analysis methods are powerful tools for such data series. A proper understanding of each of these components is used to take advantage of these changes or fluctuations and gain competitive advantage. Analysis of cycles and trend-turning points is discussed below. These are of great importance in alerting managers to the need for changes in strategy.

Cyclical Analysis

The annual cycle is the most common cycle in most time series analysis. Much time series analysis is on a short-term time horizon than we normally consider in strategic marketing. However, there are often argued to be longer time cycles such as the "business cycle" of 3 to 5 years and sometimes the "long wave" or Kondratief cycle of 35 to 50 years.

The use of longer-than-annual cycles can be unsatisfactory. For instance, the idea of the business cycle reflects the impact of the general macroeconomic environment. If this is so, then it can be argued that it is better to build a multivariate model in which key macroeconomic indicators are forecast and their impact incorporated, rather than assume that the impact will consistently be of the same order and frequency. Indeed, substantial macroeconomic data exist to indicate that such an assumption is unfounded.

Such an approach has two inevitable limitations. First, we need a reasonable number of time cycles in the data, otherwise the "degrees of freedom" in estimating the genuine cyclical effect are limited. Second, since the analysis normally starts with a "decyclical" state, there is a danger that a "later" analysis such as that for turning points in the trend will be distorted and biased by earlier modifications.

Trend Turning Points

Just as the identification of trends in the example depended on variable transformations so that a monotonic relationship could then be estimated, the analysis of turning points in trend data is most commonly undertaken with the analysis of linearity of the various order differentials of the basic data.

We know from basic calculus that if a trend line approaches a simple turning point, the slope, or the first order differential changes sign. Therefore, if the first order differential is approaching zero we can assume in many cases that a turning point should be forecast in the future trend.

However, we may need to combine such an assessment with an analysis of the higher order differentials, and more importantly, the results of the type of variable transformation analysis already discussed. For instance, the logarithmic transformation allows us to distinguish between the approach of a turning point and the asymptotic approach to a particular value.

Optimization Approaches

As we have indicated, there is an inevitable interaction among the various estimation stages in time series analysis. Powerful computers provide iterative estimation procedures that recycle the later stage estimates into the earlier ones to avoid some of the sequencing biases in estimation.

A number of such software packages are now commonly available, mainly derived from the original work of Box and Jenkins.[3] The danger with such approaches lies not in their technical validity, but in the extent to which they can be treated as a "black box" with little evaluation of the output beyond the basic forecast trend.

Multivariate Trends

If the range of techniques in univariate analysis is wide, then the range of approaches in multivariate trends is at least one order of magnitude greater! Most commonly analysis involves the use of multivariate regression on lagged variables.

The basic principle in multivariate trend analysis is that we are trying to move away from a "blind" assumption of an inevitable time pattern or trend in the variable of interest (dependent variable) to some explanation for this pattern based on the effects of various other (independent) variables. As we indicated earlier, such an approach also has to consider whether the future patterns of the independent variables are any more reliably forecast than the patterns of the dependent ones: hence the appeal of "lead" independent variables where no forecast is required.

Regression analysis is a major topic and is discussed in any number of excellent statistical texts. Here, we highlight two issues: the problems of omitted variables and the nature of causation. These issues are brought to the forefront by the concerns raised about some forms of analysis of the PIMS database (Chapter 10).

[3]Box, G. and G. Jenkins, *Time Series Analysis: Forecasting and Control*, San Francisco, Holden-Day, 1970.

Omitted Variables

By definition, the set of variables in any regression analysis is limited. Two considerations generally influence the selection of variables for the dataset: relevance and feasibility. Unfortunately, these do not always take us in the same direction: variables that might *a priori* be considered relevant are not introduced because of measurement or access problems, while other variables are sometimes included mainly because they are readily available.

Both these distortions can be severe when the dataset available has already involved the collection of substantial amounts of data over a considerable period of time.

The omitted variable problem is if this "hidden" variable has an effect on two "independent" variables within the dataset, then the regression results can be interpreted as if there were a direct relationship between these two. In this sense it is no more than an example of the general spurious correlation problem such as the oft-quoted sunspot and business activity correlation: it can be less obvious an error and therefore more likely to be wrongly incorporated in the forecast.

The Nature of Causation

Perhaps the oldest "slogan" in statistical correlation analysis is *correlation is not causality,* but often it is forgotten in practice. Regression analysis remains basically a form of correlation analysis. The issue of causality can only be addressed by structuring the forms of the correlations measured and carefully interpreting them.

The purpose of any historical data analysis, in this context, is to provide a forecast of future impact. Ideally, we wish to have causal relationship between certain current independent variables and future dependent variables. Indeed, it is argued that we cannot even address issues of causation without using time series multivariate analysis (rather than the cross-sectional form of analysis often applied to, say, the PIMS[4] data).

Besides the additional demands for data, time series analysis also introduces further complexities in the representation of time-dependent variables, particularly lag structures. To retain a reasonable degree of freedom we often resort to specific lag structure formulations such as the Koyck transformation.

Practically, in such approaches to forecast the impact of market changes, we need to retain two basic concerns amidst all the analytical complexity. First, there is the degree to which the proposed regression equation actually explains the variance in the dependent variable. Anyone using a regression–based forecasting model therefore needs to be aware of the R^2 (the usual goodness-of-fit measure) of the underlying equations.

Second, there is the "robustness" of the basic model. As we introduce more variables into the multivariable model, we must ensure that the results do not depend on a particular structure of either input variables or equations. In the regression

---

[4]An example of this is to be found in Jacobson, R. and D. A. Aaker, "Is Market Share All That It's Cracked Up To Be?" *Journal of Marketing,* 49, 4, 1985, p. 11–22.

model, part of this problem is solved by the coefficient estimation procedure, which ensures that the standard deviation of the individual coefficient estimates increase if we have substantial multi-collinearity (correlations between the "independent" variables) but this will only often be evident if we inspect more than just the mean coefficient estimates.

In many situations, a time series analysis may not be appropriate. In such circumstances qualitative and technological forecasting methods are better suited.

QUALITATIVE AND TECHNOLOGICAL FORECASTING

The terms qualitative and technological are generally used to denote forecasting techniques focused primarily on predicting the environment and technology over the longer term. They contrast with quantitative methods that are employed mainly for economic, marketing, financial and other business forms of forecasting. Technological methods are not simply an extrapolation of past data patterns, as are many of their quantitative counterparts, nor do they assume constancy of the past pattern into the future. Even though history plays an important role in these methods of forecasting, technological techniques require imagination combined with individual talent, knowledge and foresight in order to effectively predict long-run changes. The intuition, judgment, imagination, and expertise required for application of these methods are in fact more important than the methods themselves.[5]

As we indicated in the introduction to this chapter, when we move into the area of qualitative and technological forecasting, we have to consider more directly judgment and evaluation. We must also not overemphasize the differences. If we are to analyze the problem, it is reasonable to suggest that we shift our focus from method to expertise and knowledge; however, if we are to avoid mere tautology, we have to have some systematic means of assessing the latter characteristics—we still need method.

A great deal of technology forecasting begins with trend analysis which was discussed earlier. Common approaches use log-linear plots of a relevant measure of a technology (e.g., size of memory cores, speed of airplanes, etc.) and estimates of theoretical potential and use the "envelope" of S-curve approaches to forecast the overall impact of changing technologies. Both of these approaches are illustrated in Exhibit 3–5.

The next stage is to interpret the various trends that have been established. This interpretation can be merely the informal application of expertise or the use of more formal approaches such as the *Delphi Approach,* or *Scenarios.*

The Delphi Approach

The Delphi approach was developed to deal with situations in which systematic estimates are required from a diverse group or panel of "experts." The basic approach involves asking each individual to provide independent estimates for specific, identi-

[5]Makridakis, S. and S. C. Wheelwright, *Forecasting Methods for Management,* New York, Wiley, 1989.

EXHIBIT 3–5   Graphs of Efficiency of Man-Made Light and S-Curve of Transportation
Speed with Additional Comments (Makridakis and Wheelwright)

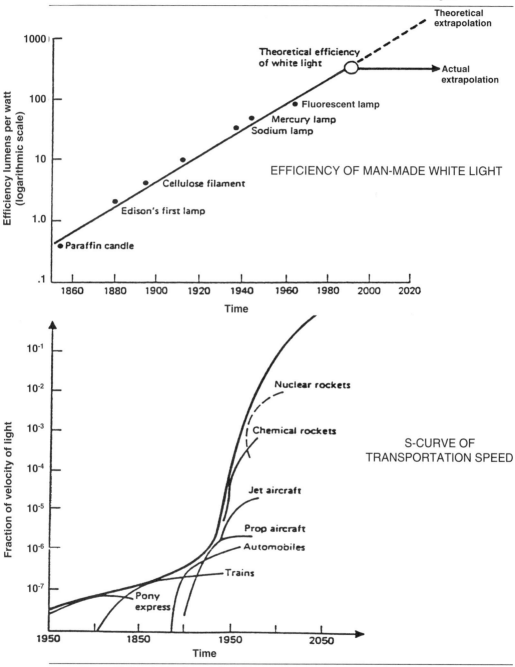

fiable events and then to obtain revised "forecasts" in light of the estimates provided by other panel members. This iterative process usually takes two to four cycles before it converges to a "forecast." The basic Delphi approach depends on two critical assumptions: first, that the necessary expertise is contained within the panel of experts and, second, that the risks of bias and dominance in a face-to-face group meeting are such that a more restricted process of feedback and revaluation is justified.

Laboratory experiments have been conducted on issues such as the most effective size of the Delphi panel, identification of other panel members, and providing alternative rationales behind the estimates, as well as the estimates themselves. A good Delphi procedure recognizes a number of basic operating rules, such as those enunciated by Glazier:

> Minimize the number of performance parameters which will be subjected to Delphi convergence, but word them in as clear and succinct a manner as possible.

> Use as broad a spectrum of experts as possible (multidiscipline) in reaching a consensus as to a parameter's value index.

> Be sure that a reasonable population of experts (multi-interests) contribute to the scoring (p. 361).[6]

The problem is that such apparently simple principles often hide intractable obstacles to effective implementation. The need to simplify performance parameters can result in oversimplified macroforecasts of little relevance to more detailed issues of specific market evolution; the need for a broadspectrum of experts often creates conflicts in defining the range of expertise or experts required and, finally, the need for a reasonable representation of the population conflicts with the practicalities of dealing with a panel of between 10 and 20 persons.

Indeed, many of these problems are well-illustrated by the example used by Glazier in which constraints on the development of a commercially viable SST (supersonic transport) plane were forecast to be technological. History now tells us that the field was left ultimately to the Concorde, which proved to be non-commercial, at least until the British and French governments wrote off its research and development costs. As Makridakis and Wheelwright comment:

> During the sixties it was continuously assumed that the problems of adoption of SST technology and aircraft were technical in nature and that once it became feasible and economical the use of such aircraft would become widespread. Again the reaction of consumers and those elements of the U.S. population associated with the SST aircraft were not considered in forecasting the adoption of this technology.[7]

[6]Glazier, F. P., "A Multi-Industry Experience in Forecasting Optimum Technological Approach," *In* J. R. Bright and M. E. F. Shoeman (eds.), *A Guide to Practical Technological Forecasting,* Englewood Cliffs, NJ, Prentice–Hall, 1973, pp. 335–361.

For information on the use of electronic mail for implementing the Delphi Method please see Husbands, B. S., "Electronic Mail System Enhances Delphi Method,'' *Journal of Business Forecasting,* Summer, 1982, pp. 24–27.

[7]Makridakis, S. and S. C. Wheelwright, *op. cit.,* p. 515.

Cross-Impact Analysis

Cross-impact analysis is a formal attempt to recognize interactions among the various parameter estimates such as those on a Delphi panel survey. The intention is to move from the single event estimates in a basic Delphi approach to conditional estimates:

> A cross-impact matrix describes two types of data for a set of possible future developments. The first type estimates the probability that each development will occur within some specified time period in the future. The second estimates the probability that the occurrence of any one of the potential developments would have on the likelihood of occurrence of each of the others. In general, the data for such a matrix can be obtained using rather subjective assessment procedures or a method such as the Delphi approach.[8]

In principle, many event forecasts involve some interaction effect. For instance, in an example used by Rochberg, et al.[9] referred to by Makridakis and Wheelwright, the occurrence of one event (limited weather control) would clearly increase the likelihood of two other events (reliable weather forecasts and reduced crop damage from adverse weather). In practice, considerable problems are encountered in getting reliable estimates for the interaction effects. This is partly because, except in obvious examples, the nature of the "question" (that of a conditional probability) may be difficult to answer for the "experts," partly because, by definition, there is no obvious historical data for validation of the estimates and partly because sequencing of events can also be at least as important as their individual occurrence. Despite these problems, this method is a key component of scenario development (discussed later).

Input-Output Analysis

A particular form of "cross-impact matrix," well-known to economic forecasters and which does not have some of these problems is an industry *input-output* matrix. An input-output matrix identifies the transaction coefficients between individual industries in the economy (the proportion of industry A's output that converts into required supplies from industry B). Such coefficients can be derived from industry surveys, although for planning they may be supplemented by forecasts of changes.

The classification is based on Standard Industrial Classifications (SIC), and the definition of the economy is national, although various attempts have been made to estimate subnational (regional) matrices.

From the specific point of view of forecasting market evolution, such matrices have limited value. In particular, the use of SICs implies a static nonmarketing viewpoint, and the various facets which could significantly alter the individual coefficients can be considerable. Such factors include changes in technology, product mix, and relative price.

[8]Makridakis, S. and S. C. Wheelwright, *op. cit.,* p. 500.

[9]Rochberg, R., T. J. Gordon, and O. Helmer, "The Use of Cross-Impact Matrices for Research and Implementation," *Journal of Forecasting,* 1970, pp. 341–358.

The intention of any form of cross-impact analysis is to create internal consistency in the set of event forecasts:

> The aim of cross-impact analysis is to refine the probabilities relating to the occurrence of the individual future developments and their interaction with other developments to the point that these probabilities can be used either as the basis for planning or for developing scenarios that subsequently can be used in planning.[10]

Recently, attention has focused on the use of planning scenarios, rather than on these individual forms of analysis.

PLANNING SCENARIOS

The Basic Concepts

In an extended series of surveys and interviews, Linneman and Klein established data about the use by U.S. corporations of planning scenarios, or in their term, "multiple scenario analysis," in the period 1977 to 1981.[11]

Their surveys showed substantial and growing use of scenario analysis, compared with a relatively low use of other related techniques, such as technological forecasting. Specifically, the median activity was scenario analysis in a five-year period, with 2 to 3 different scenarios based on 3 to 5 variables, mainly economic. The different scenarios were the "most likely, optimistic, pessimistic" variety, and were both quantitative and qualitative.

The basis of scenario planning is to ensure that the "so-called" independent input variables to the forecasting model are actually determined in a way which recognizes the actual interrelationships among them.

Specific definitions of scenarios have, however, caused some confusion. For instance, Lanzenauer and Sprung adopted the basic notion:

> A scenario is simply a general description of future conditions relevant to the planning problem at hand.[12]

Such a definition allowed them to focus on the development of scenarios relating to only one key variable: inflation.

[10]Makridakis, S. and S. C. Wheelwright, *op. cit.,* p. 501.

[11]For details, see Linneman, R. E. and H. E. Klein, "The Use of Multiple Scenarios by U.S. Industrial Companies," *Long Range Planning,* 15(4), 1982, pp. 37–44; Linneman, R. E. and H. E. Klein, "The Use of Scenarios in Corporate Planning–Eight Case Histories," *Long Range Planning,* 14(5), 1981, pp. 69–77; and Linneman, R. E. and H. E. Klein, "The Use of Multiple Scenarios by U.S. Industrial Companies: A Comparison Study, 1977–1981," *Long Range Planning,* 16(6), 1983, pp. 94–101.

[12]Lanzenauer, C. H. and M. R. Sprung, "Developing Inflation Scenarios," *Long Range Planning,* 15(4), 1982, pp. 37–44.

At the other extreme, Nair and Sarin chose to define a scenario broadly:

> A scenario in terms of these (many external) events may be thought of as a description of a certain aspect of the state of the world. A scenario consists of a combination of the occurrence and non-occurrence of all the events (p. 57).[13]

Becker, on the other hand, chooses to be esoteric:

> Scenario is defined as "Libretto of an opera, screenplay, shooting as script or account or synopsis of a projecting course of actions or events." Projecting courses of action or describing future events is not limited to contemporary authors. Ancient civilizations speculated about the future. Authors of those times depicted man's participation in flight like a bird, travelling under oceans, and other possibilities that often proved realistic visions of the future. In more recent times, Jules Verne, with his adventures of Captain Nemo in the Nautilus and his vision of travel to the Moon, probably did more to popularize what is known as science fiction—or in other terms scenarios of future human endeavor—than did previous authors (p. 95).[14]

We suggest that effective development of planning scenarios involves recognizing a number of "strands" from these definitions. Any specific scenario should deal not only with a number of interrelated events, but also be developed and presented in such form that it demands attention. To quote Pierre Wack, who, at Shell, helped develop probably the most cited system for development and use of scenarios:

> Most scenarios merely quantify alternative outcomes of obvious uncertainties (for example, the price of oil may be $20 to $40 per barrel in 1995). Such scenarios are not helpful to decision makers. We call them "first generation" scenarios . . . Even good scenarios are not enough. To be effective, they must involve top and middle management in understanding the changing business environment more intimately than they would in traditional planning process (p. 74).[15]

The proponents of scenario planning argue that it provides a means whereby the many and varied options of input variable values can be reduced to a limited set of internally consistent "scenarios," which reflect both causal and correlative relationships among the variables.

Such a justification, however, raises three further concerns: How limited can the set of futures be? How far does scenario planning go in encouraging a false division between external scenario development and internal corporate forecasting? And, how far can it effectively engage the attention of senior executives?

[13]Nair, K. and R. K. Sarin, "Generating Future Scenarios—Their Use in Strategic Planning," *Long Range Planning,* 12, June 1979, pp. 57–61.

[14]Becker, H. S., "Scenarios: A Tool of Growing Importance to Policy Analysts in Government and Industry," *Technological Forecasting and Social Change,* 23, 1983, 95–120.

[15]Wack, P., "Scenarios: Uncharted Waters Ahead," *Harvard Business Review,* 1985a, September–October, pp. 73–89.

A Limited Set of Futures

Even given the need for consistency among input variables, there remains the further problem of assuming that the relevant "future states of nature" can be reduced to a few well-defined states.

In principle, of course, the uncertain nature of the future means that the range of detailed states is infinite. In practice, we always have to approximate to a limited set, so the fact of doing this in scenario planning is less critical than the way in which it is done.

A key item, therefore, is the nature and assumptions underlying what might be called the "splitting factor" in a particular set of scenarios. The "splitting factor" is that variable or set of variables that distinguishes between the specific scenarios. As an example, one of the most sophisticated companies using scenario planning is Shell International. They have been involved in various scenario developments, some of which are described by Zenter[16] and Wack,[17] but, often, one of, if not the key splitting variables is related to the "degree of organization of the international oil market," or "the stability of the cartel (OPEC)."

Why should we regard this factor as not only an important one, which it clearly is, but also the crucial splitting factor? The term splitting factor is adopted intentionally; it comes from mathematically formulated catastrophe theory, in which the splitting factor is the one which, with small changes around the critical point, can cause catastrophic differences in outcomes. Much of the application development of catastrophe theory is from Zeeman[18] who uses the traditional "flight–fight" behavioral pattern as an example. At a certain critical point, a small difference in the critical splitting factor (fear) can result in a major difference in behavior (fight or flight).

To be effective, however, the splitting factor also needs to be near the critical point. So we have two questions: Have we reason to believe that the factors concerned are genuine splitting factors? And, are they also near what we believe to be their critical values? We can only expect in almost all cases to give qualitative rather than quantitative answers to these questions. We must not accept them implicitly and uncritically in a particular set of scenarios.

In the Shell example, it is perhaps too easy to see OPEC as a critical splitting factor. In one sense, it is obvious that we should choose it, but in another it might be that the long-term impact of "market forces" was more significant than a partial-producers' cartel. In popular thought, OPEC was the main cause of the oil crisis (rather than the supply–demand balance), and so will be a major cause of the "next one." Yet even if this is a reasonable reconstruction of history, we should not assume that history will repeat itself in so direct a way.

[16]Zenter, R. D., "Scenarios, Past, Present and Future," *Long Range Planning,* 15(3), 1982, pp. 12–20.

[17]Wack, P., "Scenarios: Shooting the Rapids," *Harvard Business Review,* 1985b, November–December, pp. 139–150.

[18]Zeeman, E. C., *Catastrophe Theory: Selected Papers,* 1972-1977, Reading, MA, Addison–Wesley, 1977.

The typical steps in scenario development are:

1. Identification of the issues.
2. Identification of the key factors.
3. Specifying major possibilities for each factor.
4. Assigning *a priori* probability to each possibility of each factor.
5. Generating scenarios as probable combinations of the possibilities of key factors, labeling the scenarios.
6. Use of scenarios.

An example of scenario analysis is that done by Batelle (a consulting firm) for a U.S. information technology (IT) company.[19] In 1988, the CEO of this company wished to know:

Step 1 • How likely was the European Common Market (EC) to reach its single market cohesion goals by the end of 1992?

• Would an integrated EC market result in a "Fortress Europe," with a policy of protectionism aimed at U.S. products?

• How might a more integrated EC affect the overall growth and competitiveness of the IT market?

This information was to be used for deciding whether or not to invest further in manufacturing facilities in Europe.

Step 2   Through several group interviews with key managers, Batelle developed 20 critical factors which were to form the basis of their scenarios.

Step 3   Available data were analyzed. An essay was written on each factor, defining it, explaining its importance, reviewing its immediate history and current situation, and conjecturing its alternative (2, 3, or 4) outcomes (or possibilities) by the end of 1992. (It is at this step that much of the time series analysis discussed earlier would be helpful.)

Step 4   For each outcome (or possibility) for each factor, an *a priori* probability was assigned by those who wrote the essays.

[19]This example has been excerpted from Millett, S. M. "Battelle's Scenario Analysis of a European High-Tech Market," *Planning Review,* March–April, Vol. 20, No. 2, pp. 20–23. The BASICS–PC program is available from the Columbus, Ohio Division of Battelle. Its price (January 1994) for a single geographic site is $9500.

Another useful example to look at is from the Southern California Edison Company. This may be found in F. Mobasheri, Z. H. Orren, and F. P. Sioshansi, "Scenario Planning at Southern California Edison," *Interfaces,* Vol. 19, No. 5, September–October, 1989, pp. 31–44. The authors report the development of 12 plausible scenarios labeled: Economic Bust, High Fuel Cost, Extensive Bypass, Expanded Environmentalism, Noncompetitive Pricing, Base Case, Economy Imports, Generation Shutdown, Conflict, Electrification, Low Fuel Cost, and Economic Boom. A thorough analysis of the resource needs of each scenario led them to develop several strategic building blocks which provided the needed flexibility to succeed in each of the scenarios.

Step 5   The cross-impact of each possibility of each factor on that of the others was judgmentally obtained from the analysts. (These are akin to conditional probabilities.) Based on these conditional probabilities, a cross-impact matrix was developed. This was reviewed and differences of judgment between the analysts were reconciled. Battelle's software program BASICS-PC combined the input on various possible starting conditions and the cross-impact matrix and provided a set of internally consistent and highly probable outcomes. These combinations led the analysts to arrive at four major scenarios.

Step 6   These steps were then followed by presentations to key managers and the subsequent use of these scenarios in planning.

The Boundary Between External and Internal

The process of scenario planning also places severe constraints on the modeling of the relationship between the external world (represented by the scenarios) and the internal corporate world (often represented by the corporate which uses the scenario output variables as input). In fact, in many cases no feedback loops are incorporated; yet, to return to our Shell example, it is difficult to believe that the external scenario for world oil prices will be totally unaffected by the moves of one of the major oil companies. Even when some form of feedback is allowed for it, by definition, it can only be in changing the outcome probabilities for the various discrete scenarios: continuous external change is inconsistent with the scenario method.

A further problem also arises in that it seems likely that part of the environment which is "coupled" to the firm's actions is most significant in influencing the future performance of the firm. We know, for instance, that as we move from world economy to national economy to industry to "strategic group," the influence of the outside world becomes more significant. But as we define the external environment around the firm more and more tightly, the logic for the clear division between external and internal that is part of the basic scenario method becomes less and less valid.

Further confusion arises in the common labeling of the limited number of scenarios. We have already noted the tendency to use "most likely, pessimistic, and optimistic," though a scenario should be defined in terms of the external environment rather than its impact on corporate performance. We should look for labels which reflect distinctly different development paths for the national or international economy or market. But again the logic of the limited number of futures intervenes: it may well be that such a range of external scenarios creates considerable problems when we look at the corporate impact (because its assessment is virtually impossible). The temptation to revert to "base sales (or market share) plus/minus 10%" is considerable, but such an approach can hardly be described as any form of planning scenario.

Influencing the Senior Executives

Wack centers much of his concern around the intended impact of scenario planning on decision makers and managers:

What distinguishes Shell's decision scenarios from the first-generation analyses is not primarily technical, it is a different philosophy, having to do with management perceptions and judgment … Scenarios deal with two worlds. They explore for facts but they aim at perceptions inside the heads of decision makers. Their purpose is to gather and transform information of strategic significance into fresh perceptions.

Scenario analysis demands first that managers understand the forces driving their business systems rather than rely on forecasts or alternatives … The foundation of decision scenarios lies in exploration and expansion of the predetermined elements, events already in the pipeline whose consequences have yet to unfold, interdependencies within the system (surprises often arise from interconnectedness), breaks in trends, or the "impossible." Decision scenarios rule out impossible developments; they deny much more than they affirm.[20]

Such concerns mean that the effective application of a scenario plan is not different from the more general issue of the effective application of strategy analysis. We need to be mindful however, of the perceptions of the decision-makers, the problems of ambiguity, and the role of the analysis itself.[21]

Beyond the essential need to involve key executives, Wack suggests that

The ideal number (of scenarios) is one plus two; that is, first the surprise-free view (showing explicitly why and where it is fragile) and then two other worlds or different ways of seeing the world that focuses on critical uncertainties. A design that includes three scenarios describing alternative outcomes along a single dimension is dangerous because many managers cannot resist the temptation to identify the middle scenario as a baseline.[22]

Specific Applications

A specific application of scenario planning is described in Exhibit 3–6. This example of scenarios illustrates many of the issues of good practice in developing planning scenarios that we have discussed previously.

In particular, we note the detailed development of only a limited number of scenarios. However, as with many examples of actual scenario development, we also note that the focus is on major global economic effects first and then on broad industry effects. This is clearly appropriate for Shell, which is a major global player in a basic industry. For many smaller firms operating in different markets, the impact of either the general global economy or broad industry performance may be less critical than the development of their specific market or customers.

CONCLUSION

As one progressed through this chapter, an important issue in forecasting the impact of market changes should have become evident. Whereas basic forms of forecasting, in par-

---

[20]Wack, P., 1985b, *op. cit.,* p. 140.

[21]This has been particularly highlighted by R. Wensley in "The Effective Strategic Analyst," *Journal of Management Studies,* 1979.

[22]Wack, P., 1985b, *op. cit.,* p. 146.

EXHIBIT 3–6   Scenario Development at Shell (1975)

A specific example of scenario development at Shell about 1975 is also given in Wack (1985b). The global economy was experiencing its most severe postwar recession, and three of the key governments (Japan, Germany, and the U.S.) were facing a general election in 1976. As a result, two scenarios were developed in detail:

- The "Boom and Bust" scenario: a vigorous recovery that contained the seeds of its own destruction.
- The "Constrained Growth" scenario: a kind of "muddling through" recovery that would differ fundamentally from earlier business cycle recoveries.

The nonrelationary ("Depression and Contingency") scenario was not viewed as probable enough for planning purposes.

In the "Boom and Bust" scenario there were a number of surprises: very rapid recovery, which would be oil-intensive with booming U.S. oil imports and little alternative energy development. Inevitably it led to a second recession.

The "Constrained Growth" scenario predicted continuing pressure on income tax to pay for social programs, slow investment in new technology, and increased friction in international trade.

---

ticular, those relating to univariate and multivariate analysis, can be applied directly to market or market-related variables, the technological forecasting inevitably encourages a technology-driven view of market evolution, while planning scenarios effectively often focus attention on the general economic forces. The problem, then, is to add to the forecast the more specific marketing dimensions, particularly of both the market and customers themselves, as well as the likely behavior of the competition.

A recently reported study[23] suggests that weighing managerial forecasts and model-based forecasts equally is the best combination. This is suggested when the "optimal weights" to be assigned to the two are not known. Managerial experts are able to incorporate "broken leg"[24] cues—signals that are informative but so seldom occur that statistical methods do not pick them up. These are akin to the metamorphosis forces discussed earlier. On the other hand, managers-experts may not be able to process the tremendous amount of information that the statistical models can. Thus, a combination is expected both to add and balance the strengths and weaknesses of the two methods to provide a better forecast.

Humans bring many biases to forecasting. These are largely based on memory (not forgetting), optimism, and need for stability and comfort. Recent psychological evidence has documented these biases.

---

[23]Blattberg and S. J. Hoch, "Database Model and Managerial Intuition: 50% Model + 50% Manager," *Management Science,* Vol. 36, No. 8, August 1990, pp. 887–899.

[24]Meehl, P. E., *Clinical Versus Statistical Prediction,* University of Minnesota Press, Minneapolis, 1954.

[25]Makridakis, S. G., *Forecasting, Planning and Strategy for the 21st Century,* New York, The Free Press, 1990.

EXHIBIT 3-7 Common Biases in Future-Oriented Decisions and Proposed Ways of Avoiding or Reducing Their Negative Impact

Type of Bias	Description of Bias	Ways of Avoiding or Reducing the Negative Impact of Bias
Search for supportive evidence	Willingness to gather facts which lead toward certain conclusions and to disregard other facts which threaten them.	Induce disconfirming evidence. Introduce role of devil's advocate.
Inconsistency	Inability to apply the same decision criteria in similar situations.	Formalize the decision making process. Create decision making rules to be followed.
Conservatism	Failure to change (or changing slowly) one's own mind in light of new information/evidence.	Monitor for changes in the environment and build procedures to take actions when such changes are identified.
Recency	The most recent events dominate those in the less recent past, which are downgraded or ignored.	Realize that cycles exist and that not all ups or downs are permanent.
Availability	Reliance upon specific events easily recalled from memory, to the exclusion of other pertinent information.	Present complete information. Present information in a way that points out all sides of the situation being considered.
Anchoring	Predictions are unduly influenced by initial information which is given more weight in the forecasting process.	Start with objective information (e.g., forecasts). Ask people to discuss the types of changes that are possible; also ask the reasons when changes are being proposed.
Illusory correlations	Belief that patterns are evident and/or two variables are causally related when they are not.	Verify statistical significance of patterns. Model relationships, if possible, in terms of changes.
Selective perception	People tend to see problems in terms of their own background and experience.	Ask people with different backgrounds and experience to independently suggest solutions.
Regression effects	Persistent increase might be due to random reasons which, if true, would increase the chance of a decrease. Alternatively, persistent decreases might increase the chances of increases.	Explain that when errors are random the chances of a negative error increases when several positive ones have occurred.
Attribution of success and failure	Success is attributed to one's skills while failure to bad luck, or someone else's error. This inhibits learning as it does not allow recognition of one's mistakes.	Do not punish mistakes, instead encourage people to accept their mistakes and make them public so they and others can learn to avoid similar mistakes in the future. (This is how Japanese companies deal with mistakes.)
Optimism, wishful thinking	People's preferences for future outcomes affect their forecasts of such outcomes.	Have the forecasts made by a disinterested third party. Have more than one person independently make the forecasts.
Understanding uncertainty	Excessive optimism, illusory correlation, and the need to reduce anxiety result in underestimating future uncertainty.	Estimate uncertainty objectively. Consider many possible future events by asking different people to come up with unpredictable situations/events.

Markidakis[25] has condensed this literature admirably (Exhibit 3–7). It tabulates the major biases, a brief description of each, and guidelines on to how to avoid or minimize their harmful consequences. In viewing forecasts, strategists should understand these biases and make sure that they do not interfere in making sense of their planning context.

Concept Questions

1. Distinguish between the two types of forces or factors related to changes in context.
2. What are the different quantitative methods of forecasting and when is each applicable?
3. What are some qualitative methods of forecasting and when are they applicable?

Discussion Questions

1. Perform a scenario analysis for a company of your choice, based on the discussion in this chapter.
2. Discuss the impact of common human biases in information collection, retrieval, and action on forecasting context changes.

Chapter 4

Product-Market Definition

Sales and market share are two key indicators of marketing performance. They are used both for choosing from a set of alternative marketing strategies, and as a signal to monitor and adjust marketing strategies and tactics. They arise from a competitive process in which customers choose from available alternatives. To calculate expected sales or expected or actual market share requires that alternatives, from which customers make their choices, be available. This situation can be confounded because of several reasons.

The first difficulty arises from the heterogeneity of customers. Different customers, for the same specific purpose, may choose from different sets of alternatives. The product-market definition problem becomes one of identifying different customers and their alternative sets and then uniting these sets. The second difficulty arises because of the possible use of a product by a customer for quite different purposes. For each purpose, this customer may choose from a different set of alternatives. The two difficulties suggest that determining a set of competitors requires knowledge of which customers might be using this product and for what purposes.

These difficulties may be the result of deliberate marketing action. For example, if a product is not advertised or distributed where a certain group of customers have access to it (perhaps because of closed international borders), then it is unlikely to be in this group's set of alternatives. Another example may be communicating that the product can be used for several purposes. Or, these difficulties may arise simply by "accident" or by the action of others. For example, the discovery by customers of new uses for a product could make the product compete with vastly different sets of alternatives. If this leads to considerable overall sales, it could easily make any market share calculations based on the original set of "competitors" quite meaningless.

The central theme of marketing competition is designated by the hyphenated term product-market—implying that both need to be jointly considered in defining a competitive boundary.

Identifying a product-market in which a company has an offering defines both its customer-oriented purpose(s) and the competition that affects the achievement of its goals. The former is achieved by a specification of the customer needs being served, and the latter by identifying competitors for each need.

The definition of product-market is also used by the regulatory system. To decide if any firm has a monopoly in a market, its ability to restrict competitive activities is evaluated. A key measure used is market share. As discussed earlier, market share cannot be measured without first defining the market in which it is being measured. In constructing a marketing strategy, the choice of whether to enter a new offering, or to merge with competitors may hinge on whether doing so results in a monopoly and thus violates the relevant law.

This chapter describes several approaches that have been suggested for defining a product-market. This permits the reader to gain detailed knowledge of the nuances of the various approaches and to be able to tackle the problem of defining the core competitive arena with greater insight. The importance of product-market definition is exemplified by the following case histories.

SUN

Sun[1] has sold computer network servers in the past, but its strength has been in individual desktop units selling for $5,000 to $25,000. The Mountain View, California company, months behind schedule in introducing new machines, was counting on them to enable it to continue its growth and to offer a more complete line of computers.

"It will allow us to attack the entire computing marketplace now, instead of just the technical," said Larry Hambly, Vice President of Marketing for Sun's computer hardware division.

The new machines, known as the Sparcserver 600 MP series, will be multi-processing, using either two or four Sparc microprocessors to obtain greater speeds.

From a product-market standpoint, the key issues here, are: (a) Who is going to be attacked by Sun? (b) Who is going to be served by Sun? (c) What is Sun providing its customers?

ARMANI

A recent article in the *New York Times*[2] is headlined "Armani Under $100 (More or Less)." The article describes the clothes that Giorgio Armani, the famous Italian fashion house, is going to carry at its new A/X: Armani Exchange boutiques. These clothes

---

[1]Pollack, A., "New Products Due From Sun and Apple," *New York Times,* September 30, 1991, C1-C2.

[2]Schiro, Anne-Marie, "ARMANI Under $100 (More or Less)," *New York Times,* September 30, 1991, B5.

will be priced between $30 to $100. Eighty percent of the merchandise at these boutiques will cost less than $100. This is a major switch for Armani whose $1,400 jackets people could only "admire from afar." This new concept is an off-shoot of Armani jeans, which is ten years old and now has annual retail sales of $160 million.

The author of the article asks: What will A/X have? Jeans and t-shirts? Or more?

How will it compare with the Gap?

How will it affect other Armani sales? (The answer might depend on "Will it become the weekend choice for the Italian designer's regular customers or whether it will attract a less affluent but equally label-conscious shopper?".)

This example touches on the following broad questions:

Who are Armani's customers?

What products are going to be offered?

What impact will this new set of products through a new channel have on the existing products and on the Armani label?

Who are the competitors and how will A/X stack up against them?

THE QUAKER OATS COMPANY

The following quotes are from the Company's 1991 Annual Report:

U.S. and Canadian Grocery Products encompasses the leading brands that are the key value generators for The Company. Eighty-five percent of the brands in our U.S. and Canadian Grocery Products business hold a number-one or number-two share position within their relevant product category. These leading brands generate strong cash flows that we are able to reinvest in marketing programs, research and development, and capital expenditures, all aimed at maximizing the value of our shareholders investment (p. 14).

In acquisitions, we look for companies with strong brand franchises positioned in growing, "on-trend" categories whose future stream of discounted cash flows exceeds the acquisition's cost in today's dollars (pp. 15–16).

Hot cereals are Quaker's oldest, best-known and most profitable products. Quaker holds the top share (63 percent) of the $770 million hot cereal market. Old Fashioned and Quick Quaker Oats are the leading "long-cooking" hot cereals, while Instant Quaker Oatmeal is the best-selling brand in the "instant" segment of the hot cereal market (p. 16).

Looking ahead, Quaker expects the hot cereal market to return to its pattern of steady, more modest sales growth experienced prior to the "oat bran boom" (p. 18).

Quaker's 7.4 percent share of the $8 billion ready-to-eat category is composed primarily of Cap'n Crunch, Quaker Oat Squares, Life and Quaker 100% Natural Cereals (p. 18).

Quaker Oat Squares is a strong competitor in the important growing "all-family" category. The brand's hearty, whole-grain taste and clear marketing proposition—a basic, wholesome, ready-to-eat cereal from Quaker intended for the entire family—have helped successfully sell the brand to value-conscious consumers (p. 19).

These selected quotations clearly indicate the importance of market-share as a benchmark or an evaluation measure for this company and that the definition of a category (essential to the determination of market share) varies even within a single company. For example, hot or ready-to-eat cereals are descriptors of the product, and the "all-family" category is a descriptor of the customer group. The quotations also show category definition is necessary to assess if an opportunity is "on-trend", that is, to forecast or understand its long-term potential, and that market share is both a matter of pride and an indicator of resources for the Company's future.

BROWN SHOE COMPANY

This is a classic example, considered to be very important in the legal definition of a product-market.

The United States Government sought an injunction to block the planned merger of the G. R. Kinney Company, Inc. and Brown Shoe Company, Inc. The basis for the action was that it would violate Section 7 of the Clayton Act.[3] The judge in this case noted that:

> The boundaries of a product market are determined by the reasonable interchangeability of use or the cross–elasticity of demand between the product itself and substitutes for it. However, within this broad market, well-defined submarkets may exist which, in themselves constitute product markets for antitrust purposes. The boundaries of such a sub-market may be determined by examining such practical indicia as industry or public recognition of the submarket as a separate economic entity, the product's particular characteristic and uses, unique production facilities, distinct prices, sensitivity to price changes, and specialized vendors.[4]

This example highlights the importance of a legally acceptable definition of a product-market.

No marketing analysis or strategic thinking can begin without at least a tentative outline of a product-market. The key issue of relationships implies a questioning of who the relevant customers and channel members are. Resource allocation across product categories requires an appropriate definition of these categories.

Decisions on the timing of resource allocation (for example, entering, increasing commitment, decreasing commitment, or exiting) are based on expectations about and knowledge of the dynamics of product-markets. A product-market is therefore a key unit of analysis for marketing strategy formulation and implementation. Its treatment by the legal system and its use for other strategic purposes are also important to market strategists.

[3]Oppenheim, S. C. and G. E. Weston, *Federal Antitrust Laws: Cases and Comments,* St. Paul, MN, West Publishing, 1968.

[4]Bourgeois, J. C., G. H. Haines, Jr. and M. S. Sommers, "Product/Market Structure: Problems and Issues," *Analytical Approaches to Product and Marketing Planning,* Conference Proceedings, Nashville, TN, October, 1981.

In the balance of the chapter, we first discuss alternative definitions of the term *product-market*. We then describe different ways product-market definitions may be arrived at and their strategic uses. The different approaches presented are the North American legal-economics based approach and the marketing approach, which we discuss at length.

DEFINITION OF PRODUCT-MARKET

Legal View—United States

In the United States, the definition of a relevant market is crucial to antitrust regulation and is based largely on economic analysis. Based on the 1966 United States v. Grinnell Corporation case, Roszkowski and Brubaker[5] point out that, according to the Supreme Court, the offense of monopolization has two distinct elements:

> (1) the possession of monopoly in the relevant market, and (2) the willful acquisition or maintenance of that power as distinguished from growth or development as a consequence of a superior product, business acumen, or historic accident.

Based on the 1956 United States v. E. I. DuPont De Nemours & Co. case, they point out that the Supreme Court defined monopoly power as "the power to control prices or exclude competition."

The courts require plaintiffs in monopolization cases to first define the relevant market. The defendant's market power is assessed by calculating its sales or output share of that relevant market, and by considering other factors such as: entry barriers, number and size of other competitors, intensity of competition, the actual ability of the firm to keep out competitors or affect prices, its ability to enforce price discrimination, its accrual of above normal profits, margins, or maintaining above normal prices, and the firm's absolute size. The key questions are: (a) What is a relevant market?, and (b) What share of a market gives monopoly power? [The answer to the latter seems to be that 90% certainty leads to an inference of market power; 75% may be sufficient, less than 50% is insufficient, and below 70% is questionable.][6]

The definition of a relevant product-market is given in the 1984 Merger Guidelines issued by the United States Department of Justice. While these guidelines provide a definition of a relevant market only for the purposes of analyzing mergers, Professor Hovencamp, a well-known scholar of antitrust law, of the University of Chicago Law School, points out that, "Many of the economic principles developed in the guidelines serve equally well in other antitrust contexts."[7]   The Department of

---

[5]Roszkowski, M. E. and R. Brubaker, "Attempted Monopolization: Reuniting A Doctrine Divorced From Its Criminal Law Roots and the Policy of the Sherman Act," *Marquette Law Review,* Vol. 73, No. 3, Spring, 1990, pp. 355–420.

[6]Hovenkamp, H., *Economics and Federal Antitrust Law,* West Publishing Co., St. Paul, MN, 1985, pp. 139–140.

[7]*Op. cit.,* p. 75.

Justice's definition of a relevant product-market is "a group of products such that a ★★★ firm that was the only present and future seller of those products ('monopolist') could profitably impose a 'small but significant nontransitory' increase in price."[8]

Also, according to Professor Hovencamp, "A relevant market for antitrust purposes includes both a product market and a geographic market."[9,10]

A definition of the relevant geographic market is also, therefore, necessary. For antitrust purposes it is defined as

> . . . some section of the country in which a firm can increase its price without 1) large numbers of its customers immediately turning to alternative supply sources outside the area; or 2) producers outside the area quickly flooding the area with substitute products. If either of these things happens when the firm attempts to charge a supracompetitive price, then the estimated geographic market has been drawn too narrowly, and a larger market must be drawn to include these outside suppliers.[11]

Marketing View

Traditionally, even in marketing, a market was defined primarily from a supply-side perspective. This entails a semantics–based approach. For example, a market for cricket (or baseball) bats, would be all cricket (or baseball) bats manufactured. This may be broken down into submarkets, for example, English or Kashmir Willow-made cricket bats (or wooden or aluminum baseball bats), and so on.

In 1966 Sissors proposed that market definition consist of delineating the market on a product-related basis and then linking this to the appropriate characteristics of buyers of the product.

The next stage saw a greater concern for consumer needs in the definition of a market. For example, in a textbook by Stanton, Sommers, and Barnes, it is defined as "an aggregate demand by potential buyers of a product or service."[12] In Kotler's textbook it is defined as "people with needs to satisfy, the money to spend, and the willingness to spend it."[13]

At about the same time, for some scholars, the notion of competition entered into the picture at two levels. At the aggregate sales level, according to Bass, King and Pessemier

> By market here is meant the interrelated class of brands or products whose relations of substitution and competition are powerful enough so that the sales of each are strongly influenced by the sales of the other.[14]

[8]*Op. cit.,* p. 75.

[9]*Op. cit.,* p. 70.

[10]*Op. cit.,* p. 70.

[11]Scissors, J. Z., "What is a Market," *Journal of Marketing,* Vol. 30, No. 3, July, 1966, pp. 17–21.

[12]Stanton, W. J., M. S. Sommers and J. G. Barnes, *Fundamentals of Marketing,* Second Canadian Edition, Ryerson, Toronto, McGraw-Hill, 1977.

[13]Kotler, P., *Marketing Management: Analysis, Planning and Control,* 2nd ed., Englewood Cliffs, NJ, Prentice-Hall, 1976, p. 7.

[14]Bass, F. M., C. W. King and E. A. Pessemier, *Applications of the Sciences in Marketing Management,* New York, John Wiley, 1968, p. 252.

At the level of the individual consumer, competition is captured in the term "evoked set," which was first defined in the seminal book on buyer behavior by Howard and Sheth. As they explained, "This concept (i.e., evoked set) is important because the brands in a buyer's evoked set constitute competition for the seller."[15,16]

Combining the supply and demand viewpoints, Abell proposed a conceptualization of a product-market as being the set of products that serve a certain need of a certain market segment with a certain technology.[17] A graphic depiction of this definition is shown in Exhibit 4–1.

Perhaps realizing that Abell's definition implicitly assumes that only products made using the same technology (assuming they serve the same needs for the same segment) are substitutes, other scholars,[18] starting with Professor Day, have brought consumer per-

EXHIBIT 4–1   A Small Lighting Company's Current Definition of Its Business Domain

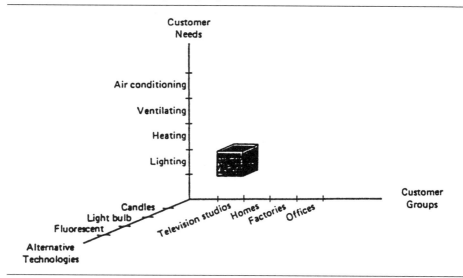

[15]Howard, J. A. and J. N. Sheth, *The Theory of Buyer Behavior,* New York, John Wiley, 1969.

[16]Howard, J. A. and J. N. Sheth, "A Theory of Buyer Behavior," *In* H. K. Kassarjian and T. S. Robertson (eds.), *Perspectives in Consumer Behavior,* Glenview, IL, Scott, Foresman, 1976, pp. 519–540.

[17]Abell, D. F., "Business Definition as an Element of the Strategic Decision," *In* A. D. Shocker (ed.), *Analytic Approaches to Product and Marketing Planning,* Cambridge, MA, Marketing Science Institute, November 1977, pp. 127–138.

[18]For details please see:

Day, G. S. and A. D. Shocker, "Identifying Competitive Product-Market Boundaries: Strategic and Analytical Issues," University of Pittsburgh, Working Paper No. 156, 1976.

Day, G. S., "Incorporating the Customer Dimension Into the Business Definition," *In* A. D. Shocker (ed.), *Analytical Approaches to Product and Marketing Planning,* Cambridge, MA, Marketing Science Institute, November, 1977, pp. 139–146.

Day, G. S., A. D. Shocker and R. K. Srivastava, "Customer-Oriented Approaches to Identifying Product–Markets," *Journal of Marketing,* Vol. 43, No. 4, Fall, 1979, pp. 8–19.

ceptions into the definition of a product-market. Consider, for example, a digital wrist-watch and a mechanical wristwatch. Under the right (perhaps price-based) circumstances, the two could be viewed as substitutes by a particular market segment to satisfy the same need. Thus Abell's definition does not seem quite adequate.

More recently, it has been pointed out that from an applications point of view

> . . . a product market can be thought of as the totality of product alternatives that could be actively considered for purchase or use by at least some minimal percentage of those people for whom such purpose or use is relevant.[19]

This is a useful point of view, and may be interpreted to capture its essential properties for marketing strategists.

First, it implies that if such a set (totality of alternatives) were to be known, then (a) the impact of a change in the marketing activities of a product (belonging to this set) can be assessed adequately by considering only this set of products, and (b) the competitive standing (e.g., via market share measurement) and financial performance of a product (belonging to this set) over time, can be adequately gauged by considering only this set of products. These implications also consider the advent of new competitors, because the products here are those that "could be actively considered."

Second, it allows for the possibility that the impact of a change in the marketing activities associated with a product (belonging to this set) may depend on a different subset of products in one customer segment (assuming such segments exist and are relevant) more than in another. For example, the impact of a change in the price of Crisco, a brand of vegetable shortening from Procter and Gamble, may result in a different impact on its market share in the vegetarian customer segment versus the non-vegetarian customer segment. The set of products it competes with in the vegetarian segment is likely to be a further subset of the set it competes with in the nonvegetarian segment. So, in considering the product-market for a given product, we need to consider all the segments it may be used by and pool all the products that could be considered by at least some members of each segment. This definition also calls for each segment to possibly use the product of focus for one or several situations. Its competitive set within each situation may be different. For example, nonvegetarians may consider choosing Crisco when they plan a dinner party for vegetarians. Thus, since a product (or a service) is chosen to satisfy some purpose(s) and thus has a usage situation associated with it, this aggregation across usage situations seems to be a useful property of this definition in that it captures the basic reason for choice.

Third, it also implies that since this set of products could be *actively* considered, buyers are aware of these products (in other words, communication advertising has reached at least some of them).

Fourth, it also implies, similarly, that these products are or could be available (distribution channel function) to buyers.

[19]Shocker, A. D., D. W. Stewart and A. J. Zahorik (1990), "Market Structure Analysis: Practice, Problems, and Promise," *In* G. S. Day, B. Weitz and R. Wesley (eds.), *The Interface of Marketing and Strategy,* Greenwich, CT: JAI Press, 1990, pp. 9–56.

In marketing strategy, this definition, along with the implications we have discussed, seems to be useful. Let us next consider in some detail the issue of identifying product-markets both from a U.S. legal view, as well as from a marketing view.

IDENTIFYING A PRODUCT-MARKET

North American Legal Context

As Professor Hovencamp points out,

> . . . the court usually 1) determines a relevant product market, 2) determines a relevant geographic market, and 3) computes the defendant's percentage of the output in the relevant market thus defined. §2 of the Sherman Act and §7 of the Clayton Act, the two statues that most often require analysis of market power, both use language that suggests such an approach.[20]

A need for such an action by a court usually comes about because of a challenge to a merger or acquisition or an investigation by the Federal Trade Commission (FTC) of anticompetitive activities. An example of a challenged acquisition was the attempted acquisition of Marathon Oil by Mobil Corporation (not allowed). An example of a merger was that between two grocery store chains in the Los Angeles area, Von's Inc. and Shopping Bag, Inc. (deemed a merger between competitors). An example of a break-up of a monopoly, albeit a regulated one, is the case of AT&T, which was broken up into various companies providing local (regional) services and the parent which was permitted to provide long-distance services. Determining the relevant market, both product and geographic, is obtained from two types of information. The first is depositional, obtained through interviews of, and presentations by, senior executives, various members of the "industry," economists, and other consultants. The second type is discovery evidence or documentary evidence. The latter includes company documents of the process of decision making and the rationale behind various decisions. The following examples provide the basis of the methods used to identify relevant markets. These examples are not exhaustive (and given this legal framework, legal advice should be sought in any litigation); rather these examples are presented as an overview to the marketing strategist.

CASE 1:   THE CIVIL AERONAUTICS BOARD (CAB) PROCEEDINGS ON CARRIER-OWNED COMPUTER RESERVATIONS SYSTEMS (CRS).

This proceeding was initiated in 1984 because of complaints by independent airlines and travel agent groups that the SABRE system of American Airlines and the

---

[20]Hovencamp, *op. cit.,* p. 59.

APOLLO system of United Airlines, were hurting their ability to compete and provide better information on prices and schedules.

The product-market was determined by the CAB to be, the "provision, in computerized form, of extensive and organized information on flights, schedules and fares on airlines, as well as other travel-related services."[21] This definition was arrived at based on extensive interviews of industry participants and examination of travel agent usage data; the CAB sought to determine first, substitutes for CRSs, and then, whether users would shift to these substitutes if the prices for the CRSs were to be raised substantially above competitive levels. Two main user groups, travel agents and airlines, were identified. The CAB obtained the cost of ticketing both for agents using CRSs and for those not having them. It was found that ticketing service (information on schedules and pricing) was better provided with a CRS than without it. Those without CRSs had to use the "Official Airline Guide" or had to telephone the various airlines to obtain the required information and had to issue tickets manually. Also, based on a cost analysis, the CAB concluded that an agent having once chosen a CRS could not easily change to another. The CAB could thus define the relevant product-market.

In defining the relevant geographic market, the CAB determined that a travel agency chose the CRS that provided the most information on the airline that had a hub in the local area (of the travel agent) or had the highest share of travel originating from that area. It was also found that airlines had to be represented in several (if not all) CRSs, in order to get seat bookings, because one CRS was not sufficient to obtain national coverage. Thus the *relevant* geographic market was defined as a local market. Based on its analysis, the CAB concluded that CRS vendors had market power.

In their defense, United Airlines (which contested the CAB's finding that CRS vendors had market power) and American Airlines (which claimed that this power, if at all, came because of the historical process of evolution of a CRS from an internal reservation system and not anti-competitive activity) both provided economic analyses to support their respective positions. United described a CRS as being a bundle of three distinct products: (a) passenger service via routing information, (b) a travel agent information, reservation and ticketing service, and (c) a marketing and distribution service of the CRS owner. United also analyzed the cost of performing these three services alone and in a bundle and showed that "economies of scope" existed for CRSs. Because of its expanded definition of the "product," United's market share figures differed from the CAB's (they were lower). This expanded definition also allowed United to claim that this market had low entry barriers.

American Airlines' analysis established the presence of "economies of scale and scope" in this industry. Contrary to United Airlines, they found that the CRS industry had a high fixed (and sunk) cost, low variable costs, and that it had a high entry barrier. AA also examined the nature of pricing and concluded that because of the bundling of product, pricing of a CRS itself was low (to gain bookings). Further,

---

[21]This example is taken from Guerin-Calvert, M. E., "Vertical Integration as a Threat to Competition: Airline Computer Reservation Systems" (1984), *In* J. E, Kwoka, Jr., and L. J. White (eds.), *The Antitrust Revolution,* Glenview, IL, Scott Foresman, 1989, pp. 338–340.

given the competition to get into CRSs (by airlines) they suggested that the CAB apply only minimal regulation, and that, too, uniformly, to all CRSs. Different definitions of "product" led to disparate findings regarding the degree of competition in this case.

This example points out that the various measures used were user costs of alternatives, entry costs, and economies of scale and scope. These varied based on market definition.

CASE 2: *MARATHON OIL COMPANY V. MOBIL CORPORATION*

This case resulted from Mobil Corporation's announcement of a tender offer to purchase sufficient outstanding common stock to gain control of Marathon. It is reported in detail by Scherer.[22]

The preliminary injunction hearings were expedited. Gasoline was identified as the relevant product-market.

The essential relevant analyses for identification of the relevant geographic market were (a) the effect of price changes in different geographic areas on inter-area product flow and (b) analysis of national and regional concentration ratios.

Detailed data on the geographic distribution of petroleum refining, transportation, and marketing in the entire United States were used.

Marathon, a regional company, operated in 21 states, particularly in the midwestern states. Its refineries were in Louisiana, Texas, Illinois, and Michigan. Mobil, a major national company, had refineries in Texas, Illinois, California, New Jersey, Washington, and Kansas.

The flow of refined petroleum between the Petroleum Allocation Districts (PAD) is shown in Exhibit 4–2. Movement across the PADs was based on cost and availability of transportation. Such cost figures were also obtained. Economists

EXHIBIT 4–2   Pattern of Refined Product Demand and Supply Flows, by Petroleum Allocation District, 1980*

Consuming PAD	Consumption (barrels/day)	Percentage of Consumption Obtained from:					
		PAD I	II	III	IV	V	Non-U.S.
I	5,630,000	26	nil	53	nil	nil	21
II	4,505,000	5	77	14	nil	nil	4
III	3,775,000	nil	nil	96	4	nil	nil
IV	507,000	nil	nil	15	85	nil	nil
V	2,570,000	nil	nil	2	3	92	3

*Defendant's Exhibit 2, "Regional Oil Dynamics," prepared by the Economics Department of Marathon Oil Company (October 1981).

From THE ANTITRUST REVOLUTION edited by John E. Kwoka, Jr. and Lawrence J. White. Copyright © 1989, Scott, Foresman and Company. Reprinted by permission of HarperCollins Publishers, Inc.

[22]This example is described in detail in Scherer, F. M., "Merger in the Petroleum Industry: The Mobil-Marathon Case (1981)," *op. cit.*, 1989, pp. 290–337.

compared the price trends, over time, in pairs of cities. This comparison defined the relevant geographic markets.

Shares and concentration ratios were used to study competitive power. Exhibit 4–3 shows these data for the entire U.S. and Exhibit 4–4 shows these data for seven midwestern states. These exhibits indicated the total share for Marathon and Mobil combined would be 8.5% and the 4-seller concentration ratio would rise from 31.4% to 34.5%. Nationallly, this merger would not impact competition significantly. However, as seen in Exhibit 4–2, this would change in a local market perspective in that concentration ratios in particular markets would go up substantially. The Department of Justice guidelines for the definition of a geographic market (see page 89) were crossed in 24 cities. Thus the relevant geographic markets were defined to be local and not national.

The District Court concluded:

> The persistence of price differentials in various areas of the nation demonstrates that motor gasoline does not move from area to area in response to price changes easily or readily as Mobil asserts. Rather, they indicate that the relevant geographic market for motor gasoline is something less than nationwide. Clearly, such an analysis must be more fully developed at a trial on the merits.[23]

This example shows how the choice of whether the relevant market is national or local was made.

FTC V. COCA-COLA COMPANY[24]

Within three-and-a-half weeks of each other in 1986, PepsiCo and Coca-Cola Company announced their intentions to acquire the Seven-Up Company and the Dr. Pepper Company, respectively. The Federal Trade Commission (FTC) decided that these mergers would be anticompetitive and announced its preliminary decision to challenge them. PepsiCo called off its proposal. Coca-Cola and Dr. Pepper carried the dispute to a trial in federal district court.

The relevant product-market debate was whether it was the carbonated soft drink market (CSD) or whether it was the beverages market that would have to be considered in demonstrating the anticompetitive outcome of the proposed merger. The FTC and the trial judge concluded that the CSD market was the relevant one.

The FTC investigation revealed that company executives were planning all their pricing and other marketing strategies at other CSDs and not other beverages. Coca-Cola argued qualitatively that it and other CSDs competed against beverages and not

---

[23]This quotation is taken from p. 35 of *op. cit.,* J. W. Kwoka, Jr., and L. J. White (eds.), *The Antitrust Revolution,* which in turn has quoted it from Marathon Oil Co. v. Mobil Corporation, et al., Northern District of Ohio, 530 F. Supp. 315 (1981).

[24]For more details see White, L. J. (1989), "Application of the Merger Guidelines: The Proposed Merger of Coca-Cola and Dr. Pepper (1986)" *In* J. W. Kwoka, Jr., and L. J. White (eds.), *The Antitrust Revolution, op. cit.,* pp. 80–98.

An excellent discussion of this case can be found in Hilke, J. C., and P. B. Nelson (1989), "Nonprice Predation and Attempted Monopolization: The Coffee (General Foods) Case (1984)," *In* J. W. Kwoka, Jr., and L. J. White (eds.), *The Antitrust Revolution, op. cit.,* pp. 208–240.

EXHIBIT 4–3   Concentration Ratios in Runs of Petroleum Through American Refineries, 1970–80*

	Year					
	1970	1975	1977	1978	1979	1980
Four–firm concentration ratio (%)	34.2	32.9	31.8	32.3	31.0	31.4
Eight–firm concentration ratio (%)	61.0	57.7	55.1	55.8	55.0	54.3
Mobil's share (%)	7.5	6.0	5.4	5.3	5.5	5.4
Marathon's share (%)	1.7	2.3	3.2	3.4	3.2	3.1

*Defendant's Exhibit 12, *Marathon v. Mobil* hearing.

From THE ANTITRUST REVOLUTION edited by John E. Kwoka, Jr. and Lawrence J. White. Copyright © 1989 Scott, Foresman and Company. Reprinted by permission of HarperCollins Publishers, Inc.

just CSDs. As evidence they claimed that CSD sales increases were coming at the expense of other beverages, notably, coffee. PepsiCo presented econometric analysis showing the existence of cross–elasticity of demand to price between CSDs and other beverages (i.e., that the demand for CSD was sensitive to the prices of the other beverages). Based on biweekly and weekly marketing data from the A. C. Nielsen Co., the FTC produced econometric studies showing that the CSD could collectively exercise market power. That is, they could collectively raise prices without a substantial decrease in their sales.

In terms of the relevant geographic market, the conclusion was that it was a national market and some individual local areas were also relevant markets. The FTC, again using marketing data, concluded that the CSD could exercise market power through pricing at the national level as well as at the local level. They could effectively charge different prices in different markets, as well as raise prices nationwide.

Cost of entry was also calculated. A high sunk entry cost (mainly advertising and promotion) was indicated by the FTC analysis of new product introduction expenditures. Limited access to distribution channels, via control of bottlers (distributors),

EXHIBIT 4–4   Concentration Data for Motor Gasoline Sales in Seven Midwestern States, 1970*

State	Four-Firm Concentration Ratio %	Mobil's Share %	Marathon's Share %	Combined PostMerger Market Rank
Ohio	53.0	1.74	13.92	2
Illinois	47.0	4.27	12.18	2
Indiana	47.0	2.47	14.53	1
Michigan	44.5	7.68	12.06	1
Wisconsin	44.1	8.14	9.15	1
Florida	41.0	4.52	7.22	1
Tennessee	n.a.	4.49	5.95	2

*Marathon complaint; Plaintiff's Exhibit E.

From THE ANTITRUST REVOLUTION edited by John E. Kwoka, Jr. and Lawrence J. White. Copyright © 1989 Scott, Foresman and Company. Reprinted by permission of HarperCollins Publishers, Inc.

was found in reaching buyers at retail outlets. It was also found to be difficult to reach consumers through vending machines and fountains, because of the limitation in the number of buttons and spigots available on them. Additional buttons and spigots could not be easily added to these vending machines and so entry was deemed to be extremely difficult.

Judge Gerhard Gessell ruled in favor of the FTC. How managers made their decisions, the high concentration (4-seller concentration ratio over 75%), difficulty of entry evaluation, and the anticompetitive consequences of the merger (even though it was felt that competition between Coca-Cola and Pepsi would not be lessened), were key to the decision.

A United States marketing strategist should (1) be familiar with Section 2 of the Clayton Antitrust Act, Section 7 of the Sherman Antitrust Act, the Celler-Kejawer Act of 1950 (which amended the Clayton Act), and the 1984 Department of Justice Guidelines for Mergers; (2) understand concentration ratios, price elasticity and cross-elasticity of demand, and ease of entry calculations; and (3) be aware that records of meetings and intent of managerial decisions could be used in assessing a relevant product-market definition.

An interesting example in which a regulatory definition of business presented a unique opportunity is the television industry. United States federal regulations bar network operators (CBS, NBC, ABC), each of which broadcasts more than 15 hours a week of its own programming, from producing and distributing original shows to others. That is, a network operator is one broadcasting more than 15 hours of its own programming. The Fox network (controlled by Rupert Murdoch) keeps its programming under 15 hours and, as a "non-network" network does not come under this regulation. This is an insightful use of the product-market definition to gain a competitive advantage.

Marketing Oriented Views

A product-market is the fundamental unit of competitive analysis. Our discussion in the legal section focused more on how competitors may be identified by using aggregate measures of substitutability like cross-elasticity of demand, and how competition may be restricted by considering cost-based barriers to entry. To gain an advantage, it is also necessary to understand why a particular set of competitors is considered as such and which product-market boundary borders are likely to be or should be breached. These issues are now discussed. The basis of the discussion is Abell's segments × needs × technologies framework.

Segments × Needs × Technologies

Professor Abell defined the scope of a business as the space occupied by it on a three-dimensional map (see Exhibit 4–1). The more space occupied by a firm, the larger its scope of business. As mentioned earlier, each box (or cube) in this map, if part of a firm's business scope, represents one of its product-markets. The three dimensions are segments, needs, and technologies.

Segments are some pre-identified groups of "homogeneous" buyers. For example, banks versus savings and loan associations, people living in Alaska versus those living in Alabama, and so forth.   These segments seem to be defined more on the ability to reach them for distribution of products and services or communication of information, as opposed to a higher commonality of needs within a segment as compared to that across segments.   Notice in Exhibit 4–1 two segments may have the same needs.   So, Abell's map allows an opportunity to view the possibilities of serving either different needs of one segment, or satisfying the same need for multi-segments, or multiple needs for multiple segments, as the scope of business.   The choice depends on the leverageable assets and skills of the firm.   If its relationship with a particular segment is strong, perhaps satisfying other needs that this segment may have would be advantageous.   On the other hand, if its ability to satisfy a particular need is its major strength and if it can be transferred to other segments, then this would be the strategy for this firm.

Coca-Cola Company, for example, used its "Refreshes You Best," slogan to add one country (segment) after another to its current position of a premier global brand. Subsequently, by introducing a line of clothing under its brand name it has leveraged its relationships with its customers.

"Technology" is probably one of the most overworked words in current business strategy literature and, because of this, it has acquired a multitude of meanings.   Abell describes technology simply as "the way, or how customer needs are satisfied."[25] This commonsense definition corresponds closely with that adopted by Day; "The Technological dimension . . . represents the various ways in which a particular function can be performed."[26]   To illustrate these definitions, Abell uses the alternative choices available in technologies for diagnostic imaging, for example, as radiographs, ultrasound, nuclear imaging, and computerized tomography (CT) and Day uses the alternative technologies for the transportation of letters and packages, for example, trucks, dedicated airplanes, and facsimile transmission.

Whereas technology is undoubtedly an important strategic decision, from a marketing standpoint, technology provides consumers with a particular functionality, in a particular form, and at a particular price.   For example, the difference between a full size camcorder and a palmcorder is seen by the consumer in its form, though the differences are created by technology.   As another example, the differences between a McDonald's hamburger and that from a local hamburger stand are also created by technology and result in differences in, say, form (looks, standardization across outlets, etc.) and price.   Thus, functionality, form, and price seem to better represent the dimensions of needs and technology from a marketing point of view.

Let us now consider in more detail these elements of product-market definition and some alternate approaches to identifying the structure of inter-product competition in a product-market.   In doing so, let us, remember that a product-market defini-

---

[25]See Abell, D. F., *Defining The Business: The Starting Point of Strategic Planning,* Englewood Cliffs, NJ, Prentice-Hall, 1980.

[26]Day, G. S., *Strategic Market Planning: The Pursuit of Competitive Advantage,* St. Paul, MN, West Publishing, 1984.

tion should allow a strategic analysis of possible outcomes over time, competitive standing, and growth opportunities.

SEGMENTS

Historically and structurally, due principally to differences in reach and cultural differences, geography and demography have been the major variables for segmenting customers. For example, the need for refrigeration in Phoenix, Arizona is different from that in Anchorage, Alaska; the need for underclothing differs between men and women; the need for water softeners varies by geographical location, and so forth.

Historically, transportation costs too have determined the trading area of a retail outlet as well as the delivery area of a manufacturing plant. International boundaries have also restricted trade flow because of each country's customs regulations. Culture has also limited the homogenization of needs and demands. Most needs and demands derive from particular rites and rituals which govern daily life. As more of these are now governed by secular rites and rituals, and with the ease and quickness of information flow and technology, growing homogenization of needs around the world is now clearly visible; albeit with some local variations. Thus, a segment is a clearly identifiable group of customers with the same generic need—although the group might vary in the details of its needs, or it can be relatively isolated in communication or distribution reach or purchasing ability.

When is a particular segmentation of a market adequate to define a product? Consider the following example.

Granny Goose is a manufacturer of potato chips on the West Coast of the U.S. Is it wise for Granny Goose to assume that it should consider only the West Coast market in its strategic analyses? To answer this question requires thought and data collection.

1. Can potato chips manufactured outside the West Coast market area be sold on the West Coast? In other words, is delivery possible? Can potato chips be transported? If so, will any local dealer or retailer carry the product (relationship), or is there an alternative (e.g., catalog sales) channel available? If the answer to the primary question is yes, then the West Coast is an adequate definition of the market.

2. Assuming that only potato chips manufactured outside the West Coast cannot be sold there, then, is there are any cost advantage based on volume of manufacture or scope of operation, even if these occur in multiple locations? If these exist, that is, if there is at least one manufacturer who also has operations outside, then there is a possibility that the West Coast is an inadequate delimiter for this market. This is because an evaluation of relative cost advantages (and therefore of pricing margins as well as resources available for R&D, etc.) also need to take into consideration outside the area operations.

3. Does Granny Goose have a relationship with its channels or its end buyers

such that they would not buy a "foreign" brand? (Another example is buyers who would only "buy American," thus obviating the need to consider imports as competitors.) If so, then despite Condition 2, the West Coast may be an adequate delimiter.

4. Whereas the West Coast may be adequate for assessing competitive standing and for assessing performance in this market, geographical boundaries may not be adequate to assess strategic growth opportunities. For example, although the Rockies may isolate the West Coast from the East Coast, the rest of the country may have to be segmented differently.

5. Any change in Granny Goose's marketing strategy, for example, repositioning of the brand, may elicit different reactions from the local and outside manufacturers. For an outside manufacturer, the West Coast market may be trivial and so not worthy of a response. Or, it may be an opportunity for the outsider to signal to competitors in other markets that it would also respond strongly to any such action by them. If the latter, then a larger view of the market may be called for, even though other brands outside the area do not directly compete with Granny Goose.

This example highlights the need for logic and a critical challenging of assumptions regarding the bases of competitive advantage and their impact on performance in deciding whether geographical boundaries are adequate or useful delimiters of segmentation.

Needs

To continue the example, the West Coast market may be a useful boundary marker. However, the West Coast potato chip market may not be adequate as a boundary definition. If customers choose between potato chips and banana chips or dry roasted peanuts, and if changes in the marketing strategy of dry roasted peanut manufacturers (for example, if they changed the form by crushing and reconstituting peanuts to make flat chips) has an impact on the sales of potato chips, then a broader view of the market is called for. But it is perhaps likely that there might be more impact by changes made in other potato chips than in peanuts. A hierarchical view of a product–market based on the satisfaction of customer needs is thus called for. In the case of CSD (as in the Coca-Cola case discussed earlier), carbonated soft drinks would be at one level of a hierarchy with fruit drinks, coffee, tea, and milk also competing but with decreasing intensity for satisfying the same needs (Exhibit 4–5). An extended discussion of hierarchical product-market definitions is provided in the appendix to this chapter.

Like geographical boundary identifiers, some other structural segmentation identifiers need to be considered. Daewoo, as mentioned in Chapter 1, is moving from manufacturing private label products to introducing name-brand products. J. C. Penney's microwave ovens (when they sold them) competed with Amana, Whirlpool, and G.E. brands. However, did Samsung (which made J. C. Penney's ovens) microwave ovens compete with these companies? Or, did Samsung compete with those manufacturers who were interested in supplying J. C. Penney? This is an example of vertical market segmentation. It is vertical in that it segments the market

EXHIBIT 4–5   A Hypothetical Market Hierarchy

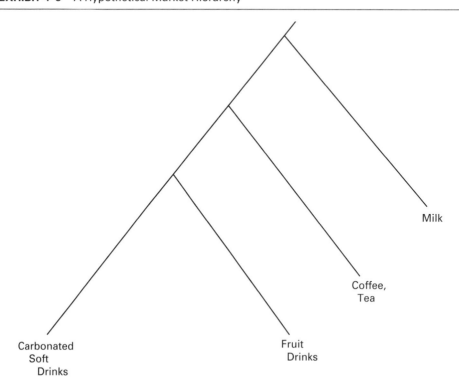

Milk

Coffee,
Tea

Carbonated
Soft
Drinks

Fruit
Drinks

according to the levels of the distribution channel, as opposed to considering the segmentation of customers at the same level of the distribution channel. For example, intermediaries would form one segment, and end consumers another.

Let us consider the U.S. white goods industry to explore such vertical segments as well as horizontal segments—the identifiers of which are related to product differences and bundling of products.

THE U.S. "WHITE GOODS" INDUSTRY: AN EXAMPLE

Function by Price Needs

The overall function by price points space in the U.S. domestic white goods market can be represented initially by a simple matrix (Exhibit 4–6). This matrix involves classifying six functional types (clothes washers, clothes dryers, dishwashers, electric ranges, refrigerators, and microwave ovens) and three "price points." The price levels are based on the customers' preferences (perhaps based on affordability) for price (and correlated with their perceived quality)—unbranded (i.e., retail or store brand) offering the lowest perceived quality and price, average quality branded, and premium quality branded. For our purposes we need only recognize that the simple assumption

EXHIBIT 4–6   White Goods Product-Market Space

	Unbranded Private	Standard	Premium
Clothes Washer			
Clothes Dryer			
Dishwasher			
Refrigerator			
Electric Range			
Microwave Oven			

of the relationship between branding and quality must be treated with caution. A number of studies have shown that consumers do not consistently perceive a simple rank ordering of generic store to manufacturer's brands, in quality perceptions. Indeed in the United Kingdom (U.K.), it is widely recognized that some store brands (particularly Marks and Spencer's "St. Michael" brand) carry a higher quality perception than nationally distributed manufacturer brands. Eckerd Drugs has attempted to pursue a similar strategy in the U.S. drug store business by promoting their "generics" as different from the rest. There are also a number of options available under the general heading of family branding that provide a mechanism for an individual manufacture to span a number of differing quality segments. This definitional space, like others we have discussed, is a simplification. We have, for instance, totally ignored the potential for segmenting the market geographically either regional or international or by purchase situation such as new construction, modernization, replacement, and industrial. Additionally, we have limited the number of white goods products to six. However, this simplified space can be used to illustrate complexities in identifying various product-market opportunities.

A viable product-market opportunity is an area of a product-market space (or subspace) which can be isolated from other areas in competitive activity and in its product offerings. As a convenient starting point for this analysis, we might try to answer the question, "Can a competitive position be defended by focusing exclusively on one cell?" For example, can a business be successful by defining its target product-market as average quality, branded clothes dryers and only offering products in this cell? (Let us assume there is only one market segment and one form for each functional product type.) One suspects that such a narrow focus will not be viable. With such a narrow product line it is difficult for the business to develop a distribution network. Retailers prefer to deal with a few manufacturers that offer broad product lines rather than many manufacturers offering narrow product lines. To illustrate, consumers typically purchase a clothes dryer and a clothes washer at the same time. Since they prefer a matching set, they will generally buy it from the same vendor.

Crossing Boundaries

In general, it is difficult to defend a position by focusing on a narrow segment of the product-market space. Given that it is necessary to have a position in more than one cell, the key issue is identifying the barriers between sets of cells. A set of cells constituting a defendable product-market position (discussed earlier) is defined so that presence in each cell within the set contributes to the overall competitive position of the firm while its competitive position is unaffected by its or others presence in other sets of cells. Thus a firm operating within a product-market (a set of cells) makes strategic decisions the impact of which cannot be influenced easily by firms in other product-markets. Further, firms in other product-markets can only initiate the decision at substantial cost or risk. The concept of product-market boundaries is, therefore, strongly interrelated to the notion of the types and forms of effective competition. In drawing a map of the product-market boundaries in the overall space, we are also attempting to draw a map of both current and "latent" competitive structure.

Vertical Segments or Market–Related Boundaries

An analysis of the simplified, white goods competitive space suggests that a vertical barrier exists among the markets for the 6 unbranded and 12 branded cells. This boundary arises because the cost structures are completely different for branded and unbranded products. To compete effectively in the unbranded cells, a firm must have tight cost control based on prespecified standards set by the customer (the retail outlet). In the branded cells, the key concern is the effective selling and marketing of the product to the consumer. Since unbranded manufacturers do not undertake marketing and sales activity, they have no expertise in these functions and would be at a severe disadvantage if they chose to enter the branded cells.

Note that the height of this barrier depends on which side of the barrier a firm is located. The barrier will probably be higher for unbranded vis-á-vis branded producers. An unbranded producer will have difficulty entering branded markets because the firm will have to acquire a new set of marketing skills and establish a distribution channel. The branded producer may find it easier to enter unbranded, private label markets. To compete effectively in these markets, the branded producer needs efficient, low cost production capabilities—capabilities that only a high volume, branded producer may have.

In addition, one could argue that another vertical boundary exists among the six standard quality, branded cells and the six premium quality, branded cells. This barrier, based primarily on customer loyalty and perceived quality, makes it difficult for a firm to compete in both standard and premium quality cells. Customers may be unwilling to believe that a standard quality producer can also make premium quality products if such information is possessed by them. In addition, the manufacture of premium quality products emphasizes quality control, while the manufacture of standard quality products emphasizes cost control. Therefore, even if a standard quality manufacturer offers a premium product under a new brand name to avoid the customer confusion concerning quality, the focus of the manufacturing processes for the two products must also be different. There appears to be a high "vertical" barrier between unbranded and branded products because of differences in cost structure and a lower, vertical barrier between standard and premium quality branded product based, primarily, on customer perceptions and loyalty toward quality products.

Need-Related Boundaries

Let us look now at potential "horizontal" barriers. As mentioned previously, the tendency to purchase clothes washers and dryers as a "unit" suggests that perhaps no horizontal barrier exists between these two products. Whereas customers prefer to buy the same brand of clothes washer and dryer, a retailer may be able to erect a barrier between these two products. Since the private label manufacturer is typically supplying products to a retailer's specification, the retailer could use different suppliers for the two products but specify compatible designs and sell them both under the same store brand. The retailer control of design would force a producer to define a position in just one product. If a retailer had not created this boundary, it might not have been sufficient to offer just a washer or a dryer either because of cost or because of joint purchasing by customers. This potential cost barrier assumes that synergies exist in cost structures and skills in the manufacture of washers and dryers.

Technology-Based Boundaries

In the white goods product-market space, unique production methods or product technologies may result in "horizontal" barriers. For example, if the technology required to manufacture dishwashers is substantially different from that needed to manufacture clothes dryers, a boundary exists between these two products. This boundary indicates that the two products can be isolated from one another in a competitive situation. A manufacturer of only one product is at no disadvantage compared with a firm that manufactures both products because there is little technical or manufacturing synergies between the products: the products have two distinct cost structures and experience curves.

In the white goods business, there are varied technology linkages among the products; one might therefore expect some barriers to arise between the products. But these barriers are not very high, because the technologies are not proprietary. It is relatively easy for a producer of refrigerators to acquire the technology and manufacturing skills to enable it to be an efficient producer of electric ranges. However, the unique technology needed to manufacture microwave ovens might result in a slightly higher barrier between this white good and the five others.

Vertical Segment-Based Boundaries

In this situation, the importance of barriers also can be affected by channel considerations. Standard brand white goods are examples of shopping goods—products for which consumers have some brand preference and for which they will typically compare several brands before making a purchase. Thus, retailers of standard brand white goods offer several brands so that a consumer can make these comparisons in one retail outlet. Since retailers prefer to develop relationships with a limited number of manufacturers, a manufacturer of standard brand white goods probably needs to offer a broad line (electric rangers, refrigerators, washers and dryers) to secure distribution. In addition, availability of a broad product line gives the producer more control over the distribution channel.

Horizontal Segment-Based Boundaries

Premium white goods are a specialty product. Since customers have much stronger brand preferences, they are willing to expend extra effort to locate a store stocking the brand. The brand decision is often made before the store is selected. For premium quality white goods, extensive distribution is not as critical as it is for standard quality brands. Thus a premium brand manufacturer does not need a broad product line. In fact, a broad product line may actually decrease the perceived quality of the individual products. Customers may be reluctant to accept that a manufacturer can make both a high quality refrigerator and clothes washer. They may feel that high quality can only be achieved by focusing on one product type.

Dynamics of Product-Markets

Our previous discussion concerning product-market boundaries in white goods is summarized in Exhibit 4–7. Because of differences in cost, there is a high "vertical" barrier between markets for branded and unbranded product. A lower, but significant, barrier caused by both quality perception and cost exists between markets for standard and premium brand products. Shallow, horizontal barriers arise among functional product types because of differences in technology. These technology barriers are highest between microwave ovens and other white goods. However, purchase patterns eliminate the barrier entirely between clothes washers and dryers. Between the set of standard products, the barriers are also reduced because of distribution and channel control. Finally, the barriers between the set of premium brands are heightened because of customer perceptions of quality. The boundaries shown in Exhibit 4–7 suggest that some positions in the product-market space are more defendable than others. It would be difficult to defend a position which focuses solely on the standard brand dryer market because there are no barriers that isolate this position from producers of standard-brand washing machines, dishwashers, refrigerators, and kitchen ranges. Based on the boundaries identified in Exhibit 4–7, a manufacturer of standard brand white goods needs to participate in all product cells to defend its position. Whereas a manufacturer of premium quality dishwashers may be able to defend its position by participating only in this one cell because of the customer loyalty and perceived quality barriers that can be built around this position and its highly credible threat of entry into other cells, if necessary. Finally, because of technology barriers it might be possible for a manufacturer to build a defendable position around the branded, microwave oven market.

EXHIBIT 4-7 Defendable Boundaries in White Goods Product-Market Space

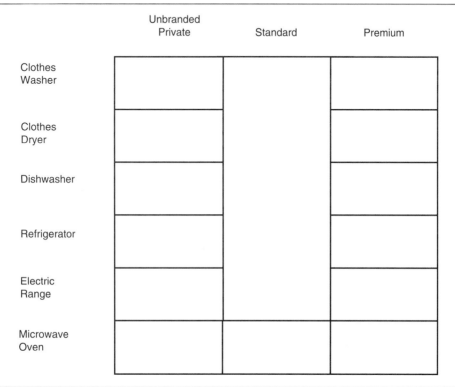

Technology can be a significant barrier to operating in a particular market. This occurs if there exists a unique technology to deliver a particular function, form, and price combination of value to channels-buyers. Possessors of this unique technology could then be expected to be the competitors in this industry (if they are not already). The importance of technology is beyond doubt; the problem is refining this concept in practice. Let us consider more carefully why and how technology is important.

In economic terms, technology is equivalent to the existence of different costs. However, the economic analysis of technology is often based on unrealistic assumptions:

> The production and utilization of technological ... knowledge is a central economic activity that is handled in a most cavalier way within economic theory. By far, the most common theoretical approach is simply to take technology as a given, ignoring entirely the fact that the options open to a manager almost always include an attempt at some degree of innovative improvement in existing ways of doing things. On the occasions when this pattern is broken

by explicit attention to technology change, the treatment of states of knowledge and the changes therein if often simplistic and undifferentiated. It is common to assume that technology is proprietary, that is, embedded in a 'book of blueprints.' However, in reality, know-how is commonly not in this form. It is often tacit, in that those practicing a technique can do so with great facility, but they may not be able to transfer the skill to others without demonstration and involvement. To assume otherwise, often obscures issues relating to the generation and transfer of 'know-how'?[26]

The notion of a "book of blueprints" does, however, help us to consider what we really mean by the role of technology in identifying and creating market boundaries. At one level, technology is simply an issue of cost competition. Different technologies are just different cost curves and the implementation of a new technology means jumping on a new cost (experience) curve. In this sense, technology is no more than a more complex model of the nature of cost competition.

At a deeper level, technology, particularly potential technological change, has an important additional effect on product-market boundaries when one considers the specific nature of the costs and benefits provided and the functions involved. In other words, a change in technology implies a change in relationship between the factor inputs and the nature of the additional benefits (functions or forms) that can be offered to customers. For example,

> The introduction of "Pringles," a manufactured potato chip, by Procter and Gamble in the U.S. did not reduce (in fact it probably increased) direct manufacturing costs. Since Pringles can be stacked in a can and has a long shelf life, this new technology for making potato chips offers substantially reduced costs of distribution. This innovation provided the option of much wider scale geographic distribution and hence, economies of scale in both selling and advertising. If consumers had evaluated Pringles to be of comparable quality to traditional potato chips, the whole competitive structure of the market could have changed from a larger number of local producers to a few, large-scale national producers.[27]
>
> By studying the nature of the technology for the efficient long distance transport of cars, the Japanese succeeded in entering the U.S. auto market with a transportation cost from their plants not significantly different from that faced by U.S. manufacturers. This substantially increased the competitive threat for an industry which had previously assumed that high transportation costs for foreign competition were a significant barrier to entry.
>
> The introduction of more and more electronics into domestic appliances makes it much easier to offer certain features in terms of automatic control both for the unit itself as well as an overall integrated system. Just as in the "office of the future" market, this convergence of technologies is changing the potential structure of the market.

In the early development of a market, access to new technology is often both critical and difficult to secure for "novice" entrants. For example, in the white goods market, the first entrants in the microwave oven market were those companies that had access to the research and development directly linked to microwave technology. As the market developed, however, the situation changed. Although access to new technology might not have

[27]"A Stubborn P&G Still Likes Pringles," *Business Week,* June 19, 1978, pp. 30.

been either cost-free or risk-free, a number of major firms in both the appliance market and the consumer electronics market acquired the technology and exploited their superior distribution and greater capabilities. As a market matures, therefore, we can often expect the technological barriers to competition to lower. Of course, there are well publicized examples in which technological barriers have remained strong, particularly when there existed efficient patent protection. Polaroid, through patent protection, delayed Kodak's entry into the instant photography market and eventually forced Kodak's withdrawal.

A number of related concerns must be considered when technology is used to justify a market barrier:

> What proportion of the total product (including physical distribution) cost does the new technology affect? For example, the introduction of electronic rather than electro-mechanical control systems in appliances was a relatively small proportion of product cost, while the use of microwave energy rather than radiant heat in a cooking oven represented a large proportion of total cost. The height of technological barriers is directly related to the proportion of total product cost related to the proprietary technology.
>
> What proportion of the total value added is attributable to product costs? For example, product costs are often a large proportion of total costs for industrial goods such as machine tools and a low proportion for consumer goods such as cosmetics and beer. Technological barriers will typically be less important when product costs represent a small proportion of the value.
>
> Does the technology result in a unique and important customer benefit? How accessible is the "technology" to enable a competitor to be effective either in production costs or marketing/distribution costs?

The real nature of the technology barrier depends on two conditions: (1) the cost involved must be significant in the overall value added chain or provide a significant and unique customer benefit, and (2) the advantage in the technology related to this cost must be difficult for a competitor to access. For instance, in a number of markets, Procter & Gamble retains a cost advantage over its competitors in marketing rather than in manufacturing technology and, as important, it is more difficult for the competition to duplicate this marketing technology advantage rather than a product technology advantage.

Our discussion so far has focused on a product-market as a unit of analysis for competition, it also permits a creative examination for the purposes of leveraging relationships. In particular, viewing both needs and segments jointly in the details of customer advice and action makes this very fruitful.

Scope Based on Customer Purchase Behavior

In the white goods example, we proposed that a significant linkage exists between the market for clothes washers and dryers because of customer purchase behavior. Specifically, consumers tend to purchase both products as a unit. Therefore, a vendor may need to offer a compatible set of products. The interrelationship among refrigerators, electric ranges, and dishwashers might be even stronger in the new house construction market in which the items might be purchased singly, in volume by a developer-builder. We need to distinguish between products which are purchased at the same time and those which are used in an integrated manner.

The common purchase situation is merely a specific example of a much wider retailing issue. After all, a coffee manufacturer would not argue that a boundary does not exist between coffee and cream just because coffee is almost always purchased along with cream. In this case, the issue can be examined in basic transaction cost terms. A joint offering to the customer of coffee and cream reduces the customer's costs compared with dealing with two suppliers. But such costs could be reduced much more significantly if a whole range (or assortment) of grocery products were made available from the same supplier. This supplier is typically an intermediary between the producer(s) and the customer. The existence of the intermediary would, of course, increase the total costs in the overall distribution channel, but often not enough to offset totally the benefits to the final customer of providing a wide assortment in one location.

The issue of integrated usage provides a stronger case for reducing the boundary between the two product markets. While U.S. consumers may want style and design compatibility, they probably do not see a need for physical compatibility between a clothes washer and dryer. In Europe and Japan, there is a slightly stronger concern about physical compatibility because it is common to stack one product on top of the other, which introduces concerns about physical as well as design compatibility. Space considerations also make miniaturization and the package of multi–function products necessary for certain segments than others.

There are a significant number of markets in which there is some customer benefit in compatible offerings and firms participating in these markets attempt to exploit this potential among their offerings. In the stereo market, the importance of compatibility to consumers has developed to such an extent that products are either sold as an integrated system of a manufacturer or retailers are buying components from multiple suppliers to provide a set of components under a common brand name.

However, it appears that there are a limited number of instances in which the concern for compatibility is so strong among customers that all competitors are forced to offer a full set of products (in both cells). For example, we might expect the forces for compatibility to be strong in the home computer market because of the relationship between computers and printers. However, a significant proportion of the printer market is supplied by firms which specialize exclusively in printers. Similarly, with large mainframe computers, there are a number of lucrative market opportunities for those smaller peripheral manufacturers who produced IBM-compatible equipment.[28]

In general, the customer concern for compatibility is often expressed as a need for reassurance about the degree to which a product will operate in a system. While such reassurances can be provided through common branding, they can also be provided by various intermediaries such as retailers and wholesalers. In many more specialized markets reassurances can be provided by consultants and advisers, rather than the manufacturer. In addition, a common purchase occasion can also occur prior to

---

[28]Abell, D. F., *Defining The Business: The Starting Point of Strategic Planning, op. cit.*

the end customer in various ways, for example, by the building contractor in the domestic appliance market.

Customer Usage–Based Substitution

The previous discussion of customer purchase behavior considered the extent to which two different product offerings are complementary. This section on customer usage looks more closely at the nature of substitutes. There is little need for a boundary between two product market cells when the offerings from both cells are highly complementary or when they are effectively direct substitutes.

Abell (see Footnote 25), in defining the use of the function dimension, attempts to make a distinction between technology, function, and benefits

> . . . products or services perform certain functions for the customer. Functions have to be separated conceptually from the way the function is performed ("technology") and the attributes or benefits that a customer may perceive as important criteria for choice. Thus transportation is a function; taxi transportation is a way of performing the function; price, comfort, speed and safety are attributes or benefits associated with the choices. Likewise, teeth cleaning is a function; flavor, brightness, decay prevention, and price are attributes associated with a particular purchase (p. 170).

However, Day emphasizes "the related benefits being provided to satisfy the needs of customers" in his definition of function.

It is often difficult to identify substitutes using a narrow, technical definition of function. For example, microwave and conventional ovens perform the same function—cooking food. However, they deliver a different set of benefits when performing this function. Microwave ovens cooked food faster but did not brown food until browning elements were added. Because of this different set of benefits, microwave ovens would never have become a substitute for conventional ovens, but would have been restricted to functions of defrosting and cooking prepackaged frozen foods—functions for which it provided benefits superior to conventional ovens. This view fits in with an anthropological view of function: the potential utility or contribution of a product to the buyer.[29] However, technology (the browning element) has considerably diminished this difference and the difference that remains is in form, not function.

VCRs provide another interesting example. VCRs can be used in two distinct ways: (1) the playback of prerecorded tapes, or (2) the recording and subsequent playback of broadcast material. Assumptions concerning the customer function that are satisfied by the VCR are critical in determining the extent to which the video-disk would be substituted for the VCR. Because of the nature of the broadcast system in different countries, the use of VCRs varies significantly from national market to national market. In markets where there is a significant level of video rentals, the video-disk player is a significant substitute for VCRs. But in markets where VCRs are used primarily to record broadcast material, there will be less substitution.

[29]For more details see the classic book on innovations by Rogers, E. M. and F. F. Shoemaker, *Communication of Innovations: A Cross-Cultural Approach,* New York, The Free Press, 1971.

A basic consideration in employing the customer use dimension to define boundaries is distinguishing between use itself and the nature of the existing product offerings. One must be careful to define use options in terms which go beyond the existing situation. For example, we can expect the emergence of facsimile systems and other forms of immediate data transfer will change the nature of the customer demand and, therefore, the uses satisfied. In a business, no one with experience needs reminding that the introduction of a "rush" service affects the deadlines (and, therefore, the requirement for the service) throughout the business. Such in-depth analyses should be used either to find new ways of breaking down the existing boundaries, or to strengthen relationships with customers and to create boundaries for others.

At an even greater level of detail, boundaries are reflected in the minds of customers in the set of products that are considered for a particular use. The set of products that buyers consider in a particular choice or purchase task are studied in marketing as *categorization*. The products that would be considered for a particular application (this is part of the definition of Shocker, et al. discussed earlier), or the consideration set (according to this definition) is the membership in the category that is most closely associated with this application. A couple might want to purchase a drink to send with their young son on a picnic. Perhaps they want a small, easy-to-open, difficult-to-spill container (form), with a sweet–flavored thirst quencher. They have thus specified the form and function desired. While several alternatives may fit this "description," this couple may consider only a small number of them. According to research on categorization,[30,31] a small number of alternatives, or a small consideration set, would be more typical for a buyer of this category of product. Ultimately, the competitors of a product at a customer level are the set of products that a customer would consider for use. To map competition at this level requires a study of the categorization by customers.

To put it more succinctly,

Consumer Choice is a function of consideration set.

Consideration Set is a function of the category evoked and affordability decision condition particulars.

Category Evoked is a function of a buyer's intended use or application and knowledge.

---

[30]In Rogers and Shoemaker, *op. cit,* form is described as dealing with directly observable physical appearance and substance of an innovation.

[31]For information in the area of categorization, see:

Nedungadi, P. and J. W. Hutchison, "The Prototypicality of Brands: Relationships with Brand Awareness, Preference and Usage," *Advances in Consumer Research,* Vol. 12, 1985, pp. 498–503.

Cohen, J. and K. Basu, "Alternative Methods of Categorization: Toward A Contingent Processing Framework," *Journal of Consumer Research,* Vol. 13, March, 1987, pp. 455–472.

Ratneshwar, S., and A. D. Shocker, "The Application of Prototypes and Categorization Theory in Marketing: Some Problems and Alternative Perspectives," *Advances in Consumer Research,* Vol. 15, 1988, pp. 280–285.

For more information on consideration sets see Howard and Sheth, *op. cit.;* Hauser, J. R. and B. Wernerfelt, "An Evaluation Cost Method of Consideration Sets," *Journal of Consumer Research,* Vol. 16, March, 1990, pp. 393–408.

Knowledge is a function of the consumer and the consumers' interaction with society, the media, and channel members.

Knowledge that is relevant pertains to the function and form suitable for this application, price, and the function and form of products available.

Categorization is likely to be dynamic, in that a consumer's knowledge may be updated by an ad or a point-of-purchase display, or a salesperson's communication. It is very much consumer–based, though it may be influenced by marketing actions, for example, advertising. Not understanding categorization could lead to gross errors. Consider a Pittsburgh brewery[32] which thought it could produce a better tasting beer by adding fruit flavoring to it. Consumers, however, did not perceive it to be a beer anymore. Consumers categorized it differently than intended by the brewer, and its purchase was not in place of "regular beer." In this case form was an effective boundary delimiter. Perhaps, communication leading to a different categorization of the product may have produced better results.

SUMMARY

In this chapter we highlighted the importance of understanding the domain of competition of a product. We discussed competition both from legal and marketing viewpoints. The former provided an opportunity to present economics–based ideas which are central to the legal view. It concentrates largely on measuring the price elasticity and cross-elasticity of demand to identify the boundaries of a market, both geographical and product. Market power was also shown to be assessed on cost based on both cost of entry and economies of scale and scope.

In discussing the marketing view, we stressed the importance of understanding the process of customer choice as well as certain structural factors. The factors discussed are geography and demography which relate to the relevance of the product and its reach to consumers in subgroups, technology representing unique barriers to satisfying consumer needs, and the presence of branded versus unbranded opportunities. Customer choice is ultimately made from a consideration set. This set is based on which category of products a consumer feels will best satisfy need. The importance of positioning a product within a consideration set is critical to marketing success. Knowledge of which consideration set a product is placed in is important in identifying its competitors.

Concept Questions

1. What are some marketing literature–based definitions of a product-market?
2. What considerations are involved in defining a relevant market from a United States legal viewpoint?
3. What are the major elements of some of the key cases from which case law on relevant market definitions has emerged?
4. What is the segments × needs × technologies view of a product-market?

---

[32]Described in Ratneshwar and Shocker, *op. cit.*

How can it be used by marketing strategists? How is this framework related to the function × form × price framework?

5. (a.) What are concentration ratios?

(b.) How can they be measured?

(c.) How can they be used?

6. What is the difference between horizontal and vertical barriers to movement in product-markets?

7. What is a market hierarchy? How can it be used?

Discussion Questions/Exercises

1. (a.) What is market share? Why is it useful? How should it be measured?

(b.) Develop alternative definitions of a product-market that lead to different market shares for the same product or service. Discuss how you would choose the right measure. Is there a correct measure?

2. Why is it important for a marketing strategist to consider the legal definitions of a relevant market?

3. For a product or service of a company of your choice, draw your perception of its competitive market hierarchy. Also, identify both horizontal and vertical barriers to movement in its relevant market. Discuss the implications of your analysis.

APPENDIX

Here are examples of methods used to determine product-market definitions (PMD) and what is referred to as market structure analysis (MSA).[33]

Methods that purport to develop a PMD typically rely on obtaining consumer judgment regarding the following:

a. Ratings of a large set of products on a predetermined set of product attributes (e.g., ratings of cars on MPG, comfort, sportiness, etc.). Products are then grouped according to the similarity of their attribute ratings. More "similar" products are closer competitors then less similar ones.

b. Evoked on consideration sets. The more sets in which two products jointly occur is said to represent the closeness of substitution between these products. Thus common presence across consideration sets is used to infer closeness of products.

c. Product deletion. Which product would not be bought if a consumer had a particular one? This question is representative of this method. Closeness is defined as an affirmative answer for a particular candidate product.

---

[33]An extensive critical review of these methods may be found in Shocker, A. D., D. W. Stewart and A. J. Zahorik, "Market Structure and Analysis: Practice, Problems and Promise," *In* G. Day, B. Weitz, and R. Wensley (eds.), *The Interface of Marketing and Strategy,* Greenwich, CT, JAI Press, 1990, pp. 9–56.

d. Overall similarity. For example, asking consumers to rate or rank the overall similarity of pairs of a large set of products. These similarity scores are then used to develop multidimensional scaling (MDS) based on maps of this set of products. In these methods, the attributes of the products do not have to be prespecified—they emerge as a product of the analysis and must be interpreted carefully. Closeness in such a map is interpreted as closeness in substitutability.

e. Substitution in use. In this set of methods, a product-market definition is arrived at by considering the similarity of use for which members of a set of product are individually felt to be suited. A map of these products, reflecting the situations for which they are suitable and a hierarchy of competition, results from each approach.

EXHIBIT A4–1   Hierarchical Clustering of Financial Services

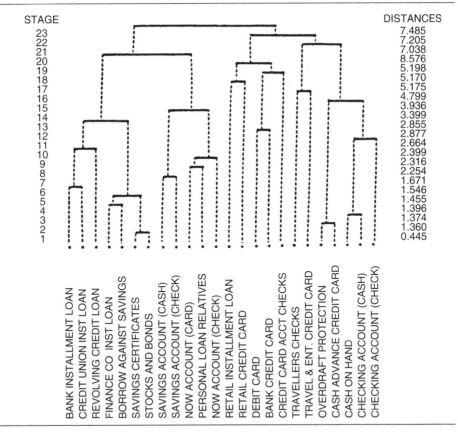

From Srivastava, R. K., M. J. Alpert and A. D. Shocker, "A Customer-Oriented Approach for Determining Marketing Structures," *Journal of Marketing,* Vol. 3 No. 2, Spring, 1984, p. 40. Reprinted by permission of the American Marketing Association.

An example of this approach is next presented.[34]   The data collection for this study was done in two stages.   In the first stage, a sampling of customers was asked to suggest as many uses as possible for a product (brand), for example, a bank credit card.   Then, for these uses, the customers were asked to suggest other possible products or brands.   As a follow-up, uses for these products were obtained.   The result was a large set of products and uses.   An independent sample then rated the suitability of each product for each use.   These data were analyzed using principal components analysis with use variables.   The resulting map of factor scores and loadings was used to develop a taxonomy of use.   In the second stage, hypothetical uses were created based on this taxonomy.   Twenty-four services were evaluated for their appropriateness in 12 different uses by a sampling of consumers.

These data have been analyzed in many different ways by Srivastava of the

EXHIBIT A4–2   Financial Services Market Structure (Overlapping Clusters)

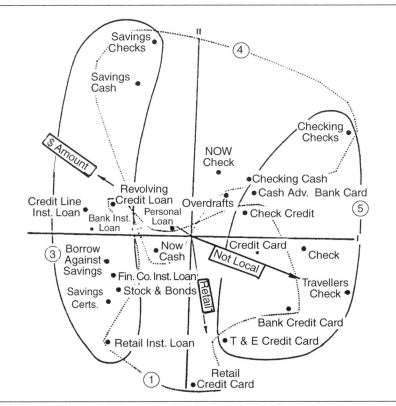

From A Customer Approach for Determining Structures. Srevastra, R. K., M. I. Alpert, and A. D. Schocker, *Journal of Marketing,* Vol. 3 No. 2, Spring, 1984 p. 41. Reprinted by permission of the American Marketing Association.

[34]This example is taken from Srivastava, R. K., M. I. Alpert, and A. D. Shocker, "A Customer–Oriented Approach for Determining Market Structures," *Journal of Marketing,* Vol. 48, Spring, 1984, pp. 32–45.

EXHIBIT A4–3   Testing Competitive Market Structure

Alternative _a_: Brand

$$\dot{p}* = 0.07$$
$$p* = 0.12$$
$$z = -2.7$$

	Maxwell House	Tasters Choice	Sanka	Brim	Folgers	Nescafe
Brand Structure:	$\dot{p}(s) = 0.07$	$\dot{p}(s) = 0.05$	$\dot{p}(s) = 0.03$	$\dot{p}(s) = 0.09$	$\dot{p}(s) = 0.04$	$\dot{p}(s) = 0.06$
No structure:	$p(s) = 0.18$	$p(s) = 0.11$	$p(s) = 0.12$	$p(s) = 0.04$	$p(s) = 0.02$	$p(s) = 0.04$
	$z = -2.9$	$z = -1.3$	$z = 0.8$	$z = 1.3$	$z = 0.9$	$z = -0.5$

Alternative _b_: Product Attribute

$$\dot{p}* = 0.32$$
$$p* = 0.11$$
$$z = 11.3$$

Ground Caffeinated	Ground Decaffeinated	Instant Caffeinated Regular	Instant Caffeinated Freeze Dried	Instant Decaffeinated Regular	Instant Decaffeinated Freeze Dried
$\dot{p}(s) = 0.47$	$\dot{p}(s) = 0.19$	$\dot{p}(s) = 0.37$	$\dot{p}(s) = 0.23$	$\dot{p}(s) = 0.23$	$\dot{p}(s) = 0.25$
$p(s) = 0.11$	$p(s) = 0.03$	$p(s) = 0.13$	$p(s) = 0.09$	$p(s) = 0.09$	$p(s) = 0.13$

Alternative _c_: Use

$$\dot{p}* = 0.40$$
$$p* = 0.46$$
$$z = -1.5$$

	Morning	Afternoon & Evening (P.M.)
Use Structure:	$\dot{p}(s) = 0.40$	$\dot{p}(s) = 0.41$
No Structure:	$p(s) = 0.44$	$p(s) = 0.48$
	$z = -1.5$	$z = -2.8$

Alternative _d_: Users

$$\dot{p}* = 0.23$$
$$p* = 0.59$$
$$z = -8.69$$

	Heavy	Light
Use Structure:	$\dot{p}(s) = 0.34$	$\dot{p}(s) = 0.11$
No Structure:	$p(s) = 0.75$	$p(s) = 0.18$
	$z = -9.3$	$z = -1.2$

From Urban, G. L., P. L. Johnson and J. R. Hauser, "Testing Competitive Marketing Structures," _Marketing Science,_ Vol. 3, No. 2, Spring, 1984. Reprinted with permission of The Institute of Management Sciences.

EXHIBIT A4–4   Brand Offerings by Selected Firms (1977)

	Ground		Instant			
	Caffeinated	Decaffeinated	Caffeinated		Decaffeinated	
			Regular	Freeze–Dried	Regular	Freeze–Dried
Nestle	No Brand	No Brand	Nescafe	Tasters' Choice	Nescafe	Tasters' Choice
General Foods	Maxwell House, Yuban	Sanka, Brim	Maxwell House, Yuban	Maxim	Sanka	Sanka, Brim
Procter & Gamble	Folgers	No Brand	Folgers	No Brand	High Point	No Brand

From Urban, G. L., P. L. Johnson and J. R. Hauser, "Testing Competitive Market Structures," *Marketing Science,* Vol. 3, No. 2, Spring, 1984. Reprinted with permission of The Institute of Management Sciences.

University of Texas at Austin and Shocker of the University of Minnesota and their colleagues. Recently, they recommended the use of overlapping cluster analysis to develop a product-market map. Their hierarchical clustering, showing the closeness of the different products is reproduced in Exhibit A4-1. Their overlapping cluster solution is shown in Exhibit A4-2. These exhibits can be used for many strategic purposes: (1) a manager could determine if any uses are underserved, implying an opportunity, (2) if a firm has more than one product to serve a particular use, then this should raise the likelihood of product cannibalization—which may be a problem, (3) if the use for which a product is best suited is decreasing, then it highlights a potential threat, and (4) it has possible implications for product redesign and repositioning.

Methods for determining a market structure rely on measures of actual purchasing behavior (or laboratory behavior). An example of these methods and a comparison, based on a paper by Urban, Johnson and Hauser, is discussed below.[35]

They assumed a market structure based on the following breakdowns (Exhibit A4–3): (1) by brand name, assuming that consumers' choice is based on brand name and that all brands are equally competitive, (2) by product attribute—ground or instant, caffeinated or not, and regular or freeze dried, (3) by use—in the a.m. or p.m., and (4) by heavy versus light users. They compared the market shares predicted by each of these structures with that obtained from a panel of coffee users. They found that the product attribute breakdown was the best of the four tested.

The coverage of the various submarkets (Exhibit A4–4) by the three major competitors indicates possible cannibalization and dissipation of energies by General Foods because of the presence of several brands in the submarket. However, such a multiplicity of brands in a submarket might be necessary to preempt entry into that submarket. Nestle does not have any brand in the ground coffee submarket, indicating a potential opportunity, or indicating the effectiveness of General Foods' product proliferation strategy in this submarket.

[35]Urban, G. L., P. L. Johnson, and J. R. Hauser, "Testing Competitive Market Structures," *Marketing Science,* Vol. 3, No. 2, Spring, 1984, pp. 83–112.

Part 2

RELATIONSHIPS WITH KEY PUBLICS

Chapter 5
Relationships With Channels of Distribution*

In Chapter 4 we discussed the core domain of marketing competition: the product-market. This chapter focuses on relationships with intermediaries (channel members) who help a firm reach its ultimate customers. Chapter 6 examines the development of long-term relationships with customers.[1]

We begin by examining why channel relationships play such a strategic role. We then review the activities performed by channel members and the types of structures used for organizing these activities. Next, we discuss an economics-based framework—transaction cost analysis—to determine strategic advantages that arise from alternative channel structures. We conclude with a discussion of how strong channel relationships are developed, even when the firm does not have direct control over the channel members.

STRATEGIC IMPORTANCE OF CHANNEL RELATIONSHIPS

In most marketing management textbooks, channels of distribution are treated as one of the four Ps in a marketing mix of product, price, promotion, and place. Both students and teachers pay considerably more attention to the product and promotion mix

*Used with the permission of the Authors, Bart Weitz and Robin Wensley.

[1]In this text we focus on market relationships with customers and channels as sources of competitive advantage. Clearly, firms have many relationships that can result in sustainable competitive advantage such as relationships with sources of capital (financial institutions, investors), suppliers of goods and services, and government agencies. However, we consider these relationships to be in the domain of strategic management, *not* marketing strategy.

than to price and place. Many business schools do not even offer a course in channel management. Given this lack of attention to channels of distribution, why do we devote an entire chapter to competitive advantages based on channel relationships?

Channel relationships play a strategic role for the following reasons. First, channel activities provide an excellent opportunity to develop a superior offering from the customer's perspective, because distribution functions add significantly more value to a firm's offering than product development, manufacturing, and advertising. Second, enduring channel relationships are difficult to achieve and even more difficult to alter. Third, one of the critical steps to achieve cooperation is credibility through commitment (discussed in Chapter 2), and careful development of channel relationships establishes commitment. Thus, advantages based on channel relationships are not easily usurped by competition.

Customer Value Created in Distribution Channels

Through research and development (R&D) and manufacturing, firms add value by assembling raw materials and components into a useful product. A finished product does a better job of satisfying customer needs than a bag of components. However, channel members—retailers and wholesalers—also add value. They increase the place, time, possession, and form utility of the product.

Consider an Apple Computer sitting on a shelf in a warehouse in Cupertino, California. This computer does not offer much value to a customer because it is not available at a location convenient to the customer (*place utility*), when the customer wants it (*time utility*), and the customer does not have exclusive, convenient use of the computer (*possession utility*). The local computer store increases the value of the Apple Computer by stocking it in inventory so that it is available when customers want it, by showing customers how to use the computer, matching the computer with peripheral equipment and software to provide an entire system for solving customer problems, offering payment terms that facilitate customer purchase, and providing service should any problems arise after the computer is purchased.

The value added by channel members is reflected in the channel margin—the percent of the retail selling price paid to channel members to provide services that facilitate the flow of goods from producers to ultimate customers. Typically, these channel activities account for 25% to 50% of the ultimate product value delivered to the customer. Advertising accounts for less than 3% of the value added, while personal selling accounts for less than 6%.

Cost Advantage. The significant value provided by channel activities and associated costs offer many opportunities for firms to create a differential advantage. Cost advantages can be established by performing channel activities more efficiently than competitors. For example, Gallo has achieved a distribution cost advantage over its competitors by emphasizing the supermarket versus the higher cost liquor store channel. However, to develop this lower cost channel, Gallo had to use extensive advertising to pull its products through supermarkets since supermarkets offer less services to the wine consumer than liquor stores. In addition, the "pull through" advertising created faster turnover which resulted in supermarkets accepting lower margins from Gallo than from its competitors.

A cost advantage can also be achieved through scale economies resulting from distributing many products through the same channel. For example, GE and Whirlpool are able to reduce distribution costs by offering a full line of major appliances (ranges, refrigerators, dishwashers, washing machines, and dryers) to the new construction market.

Unique Customer Benefits.   Through distribution activities a firm can offer a unique set of benefits to customers—benefits which may be very costly for competitors to imitate. For example, Cole National has developed a program that enables retailers to offer key duplication with minimal investment. The program includes providing a key duplicating machine, an appropriate set of blank keys (made by Cole National), and training for retail employees. By offering this program, Cole National enables consumers to purchase high quality, duplicate keys conveniently from a broad selection of retail outlets. Because of the limited size of the key duplicating market and the limited benefits to retailers from switching to another key duplicating program, competitors would have difficulty challenging Cole National's position in supplying blank keys.

L'Eggs hosiery by Hanes is another example of offering customer benefits through distribution. Hanes dramatically improved the convenience in purchasing hosiery by developing a unique system for distributing hosiery through supermarkets. Through innovative packaging and displays and a program of direct delivery to supermarkets, Hanes was able to offer more value to its customers, both retailers and consumers.

Channel Structures

(This section may be omitted by those already familiar with the alternative types of channel structures.) Exhibit 5–1 illustrates the wide variety of channel structure used to distribute products. Producers, who sell directly to consumers or industrial customers, perform all the channel activities themselves. They break bulk, offer assortments, carry inventory, finance sales, advertise, and provide after-the-sale services. However, most products and services are not sold directly to end users. For over 90% of the products sold, some of these functions are performed by channel intermediaries—agents, wholesalers, and retailers. Thus, developing a competitive advantage through distribution often involves coordinating activities performed by a diverse group of organizations.

Throughout this chapter we take the perspective of a producer of goods or services coordinating distribution activities to provide benefits associated with its products to its ultimate customer. However, one must recognize that channel members are independent business firms with their own marketing strategies. They are also attempting to develop competitive advantages in their markets by developing customer loyalty through differentiation of their offering. Sears tries to coordinate activities of its suppliers to achieve an advantage over other retailers such as Kmart and J. C. Penney. Rexall tries to coordinate producers and retail outlets to achieve an

EXHIBIT 5-1   Channel Structures

Consumer Products

Producer	Producer	Producer	Producer	Producer	Producer
↓	↓	↓	↓	↓	↓
Agent	Agent			Agent	
↓	↓	↓	↓	↓	↓
Wholesaler			Wholesaler		
↓	↓	↓	↓		
Retailer	Retailer	Retailer	Retailer	↓	↓
↓	↓	↓	↓		
Consumer	Consumer	Consumer	Consumer	Consumer	Consumer
				Avon,	L.L. Bean
				Mary Kaye	direct
				cosmetics	mail

Industrial Products

Producer	Producer	Producer	Producer
↓	↓	↓	↓
Agent		Agent	
↓	↓	↓	
Wholesaler	Wholesaler		↓
↓	↓	↓	↓
Customer	Customer	Customer	Customer

advantage over other drug–wholesalers such as Sentry.   Even though the discussion focuses on the producer, the concepts can be easily translated into marketing strategy issues confronting distributors or retailers.   Moreover, it is important to recognize that strategic decisions made by any one channel member are not made in isolation, because each channel member is developing its own marketing strategy.

The independent pursuit of strategies can introduce problems for each independent channel member.   For instance, over an extended period, Marks and Spencer, in the U.K., became a dominant competitor in the adult clothing market.   A number of its suppliers achieved substantial and profitable growth because of this position. This also meant that they came to rely on M&S as effectively their sole "marketing" activity.   As potential markets developed in which M&S's position was less strong (Europe and North America), they had neither the knowledge nor the resources to respond effectively to such opportunities.   Recently such problems have been exacerbated by the increased pressure of M&S's position in the U.K. market because of the emergence of revitalized retail competition.

Conventional System.   In a conventional channel, the functions are provided by independent channel intermediaries.   The agents, wholesalers, and retailers in conventional channels distribute products offered by a number of producers. Each intermediary is primarily concerned with managing its immediate suppliers and customers to maximize its profits.   Thus, a conventional channel involves a number of independent decision makers who focus on only one stage of the distribution process.

Coordination of distribution functions is provided by market forces via price. Producers compete by offering products at attractive prices (margins) to secure the services of channel intermediaries. Conventional channels are characterized by a low level of coordination among channel members and limited control by the producers over activities performed by the channel members.

However, market forces can result in very efficient distribution functions. If a distributor fails to perform efficiently, producers and retailers will use other available distributors to provide services at lower costs.

Administered System.   In an administered system, a producer coordinates the distribution function by offering a program for a specific line of merchandise. The channel members are independent and can accept or reject the program. In addition to the Cole National key and L'eggs pantyhose examples, Sealy (mattresses), Scott (lawn care products), and Villager (women's sportswear) use programs to coordinate channel activities.

The typical program involves the producer offering guaranteed prices and delivery, customized sales aids (catalogs, point-of-purchase displays, demonstration equipment), advertising support, sales training, and assortment and floor plans. In exchange, the retailer agrees to display the products in the suggested manner, maintain a specified level and assortment of inventory, and undertake appropriate advertising. Producers using an administered system to achieve control over distribution are exploiting their expertise in merchandising their products. Even though the producer can not force the channel member to participate in the program, the program is designed so that it is in the channel members' economic interest to adopt it.

Contractual System.   In a contractual system, the activities to be performed by channel members and the producer are formalized in a contractual agreement. Through this agreement, independent firms have a greater impact on the market than they could realize unilaterally.

Although there are many types of contractual systems, franchising is the most pervasive contractual system in the U.S. Over 30% of all U.S. retail sales are made by franchise chains. Franchise contracts coordinate activities between producers and retailers (General Motors and Ford automobile dealerships), producers and wholesalers (Coca-Cola and Pepsi-Cola soft drink bottlers), wholesalers and retailers (Rexall drug stores), and developers of services and retailers (AAMCO transmissions, Midas mufflers, Holiday Inn, McDonald's, Kentucky Fried Chicken, and Kelley Girls).

Corporate System.   A corporate channel represents forward vertical integration by producers. All channel functions are performed by organizational entities owned and operated by one firm. Singer (sewing machines), Sherwin-Williams (paints), and Hart, Schaffner & Marx (men's clothing) are examples of corporations which perform the production, wholesaling, and retailing functions for their products. By virtue of ownership, these firms maintain absolute control over the distribution of their products and have an opportunity to coordinate these activities to achieve a competitive advantage. However, significant administrative cost may be involved to effectively coordinate distribution.

Control, Coordination, and Costs. In Exhibit 5–2, the four channel systems are arrayed along a control dimension. The producer has the greatest control over channel activities under the corporate system and the least control under the conventional system. The contractual and administered systems represent intermediate levels of control.

EXHIBIT 5-2 Producer Control and Channel Systems

Corporate	Franchiser	Administered	Conventional
Singer	Midas	Cole National	Most
Sherwin-Williams	Rexall	L'Eggs	firms
Hart, Schaffner & Marx	McDonald's	Sealy	

Greater			Less
			---->
	Producer Control		

Many marketers feel that greater control automatically leads to more efficiency in coordinating channel activities. Often, however, the conventional systems using the "invisible hand" of the marketplace can be more cost efficient than corporate systems. In the next section we discuss conditions under which vertical integration (corporate system) results in a more cost effective channel than a conventional system.

VERTICAL INTEGRATION AND CHANNEL EFFECTIVENESS[2]

Economic theory suggests two reasons for vertically integrating the performance of channel functions: (1) cost reduction and (2) strategic control.[3] The need for vertical integration to reduce costs arises when the efficient performance of a business requires close coordination. Steel manufacturing is a classic example of advantages gained by one firm operating blast furnaces, converters, and primary reduction mills, thereby eliminating the need to reheat material between production stages. Conceptually these activities could be performed by independent firms using adjacent facilities. A steel processing firm might negotiate with a blast furnace firm to build an adjoining plant. The processing company would be able to reach a favorable contract price because a number of blast furnace companies would compete for the opportunity to provide molten steel. However, once the contract is drawn and the blast furnace is built, the processing firm no longer faces a competitive market for molten steel. The firm initially selected to provide the molten steel has an advantage over

[2]This section is based on Barton A. Weitz and Erin Anderson, "Make-or-Buy Decisions: Vertical Integration and Marketing Productivity," *Sloan Management Review,* 27 Spring 1986, pp. 3–20.

[3]Scherer, F. M. *Industrial Market Structure and Economic Performance,* 2nd Ed, Chicago, Rand-McNally, 1980, p. 78.

other competitors because of its location. Because of this unique locational asset, the blast furnace company has realized a quasi–monopolistic position and can charge excessive prices for molten steel, raising the processing company's costs. To prevent this possibility, firms either vertically integrate or develop complex contingent claim contracts and cost monitoring systems. Through vertical integration or contracting, the processing firm prevents a competitive market, *ex ante,* from degenerating into a noncompetitive, *ex post,* market.

Firms also vertically integrate to gain strategic control over their environment.[4] Backward integration ensures the supply of scarce raw material, while forward integration ensures access to markets through limited distribution channels. By controlling an important distribution channel, the firm reduces the risk of channel members or other producers from exerting monopolistic power and charging excessive prices to perform distribution functions. In addition, the control may enable the firm to offer a unique set of benefits—differentiate its product—or provide more customer value by reducing costs and lowering prices.

The cost reduction and strategic control motives suggest that the primary reason for vertical integration is to protect the firm from adverse effects which occur when there are no competitive markets for goods and services needed by the firm. If the markets for providing distribution services were perfectly competitive, there would be no need to vertically integrate to assure low-cost distribution. Because of scale economies realized through performing distribution activities for many producers, channel members would be able to provide these functions at a lower cost than any one producer. Additionally, the competitive forces in the marketplace would prevent excessive prices (margins) for the distribution services. The "invisible hand" of the marketplace places substantial pressure on independent channel members to perform efficiently, offering services at a fair place. Therefore, when competitive markets exist for distribution services, producers are assured of a low-cost supply of these services. In practice, producers face markets which are competitive. In most situations there are not enough suppliers that we can presume the operation of Adam Smith's "invisible hand" automatically. We therefore need a more refined framework in which to evaluate the arguments for and benefits of external distribution services. Such a framework is provided by transaction cost analysis.

Transaction Cost Analysis

Transaction cost analysis, developed by Oliver Williamson,[5] identifies specific conditions under which markets become noncompetitive, necessitating vertical integration to contain costs. The theory addresses the question: Under what conditions are transactions performed more efficiently within an organization under bureaucratic control

---

[4]Harrigan, Katherine, "A Framework for Looking at Vertical Integration," *The Journal of Business Strategy,* February 1983, pp. 30–37.

[5]See Oliver Williamson, *Markets and Hierarchies: Analysis and Anti-Trust Implications,* New York, Free Press, 1975; "Transaction Cost Economics: The Governance of Contractual Relationships," *Journal of Law and Economics,* October 1979, pp. 233–262; "The Economics of Organization: The Transaction Cost Approach," *American Journal of Sociology,* 87, 1981, pp. 547–577.

(corporate channel system) versus independent entities under market control (conventional channel system)? A transaction, in this context, is the payment of compensation in the form of a margin to a channel member in exchange for services to be performed by the channel member. Based on transaction cost analysis, the efficiency of performing distribution functions through a corporate system as opposed to a conventional system increases as

1. the degree to which idiosyncratic assets are required to perform channel function increases;
2. the environment in which the channel functions are performed becomes more unpredictable and volatile;
3. the assessment of channel member performance becomes more difficult;
4. the potential for free-riding increases; and
5. the scale on which the distribution activities are performed increases.

Idiosyncratic Assets. Idiosyncratic assets arise when producer-specific capabilities are needed to distribute effectively a product or service. Producer-specific capabilities are specialized knowledge and skills or specialized equipment required to perform distribution functions. For example, to perform distribution functions effectively, a channel member may need to use a unique storage facility, to develop a good working relationship with producer personnel, to adjust its order processing system to the producer's system, or to learn unique terms and procedures used by the producer. These capabilities are considered assets because they either added value to the producer's offering by reducing distribution costs or increasing product performance. These assets are idiosyncratic when they are useful only for performing distribution functions for one producer.[6]

Why does the need for idiosyncratic assets suggest that producers should vertically integrate and perform distribution functions within the same corporate structure? Consider the following. Special facilities are needed to store a producer's products. Distributors are unwilling to pay the cost for these facilities, so the producer agrees to pay a substantial portion of the cost for constructing the specialized facility for one distributor in each geographic area. This distributor now possesses an idiosyncratic asset. The distributor can demand a greater margin to perform distribution functions for the producer, withhold or distort relevant information, favorably reinterpret implicit or explicit agreements, or simply devote inadequate (from the producer's perspective) effort and resources toward distributing the producer's products. The producer will be willing to tolerate some of this opportunistic behavior because it is reluctant to incur the cost of building a new storage facility for a competitive distributor. Thus, the producer is forced to tolerate some inefficiencies because of the high cost of switching from one distributor to another. The market for performing

---

[6]Note that idiosyncratic assets are not the same as unusual or rare capabilities. For example, only a few retailers may have the capability of servicing microcomputers, but this capability is only idiosyncratic if it is germane to the computers manufactured by one firm.

distribution functions for the producer's products is no longer competitive as a result of the idiosyncratic asset, the storage facility, required to distribute the product.

In the specialized storage situation, the producer must guard against the distributor taking advantage of an idiosyncratic asset or capability. However, producers often deliberately develop and take advantage of idiosyncratic assets to "lock in" customers or distributors. For example, government contractors may submit bids below cost for an initial order of equipment. While they lose money on the initial order, they develop *unique* know-how and production equipment (idiosyncratic assets) that will give them advantage when bidding for follow-on orders. They "get well" by charging high prices for follow-on equipment orders.[7]

Computer airline reservation systems were used by airlines to "lock-in" travel agents. Agents were trained to use a system developed by one airline—a system that highlights flights offered by that airline. After learning one system, the agents were reluctant to switch to another system, even if the new system reduced their costs, because they did not want to invest in learning a new system.

Thus, idiosyncratic assets can be a double-edged sword—they can enable a distributor to take advantage of a producer or enable a producer to take advantage of a distributor. By vertically integrating distribution, the firm can control the potential problems arising from idiosyncratic assets by using its authority to direct behavior of groups within the corporation; however, vertical integration is not without cost, as we shall discuss later.

Another approach in preventing problems arising from idiosyncratic assets is to write a complex contract between the producer and channel member defining each organizations' responsibilities and prices that are to be charged for services performed. To be effective, this contract must define how contractual terms will change if factors in the environment change and how the performance of parties covered by the contract will be monitored. Often, such contingent claims contracts become so complex that they are not a cost effective control mechanism.

Environmental Uncertainty. Corporate systems (vertical integration) are appropriate when the environment in which channel functions are performed is complex, turbulent, and unpredictable. In unpredictable and uncertain environments, producers fre-

---

[7]See R. E. Weigand, "Buying In To Market Control," *Harvard Business Review,* November–December, 1980, pp. 141–149.

The economic analysis of this problem is more complex than this presentation suggests. For instance, if we consider the nature of the total costs for both the initial and follow-on orders and presume that the initial order is subject to competitive bidding, then the net effect may be no more than that the supplier receives a "fair" return in the total contracts. The problem arises if there is no clear contractual link between the initial and follow-on prices and when it is not feasible for a competitor to bid against the follow-on contract only. In a recent EEC case, Rover group attempted to argue that it had exclusive copyright for replacement exhaust (muffler) designs for its cars. Therefore any distributors would either have to purchase directly from Rover or from suppliers who had been licensed. This situation was seen by the courts as an attempt to reinforce what might well be a simple investment advantage over competition (DEM suppliers to Rover would obviously already have the facilities available to produce replacement parts) with a restraint that would restrict competition, and was therefore dismissed. This result did not, however, mean existing suppliers might still not be in a "justified" advantageous position in bidding to supply replacement orders.

quently make adjustments in prices, product mixes, and services which impact distribution activities. Uncertain environments often involve reinterpreting what and how distribution activities should be performed. This reinterpretation can be difficult to manage with independent distributors, who are primarily interested in the impact of the changes on their performance rather than the performance of the whole system.

However, uncertainty also creates problems for vertically integrated organizations. When a change in distribution tactics is required, it may be easier to negotiate or even terminate, an independent distributor than pressure an entrenched distribution division to adopt a new program.[8] Obviously, the potential flexibility, provided by the independent distributor approach can only be realized if the cost of replacing distributors is minimal—if there are no idiosyncratic assets required to perform the new distribution function.

Difficulty in Assessing Performance. When it is difficult to assess the performance of distribution activities using output measures such as sales, the effectiveness of independent distributors may decline because inefficiencies or even deliberate shirking may go unnoticed. In principle, through vertical integration these assessment problems can be minimized, since the vertically integrated firm has greater access to information on distributor performance. It can monitor inventory levels, service provided, and sales calls to assess performance when output measures are inadequate.

Difficulty in assessing performance using outputs often arise when close coordination is required to perform an activity. For instance, when a distributor needs factory support to make a sale, it is difficult to determine the contributions of the factory support staff and distributor personnel to the eventual sale.

"Free-Riding" Potential. When distributors can "free-ride," there is a tendency for distribution effectiveness to decline. The classic example of free-riding is a McDonald's fast food franchise located on a highway. Through the efforts of McDonald's and its franchises, the McDonald's name has a good reputation for fast food. The individual highway franchise enjoys the benefits of this reputation, but may not have to pay the costs. It can cut costs and provide substandard service, but not suffer a significant loss in sales because its customers are transient—they have little opportunity to repeat purchases. However, other McDonald's franchises may suffer because the substandard service provided by the highway franchise has degraded the image of McDonald's and all its franchises. While it is difficult to control free-riding by independent channel members, by vertically integrating, a firm can use its authority to prevent free-riding. In addition, in the vertically integrated firm, the people performing distribution activities are employees of the firm and often do not benefit directly from the rewards of free-riding.

Scale. Vertical integration is an organizational method for dealing with problems that arise from idiosyncratic assets, uncertain environments, performance assessment difficulty, and free-riding. However, an administrative staff is needed to

[8]See K. J. Arrow, *Limits of Organization,* New York, Norton, 1974 and R. H. Miles, *Macro Organizational Behavior,* Santa Monica, Goodyear Publishing, 1980.

coordinate activities when distribution functions are performed in a corporate system. This fixed administration cost is only justified when distribution functions involve a significant level of activity. Even when distribution costs are substantial, administrative costs associated with vertically integrating may be greater than efficiency losses because of noncompetitive markets, uncertainty, assessment problems, and free-riding.

Benefits.   Vertical integration reduces inefficiencies resulting from idiosyncratic assets, performance assessment difficulties, environment uncertainty, and free-riding by (1) using the authority of the firm, (2) having access to more and better information, (3) reducing the potential gains of people engaging in improper activities, and (4) being more flexible in response to a changing environment. The firm can resolve disputes by fiat and dictate the activities of employees through rules and procedures. Although the authority of the firm is limited, the firm certainly has more control over its employees than it does over independent distributors.

Firms have a greater opportunity to access information and audit activities (inputs) and performance (outputs) of their employees. The producers in corporate systems are not constrained by written documents on relevant issues such as sales. They can undertake informal reviews of poor performance and delve into side issues that might reveal distribution problems. Finally, employees readily yield more and better information than an independent distributor.

In corporate channels, firms can prevent behaviors such as free-riding because employees, unlike independent channel members, do not directly benefit from these improper activities. Employees are paid by management and thus cannot benefit directly from profits gained through free-riding.

Finally, the firm can offer a broader range of incentives than those offered to the independent channel member through the marketplace. Through these incentives, such as job security and status, employees identify with goals of the company, while independent channel members are primarily guided by the goals of the firms.

Costs.   Based on earlier discussions, you might believe that the vertically integrated, corporate channel always outperforms the conventional channel. However, there are disadvantages to the corporate channel, beyond the required administrative costs. Large, vertically integrated organizations are often inefficient since managers are reluctant to end inefficient internal programs and to terminate employees. Employees, unlike independent channel members, are sheltered from the competitive forces of the marketplace, and become inefficient. The goals of individual managers may not be related to the performance of the firm, since large organizations breed alienation among employees. Problems of control can arise in vertically integrated functions, but responsiveness to market pressure is lost.

On the other hand, the "invisible hand of the competitive market" places substantial pressure on independent distributors to provide effective service or be replaced. In addition, the fact that we have recognized that relationships between such independent channel members are governed by economic forces does not mean that they are always impersonal as might first appear. Channel members are concerned with their own self-interest, but except in exceptional circumstances, they have considerable interest in building their own reputation (trust is key in dealing with uncertainty), as well as maintaining the level of performance of the channel as a whole.

Because of the inefficiencies of large bureaucracies and the inherent efficiencies of market transactions, economists suggest that conventional channels are more efficient than corporate channels. In fact, many U.S. corporations are restructuring, particularly in manufacturing, to reduce costs and increase flexibility (Exhibit 5–3). However, Exhibit 5–4 shows conditions under which this trend is applicable—the conditions under which a market mechanism is likely to fail and channel efficiency therefore is increased through vertical integration.

INTERMEDIATE FORMS OF CHANNEL CONTROL

In the previous section, we examined the issue of channel organization and control as if there were only two options—corporate or conventional. However, Exhibit 5–2 suggests that a variety of options exist for achieving channel control. The corporate and conventional systems represent extreme points on the control continuum. The need for intermediate forms becomes apparent when one attempts to use the questions in Exhibit 5–4 to analyze a specific situation. Only in rare instances will the answers uniformly point to a conventional or corporate channel system. Most situations are a

EXHIBIT 5-3   The Network Organization

A special report in *Business Week* (March 3, 1986, pp. 60–71) describes the growth of a new corporate form—the network. As corporations began to vertically integrate in the 1850s, management levels were added to oversee each stage in the production process from purchasing raw materials to marketing finished products. In the 1900s, corporations formed divisions, with their own set of functional managers, to cope with the expansion in the number of products being made and marketed by the corporation. By the 1950s, large, vertically-integrated firms had difficulty exploiting synergies and coordinating the efforts of separate divisions. To overcome these coordination problems, a more complex, matrix organization structure was created by adding another layer of managers who were responsible for informally linking groups with complementary responsibilities. By the 1980s, the bureaucracies in many large corporations stifled manufacturing and flexibility, and significantly increased the cost of manufacturing products. The network corporation is a response to these problems associated with large, vertically-integrated firms.

The network corporations are "vertically disaggregated." They rely on other corporations to perform many of the functions performed by a business such as manufacturing, research and development, or marketing, but continue to perform specific functions for which they have a competitive advantage. For example, many firms (Liz Claiborne, Nike, Schwinn Bicycle, Esprit) use non-U.S. contract manufacturers to produce their products at low cost while they concentrate their efforts on design and marketing. Convergent Technology concentrates on designing and manufacturing computer work stations, whereas AT&T and Unisys perform the marketing and distributing functions for their products. In fact, some toy manufacturers are actually "hollow corporations," and only perform a coordinating function internally and contract a number of other firms to design, manufacture, advertise, distribute, and collect accounts receivable.

EXHIBIT 5-4   Factors Affecting Vertical Integration Decisions

Variable	Conventional Channel	Corporate Channel
Idiosyncratic Assets		
How many firms could satisfactorily perform the channel activities satisfactorily?	Many	Few
How costly would it be to replace a firm presently performing channel functions?	Not very	Very
How long does it take a new distributor with experience in the industry to achieve the performance level of your existing distributors?	Short time	Long time
Does the producer use terms and manufacturers not used by other firms in the industry?	No	Yes
Are the products or services:	Standard	Highly differentiated
Are customer loyalties directed primarily toward:	Producers	Distributors
Environmental Uncertainty		
How accurately can the producer forecast sales?	Accurately	Not accurately
How frequently does the producer need to react to competitive activity?	Infrequently	Frequently
Difficulty in Assessing Performance		
Can the producer accurately evaluate the performance of channel members using output measures?	Yes	No
How much coordination is required between channel members and the producer?	Little	A lot
Free-Riding Potential		
How frequently do customers purchase from the same distributor?	Frequently	Infrequently
Are all distributors required to provide the same level of support and service?	No	Yes
Is the reputation of the channel member more important than the reputation of the firm?	Yes	No
Scale of Channel Activities		
What is the average order size?	Small	Large
How many products from the producer are ordered at one time by customers?	Many	Few

mix of answers—some suggesting a corporate system, others indicating a conventional system. In this section we discuss some intermediate forms of control based on contractual agreements between producers and channel members—franchising and the use of vertical market restraints.

Franchise Systems

The Franchising Agreement.   In a franchise system, one firm (the franchisor) licenses an entire business format to a number of outlets (franchises) to market a product or service. The business format may include the franchisor's brand names, trademarks, know-how, and method of doing business. Franchise contracts typically include the following elements:

1. The franchisor provides managerial assistance to the franchisee, which may include site selection, training programs, operating procedures, advice on ongoing operations, design of physical layout, and advertising materials. In addition, the franchisor may offer group insurance, centralized purchasing, and national advertising.

2. The franchisee agrees to operate the franchise in the prescribed manner. The contract may specify the products to be sold, prices, hours of operation, condition of the facility, and inventory levels. The franchisor audits its franchises to ensure that these provisions are met.

3. The franchisee agrees to pay a royalty, usually a percentage of sales, to the franchisor, plus an initial franchise fee. In addition, the franchisee may be required to purchase products from the franchisor, and pay rental, lease, license, or management fees.

***Rationale for Franchising.*[9]**   The franchise system enables the franchisor (producer) to achieve a high degree of control without actually owning the retail outlets. The common explanation for use of a franchise system is that it enables a franchisor to raise capital (through the franchise fee) and expand its business more quickly than it could by other means. However, capital theory indicates that this argument is questionable, because the franchisee faces higher risk since it owns only one location. Therefore the cost of capital to the franchisor should be lower than the cost to the franchisee because the franchisor is able to reduce its risk through participation in multiple locations. If the franchisor is unable to raise money in capital markets, it will probably be unable to raise capital by selling its franchises as well.

An alternative explanation of franchising is based on the problem firms have in monitoring and controlling distribution activities. Typically, franchising is used when the franchises are relatively small and spread over a wide geographic area. In this situation, if the outlets were owned by the producer, the costs of effectively supervising managers would be extremely high. The franchise contract minimizes this administrative expense by motivating remotely located managers to operate efficiently. The franchisee managers are given a major share of the proceeds from the operation; however, the opportunities for free-riding are so great, that a high degree of control over operations is needed.

Franchising is an example of assigning specific business functions to the organizations which are most efficient at performing the functions. The franchisor through scale economies is most efficient at developing the format and providing training and advertising support; whereas the franchisee is most efficient at managing day-to-day operations with low cost, low overhead.

[9]Rubin, Paul H., "The Theory of The Firm and The Structure of Franchise Contracts," *The Journal of Law and Economics,* Vol. 21, April, 1978, pp. 223–233.

Vertical Market Restrictions

Types of Restraints.   Franchising involves a complex contract for an entire business format.   Producers also use contracts to control specific elements of a channel member's activity.   Some common restrictions which have been or are used are:

1. *Exclusive Dealing*   The producer requires that the channel member sell only its products and not products offered by competitors.

2. *Territorial and Customer Restrictions*   The producer restricts the geographic region or type of customer to which the channel member can sell the producer's products.

3. *Resale Price Maintenance*   The producer specifies a price below which retailers may not sell the product.

4. *Full-Line Forcing*   The producer insists that a channel member stock or sell the complete product line offered by the producer.

5. *Refusal to Deal*   The producer typically establishes a set of conditions and refuses to deal with channel members who do not follow these conditions.

Rationale for Vertical Restraints.   The societal and legal implications concerning vertical restraints are hotly debated among marketers, lawyers, and economists.   Some commentators[10] feel that all vertical restraints should be *per se*[11] illegal because they decrease *competition* among channel members selling the same brand (intrabrand competition).   For example, granting exclusive territory to a distributor enables the distributor to secure a monopoly position in its territory for that brand and shield itself from competition related to the producer's products.   The distributor could charge excessive prices to its customers and the social welfare would be sacrificed.   (It is interesting to note that in general producers favor the use of vertical restraints.   However, the contention that vertical restraints result in excessive profits for the distributor suggests that producers should voluntarily abandon restraints to increase their sales and profit, as distributors prices are reduced through competition.)   Others[12] argue that, in general, vertical restrictions promote competition between brands (interbrand competition) resulting in greater economic efficiency.

To understand the reasons that favor vertical restraints from the point of view of the producer and economic theory, consider this example.   A producer of high performance, expensive audio speakers is interested in selling its speakers through retail stores specializing in audio equipment.   The producer needs to educate the retail

---

[10]Meehan, James and Robert J. Larner, "A Proposed Rule of Reason for Vertical Restraints on Competition," *The Anti-Trust Bulletin,* Summer 1981, pp. 195–225 and Louis W. Stern and Thomas L. Eovaidi, *Legal Aspects of Marketing Strategy: Anti Trust and Consumer Protection Issues,* Englewood Cliffs, Prentice-Hall, 1984.

[11]*Per se* illegal means that the practice is illegal *under all circumstances*.

[12]Pitotsky, Robert, "The *Sylvania* Case: Antitrust Analysis of Non-Price Vertical Restrictions," *Columbia Law Review,* 78, 1978, pp. 1–38 and Martin B. Louis, "Vertical Distributional Restraints under *Schwinn* and *Sylvania*: An Argument for Continuing Use of Partial *Per se* Approach," *Michigan Law Review,* 75, 1976, pp. 275–311.

salespeople about the unique design features so that the salespeople can inform customers about the performance and justify the high selling price. Additionally, the producer would like the retailers to build a special soundproof room so that the quality of the speakers can be demonstrated to potential customers.

However, the audio retailers are reluctant to invest in training their salespeople and building a soundproof listening room because the producer has placed no restrictions on distribution. A customer might learn about the speakers in their audio store, but buy the speakers at a discount store. The discount store can offer lower prices than the audio store because the discounter does not have to invest in training salespeople or building special listening rooms. The discount store would be free-riding on the services provided by the audio store.

How can the producer get the audio stores to provide the services needed to sell its products? The producer needs to restrain competition among retailers for its speakers so that the audio store makes enough profit to justify the necessary investment. One method for protecting the audio store is to grant the store the exclusive right to sell the speakers in a geographic region (exclusive dealing). Another method is to place a restriction that no retailer can sell the speaker below a specified price (resale price maintenance). If a minimum price is established, customers tend to purchase the speakers from the outlet offering the greatest service— the audio store. Finally, the producer can refuse to sell to any retailer who does not agree to install a listening room and to train its salespeople (refusal to deal). By reducing intrabrand competition for the speakers using vertical restraints, a new high performance speaker that requires special investment can be presented effectively to the public and thus competition among brands (interbrand) of speakers is increased.[13]

The use of contracts, either vertical restraints[14] or franchising, enables a producer to gain control over the performance of channel functions without resorting to vertical integration.

ACHIEVING CONTROL OF CONVENTIONAL DISTRIBUTION CHANNELS

Conventional distribution channels (independent distributors and retailers who sell products from many producers) historically have been and continue to be the most common method for distributing goods and services. As shown in Exhibit 5–4, the use of independent channel members is expected to increase. Firms attempting to

[13]Williamson, Oliver E., "Assessing Vertical Market Restrictions: Antitrust Ramifications of a Transaction Cost Analysis Approach," *University of Pennsylvania Law Review,* 127, 1979, pp. 953–993. Robert H. Bork, *The Anti Trust Paradox: A Policy at War with Itself,* New York, 1978, Chapter 14; and Richard A. Posner, "The Rule of Reason and the Economic Approach: Reflections on the Sylvania Decision," *University of Chicago Law Review,* 45, 1977, pp. 1–20.

[14]In the United States, the antitrust implications of vertical restraints are an important and volatile legal issue. Presently, resale price maintenance is *per se* illegal. The rule of reason applies to exclusive dealing and refusal to deal. Each case is decided on its own merits to determine whether competition is diminished because of the restraint.

develop strategic advantages will have to learn to deal with independent channel members. However, control of an independent channel member is difficult since by definition it cannot be achieved through elaborate contracts (franchising agreements) or vertical integration. Producers need to seek alternatives to achieve a strategic advantage when using conventional channels.

Sources of Conflict Among Producers and Independent Channel Members

Problems in coordinating the activities of independent channel members frequently arise from (1) goal incompatibility, (2) disagreements concerning the scope of the channel members' activities, and (3) differences in perceptions of the activities under-taken by channel members. Frequently, producers and distributors have conflicting goals and objectives. For example, executives of a large, publicly-owned producer may be risk-neutral with the objective of increasing stockholder wealth through growth in sales and profits; whereas a small, privately-held retailer may be highly risk-aversive with the objective of maintaining current income rather than increasing income. In addition, conventional channel members must deal with the potentially conflicting goals and objectives of many producers and may not be able to undertake all of the activities expected by each producer.

Conflicts between producers and distributors can also arise because of disagree-ments concerning the role of the channel member in the producer's distribution pro-gram. For example, a producer may feel that it can handle large customers more effectively than a distributor, whereas the distributor is reluctant to have the producer "skim the cream off its market" by handling large customers directly. Or, a producer may feel that a distributor is not actively pursuing new customers, but simply selling its products to customers who were presold on the product by the producer's advertising.

Such conflicts about roles frequently arise when producers use multiple channels of distribution. A manufacturer of uniforms may use a direct sales force to sell large hospitals, direct mail to sell to private nurses, and distributors to sell to nurses in doc-tor's offices. The distributor may define its domain as all potential customers within its geographic region, whereas the manufacturer wishes to confine the distributor's activi-ties to a subset of these customers that it wishes to service through distribution.

Use of Power to Control Independent Channel Members[15]

Power is the ability of a producer to get a channel member to do something that the channel member would not normally do. For example, Procter & Gamble may use its power to get small grocery stores to sell three brands of its detergents, even though the grocery store prefers to carry only one brand. More formally stated, the producer's (A's) power over a channel member (B) is the difference between the probability of B's

---

[15]See Louis W. Stern and Adel I. El-Ansary, *Marketing Channels,* 2nd Ed., Englewood Cliffs, NJ, Prentice-Hall, 1982, Chapter 6.

undertaking a behavior after A has intervened and the probability of B undertaking the behavior without A intervening.

Note that the concept of power describes a relationship between two parties. A firm is only powerful with respect to another firm. Thus Levi's may be powerful with respect to a small retailer, but much less powerful with respect to Sears. Also, power can be implicit. The channel members do not have to take overt action to demonstrate the power of a producer. An increase in the popularity of the channel member acting in accordance with the producer's wish indicates relative power.

Power can also be viewed in terms of dependency. When a producer is highly dependent on a channel member, the channel member is more powerful. Carrefours, a chain of French supermarkets, may represent 80% of the sales made by a producer of men's shirts. The shirt manufacturer is dependent on Carrefours and thus Carrefours is powerful and has great influence over the manufacturer. Dependencies arise when the number of potential distributors or the number of potential suppliers is limited. When only one effective distributor exists in a territory, the producer wishing to sell through a distribution channel is highly dependent on the distributor. The impact of dependency is heightened when the territory accounts for a sizeable portion of the producer's sales.

Sources of Power

Firms have a number of sources or bases of power available to them to facilitate their attempts to influence the activities of channel members. Some of the power sources are:[16]

1. *Rewards*   Reward power arises when a channel member believes that if it undertakes an action it will receive a reward from the producer. For example, a producer might use reward power by granting an exclusive territory to a distributor that agrees to stock and sell its products.

2. *Coercion*   Coercive power is based on the expectation of a channel member that it will be "punished" if it does not undertake an action asked for by the producer. At one time, General Motors would terminate a dealer that sold automobiles manufactured by other companies.

3. *Knowledge*   A channel member may tend to agree to an action requested by a producer because it views the producer as an expert. For example, a distributor might stock the assortment of drills suggested by the producer because it feels the producer has more knowledge of the drills required by end users.

4. *Identification*   Reference or identification power arises when a producer has an image with which a channel member would like to identify. For example, a producer of high quality products may be able to influence a discount store's buying decision simply because the discount store would like to be identified with the producer.

All of these sources of power can be translated into economic terms. Clearly,

[16]French, John R. P., and Betram Raven, "The Bases of Social Power" *In* D. Cartwright (ed.), *Studies in Social Power*, Ann Arbor, MI, University of Michigan Press, 1959.

the use of rewards and punishments has economic consequences, just as the use of knowledge and identification can also increase the rewards accruing to channel members. Although all bases of power have the potential to influence a channel member's actions, coercion is unique in that it often results in channel members doing something that is not in their own economic best interest.

Long-Term Effects of Power

While the threat or use of power can be an effective method for influencing the actions of channel members, power can accentuate conflict in the producer-channel member relation.[17] When producers use power to force channel members to act in a way that is not in their economic best interest, channel members will redress the power imbalance and realize acceptable financial returns.

The actions of franchised automobile dealerships in the United States illustrate the potential long-term instability of using power to control channel members. Traditionally, U.S. automobile manufacturers used their superior power to control franchise dealers. Since dealers depended on the manufacturers, the manufacturers could force the dealers to take excessive inventory and incur high service cost. The dealers at first lobbied for legislative protection to shield them from the adverse economic consequences of their power imbalance. Recently, the imbalance of power has been minimized by the emergence of super dealers who leveraged multiple dealerships, often including foreign producers, to diminish the ability of U.S. manufacturers to control channel activities.[18]

DEVELOPMENT OF LONG-TERM CHANNEL RELATIONSHIPS

Continuum of Channel Relationships

Relationships among producers and channel members can be along a continuum ranging from short-term, discrete relationships involving a single market transaction to long-term relationships. To create a sustainable competitive advantage based on control of a conventional channel, producers need to develop stable, long-term relationships with channel members. Some characteristics that can be used to describe channel relationships along with a characterization of the extreme points on this continuum are shown in Exhibit 5–5.

Stable, long-term channel relationships evolve over time. Each interaction between a producer and a channel member is viewed in light of both past and future interactions. The relationship is sustained by implicit and explicit assumptions and cooperative planning. The cornerstone of such relationships is mutual trust.

Trust is the belief by each party that its needs will be fulfilled in the future by

---

[17]For more details please see G. L. Frazier, "The Design And Management of Channels of Distribution, *In* G. Day, B. Weitz, and R. Wensley (eds.), *The Interface of Marketing and Strategy,* Greenwich, JAI Press, 1990, pp. 255–304.

[18]*Business Week,* "The New Super Dealers," June 25, 1986, pp. 53–60.

EXHIBIT 5–5   Characteristics of Channel Relationships

Relationship Characteristics	Short-Term Market Relationship	Long-Term Trusting Relationship
Time period of relationships	Discrete beginning, short duration, sharp ending	Previous history, enduring, on-going
Number of parties involved	Two	Often more than two involved in process and governance
Terms	Specific, based on contract and legal enforcement	General agreement about obligations
Expectation from relationship	Conflict of interest assumed, but causes minimal problems	Conflicts resolved by trust and mutual efforts to resolve problems
Communication	Minimal personal interaction	Extensive formal and informal interaction
Regulation or governance of relationship	Social norms, low prospect for self-gain	Self-regulation by members
Cooperation	No joint effort	Joint effort for planning, assessing performance, and making adjustment over time
Power	Balanced or unbalanced	High level of interdependence
Division of benefits	Precisely defined	Sharing of benefits adjusted over time

Adapted from F. Robert Dwyer, Paul H. Scharr, and Sejo Oh, "Developing Buyer–Seller Relationships," *Journal of Marketing,* April, 1987, pp. 11–27. Used with permission from the American Marketing Association.

actions undertaken with the other party.   Trust is critical because short-term inequities are inevitable in all relationships.   At the most basic level, one party must undertake actions before the other party, and must rely on the other party to honor its commitments.   For example, Phillips must ship light bulbs to a retailer and trust the retailer to pay for them.   Any attempt to coordinate activities makes the parties in the relationship vulnerable to exploitation.   Through trust, the producer and channel member develop confidence that short-term inequities will be adjusted over the long-run to yield a high level of mutual benefit.   For example, a fashion apparel manufacturer and retailer that have a trusting relationship will maintain that relationship through difficult periods.   The retailer will continue to stock the manufacturer's line even when the line for a particular season is not in strong demand and the producer will favor the retailer when demand for its line during the next season exceeds supply.[19]

[19]See F. Robert Dwyer, Paul H. Scharr, and Sejo Oh, "Developing Buyer–Seller Relationships," *Journal of Marketing,* April 1987, pp. 11–27; Ian R. Macneil, "Contracts: Adjustment of Long-Term Economic Relations Under Classical, Neoclassical, and Relationship Contract Law," *Northwestern University Law Review,* 72, 1978, pp. 854–902.

EXHIBIT 5–6   Types of Producer-Channel Member Relationships

	Producer Power Channel Member Dependency	
	LOW	HIGH
LOW Producer Power	Relationships based on producer domination	Long-term relational exchange. Requires development of trusting relationship
HIGH	Short-term Discrete Market-based	Relationships based on channel member domination

The nature of relationships arises from different levels of producer and channel member power (Exhibit 5–6). High levels of interdependencies and mutual benefits can arise when a trusting relationship develops between a channel member and a producer. These relationships exhibit the highest degree of stability over time. Through such relationships a producer can develop a sustainable competitive advantage because it has access to a channel member not available to a competitive producer.

When asymmetries in power (or dependence) exist—when a producer is more powerful than a channel member, or vice versa—relationships will not be mutually beneficial and will be unstable. Low levels of interdependency result in short-term, market-based relationships—relationships through which a producer cannot achieve a competitive advantage because all competitive producers have equal access to the channel member.

SUMMARY

We have discussed four approaches for achieving a sustainable competitive advantage through channel control: (1) the use of authority to control channel activities through vertical integration, (2) the use of contracts enforced by the legal system, and (3) the development of long-term, trusting relationships that facilitate cooperation and encourage mutual investments, and (4) the use of market power to secure support through market exchanges.

Each of these approaches has advantages and disadvantages. Potentially, the greatest degree of control can be achieved through vertical integration; however, the bureaucracy required to control a large corporation may be costly and inefficient. Vertical integration may be useful in tailoring the performance of a channel to meet customer needs, but it might also increase prices.

Market exchanges are typically very efficient, but decrease a firm's ability to tailor its channel to satisfy unique customer needs. In market exchanges characterized by conventional channels, all producers have equal access to channel members. The performance of channel functions cannot be developed into a sustainable advantage.

The development of a competitive advantage through channel controls requires a series of tradeoffs—tradeoffs that need to be consistent with the firm's target markets and competitive strengths.

Concept Questions

1. How do distribution channels create customer value?
2. (a.) What are the main types of distribution channels?
   (b.) From a manager's viewpoint, what are the key points of difference between the various types of distribution channels?
3. (a.) What is Transaction Cost analysis?
   (b.) How does it help to decide whether or not to vertically integrate forward?
4. (a.) What is a Franchise System?
   (b.) What is the rationale for such a system?
5. What are the main types of vertical market restrictions? What is the rationale for their presence?
6. (a.) What are some of the main sources of conflict between producers and independent channel members?
   (b.) What are the mechanisms for managing such conflicts?

Discussion Questions

1. A joint venture was announced by IBM and Blockbuster Entertainment Corp. on Tuesday, May 12, 1993. This venture serves customers by allowing them to name the music title desired on a store computer. This computer, using fiber optic telephone lines from a database perhaps thousands of miles away, copies it almost instantaneously onto a compact disc, along with the glossy jacket art and liner notes!
   (a.) What value(s) will such a channel provide to customers?
   (b.) Why could not IBM have set up its own channel for this market?
   (c.) Which product-markets need to be redefined because of this innovation?
2. Why does Power play such an important role in managing distribution channels
3. When, in your opinion/experience, will a franchise system not work?
4. Does the Transaction Cost Analysis of the vertical integration decision apply to a business just getting started? Discuss.

Chapter 6

Relationships with Customers

Customer Satisfaction as a Motivating Force

A recent *Fortune* magazine article, "Getting Customers to Love You," advises "It takes more work than most managers think, but the payoff comes in building loyal repeat buyers. Holding on to them costs one-fifth as much as acquiring new ones."[1] Remember this: a customer in hand is worth five in the bush!

Tod Johnson, president of NPD Group, a major marketing research company, presented evidence[2] that of 60 brands that comprise the top three brands in each of 20 consumer product categories in 1975, 40 maintained their standing in the top three in 1989. Two-thirds maintained their top positions over 15 years! A similar finding for British brands is reported by Doyle.[3] This is amazing, considering the extent of new product activity in both markets!

Finally, consider the results of a national survey conducted for the United States Office of Consumer Affairs (USOCA): Sixty-three percent of the consumers who

[1]Sellers, Patricia, "Getting Customers to Love You," *Fortune,* March 13, 1989, pp. 38–49.

[2]Johnson, Tod, "15 Years of Brand Loyalty Trends," *In* Eliot Maltz, *Brand Equity,* Cambridge, MA, Marketing Science Institute, 1990.

[3]Doyle, P., "Building Successful Brands: The Strategic Options," *Journal of Consumer Marketing,* Vol. 7, Spring, 1990, pp. 5–20.

Sheth, Jagdish N., "Presidential Address: Broadening the Horizon of ACR and Consumer Behavior," *In Advances in Consumer Research*, Elizabeth C. Hirschman and Morris B. Holbrook (eds.), Vol. 12. Provo, Utah, Association for Consumer Research, 1985, pp. 12.

Holbrook, Morris B., "O, Consumer, How You've Changed: Some Radical Reflections on the Roots of Consumption," *In* A. Fuat Firat, Nikhilesh Dholakia and Richard P. Bagozzi (eds.), *Philosophical and Radical Thought in Marketing,* Lexington, Lexington Books, 1987, pp. 157–178.

experienced a perceived loss of between $1 and $5 and did not complain, said they would not buy that brand again. Fifty-four percent of those whose complaints were not satisfactorily resolved said they would not purchase that brand again. On the other hand, 30% of consumers with resolved complaints would be lost to that brand.

These three facts suggest reasons why companies are intently pursuing customer satisfaction today. Customers are satisfied when there is no gap between their expectations and their experience. Their expectations can best be met if they are understood. The cornerstone of consumer satisfaction is a thorough understanding of customer commercial relationships.

Building appropriate relationships with customers allows this understanding to continue to evolve dynamically since both competition and customer expectations change. It provides vital feedback and learning that are necessary to manage survival and growth in complex environments. Knowledge for such environments cannot be totally "preprogrammed," but must be developed and based on context. This theme is addressed more fully in Chapter 14. Learning about customers only occurs through appropriate relationships. Further, these relationships may be key in signaling the credibility of commitment. As discussed in Chapter 2, this is central to strategic planning.

Building relationships should not be taken to mean the building-in of rigidity. To the contrary, relationships should be built to permit flexibility in response to contextual changes. For example, in the early days of computerized reservation systems (CRS) in the airlines industry (e.g., American Airlines' SABRE), this channel could have been viewed as a biased sales channel: biased in favor of American Airlines SABRE. However, with the rapid developments in communication technology, information systems are not the insurmountable barriers that they once were. Electronic distribution does not seek to bind customers—but to increase exchange and choice. For example, American Hospital Supply Corporation's ASAP system is open to competitors' products. A reservation and yield management system, CONFIRM (developed by AMRIS, a subsidiary of American Airlines), was designed to be jointly marketed by Amris, Marriott, Hilton, and Budget Rent-A-Car and to be available for purchase by competitors.

Electronic commerce is not creating entry barriers through structure. However, it is shifting the possibility of success to those who possess the ability to speedily analyze and interpret customer needs as they appear in the electronic marketplace and to respond to the diverse requirements.[3a]

In this chapter a framework for understanding customer relationships is introduced. Next, the key elements of this framework are elaborated and various types of relationships based on sociopsychological knowledge are discussed. For branded goods, customers are provided and often use brand names as cues and "handles" through which their consumption experiences may be categorized, stored, and retrieved. Therefore, a discussion of branding is necessary. The role of branding in customer relationships is discussed in the last part of the chapter, using concepts from the field of social cognition.

[3a]Hopper, Max D., "Rattling SABRE—New Ways to Compete on Information," *Harvard Business Review,* May–June, 1990, pp. 118–125.

A GENERAL OVERVIEW OF CONSUMPTION RELATIONSHIPS

The customer is fundamental to a marketing relationship. Marketing exists to make the satisfaction of customer needs, as well as those of the marketing organization, efficient and possible. There is a considerable body of knowledge in the social sciences that sheds light on the many facets of human relationships. We draw from these sources to further our understanding of consumer relationships.

Marketing exchange seeks to achieve satisfaction for the consumer and the marketing organization (or company). In this latter group we include employee, shareholder, and managerial satisfaction. Other stakeholders are also important; however, our focus is on customers and the marketing organization.

A Customer-Relationships Model

A general model of customer-relationships is shown in Exhibit 6–1.

The key ideas highlighted in this model are:

1. Customer satisfaction or delight is based on the gap between expectations and experiences.

EXHIBIT 6–1   A General Model of Customer Relationships

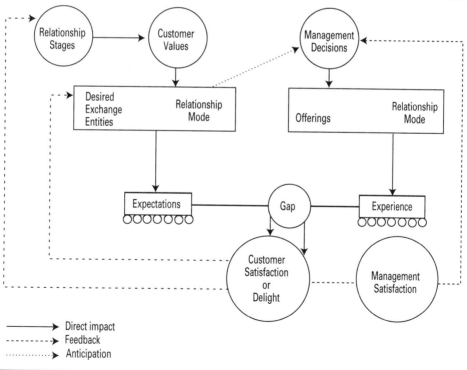

2. Customer expectations have two broad components—an expectation of the exchange entities (EE) to be obtained and an expectation of how they should be treated (relationship mode [RM]).

3. These expectations are formed to satisfy the values (CV) desired by customers.

4. These values depend on the stage (S) of the relationship with respect to the product, service, or marketing organization.

5. Customer satisfaction provides feedback to change (e.g., to terminate, or progress) the stage of relationship as well as the expectations.

6. Marketing management anticipates customer expectations (explicitly or implicitly).

7. Based on this anticipation and its needs, management decides and makes available a set of offerings in a particular relationship mode.

8. This decision and corresponding action lead to customer experience.

9. The experience compared with expectations leads to customer satisfaction or delight (same as in [1]).

10. When fed back to marketing management, this customer reaction leads to any necessary change in management satisfaction.

11. This change (if any) in management satisfaction along with new anticipation of customer expectations leads to a change in management decisions, and so the cycle continues.

As you examine Exhibit 6–1, remember the solid lines refer to direct impact, the dashed lines refer to feedback routes, and the dotted lines refer to routes of anticipation.

The important steps of this model are stage(s) of relationships, customer values (CV), exchange entities (EE), and relationship modes (RM). These are now discussed in detail.

Examples

Ms. Anita Commonuser has just been accepted in the MBA program at a major university. During orientation she hears names like dBase, Lotus 1-2-3, Quattro Pro, and so forth. She realizes she needs a personal computer and accoutrements but is on a limited budget and must use her funds wisely. She is now at a very early stage in the process of acquiring a computer and of forming a relationship with computer marketers.

In contrast Ms. Susan Prouser has two personal computers at home. She uses Prodigy daily to get stock quotes and to arrange her travel itinerary. She is thinking of adding a fax/modem board to her computers. She contacts the company where she purchased her add-on hard disk drive, a year ago, rather than the company where she bought her new mouse a month ago, despite that company's lower prices. She is clearly at the same stage in the purchase process (need arousal) as Ms. Commonuser, but, is at different stages in her relationship with the vendors of her mouse and disk drive. She has decided to dissolve one relationship and is maintaining/reinforcing the other (she is "loyal" to one and not the other).

Do Ms. Commonuser and Ms. Prouser have the same needs? Do they seek the same values from their purchases? The exchange entities they seek are different in the level of information, and in the amount of "coaching" necessary. Ms. Commonuser has to initiate a new relationship; Ms. Prouser has to continue one. She probably does not need to provide her address, credit card number, and so forth, if she orders by telephone or Prodigy and wants all the transaction details (except for the product) to be exactly as before. (The vendor probably has this information on a database.)

Ms. Prouser has had a long day and wishes to treat herself to dinner. She is tired of Chinese, Indian, TexMex and Thai food and wishes to try something new. She is seeking variety as a primary value and might wish to find a restaurant where she has to dress up, make a reservation, and be served by a suitably attired, *proper* waiter. Or, she might wish to dress casually and dine in an informal atmosphere. Her desired values, and the formality of the interaction wanted not only dictate her choice of restaurant, but her satisfaction depends on how closely her wishes were met.

Managerial Viewpoint

A marketer has to choose a set of offerings to be provided as well as the relationship mode to be established.

Often, as soon as a purchase is made, the seller realizes an immediate financial gain. (Note that an invoice is sufficient to register a sales increase, even though cash flow is affected only after payment has actually been received. Also an invoice may be sold to "factors" in international trade or used to obtain credit from banks or to obtain immediate reimbursement from credit card organizations, if a credit card was used.) A customer only achieves final satisfaction through consumption (either directly, or perhaps after the purchase is given as a gift and "appreciation" received). There is likely to be much more uncertainty on the part of the customer at the point of purchase in the value to be gained and satisfaction obtained. This has direct implications for the relationship mode that may be needed. For example, should a jeweler allow a prospective customer to take a ring on "trial" with just a handshake or require a formal contract? This depends on the stage of the customer-vendor relationship and would imply the degree of trust established, the power to enforce punitive measures in case of a dispute, and so forth. Besides these choices, the strategist has also to ensure the satisfaction of managerial goals. The strategist must analyze the requirements of prospective markets, design the best strategy for the market, and decide whether it satisfies managerial goals. If not, the market may not be worthy of further resource allocation.

The strategist has to have an understanding of how to use the consumer relationships. It is an essential part of strategy development to consider what options are opened up by the evolution of relationships through different stages. The appropriateness of offerings (e.g., the range of computer accessories provided as a consumer begins to use the computer more extensively, or a person's wardrobe as he or she grows more successful) may also evolve relationships in desired directions, for example, the change in offerings from The Limited Company as its customers' needs change.

The timing of new offerings is tied into relationship stages. The mode of relationship might constrain the offerings and vice versa. In order to build the best strategy for a market or to build a strategy for a portfolio of products, an understanding of the various components shown in Exhibit 6–1 is useful. We shall discuss each of the components separately and then put them together in a marketing strategy.

Relationship Stages

In marketing literature, the hierarchy-of-effects model is well known.[4] Several variants of this model exist. Some common forms of this model are shown in Exhibit 6–2. The basis of this model is that consumers follow a stage-by-stage process in making a choice. These stages are Awareness, Knowledge, Liking, Preference, Conviction, and Purchase. (Interest is related to attitude.) Innovation-Adoption has been a useful model to estimate sales[5] and to determine if the gap between expected and achieved sales is caused by advertising (low awareness), or by product (low trial-

EXHIBIT 6–2   Hierarchy-of-Effects Model

		Model		
Stages	"ALDA"	"Hierarchy-of-Effects"	"Innovation-Adoption"	"Communications"
Cognitive	Attention	Awareness ↓ Knowledge	Awareness	Exposure ↓ Reception ↓ Cognitive response
Affective	Interest ↓ Desire	Liking ↓ Preference ↓ Conviction	Interest ↓ Evaluation	Attitude ↓ Intention
Behavior	Action	Purchase	Trial ↓ Adoption	Behavior

[4]Kotler, Philip, *Marketing Management,* 7th ed., Englewood Cliffs, Prentice-Hall, 1991, p. 342.

[5]Parfitt, J. H. and B. J. K. Collins, "Use of Consumer Panels for Brand Share Prediction," *Journal of Marketing Research,* Vol. 14, No. 1, February, 1977, pp. 22–23.

to-adoption conversion rates), and so on.   Although this has been a useful model, considerable debate, starting with Krugman,[6] has questioned this stage-by-stage process, especially for low-involvement products.   It has been pointed out that in the case of low-involvement products (like chewing gum), a consumer may simply try it, without there having been any significant passage of time or significant information processing between awareness and trial, to say nothing of developing an attitude toward the brand in question.   Further, interest in the brand, or an attitude toward it may only result after purchase.   This model shows the situation when a consumer first chooses a brand.   In social psychology (like the AITA model), there has been considerable work in the area of relationship development (rather than only on the first choice) *between individuals and between individuals and organizations*.   A study of this literature provides a basis for understanding the different stages in the relationship between a consumer and a brand (or a provider).   Each stage implies a difference in information requirements as well as in other requirements (CEE) in order to create ongoing (brand) loyalty.   It also provides direction to breach an ongoing loyal relationship between a customer and a competitor and to develop a new relationship.

Implications of Each Stage

As postulated by Scanzoni,[7] the three stages in the development of a relationship are exploration, consolidation and commitment.   Dwyer, Schurr and Oh[8] add two more stages: awareness and dissolution.   Park, Jaworski and MacInnis[9] provide a similar framework for the management over time of a brand concept.   This stage-by-stage approach is useful in managing one-on-one relationships as discussed by Scanzoni and Dwyer, Schurr and Oh (Exhibit 6–3).   However, in consumer products, for example, consumer electronics like VCRs, this approach might seem irrelevant.   But, if the desire is to establish a relationship which allows leveraging the value delivered by the

EXHIBIT 6–3   Development Phases in Relationships

Scanzoni	Dwyer, Schurr and Oh	Park, Jaworski and MacInnis
	Awareness	Introduction
Exploration	Exploration	
Consolidation	Expansion	ELABORATION
Commitment	Commitment	FORTIFICATION
	Dissolution	

[6]Krugman, Herbert E., "The Impact of Television Advertising: Learning Without Involvement," *Public Opinion Quarterly,* Fall, 1965, pp. 349–356.

[7]Scanzoni, John, "Social Exchange and Behavioral Interdependence," *In* Robert L. Burgess and Ted L. Huston (eds.), *Social Exchange in Developing Relationships,* New York, Academic Press, 1979, pp. 61–98.

[8]Dwyer, Robert F., Paul H. Schurr, and Sejo Oh, "Developing Buyer-Seller Relationships," *Journal of Marketing,* April, Vol. 51, No. 2, 1987, pp. 11–27.

[9]Park, C. Whan, Bernard J. Jaworski and Deborah J. MacInnis, "Strategic Brand Concept–Image Management," *Journal of Marketing,* October, Vol. 50, No. 4, 1986, pp. 135–145.

satisfactory VCR, then it has application here too. Homans[10] points out that a relationship does not come into being until several exchanges take place. At the very least, there needs to be an opportunity for such multiple exchanges to build a relationship. As we saw in Chapter 1, Daewoo's move to build relationships directly with end users has to involve a branded entry along with a product line and service arrangements to establish this relationship. Strategically, an important implication is that a single entry in a category which is purchased at very long intervals does not build a relationship and does not provide adequate leverage. An exception is probably the category of extremely expensive, high margin products like Rolls Royce automobiles (Rolls Royce even has several models, allowing consumers a chance to "move up").

Relationship Stage Variation Across Customers

For frequently purchased consumer goods, a different issue arises, that is, stages of relationship development may vary considerably among consumers. And, advertising, product offerings, and other exchange entities may not be attuned to each individual or even to different stages. The solution is to recognize the mix of stages and to develop advertising and the exchange entities to satisfy to the maximum the appropriate requirements while offending the least number of consumers. This involves understanding the different values being sought and, if possible, finding distinctive media outlets to reach each group. This also has implications in allocating resources. Consumer uncertainties are greater at early stages of building relationships, which is precisely when most of the resources (including managerial emotion) are committed (even if not spent). This implies the need for a diversity of options to bring in large enough numbers of appropriate consumers. Among such options are perhaps a variety of message formats or flexibility in the type of product or service possible as well as the ability to obtain quick feedback on what consumers seek based on what is available. All these are not only sensible actions to take, but also are more feasible because of new technology.

Middle Stages

In the middle stages, when customers already have positive feelings about a brand (or company) and are ready for consolidating ties and developing commitment, the investment risks are considerably lower and these customers are not only better known, but also willing to provide help in developing a more diverse set of offerings that they would purchase. By preemptively committing to provide appropriate offerings, customers may be moved to "deciding" to purchase the new offerings—thus making it a strategic move.

Final Stages

The dissolution stage may occur either because of dissatisfaction or change in the values sought by a consumer. Once dissatisfaction reaches a certain level, it is difficult to rebuild the relationship. (Recall the survey mentioned earlier.) If the

[10]Homans, George C., Foreword to Robert L. Burgess and Ted L. Huston (eds.), *Social Exchange in Developing Relationships,* New York, Academic Press, 1979.

product is such that consumers seek a different kind of value as their situation evolves, a marketing strategist should consider developing proactively the next stage product. For example, a range of cars that allows the leveraging of past success is available from most automobile manufacturers. In fact, an automobile salesperson's pay depends on how much repeat business can be generated. For example, Mr. Otis Ewing, a salesperson in suburban Detroit, made $75,000 in 1991. Seventy percent of his sales came from a loyal clientele. On the other hand, Mr. Robert Williams of suburban Chicago who has changed dealerships six times in less than three years made only $10,000 in 1991. Mr. Ewing works to prevent the dissolution stage from occurring by staying with one dealership and developing a loyal clientele. If a dissolution is inevitable, then it should be done in a way that allows a fresh start.[11]

Summary

A marketing strategist must understand the requirements of each relationship development stage. Such understanding permits an examination of the resource allocation necessary, risk levels, and planning options. Resource allocations per sales unit are high at the early stages and then decline. Risk follows the same pattern. Options increase with advances in relationship development if they are used to obtain ideas for the expansion of product-markets, but may decline at the final stage. These stages must be planned for as part of marketing strategy.

Consumption Values

Holbrook says, "As our intellectual forbearers in consumer research fully recognized, consumer behavior rests on value, and all customer value inheres in the consumption experience."[12] At the early stage of a relationship (before consumption), all that the customer has is an expectation of possible values to be gained. Customer risk is also highest at this stage. Satisfaction comes from fulfilling the marketing promise by delivering the expected values. In this section we summarize the values that customers seek. This section builds on the discussion of consumer values in *Consumption Values and Market Choices* by Sheth, Newman and Gross.[13]

Five Value Drivers

Five fundamental types of value are said to drive market choice behavior (Exhibit 6–4). The Sheth, Newman and Gross model brings together research and writing in many fields: sociology, social psychology, humanistic psychology, consumption economics, clinical psychology, and experimental psychology. The authors claim their

[11]Patterson, Gregory A., "A Car Salesman Finds It's Also Hard For Him To Get A Good Deal," *The Wall Street Journal,* Tuesday, March 10, 1992, A1, A7.

[12]Holbrook, Morris B., *op. cit.,* p. 1987, 161.

[13]Sheth, Jagdish N., Bruce I. Newman, and Barbara L. Gross, *Consumption Values and Market Choices: Theory and Applications,* Cincinnati, South-Western Publishing, 1991.

EXHIBIT 6–4   The Five Value Drivers of Market Choice Behavior

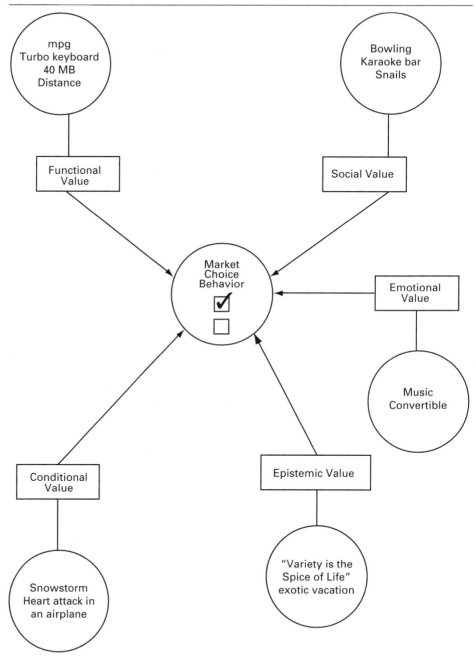

Adapted from Sheth, Jagdish N., Bruce A. Newman, and Barbara L. Gross, *Consumption Values and Market Choices: Theory and Applications,* Cincinnati, South-Western Publishing, 1991, Figure 1–1.

method allows a marketing researcher to identify the values important to consumers in three situations: (1) to buy or not to buy choice, (2) product type choice, and (3) brand choice.

It is vital for a product strategist to know the values which consumers consider important so that a strategy can be devised. The particular values not only shape the exchange entities required, but knowledge of the offered values also allows an appraisal of the size of the market and the pattern of demand. A description of the five types of values and their role in strategy development follow (quoted from Footnote 13).

> *Functional Value.* The perceived value acquired by an alternative as the result of its ability to perform its functional, utilitarian, or physical purposes. Alternatives acquire functional value through the possession of salient functional, utilitarian, or physical attributes (p. 18).

(For example, performance, reliability, durability, and price.)

> *Social Value.* The perceived utility acquired by an alternative as a result of its association with one or more specific social groups. Alternatives acquire social value through association with positively or negatively stereotyped demographic, socioeconomic, and cultural ethnic groups (p. 19).

(Social values are most frequently important for very visible items of consumption.)

> *Emotional Value.* The perceived utility acquired by an alternative as a result of its ability to arouse feelings or affective states. Alternatives acquire emotional value when associated with specific feelings or when they facilitate or perpetuate feelings (p. 20).

(Examples of emotional values include: comfort, security, excitement, romance, passion, anger, fear, guilt, friendship, loyalty, trust.)

> *Epistemic Value.* The perceived utility acquired by an alternative as a result of its ability to arouse curiosity, provide novelty, and/or satisfy a desire for knowledge. Alternatives acquire epistemic value through the capacity to provide something new or different (p. 21).

> *Conditional Value.* The perceived utility acquired by an alternative as a result of the specific situation or the context faced by the choice maker. Alternatives acquire conditional values in the presence of antecedent physical or social contingencies that enhance their functional or social value, but do not otherwise possess this value (p. 22).

Competitively, the first three differ from the other two. Functional, emotional, and social values can be built into the exchange entities or market offerings. Epistemic and conditional provide opportunities to enter a consumer's consideration set, or to take advantage of whims or unusual circumstances. Each of them provides a way to build in uniqueness.

Functional Values

For example, if functional values are important in the purchase of a home computer, then providing the speed, the hard disk capacity, and so forth, may dominate both product design and product communication. Dominance in functional prowess and constantly upgrading may afford a unique and possibly sustainable advantage. In fact, if a functional advantage is sought, a constant process of functional renewal is dictated.

Emotional Values

If the values emphasized are emotional (assuming these are being sought and impor-tant), for example, a need to feel greater self-worth in the choice of exercise programs, then these emotions have to be reinforced. It is relatively easy to assess objectively functional promises, but to assess those pertaining to emotion is likely to be more dif-ficult. Emotional value has implications for the mode of relationship between the consumer, the vendor, and the consumption process. Tying in emotions to offerings (e.g., Hallmark cards as a symbol of love on birthdays) may provide unshakable bonds with consumers. This provides the unique and sustainable competitive edge that can be exploited.

Social Values

Social values must be treated differently from emotional and functional values. Social values arise over time in society. For example, the switch in southern India by women wearing sarees to wearing the salwaar-kameez of the north, or to the skirts and pants of the Western world, required a change in mores. The building of social values requires an enabling condition—the tie between the product-service-brand and the norms of the consumer group targeted. Cultivating and building new social values have been traditionally risky and taken place over the long-term. (In societies, or in social groups trying to renew or transform themselves, the pace of change may be much quicker.) The rewards of change could, however, be significant well into the future. For example, persuading consumers to smoke, to wear pants, to eat sushi, to switch to infant formula food, might provide payoffs, but only long-term.

Epistemic Values

Why do some vacationers seek *different* exotic locales for each vacation? Certainly not only for rest or for the price (function), or to be like their socioeconomic group (social), or because it happened to be convenient (conditional), but rather to satisfy their epistemic value desires. Is it possible to build a unique and sustainable advan-tage by focusing on consumers' epistemic needs? Yes! Consider Club Med with its consistency of service. Consider also the ready-to-eat (RTE) cereal category, Kelloggs alone has over 20 different types of children's cereals. Although each pro-vides a different functional value, the whole product line satisfies epistemic value. If children did not seek a variety of cereals (consider the parent who has to feed the children and get them out to school in the morning and has to entice the child to eat—variety is the "ace-in-the hole"!), then perhaps this product line would not have as many new variations as now exist. A common tactic to decrease the importance of epistemic value is to provide an incentive not to change, for example, providing coupons for the next purchase. In other words, the cost of change is increased. Epistemic values force customers to change and create an environment of uncertain demand.

Conditional Values

By definition, conditional value is unplanned on the customer's part and is also likely to change the prior decision, if any.

For example, consider a shopper who finds a brand of tortilla chips on sale. Having decided to buy these chips now makes salsa dip (perhaps) have a higher value. Prior to seeing the chips on sale, there might have been no intention to buy a salsa dip, and the value attached to buying a salsa dip may have been very low. Its value has now been enhanced because of another condition in the store. In marketing strategy, if a product is expected to attract conditional value, then these conditions should be designed. For example, this may be done by providing an incentive to the chips manufacturer to promote the product, or by having the dip placed next to the chips on the store shelf, or by having cross-promotions, and so forth. By making a move that encourages others to act "cooperatively," gain may be realized. Finally, the importance of conditional value could be determined and used to discover market opportunities for new offerings. Examples of such possibilities are (1) infrequent air travelers who need air travel insurance at the airport, (2) the needs of families with babies who are traveling long distances and require play areas for children at airports, (3) accessories and other products carrying the theme or name of a successful movie or personality, sales of which are contingent on the success of the theme, movie, or personality.

Summary

Exhibit 6–5 summarizes the key strategic implications of stressing different value types. As a relationship develops, the importance of different value types might change because (a) the needs change and (b) the presence or delivery of certain values is taken for granted. Some values become more transparent and others more

EXHIBIT 6–5   Value-Strategy Key Links

Type of Value	Key Strategic Features for Sustained Advantage
Functional	Continuous upgrading required
Social	Long-term relationships, uncertain in the beginning—stable once established, visible reinforcement required
Emotional	Periodic reinforcement required because of need for intimate relationships
Epistemic	Variety required to take advantage of uncertainty
Conditional	Niche opportunities to take advantage of happenstance, cross-promotions possible, quick response desired

salient. Functional values may dominate the beginning of a relationship. Variety and high touch may become more important as consolidation and commitment develop.

The importance of various values to consumers and their provision by existing and potential competitors are important considerations in building the exchange entities and relationships with others in the marketing process that lead to satisfied consumers.

Exchange Entities

Central to the marketing concept is exchange. What are exchanged are called exchange entities. The entities exchanged depend, for the consumer, on the values sought. For the manager they usually provide financial gain or the possibility of use of this exchange as a basis for future transactions with the same or other consumers. The principal exchange entities, based on Foa and Foa's[14] theory of resource exchange are: (a) Goods, (b) Services, (c) Money, (d) Information, (e) Status and (f) Love (Exhibit 6–6). Of these, goods, services, and information are provided to the con-

EXHIBIT 6–6   Exchange Entities

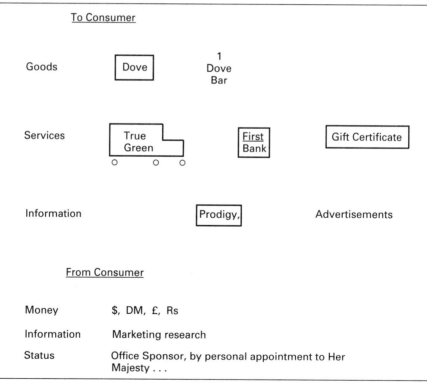

To Consumer

Goods

Dove

1
Dove
Bar

Services

True
Green

First
Bank

Gift Certificate

Information

Prodigy,

Advertisements

From Consumer

Money $, DM, £, Rs

Information   Marketing research

Status   Office Sponsor, by personal appointment to Her
              Majesty . . .

[14]Homans, George C., *op. cit.,* 1979, p. xvii.

Foa, Uriel G. and Edna B. Foa, *Societal Structures of the Mind,* Springfield, Charles C Thomas, 1974.

sumer by a marketing organization. Money, information, and status are entities obtained by the marketer.

The particulars of the goods, services, and information to be provided to consumers clearly depend on the values sought by them. For example, the products likely to be bought for Halloween, in the U.S. are different from those bought for Valentine's Day. The same candy is bought both on usual days and for Valentine's Day in terms of its function (sweetness, chocolate taste, etc.), but its form changes substantially (heart-shaped, different packaging, etc.) for Valentine's Day. Social and conditional values dominate the form of candy to be purchased on special occasions. Such knowledge is essential to develop resource allocation plans for seasonal markets. The same is true for services. The type and amount of information required by consumers at different stages of relationship development vary. For example, at the consolidation and commitment stages, more information on system upgrades, or availability of variations, or continuity and less information on a need to establish superiority are perhaps in order. The choice of goods, services, and information to be provided should match the values desired and the stage of the relationship. The offerings to be provided as exchange entities are described at greater length in Chapter 13. They are considered as function, form, price, and transaction facilitators necessary to sustain relationships with customers. This discussion, therefore, includes one of being successful in competing for the opportunity to satisfy customers.

Relationship Mode

The ability to build a positive, sustainable customer relationship depends on how you treat the customer. According to Professor Kotler,[15] the favored mode of relating to consumers should be chosen after considering their lives. It is to practice a philosophy, "... that takes as its central objective the earning of profit through the enhancement of the customers' long-run well-being. It assumes that: the customer is active and intelligent; seeks satisfaction of both immediate and larger interests; and favors companies that develop products, services, and communications that enrich the customer's life possibilities" (p. 272). He calls this philosophy "humanistic marketing."

Examples of Humanistic Marketing

1. *Avon:* It recruits neighbors to sell excellent products to neighbors. This provides a long-term relationship and exploits the already developed credibility and mutuality of interest of neighbors, along with an implied continuity in relationships.

2. *Marks & Spencer:* It developed the ability to provide quality merchandise at a low cost. Customers depend on Marks & Spencer's quality at reasonable prices at any time.

3. *Carrefours:* This French *hypermarché* focused on providing consumers a

---

[15]Kotler, Philip, "Humanistic Marketing: Beyond the Marketing Concept," *In* A. Fuad Firat, Nikhilesh Dholakia and Richard P. Bagozzi (eds.), Philosophical and Radical Thought in Marketing, Lexington, Lexington Books, 1987, pp. 271–288.

mix of brand and price choice. It displayed comparable quality house-brands at low prices next to branded products. It exploited existing relationships to gain customers who also wished to use lower priced products for some categories and not for others.

4. *Whirlpool Corporation:*   To prevent consumer dissatisfaction and to maintain and encourage relationships with consumers, Whirlpool introduced a toll-free telephone service. Its warranty and instructions to customers were rewritten in easy-to-understand language. Its three-story customer service operation is always busy and, along with improvements in product design, has helped Whirlpool's success.

Buyers' Views of Sellers

According to Kotler, buyers view sellers as foes, strangers, helpers, or friends. These first two are hardly the basis for any positive relationship or for developing loyalty. It is important to know how a corporation is viewed by its customers and then to develop the strategy that provides an appropriate platform for the building of meaningful relationships. Loyalty does not mean exclusivity. When epistemic values are to be satisfied, a corporation should allow for such needs to be satisfied, either by developing the variety itself, by building partnerships, or by providing a mechanism for coming back "into the rotation" (to use a baseball term).

Sellers' Views of Customers

Unfortunately, marketers often view customers as targets, rather than as neighbors and friends. To illustrate, the terms "target marketing" or "target segments" are commonly used in marketing. Managers are often at a distance from customers and so are mentally separated from them (this is especially true in international markets). Thinking of customers, even metaphorically, as "targets" could, because of this distance, become a problem. A "target" or prey-oriented view of customers cannot be the basis for building a meaningful relationship. Better metaphors are called for and a different framework is necessary to understand and approach customers properly.

A Framework for Viewing Customers

Wiggins[16] provides a more formal view of relationships. For him, any relationship can be placed in a three-dimensional space, whose dimensions are (a) reward-punishment, (b) power-dependence, and (c) intimacy-formality. Most marketing literature has focused on the first two dimensions, especially in industrial marketing relationships. These were discussed in Chapter 5. We provide more detail in Chapter 12. Although these are pertinent in managing other channel members and in keeping with Kotler's proposed humanistic marketing concept, the intimacy-formal dimension perhaps provides the best base for viewing consumer relationships. The key to success

---

[16]Wiggins, James A., "Dynamic Theories of Social Relationships and Resulting Research Strategies," *In* Robert L. Burgess and Ted L. Huston (eds.), *Social Exchange in Developing Relationships,* New York, Academic Press, 1979, pp. 381–407.

EXHIBIT 6–7   Map of Relationship Modes

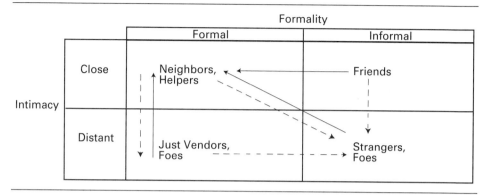

is in conceiving new ways to bring about desired levels of intimacy, while maintaining formal consumer relationships. In consumer marketing, perhaps Wiggins' intimacy-formal dimension is more than one dimension. Exhibit 6–7 "maps" Kotler's description of how buyers view sellers onto the dimensions of intimate-distant and formal-informal exchange. Although this exhibit is a simplified view of all the possible complexities, it captures the essential elements. The solid lines show the directions of change leading to the strengthening of relationships. The dotted lines show the directions leading to a weakening and dissolution of relationships. To build long-term relationships, marketing strategy should move the exchange process to the Formal-Close quadrant. The Informal-Close quadrant is unlikely (or at least unlikely to be sustained) in the type of relationships common to organized marketing. Such positive moves show credibility in commitment to customers, view them humanistically, and lead to strong relationships as well as being strategic.

Strategic Action

How customers view a marketing organization is based on how they are treated by it and their experience with its product(s). Customer satisfaction depends on the gap between expectations and experience (see Exhibit 6–1). These are principally in their expectations and experience of desired exchange entities and relationship modes. If the marketing organization views customers as friends or helpers or neighbors, and not as targets or prey (or foes), then the first step in establishing meaningful and sustainable relationships is in place. This view is reflected in the enormous effort being made by companies to use Total Quality Management (TQM) principles and to carry out customer satisfaction surveys, and the like. These reinforce the fact that customer satisfaction is key to marketing success. Along with customer satisfaction comes incentive systems (commitment by top management) to marketing personnel to ensure customer satisfaction. Besides these incentives, an "organization culture" that reflects these new views of customers is being put into place. This, of course, means a change in the way employees themselves are viewed internally. Some positive changes are the new "empowerment" of employees, creation of team-oriented incentives, incentives for helping customers, on-premise day-care centers for employees' children, and so forth.

Finally, referring again to Exhibit 6–1, managers also need an information system that provides them with an accurate assessment of evolving consumers' values, desired exchange entities, and preferred relationship mode in order to build a lasting, mutually advantageous relationship. There should also be available a system that monitors their views of customers, their relationship modes, and brings them into agreement with those of the customers.

BRANDING

A sustained relationship on the part of customers is typically referred to as *brand loyalty*—even if it might really be "salesperson" loyalty or "store" loyalty. A name is a taxonomic device used to distinguish one product (or entity) from another. A name is also a cue or label around which consumption-related experiences and information are stored for future choice making. A discussion of customer relationships must include branding.

The concept of consumer loyalty is intimately related to branding, because loyalty and repeat purchase behavior can only arise when consumers can easily identify the products they prefer. Brand names and trademarks enable consumers to identify the manufacturer of a product.

As far back as 5000 B.C. identity marks were used on pottery. However, these ancient marks identified the owner of the goods rather than the "manufacturer." These marks did not serve the business function of modern brands and trademarks. In the 12th century the use of trademarks became widespread. Craft guilds required that members mark their goods so that the quantity and quality of products could be controlled. When the product quantity needed to be reduced because of decline in demand, the guild could use the marks to verify that each producer had reduced production. In addition, the marks readily identified the craft people who were providing inferior goods.

Brand names and trademarks guarantee that products bearing the mark will be of uniform quality. Through branding, producers have an incentive to maintain the quality of their products. Branding enables a producer to obtain the benefits of offering products with unique or superior qualities, and provides an opportunity to transfer this identifiable relationship to other products or services.

Branding makes a wide range of products available to consumers and offers a method for consumers to reduce their risk when making complex purchase decisions. Consumers' responses to the benefits of branding have resulted in the introduction of branding into many new product categories that were previously treated as commodities. For example, consumers no longer purchase tennis shoes or sneakers; they buy Adidas, Nikes, Reeboks, and so forth. Produce, meat, and poultry are now branded in U.S. supermarkets.

The competitive advantage from a successful brand name is a valuable asset for the firm owning the brand. The value of this asset is indicated by the money paid by firms that have acquired consumer packaged goods with strong brand names. Procter

EXHIBIT 6–8   Enduring Brand Names

Product	Leading Brand (1925)	Current Position (1985)
Bacon	Swift	Leader
Batteries	Eveready	Leader
Biscuits	Nabisco	Leader
Breakfast cereal	Kellogg	Leader
Cameras	Kodak	Leader
Canned fruit	Del Monte	Leader
Chewing gum	Wrigley	Leader
Chocolates	Hershey	No. 2
Flour	Gold Medal	Leader
Mint candies	Life Savers	Leader
Paint	Sherwin-Williams	Leader
Pipe tobacco	Prince Albert	Leader
Razors	Gillette	Leader
Sewing machines	Singer	Leader
Shirts	Manhattan	No. 5
Shortening	Crisco	Leader
Soap	Ivory	Leader
Soft drinks	Coca-Cola	Leader
Soup	Campbell	Leader
Tea	Lipton	Leader
Tires	Goodyear	Leader
Toothpaste	Colgate	No. 2

From: Wurster, Thomas S., "The Leading Brands: 1925-1985," *Perspectives,* The Boston Consulting Group, 1987.

& Gamble paid 2.6 times Richardson-Vicks' book value, Nabisco sold for 3.2 times book value, and General Foods for 3.5 times book value.[17]   The enduring nature of brands is illustrated by the brand names that were among the leaders in their product category in the United States (1923) in both 1925 and 1985 (Exhibit 6–8).

Coca-Cola's experience with new *Coke* further shows how brand loyalty can have more influence than product performance.   Faced with declining market share caused by consumer preference for the sweeter *Pepsi-Cola, Coca-Cola* spent $4 million to taste test (200,000 consumers) a new formulation of *Coke.*   It learned conclusively that consumers preferred the new, sweeter formula; however, it failed to estimate consumers' reaction to changing *Coke.*   When it introduced the new Coke in April 1985:

> … (the) consumer felt that the company had broken the first promise of branding; that what you get today will be what you got yesterday. "All of the time and money and skill poured into consumer research on the new *Coca-Cola* couldn't measure or reveal the deep and abiding emotional attachment to original *Coca-Cola,*" says Donald R. Keough, Coke's President and Chief Operating Officer.

[17]"New? Improved?" The Brand Name Mergers," *Business Week,* October 21, 1985, pp. 108–110.

What is Brand Loyalty?

Even though the development and maintenance of brand loyalty is a central thrust of consumer marketing programs, there is no well-accepted definition of what brand loyalty is. In a review of brand loyalty research, Jacoby and Chestnut[18] cite 53 different definitions.

Purchase Behavior. Most of these definitions define brand loyalty by examining a sequence of purchase decisions made by a family or a person. To illustrate these brand loyalty definitions based on purchase behavior, consider a person who eats at a fast food restaurant once or twice a week. The sequence of fast food restaurants at which the individual has eaten during the last three months is:

McD, McD, BK, McD, McD, BK, McD, McD, McD, BK, BK, McD
[McD = McDonald's   BK = Burger King]

Definitions based on percent of purchases criteria would consider this person to have brand store loyalty to McDonald's. However, other definitions which require four or five consecutive purchases of one brand would indicate that this person is loyal neither to McDonald's nor Burger King.

Assessment of loyalty based solely on purchase behavior can be misleading. People may purchase only one brand and appear to be loyal because the store at which they shop stocks only one brand. If the store were to stock another brand, they might shift to the new brand or split their purchases between two brands. Alternatively, inconsistent purchases may reflect different users or usage situations. Purchase of breakfast cereal by a family may include a number of brands; however, each member of the family may be loyal to one brand or a limited set of brands (multi-brand loyalty). An individual may use multiple brands but be loyal to specific brands in different usage situations. For example, even though the fast-food purchases described seem to indicate limited loyalty, these purchases may simply reflect individual loyalty in going to McDonald's when accompanied by the family and loyalty in going to Burger King when he/she is eating alone. Finally, some consumers might use a decision rule such as "buy the lowest price brand" which results in repeat purchase of one brand that has been on sale regularly; however, these consumers will quickly switch to another brand when it goes on sale.

Psychological Considerations

Observations of past behavior do not accurately assess the degree to which consumers are committed to a brand. Brand loyalty is a multidimensional concept that includes a consideration of the consumer's state of mind as well as purchase behavior to assess

---

[18]Please see Jacoby, J. and R. W. Chestnut, *Brand Management,* New York, Wiley, 1978; George Day, "A Two Dimensional Concept of Brand Loyalty," *Journal of Advertising Research,* 9, September, 1969, pp. 29–35; Jacob Jacoby and David B. Kyner, "Brand Loyalty Versus Repeat Purchase Behavior," *Journal of Marketing Research,* 10, February, 1973, pp. 1–9; Jagdish Sheth and C. Whan Park, "A Theory of Multidimensional Brand Loyalty," *In* Scott Ward and Peter Wright (eds.), *Advances in Consumer Research.* Vol. 1, Ann Arbor, MI, Association for Consumer Research, 1974, pp. 449–459; Richard Lutz and Paul R. Winn, "Developing a Bayesian Measure of Brand Loyalty: A Preliminary Report," *In 1974 Combined Proceedings,* R. C. Curhan (ed.), Chicago, American Marketing Association, 1975, pp. 104–108.

the degree of commitment. True brand loyalty only arises when consumers hold a highly favorable attitude toward the brand. Day found that 70% of consumers in his study would be considered brand loyal using data on past purchases; however, only 50% were loyal when measures of attitude were also considered.[19]

To incorporate commitment into the concept of brand loyalty, we need to consider other properties of brand attitude and aspects of consumer decision making.[20] Three properties of an attitude related to its stability and the degree to which the attitude results in consistent behavior are confidence, centrality, and accessibility.

Confidence. Confidence is the degree of certainty that consumers have in a brand attitude. One can view an attitude as a probability distribution of levels. The mean of the distribution is the attitude magnitude—the value that a consumer would circle on a 1 to 7 attitude scale measure—and the variance of the distribution is the confidence or certainty that the consumer has in the attitude measure. Some consumers may have a favorable attitude toward a brand, but not be confident in this attitude because the attitude is based on seeing an ad on TV. When consumers are confident in their brand attitudes, they will be interested in searching for additional information about brands and will be susceptible to influence by marketing activities of competitive brands. When consumers are highly confident in their brand attitudes, they will tend not to search for new information and demonstrate loyalty to the brand.[21]

Centrality. Centrality is the degree to which the brand attitude is related to other consumer attitudes and values. For example, a brand such as Charlie perfume might be intimately connected to a consumer's value system. Charlie may epitomize the consumer's self-concept of an active, self-reliant woman encountering many interesting experiences. Such a highly centralized brand attitude is stable because changing the attitude toward the brand also involves changing a number of other beliefs and attitudes that the woman holds about herself. Because of this stability, the centrality of a brand attitude is related to the commitment toward the brand.[22]

Accessibility. Accessibility is the ease with which an attitude and associated beliefs and attitudes can be retrieved from memory. Brand names are accessible when they are strongly associated with product categories or usage situations. For

---

[19]Day, *op. cit.,* 1969.

[20]The following discussion is based on Allan Dick, Kunal Basu and Barton Weitz, "Consumer Loyalty: Toward An Integrated Framework," Working Paper, University of Florida, 1986.

[21]See Barbara E. Kahn and Robert J. Meyers, "Modeling Customer Loyalty: A Customer Based Source of Competitive Advantage," *In* G. Day, B. Weitz, R. Wensley (eds.), *Contributions of Marketing to Corporate Strategy,* Greenwich, CT, JAI Press, 1989.

[22]For research relating to self-image, store image, and store loyalty see Danny N. Bellenger, Earle Steinberg and Wilber W. Stanton, "The Congruence of Store Image and Self Image," *Journal of Retailing,* 52, Spring, 1976, pp. 17–32. Bruce L. Stern, Ronald F. Bush and Joseph F. Hair, Jr., "The Self-Image Store-Image Matching Process: An Empirical Test," *Journal of Business,* 50, January, 1977, pp. 63–69. M. Joseph Sirgy and A. Coshun Samli, "A Path Analytic Model of Store Loyalty Involving Self-Concept, Store Image, Geographical Loyalty and Socioeconomic Status," *Journal of the Academy of Marketing Science,* 13, Summer, 1985, pp. 265–291.

example, the brand name, Xerox, may come to mind immediately when someone wants to make a copy of a document, or Kleenex might be thought of whenever a person has a cold. Because brand names and associated attitudes are readily accessible, they have a strong influence on repeat purchase behavior—they reduce the need for a consumer to think about which brand to purchase.

Brand loyalty arises when brand attitudes are favorable and are held with confidence, are central to a consumer's value system, and are highly accessible. Under these conditions, consumers have little incentive to do a lot of thinking before purchasing a brand. They are unlikely to seek out information about alternative brands and may not even consider alternative brands when making a purchase. Since marketing efforts undertaken for competitive brands will have limited influence on these brand attitudes, consumers possessing these brand attitudes will be quite loyal.

Brand Experience. The repeated purchase and use of a brand have a reinforcing effect on brand loyalty. Research suggests brand use increases the magnitude, confidence, centrality, and accessibility of brand attitudes.[23] In fact, brand use experience has a much stronger impact on attitudes than advertising about the brand.[24] Consumers who have strong attitudes toward a brand are likely to search for and pay attention to information which confirms their attitude and avoid information which fails to confirm their attitudes.[25]

How Do Firms Develop Brand Loyalty?

Developing a strong brand name is quite costly. "Just take advertising alone. Ten years ago, $5 million to $20 million could establish a brand. Today you are talking about $50 million to $100 million annual investment."[26] Some common traits shared among brands that have been leaders in their product categories for over 50 years are: (1) uniquely superior performance, (2) consistent and continually improving quality and taste, (3) consistent positioning, (4) massive exposure to brand name and broad distribution, (5) linking of brand name to symbols, (6) emotional associations with a brand, and (7) concentrated use of brand name.[27]

[23]Fazio, Russell, "How Do Attitudes Guide Behavior?," *In* R. M. Sorrentino and E. T. Higgins (eds.), *The Handbook of Motivation and Cognition; Foundations of Social Behavior.* New York, Guilford Press, 1986, pp. 204–243.

[24]Smith, Robert E., and William Swinyard, "Attitude Behavior Consistency: The Impact of Product Trials versus Advertising," *Journal of Marketing Research,* 20, August, 1983, pp. 257–267.

[25]Brehm, J. E., "Post-Decision Changes in the Desirability of Alternatives," *Journal of Abnormal and Social Psychology,* 52, July, 1956, pp. 384–389; Harold Kassarjian and Joel B. Cohen, "Cognitive Dissonance and Consumer Behavior," *California Management Review,* 8, Fall, 1965, pp. 55–64; Charles G. Lord, Lee Ross and Mark R. Lepper, "Biased Assimilation and Attitude Polarization: The Effects of Prior Theories on Subsequently Considered Evidence," *Journal of Personality and Social Psychology,* 37, 1979, pp. 2098–2109.

[26]"New? Improved? The Brand Name Mergers." *Business Week, op. cit.,* p. 109.

[27]The information in the remaining portion of this section is based on David Clearly, *Great American Brands: The Success Formulas That Made Them Famous.* New York, Fairchild Publications, 1981.

Superior Performance. Perhaps the key ingredient to developing a product with high loyalty is simply to satisfy customer needs better than the competition.[28] Many people feel that successful brands are created simply by massive advertising. However, leading brands consistently outperform competitive brands in blind taste tests. A former chairman of Procter & Gamble, the world's largest advertiser, said:

> The key to successful marketing is superior product performance ... if the consumer does not perceive any real benefits in the brand, then no amount of ingenious advertising and selling can save it.

To which David Ogilvy, one of the most distinguished practitioners in advertising, responded:

> The best way to beat P&G is, of course, to market a *better product.* Bell Brand potato chips defeated P&G's Pringles because they tasted better. And Rave took over Lilt in less than a year because, not containing ammonia, it was a better product.[29]

Although some enduring brand leaders appear to offer few benefits over competitive brands now, when they were first introduced they did provide unique benefits. Gillette and Gerber offered considerable convenience to their customers. Gillette safety razors (first marketed in 1903) significantly reduced the likelihood of cuts when shaving and eliminated the need to strop and hone a razor before shaving. Gerber baby food (1928) freed families from spending time preparing strained vegetables when they wished to feed solid foods to their babies.

Budweiser beer (1876), Maxwell House coffee (1870), and Hershey chocolate (1900) provided unique tastes by using special processes and techniques. Budweiser used the centuries-old European Kraeusening process coupled with beechwood aging and the finest barley, malt and rice (rather than the cheap corn) to produce a beer of unique taste and quality. Maxwell House offered a unique blend of coffee beans, and Hershey improved the taste of chocolate by using costly fresh milk.

Ivory soap (1879) provided a low-priced, hard, white soap that was as pure as imported castile soaps and was marketed as the first dual-purpose soap for bath, toilet, and laundry use. To dramatize these two uses, the laundry size soap bar had a notch on each side so that it could be easily divided into smaller bars for toilet use. By using heavy cotton and riveted pockets, Levi denim jeans (1853) enabled its pants to withstand the harsh environment experienced by California gold miners. Goodyear (1905) introduced a tire with a braided wire bead that increased the air capacity and cushioning of automobile tires, and even more importantly, made changing tires much easier.

By offering unique benefits valued by customers, favorable attitudes and strong preferences were developed for these brands when first introduced.

[28]Davidson, J. Hugh, "Why Must Consumer Brands Fail?" *Harvard Business Review,* 54, March–April, 1976, pp. 117–122.

[29]Ogilvy, David, *Ogilvy on Advertising.* New York, Crown, 1983, pp. 156–157.

However, the marketing efforts for these brands went beyond product performance to develop loyalty.

Consistent and Continually Improved Quality.   In addition to providing unique benefits when initially introduced, enduring brands emphasized consistent product quality.   As Coca-Cola (1886) began to expand nationally, it developed the technology to purify economically local water to absolute neutral before mixing with Coca-Cola syrup.   Thus, a Coke tastes the same across the world, even though it is bottled locally.

Brewery wagons have been replaced by trucks, and wooden barrels and vats are now stainless steel, but the formula, ingredients, and process for brewing Budweiser beer have not changed in 100 years. Similarly, Ivory soap, Hershey candy bars, and Levi jeans are virtually identical to products sold over 100 years ago.   Over the years, firms have been particularly aggressive in using new technology to improve the performance of their brands such as Goodyear tires, Gillette razors, and Tide laundry detergent.

Consistent Positioning.   Even though the formulation of some enduring brands has changed, the positioning of many brands has been remarkably consistent. Budweiser's advertising always stressed, "If you drink beer, this beer is the best," and did not associate itself with a more exciting life, attraction to the opposite sex, or acceptance by one's peers.   Singer sewing machines have emphasized economy and durability rather than special features.   *99 and 44/100 pure* has been the central concept in positioning Ivory soap since its introduction. Maxwell House has emphasized its tastes with the slogan "Good to the last drop"—a quote attributed to President Theodore Roosevelt after finishing a cup of coffee during a visit to Joel Cheek's (the founder of Maxwell House) home in 1907.   Camel cigarettes also emphasized a unique taste by using the slogan, "I'd walk a mile for a Camel," for 35 years.   The Coca-Cola slogan, "Delicious and Refreshing," first appeared in the *Atlanta Constitution* in 1876.

Consistent product quality and positioning reduce consumer uncertainty about the brand and result in confident attitudes—a property that increases the stability of the brand attitude.

Massive Exposure and Broad Distribution.   The marketing programs for enduring brands have included building extensive exposure for the brand name and intensive distribution.   Most leading brands are supported by extensive advertising. However, intense distribution and promotion campaigns do more than increase brand awareness.

Singer sewing machines were perhaps the first global brand.   In 1861, Singer sold more sewing machines in Europe than in the United States. Singer's salespeople have since promoted their products in every inhabited spot on the world, from igloo settlements in the Arctic to Kraals in Equatorial Africa.

Coca-Cola offered fountain operator signs, souvenir fans, calendars, clocks, serving trays, and glasses so that consumers would constantly be exposed to the brand name. Thousands of small establishments which had never displayed a sign were given metal posters proclaiming "Ice cold Coca-Cola sold here" and coolers to make sure the promise was fulfilled. Gillette razors and Hershey candy bars have the broadest distribution of any products in the United States.

Budweiser became America's first national brand by using the relatively new pasteurization process, by setting up ice houses on rail sidings, and by acquiring a fleet of refrigerated rail cars. In 1876, Anheuser-Busch distributed one million reproductions of a painting, "Custer's Last Stand," to tavern keepers, putting the Budweiser name in front of tavern goers throughout the U.S. The Budweiser label has become a popular form appearing on t-shirts, caps, and sail boat spinnakers. Three hitches of eight Clydesdale horses make over 300 appearances yearly at state fairs and shopping centers. Budweiser's name appears on racing hydrofoils and cars sponsored by Anheuser-Busch.

Symbols.   Many enduring brands have symbols that have been consistently linked to the brand. The script logo, unique bottle, and glasses are associated with Coca-Cola. The Gerber baby and Campbell kids are a part of Americana. The design and colors of the Budweiser, Campbell's, and Levi's labels and Hershey bar wrapper have not changed significantly in 50 years.

The wide exposure to brand names and linking of these names to symbols increase the accessibility of the brand names, beliefs, and attitudes. It also increases their social value. Some brand names have become so closely linked to product categories that they are used generically to identify the category such as Kleenex, Saran Wrap, and Xerox.

Emotional Aspect.   Over time, consumers have developed a strong emotional response toward brands. These brands have become part of the lifestyle and culture of individuals. For example, AT&T's long distance telephone theme of "Reach out and touch someone" appeals to our social needs. Michelin's advertising that stresses safety, uses babies to make a strong emotional statement. In the early 70s, Coca-Cola used a television commercial featuring a young choral group that sang, "I'd like to teach the world to sing in perfect harmony . . . I'd like to buy the world a Coke to keep it company." This campaign emphasized that Coke is part of our cultural heritage—the brand itself is a symbol of peace and friendship.

These emotional links toward brands increase the centrality of brand attitudes to consumer values and, thus, result in stable attitudes and repeat purchase behavior.

Limited Use of Brand.   Even though the brand names discussed are a valuable asset, many of the firms owning these names have been reluctant to use the names on multi-products. Only recently have the brand names Coca-Cola, Budweiser, Tide, and Ivory been extended to diet cola drinks, light beer, liquid detergents, and shampoo. Even these extensions have been limited, using abbreviations of Diet *Coke* and *Bud* Light. Campbell and Gillette offer many products but continue to link the brand names Campbell with soup and Gillette with the safety razor. New brand names have been developed for other products such as Swanson, Le Menu, Right Guard, Cricket, Adorn, and Foamy.

The limited use of brand names increases the confidence and accessibility of brand attitudes. By associating a name with one specific product, the consumer is able to develop a distinct image of the brand and associate this image with one product.

Besides increasing the positive aspects of the relationship, it might also be necessary to minimize the possibility of its dissolution as is discussed next.

SWITCHING COSTS

Consumers become brand loyal because they perceive that the cost of switching to a new brand is greater that the potential benefits. These switching costs in consumer choice situations are largely psychological, such as the mental energy to search for evaluation information about a new brand and the risk of being dissatisfied with the new brand. In many situations, consumers and industrial customers become committed to a product, because real costs will be incurred if they switch to a new product. Note that often there is little distinction between real and psychological switching costs. In many situations both occur. We next explore some aspects of switching costs that confront industrial customers and, in some situations, consumers.

Types of Switching Costs

The investment and benefit patterns over time for the three basic types of switching costs are shown in Exhibit 6–9. In the first situation customers make an initial purchase or investment from which they receive a flow of benefits. However, the initial investment commits the customers to make subsequent purchases from the supplier or incur high cost if they switch to a new supplier.

A consumer service example of this type of switching cost is the initial fee to join a health club. After paying the initial fee at one health club, the consumer incurs a high switching cost (another initial fee) if he or she wishes to go to another health club.

The second type of switching involves a series of investments decreasing over time with a sequence of benefits that increase over time. An example of this pattern of investment and benefits in a consumer setting is learning the location of items in a supermarket or department store. After shopping at one store, the consumer can learn about the store and spend less time looking for items. If the consumer switches to a new store, he or she incurs these learning costs again.

The final type of switching cost involves making a sequence of investments purchases which result in future payoffs. For example, a customer may get a discount on future purchases after reaching a specific cumulative level of purchases from a supplier. Similarly, consumers may get a free air ticket after they have flown 20,000 miles with an airline. After making a few purchases or flying a few miles with an airline, the customer is committed to continue to make purchases from a supplier or risk delaying or losing future payoffs.

EXHIBIT 6-9   Types of Switching Costs

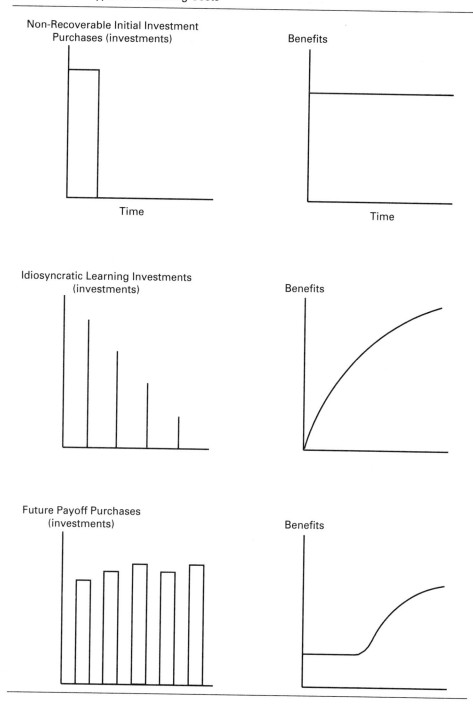

Idiosyncratic Investment

The switching cost scenarios described previously only commit customers to a supplier when the investments made by the customer are idiosyncratic to one supplier. For example, to a purchaser of a shaving razor, switching costs would be reduced if razor blades designed for one razor worked equally well with razors made by other firms.

Switching costs associated with learning only arise when the learning is idiosyncratic to one supplier's offering. If all word processors were identical in operation and maintenance, then any investment in learning about one word processor would be readily transferable to another word processor. No switching costs (in terms of learning) would prevent a customer from switching to a new supplier of word processors.

Finally, if all airlines accepted each other's mileage, a consumer would not feel a commitment to continue to fly with one carrier.

Standardization and Modularity.

The standardization of interfaces to equipment and operating procedures reduces or eliminates switching costs. If all personal computer manufacturers used identical operating systems, software developed for one computer could be used on all computers. Users would no longer have to learn a new system or buy new software if they switched to a new supplier. Thus, standardization reduces the commitment of customers to the offering of one supplier. By adhering to an industry standard, a new entrant has an opportunity to gain market share quickly, because customers can switch to its product at low cost. However, adhering to the industry standard is a two-edged sword. By standardizing an offering, the supplier has more difficulty committing customers to its offering and, thus, creating sustainable competitive advantage.

Consider IBM's entry into the personal computer market. By using an open architecture, a nonproprietary operating system, and standard components, IBM was able to develop and produce the PC quickly. The use of an open architecture enabled software and peripheral manufacturers to easily provide compatible products and resulted in the PC becoming the "standard" personal computer. However, competitors were also able to make "clones" (compatible personal computers), and offer them at lower prices thereby eroding IBM's margins and market share. From 1985 to 1986, the market share for the IBM PC dropped from 42% to 31% whereas the share for PC clones rose from 18% to 38%. During this period, the average price paid for an IBM PC dropped from $2300 to $1650.[30]

In contrast, Apple computers used a proprietary architecture. Although their computers have not become industry standards, they have not been copied by competitors and, thus, have a greater percentage of "commitment" to customers. This commitment is reflected in the higher profit margins that Apple is able to realize compared to IBM (51% versus 42%). However, customer usage, especially in corporations, has prompted Apple to develop partnerships and allow its machinery to work in conjunction with others.

Modularity in product design and use enables customers to make small initial

[30]"The PC Wars: IBM vs the Clones," *Business Week,* July 28, 1986, pp. 62–68.

purchases from a supplier. Customers can try a product at low cost and then expand their use of the product if they are satisfied. Since a major initial commitment is not required, a vendor offering a modular product has an easier time selling to a new customer. However, modularity, like standardization, has its drawbacks. Although it offers an easier entry for a new vendor, it also reduces the customer's commitment to the vendor.

Suppliers must always confront the tradeoff between the use of modularity and standardization to win new customers and the danger of these tactics to reduce the long-term commitment by customers.

Sunk Costs. Note that the initial idiosyncratic investment made when purchasing a vendor's product is a sunk cost and, normally, should not be considered in subsequent purchase decisions. Subsequent decisions should simply consider the net present value (NPV) of buying from a new vendor—the cost of making a new initial investment compared to the potential increase in cash from the new investment versus the original investment. However, few, if any, consumers use NPV to make product choice decisions.

SUMMARY

This chapter focuses on understanding consumer relationships and loyalty and on building sustaining relationships.

The basis for forming sustaining relationships is to satisfy or delight customers. Satisfying customers requires matching or exceeding their expectations of exchange entities and relationship modes. Customer expectations are based on the values they desire and the stage of the relationship process (and their past experience). The five key drivers of customer values are functional, social, emotional, conditional, and epistemic values. Each requires a different approach to its satisfaction. Similarly, customers at different stages of relationships have different expectations.

The development of sustaining customer relationships is aided by having a humanistic customer perspective. A framework within which to place the current status of the customer relationship and to use in identifying its change is two dimensional: degree of formality and degree of closeness.

Information and experience about a brand are often associated by customers with the brand name as a cue. Branding is an important strategic activity. It signifies a commitment and symbolizes the values that are being offered.

Customer commitment increases when customers perceive that the costs of switching to an alternative supplier are greater than the benefits. In consumer markets, such perceptions also result in brand loyalty. Firms attempt to build brand loyalty by increasing the favorableness of consumer attitudes toward their brand, by increasing confidence in the brand attitude, by making the brand attitude more central to the consumer's value system, and by making the attitude more accessible.

Firms can build mutually advantageous relationships if they carefully match their market offerings to the vendors and relationship modes desired by consumers.

Concept Questions

1. What is a marketing relationship?
2. What are the key elements of the various types of customer values?
3. What are the relationship stages, and what are the key features of each stage?
4. How does customer satisfaction arise? How is it different from customer delight?
5. (a.) Explain humanistic marketing to your Marketing VP.
   (b.) Describe the dimensions along which customer relationships may be viewed and analyzed.
6. (a.) Distinguish between inertial and attitudinal brand loyalty.
   (b.) What is the relationship between brand loyalty and positioning?

Discussion Questions

1. (a.) How would you identify a customer's stage of relationship?
   (b.) How would you use this information?
2. (a.) Compare and contrast the different types of customer values.
   (b.) How would you assess (a) what values your current customers seek, and (b) what values you currently best provide?
   (c.) How would you use the knowledge gained in 2b, to your advantage?
3. Share-of-mind (SOM) and share-of-market are two important constructs that you would have discussed in introductory Marketing. How do these constructs relate to the customer-relationships model in this book?
4. Customers rarely seek only one type of value. Further, customers typically vary according to their stage of relationship. Given this, should you have a portfolio of customers at different stages? How would you develop a balance within this portfolio? Will this portfolio be stable? Discuss.
5. Discuss the relationship between branding and switching costs.
6. Discuss whether humanistic marketing is a stable concept for free markets.

Chapter 7

Competitive Analysis

As discussed in Chapter 1, marketing strategy is creating a pathway to attain desired marketing goals. Whether these goals are attained depends on implementing the chosen strategy as well as on the context in which the strategy needs to operate.

Given a goal, which strategy will enable it to be attained? Given a strategy, what will be its outcome? These fundamental questions need to be answered when choosing a strategy. To answer them requires an analysis of the competitive conditions or context in a product-market.

Context mediates the outcome of implementing a strategy. It also defines the degree of difficulty in achieving a particular outcome in a product-market. In this chapter, we discuss the seven factors that affect competitiveness or rivalry in a product-market. Some generalizations about the relationship among each of these factors and the competitiveness or rivalry in a product-market are also discussed. However, because they are generalizations, they need to be carefully examined for each product-market.

One of the factors affecting rivalry is the nature of competitors. Strategic moves should (as discussed in Chapter 2) be based on what the competition will do and also on ways to change what they might do. To do so requires understanding these competitors and their strengths and weaknesses. Two broad frames of reference—the competitive advantage and the value-chain—are discussed as being useful in doing so. A detailed understanding of individual competitors is often desirable. Finally, a point of reference that combines the characteristics of the competitors and the impact of the other factors is also discussed.

The firm for which a marketing strategy is being developed is also a competitor or a potential competitor. The methods of analysis and the factors to be considered for this firm are the same as those discussed in the general context of competitors.

Motivating Situations

Bosch GmbH: Auto Components

Germany's Robert Bosch GmbH will sell $10 billion in car parts this year, making it the world's largest independent manufacturer of auto components. It is solidly profitable back at home, but in the U.S., where it books around $800 million of its sales, Bosch has swerved into the red.[1]

Federal Express: Air-Express Mail

It has taken Federal Express Corp. more than a year of soul-searching, analysis and negotiations to come up with a new European strategy.

The question now is whether the plan will work.

The air-express giant, which tried and failed to build a package-delivery franchise in Europe from the ground up, now faces big hurdles in its attempt to cut losses by relying on local partners to deliver packages within Europe.

… The restructuring could aggravate what is already a big problem for Federal Express: too little volume on the return trip from Europe to the U.S. And it could make it more difficult for Federal Express to beat its rivals' prices in a fiercely competitive and recessionary world market.[2]

U.S. Ready-to-Eat (RTE) Cereal Market

"We're seeing aggressive pricing," says a spokesman for Dominick's Finer Foods, a Chicago-based supermarket chain. Promotions, he adds, are "more frequent and deeper."

… The explanation is simple: A single share point, or 1 percent of total sales, means $75 million in revenue. Brands can thrive on less than that. And where profit margins run 20 percent and more, incremental sales mean bottom line gains.[3]

A *Forbes* article[4] reports that a new cereal costs $20 to $40 million in advertising and merchandising in the first year and in order to make money a new cereal needs about 0.6% or 0.7% market share. The article also provides the following, indicating that while the incremental share obtained in introducing a new cereal decreases each year, it is still, nevertheless, on average, profitable.

Year	Number of New Brands	Average Share (%)
1984	11	0.41
1989	32	0.23
1990	11	0.18

[1]Fuhrman, P., "Euro–Thrash," *Forbes,* July 22, 1991, pp. 66–67.

[2]Pearl, D., "Federal Express Pins Hopes on New Strategy in Europe," *The Wall Street Journal,* March 13, 1992, A 3.

[3]Gibson, R., "Cereal Giants Battle Over Market Share," *The Wall Street Journal,* December 16, 1991, B1.

[4]Levine, J., "Why 'New' Is Old Hat," *Forbes,* July 22, 1991, pp. 302–303.

Questions Raised by These Examples

These examples demonstrate how context affects performance. The Bosch example leads us to ask: What makes the U.S. market for auto parts different from the European market?

The Federal Express example points out that the problem of flow of air-express mail is an important contextual factor that could potentially impact Federal Express's performance.

The U.S. RTE cereal market example shows an industry in which total demand is very high, making small shares profitable. This same factor, however, brings competition, thus making competition intense.

Although structural factors unique to a product-market contribute to the intensity of competition, differences are found in the strategies as well as the intensity of competition adopted by different firms. For example: in the European auto parts market, although major players like Bosch largely "go it alone," Japan's Nippondenso Co., which is the world's second largest parts-maker, "has moved stealthily into Europe, acquiring a small British partsmaker and establishing a joint venture with an Italian firm."[5]

Joseph Stewart, Senior Vice President of Kellogg, has said, "As the market leader, we are going to protect and increase that leadership doing whatever it takes."[6]

In Chapter 1, we alluded to the strategic planning process as incorporating a simulation-like exercise in which the consequences of each possible strategy need to be carefully evaluated. Such evaluations must include potential reactions by existing and potential competitors in each product-market that would be affected by the strategy being considered. Such reactions are based both on overall industry structure as well as on the capabilities and aspirations of the participants (current and potential) in each product-market. Keep this goal-driven process in mind as you read this chapter. The structural factors related to competitiveness are discussed next.

Factors Determining the Level of Competitiveness in a Product-Market

As Michael Porter put it:

> Moreover, in the fight for market share, competition is not manifested only in other players. Rather, competition in an industry is rooted in its underlying economics, and competitive forces exist that go well beyond the established combatants in a particular industry. Customers, suppliers, potential entrants, and substitute products are all competitors that may be more or less prominent or active depending on the industry.[7]

This paragraph succinctly captures the essence of his *drivers of competition* diagram (Exhibit 7–1).

[5]Fuhrman, P., *op. cit.,* 1991.

[6]Gibson, R. *op. cit.,* 1991.

[7]Porter, M. E., "How Competitive Forces Shape Strategy," *Harvard Business Review,* March–April, 1979, pp. 137–165.

Insight into the underlying economics and competitive forces is provided by research in *evolutionary economics* and in *transaction-cost economics*. The former deals with organizational adaptations and the latter with organizational relationships. In Chapter 5 we discussed key facets of transaction-cost economics and its relevance to understanding relationships among members of a distribution channel.

In marketing strategy, assessment of the competitiveness or rivalry within a product-market is critical in making resource allocations. These decisions include whether to enter or exit a product-market, and whether or not to increase or decrease resources allocated to a product-market. If rivalry is to be of use in understanding the multifaceted nature of competitiveness in a market, it needs to be adequately defined.

EXHIBIT 7–1   Elements of Industry Structure

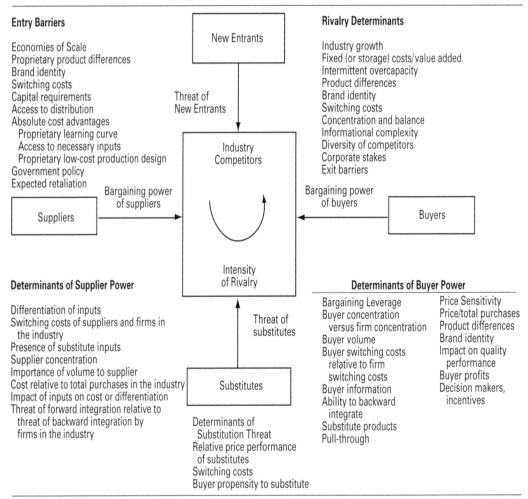

Entry Barriers

Economies of Scale
Proprietary product differences
Brand identity
Switching costs
Capital requirements
Access to distribution
Absolute cost advantages
  Proprietary learning curve
  Access to necessary inputs
  Proprietary low-cost production design
Government policy
Expected retaliation

Rivalry Determinants

Industry growth
Fixed (or storage) costs/value added
Intermittent overcapacity
Product differences
Brand identity
Switching costs
Concentration and balance
Informational complexity
Diversity of competitors
Corporate stakes
Exit barriers

Determinants of Supplier Power

Differentiation of inputs
Switching costs of suppliers and firms in
  the industry
Presence of substitute inputs
Supplier concentration
Importance of volume to supplier
Cost relative to total purchases in the industry
Impact of inputs on cost or differentiation
Threat of forward integration relative to
  threat of backward integration by
  firms in the industry

Determinants of Buyer Power

Bargaining Leverage
Buyer concentration
  versus firm concentration
Buyer volume
Buyer switching costs
  relative to firm
  switching costs
Buyer information
Ability to backward
  integrate
Substitute products
Pull-through

Price Sensitivity
Price/total purchases
Product differences
Brand identity
Impact on quality
  performance
Buyer profits
Decision makers,
  incentives

Determinants of
  Substitution Threat
Relative price performance
  of substitutes
Switching costs
Buyer propensity to substitute

Definition of Rivalry

Rivalry or competitiveness faced by a firm in a product-market is an indicator of the resources required for it to attain its goals in that product-market.

To be precise and to provide a standard measure across product-markets, we need to specify some standard goal, for example, an increase in market share of 1%, up from 20%, or a 1% increase in return on sales from a return on sales of 15%, or to profitably introduce a new product, and so forth. However, given that different firms have different objectives, and given our state of knowledge, such a standard measure is perhaps not useful or even possible. On the other hand, for one firm it may be useful to understand the rivalry or competitiveness of various product-markets in our definition. This view of rivalry is reflected in the following excerpt from *Business Week*:

> Robert Iverson (CEO of Kiwi International Airlines) "recognizes the danger in challenging the majors, but says he isn't worried. As long as an upstart doesn't garner more than 10% of the market on any given route, the powerful airlines won't go after it. In fact, as worries mount about the threat of oligopoly, the big airlines will have strong incentive to tolerate upstarts. Says Iverson: "We're more help to them alive than dead."[8]

In economics, all firms have profit maximization as their objective and rivalry is conceived of as price competition only. Thus the definition of rivalry is not a problem. In economics, rivalry is also common to all firms. That is, it is an industry- (product-market) level indicator. In marketing strategy, given differences in firms and their relative strengths and weaknesses, as well as differences among product-markets, rivalry has to be both specific to a firm (or at least to an objective) as well as to a product-market industry.

Seven Competitiveness Factors

The factors that influence differences in competitiveness or rivalry between product-markets are:

- Growth Rate
- Regulatory Status
- Information Status
- Cost Structure
- Market Structure
- Customer Preference Structure
- Nature of Product-Market Players

Of these, the last is different from the others and requires an examination of the individual players. It is discussed separately.

Growth Rate.   Rivalry is expected to vary during the different stages in the life cycle of a product—from introduction through growth through maturity and finally *decline*. It is normally expected that rivalry follows the same pattern as that

---

[8]Rothman, A., G. DeGeorge, E. Schine, "The Season of Upstart Startups," *Business Week,* August 31, 1992, pp. 68–69.

followed by the sales volume of a market over time. Sales volume increases modestly, then rapidly, then flattens out at some peak level, and then drops off.

With a vibrant growth of the overall market, sales growth does not have to come at the expense of the other factors. (Even in a growth market, if the objective of a firm is to increase considerably its market share, it may face intense rivalry if its competitors are able and so inclined.) In the initial (or introductory) stage, there may be fewer major players, but rivalry among them may be high. For example, when video cassette recorders were first introduced there was a major confrontation between Sony, which used the BETA format, and JVC which introduced the VHS format. Sony licensed its technology for $50 per machine, whereas JVC's license fee was $1.50. Thus, despite the technological superiority of the BETA format, JVC has become a dominant seller. The U.S. domestic airline industry, which may be said to be exhibiting low growth, if at all, is highly competitive, with low efficiency in obtaining incremental market share. However, acquiring other airlines may allow considerable gain in market share, perhaps efficiently. When the personal computer market in the United States was growing rapidly, many small companies entered the market. Now, with considerable slowing in growth in this product-market, competition for market share, profitability, technology edge, and so forth, is severe. Clearly, as these examples show, looking at each type of factor is useful, but *the interaction among these factors dominates the extent of rivalry to be faced in a product-market.*

Regulatory Status.   Regulations vary across countries as well as across product-markets in a country. The long distance telephone market in the United States has been changed from a regulated monopoly to a partially regulated market. Certainly the nature of competition has changed dramatically in this market. Formerly, a firm wishing to enter this market could not do so (until MCI challenged AT&T in court, incurring considerable cost); there are now several competitors in this market and market share is fiercely contested. Antitrust regulation may prevent entry (either directly or via acquisition) into a market by a firm which already has a certain market share in it. The impact of regulation may be that entry is or is not permitted, or may change the degree of present competitiveness.

Information Status.   This is how quickly competitive actions are known by other players in a product-market. For example, if customers respond positively to a reduction in price, then a firm, by reducing the cost of its product might be able to obtain market share. However, the price cut it needs to make to gain a certain share could be very different if its competitors reacted with price cuts (or other competitive reactions) of their own. Such reactions by competitors could occur if, and only if, they knew that a price cut had occurred. Even if there is a delay in transmitting the price cut information to competitors, the market share gain may be only short-lived because there might be a lag in knowing the competitors' reactions as well. So, while there may be short-lived gains, the long-term gains may be lower. If there is a competitive first-mover advantage, then such a product-market exhibits less competitiveness for this first-mover firm than another product-market when such is not the case. *This means that when a first-mover advantage exists, a later competitor is at a disadvantage and is less likely to threaten the first-mover.*

Another aspect of the information status of a product-market is uncertainty regarding various costs (or for that matter the other types of factors discussed in this section). For example, uncertainty about exit costs might encourage (wrongly) entry into a market, thereby increasing the competition for market share. (Of course, this might affect products that are similarly perceived by customers than other products.) Probably, though, it might discourage entry because of the high uncertainty that is associated with the success of an entry.

In general, it appears that *lack of information* (or slowness of its transmission) *and uncertainty both seem to indicate lower rivalry* and an opportunity to make strategic moves in a product-market.[9]

Cost Structure.   This refers to mobility barriers (entry and exit costs), economies of scale and scope, asset specificity and transaction costs. Entry and exit costs are the fixed costs required for entry and exit. If unit marginal costs decline with total volume of production it implies that economies of scale exist (either because of experience, plant size, or both). Economies of scope refer to the relationship between costs and the variety (or diversity) of the firm's operations. Finally, transaction costs are the costs of carrying out the various functions (distribution, etc.) required in the movement of a product from its raw material stage to its sale to consumers. Companies from France, Spain, Germany, and Britain formed a consortium to create Airbus Industrie. This was necessary because of the high entry costs in the commercial airplane market. Their airplanes compete mainly against Boeing, which dominates the commercial aircraft market. Entry into this market is difficult because of the need for exceptional technology, close relationships with governments of various countries (most countries have national airlines which, even if privately held, still have to obtain government approval for placing the high-priced orders with airline manufacturers because of foreign exchange rates, negotiated credit terms, etc.), relationships with banks and other financial institutions and a high fixed cost of entry. This is a product-market with both high entry costs and high transaction costs. There is a high importance placed both on every order as well as on market share. For example, United Airlines recently leased 50 A320 airplanes from Airbus.[10] Boeing received an order valued at $320 million for two Boeing 747-400s from Singapore Airlines, increasing its total of confirmed orders in 1992 to 111 and valued at $9.4 billion.[11]

In markets with higher entry costs there is likely to be greater rivalry than in markets with lower entry costs. High entry costs require higher market share for their recovery, thus leading to higher rivalry. This is especially true if the costs are in assets specific to this product-market and thus act as high exit costs. Higher exit costs or asset specificity also lead to greater rivalry. Exit costs in unemployment also need to be considered when looking at government-backed consortia like Airbus Industrie. This raises rivalry still higher, with different levels and forms of competitive activity (e.g., governmental bans on foreign companies, etc.) than are typical.

[9]For an in-depth treatment see Oster, S. M., *Modern Competitive Analysis,* New York, Oxford University Press, 1990. In particular see pages 208 and 255.

[10]Salpukas, A., "Lease Deal by Airbus and United," *The New York Times,* July 9, 1992, C1.

[11]"Boeing Gets $320 Million Order from Singapore," *The New York Times,* July, 1992, C3.

If there is a greater possibility for economies of scale in one product-market than in another, then there is likely to be greater rivalry in the market with the greater possibility for economies of scale. Consider the semiconductor market. The effects of cumulative production volume (experience) in this industry are considerable. (Exhibit 7–2 shows an experience curve in this industry and in some others.) Increasing the volume of production (of standard chips) leads to higher profits, than without increasing production volume. Thus in such an industry, as opposed to, say, a chemical process plant, there may be greater opposition to a competitor's attempts to gain sales or market share. The effects of economies of scale and entry costs are reflected in a ratio of minimum efficient scale of production to market size. *Minimum efficient scale* is the smallest volume of production which results in the lowest unit cost. The ratio of the minimum efficient scale to the market size provides *one* indicator of the minimum market share required in a market. The higher it is, the greater will be efforts to protect its erosion; if it is smaller, there may be more margin for competition. Exhibit 7–3 shows the minimum economic size as calculated for some industries.

EXHIBIT 7–2   Sample Experience Curves

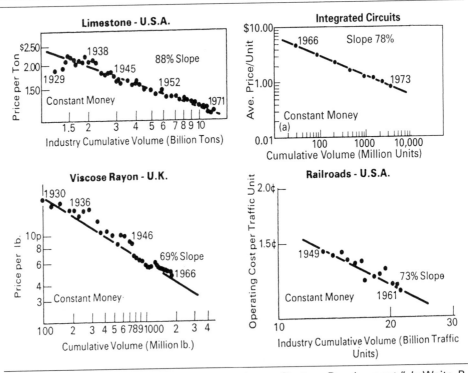

From Hedley, B., "Fundamental Approaches to Strategy Development," *In* Weitz, B. A., and R. Wensley (eds.), *Strategic Marketing: Planning, Implementation, and Control,* Boston, Kent Publishing, 1984, pp. 149–165.

EXHIBIT 7–3 Minimum Efficient Scale Estimates

(Minimum Efficient Firm Size as Percentage of Industry Capacity)			
Fruit and vegetable canning	0.5	Rayon	6.0
Oil refining	1.75	Farm machinery	6.0
Meat packing	0.2	Automobiles	10.0
Meat products	2.5	Tractors	15.0
Fountain pens	10.0	Shoes	2.5
Copper	10.0	Cement	10.0
Typewriters	30.0	Steel	20.0
Flour milling	0.5	Gypsum products	33.0
Liquor distilling	1.75	Soap	15.0
Metal containers	3.0	Cigarettes	20.0
Tires	3.0		

Reprinted with permission from Oxford University Press, Oster, S. M., *Modern Comparative Analysis,* 1990, p. 4.

When substantial economies of scope are obtainable either through the offering of a product line in a product-market or that of several products in various product- markets, then greater protection may be exhibited by the firms in a product-market. *Synergy in production or marketing or other activities may increase profitability by lowering costs.* Any challenge to even a single product may lead to a more vehement reaction, when such synergies are present compared with when they are not.

There are costs associated with business transactions. In fact, whether vertical integration is seen in an industry may depend on if it is cheaper to perform the other activities in-house, or to have them performed by another party. Besides transaction costs, issues of control, flexibility, speed, and information availability also influence decisions to vertically integrate. (This is discussed in Chapter 5.) In comparing two product-markets with different transaction costs associated with reactions, the one with greater transaction costs may actually exhibit less competitiveness. If it costs more to react, then this is likely to place a damper on hasty reaction. On the other hand, higher (noncompetitive reaction-specific) transaction costs should also be associated with greater attempts to protect returns on sales and for investments, market share, and so forth. *The relationship between rivalry and transaction costs is not always one of positive correlation.*

Market Structure. Typically, market structure is the number of firms (products) in a market, the distribution of shares across these products and the substitutability among these products (as captured through cross-elasticities or brand switching).[12]

Two common ways to view the products in a product-market are product-positioning maps, and product-market hierarchies.

Product-positioning maps show the location of the products in a product-map based on either physical characteristics (in discussions in economics), space, or perceptual

[12]A discussion of substitutability may be found in Chapter 7. Also see the Appendix.

dimensions (based on psychometric measurement). An example of such a perceptual map used by Chrysler and reported in the *Wall Street Journal* is shown in Exhibit 7–4. In such maps, the closer two products are, the more similar they are inferred to be and thus more competitive. A higher number of products in a product-market may lead to greater competitiveness. For example, an antitrust suit was brought against Kellogg, General Foods, General Mills and Quaker Oats, the four major manufacturers of ready-to-eat cereal, based on product proliferation leading to entry deterrence and thus lowered competitiveness.[13] When drawing such inferences from product-positioning maps, a word of caution is needed. The scales on such maps are arbitrary and the *density of such maps*

EXHIBIT 7–4   Perceptual Map-Brand Images

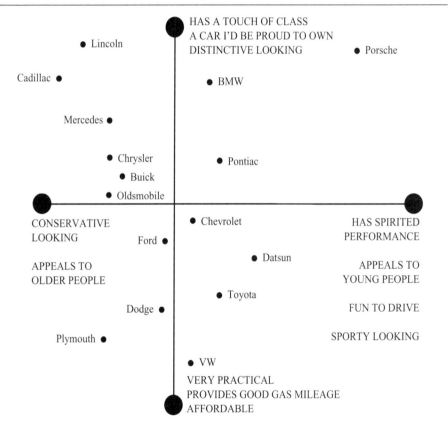

[13]Schmalansee, R., "Entry Deterrence in the Ready-to-Eat Breakfast Cereal Industry," *The Bell Journal of Economics,* 9, Spring, 1978, pp. 305–327.

cannot be unambiguously ascertained by inspection (eye-balling). However, for two markets which are otherwise similar (easier to think of conceptually than to do practically—for each market is different!), the one with more products is likely to exhibit greater rivalry.

Hierarchical product-maps, based on brand-switching or cross-price-elasticity data, allow a simpler understanding of the submarkets within a product market. Exhibit 7–5 provides an example of such a map.[14] For the current discussion, the number of branches of such a map is an indicator of overall rivalry. The more branches, the more competition will be localized. The flatter the structure, or fewer branches, the more the products are closely competitive. The former condition is associated with greater differences across products and the latter with fewer differences (or less product differentiation). And, *increased differentiation may be linked to lower competitiveness in rivalry.*

Two indices are available for capturing the size distributions of firms in an industry: the *four-firm concentration ratio* (C4) and the *Herfindahl Index* (HI). C4 is calculated for the United States by the government and published in the *Census of Manufacturing*.[15] C4 is the market share of the four largest firms (not products) in an industry. The Herfindahl Index is given as $HI = 10,000 \sum_i s_i^2$, where s_i refers to the share of the ith firm. Note that these indices, or suitable versions of them, may be used at each level of a product-market hierarchy to denote the possible intensity of competition at that level.

EXHIBIT 7–5   Two Alternative Hierarchies for Selected Deodorant Brands

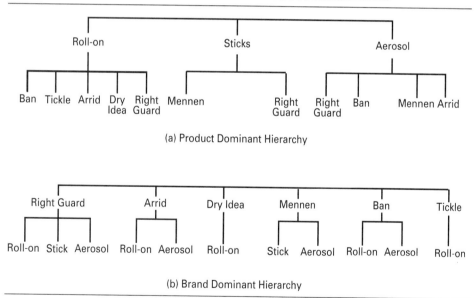

(a) Product Dominant Hierarchy

(b) Brand Dominant Hierarchy

Reprinted with permission from Prentice-Hall, Urban, G. L. and J. R. Hauser, *Design and Manufacturing of New Products*, 1980, p. 92.

[14]From Urban, G. L., and S. H. Star, *Advanced Marketing Strategy: Phenomena, Analysis and Decisions*, Englewood Cliffs, NJ, Prentice-Hall, 1991.

[15]Note that C4 is provided on an industry basis, in which industry is defined by the *Standard Industrial Classification* (SIC) code of the U.S. government. It is not calculated on a product-market basis.

In general, *industries with higher concentration seem to be associated with increased chances for coordination or collusion.* Such an industry (or product-market) is thus likely to be more hostile to an outsider, than ones with lower concentration ratios. If collusion exists and can be monitored, then rivalry among the colluders is self-defeating, and the question of degree of rivalry is moot. If there is no collusion, then the degree of rivalry is likely to be higher in markets with higher concentration ratios, with the major players jockeying for leadership and cash flow.

Exhibit 7–6 is a graph that shows the distribution of the number of firms in an industry, as well as the distribution of the number of firms in industries prosecuted by the government for price conspiracies. The RTE[16] cereal market in the United States had a C4 of 84% (Kellogg 38%, General Mills 28%, Post 11%, and Quaker 7%) and rivalry in this industry is very high. So much so, that it has been said that: "For knockdown rivalry, forget the Rose Bowl or the Cotton Bowl. This year's toughest competition is taking place in the cereal bowl."

The greater the Herfindahl Index, the lower the expected rivalry among incumbents, because of the existence of a monopoly or of collusion. An HI of 1800 or higher signals a dangerous possibility of collusion to the U.S. Department of Justice. For example, in the U.S. beverage market example (Chapter 7), the HI was calculated to be 2362.[17] If the proposed acquisitions of 7-Up by PepsiCo and Dr. Pepper by Coca-Cola had gone through, the HI would have become 3258. As noted earlier, these acquisitions were blocked by the Federal Trade Commission.

Two other market conditions need to be discussed under market structure: excess capacity and inventory level. *The existence of considerable excess capacity signals the potential for significant rivalry.*[18] This is especially true if it is coupled

EXHIBIT 7–6   Frequency Distribution of Industry Conspiracies

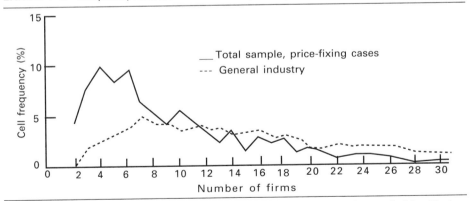

Reprinted with permission from Oxford University Press, Oster, S. M., *Modern Comparative Analysis,* 1990, p. 212.

[16]Data from Gibson, R. *op. cit.,* 1991. The quotation is also from this source. Rose Bowl and Cotton Bowl refer to two major intercollegiate football championships in the United States.

[17]These numbers are from Oster, S. M., *op. cit.,* 1990, p. 213.

[18]For example, see Milgrom, P. and J. Roberts, "Predation, Reputation and Entry Deterrence," *Journal of Economic Theory,* 27, 1982, pp. 280–312; and Kreps, D. W. and R. Wilson, "Reputation and Imperfect Information," *Journal of Economic Theory,* 27, 1982, pp. 253–279.

with high exit costs. High excess capacity signals a preemptive strategy that seeks to keep out potential entrants and indicates "significant" rivalry. Excess capacity also leads to increased rivalry among incumbents, as they seek to retain economies of scale and increased return through share gains. High levels of inventory are likely to be short-term situations. When present, high levels of inventory are likely to make their holders anxious to dispose of them, again implying high rivalry in such markets.[19]

The structure of products and the structure of buyer demand are highly related, as we shall see.

Customer Preference Structure. Product-markets differ in (a) total demand size, (b) the distribution of buyer preferences, and (c) the distribution of information possessed by buyers.

Higher demand (in units especially) is usually associated with more products or firms satisfying this demand. And thus it *is associated with lower rivalry.*

Preference distributions are typically incorporated into product positioning maps— leading to what are called joint- (perception and preference) space maps. An example of such a map is shown in Exhibit 7–7. Preferences are shown in such maps as *ideal-points* (representing the ideal combination of the important product attributes, closeness to an ideal point represents a higher preference than otherwise), or *ideal-vectors* (representing the most desired ratio of the important attributes). The more the ideal-points and the greater their spread indicate a greater desire in this market for variety and product differentiation. As we saw earlier, the strength of local submarkets is likely to be higher. Rivalry is likely to be localized in submarkets and may be easier to combat by a strong entrant (the effects of scope may be vital to this implication, however). Greater variety of tastes/preferences also might indicate opportunities for niching—satisfying an otherwise unserved segment of the market.

EXHIBIT 7–7   Illustration of Joint Space of Ideal Points and Stimuli

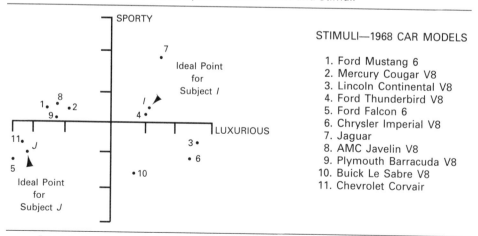

Reprinted with permission from Prentice-Hall, Green, P. E., and D. Tull, *Research for Marketing Decisions,* 1975, p. 469.

[19]If such a building-up of inventory is from illegal hoarding, then rivalry may be of a different form altogether!

If this segment is not large enough or not viewed by another competitor as being necessary for its survival, then rivalry may be low. (This argument is also a submarket rivalry argument.)

If the buyers in a market exhibit considerable uncertainty, then it implies that they are not yet set in their buying patterns in this product-market. This implies that there is not a high advertising barrier erected by industry participants which in turn, implies lower rivalry. Further, if buyers do not have access to (or it is costly to obtain) comparative information about the competitors' offerings, then competitive reactions may bear little fruit and lower rivalry is implied. Thus, the structure of buyer demand and preferences may provide some general indications of rivalry in a market.

Gross Input Analysis.   We have stressed that the six factors discussed so far interact and jointly influence rivalry. A possible way to assess their overall impact may be via a cross-impact analysis. This method of analysis was discussed in Chapter 2 in scenario development.

Implicit in the preceding discussion is the impact of the firms participating in a product-market on the rivalry exhibited in it. This is examined next.

Nature of Product-Market Players

Competitiveness of Players or Competitor Analysis.   Understanding the competitiveness of a competitor is often a pragmatic issue for marketing strategists. Often marketing strategists are particularly interested in monitoring and predicting the behavior of a limited group of specific competitors. After all, the greatest influence on the achievement (and the efficiency of such achievement) of a firm's goals is held by competitor's actions and reactions, and the response to such by buyers, channel members, and other relevant publics. Thus, how competitive a firm will be in a market is of great relevance. What makes one firm demonstrate greater competitiveness than another? The same methods of analysis are also applicable to self-assessment.

It should have both the intention and resources to do so. For example, in the third quarter of 1991 alone, Kellogg poured in approximately $100 million more marketing than it had in 1990 in its implementation of its intention to " . . . protect and increase the leadership—doing whatever it takes."[20] Ambition should indeed be made of sterner stuff. Thus differences in firms' competitiveness may be found based on intentions or motivations, and the "sterner stuff" that allows them to render possible their intentions. Let us look at these. This sequential discussion is mainly for instructional purposes. In reality, intentions and the underlying core competencies are (or should be) symbiotically linked.

Consider these quotes from the 1991 Annual Report of Philip Morris Companies Inc. (The cover of this report is peppered with their brand names: Jell-O, Marlboro, Kraft, Maxwell House, Kool-Aid, Miller, Toblerone, Velveeta, Oscar Mayer, Post, Merit, Jacobs Café, and Breyers. They own many more such well-known brands. And, the words, "The strength of our brands begins with our people" is emblazoned across the center of the front cover.)

Philip Morris U.S.A. has a unique and powerful portfolio of trademarks, and we are committed to competing vigorously in every market segment offering opportunities for

[20]Gibson, R., *op. cit,* 1991.

profitable growth or strategic advantage. At the same time, with improvements in productivity and efficiency, we are moving toward our goal of becoming the low cost producer in each category (p. 6).

We are continuing to invest in the tobacco industry in Eastern Europe. We purchased an 80 percent stake in Egri Dohangyar, our licensee in Hungary. Egri is one of the highest-quality cigarette manufacturers in Hungary (p. 9).

As worldwide demand for Philip Morris brands continues to rise, we are upgrading and expanding our manufacturing facilities around the world (p. 10).

To build on our presence in the $2.8 billion European process cheese category, we are introducing a variety of low calorie and reduced fat cheeses throughout the region (p. 16).

In 1991, despite difficult economic conditions, Kraft General Foods made clear progress toward fulfilling its mission of becoming the world's leading food company (p. 18).

Motivations.   The intentions of the above corporations are clear. Motivations for exhibiting significant competitiveness in a product-market derive from its importance. For example, Kellogg's (38% share) principal business is the ready-to-eat cereal market. For Philip Morris, this market is a trivial part of its business portfolio (its Post brand holds an 11% share of this market, with an approximate sales value of $825 million for a company with consolidated operating revenues of $56.5 billion in 1990). But, changing environmental pressures on its tobacco business have led Philip Morris to strengthen its food business and so now Post is perhaps a strategically important brand. This market, although quite profitable for Nabisco (4% share), is not a particularly major one in its portfolio. In summary, the resources and skills expended in competing in a market depend on what is at stake in it, and the strategic role of such a market in a company's portfolio. (Portfolio analysis is discussed in detail in Chapter 9.)

Dominant Culture.   Firms also differ in their competitive culture. Miles and Snow[21] in 1983 proposed a classification of firms based on their business strategies. Exhibit 7–8 briefly describes the strategy of each of their types. They propose that firms can be identified as one of four types of business: *Prospector, Defender, Analyzer,* and *Reactor.* Some recent studies[22] have further validated this classification and found it to be robust over different product lines within a company. This classification seems to capture an inherent dominant world view within a firm; it captures the dominant corporate culture.

The rivalry displayed by each of the above types of firms in a given product-market may be different. Prospectors exhibit considerable rivalry at the early

[21]Miles, R. E. and C. C. Snow, *Organizational Strategy, Structure and Process,* New York, McGraw-Hill, 1978.

[22]For example, see Hambrick, D. C., "Taxonomic Approaches to Studying Strategy: Some Conceptual and Methodological Issues," *Journal of Management,* 10, 1, 1984, pp. 27–41; and McDaniel, S. W. and J. W. Kolari, "Marketing Strategy Implications of the Miles and Snow Strategic Topology," *Journal of Marketing,* 51, October, 1987, pp. 19–30.

EXHIBIT 7–8   Summary of Miles and Snow's Four Business Strategies

Prospector

- Operates within a broad product-market domain that undergoes periodic redefinition.
- Values being a "first mover" in new product and market areas, even if not all efforts prove to be highly profitable.
- Responds rapidly to early signals concerning areas of opportunity; these responses often lead to new rounds of competitive actions.
- Competes primarily by stimulating and meeting new market opportunities, but may not maintain strength over time in all markets it enters.

Defender

- Attempts to locate and maintain a secure position in relatively stable product or service areas.
- Offers relatively limited range of products or services compared to competitors.
- Tries to protect its domain by offering lower prices, higher quality, or better service than competitors.
- Usually not at the forefront of technological-new product development in its industry; tends to ignore industry changes not directly related to its area of operation.

Analyzer

- An intermediate type; makes fewer and slower product-market changes than prospectors, but is less committed to stability and efficiency than defenders.
- Attempts to maintain a stable, limited line of products or services, but carefully follows a selected set of promising new developments in its industry.
- Seldom a "first mover," but often a second or third entrant in product-markets related to its existing market base—often with a lower cost or higher quality product or service offering.

Reactor

- Lacks any well-defined competitive strategy.
- Does not have as consistent a product-market orientation as its competitors.
- Not as willing to assume the risks of new product or market development as its competitors.
- Not as aggressive in marketing established products as some competitors.
- Responds primarily when it is forced to by environmental pressures.

As adapted with permission from Miles, R. E. and C. C. Snow, *Organizational Strategy, and Process,* 1979, McGraw-Hill, Inc.

stages of the life cycle of a product-market or when the market is jolted by massive environmental change (e.g., the RC brand of soft drinks pioneered the diet and decaffeinated carbonated soft drink markets, but did not maintain its strength subsequently). Defenders like to find limited domains that they can more easily protect, and are not easily challenged in. Preferring stability, they fight to get back into equilibrium and do not react to nondirect attacks or competitive actions. A prime example of a Defender is the Rolls Royce automobile company. Unlike Defenders, Analyzers protect their core business, but do venture into new territories. Thus in and for their core products they exhibit considerable competitiveness, but much less so in others. Finally, Reactors, as the name implies, are not proactive but respond to environmental changes. (In a study[23] of 232 businesses 50 were classified as Reactors.) Their performance is not very sound and so they have even less resources to plow back into business development. They are likely to be the least competitive.[24] A new product is likely to face intensity of competition from incumbents in decreasing order from Defenders, Analyzers, Prospectors, and Reactors. The order of the types of competitors in decreasing competitiveness to existing brands from new products threats is Prospectors, Analyzers, Defenders, and Reactors. For competitive moves by an existing product, the expected order of decreasing competitiveness is Defenders, Reactors, Analyzers, and Defenders, unless it is against an Analyzer's core product, in which case Reactors and Analyzers trade places in the above order.

Although these types seem to be quite consistently identifiable by managers (see Footnote 23), they can change as corporate cultures change. For example, Jack Welch is engineering major changes in GE's various business units.[25]

Strategic Intent. Continuing to look at generic indicators of competitive intent and thus the expected rivalry from individual competitors, we come to the concept of Strategic Intent. In an award winning article,[26] Hamel and Prahalad propose that looking at what a competitor is currently doing is like looking at a snapshot. History and the future are both not in the picture. Hamel and Prahalad recommend an analysis of the strategic intent of a competitor (and they recommend building strategies around Strategic Intent). We shall extend this idea shortly in our discussion of the classical Strength-Weakness Opportunity-Threat (SWOT) analysis. As they put it,

> Think back. In 1970, few Japanese companies possessed the resource base, manufacturing volume, or technical prowess of U.S. and European industry leaders. Komatsu was less than 35 percent as large as Caterpillar (measured by sales), was scarcely respected outside Japan, and relied on just one product line—small bulldozers—for most of its revenue. Honda was smaller than American Motors and had not yet begun to export cars to the United States. Canon's first halting steps in the reprographic business looked pitifully small compared with the $4 billion Xerox powerhouse.
>
> If Western managers had extended their competitor analysis to include these companies, it would merely have underlined how dramatic the resource discrepancies between them were. Yet by 1985, Komatsu was a $2.8 billion company with a product scope encompassing a broad range of earth-moving equipment, industrial robots and semicon-

---

[23]Snow, C. C. and L. G. Hrebiniak, "Strategy, Competence and Organizational Performance, *Administrative Science Quarterly,* 25, 1980, pp. 317–335.

[24]This result is also in keeping with a finding from the PIMS start-up database that only 50% of the brands were reported to have reacted to new product entry in their markets. See Robinson, W. T., "Marketing Mix Reactions by Incumbents to Entry," *Marketing Science,* 7, Fall, 1988, pp. 368–385.

[25]For example, see Stewart, T. A., "GE: Keep Those Ideas Coming," *Fortune,* August 12, 1991, pp. 41–49.

[26]Hamel, G. and C. K. Prahalad, "Strategic Intent," *Harvard Business Review,* May–June, 1991, pp. 63–76.

ductors.   Honda manufactured almost as many cars worldwide in 1987 as Chrysler.
Canon had matched Xerox's global unit market share.

The lesson is clear: assessing the current tactical advantages of known competitors
will not help you understand the resolution, stamina and inventiveness of potential competitors (p. 64).

Exhibit 7–9 briefly summarizes the key elements of what constitutes Strategic Intent
and its implementation.   By monitoring the activities of a competitor, if the steps out-
lined in Exhibit 7–9 are observed, then analysis of these actions provides the Strategic
Intent that underlies them.   For example:

Komatsu set out to 'Encircle Caterpillar.' Canon sought to 'Beat Xerox.' For Coca-
Cola, strategic intent has been to put Coke within 'arm's reach' of every consumer in the
world (Hamel and Prahalad, p. 64).

The strategic intent of Komatsu and Canon was deducible from public speeches,
company slogans, advertising and internal directives, and observable intelligence
actions.   Although much of this information may be sensitive and private, rather than
publicly available, astute managers can obtain valuable information from a variety of
sources.[27]   For example, Dr. Koji Kobayashi, in October 1977 (when he was the
Chairman of NEC), introduced the so-called C&C (Computers and Communication)

EXHIBIT 7–9   Strategic Intent (SI)

WHAT IS SI?
- Strategic intent captures the essence of winning.
- Strategic intent is stable over time.
- SI sets a target that deserves personal effort and commitment.

HOW TO IMPLEMENT SI
- Create a sense of urgency.
- Develop a competitor focus at every level through widespread use of competitive intel-
  ligence.
- Provide employees with the training they need to work effectively.
- Give the organization time to digest one challenge before launching another.
- Establish clear guidelines and review mechanisms.

Adapted from Hamel, G. and C. K. Prahalad, "Strategic Intent," *Harvard Business
Review,* May–June, 1989, pp. 63–76.

[27]See Sutton, H., "Keeping Tabs on the Competition," *Marketing Communications,* January, 1989,
pp. 42–45. Sutton reports on a study of 315 companies conducted for The Conference Board, New York.
"AT&T has created a sophisticated electronic intelligence network to track its competition.   More than
two years in the making, it provides information on 1,400 products, 580 companies and 180 different
industries.

- Motorola hired a former CIA agent to organize and beef up its competitive intelligence operations.
- Kraft has developed a worldwide network of about 40 managers who sift through business journals,
  newspapers and magazines and prepare quick reading summaries for key corporate executives on what
  the competition is doing."

From this 1989 report, it appears that intelligence gathering is more the rule than the exception.

EXHIBIT 7–10

There's so much to be gained by removing the communication barrier.

A world where no communication barriers exist, and where technology works to bring people closer. NEC is making it happen through constant development of our C&C concept — the merging of computers and communications to help remove forever the barriers of language, time and distance. And make the world a closer, more productive place. For global and local solutions that make a difference, rely on NEC.

One world through C&C.

C&C Computers and Communications

NEC

Courtesy NEC Corporation.

concept at the INTELCOM 77 international conference in Atlanta, Georgia. This concept continues to drive NEC today.[28] The NEC ad (Exhibit 7–10) is a reminder of this theme. In Exhibit 7–11 we reproduce a chart developed by Rothschild[29] that provides a generic listing of sources of information on competitors. Besides this list, many books are available on competitor intelligence. These sources are important in bringing in information. Such information is virtually useless, however, without an appropriate framework (or machinery) with which to process it and draw conclusions. A useful framework was presented by Day and Wensley in 1988.[30] It captures the dynamic nature of the elements of competitive advantage (Exhibit 7–12).

Competitive Advantage Framework The Day and Wensley framework stresses sustainability of advantage through renewed investment. The ability to do so rests on superior performance. Superior performance is obtained through positional advantages of superior customer value and lower relative costs. In other words, a superior position relative to competitive offerings leads to superior performance. Such a superior positioning is a derived from superior skills and resources.

EXHIBIT 7–11   The Identification of Strategic Opportunities

	Public	Trade professionals	Government	Investors
What competitors say about themselves	• Advertising • Promotional materials • Press releases • Speeches • Books • Articles • Personnel changes • Want ads	• Manuals • Technical papers • Licenses • Patents • Courses • Seminars	• SEC reports • FTC • Testimony • Lawsuits • Antitrust	• Annual meetings • Annual reports • Prospectuses • Stock/bond issues
What others say about them	• Books • Articles • Case studies • Consultants • Newspaper reporters • Environmental groups • Consumer groups • Unions • "Who's Who" • Recruiting firms	• Suppliers/vendors • Trade press • Industry study • Customers • Subcontractors	• Lawsuits • Antitrust • State/federal agencies • National plans • Government programs	• Security analyst reports • Industry studies • Credit reports

Reprinted by permission of publisher, from *Management Review,* July, 1979 © 1979. American Management Association, New York. All rights reserved.

[28]Reported in Uenohara, M., "Strategic Management of Innovation in the Global Scale—The Experience of NEC," *Management Japan,* Vol. 24, No. 1 Spring, 1991, pp. 3–7.

[29]Rothschild, W. E., "Competitor Analysis: The Missing Link in Strategy," *Management Review,* July, 1979, pp. 22–28, 37, 38.

[30]Day, G. S. and R. Wensley, "Assessing Advantage: A Framework for Diagnosing Competitive Superiority," *Journal of Marketing,* April, 1988, pp. 1–20.

EXHIBIT 7–12   The Elements of Competitive Advantage

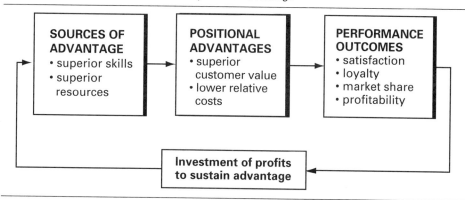

From Day, G. S. and R. Wensley, "Assessing Advantage: A Framework for Diagnosing Competitive Superiority," *Journal of Marketing,* April, 1988, p. 3. Reprinted by permission of the American Marketing Association.

This is a sound perspective. From the perspective of strategic superiority (and not just competitive superiority), as we discussed in Chapter 1, and in keeping with Hamel and Prahalad's comments, we need to consider specifically relationships that are being established, the trajectory of a competitor's offerings, and the trajectory of resource allocations. Together, these three elements provide a picture not only of the strategic intent of a competitor, but also of its realizable strategic intent. The fourth element we referred to as part of the strategic choice set, timing, is different from the other three elements. It does capture the nature of the competitor and includes the speed with which a competitor may react to threats or exploit or create new opportunities.

These four elements of the marketing strategy choice set result from an interplay between the skills and resources that have been assembled by a competitor. However, identical sets of skills and resources do not lead to identical strategy choice sets. This may be because creative thinking is idiosyncratic and differs widely even among those with otherwise similar skills.[31] This combined with chance and the critical human dimension involved in the interplay between resources and skills makes strategic choices idiosyncratic. It is not enough to monitor just the skills and resources accumulated by competitors, it is also necessary to monitor the trajectory of the interplay of the resources and skills assembled by them. Further, since these resources and skills include the relationships necessary to serve customer needs and the survival of a competitor, they need to be considered as part of the interlink of organizations to do so. An assessment (or inventory) of the existing skills and resources of a competitor in the context of the entire system of businesses that form the link from raw material subcomponents to the satisfaction of customer needs can be made using a value chain or a business system framework. This framework is attributed to McKinsey and Co.

[31]Even if the level (volume or importance) of creative activity is the same, the outcomes could be very different. Think about it!

but has been developed into a management tool because of the efforts of Michael Porter.[32]

  The Value Chain Framework.   Developing the value chain for a competitor forces an integrated or systems view of the process by which the competitor serves the end buyers and consumers. It also provides a comprehensive view of how the competitor fits into the overall system through which materials or concepts are transformed (production, value addition) and transferred (value and title transferring) through a sequence of chains.[33]   These chains are: the value of chains of suppliers, the competitor itself, its channel and perhaps the buyer's consumption chain (e.g., gift giving involves a consumption chain from buyer to gift-giver to gift-receiver to perhaps gift-user as in the case of a promotional cap given to a client's staff person who in turn gives it to his daughter, or an industrial buying situation, in which a buying center is often involved and where the buyer and the user could be quite different persons or even organizational entities as in the case of U.S.A.I.D.'s buying processed food for providing aid to needy countries).   A generic value chain is shown in Exhibit 7–13.

EXHIBIT 7–13   The Value System[32]

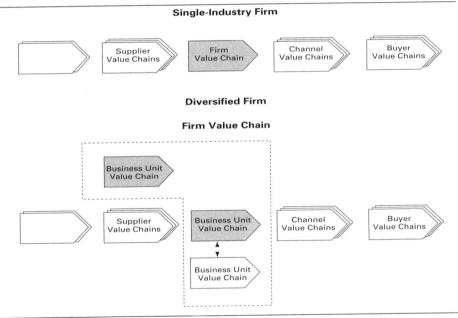

Reprinted with the permission of the Free Press, a Division of Simon & Schuster from *Competitive Advantage: Creating and Sustaining Superior Performance* by Michael E. Porter. Copyright © 1985 by Michael E. Porter.

[32]Porter, M. E., *Competitive Advantage: Creating and Sustaining Superior Performance,* New York, The Free Press, 1985.
[33]Transformation is used as a general term. It includes a manufacturing operation or integration (for example, Johnson & Johnson's assembling the necessities for a surgical procedure and marketing this packaged unit), or packing a travel package by a travel agency or conversion of insurance policy availability and pricing (premium) data into a tailor-made insurance policy, and so forth.

To discern an overall view of a competitor, as shown in Exhibit 7–13, is time consuming. On the other hand, if done, it quickly presents a detailed account of the relationships and offerings that it has assembled. The existing momentum in relationships and offerings may be most readily exploited by providing more of the existing offerings to more of the members with whom current relationships exist (e.g., a firm manufacturing hot chocolate mix for institutional use and candy for the retail trade may perhaps offer candy to its institutional links and hot chocolate mix to its retail trade links.). Certainly new relationships and offerings may be developed. But as a first approximation, expansion of activities might begin with either existing relationships or existing offerings. Competitive advantages may also be arrived at by replacing certain elements of the volume chain, for example, using telemarketing instead of a retail channel (in which case telemarketing organizations and mail processing and delivery organizations replace the traditional retail trade channel members) or performing these activities alone (vertical integration). An example from Australia is the joint ownership by Ansett and Australian Airlines of Queensland Resort Islands to provide an integrated vacation package.[34] In the United States, a similar attempt by United Airlines through acquisition and by converting itself to a new corporation called Allegis, was terminated by its shareholders and employees.

Synergies and Multipoint Competition. The value chain allows an understanding of the competitor's cost structure. The transfer margins across various interfaces are often known in an industry. Knowing the value chain of a competitor allows an assessment of whether any synergies might be present across its various activities, and thus allows an adjustment of its cost structure accordingly. (We discuss cost analysis in more detail later.) In the same way, a value chain allows a quick determination of whether there is or a potential for multipoint competition. The following quote from Hamel and Prahalad is appropriate.

> Contrary to tried-and-true MNC policy, a subsidiary should not always be required to stand on its own two feet financially. When a company faces a large competitor in a key foreign market, it may make sense for it to funnel global resources into the local market share battle, especially when the competitor lacks the international reach to strike back.
>
> Money does not always move across borders, though this may happen. For a number of reasons (taxation, foreign exchange risk, regulation) the subsidiary may choose to raise funds locally. Looking to the worldwide strength of the parent, local financial institutions may be willing to provide long term financing in amounts and at rates that would not be justified on the basis of the subsidiary's short-term prospects.
>
> Such cross-subsidization is not dumping. When a company cross-subsidizes it does not sell at less than the domestic market price. Rather than risk trade sanctions, the intelligent global company will squeeze its competitors' margins just enough to dry up its development spending and force corporate officers to reassess their commitment to the business.
>
> With deteriorating margins and no way of retaliating internationally, the company will have little choice but to sell market share. If your competitor uses simple portfolio management techniques you may even be able to predict how much market share you may have to buy to turn the business into a "dog" and precipitate a sell-off. In one such case a beleaguered

---

[34]Cited in Brown, L., "Competitive Marketing Strategy," Melbourne, Australia, Thomas Nelson Australia, 1990, p. 258.

business unit manager, facing an aggressive global competitor, lobbied hard for international retaliation. The corporate response: "If you can't make money at home, there's no way we're going to let you go international!" Eventually, the business was sold.[35]

The Value Wheel. Among organizations which have a marketing orientation and are driven by the market, a value wheel represents the process of transformation and transference (Exhibit 7–14). The resources allocated to each of the elements of this wheel provide an indication of the speed of reaction and creation and fit to market needs that this competitor may use as a competitive leverage point. As a tool for self-analysis, it brings a market-focused and market-driven viewpoint to management activities.[36]

Analyzing Competitor Costs

The discussion in the last several sections focused on the bases of rivalry in a product-market and on understanding the competitive intent of individual firms in a product-market. The economic consequences of a firm's competitiveness, is, in part, related to its costs (or expected costs)—which may be related to its strategic choices of relationships, offerings, resource allocation, and timing. An understanding of a competitor's costs is essential. We next describe and discuss two traditional perspectives-frameworks of the strategic management accounting systems and also a more contemporary approach, Activity Based Costing.

EXHIBIT 7–14   Value Wheel

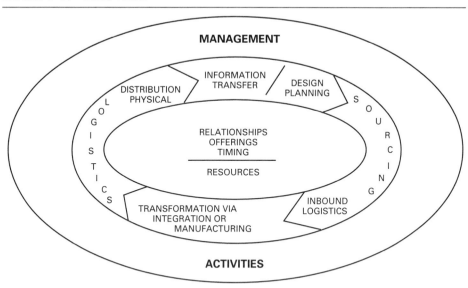

[35]Hamel, G. and Prahalad, C. K., "Do You Really Have A Global Strategy," *Harvard Business Review,* July–August, 1985, pp. 139–148.\

[36]A useful process for value mapping (either chain or wheel) is perhaps the old Process Mapping technique. This technique has been reintroduced at GE. Used on a production line at its Evendale, Ohio plant, it is reported (T. A. Stewart, *op. cit.,* 1991) to have resulted in a 50% time saving in 1991, a $4 million inventory savings and at increasing more than threefold the inventory turns.

Strategic Use of the Management Accounting System

In many firms, the management accounting system has developed in response to a number of conflicting pressures. In particular, the early development of management accounting systems was an attempt to attribute costs and revenues to individual products as a guide to pricing policy in a market downturn and overall financial pressure.[37]

The development of manual systems, however, meant that early and virtually irreversible decisions had to be made in both the unit-of-analysis to which costs would be attributed (most often the product) as well as the basis on which costs themselves would be allocated. Much debate took place regarding the problems and ambiguities of such an approach, particularly in cost allocation, but it was often argued that the inevitable requirement would be for one single, if imperfect, method.

Recently, the widespread use of initial computer entry of base data and the possibility of multiple forms of analysis have raised the possibility of more flexible management accounting systems able to overcome the traditional single unit-of-analysis, single method of allocation approach. However, it should be recognized that for many organizations developing such a system from the beginning is still costly and it may often remain cost effective to rely on ad hoc adjustments, even if only approximate, to the existing accounting data.

From a strategic marketing perspective, there have been two forms of development proposed. First, a so-called modularized contribution approach to existing cost and revenue data; second, an integration of comparative competitor data to provide a more strategically relevant measure of performance. We mention a third approach, that of activity-based costing which adds to the strategic understanding of a competitors' (as well as for a self-analysis) points of leverage.

The Modularized Contribution Approach

Dunne and Wolk[38] proposed a "modularized contribution approach" with particular reference to marketing cost analysis. The basic approach is one which attempts to distinguish between the fixed and variable elements of cost at different levels: in particular in their case, product and segment. Their approach also involves the allocation of revenues to the various cost groupings so that relative margins and contribution levels can be established. They argue that such data can then be used for a more focused analysis of both problems and opportunities.

In the actual example they use, the analysis is segregated by product, then by sales territory and, finally, by channel and order size. Their example of the results of such an analysis is shown in Exhibit 7–15. Of course, in their approach, they recognize that the new accounting system will involve additional costs, but they claim:

> While the benefits of segmental statements must exceed the costs of preparation, the power of a computer should lessen costs enough to make segmental analysis beneficial to an increasing number of companies.

[37]Hopwood, A., M. Page, and S. Turley (eds.), *Understanding Accounting In a Changing Environment,* Herfordshire, United Kingdom, Prentice-Hall, International (UK), 1990. Provides an analysis of changes in accountancy. In particular, it provides another example of the use of scenarios in understanding context changes for an entire service industry.

[38]Dunne, P. M. and H. I. Wolk, "Marketing Cost Analysis: A Modularized Contribution Approach," *Journal of Marketing,* July, 1977, pp. 83–94.

EXHIBIT 7-15 Marketing Cost Analysis: A Modularized Contribution Approach

Segmental Contribution Income Statements: D-W Appliance Company

FIGURE 5.5 BUDGETED INCOME STATEMENT CORPORATE LEVEL, 1977

Revenues	$2,984,000
Variable Costs, Total	2,205,695
Contribution Margin	778,305 (26.1%)
Fixed Costs, Total	787,000
Net Loss	($8,695) (0.3%)

Percentages shown are based on revenues

FIGURE 5.6 BLENDERS (BOTH TERRITORIES)
Contribution Margin $392,705
Segment Income $157,705

FIGURE 5.13 MIXERS (BOTH TERRITORIES)
Contribution Margin $385,600
Segment Income $263,600

FIGURE 5.7 BLENDERS — EAST TERRITORY
Contribution Margin $224,256
Segment Income $104,256

FIGURE 5.10 BLENDERS — WEST TERRITORY
Contribution Margin $168,449
Segment Income $53,449

FIGURE 5.14 MIXERS — EAST TERRITORY
Contribution Margin $183,900
Segment Income $133,011

FIGURE 5.17 MIXERS — WEST TERRITORY
Contribution Margin $201,700
Segment Income $130,589

FIGURE 5.8 WHOLESALER CHANNEL
Contribution Margin $150,728
Segment Income $76,148

FIGURE 5.9 LARGE RETAILER CHANNEL
Contribution Margin $73,528
Segment Income $28,198

FIGURE 5.11 WHOLESALER CHANNEL
Contribution Margin $63,838
Segment Income $14,751

FIGURE 5.12 LARGE RETAILER CHANNEL
Contribution Margin $104,611
Segment Income $38,698

FIGURE 5.15 WHOLESALER CHANNEL
Contribution Margin $120,000
Segment Income $87,000

FIGURE 5.16 LARGE RETAILER CHANNEL
Contribution Margin $63,900
Segment Income $46,011

FIGURE 5.18 WHOLESALER CHANNEL
Contribution Margin $64,300
Segment Income $34,689

FIGURE 5.19 LARGE RETAILER CHANNEL
Contribution Margin $137,400
Segment Income $95,900

FIGURE 5.8A SMALL ORDERS: WHOLESALERS
Contribution Margin $75,761
Segment Income $37,534

FIGURE 5.8B LARGE ORDERS: WHOLESALERS
Contribution Margin $74,967
Segment Income $38,614

FIGURE 5.9A SMALL ORDERS: LARGE RETAILERS
Contribution Margin $34,048
Segment Income $12,565

FIGURE 5.9B LARGE ORDERS: LARGE RETAILERS
Contribution Margin $39,480
Segment Income $15,633

FIGURE 5.11A SMALL ORDERS: WHOLESALERS
Contribution Margin $29,386
Segment Income $5,867

FIGURE 5.11B LARGE ORDERS: WHOLESALERS
Contribution Margin $34,452
Segment Income $8,884

FIGURE 5.12A SMALL ORDERS: LARGE RETAILERS
Contribution Margin $52,195
Segment Income $18,318

FIGURE 5.12B LARGE ORDERS: LARGE RETAILERS
Contribution Margin $52,416
Segment Income $20,380

FIGURE 5.15A SMALL ORDERS: WHOLESALERS
Contribution Margin $64,000
Segment Income $45,666

FIGURE 5.15B LARGE ORDERS: WHOLESALERS
Contribution Margin $56,000
Segment Income $41,334

FIGURE 5.16A SMALL ORDERS: LARGE RETAILERS
Contribution Margin $17,700
Segment Income $12,333

FIGURE 5.16B LARGE ORDERS: LARGE RETAILERS
Contribution Margin $46,200
Segment Income $33,678

FIGURE 5.18A SMALL ORDERS: WHOLESALERS
Contribution Margin $31,500
Segment Income $15,824

FIGURE 5.18B LARGE ORDERS: WHOLESALERS
Contribution Margin $32,800
Segment Income $18,865

FIGURE 5.19A SMALL ORDERS: LARGE RETAILERS
Contribution Margin $67,200
Segment Income $45,682

FIGURE 5.19B LARGE ORDERS: LARGE RETAILERS
Contribution Margin $70,200
Segment Income $50,218

From Dunne, P. M. and H. I. Wolk, "Marketing Cost Analysis: A Modularized Contribution Approach," *Journal of Marketing*, July, 1977. Reprinted by permission of the American Marketing Association.

In fact, the general approach they recommend is capable of further extension. The notion of "fixed" costs merely reflects that certain costs are "lumpy" in terms of scale or time; in particular, we tend to treat those costs which are lumpy in both scale and time as "investments." In principle, therefore, we can take a cost item and identify it in the structural component to which it refers as well as in its longevity in either scale or time. We can then build up a cost (and related revenue) analysis in various ways depending on the structural relationships that are assumed.

For example, the Dunne and Wolk approach presumes a certain structural relationship: product-territories-channel-order size, but we could consider a very different structure which, for instance:

1. Looked more closely at the fixed (investment and overhead) costs of maintaining a presence in certain territories and channels;
2. Considered long-term "profitability" of individual key customers;
3. Tested the interactions between plant location and logistical choices (certain costs will be site- or distribution-system specific) against various production and demand mixes.

Strategic Management Accounting

Simmonds[39] has proposed that the activity fundamental to management accounting of monitoring performance should be extended so that the ratios and indices used are derived on a relative rather than an absolute basis. He proposes that competitors' costs should be estimated so that the business unit performance data can be presented in a way that allows direct competitor comparisons. He also suggests that more market-based measures of competitive performance, such as market share, be integrated into the management accounting data.

Accounting for Strategic Management

Hiromoto,[40] of the leading Hitotsubashi University in Tokyo, provides thrilling (or chilling, depending on your viewpoint!) examples of how accounting measures are

---

[39]Simmonds, K., "Strategic Management Accounting," *Management Accounting,* Vol. 58, April, 1981, pp. 26–29.

[40]Hiromoto, T., "Another Hidden Edge—Japanese Management Accounting," *Harvard Business Review,* July–August, 1988, pp. 22–26.
A numerical example that is particularly insightful is:

Consider a factory building several different products. The products all use one or both of two parts, A and B, which the factory buys in roughly equal amounts. Most of the products use both parts. The unit cost of Part A is $7, of Part B, $10. Part B has more capabilities than Part A; in fact, B can replace A. If the factory doubles its purchases of Part B, it qualifies for a discounted $8 unit price. For products that incorporate both parts, substituting B for A makes sense to qualify for the discount. (The total parts cost is $17 using A and B, $16 using B only). Part B, in other words, should become a standard part for the factory. But departments building products that use only Part A may be reluctant to accept the substitute Part B because even discounted, the cost of B exceeds A.

This factory needs an accounting system that motivates departments to look beyond their parochial interests for the sake of enterprise-level cost reduction.

derived from strategic objectives and not vice versa. In the fashion of reverse engineering, strategic objectives may be inferred from these accounting measures. Let us consider the following examples described by Hiromoto:

- For the world's largest factory devoted to the manufacturing of videocassette records (VCRs), Hitachi still uses direct labor to allocate manufacturing overhead. This is an already highly automated plant! The natural question is why? Management had decided that even more automation would provide long-term competitive strength and so adopted this allocation measure. So the allocation measure used was from the strategic objectives of this division of Hitachi.

- In another factory producing refrigeration and air conditioning equipment, Hitachi allocates overhead based on the number of parts used in a product. It also adds a surcharge to products that use nonstandard parts. Of course, the objective is to reduce the number of parts, especially parts unique to a product. Significant cost savings[41] are reported by reducing the number of parts used in a factory. (Another example of synergy built-in, in this case, by designers.)

EXHIBIT 7–16   Activity-Based Cost System

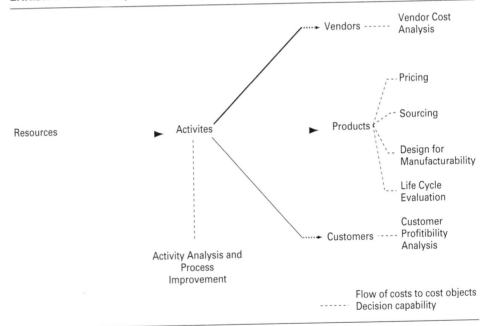

From Cooper, R. and R. S. Kaplan, "Measure Costs Right: Make the Right Decisions," *Harvard Business Review*, September–October, 1985, pp. 102–103. (© 1985 by the President and Fellows of Harvard College; All Rights Reserved.)

[41]Hitachi has adopted such an approach by adding overhead surcharges to products that use nonstandard parts. The more custom parts in a product, the higher the overhead charge.

- Production, marketing and sales departments are treated as separate profit centers in a U.S. subsidiary of a Japanese electronics firm. The transfer price between production and marketing and the sales commission are both negotiated. Thus, the marketing department makes product decisions without being constrained by a fixed sales commission. This motivated the sales department to increase its operating efficiency. The whole system is thus more readily able to be proactive to market needs.

The above examples are best summarized by Hiromoto's own words: "In general, Japanese management accounting does not stress optimizing within existing constraints. Rather, it encourages employees to make continual improvements by tightening these constraints."[42]

These ideas, as presented by Hiromoto, of choosing the right allocation measures, should be carried out after deciding which products should be offered and how. The latter requires the ability to "measure costs right," the former requires that "the right costs be allocated."

Activity Based Costing (ABC)

To measure costs correctly in the United States, the Activity Based Costing (ABC)[43] system has been developed. As stated by Cooper and Kaplan,[44] the basic idea behind it is:

> Virtually all of a company's activities exist to support the production and delivery of today's goods and services. They should therefore all be considered product costs. And since nearly all factory and corporate support costs are divisible or separable, they can be split apart and traced to individual products or product families.

Exhibit 7–16 provides a graphic representation of this idea.

Consider the example provided by Cooper and Kaplan of a building supply company that uses six distribution channels. Its profits from each of these channels using a standard cost allocation system ("old system") and using ABC are shown in Exhibit 7–17. The average gross margin for all six channels is 34%. Marketing costs averaged 16.4% of sales and general and administrative expenses averaged 8.5%. The company, seeking to improve its profitability, targeted SG&A expenses. These expenses were previously assigned as (the company average) 25% of sales to each channel of distribution. The OEM channel, under the old system, produced 27% gross margin and a 2% operating merger—making it a prime target of concern. But imagine assigning 25% of sales as SG&A expense to business from a channel on which almost no advertising, promotion, warranty, and so forth, resources were

---

[42]This concept of constraint tightening is similar to the idea of assumption surfacing and management that we talked about in Chapter 1, and which we shall discuss again.

[43]For a simple short introduction to ABC and for an important application area see Menzo, R. J., "Activity-Based Costing for Information Systems," *Cost Management,* Spring, 1991, pp. 35–39. Other relevant sources are: Cooper, R. and R. S. Kaplan, "Measure Costs Right: Make the Right Decisions," *Harvard Business Review,* September–October, 1988, pp. 96–103; and Kaplan, R. S. and H. T. Johnson, *Relevance Lost: The Rise and Fall of Management Accounting,* Boston, Harvard Business School, 1987.

[44]Cooper, R. and R. S. Kaplan, *op. cit.,* 1988, pp. 96–97.

EXHIBIT 7–17   Measuring Costs

OEM Changes from a Laggard . . .
Profits by Commercial Distribution Channel (Old System)

	Contract	Industrial Suppliers	Government	OEM	Total Commercial
Annual Sales *(in thousands of dollars)*	$79,434	$25,110	$ 422	$ 9,200	$114,166
Gross Margin	34%	41%	23%	27%	35%
Gross Profit	$27,375	$10,284	$ 136	$ 2,461	$ 40,256
SG&A Allowance* *(in thousands of dollars)*	$19,746	$ 6,242	$ 105	$ 2,287	$ 31,814
Operating Profit *(in thousands of dollars)*	$ 7,629	$ 4,042	$ 31	$ 174	$ 11,876
Operating Margin	10%	16%	7%	2%	10%
Invested Capital Allowance† *(in thousands of dollars)*	$33,609	$10,624	$ 179	$ 3,893	$ 48,305
Return on Investment	23%	38%	17%	4%	25%

*SG&A allowance for each channel is 25% of that channel's revenues.
†Invested capital allowance for each channel is 42% of that channel's revenues.

. . . to a Solid Performer
Profits by Commercial Distribution Channel (New System)

	Contract	Industrial Suppliers	Government	OEM	Total Commercial
Gross Profit *(from previous table)*	$27,375	$10,284	$136	$2,461	$40,256
Selling Expenses* *(in thousands of dollars)*					
Commission	$ 4,682	$ 1,344	$ 12	$ 372	$ 6,410
Advertising	132	38	0	2	172
Catalog	504	160	0	0	664
Co-op Advertising	416	120	0	0	536
Sales Promotion	394	114	0	2	510
Warranty	64	22	0	4	90
Sales Administration	5,696	1,714	20	351	7,781
Cash Discount	892	252	12	114	1,270
Total	$12,780	$ 3,764	$ 44	$ 845	$17,433
C&A *(in thousands of dollars)*	$ 6,740	$ 2,131	$ 36	$ 781	$ 9,688
Operating Profit *(in thousands of dollars)*	$ 7,855	$ 4,389	$ 56	$ 835	$13,135
Operating Margin	10%	17%	13%	9%	12%
Invested Capital*	$33,154	$10,974	$184	$2,748	$47,060
Return on Investment	24%	40%	30%	30%	28%

*Selling expenses and invested capital estimated under an activity-based system.

From Cooper, R. and R. S. Kaplan, "Measure Costs Right: Make the Right Decisions," *Harvard Business Review,* September–October, 1985, pp. 102–103. (© 1985 by the President and Fellows of Harvard College; All Rights Reserved.)

expended! When the analysis was done using ABC, as shown in Exhibit 7–17, it shows an OEM segment operating margin of 9%, not 2%!

An ABC analysis of a competitor, albeit using second-hand information, is likely to show possible threats from certain product lines, which might become more attractive, or an opportunity if it might be a product that is "actually" less beneficial to the competitor than under the old system. The latter is, of course, true if the competitor uses ABC. The former is a threat if the competitor were to adopt ABC. The value of ABC, like most management tools, is often much more in the *process* it forces management to engage in than it is in the document(s) it produces.

Any such analysis can be onerous. Thus it must be carried with a sense of priority. Cooper and Kaplan[45] suggest three rules that should provide such priority.

1. Focus on expensive resources.

2. Emphasize resources whose consumption varies significantly by product and product type; look for diversity.

3. Focus on resources whose demand patterns are uncorrelated with traditional allocation measures like direct labor, processing time, and materials.

These same rules for ABC provide the basis for a strategic cost analysis of competitors.

In assigning particular values to a competitor, special care must be taken to account for any special synergies that might be unique to the competitor. For example, in a study of the relative advertising efficiency of new brands versus brand extensions, Daniel Smith found that, on average, the advertising to sales ratio for newly launched brand extensions is 10% compared to 19.3% for completely new brands.[46] This is the type of synergistic impact on cost that we are discussing. Less well investigated perhaps, but clearly obvious, is the possibility of synergy through the sharing of distribution channels. This list can be expanded, but priorities must be set (perhaps using Cooper and Kaplan's three rules), and then implemented.

ABC performed in a modular fashion (Dunne and Wolk, Footnote 38), and then implemented using Hiromoto's "hidden edge" approach can be powerful. A competitor's business needs to be analyzed this way for a true picture of potential competitive activity.[47]

The SWOT Framework

Several individual frameworks have been described. A candidate for an integrative framework within which these can be brought together is the Strengths-Weaknesses-Opportunities-Threats (SWOT) framework.[48]

[45]Cooper, R. and R. S. Kaplan, *op. cit,* 1988, p. 98.

[46]Smith, D. C., "Brand Extensions and Advertising Efficiency: What Can and Cannot Be Expected," Working Paper, February, University of Wisconsin, Madison, 1992.

[47]This requires that the appropriate competitiveness intelligence be collected and suitable assumptions be made to understand competitors at this level of detail.

[48]Learned, E. P., C. R. Christenson, K. R. Andrews, and W. D. Guth, *Business Policy: Text and Cases,* Homewood, IL, Richard D. Irwin, 1965, p. 21. See also Ansoff, H. I., *Corporate Strategy,* New York, McGraw Hill, 1956, p. 92; and Golde, R. A., "Practical Planning for Small Businesses," *Harvard Business Review,* September–October 1964, p. 147.

Two fundamental premises lie behind the SWOT framework. The first, "know thyself" is essential for effective planning and strategy development. This entails a thorough appraisal of a business unit's (or a firm's, or a product line's) inherent skills and resources. The second is the notion that success follows from finding the right environmental opportunities to exploit and the threats to avoid or thwart. This equates with "fit into the right niche."

To carry out a SWOT analysis requires an internal appraisal, scanning of the external environment, and then combining the two. In Exhibit 7–18 we reproduce a flow chart from Stevenson[49] for carrying out a SWOT analysis.

A key issue often overlooked in any Strengths-Weaknesses analysis is the definition of the factors to be assessed. It is also possible to conduct an unstructured analysis of different types and relationships without any explicit consideration of either the criteria or the interactions.

We can broadly define the usual forms of analysis of strengths and weaknesses for the individual firm as either "free-form" or "checklist driven." In the former, we need to consider the process whereby different "free-form" answers from different sources can be compared; in the latter, we start by considering a suitable checklist.

A Useful Checklist

Exhibit 7–19 is a checklist derived from the work on strengths and weaknesses analysis done by Stevenson. It is particularly useful because it is derived from managerial responses in the companies that he has surveyed. Even so, we must be wary, as Stevenson himself cautions: "The individual attributes listed are neither mutually exclusive nor collectively exhaustive in partitioning each of the general categories."

The list also focuses clearly on what might be termed "functional" strengths and weaknesses. This has significant implications for the interpretation of the results as will be discussed shortly.

The Free-Form Process

To use an effective free-form process we need to have a way of characterizing responses which allows for comparison and contrast. However, any such development also raises valuable questions about the analysis itself such as how far the dimensions chosen are really independent, and how far they effectively discriminate between different entities (i.e., either different divisions or units within the same firm or between the firm and its competitors).

In general, it is likely that this free-form approach focuses the analysis on critical issues rather than on the functional elements in a standard checklist approach. Between these two groups are the basic resources and capabilities of the firm itself. The free-form approach has the advantage in that the issues under discussion are

[49]Stevenson, H. H. , "Defining Corporate Strengths and Weaknesses," *Sloan Management Review* Spring, Vol, 17, No. 3, 1976, pp. 51–68.

EXHIBIT 7–18   A Process Model of Strategy Formulation

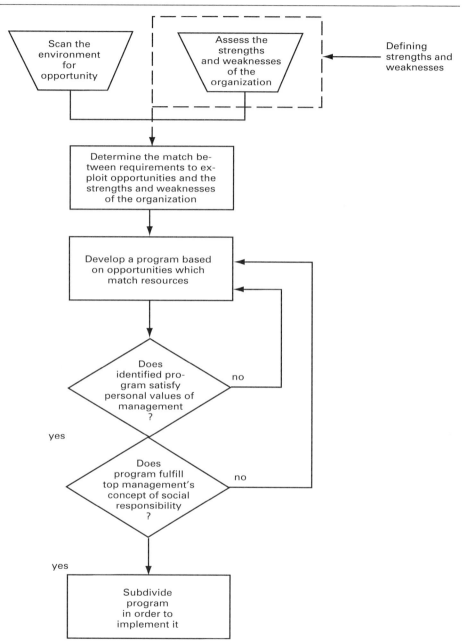

From Stevenson, H. H., "Defining Corporate Strengths and Weaknesses," *Sloan Management Review,* Spring, Vol, 17, No. 3, 1976. Reprinted with permission by the Sloan Management Review Association.

EXHIBIT 7–19   Defining Corporate Strengths and Weaknesses

Which attributes can be examined?	What organizational entity is the manager concerned with?	What types of measurements can the manager make?	What criteria are applicable to judge a strength or a weakness?	How can the manager get the information to make these assessments?
Organizational structure	The corporation	Measure the existence of an attribute	Historical experience of the company	Personal observation Customer contacts
Major policies				Experience
Top manager's skills Top manager's experience	Groups Divisions	Measure an attribute's efficiency	Intracompany competition	Control system documents Meetings
Information system Operation procedures	Departments	Measure an attribute's effectiveness	Direct competitors	Planning system documents
Planning system			Other companies	Employees
Employee attitudes	Individual employees			Subordinate managers
Manager's attitudes Union agreements			Consultants' opinions	Superordinate managers
Technical skills Research skills New product ideas Production facilities			Normative judgments based on management's understanding of literature	Peers Published documents Competitive intelligence
Demographic characteristics of personnel			Personal opinions	Board members Consultants
Distribution network				Journals
Sales force's skill Breadth of product line Quality control procedures Stock market reputation			Specific targets of accomplishment such as budgets, etc.	Books Magazines Professional meetings Government economic indicators
Knowledge of customer's needs Market domination				

Adapted from Stevenson, H. H., "Defining Corporate Strengths and Weaknesses," *Sloan Management Review,* Spring, Vol. 17, No. 3, 1976. Reprinted with permission by the Sloan Management Review Association.

likely to be of high salience to the participants; the potential disadvantage is the loss of a long-term perspective.

Strengths and Weaknesses of Analysis in Practice

Whether a "checklist" or "free-form" approach is adopted, the inevitable issue arises as to how different evaluations by different respondents are to be handled.

The first question to be considered is the validity of any "claims" made by respondents in a Strengths-Weaknesses analysis.   To discuss this issue of validation further, we need to distinguish among element claims, system claims, and expertise.

Element claims refer to any suggestion of specific strengths and weaknesses. We expect that any specific claim would be justified with some empirical evidence. For those who have been previously involved in such studies, even this limited validity criterion may have been ignored, but most would find it difficult to take the outcome of such an analysis seriously.

More difficult to assess are system claims, in which statements are made about the net effects of the interaction among a number of factors at the system or subsystem level. At this level the validation problem is much more complex, particularly if it involves the relative weighting of various composite factors.

The solution in the latter case is often to rely on the expertise of either the individual provider or else subject any claim to challenge from key individuals and their collective expertise. The problem with such an approach, however practical, is that it raises the question of the actual expertise for the specific task as well as, in many cases, the criterion of consensual validity. There is considerable similarity between such questions in this context and the problem inherent in the Delphi forecasting method that was discussed in Chapter 3. We need to recognize that expertise itself may not be hierarchically related and that surprise may be a more important criterion than consensus.

As we have discussed, much of the process of a Strengths-Weaknesses analysis can be seen in the simultaneous activity to define both the relevant dimensions as well as the relative corporate or unit performance along these dimensions. In analogous forecasting processes, particularly when based on the expertise of a limited number of contributors, it is often useful to provide not only the estimates for the other participants, but also a summary of their estimates. It might often be appropriate to adopt such a procedure on a more formal basis in the case of a Strengths-Weaknesses analysis.

The problem of the structure of the elements in a SWOT analysis is more complex. The process development in this area uses systematic procedures to enable contributors to exchange views as to the significance or interpretation of the issues in strengths and weaknesses.

Experimental Evidence

Few systematic surveys of the process of Strengths-Weaknesses analysis have been conducted. One notable example, despite the small sample, is that conducted by Stevenson. We have already mentioned that the approach adopted was one which focused on functional elements. As such it should come as no surprise that not only were the individual elements rated differently by the participants but also that a major explanatory variable was the functional area to which they belonged.

Some of his results, however, do raise general concerns about any S&W process. For instance, Stevenson concluded that:

> Managers tend to treat strengths differently from weaknesses . . . (and) . . . The manager's position and responsibility in the organization are crucial influences on the way in which he carries out the process of defining strengths and weaknesses.

Indeed he looked more closely at the broad criteria underlying the assessment of strengths and weaknesses (Exhibit 7–19), which emphasized the extent to which strengths were defined by historical evidence, and weaknesses by external "norms."

Further, his own results suggested that:

> There are some aspects of a company that are of concern in all companies (and) . . . managers within any company examine a broad range of attributes (but) . . . there is no consensus on "the corporation's strengths and weaknesses."

As a result of these problems, Stevenson's conclusion as to the value of strengths and weaknesses analysis is ambivalent:

> Definitions of strengths and weaknesses generally applicable for whole organizations were not found. However, there appear to be definitions which can aid the individual manager in doing his own job. The use of a formal assessment program developed from the budgeting process seems unlikely to succeed because the information gathered at one organizational level is not directly additive with information from other levels. A program which carefully defines the relevant attributes to be examined and which imposes rigorous and consistent criteria may provide important assistance in the strategic planning process.

As we have suggested, there are some further ways forward along the direction suggested by Stevenson. The development of "relevant attributes" can itself be seen as a process of redefinition among the various participants. The "usefulness" of such attributes, in their meaning and potential for action, can also be integrated into the process of redefinition. Finally, we can relate such an analysis to the restructuring of the management accounting system in a way that avoids or at least overcomes some of Stevenson's correct concerns about overreliance on historic, aggregated data.

An Extended SWOT Framework

The first major corrective issue that would make it easier to carry out a SWOT dialogue is to express both Strengths and Weaknesses in the same units as those in which Opportunities-Threats are typically obtained. At the level of marketing strategy, particularly, this is problematic. For example, an environmental analysis may reveal that in the cola market, because of shifting demographics, there is an increased preference for sweetness. Strengths could be: excellent distribution channel access, manufacturing ability, and consumer marketing skills. How should these strengths be deployed to exploit the opportunity? The problem arises essentially because of a lack of action focus in the analytical framework. Thus there is a need to introduce intermediate constructs to make the units of thought of the S-W and O-T axes (if you will) match up.

The second major issue is that the typical SWOT analysis with its largely historical focus prevents a formulation of strategy in changing strengths and weaknesses; this despite the following early observation by Andrews.[50]

> The match is designed to minimize organizational weaknesses and to maximize strength. In any case, risk attends it. And when opportunity seems to outrun present distinctive competence, the willingness to gamble that the latter can be built up to the required level is almost indispensable to a strategy that challenges the organi

[50]Andrews, K. R., *The Concept of Corporate Strategy,* Homewood, IL, Dow-Jones-Irwin, 1971, p. 97.

zation and the people in it. It appears to be true, in any case, that the potential capability of a company tends to be underestimated. Organizations, like individuals, rise to occasions, particularly when the latter provide attractive reward for the effort required.

EXHIBIT 7–20   Extended SWOT Framework for Marketing Strategy

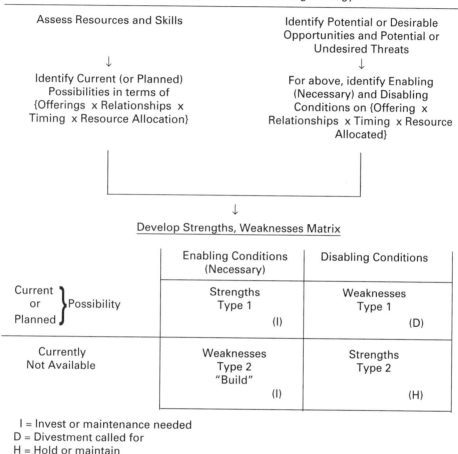

I = Invest or maintenance needed
D = Divestment called for
H = Hold or maintain

This contention (the second issue) is borne out by the statements of other management scholars, for example, Hamel and Prahalad,

> As "strategy" has blossomed, the competitiveness of Western companies has withered. This may be a coincidence, but we think not. We believe that the application of concepts such as "strategic fit" (between resources and opportunities), "generic strategies" (low cost vs. differentiation vs. focus), and the "strategy hierarchy" (goals, strategies and tactics) have often abetted the process of competitive decline.[51]

[51]Hamel and Prahalad, *op. cit.,* 1989, p. 63.

The framework shown in Exhibit 7–20 incorporates this action orientation into competitor (other or self) and competitive analysis.

The first steps of the process consist of taking inventory of resources and skills, and an environmental scanning input of opportunities and threats. From these current or planned possibilities and enabling and disabling conditions[52] are to be arrived at. The units of thought are the marketing-strategy set elements of (Offerings × Relationships × Timing × Resource Allocation). For example, it might be desirable to introduce products into an Arab country. However, having relationships with Israeli markets could make this a disabling condition. Similarly, having an exclusive trade agreement could be disabling in using a new technology for another purpose or entering a new market, and so forth. Examples of enabling conditions should be obvious. Of course, any of these conditions either on the possibilities side or the environmental side could be changed and therefore must be reviewed periodically and as major changes are perceived.

A key part of this process (in keeping with the 4A + 3I framework suggested

[52]An interesting study on success producers and failure preventers was carried out using the PIMS database. The conceptual discussion in the paper shows the identification of the principal success producers and failure preventers. The results of the PIMS-based study are summarized below.

Factors Considered (All in relative terms)	Consumer Non-Durable Businesses	Capital Goods Businesses
Breadth of Product Line	SP[a]	SP
Product Quality	SP	(SP)
New Product Activity	(SP)[b]	(SP)
Quality of Customer Services	FP	FP
Sales Force Expenditure Level	(FP)	(SP)
Advertising Expenditure Level	(SP)	(FP)
Sales Promotion Expenditure Level	(FP)	(FP)
Relative Price	—[c]	—
Degree of Forward Vertical Integration		FP
Number of Businesses in Sample	157	161

[a]= Significant as per regression analysis.

[b]= Expectation.

[c]= Not classifiable, according to the author.

SP = Success Producer.

FP = Failure Prevention

Year of data: 1973
Database: PIMS
Dependent Variable: Market share
Derived from: Vardarajan, P. R., "A Two-Factor Classification of Competitive Strategy Variables," *Strategic Management Journal,* Vol. 6, 1985, pp. 357–375.

in Chapter 1) is an effort to examine critically the assumptions being made about a competitor's (other or self) aspirations and capabilities, as well as about the environment.[53]

The strengths-weaknesses matrix in Exhibit 7–20 points out the existence of two kinds of weaknesses. They correspond roughly to those of commission and those of omission. Type 1 strengths are immediately usable and must be reinforced if necessary. Type 2 strengths exist because the disabling conditions or factors do not exist. For example, not having an exclusive agreement, or supplying a competitor, or even not being wedded to a quality control system quite different from that needed by the key client being pursued. Type 1 weaknesses should be targeted for removal. For example, having an exclusive agreement, not having the appropriate resources, and so on. Type 2 weaknesses require investment. These are likely to be the so-called "chinks in the armor" and need to be attended to promptly.

A Type 1 weakness played a dramatic role in the battle for fountain sales between Coke and Pepsi as captured by the following quotation. "Fountain sales account for almost $10 billion in retail soft-drink sales annually. That translates into 31% of Coca-Cola's U.S. volume and about 21% of Pepsi's."[54]

> Coke has built up a commanding advantage in the fountain business, with 63% of the market, leaving Pepsi with 25%.
>
> Having Coke or Pepsi exclusively on the menus of McDonald's or Burger King is a potent tool for building brand strength.
>
> Unfortunately for Pepsi, its diversification strategy has played right into Coke's hands. PepsiCo Inc., Pepsi Cola's parent, owns the Pizza Hut, KFC, and Taco Bell fast food chains. So buying Pepsi's syrup, argues Coke, is putting money into a competing restauranteur's pocket.
>
> "Suddenly, we looked around, and we were surrounded by Pepsi restaurants," says Thomas H. Hensley, Chief Executive of Druther's Systems Inc.,

[53]In this context it is perhaps helpful to bear in mind the six broad principles suggested by Ian Mitroff to challenge the so-called "unchallengeable" assumptions-practices. These principles are:

1. Seek the obvious, but do everything in your power to challenge and even to ridicule it (e.g., challenge the enabling conditions and the obvious strategy sets).

2. Question all constraints. The most limiting constraints are usually imposed not by the problem but by the mindset of the problem solver (e.g., in this application, question the impossibilities).

3. Challenge as many assumptions about the problem as possible. Remember that what seems self-evident to you is not always evident to others (e.g., challenge the disabling conditions).

4. Question the scope or definition of a problem. Frequently, what is omitted from the statement of a problem is as critical as what is included (Is the thinking broad enough?).

5. Question whether a problem is to be "solved," "resolved," or "dissolved."

6. Question logic. Being logical and being right are not always the same. The more logical a solution to a complex problem sounds, the more it deserves to be challenged.

Source: Mitroff, I. I., *Business Not As Usual: Rethinking Our Individual, Corporate, and Industrial Strategies for Global Competition,* San Francisco, Jossey-Bass, 1987.

[54]Konrad, W. and G. DeGeorge, "Sorry, No Pepsi. How 'Bout A Coke?" *Business Week,* May 27, 1991 p. 71.

a 65-unit restaurant chain based in Louisville, that also owns some 68 Dairy Queens. Druther's switched over to Coke in April, in part because of the competition issue.

An analysis of the type indicated in Exhibit 7–20, by product-market, by identifying the enabling and disabling conditions, and by matching it to potential and current competitors provides a picture of the expected competition. The expected resource allocations by a competitor are based on the nature of the product-market as discussed earlier, the motivation of the competitor, as well as the resources and skills it possesses. The extended SWOT framework focuses the major elements discussed so far in creating an action and future-oriented marketing strategy.

SUMMARY

This chapter provides an overview of competition in a product-market. The factors influencing overall competitiveness of rivalry: growth rate, regulatory status, information status, cost structure, market structure, customer preference structure, and nature of product-market players are discussed. This discussion centered on an application-oriented definition of rivalry. Initial intensive discussion on the nature of product-market players included discussion on motivation based on understanding the concepts of dominant culture via the Analyzer, Prospector, Defender, Reactor classification and strategic intent. Further discussion on the resources for competition was presented using the frameworks of competitive advantage, value chain analysis, strategic cost analysis (including activity-based costing) and SWOT analysis. Finally, a new framework, called the extended SWOT framework making the SWOT framework more action-oriented, strategic, and "take charge" was discussed.

Concept Questions

1. What is rivalry or competitiveness?
2. Describe the effects that each of the seven competitiveness factors have on rivalry.
3. Interpret the nature of competitiveness (a) overall and (b) by each of the products in Exhibit 7–7.
4. Describe the key elements of the competitive-advantage framework.
5. Describe the value chain framework and its application to the analysis of a competitor.
6. What are the key benefits of using
   (a.) the Dunne-Wolk approach, and
   (b.) the ABC approach for analyzing competitors?
7. Describe the extended SWOT analysis approach to assessing strengths and weaknesses.

Discussion Questions

1. Devise a scoring scheme (or an integrative mathematical model) to:
   (a.) Measure (capture) the rivalry in different product markets.
   (b.) Characterize the rivalry expected from a given competitor.

2. Identify the sources of information that will permit you to perform (a) a Dunne-Wolk analysis, (b) an ABC analysis, and (c) an extended SWOT analysis of a company that you plan to interview with and of its key competitor. (Note: first, carefully ask yourself: what does it mean to say that one firm is another's key competitor?)

3. Discuss how you would use the various concepts presented in this chapter in conjunction with the various strategy lenses from Chapter 2.

4. Perform an extended SWOT analysis for your (a) program of studies and (b) yourself.

Part 3

ANALYTICAL TOOLS

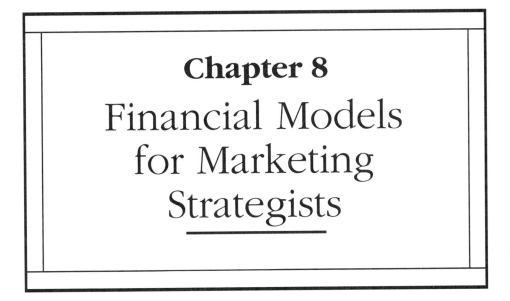

Chapter 8
Financial Models for Marketing Strategists

INTRODUCTION

Karen M. Tibus ought to be delighted. While her rivals are offering steep discounts to move their metal, Tibus, a Plymouth (Michigan) Saturn dealer, is able to charge full price . . . Saturn dealers in July sold 22,305 cars—an average of 115 apiece. That's twice the rate per dealer for the nearest competitor, Toyota Motor Co. . . . Saturn's growth spurt is forcing some tough decisions at GM's Detroit headquarters. Already, Saturn President Richard G. "Skip" Le Fauve is clamoring for money to increase Spring Hill's assembly capacity, to 500,000 cars a year.[1]

- Will "Skip" get his money?
- Clearly the increased capacity has to be moved by sales—so what is the marketing analysis backup for this request? Will the demand "picture" be sufficient?

These are just two examples of questions that a marketing strategist at Saturn would naturally ask. The decision is one of capital budgeting. The basic principles of capital budgeting are of interest to a marketing strategist to understand how resources are allocated in organizations. Resources and action go hand-in-glove. The right strategy makes sure they match!

Financial strategy and marketing strategy decisions are intertwined. The following example lays out this intertwining and the possible mishaps caused by the two being out of step.

[1]Excerpted from the cover story in *Business Week,* August 17, 1992, p. 86.

Reacting to a hostile takeover attempt in 1986, Revco Drugstore's Chairman Sidney Dworkin led a $1.3 billion leveraged buyout, financed largely by junk bonds bearing interest rates above 13 percent. Revco's corporate restructuring strategy, which included this leveraged buyout, placed a heavy debt burden on the company. This left Revco with a dangerously small cash balance.

To avoid this risky position, most LBO strategies call for conservative long-range plans that will generate steady cash flows to provide funds for debt service. However, instead, Revco adopted a very aggressive marketing strategy: It broadened product lines, intensified advertising, and emphasized cut-rate store brands. While this marketing strategy was expected to increase costs, Revco should also have anticipated that these tactics might not increase sales volume enough to create the needed cash flow. The company was well aware that the profit margin on store brands is quite narrow. All too soon, Revco was plagued by cash shortages, had trouble maintaining adequate inventories, and missed deadlines for debt payments. The company filed for bankruptcy in July 1988.[2]

Capital budgeting decisions involve balancing the risks and returns presented by various alternatives. The seizing of any such opportunity also requires a financing decision; that is, should this opportunity be funded through debt or equity? Use of debt requires its repayment be considered in evaluating the net benefits to be obtained from the opportunity.

In this chapter both capital budgeting and financing decisions are discussed. In particular, traditional capital budget models are reviewed, the concept of shareholder wealth is discussed, methods for joint consideration of both the return and risk of an investment opportunity are summarized, and the concept of self-sustaining growth rate is discussed. We also provide an Appendix that briefly discusses the possible use of option pricing theory in marketing.

The Intellectual and Practical Aspects of Financial Decision Making

Changes in world economic conditions have radically changed the availability of capital and along with it decision making within the corporation. Decentralized decision making and centralization continue to alternate as dominant styles as organizations respond to environmental buffeting. Before the 1974 OPEC crisis, divisional managers usually got the funds they wanted from top management. Decision making was theirs. Scarcity of capital (or at least its cost) changed the situation. Divisional financial autonomy became history. It was replaced by centralized strategic decision making. The emergence of strong corporate leaders like Jack Welch and the growth in power of leverage buyout (LBO) powerhouses like Kohlberg, Kravis, Roberts & Company (KKR) are evidence of such changes. KKR representatives, sitting on the boards of directors of companies in which they are active, get involved in selecting and closely monitoring the Chief Financial Officers. For example,

Prior to the RJR Nabisco leveraged buyout, managers of the food and biscuit operations were content with earnings growth of about 10% to 15% a year . . . Immediately after the

---

[2]The Revco example is used in both Newport, S., G. G. Dess and A. M. A. Rasheed, "Nurturing Strategic Coherency," *Planning Review,* November-December, Vol. 19, No. 6, 1991, pp. 18–22, 26, 27, 47; and in Jensen, M. C., "Eclipse of the Public Corporation," *Harvard Business Review,* September–October, Vol. 67, No. 5, 1989, pp. 61–75. This quote is from Newport, et al., p. 19.

buyout, KKR encouraged Nabisco managers to draft plans for a 40% increase in operating earnings for 1989, taking advantage of long-dormant opportunities for price increases and the introduction of new, higher-margin products.[3]

How, then, do capital allocation decisions get made, given this centralization of strategic capital decisions? There certainly is not a "magic" formula to produce the "optimal decision." Professors Donaldson and Lorsch of Harvard University conducted an in-depth study[4] of strategic and financial decision making in 12 major industrial firms.

> What we have observed in these records leads us to challenge those who argue that corporate managers consider only the bottom line and the shareholders associated with it. These executives may not always be even handed statesmen; but neither are they single-minded. Concerned, above all, with the long-term survival of their enterprises, they cannot afford to be parochial in their views. Instead they must balance the demands made on them by three competing constituencies, whose cooperation is vital for their firm's success. These are the capital market, the product market, and the organization (p. 34).

(Note the term product-market as used by Donaldson and Lorsch is different from than used by marketing writers. To them it means the firm's major customers, unions, suppliers, and host communities.)

Their "three competing constituencies," as descriptive of organizational decision making, is evocative of the notion of coalitions and subcoalitions put forth by eminent scholars such as the Nobel laureate Herbert Simon and Cyert and March[5] in the fifties and sixties. Referring to the KKR example, the coalitions may change, but the organizational process is one of managing the conflict among the coalitions. The work of Pfeffer and Salancik relates why certain coalitions develop influence and control over organizational goals and other issues. Not surprisingly, the coalitions that possess "behaviors, resources and capabilities that are most needed or desired by other organizational participants come to have more influence and control over the organization."[6] Although not surprising now, these studies provided a dramatic departure from the reigning "profit-maximization" paradigm of the then existing economic schools.

[3]George Anders, a senior special writer at the Wall Street Journal, recently wrote a book on KKR titled *Merchants of Debt: KKR and the Mortgaging of American Businesses* (Basic Books, 1992). This quote is taken from p. 17 of the article by Anders, based on this book. Anders, G., "The 'Barbarians' in the Boardroom," *Harvard Business Review,* July–August, 1992, pp. 79–87. On page 82 of the same article Anders says, "Most of KKR's own revenue comes from stock appreciation of the equity stakes that it owns in concert with passive limited investors. KKR partners and associates thus have powerful economic incentives to maximize the value of the partnership holdings." This is an important theme which shall be discussed later. Studies on the process of marketing budgeting are summarized and presented in Pierce, N. F., "The Marketing Budgeting Process: Marketing Management Implications," *Journal of Marketing,* 51, October, 1987, pp. 45–59. This study also includes European research.

[4]Donaldson, G. and J. W. Lorsch, *Decision Making At The Top: The Shaping of Strategic Direction,* New York, Basic Books, 1983.

[5]For example see March, J. G. and H. A. Simon, *Organizations,* New York, John Wiley, 1958; Cyert, R. M. and J. G. March, *A Behavioral Theory of the Firm,* Englewood Cliffs, NJ, Prentice-Hall, 1963.

[6]Pfeffer, J. and G. R. Salancik, *The External Control of Organizations,* New York, Harper and Row, 1978, p. 27.

This understanding is critical to marketing strategists because each plays an advisory role to the chief executive (or division manager), an advocacy role for staff, customers, and channel members, and each has a personal goal as well as a goal for their families. Even if no financial goal is maximized, financial goals are set and used in corporate decision making. Shareholder wealth has become the dominant driving force (see KKR example, footnote 3) at companies such as Coca-Cola, Westinghouse, and RJR Nabisco. A marketing strategist who not only is able to understand and present the marketing point of view in the "language" of senior financial executives, but who also grasps and can advise on the links between marketing and financial strategy is a valuable asset to the organization. Having the information required and anticipating questions in light of the overall corporate or organizational plan is a source of influence (according to Pfeffer and Salancik). The language and concepts of capital budgeting are now discussed.

Capital Budgeting Approach

Financial theory provides some classic capital budgeting methods used to evaluate investment opportunities. Typically, these methods are applied to decisions that concern the purchase of revenue-producing assets. For example, financial evaluation models are used to determine if the cost of a computer-controlled production system is justified by the potential decrease in labor costs. Moreover, these financial models are also used to evaluate strategic marketing decisions. For example, should a business strengthen its position in a product-market by increased advertising and the introduction of product-line extensions or should it direct its resources toward a new, fast growing product-market opportunity?

In a business the conventional method for allocating resources is for operating managers to make investment proposals to a person or group responsible for capital budgeting. Each proposal contains an estimate of the investment required and the expected cash flow to be generated. These proposals are evaluated using financial criteria and funds are allocated to promising proposals.

Strategic marketing decisions parallel investment decisions that arise in preparing a capital budget. Businesses, facing a number of product-markets or channels, or customers so they can allocate resources, must decide how much of their resources to allocate to each product-market. The basis for making these allocation decisions should be the expected long-term yield from the resources invested in order to maximize shareholder wealth. Investments should be made in all opportunities which are projected to yield at least a fair market return—a return equal to or greater than the cost of capital (adjusted for the project risk) required.

Wenner and LeBer[7] of McKinsey & Co., writing in the *Harvard Business Review,* provide an example of the newly-appointed CEO of a $3 billion, multibusiness company who, upon taking over, found, much to his chagrin, that ". . . three businesses accounted for more than 90% of the corporation's total economic value. Yet the other 12% of the value consumed 30% of corporate assets and roughly half of

---

[7]Wenner, D. L. and R. W. LeBer, "Managing for Shareholder Value—From Top to Bottom," *Harvard Business Review,* November–December, 1989, p. 54.

the management's attention." You can imagine what needed to be done with the other 12 businesses! The point is that the use of total economic value (or shareholder value) as a gauge for the strategic evaluation of businesses is growing. Its use in evaluating projects, customers, channels, product-markets, and other areas calling for major resources in corporations is also expected to grow. The next section describes and compares different criteria used for making financial investment decisions.

Alternative Investment Criteria

Consider the following example. Fun Time manufactures toys and games for children and adults. The capital structure of the firm consists of 100% equity—no debt. A product manager is responsible for building blocks, a product line in a mature market. The product line has a 20% market share with annual sales of $10 million. The profit margin is 10%. Assuming that all the assets needed to produce the building blocks have been paid for and depreciated and that there is no resale value of the assets, the cash flow generated by the product line is one million dollars per year. The product manager feels that the competition is particularly vulnerable now. By launching some product line extensions and increasing the level of advertising over the next two years, she is confident that the product line can achieve a sustainable 30% share by strengthening consumer loyalty and improving channel relationships. The financial implications of the product manager's plan are shown in Exhibit 8–1.

EXHIBIT 8–1 Building Blocks—Gaining Share in a Mature Market
Position at End of Year (figures in thousands of $)

Year	1	2	3	4	5	6	7	8
Present Plan								
Sales	10,000	10,000	10,000	10,000	10,000	10,000	10,000	10,000
Cash flow	1,000	1,000	1,000	1,000	1,000	1,000	1,000	1,000
Increased Advertising plus Product Line Extension*								
Projected sales	10,000	12,500	14,000	15,000	15,000	15,000	15,000	15,000
Projected cash flow (before advertising and product extensions)	1,000	1,125	1,400	1,500	1,500	1,500	1,500	1,500
Additional advertising	0	500	200	100	0	0	0	0
Development of line extension	500	0	0	0	0	0	0	0
Net cash flow	500	625	1,200	1,400	1,500	1,500	1,500	1,500
Net incremental cash flow	(500)	(375)	200	400	500	500	500	500

*Assumes $500,000 to develop product line extensions during year 1; additional advertising of $500,000, $200,000, and $100,000 during year 2, 3, and 4, and a build-up of market share of 20%, 25%, 28%, and 30% in year 2, 3, 4, and 5.

Another product manager proposes launching a line of remote controlled robots—a new, fast growing market. This new product launch requires a significant investment during the next three years, but provides substantial returns. The financial implications of this opportunity are shown in Exhibit 8–2.

Three financial criteria used to evaluate these alternatives are (1) net return on capital employed, (2) payback period, and (3) the net present value (NPV).[8]

Net Return On Capital Employed. Net return is the total incremental return over the planning horizon; net return on capital employed is the ratio of net return to investment. For the building blocks project the net return is $1,725,000 ($3,025,000 − $1,300,000) and the net return for the household robots project is $6,300,000 ($9,300,000 − $3,000,000). Based on net return and ignoring risk, the household robots project is clearly the more attractive opportunity. For building blocks, the net return of initial capital employed is 345% and for household robots, 630%. However, the net return criteria fail to consider the timing of cash flows, the time value of money, and the potential differences in risk between the opportunities. Note that the returns for the building block proposal are realized more quickly than the returns for the robots. In addition, investments in building blocks are probably less risky than investments in robots because Fun Time has considerable experience competing in the market considered in the building blocks project, while the robots in the household robots project involve a new direction for the firm's production and engineering departments.

Payback. A simple method which considers aspects of the time value of money is the payback period—the number of years required for the net cash flow to become positive. The payback period for the building block proposal is 4.25 years and for the robots, 6.2 years. However, the payback method can be misleading because it ignores the overall magnitude of the returns and the riskiness of the investments. As Brealy and Myers[9] in their classic textbook on corporate finance put it,

> Some managers talk casually about 'quick payback' projects in the same sense that investors talk about 'high PIE' common stocks. The fact that managers talk about the

EXHIBIT 8–2   Household Robots—New Product Launch into Growing Market

Year	1	2	3	4	5	6	7	8
Projected Sales	0	0	0	5,000	8,000	12,000	18,000	20,000
Projected Cash Flow	0	0	0	0	800	2,000	3,000	3,500
Development Costs*	1,000	1,000	1,000	0	0	0	0	0
Net Cash Flow	(1,000)	(1,000)	(1,000)	0	800	2,000	3,000	3,500

*Assume the project requires no new investment in production facilities.

[8]For an example of financial methods of analyzing marketing investments see Paul F. Anderson, "Marketing Investment Analysis" *In* J. Sheth (ed.), *Research in Marketing.* New York, JAI Press, Volume 4, 1981, pp. 1–37.

[9]Brealy and Myers (1981), *op. cit.,* p. 77.

payback periods of projects does not mean that payback periods govern their decisions. Some managers do use payback in judging capital investments. Why they rely on such a grossly oversimplified concept is a puzzle.

Net Present Value (NPV). Discounted cash flow techniques consider the magnitude of the returns, the time value of money, and the risk in the assessment of investment opportunities. The financial criterion used to evaluate an investment, net present value (NPV), is calculated as follows:[10]

$$NPV = \sum_{i=1}^{n} \frac{CF_i}{(1+R)^i} \tag{1}$$

where:

NPV = net present value of opportunity
CF_i = net cash flow resulting from opportunity in year i
n = expected life of investment opportunity
R = the risk-adjusted cost-of-capital to fund the opportunity

The decision rule is to invest in all opportunities that have a positive net present value. In other words, invest in opportunities whose returns are greater than the cost of capital to fund the opportunity.

NPV and Maximizing Shareholder Wealth

In addition to the considerations of time and risk, the NPV criterion is appealing because, theoretically, a business will maximize stockholder wealth by applying it. Most financial theorists feel that maximizing stockholder wealth is the appropriate objective for a company because it is seen as consistent with maximizing social welfare.[11] In this view, the use of any other objective by a firm "is likely to result in the suboptimal capital formation and growth in the economy as well as less than optimal economic want satisfaction."[12]

Maximizing stockholder wealth is superior to traditional profit maximizing because profit maximization fails to consider the timing of investments and returns. In addition, the measurement of profits is affected by accounting procedures.

[10]An alternative is to solve equation (1) for R assuming that NPV equals zero. Discount rate (DR) is then the internal rate of return (IRR) and the decision rule would be to fund opportunities with an IRR greater than the risk-adjusted cost of capital. When properly stated and when NPV declines as the discount rate increases, IRR and NPV lead to identical project decisions. The NPV calculation is considered to be theoretically superior to the IRR calculation because there can be (1) multiple solutions for IRR, (2) IRR assumes that the projects are mutually exclusive, and (3) the term structure of interest rates is finessed in IRR calculations.

[11]Fama, Eugene and Merton Miller, *The Theory of Finance,* Hinsdale, IL, Dryden Press, 1972.

[12]Van Horne, James C. *Financial Management and Policy,* 4th Ed., Englewood Cliffs, NJ, Prentice-Hall, 1977, p. 98. Alternative perspectives concerning the theory of the firm can be found in Anderson, Paul F. "Marketing Strategic Planning and the Theory of the Firm," *Journal of Marketing,* 42, Spring, 1982, pp. 15–26.

Different accounting procedures can produce a variety of profit levels. Accounting profit is based on invoices and not on actual cash transfers. Thus as Dobbins and Witt put it, "Profit flow is an opinion, cash flow is a fact." Cash flow is the recommended basis for fact-based wealth evaluation.

The popularity of this approach is pointed out by Wenner and LeBer,[13] when they say, "Shareholder value is now widely accepted as an appropriate standard for performance in U.S. business. . . . What matters is long-term stock performance, and that's how we should manage." While rigorous research on the value of this approach is lacking, indications are that it is beneficial. For example, based on the returns received from 70 Fortune 500 firms, the consulting firm, Marakon Associates, reported[14] that:

1. Firms using value-based management concepts had an average total annual return to shareholders of 21% as opposed to 14% by those who did not, and

2. The average annualized return over a 10-year period was 25% for the 12 early adopters (in the sample) of shareholder value methods, whereas that for the S&P 400 was only 16%. (The early adopters include Coca-Cola, Wells Fargo, Marriott, and Westinghouse.)

At Westinghouse,[15] which was a pioneer in the use of value-based management, a process called VABSTRAM (Value Based Strategic Management) is used. Westinghouse's dramatic performance improvements lately have been attributed by its management to the systematic use of VABSTRAM in both portfolio restructuring and in investment decisions at all levels, including the plant level.

The value-based approach is shown in Exhibit 8–3 which combines the spread and growth elements inherent in the value of common stock.[16] While an analytical construct is useful for an accurate measure of investor wealth, implementing it requires active management and considerable judgment. As summarized by Wenner and LeBer, the implementation process needs top management commitment and development of skills throughout the company as well as an active program for staff motivation. The skills required are *expertise* in performing the elaborate calculations and *judgment* in making forecasts. The ability of the managers to discern and understand the nuances is also required. They should have a thorough *understanding* of the process in order to detect possible problems and to develop the "value drivers" for the particular project being considered—channel relationships, customer usage patterns, and so on. From Wenner and LeBer's experience and observation,

---

[13]Wenner, D. L. and R. W. LeBer, "Managing for Shareholder Value—From Top to Bottom," *Harvard Business Review,* November–December, 1989, 52–66.

[14]Reiman, B. C., "Shareholder Value and Executive Compensation," *Planning Review,* 1992, pp. 41–48.

[15]Newport, Dess and Rasheed, *op. cit.,* 1991; Rappaport, A., *Creating Shareholder Value: The New Standard for Business Performance,* New York, MacMillan, 1986.

[16]Arzac, E. R., "Do Your Business Units Create Shareholder Value?" *Harvard Business Review,* January–February, 1986, pp. 121–126.

EXHIBIT 8–3   The Value Creation Model

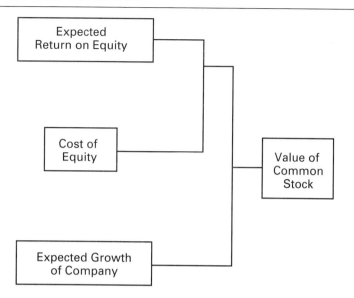

the motivation required seems to work if the shareholder value measures and process are made part of the planning process. Furthermore, developing "user-champion" line managers speeds implementation. Symbolic actions, new awards, persistent assurance, and proof of "no-penalty for past performance" are necessary to convert the naysayers to doers and believers. It requires commitment on the part of the line managers to:

1. Estimate basic data (base line) for each unit,
2. Set performance standards and evaluate them against projected performance,
3. Estimate value created, and
4. Evaluate and update decisions.

Similarly, Wenner and LeBer point out that implementation must begin with an agenda set by top management that asks:

1. How have we been doing?
2. Do our plans make sense?
3. How much better could we do?
4. What should our priorities be?

They also point out that in evaluating what the best performance could be, management should imagine that the best possible "owners" are "running the show." For example, an automobile parts business might be assumed to be run by a firm with the widest aftermarket parts distribution network.

To continue with the example of the newly-arrived CEO, Wenner and LeBer provide an example of the "value driver" analysis required. This fits nicely with the "mental simulation" orientation and the assumption surfacing and evaluation perspectives discussed earlier.

Exhibit 8–4 is a graph that relates cash flow over time, for the computer subsidiary, to different levels of sales force productivity and to whether an aggressive growth or slow growth strategy was chosen. Sales force productivity was a "value driver" in this case because the strategy to be chosen depended on its level. (Other potential drivers would also have to be analyzed to identify the real "value drivers.") In our example, an aggressive-growth approach added the most value if sales force productivity was high, otherwise a low-growth strategy was the better choice. The strategic focus then became: Could sales force productivity be improved? How? At what cost? Such an analysis in shareholder wealth helps management isolate the true value drivers of focus and possible control.

Given the focus on the "flow" of the value of money, interest rates, and risk, this form of analysis makes the issue of timing even more salient. Should a product be introduced earlier? Should marketing expenditures be made early or later? and so forth.

EXHIBIT 8–4

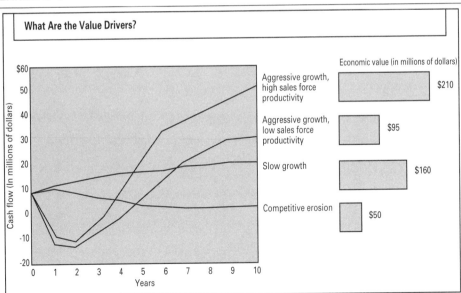

From Wenner, D. L. and R. W. LeBer, "Managing for Shareholder Value—From Top to Bottom," *Harvard Business Review,* November–December, 1989, p. 58. (© 1989 by the President and Fellows of Harvard College; All Rights Reserved.)

CAPITAL ASSET PRICING MODEL

Calculating the NPV for a strategic marketing opportunity using equation (1) is straightforward. However, determining the appropriate discount rate—the risk adjusted cost of capital to fund the project—requires some understanding of how a firm's shareholders evaluate risk and return. In 1952, Markowitz developed a normative model of investor behavior which revolutionized financial theory and for which he received a Nobel prize in economics in 1991.[17]

This financial portfolio model indicates that risk-averse investors consider both the expected returns and the corresponding variances in returns when buying stocks. The variance in return indicates the riskiness of the stock. The expected return of a stock portfolio is the weighted average of the expected return of each stock. However, the variance of the portfolio's return is a complex function of the variance of the return distribution for each stock in the portfolio and the correlations among the return series of the stock. Markowitz demonstrated that by considering these correlations the investor can select a diversified portfolio providing the minimum variance at each level of return. If investors believe their assessment of risk is directly equivalent to the statistical measure of variance, the portfolios based on Markowitz's model represent an optimal investment. Through diversification, the variation in return from specific events associated with companies represented in the portfolio, such as new product failures, strikes, product recalls, and competitive securities, can be minimized. This happens because diversification reduces the impact of events that only affect specific companies in the portfolio. The remaining variation in portfolio return is because of events which affect all companies, such as the business cycle. Thus, the variation (or risk) in an optimally-diversified portfolio can be divided into: (1) systematic risk which cannot be reduced through diversification because it is common to all firms, and (2) unsystematic risk which can be significantly reduced through diversification because it is idiosyncratic to each firm. The systematic risk of a stock is critical in determining the stock price because it cannot be controlled through diversification.

The systematic risk of companies varies considerably. For example, overall economic conditions have a significant impact on the sales of companies manufacturing consumer durables, while manufacturers of stable food products are largely unaffected by business cycles. The systematic risk of companies offering durables is likely to be much larger than the systematic risk of firms selling nondurables.

The measure used to assess the systematic risk for a firm's stock is the *beta coefficient*. Beta, β_j, is estimated by regressing the returns from the company's stock on the returns for the entire market over time. Thus,

$$R_{ij} = \overline{\alpha}_j + \beta_j R_{im} \qquad (2)$$

where R_{ij} = return from stock j during period i
β_j = Beta coefficient for stock j
R_{im} = average   return   for   all   stocks   (usually   measured   by the S&P 500 index)
$\overline{\alpha}_j$ = a constant

[17]Markowitz, Harry M. "Portfolio Selection," *Journal of Finance,* 7, March, 1952, pp. 77–91.

For example, the beta for Chrysler Corporation (1959 to 1969) was 2.94, whereas the beta for General Motors was 1.09.[18] Thus a 1% change in the returns for the entire stock market cause a 2.94% change in the return from Chrysler, but only 1.09% change in General Motors' stock. Because of Chrysler's high systematic risk (beta), its stock is unattractive compared to General Motors. Chrysler's high systematic risk (beta) means that investors require a higher rate of return from Chrysler's stock, which is reflected in the relationship between the stock price and earnings.

Equation 2 indicates that the relationship between systematic risk, beta, and returns of firm's stock is linear.[19] This linear relationship, the standard market line (SML) shown in Exhibit 8–5, represents:

EXHIBIT 8–5   Illustration of CAPM Example

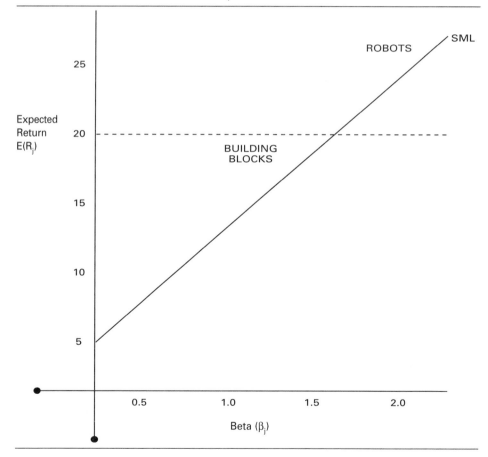

[18]Weston, J. Fred "Investment Decisions Using the Capital Asset Pricing Model," *Financial Management,* 2, Spring, 1973, pp. 25–33.

[19] Sharpe, William F. "Capital Asset Prices: A Theory of Market Equilibrium Under Conditions of Risk," *Journal of Finance,* 19, September, 1964, pp. 425–442.

$$E(R_j) = R_F + [E (R_m) - R_F] \beta_j \qquad (3)$$

where:

$E(R_j)$ = expected return of stock j

R_F = risk-free return (usually determined by the interest on U.S. Treasury bills)

$E(R_m)$ = expected return of the stock market (usually determined by the return on the S&P 500 stock index)

β_j = Beta coefficient for firm j

Theoretically when the stock market is in equilibrium, all individual stocks plot on the SML. The SML model indicates the tradeoff that investors make between expected returns and systematic risk. This model is frequently referred to as the Capital Asset Pricing Model (CAPM).

Using the Capital Asset Pricing Model for Evaluating Strategic Marketing Decisions

From an investor's perspective, a firm, such as Fun Time, is simply a collection of tangible and intangible assets (e.g., brand franchises, channel relationships, patents, plant and equipment, managerial expertise, etc.). In Exhibit 8–5, Fun Time's position is located on the SML. Its expected return, $E(R_j)$, is 20.3% and its systematic risk, β_j, is 1.7. (Assume the overall market return is 14.0% and the U.S. Treasury bill rate is 5.0%.)

As discussed previously, Fun Time is considering two strategic investments— building blocks and robots. These investments, as plotted in Exhibit 8–5, are both above the SML. The anticipated return from these projects is greater than investors expect when confronting investments with similar levels of risk. Therefore, Fun Time should undertake both projects. By combining these two projects with its other assets, Fun Time's risk-return profile will be in temporary disequilibrium—it will plot above the SML. When investors learn of these projects and if they feel confident that the projects have the projected risk-return tradeoff, investors will restore Fun Time to equilibrium in the SML by bidding up the price of Fun Time's stock and thus reducing its expected return.

Determining the Appropriate Discount Rate

The appropriate discount rate for evaluating a strategic opportunity is determined using equation (3). The market return (R_m) and risk-free return (R_F) can be estimated from readily available data. However, determining the level of systematic risk associated with an investment is more difficult. Unlike company stocks, these strategic investment opportunities, such as Fun Time's robots and building blocks, are not traded on a stock exchange. A beta for a specific opportunity cannot be estimated by simply regressing returns from the stock market on returns from the strategic opportunity.

An appropriate estimate of the beta associated with a strategic alternative can often be obtained by averaging the betas of firms engaged exclusively, or almost exclusively, in the area of business associated with the strategic alternative. For example, IBM could use the beta for companies such as Ashton-Tate, Microsoft, and Lotus when evaluating a proposal to increase development and marketing effort of microcomputer software.

CAPM and Product-Market Diversification

An interesting aspect of the CAPM approach is its implications concerning the diversification of a business portfolio of product-market investments. Frequently, the strategic investment decisions made by a firm are related to investments made in securities traded on capital markets.[20] The use of this analogy suggests applying the Markowitz portfolio model to the business' strategic investment decisions—an application which suggests that business should seek diversification in product-market investments to reduce the systematic risk confronting the firm. However, this perspective fails to recognize that stockholders can diversify their portfolios more easily and efficiently than corporations. Diversification by a firm is not a value-creating activity as long as investors have no shortage of investment alternatives and no synergies between the new set of activities. In fact, such diversification may reduce the firm's stock price because of (1) the inefficiencies associated with diversifying a portfolio within the corporation, and (2) the limited option of the corporation as compared to the stock investor.

Consider the case of a commercial airline that wishes to expand its travel-related consumer services by providing hotel accommodations. The airline decides to enter the hotel market by acquiring a hotel chain. How will this acquisition be valued by the airline's stockholders? Will the airline's stock price increase after the acquisition?

The acquisition, even if it reduces the corporation's systematic risk, does not provide any benefit to the airline's stockholders. The airline's stockholders could have purchased shares directly in the hotel chain if they had wished to reduce the risk and increase return on their individual portfolios. The hotel chain acquisition will only provide benefits to the airline's shareholders, if the acquisition results in synergistic benefits that shareholders cannot realize by buying the stocks of individual companies. Thus, if the hotel chain acquisition increases hotel *and* airline sales by providing unique benefits to travellers by providing flight and accommodation packages, then the acquisition increases shareholder wealth. Stockholder wealth is increased by exploiting synergies among strategic opportunities. Firms should be concerned with maximizing return for a given systematic risk level, and not with minimizing covariance among strategic opportunities. However, rigorous application of the CAPM to intrafirm investments must not result in minimizing synergies by ignoring specific cost reductions (or revenue increases) caused by the existing asset position.

The marketing strategy undertaken by the Kellogg Company emphasizes the importance of maximizing returns at a specific systematic risk level rather than

[20]See Phillip Kotler, *Marketing and Decision Making,* New York, Holt, Rinehart and Winston, 1971. Mahajan, Vijay, Yoram Wind and John Bradford, "Stochastic Dominance Rules for Product Portfolio Analysis," *In* A. A. Zoltners (ed.), *Marketing Planning Models,* New York, North Holland.

diversification to reduce total risk. In 1978, 75% of Kellogg's revenues and 80% of its profits came from producing and marketing ready-to-eat breakfast cereal, mainly to children.   At this time, this product-market faced an uncertain future. Consumers were becoming aware of the health risks associated with presweetened cereals; the proportion of children in the general population was decreasing; the Federal Trade Commission was mounting antitrust legislation against the four major cereal manufacturers; and consumer advocates were suggesting strict limitations on advertising to children—the major promotion vehicle for cereals. Because of this increasing level of environmental uncertainty, General Mills and General Foods diversified into other product-markets.   These risks were specific to Kellogg's product-market and therefore almost exclusively nonsystematic.   However, Kellogg continued to make major investments in its cereal business and outperformed its competitors.   Kellogg was able to realize high return in its cereal investment strategy—returns that more than compensated for the systematic risk to which it was exposed.[21]

Criticism of Discounted Cash Flow Evaluation Models

Recently, Professors Hayes and Garvin[22] suggested that using the discounted cash flow techniques (discussed previously) has a conceptual weakness resulting in underinvestment in capital stock and unintentionally jeopardizing the future of companies. They suggest these factors that are causing underinvestment in existing businesses:

1. A perception that returns from present businesses have declined because of global competition, the nature of industry, and government intrusion. This perception is exacerbated by corrections for inflation which reduce profits, increase inventory and depreciation based on replacement costs, but fail to reduce the cost of debt. (There is debate in financial circles regarding whether the *risk-free* discount rate has genuinely risen [in real terms] and what the implications of such a rise are.)
2. A recognition that the value of present assets is declining rapidly because of the development of more energy efficiency.
3. An overestimate of the discount rate commensurate with the increasingly risky business environment.

   Although these factors reduce the level of investment in present business, based on discounted cash flow analysis, they do not indicate that the analysis technique itself is flawed. They simply indicate that the techniques are not being used properly. The discount rate is inappropriate and the cash flow projections from disinvestment or maintenance investment strategies are overestimated.

[21]"Kellogg Still the Cereal People," *Business Week,* November 26, 1979, pp. 80–93.

[22]Hayes, Robert H. and James Garvin, "Managing As If Tomorrow Mattered," *Harvard Business Review,* May–June, 1982, pp. 71–79.

Issues in Applying Financial Evaluation Models

The Hayes and Garvin critique reemphasizes that care must be taken in using financial models to evaluate strategic investment decisions. Four important issues to be considered are: (1) defining the base case, (2) using economic versus accounting evaluation of assets, (3) "unbundling" the costs and benefits of an investment alternative, and (4) distinguishing between direct and indirect costs and benefits.[23]

Base Case. Financial theory emphasizes that the basis for evaluating an investment opportunity should be *incremental* cash flow. One should spend as much time assessing the likely outcome if the investment were not made (the base case) as assessing the outcome if the investment were made. Frequently, managers implicitly assume that the base case is simply the continuation of the status quo. For example, the base case for the building block investment (Exhibit 8–1) was simply a projection of the present annual cash flow of $10 million eight years into the future.

A base case built simply on projections of the status quo often means that competitive behavior or projections of the market evolution are not being assessed correctly. In the building block example, the base case projection assumes that competitors will not invest in the line extensions and the advertising campaign and the market will not decrease.

Economic vs. Accounting Asset Evaluation. Accounting systems are designed to report and control the use of existing capital assets—not to make investment decisions in new assets. Although there are some differences between the accounting treatment of operating costs and revenues and the investment analysis of incremental cash flows, the major differences are in the treatment of capital assets.

In financial investment analysis, the value of a capital asset is a function of the present value of the cash flow it is expected to generate. In contrast, the accounting or book value of an asset is its initial cost reduced by depreciation. When investment decisions involve intangibles such as R&D, customer franchise (brand loyalty), or relationships with distribution channels, the differences between economic and accounting evaluation become extreme. Investments in these revenue-producing assets have no accounting value since they are typically treated as an expense.

Over time, all assets (both tangible and intangible) change in value. From an economic perspective, these changes are caused by changing technology, customer needs, and competitive activities—factors which alter the anticipated cash flows. However, from an accounting perspective, the value of an asset is altered by a predetermined depreciated schedule (with possibly some inflation adjustments)—an alteration that does not consider anticipated cash flows. These differences in asset evaluation arise because the accounting conventions are established to report and control, not to make, investment decisions.

Assets such as brand names, or plants acquired or disposed of as part of a

[23]Barwise, P., P. R. Marsh, and R. Wensley, "Must Finance and Marketing Clash?," *Harvard Business Review,* Vol. 67, September–October, 1989, pp. 85–90.

strategic investment decision should be evaluated on their market value, *not* their book value. However, markets for such assets are often imperfect and thus the market value considers what the "highest alternative bidder" would pay for the asset.

Unbundling Costs and Benefits.

Unbundling Costs and Benefits. Many strategic investment decisions involve a group of subinvestments. For example, a firm contemplating entering a new product market may consider subinvestments in a new sales force to develop and service a new distribution channel, R&D to design the product line, a new plant to manufacture the product, and training the service personnel.

Often these subinvestments are lumped together and not analyzed as separate investment decisions. This lumping together is appropriate in some cases because of savings resulting from joint costs or inherent indivisibilities. However, many investments can be unbundled. For example, in a new product-market entry situation, examination of subinvestments may indicate that a smaller investment in using independent agents rather than a direct sales force increases the overall attractiveness of the strategic opportunity.

Indirect and Direct Costs and Benefits. Many strategic investments offer returns over and above the specific opportunity being considered. For example, Renault argued that their investment in AMC in the United States would provide a basis for future expansion of U.S. sales through the AMC distribution channel. Thus the assets acquired by investing in AMC were not only just the cash flow from AMC's present product line but also the intangible assets (or synergies) involving AMC's relationships with its franchised dealers. The value of the intangible asset needs to be assessed in its impact on future sales of Renault cars in the United States. In making the analysis, the base case needs to be considered—what would Renault car sales be with and without the AMC distribution network?

Note that the common feature of these four issues is *incremental* cash flow. Each issue is related to the need to estimate the specific incremental value of an alternative and to relate this incremental value to its specific capital cost.

Financing Decisions and Sustainable Growth

The capital structure of a company is the balance between its debt and equity. This structure is based on financing decisions. From a financial analysis standpoint the debt-to-equity ratio is important because it summarizes the business risk (based on equity) relative to the financial risk (based on debt). Increasing debt may lead to higher after-tax cash flows, if low-cost debt is used. On the other hand, debt needs to be serviced and investors require a risk premium for it. This debt service has to come from cash flows. Also, growth is funded out of retained earnings and debt. Thus, the debt-equity ratio and the earnings-retention rate (dividend payment and thus earnings retention rate is also a major financing decision) impose a constraint on the growth that can be funded.

A simple formula for self-sustaining growth, assuming that the ratio of sales to investment is relatively stable, as well as a constant debt-equity ratio, a fixed overall rate of return on assets, and cost of capital, is given by Donaldson as:

$$g(s) = \gamma \, [RONA + d \, (RONA-i)] \qquad\qquad\qquad (4)$$

where:

$g(s)$	is the rate of monthly sales,
γ	is the rate of earnings retention,
d	is the debt-equity ratio,
i	is the after-tax rate of interest on debt, and
RONA	is the return on net assets or the return on investment.

The derivation of this formula is:

Total assets (A) are made up of total debt (D) and total equity (E).

$$A = D + E \qquad\qquad\qquad\qquad (5)$$

After-tax profits may be obtained by

$$\pi = (D + E) \bullet RONA - D \bullet i \qquad\qquad\qquad (6)$$

This may be rewritten as:

$$\pi = E \bullet RONA + D \, (RONA - i) \qquad\qquad\qquad (7)$$

Defining equity growth rate as the ratio of retained earnings to equity, it can be obtained as:

$$\frac{\gamma\pi}{E} = \gamma . RONA + \gamma \bullet \frac{D}{E} RONA - \gamma \frac{D}{E} i \qquad\qquad (8)$$

$$= \gamma \, [\, RONA + \frac{D}{E} (RONA - i)]$$

$$= \gamma \, [\, RONA + d \, (RONA - i)]$$

Given γ, d, i and RONA, the maximum growth rate that can be financed is given by the above formula (of these γ and d are financial decision variables). Thus an accurate forecast of sales from marketing is necessary for appropriate financing decisions and marketing strategy objectives are affected by financial strategy.

In the Donaldson and Lorsch study they found that six of the 12 companies studied used a formula related to the one given above. This indicates the appreciation by management of imposing a coherent discipline across the firm's various functional areas. They also report that many executives set market-share goals justified largely on the necessity of taking advantage of economies of scale. (However, they found that the key driver for this goal was really a desire to be seen as a winner, rather than the existence of economies of scale. In many cases the economies of scale were vague, if at all.) Setting a market-share goal automatically sets up a growth-rate goal, because to achieve a certain share gain (or to maintain it) implies a growth rate greater (or the same for maintaining position) than industry growth rate. This focus on market share and on being self-sustaining leads automatically to seeking an investment with a target rate of return, instead of an attempt to maximize shareholder wealth.

Joint Investment and Financing Decision

Investment and financing decisions are often made simultaneously and certainly interactively. An approach that allows the two to be combined is the adjusted present value (APV) technique. APV is given by adding the NPV of an investment, assuming that it is to be fully financed only through equity (or base-case NPV) and the net present value of the financing decision. Or,

$$\text{APV} = \text{base-case NVP} + \text{net present value of (benefits} - \text{costs)}$$
$$\text{of financing decisions caused by project acceptance}$$

Using this approach, only projects or marketing investments with a positive APV will be accepted. This rule captures both the investment and financing decisions and includes both the worth of the opportunity and its incremental financing costs and benefits. A simpler alternative to APV, used by some firms, is the use of an adjusted cost of capital for NPV calculations. The adjustment made to the cost of capital accounts for the project's financing costs also.

LIMITATIONS OF FINANCIAL EVALUATION MODELS

Financial evaluation models have strong conceptual support. The NPV criterion is consistent with the objective of maximizing stockholder wealth. The optimization procedure in the decision calculus models maximizes cash flow by allocating investments based on microeconomic principles. However, some practical problems arise when these approaches are used as the sole guide for strategic investment decisions.[24]

First, the uncritical use of these evaluation models often ignores important synergies between investment opportunities. Second, the models focus attention on the calculation of results rather than on the assumptions underlying the calculation.

Synergy

Synergies often arise between strategic opportunities. When a set of opportunities is funded, sales from the set may be higher or costs and investments lower than perhaps may be obtained from each opportunity individually.

Conceptually, discounted cash flow (DCF) and decision calculus can consider these potential synergies. The cash flows for investment opportunities could be

[24]Tilles, Seymour "Strategies for Allocating Funds," *Harvard Business Review,* January–February, 1966, pp. 72–80.

adjusted based on the set of opportunities funded, or opportunities that are highly synergistic could be combined and evaluated as a set. However, DCF evaluations typically examine one proposal at a time. Often, the proposals are generated by operating managers and tend to be narrowly focused. For example, a brand manager may suggest a significant increase in support for his or her brand, without considering the positive or negative impact on other brands in the firm's product line. The examination of individual proposals may not reveal broader strategic options such as divesting an entire group of brands.

STRATPORT, the decision calculus model to be discussed in the next chapter, takes a broader perspective; however, the model assumes that the activities of the business units are independent of each other. By incorporating interdependencies between units, the response functions become so complex that managerial judgment can no longer be used to measure the curves.

Inattention to Assumptions

To develop the cash flow estimates for a proposal, all of the benefits and costs of the proposal must be quantified. The mere process of summarizing each proposal with a calculated NPV may focus attention on selecting alternatives with favorable NPVs rather than on questioning the assumptions used to define the cash flows.

These assumptions in developing cash flows or estimating functional relationships are critical. There are significant uncertainties in forecasting cash flows and relationships over the investment planning time span. In addition, there are likely to be biases in these forecasts when proposals are generated by managers with a vested interest in the strategic decisions.

Any manager can develop a proposal that shows a positive net present value or provide input to a decision calculus model which will increase the level of funding for a business unit. The crucial questions are not whether the NPV (or APV) is positive or whether more funds should be directed to a business. The critical issue is what justifies the positive NPV (or APV) or the shape of response function? What is the strategic advantage supporting the financial evaluation? A critical examination of the key drivers and assumptions behind the decision is essential in making a strategically viable decision.

Concept Questions

1. Describe the financial models used for making capital allocation decisions.
2. What are the different investment criteria and how do they differ?
3. How is Net Present Value (NPV) related to shareholder wealth?
4. What is understood by the term value-drivers?
5. Describe the Capital Pricing Model (CAPM).
6. How are capital budgeting (allocation) decisions related to financing decisions?
7. What is understood by the term "real options"?

Discussion Questions

1. How would you choose a criterion for making financial investment decisions? Assuming that what you have chosen deviates from standard practice in your firm, how would you proceed?
2. Suggest and justify a method to identify the marketing value drivers. How would you suggest this information be used?
3. Discuss how you could use the concept of "real options."

APPENDIX: REAL OPTIONS

In stock market investing, an alternative to the purchase of shares is to purchase options on shares. In strategic marketing investments, and when faced both with limited windows of opportunity and considerable uncertainty, for example, in the semiconductor and electronics industries, investments may also be considered as options. Investments in "public relations" (lobbying groups, developing contacts with influential agents, and so on), test marketing, building pilot distribution channels, building multiple versions of product, building brand loyalty or equity, are also examples of options. Early investment buys time before the major commitment has to be made.

In financial management, two types of options are available. The first is the *put* option, or the selling option. This option gives the purchaser a contracted right to acquire from the seller (or writer of the option) the specified number of shares at the contracted price on or before a fixed time. (In Europe, the call and put options can be exercised only at the contracted time, whereas in the United States they can be exercised any time up to the expiration of the contract.)

In the marketing investment contract the relevant option is the *call* option or the option to enter a market, to use an agent, to obtain distribution, and so on.

The market price of a financial option is determined by:

1. The current price of the share under negotiation.
2. The price at which it is to be transferred.
3. The period of the option.
4. The underlying risk.
5. The prevailing risk-free rate of interest.

In marketing investment there is no current value like the current share price. However, the price of entry is expected to be a time variable which provides the risk. The rewards of entry may also be time variable and so also the risk. For the European call options and United States markets, precise mathematical valuation formulas have been derived by Black and Scholes. For details please see Black, F. and M. Scholes, "The Valuation of Option Contracts and a Test of Market Efficiency," *Journal of Finance,* Vol. 27, May, 1972; and Black, F. and M. Scholes, "The Pricing of Option Contracts and Corporate Liabilities," *Journal of Political Economy,* Vol. 81, May–June, 1973.

Marketing Example

Let us consider the decision by Mr. Kim Woo-Chung, of Daewoo, to enter the European market with PCs branded under Daewoo's own name (Chapter 1). The numbers used in our example are purely hypothetical and are not related to Daewoo's considerations.

Say Daewoo has forecast the after-tax operating cash flow and the capital investment needed to introduce the Daewoo line of PCs in Europe in 1994. These figures are provided in the following table.

Year	1994	1995	1996	1997	1998	1999
After-tax operating cash flow (1)	−200	+110	+159	+295	+185	0
Capital investments (2)	250	0	0	0	0	0
Increase in working capital (3)	0	50	100	100	−125	−125
Net cash flow (1)–(2)–(3)	−450	+60	+59	+195	+310	+125

NPV at 20% = −$46.5 million

From the net cash flow figures in this table, the NPV for a 20% hurdle rate comes to approximately −$46 million.

Considered alone, this certainly would not meet Daewoo's hurdle rate of 20%! However, consider that having introduced and built up the Daewoo brand of PCs would make it possible for Daewoo to introduce its Daewoo Plus brand of integrated communications and computing gear to other organizations and communication-computing and entertainment gear to individual consumers. If the decision of whether or not to invest in the introduction of Daewoo Plus has to be made in 1997, that is, in three years, then the current investment in Daewoo PCs can also be thought of as an option to introduce Daewoo Plus later. The value of this option is obtained as follows:

Assumptions

1. The decision to introduce a new series of integrated communication-computers (Daewoo Plus) and communication-computers-entertainment products would be made after three years—in 1997.

2. The Daewoo Plus investment is double the size of the initial Daewoo investment in building a brand in Europe. The investment required is, say, $900 million.

3. Forecasted cash inflows of the Daewoo Plus are also double those of the initial entry, with present value of about $800 million in 1997 and $800 m/$(1.2)^3$ = $463 in 1994.

4. The future value of the Daewoo Plus cash flows is highly uncertain. This

value evolves like a stock price does with a standard deviation of 35% per year.

Interpretation

The opportunity to invest in the Daewoo Plus is a three year call option on an asset worth $463 million with a $900 million exercise price (investment necessary to introduce Daewoo Plus).

Valuation

$$\text{Standard deviation} \times \sqrt{\text{time}} = .35 \times \sqrt{3} \tag{1}$$

$$\frac{\text{Asset Value}}{\text{PV (exercise price)}} = \frac{463}{900/(1.1)^3} = 0.68 \tag{2}$$

Based on (1) and (2) from a call options value table based on the Black-Scholes model, obtain the following ratio:

$$\frac{\text{Call Value}}{\text{Asset Value}} = 0.119 \tag{3}$$

$$\text{Call Value} = 0.119 \times 463 = 55.1 \text{ or} \tag{4}$$
$$\text{approximately \$55 million}$$

Assuming that Daewoo Plus cannot be introduced in 1997 without Daewoo PCs having been introduced in 1994, under the above conditions, the call option value to invest in Daewoo Plus is worth $55 million. The total value of Daewoo Plus is approximately $55 million − $46 million, or approximately $9 million. This makes the decision to invest in Daewoo PC for Europe a strategically sound one.

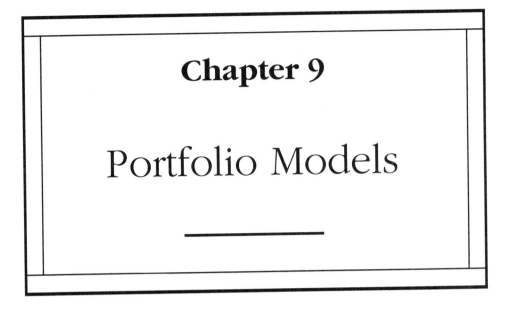

Chapter 9

Portfolio Models

INTRODUCTION

Most firms have a variety of financial opportunities in which they can invest. In the previous chapter, we discussed how financial analysis and value-based planning are used to evaluate opportunities and to determine the appropriate level of resources to allocate to a given opportunity. Although the discounted cash flow (DCF) approach has strong theoretical support, managers have recognized that problems arise when NPV calculations are used as the sole criterion for making strategic investment decisions.

To evaluate an investment using DCF, all the associated benefits and costs need to be quantified and an NPV calculated. This quantification process often focuses on the relative NPV of the opportunity rather than on stimulating an analysis on the underlying assumptions used to generate the numbers. These supporting assumptions are crucial because significant uncertainties exist in forecasting investment levels, revenues, and costs over the long-term. There are also likely to be biases in these forecasts when the financial analysis is done by managers with a vested interest in the strategic decision.

Another limitation of DCF is that the analysis often fails to consider potential synergies between opportunities, particularly when the analysis is performed by operating managers. For example, a brand manager may be able to justify financially a significant increase in support for the brand, without having considered the negative impact on other brands.

Even managers with limited experience in finance know how to adjust their forecasts to get a positive NPV. The crucial issue is not whether the NPV is positive but rather what *justifies* the positive NPV. What is the strategic opportunity that enables a firm to realize a positive NPV? The limitations of the DCF model were particularly apparent to corporate executives of large, diversified firms in the early 1970s. Many firms had acquired an array of businesses but because of a recession, they also faced financial problems. Corporate strategists were anxious to find approaches that enabled them to evaluate various opportunities and to determine which businesses should receive funds and which should be divested. Portfolio models provide a convenient method to evaluate available investment opportunities as well as factors associated with superior long-term performance. By 1979, 36% of the Fortune "1000" and 45% of the Fortune "500" companies were using some form of portfolio models in developing corporate strategy.[1] Portfolio models spawned a new vocabulary for strategic planners, introducing terms such as "cash cows," "dogs," and "harvesting." Although the usefulness of these models has been questioned over the last ten years, portfolio models continue to be used in developing marketing strategy. They are generally used in two ways. The first as a framework in developing priorities among product lines. The second is in understanding or anticipating the priorities attached by competitors to their products. The latter requires knowing the priority allocation mechanism used by competitors and then using this mechanism on their product portfolios.

We concentrate here on the two most widely used portfolio models—the Boston Consulting Group (BCG) market growth–market share matrix and the market attractiveness-business competitiveness matrix developed jointly by McKinsey and General Electric—and briefly discuss other portfolio models. We also discuss some limitations of each. Finally, we describe an operational model for resource allocation called STRATPORT (developed by Professors Srinivasan and Larreche) which uses the BCG framework as its core. This model illustrates how such models may be built and used.

USING PORTFOLIO MODELS FOR STRATEGY DEVELOPMENT

Using a portfolio model to make strategic decisions involves (1) defining the set of strategic alternatives to be considered, (2) assessing each alternative for long-term performance potential, and (3) classifying each alternative based on this assessment and allocating sufficient resources based on the classification.[2]

Defining Strategic Alternative

The definition of opportunities depends on the level in the firm at which the portfolio analysis is being applied. At the corporate level, the opportunities might be defined in organizational units associated with different product categories or market segments. For example, Procter & Gamble might define its opportunities as paper products, coffee,

---

[1]Phillippe Haspeslagh, "Portfolio Planning: Uses and Limits," *Harvard Business Review,* January–February 1982, pp. 58–61.

[2]See Yoran Wind and Vijay Mahajan, "Designing Product and Business Portfolios," *Harvard Business Review,* January–February 1981, pp. 155–165.

cake mixes, toothpaste-mouthwash, soaps-shampoos, and detergent-cleansers. As a
multinational firm, P&G might supplement this product-based definition with opportunities in different markets in the United States, Europe, Japan, Africa, and Asia. At a lower
organizational level, the manager of P&G's detergent and cleansers might define opportunities as brands such as Tide, Ivory Snow, and Cheer; forms such as liquid, powder, and
tablets; or usage such as laundry, dishwashing, and household cleaning.

Traditionally, generating alternative opportunities has been aided by a market product two-by-two matrix (Exhibit 9–1).[3] The four boxes (cells) of this matrix represent the
four strategic growth alternatives of Product Development (new product for an existing
market), Market Development (an existing product launched into new markets), Market
Penetration (old products more intensively marketed in existing markets), and
Diversification (new product in a new market). New markets mean new customers.
They can be new international markets, new segments, and so forth. An example of a
more elaborate version of such a two-dimensional portrayal of opportunities is shown in
Exhibit 9–2.[4] The axes are labeled as Product Differentiation and Market Differentiation.
Differentiation refers to differences from (or with) existing products-markets. Increasing
differentiation is more risky but with possibly higher rewards. In portfolio building and
resource allocating, this matrix considers the risk-reward trade-offs of pursuing alternative
growth paths. It has not been formally analyzed, nor has it been viewed traditionally in
building a portfolio. Guidelines do not exist regarding the mixture of efforts in each box
of Exhibit 9–1. However, it forces a choice to see if offering strengths, or existing marketing relationships should be built or whether skills at both innovating offerings and relationships should form the basis of growth.

Defining strategic opportunities for portfolio analysis is more art than science.
Although the analysis can be performed at all corporate levels, one needs to avoid levels of aggregation which combine unrelated and dissimilar products—market opportunities are considered together and levels of disaggregation in which highly related,
synergistic product-markets are treated as separate opportunities.

EXHIBIT 9–1   Traditional Growth Opportunities Matrix

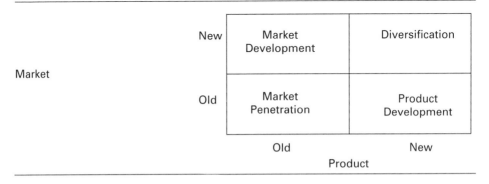

[3]Ansoff, I., "Strategies for Diversification," *Harvard Business Review,* September–October, 1957,
p. 114.

[4]Alterowitz, R. and Zonderman, J., *New Corporate Ventures,* New York, Wiley, 1988.

Evaluation of Alternatives

Each portfolio model specifies two or three dimensions on which the alternatives are evaluated and eventually classified.   These dimensions are used to assess the long-term profit potential of the alternatives.   Although the various models incorporate different dimensions, each model suggests that the factors used to assess the position of an alternative on a dimension are useful predictors of the alternative's future performance.[5]

EXHIBIT 9–2

IBM New Business Activity

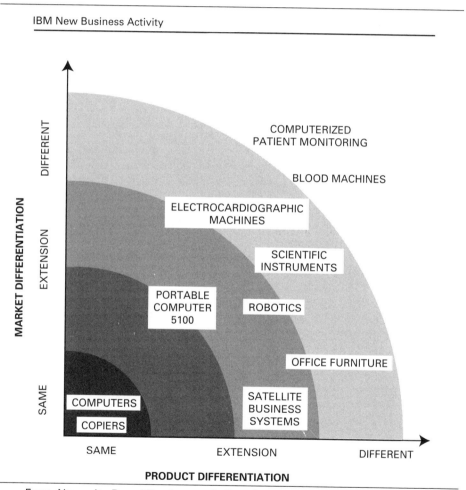

PRODUCT DIFFERENTIATION

From Alterowitz, R. and Zonderman, F. *New Corporate Ventures,* 1988. Reprinted with permission by John Wiley & Sons.

[5]See Bruce D. Henderson, *The Product Portfolio,* Boston, Boston Consulting Group, 1970 and Barry Hedley, "Strategy and the 'Business Portfolio,'" *Long Range Planning,* 10, February 1977, pp. 9–15.

Classification of Alternatives

Based on the evaluation, each alternative is positioned in a two or three dimensional space. Based on the position, the alternatives are classified in four to 16 categories. The appropriate level of investment and strategic objective are matched with each category. Therefore the portfolio model shows a resource allocation pattern across alternatives based on the classification of the alternatives.

BCG GROWTH-MARKET SHARE PORTFOLIO MODEL

History

The genesis of the BCG matrix is traced to a consulting project done by Alan Zakon of BCG for the Mead Paper Corporation in the late 1960s.[6] Zakon was concerned with the nature of Mead's paper business. He assessed this business as having high growth potential. However, to realize this potential would require a considerable infusion of cash. He conceived the need for a balance in businesses that were "cash deficient" and "growth deficient." Mead's William Wommack, to whom the ideas were first presented, liked them but asked for an elaboration. In discussions with a financial specialist, Zakon realized a link existed between his idea and different financial instruments. Thus was born the first BCG portfolio matrix, albeit without names for the two dimensions and the categories. Bruce Henderson, the founder of BCG, saw a link between this matrix and the experience curve concept he had developed based on his work with the Norton Company in the late 1960s. This was the beginning of the BCG portfolio matrix as it is popularly taught and used.

Dimensions

The growth-share portfolio model (Exhibit 9–3) focuses on the cash generating and cash use of strategic alternatives. In this model each strategic alternative is classified using market growth and relative market share.

   Relative Market Share. Relative market share, the horizontal axis in the growth-share matrix, represents the degree to which the firm has a cost advantage over its competition with respect to opportunity. High relative share indicates greater cumulative experience and lower cost. Relative share indicates position on the experience curve of relative competition. When experience-curve effects are important, alternatives with high share will have high positive cash flows because of their low-cost position.

   Relative share as used in the growth-share matrix is the strategic alternative's share divided by the share of its largest competitor. Based on this definition, if the alternative is not number one in its market, its relative share will be less than 1.0; if it is number one, its relative share will be greater than 1.0. For example, the market

[6]This story is detailed in Morrison, A. and R. Wensley, "Boxing Up or Boxed In?: A Short History of the Boston Consulting Group Share/Growth Matrix," Coventry, United Kingdom, Warwick Business School, 1990.

EXHIBIT 9–3   Henderson's Growth-Share Matrix

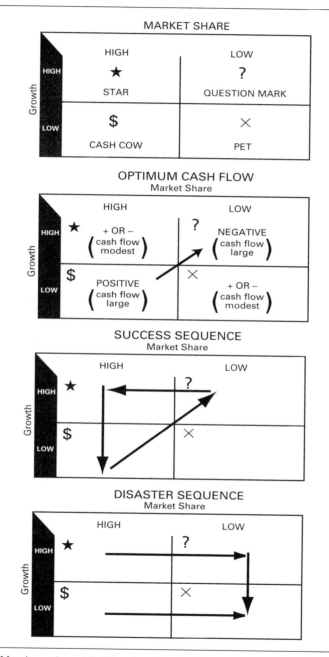

From Morrison, A. and R. Wensley, "Boxing Up or Boxed In?: A Short History of the Boston Consulting Group Share/Growth Matrix," Coventry, United Kingdom, Warwick Business School, 1990.

share for the three leading brands of ready-to-eat breakfast cereal are: Kellogg's Corn Flakes 16%, Wheaties 9%, and Cheerios 6%. The relative share of Kellogg's Corn Flakes is 1.8 (16% ÷ 9%) and the relative share of Cheerios is .38 (6% ÷ 16%). When an alternative is number one in a market, the largest competitor is number two. When an alternative is not number one, the market leader is the largest competitor.

Typically, relative market share (the horizontal axis) is plotted on a logarithmic scale. A log scale is used so that comparisons between alternatives are shown in percentages rather than in absolute differences. Thus, the movement of equal distances along the horizontal axis represents equal percentage gains or losses in relative market share.

Market Growth Rate.   Market growth rate (the vertical axis) is a rough indicator of product life-cycle stage. Alternatives in high growth markets typically consume large amounts of cash because they build new facilities and finance inventory and receivables to supply a growing market. Strategic alternatives in mature, low-growth markets demand additional working and fixed capital.

Market growth rate may also affect the ease with which firms can gain market share. Alternatives in high-growth markets may be able to increase share because of the general instability in the market. Also, competitive reactions might not be as strong, because competitors are still growing even though a firm that is increasing share will be growing at a greater rate. In low-growth markets, any increase in share often results in a decline in competitor's sales because the size of the market is relatively stable. Competitors faced with a decline in sales and lower capacity use will probably react vigorously, making it costly to continue increasing share.

Each alternative is plotted on the matrix based on relative market share and market growth rate. Frequently, the alternatives are represented as circles with the area of the circle proportional to the sales volume of the alternative. The size of the circle gives an indication of the importance of the alternative to overall firm sales.

Classification of Alternatives

The matrix in the top panel of Exhibit 9–3 is divided into four quadrants. Alternatives falling into these quadrants are referred to as stars, problem children, dogs, and cash cows. The horizontal line divides the alternatives plotted in the space into high- and low-growth markets. Typically, this line is set at 10%—the nominal level for GNP (Gross National Product) growth (inflation rate plus real GNP growth rate). However, placement of this line can be modified by unique characteristics confronting the firm such as industry growth rate or company growth objectives. For example, an analysis of pharmaceutical alternatives might use 15% as a dividing point, while Eastman Kodak might use 6%.

The vertical line is typically set at 1.0 relative share and thus divides the alternatives that are market leaders and followers. Often, another vertical line is placed to a 1.5 relative market share based on the assumption that market dominance (and a sustainable cost advantage) is only achieved by opportunities with at least 50% greater share than their largest competitor.

Cash Flow Patterns.   Based on the implications of market growth and relative market share, the expected cash flow pattern depends on the quadrant in which the alternative is classified.   Alternatives are classified as cash cows if they have the largest market share in a low growth market.   These alternatives should generate significant cash flow because their need for cash to support growth is limited but they generate substantial cash because of their low costs and high margins.   Stars dominate alternatives in high growth markets and also generate substantial cash, but their net cash flow is usually zero because they use considerable cash to fund their growth.

Both problem children and dogs generate limited cash because of their poor cost position relative to competition.   Dogs have a zero net cash flow because they do not need much cash since they are not growing.   However, problem children have a substantial negative cash flow because they use considerable cash to maintain their position in a growing market.   This negative cash flow is even greater when additional resources are being used to increase market share.   Even though dogs have a zero net cash flow, they are considered to be cash traps[7] because they are unlikely ever to become significant cash generators because of difficulty of gaining share in mature markets.   However, problem children may become cash cows eventually if they achieve a dominant position while the market is growing rapidly.

It is important to recognize that the classification of an alternative suggests its cash flow pattern.   However, the firm's investment decision can result in the actual cash flow differing from the typical pattern.   For example, a firm realizes a positive cash flow from a problem child if it decides to liquidate the business.   The cash flow from a cash cow would be significantly below expectations if a firm decided to invest in the opportunity to gain share.

Strategic Guidelines Based on the Growth-Share Matrix

The fundamental objective of the BCG growth-share model is to maintain a portfolio of strategic opportunities which balances the cash flow of a firm.   Some opportunities, for example, cash cows, generate cash which is used to fund the growth of opportunities that need cash—problem children.

Over time, the position of all opportunities moves from the top to the bottom of the matrix.   This movement represents the decline in market growth as a market progresses from the growth stage in the product life cycle through maturity to decline.   Given this inevitable decline in market growth, it is critical to maintain or achieve a dominant position in a market.   A successful strategic sequence for a problem child is shown in the lower panels of Exhibit 9–3.   In this sequence, cash generated by a cash cow is used to increase the relative market share of a problem child.   The problem child eventually achieves a dominant share while the market is still growing and becomes a star.   As the market growth rate declines, the star becomes a cash cow if its dominant position is maintained.   A disaster sequence arises when the market share of a star erodes when the star becomes a problem child and eventually a dog.   This sequence is a disaster because the investment opportunity never achieves a position in which it can generate cash to fund the growth of the firm.

[7]Henderson, Bruce "Cash Traps," Boston, Boston Consulting Group, 1973.

To plan for and achieve a positive cash flow, the firm should have a balanced portfolio of some cash cows to generate cash which will be used to fund the growth of stars and the share-gaining activities of some problem children. Most balanced portfolios also have some dogs because these alternatives represent investments in risky opportunities that have been unsuccessful. The absence of dogs indicates an inappropriately conservative bias in making strategic investments. Based on the objectives that underlie the BCG growth-share matrix, the specific strategic objectives for opportunities in each category are discussed.

Cash Cows-Leaders in Low-Growth Markets. The primary objective for a cash cow is to maintain its dominant position, thus ensuring cash flow generating capabilities. The term "cash cows" suggests that these businesses are "milked." The firm also must realize that these cows have to be fed or else the milk will stop. For example, the passenger tire business is a cash cow in Goodyear's portfolio, but Goodyear continues plant modernization to improve tire performance so that it can maintain its dominant position.

Although some level of investment in cash cows is required, firms should resist the temptation to overinvest. Because it is both costly and difficult to gain share in low-growth markets, excessive investment may not produce commensurate returns. In managing a cash cow one is constantly faced with balancing the need to invest adequately to maintain dominant share against the need to avoid overinvestment which reduces cash flow needed to support stars and problem children.

Stars—Leaders in High-Growth Markets. The primary objective of a star is to maintain or improve its dominant position. Because stars are in high-growth markets, there is little danger in overinvesting in this type of opportunity.

Problem Children—Followers in High-Growth Markets. The firm can go in either of two directions concerning problem children—invest heavily enough in a problem child to gain a dominant position or phase out the business. The phase out may be accomplished by selling the business or realizing a temporary increase in cash flow as market share is allowed to decline. The later pattern of resource allocation and share objectives over time is referred to as a harvesting strategy.

Dogs—Followers in Low-Growth Markets. Since dogs have little opportunity to achieve a dominant position, the strategic directions for dogs are (1) divest the business, (2) harvest the business, or (3) reposition the business. Repositioning involves reducing the scope of the business—redefining a narrower target market opportunity that the firm can dominate. For example, a dog can become a star by focusing on and achieving dominance in a fast-growing regional market rather than by continuing to be a follower in a mature national market. The issues discussed earlier concerning defendability must be considered. This narrowing of focus can only be effective if the position in the new target-market can be defended against competition operating with a broader focus.

Empirical Research Concerning the Growth-Share Matrix

A study by Hambrick, MacMillan, and Day[8] of 1028 businesses supports the primary theme of the BCG growth-share matrix. The four types of investment opportunities have significantly different cash flow patterns (Exhibit 9–4). Cash cows are the largest net generators of cash, while problem children are the largest net users. Surprisingly, the typical dogs seem to generate as much cash (3.4%) as the typical problem child uses (–2.7%). The standard deviation of cash flow-investment for dogs indicates that about 15% of the dogs generate significant cash—greater than 18% of sales. This finding does not support the prescription that dogs should be divested or harvested.

Dominant businesses (stars and cash cows) clearly have greater ROIs than follower businesses (problem children and dogs). However, ROI is measured as current profits divided by current assets and may not reflect the anticipated return based on projected cash flows. Exhibit 9–4 also indicates that firms make their greatest investments in assets, marketing expenses, and R&D in businesses in high growth markets.

Although this study supports the contention that the four BCG categories differ in cash flow generation and use, on average the standard deviations for the performance measures are quite high. The variables used to classify strategic opportuni-

EXHIBIT 9–4   Performance of Four Categories of Businesses in BCG Matrix

Performance Measure	Cash Cows (%)	Stars (%)	Problem Children (%)	Dogs (%)
Return on Investment (ROI)	30.0* (22.7)*	29.6 (22.6)	20.6 (24.5)	18.5 (21.7)
Cash Flow/Assets	10.0 (17.0)	0.7 (18.3)	–2.7 (18.8)	3.4 (16.2)
ROI/ROI Variability	4.6 (4.1)	4.0 (5.2)	2.4 (3.6)	2.8 (4.7)
Market-Share Change	0.4 (2.3)	0.7 (3.0)	0.4 (1.8)	0.1 (1.6)
Business Attributes				
Process and Product R&D Sales	2.3	3.9	3.5	2.3
Sales Force & Advertising/Sales	5.7	6.3	7.5	6.1
Investment/Sales	51.4	63.2	63.9	56.1

*mean (standard deviation)

Adapted from Donald C. Hambrick, Ian C. MacMillian and Diana Day, "Strategic Attributes and Performance in the BCG Matrix—A PIMS-Based Analysis of Industrial Product Businesses," *Academy of Management Journal*, Vol. 25, No. 3, pp. 510–531.

[8]Hambrick, Donald C. Ian C. MacMillian and Diana L. Day, "Strategic Attributes and Performance in the BCG Matrix—A PIMS-Based Analysis of Industrial Product Businesses," *Academy of Management Journal*, Vol. 25, No. 3, 1982, pp. 510–531.

ties—market growth and relative share—account for only a limited amount of variance in business performance.

Criticism of the Market Growth-Market Share Matrix

The market growth-market share matrix has received substantial acceptance and has spawned a new vocabulary for marketing strategy; but it is not universally accepted.[9] Concerns about the validity of the model center on the following basic premises to the model.

Factors.   The matrix assumes that relative market share and long-term market growth are the most important considerations in making strategic marketing decisions. By focusing on these factors, the BCG product portfolio approach ignores factors related to performance such as risk, customer loyalty, channel control, and market structure.

Cash Flow and Market Share.   Cash flow is assumed to be a function of relative market share. Relative market share represents competitive position on the relevant experience curve. Although there is empirical support that a business with the most experience in a product-market has lower costs, there are a number of product-markets in which the effects of experience are quite weak. There are also situations in which market share is a poor indicator of relative cost. For example, Apple had the largest market share in personal computers, but when IBM entered the market it may have had the lowest cost because of experience gained through manufacturing larger computers.

Gaining Share.   It is assumed to be "easier" to gain share in high-growth markets. This premise is based on the assumption that competitive reaction is greater in a mature market. Building on this assumption, the prescriptions of the market growth-market share matrix indicate that strategic investments be restricted to high-growth product-markets (stars or problems). But there is little evidence to support this premise. Many managers are wary of restricting investments to high-growth markets. Roy Ash followed a course of investing in high-growth, high-technology businesses when he was CEO of AM International. This strategy resulted in the near collapse of AM. Richard Black, who replaced Ash,

> . . . favors a slower, more methodical growth strategy. He sees great appeal in businesses that operate in markets growing at a 3 percent to 5 percent annual rate. "If you've got a 30 percent to 40 percent growth business, you've got everybody looking at the business and jumping in," he explains. "I have nothing against high technology, but why do I want to get into a pot-limit poker game (such as word processing) with giant companies that have money coming out of their ears?. . ."[10]

Cash Balance.   The model emphasizes that a company should be in cash balance. Although the market growth-market share model does not preclude raising cash

[9]Wind and Mahajan, *op. cit.,* 1981.
[10]*Business Week,* January 25, 1982, p. 63.

externally, there is an implied assumption that cash must be generated from some product-markets (cash cows) to fund growth and share-gaining activities in other product-markets (problems and stars). Thus the portfolio of product-market opportunities needs to be balanced between problems, stars, and cash cows. However, many companies make strategic investments with funds raised externally rather than internally.

Synergies. Interdependencies among product-markets are limited to the generation and use of cash. The product portfolio approach treats each strategic alternative as an independent unit. The business unit manager manages a portfolio of product-markets just as a mutual fund manager manages a portfolio of stocks. This perspective ignores potential synergies among product-markets, such as shared experience. Such synergies often are the basis of unique competitive advantages that determine why one company is successful in a product-market and another is not.[11]

In addition to these conceptual concerns, there are implementation problems in using portfolio models to classify products. It is often difficult to define the unit of analysis and measure its position. There are also administrative problems in aligning the objective for the product managers with their rewards. The manager of a cash cow should not be rewarded on the basis of growth. The manager of a problem child should not be rewarded on the basis of profitability. Such reward structures result in managerial decisions that run counter to the generation of cash or to the achievement of a dominant market position. Finally, assigning labels to product-markets may lead to a self-fulfilling prophecy which precludes investigating new directions which might alter the long-term prospects in the product-market.[12]

To manage in a changed business environment and in response to the possibilities for misuse inherent in their earlier matrix, BCG developed a new matrix.[13] The new focus was to gain competitive advantage. This is reflected in the dimensions of the new matrix: size of the advantage that a firm would have in a particular business or opportunity, and the number of approaches available to achieve advantage. These two dimensions describe the possible competitive structures that would emerge. The relationship between return on investment (ROI) and market share could be predicted based on the competitive structure for businesses in each of the four boxes of Exhibit 9–5A. These relationships are shown in Exhibit 9–5B. Note that only for the large-size advantage and few-approaches-to-achieving-advantage box would the market-share leadership and cost-reduction strategies still be meaningful.

[11]See Robin Wensley, "Strategic Marketing: Betas, Boxes, and Basics," *Journal of Marketing,* Vol. 45, Summer, 1981, pp. 173–182.

[12]See George Day, "Diagnosing the Product Portfolio," *Journal of Marketing,* Vol. 41, April, 1977, pp. 29–38.

[13]This discussion is based on Hax, A. C. and N. S. Majluf, *Strategic Management: An Integrative Perspective,* Englewood Cliffs, NJ, Prentice-Hall, 1984, pp. 151–152.

EXHIBIT 9–5A   The New BCG Matrix

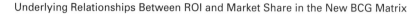

Number of approaches to achieve advantage	Many	Fragmented	Specialization
	Few	Stalemate	Volume

Small   Large

Size of the Advantage

EXHIBIT 9–5B   Concept Tools for Strategic Planning

Underlying Relationships Between ROI and Market Share in the New BCG Matrix

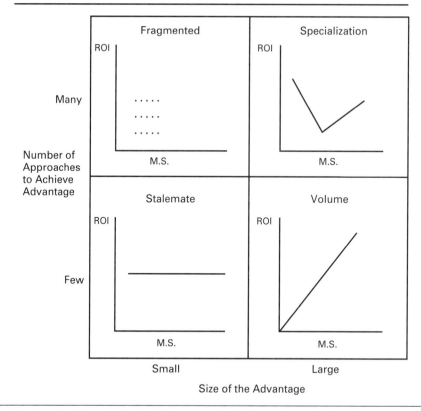

Size of the Advantage

Reprinted with permission from Prentice-Hall, Inc., Hart, A. C. and N. S. Majlof, *Strategic Management: An Integrative Perspective,* 1984, p. 152.

In closing, we add the results of a recent survey by Professors McCabe and Narayanan[14]

> Thus even though the formal use of portfolio models is on the decline in our sample, almost one in four of the companies surveyed (24%) continue to use an explicit portfolio model and perhaps as many as another one in four use portfolio logic implicitly in their planning.

MARKET ATTRACTIVENESS–COMPETITIVE POSITION MATRIX

The market attractiveness-business strength matrix was developed by General Electric Company (GE) and McKinsey & Company, a management consulting firm. GE corporate planners felt it was simplistic to make important investment decisions based on only two factors—market growth and relative market share. They therefore developed the matrix shown in Exhibit 9–6. Variations of this model have been developed by Royal Dutch Shell (Directional Policy Matrix) and Arthur D. Little (Industry Maturity–Competitive Position Matrix).

EXHIBIT 9–6   General Electric's Multifactor Portfolio Matrix

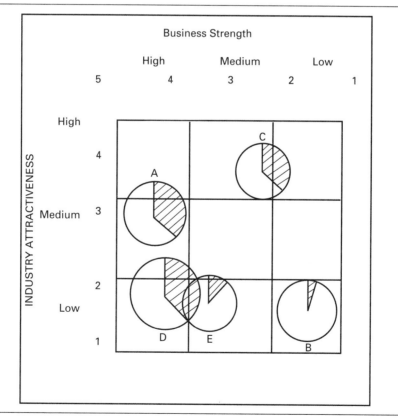

---

[14]This survey is reported in McCabe, D. L. and V. K. Narayanan, "The Life Cycle of the PIMS and BCG Models," *Industrial Marketing Management,* Vol. 20, 1991, p. 351.

Dimensions.   The basis of this matrix is that the long-term profitability of an investment alternative is a function of the attractiveness of the market in which the business operates.   This and the business position relative to other competitors' position are assessed using multiple factors.   For example, in 1981, GE used the following factors to assess each of their businesses on these two dimensions.

Market Attractiveness	*Competitive Position*
Market size	U.S. share of market
Market growth	World share of market
Profitability	Share growth
Cyclability	Relative market share
Ability to recover from inflation	Relative quality
World scope	Relative technology
	Relative costs
	Relative marketing
	Relative profitability

Evaluation and Classification of Alternatives

Evaluation.   The market attractiveness-competitive position matrix does not prescribe the factors to be used to evaluate each alternative on the two dimensions. Each firm determines the specific factors to be used based on the markets, competition, and elements critical to performance of the set of alternatives being considered. The factors and scoring scheme used by Shell to evaluate international opportunities for chemicals in Western Europe are shown in Exhibit 9–7.

These examples illustrate the variety of applications and considerations that can be incorporated into a market attractiveness–competitive position matrix.   In the Shell example, the unit of analysis is different petroleum-based chemical products sold in the Western Europe market.   The Ford example considers only one product, tractors, and treats each country in Western Europe as a different market. Since both examples deal with export markets, the regulatory environment was a factor used to evaluate market attractiveness.   However, some factors were idiosyncratic to the particular alternatives being considered.   The availability of feedstock is particularly important to a chemical manufacturer, whereas quality and quantity of distributors and service are important to a manufacturer of agricultural equipment.

Although the factors used to evaluate market attractiveness and competitive position vary, managers need to consider carefully which factors to include and how to weight them.   The choice of factors reflects management views of the key market and business factors influencing long-term profitability.

EXHIBIT 9–7   Factors Used by Shell to Evaluate Chemical Products in Western Europe

Market Attractiveness (weight)		*Competitive Position* (weight)	
Growth Rate (% per year)	(weight=5)	Market Position (9)	
0–2	0 (minimum)	leader	4
2–4	1	one of two to four major producers	3
4–5	2 (average)	strong stake, but below top producers	2
5–7	3	minor share	1
7 and over	4 maximum	no current position	0

Market Quality (5)

a. Has the business sector a record of high and stable profitability?

b. Can margins be maintained when there is an excess of manufacturing capacity over demand?

c. Is the product such that it is not susceptible to commodity pricing behavior?

d. Is the technology of production restricted to those who developed it?

e. Is the market supplied by relatively few producers?

f. Is the market free from domination by a small group of powerful customers?

g. Has the product high added value when converted by the customer?

h. In the case of a new product, is the market destined to remain limited in absolute magnitude such that it will not attract too many producers?

i. Is the product one where the customer has to change formulation or even machinery if he changes supplier?

j. Is the product free from the risk of substitution by an alternative synthetic or natural product?

Zero to four points based on number of "yes" responses.

Industry Feedstock (5)

a. Is the feedstock in balance with demand?

b. If additional feedstock is available, is it widely scattered in less than economic quantities?

c. Is the feedstock difficult to transport?

d. Is the feedstock likely to be a surplus by-product?

e. Is there a strong alternative use for it?

f. Is the technology of producing the feedstock restricted?

Zero to four based on the number of "yes" responses.

Regulatory Aspects (5)

As with the other criteria the scale of points runs from zero to four with two points for cases in which there is no regulatory influence or in which any influences are fully incorporated in market growth, research effort and price-cost relationships.

Marketing Capability (4)

0 to 4 points based Distribution channels, commercial relationships with customers, and credit control.

Production Capabilities (4)

a. Does the producer employ a modern economic production process?

b. Does the producer own the process?

c. Has the producer the R&D capability or licensing relationships that will allow keeping up with advances in process technology.

(Cont. on next page)

d. Is current capacity, plus any new capacity announced-building, commensurate with maintaining present market share?

e. Does the producer have several plant locations to provide security to customers against breakdown or strike action?

f. Are the producer's logistics to principal markets competitive?

g. Has the producer secure access to enough feedstock to sustain present share?

h. Does the product have a favorable cost position on feedstock?

Zero to four points based on number of "yes" responses.

Product R&D

Much better than competition	4
Better	3
Same as	2
Worse	1
Much worse	0

Classification.   Each alternative is evaluated on each factor, evaluations are multiplied by the weight assigned to the factor, and an overall score is calculated on the two dimensions.   For example, the weights used for calculating the score on business attractiveness for Ford tractors in a country are:

Country Attractiveness = Market Size + 2 × Market Growth + (.5 × Price Control/ Regulation) + .25 × Homologation Requirements + .25 × Local Content and Compensatory Report Requirements) + (.35 × Inflation + .35 × Trade Balance + .3 × Political Factors).

The alternatives are then plotted on the matrix.   Exhibit 9–8 illustrates the position of country alternative for Ford tractors.

Strategic Directions.   Strategic prescription alternatives falling into each of the nine cells are shown in Exhibit 9–8.   The highest levels of investment are directed toward opportunities classified in the three upper left cells—the opportunities with a stronger competitive position in attractive markets.   Opportunities falling in the upper right hand corner receive limited investment to maintain position and maximize cash flow.   Investments for opportunities in the other two diagonal boxes are directed toward locating and dominating market niche.   Minimal investments are made in opportunities that fall in the three lower right cells.

Limitations of Market Attractiveness-Competitive Position Matrix

The market attractiveness-competitive position matrix considers a broader range of variables for evaluating strategic alternatives.   In using this matrix many market and environmental characteristics in addition to long-term growth are used to assess the attractiveness of a market. Similarly, the assessment of competitive position canin-corporate technological, financial, management, and marketing capabilities in addition to relative market share and its related cost advantage. However, the assessment of position along the two dimensions is highly subjective. The set of variables to be considered are determined by the firm, thus the ultimate classification may simply reflect preconceived evaluations. While this approach can be useful in evaluating alternatives, the strategic insight provided may be limited to a rather mundane conclusion that a firm should invest heavily in attractive product-markets in which the firm possesses a strong competitive advantage.

COMPARISON OF FINANCIAL ANALYSIS AND PORTFOLIO MODELS

An evaluation of the resource allocation models discussed is shown in Exhibit 9–9. Each approach is evaluated on: (1) the quality of the theoretical support for the model, (2) the empirical evidence supporting critical assumptions, and (3) the degree to which the model focuses on the critical issue of making investment opportunities in which the firm has or can develop a sustainable competitive advantage.

Although the dimensions of the market growth-market share matrix are based on a theory defining a basis of competitive advantage and competitive market behavior, the assumptions of the theory are questionable and the empirical support limited. Whereas the discounted cash flow analysis and the market attractiveness-competitive advantage matrix focus on issues of competitive advantage, neither model assists a manager in identifying the basis of competitive advantage or in assessing the degree to which competitive advantage can be exploited.

There is considerable difference among the portfolio models and the discounted cash flow model in the unit of analyses. Typically, discounted cash flow models are used to evaluate individual projects whereas portfolio models are applied to higher levels of aggregation. For example, Eastman Kodak considered still cameras as a single opportunity rather than breaking down this product category into various product types and market segments. Because still cameras are mature products, an analysis at this level suggests that few, if any, worthwhile investment opportunities exist in this product category. However, an analysis at the product-market level may reveal attractive opportunities in disposable cameras for children or 35mm cameras for adults.

The marketing strategist cannot avoid assessing each strategic investment opportunity individually. This individual assessment considers how the specific opportunity is related to other current or potential projects. The portfolio matrix models do consider this interrelatedness between opportunities, while these interrelationships are explicitly incorporated in the revenue, cost, and investment estimates in a discounted cash flow analysis.

This chapter closes with a discussion of a decision support system for strategic portfolio management developed by Professors Srinivasan and Larreche. This dis-

EXHIBIT 9–8   Ford's Multinational Portfolio

cussion also highlights using managerial judgment in analytical models along with objective or hard data. This approach, developed by Professor Little, is called the decision-calculus approach. It is useful when all the data required cannot be ascertained directly.

DECISION-CALCULUS MODELS FOR ALLOCATING STRATEGIC INVESTMENTS

The financial evaluation models, discussed earlier are used to evaluate strategic investment decisions which are formulated as discrete choices. For example, (1) should some production equipment be purchased?, (2) should an R&D project be launched to develop products targeted for a market opportunity?, and (3) should a specialized sales force be developed to exploit a product-market opportunity? The analysis of these investments is formulated as a specific level of investment which results in a stream of future cash flows.

However, some strategic investment decisions, particularly at the corporate level, involve allocating resources across product-markets. Rather than making discrete choices among a set of opportunities, management must decide the level of funding for activities associated with each product-market. Such choices are often made in revenue or expenditure budgets rather than through a formal capital budget. In marketing, decision calculus models have been developed to assist managers in making such allocation decisions. These models have been used on tactical decisions

EXHIBIT 9–9   Evaluation of Resource Allocation Models

Model	Theoretical Support	Empirical Support	Focus on Basis of Sustainable Advantage
Discounted cash flow analysis	OK	OK	No, because focus is on numbers which are less important than market assumptions
Market growth-Matrix share	Questionable assumptions about ease of gaining share in high-growth markets and need for internal cash generation	Limited	No, because approach only considers cost advantages gained through experience effects.
Market Attractiveness Competitive Position Matrix	No clear theoretical or empirical supportsince variables considered are idiosyncratic to each firm.		Potentially focuses on bases of competitive advantage, but may add little to present procedures.

Adapted from: Robin Wensley, "Strategic Marketing: Betas, Boxes, and Basics," *Journal of Marketing,* Summer, 1981, pp. 173–183.

such as allocating selling time across customers,[15] selling time across products,[16] and promotional budget for a brand across elements of the promotional mix.[17]

     STRATPORT (*Strategic Portfolio* Planning) addresses the issue of allocating resources across the firm's portfolio of strategic opportunities. We first discuss the general concept of decision calculus models, and then the STRATPORT is reviewed.

Decision-Calculus Models

In 1970, John Little proposed an approach for building management decision support models which would be detailed enough to represent the environment confronting managers yet simple enough so that managers could understand the models.[18] Using this approach, referred to as decision calculus, over 20 models have been developed, many of which are available commercially.

     The decision calculus approach consists of:

1. Managers indicate their implicit model of the situation. They specify the key variables to be considered and the general nature of the relationship between these variables.

2. The model builder translates this description into a set of mathematical relationships.

3. The parameters specifying the relationships are estimated. Often managerial judgment is used to develop these parameters. For example, the exact functional relationship between the sales from a customer and the number of calls made on the customer is determined by fitting a curve through a set of points indicated by a salesperson's responses to the following questions:

    (a) What do you anticipate sales to this customer will be over the next 12 months if you continue to make the same number of calls on the customer?

    (b) What would sales be if the number of calls made on this customer during the coming year were doubled?

    (c) What would they be if you decreased the number of calls by 50%?

    (d) What is the maximum level of sales you could get if you devoted all of your time to this customer?

    (e) What would you expect sales to be if you made no calls on the customer during the next year?

[15]Lodish, Leonard "CALLPLAN: An Interactive Salesmen's Call Planning System," *Management Science,* Vol. 18, December, 1971, pp. 25–40.

[16]Montgomery, David, Alvin Silk, and Carlos Zaragoza, "A Multiproduct Sales Effort Allocation Model," *Management Science,* Vol. 18, December, 1971, pp. 3–24.

[17]Little, John D. C. "BRANDAID: A Marketing Mix Model, Part 1, Structure; Part 2, Implementation," *Operations Research,* Vol. 23, July–August, pp. 628–673.

[18] Little, John D. C., "Models and Managers: The concept of a Decision Calculus," *Management Science,* Vol. 16, April, 1970, pp. B466–485.

4. An interactive computer program is developed to derive the optimal allocation pattern based on the relationship specified. The interactive program
enables the manager to examine the results of alternative responses to the
questions used to set parameters regarding the key relationships.

Decision calculus models break down a complex decision (e.g., the amount of
sales time to allocate to each customer) into a set of simple relationships (e.g., the
sales realized for a given level of sales time allocated). A computer program integrates the information contained in the relationships to determine the best allocation.
Implicit in these models is the assumption that managers have an understanding of the
relationship among key variables, but need help to arrive at the best solution consistent with these relationships.[19]

STRATPORT

Overview.   STRATPORT is a decision calculus model developed to assist managers in allocating resources across strategic opportunities (Exhibit 9–10).[20]   In the
model, the firm is characterized as developing cash resources from internal operations
and external financial sources. These cash resources are allocated across the N business units (product-market opportunities) in the firm's portfolio. These business
units represent strategic opportunities, including ongoing operations as well as potential new businesses that might be developed internally or through acquisition. Within
each business unit, the investment resources allocated are used for production capacity, working capital, marketing, and R&D. Each business unit generates profits and
cash flows which, in turn, affect the amount of cash available for allocation.

The time horizon considered in the model is divided into two periods—planning
and post-planning. The resources allocated affect the performance of the business
unit during the planning period, whereas the post-planning period is used to evaluate
the long-term impact of the allocations. Thus market shares change during the planning period in response to resources allocated.[21]   Market shares are assumed to be
constant during the post-planning period because marketing investments are set at a
maintenance level. This distinction is illustrated in Exhibit 9–11.

Business Unit Module.   The core of STRATPORT is the business module
that models the cash flow and profit implications for marketing investments in a specific business unit. This module is used for all business units; however, the parame-

---

[19]For a discussion of the validity of this assumption, see Dipankar Chakravarti, Andrew Mitchell,
and Richard Staelin, "Judgment Based Marketing Decision Models: Problems and Possible Solutions,"
Journal of Marketing, Vol. 45, Fall, 1981, pp. 13–23; John D. C. Little and Leonard M. Lodish,
"Commentary on Judgment Based Marketing Decision Models," *Journal of Marketing,* Vol. 45, Fall,
1981, pp. 24–29.

[20]Larreche, Jean-Claude and V. Srinivasan, "STRATPORT: A Decision Support System for
Strategic Planning," *Journal of Marketing,* Vol. 45, Fall, 1981, pp. 39–52.

[21]See Seymour Tilles, "Strategies for Allocating Funds," *Harvard Business Review,* January–February,
1966, pp. 72–80.

EXHIBIT 9–10   Overview of the STRATPORT Model

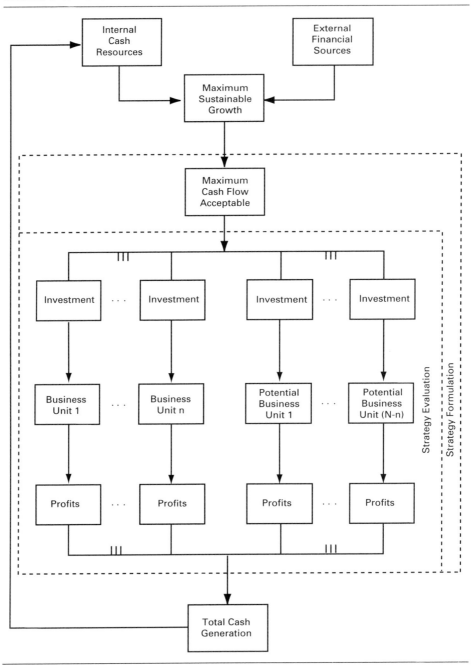

From *Journal of Marketing,* Larreche J. C. and V. Srinivasan, Fall, 1981, p. 42. Reprinted by permission of the American Marketing Association.

EXHIBIT 9–11   Planning and Post-Planning Periods

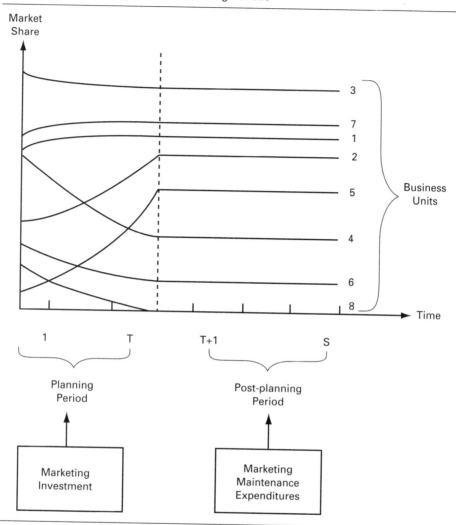

From *Journal of Marketing,* Larreche, J. C. and V. Srinivasan, Fall, 1981, p. 43. Reprinted by permission of the American Marketing Association.

ters of the response functions in the module are different for each business unit (Exhibit 9–12).

The level of marketing investments in the planning period determines the unit's market share. Unit sales are calculated by multiplying market share by the size of the market. The unit sales of the business unit affect revenues and costs during the planning and post-planning period and capacity expenditures and working capital during

EXHIBIT 9–12   Structure of STRATPORT for a Single Business Unit

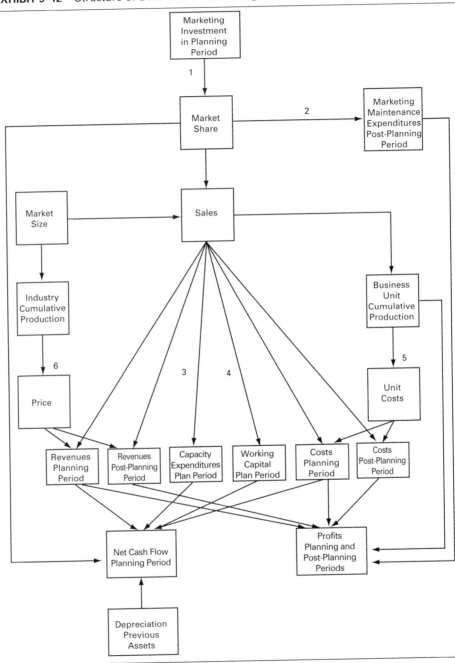

From *Journal of Marketing*, Larreche, J. C. and V. Srinivasan, Fall, 1981, p. 45.
Reprinted by permission of the American Marketing Association.

EXHIBIT 9–13   Main Functional Relationships

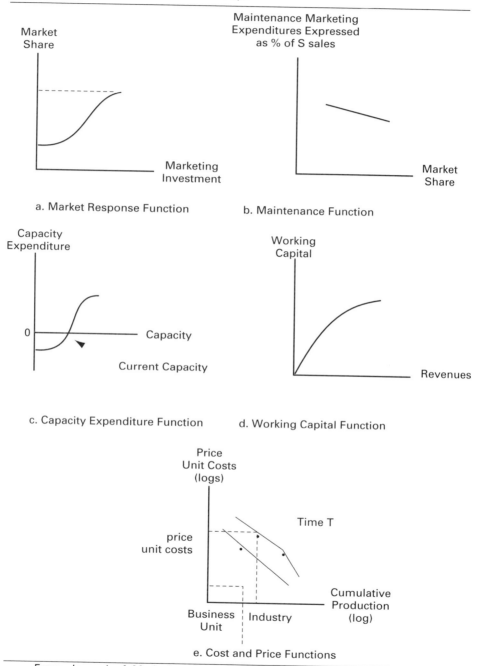

a. Market Response Function

b. Maintenance Function

c. Capacity Expenditure Function

d. Working Capital Function

e. Cost and Price Functions

From *Journal of Marketing,* Larreche, J. C. and V. Srinivasan, Fall, 1981, p. 46. Reprinted by permission of the American Marketing Association.

EXHIBIT 9–14   An Illustrative Run of the STRATPORT Model

INDICATE MARKETING INVESTMENT FOR
   BUSINESS UNIT 1 : 45
   BUSINESS UNIT 2 : 150
   BUSINESS UNIT 3 : 40
   BUSINESS UNIT 4 : 30
   BUSINESS UNIT 5 : 0
   BUSINESS UNIT 6 : 0
OUTPUT SAVED IN FILE FOR OFF-LINE PRINTING
DO YOU WANT TO PROCEED (0), OR TO DISPLAY RESULTS (1)? 1

EVALUATION OF PORTFOLIO STRATEGY

CASH NEEDS	−297.
PROFIT LEVEL	1366.
MARKET SHARE	
B. U. 1	.202
B. U. 2	.300
B. U. 3	.050
B. U. 4	.050
B. U. 5	.000
B. U. 6	.000

SOURCES AND USES OF FUNDS

B.U. NUMBER	1	2	3	4	5	6
CASH NEEDS						
REVENUE PL.	824.	1372.	345.	190.	0.	0.
COSTS PL.	551.	1082.	295.	127.	0.	0.
MKTG.IN.PL.	45.	150.	40.	30.	0.	0.
CAPA.IN.PL.	25.	79.	−11.	23.	0.	0.
TOTAL	−204.	−61.	−21.	−10.	0.	0.
PROFITS						
REVENUE PL.	824.	1372.	345.	190.	0.	0.
COSTS PL.	551.	1082.	295.	127.	0.	0.
MKTG.IN.PL.	45.	150.	40.	30.	0.	0.
REVENUE PP.	1623.	3838.	623.	468.	0.	0.
COSTS PP.	1089.	2969.	530.	302.	0.	0.
MKTG.IN.PP.	98.	460.	67.	84.	0.	0.
TOTAL	665.	550.	37.	115.	0.	0.

INPUT MINIMUM AND MAXIMUM LEVELS OF EXTERNAL CASH AVAILABILITY: -600.200
OUTPUT SAVED IN FILE FOR OFF-LINE PRINTING.
DO YOU WANT TO PROCEED (0), OR TO DISPLAY KEY RESULTS (1).
PROFIT CONTRIBUTIONS (2), OR CASH FLOWS (3) 1

KEY OPTIMIZATION RESULTS

OPTIONS	1	2	3	4	5	6
CASH NEEDS	206.	195.	185.	175.	165.	106.
PROFIT LEVEL	2911.	2894.	2877.	2860.	2842.	2735.
MARG. % YIELD	19.53	20.26	21.00	21.73	22.46	23.19
MARKET SHARE						
B.U.1	.203	.201	.198	.195	.193	.150

B.U.2	.394	.393	.391	.390	.389	.387
B.U.3.	.010	.010	.010	.010	.010	.010
B.U.4.	.171	.170	.170	.169	.169	.168
B.U.5.	.360	.358	.355	.353	.351	.349
B.U.6.	.000	.000	.000	.000	.000	.000
OPTIONS	7	8	9	10	11	
CASH NEEDS	−383.	−386.	−389.	−393.	−609.	
PROFIT LEVEL	1813.	1807.	1801.	1793.	1330.	
MARG. % YIELD	23.92	24.66	25.39	26.12	26.85	
MARKET SHARE						
B.U.1	.150	.150	.150	.150	.150	
B.U.2.	.050	.050	.050	.050	.050	
B.U.3.	.010	.010	.010	.010	.010	
B.U.4.	.168	.167	.167	.166	.166	
B.U.5.	.346	.344	.342	.339	.000	
B.U.6.	.000	.000	.000	.000	.000	

PL. = Planning Period   B.U. = Business Unit
PP. = Post-Planning Period   IN. = Investment

From *Journal of Marketing,* Larreche, J.C. and V. Srinivasan, Fall, 1981, p. 48. Reprinted with permission of the American Marketing Association.

the planning period. Sales increase the cumulative production of the business unit and decrease unit costs through an experience curve effect. Unit prices are derived from cumulative history experience. The maintenance marketing expenditures used in the post-planning period are based on the level of market share realized from the resources allocated during the planning period. Finally, the net cash flow during the planning period and the profits in the planning and post-planning period are calculated from projected revenues, costs, marketing capital, and capacity expenditure. The appropriate risk-adjusted discount rate is used to determine the net present value of investments in the business unit.

Functional Relationships. The six key relationships in the business module (see Exhibit 9–12) are shown in Exhibit 9–11. The market response function (Exhibit 9–13a) relates the expected market share at the end of the planning period to the level of marketing investment. The exact shape of this curve is estimated using four managerial inputs: (1) the expected market share if no investment is made, (2) the investment required to achieve a reference market share, (3) the expected share if the level of marketing investment is increased, and (4) the maximum market share that can be achieved with unlimited marketing investment.

The maintenance marketing function (Exhibit 9–13b) relates marketing expenditures as a percent of sales needed to maintain the share achieved at the end of the planning period and throughout the post-planning period. Managerial input is used to estimate this linear relationship; however, the curve has a negative slope indicating that as share increases, the maintenance marketing level decreases because of loss of economies.

The capacity expenditure function (Exhibit 9–13c) describes the additional investment in capacity required to provide the units indicated by the projected market share. This function is estimated using the following managerial inputs: (a) the cash flow that could be realized by selling the current capacity, (b) the cash needed to expand capacity to two higher levels of production, and (c) the investment required for a marginal expansion over the high level. The working capital function (Exhibit 9–13d) indicates the working capital (cash + inventory + equipment leases + accounts receivable – accounts payable) needed at various sales levels.

Unit cost and unit price functions (Exhibit 9–13e) are based on the experience curve concept. All real costs (except marketing expenditures) are assumed to be an exponential function of cumulative production by the business unit. The price function assumes a decline in average price based on cumulative production in the industry.

Illustration of STRATPORT Model

An illustration of the computer output from the STRATPORT model is shown in Exhibit 9–14. In this example, six business units (strategic opportunities) are considered. The first four units are ongoing businesses, whereas units 5 and 6 are new opportunities that the firm is considering. The top part of the output shows the implications of continuing the present levels of investment in each of the six business units ($45, $150, $40, $30, $0, $0 million). This level of investment generates $297 million in cash, maintains the present market shares (20%, 30%, 5%, 5%, 0%, 0%), and provides $1300 million in profit. These results are before taxes and without discounting.

The second part of the output, the STRATPORT model, uses an optimization routine to determine the implications of 11 portfolio strategies ranging from $200 million cash investment to $600 million cash generation. Strategy #1 requires an investment of $206 million but results in total profits of $2,911 million. At the other extreme, Strategy #11 generates $609 million cash flow but only results in $1,330 million profits. Over this range of cash flows, business unit 6 does not appear to be an attractive opportunity. Business unit 3 warrants only a minimal marketing investment, which results in a loss in share. However, business unit 4 experiences a substantial increase in market share as more resources are directed toward it.

The STRATPORT model breaks down the estimated cash flows used in calculating net present values into a set of relationships among key variables, such as units sold (market share), unit price, unit cost, maintenance level of marketing expenditures, and investments in marketing, working capital, and capacity. In this model, a computer program determines the cash flow implications of these relationships. In contrast, managerial judgment implicitly integrates this information when generating cash flow projections for the net present value calculations discussed at the beginning of this chapter.

SUMMARY

We have described and discussed some key portfolio models that form the basis for the allocation of resources. Once the relationship among the key performance measure (e.g., cash flow) and market or context factors (e.g., relative market share and growth rate) has been identified, and having performed a competitive analysis, several creative options may be considered. These include the development of relationships that might increase market share (e.g., through alliances with specific channels, thereby insulating these "markets" and leading to an opportunity for "monopoly rents"), or offerings (proliferation of products) to either increase share or to change the immediate growth rate of a market. Understanding the rules of the game and anticipating competitive moves permit development of creative alternatives and their attendant resource allocation to achieve specified goals.

Concept Questions

1. (a.) What is the logic behind the BCG matrix?
   (b.) What differentiates the four types of product-markets in the BCG classification?
   (c.) How was the BCG matrix intended to be used?
2. (a.) Describe a market attractiveness-market position matrix.
   (b.) Describe the strategy prescriptions for different classifications based on this matrix.
3. (a.) What is meant by the term decision-calculus?
   (b.) Describe its use for portfolio analysis.

Discussion Questions

1. Discuss why the BCG matrix should or should not be recommended for resource allocation decisions. Discuss issues related to its underlying objective, its underlying relationships, and its application to product markets.
2. Discuss the quote from Mr. Black of AM International on page 250.
3. Discuss the problems that might occur in the use of the attractiveness–position matrix for a mixture of global and domestic produce–markets.
4. Given the following financial criteria, build a framework for the allocation of resources.

   Economic Value Added (EVA) is a popular concept in finance today. The key is that the cost of equity capital should also be used in calculating return on capital. It forces companies to be aware of all resources that are used in serving each product-market.

$$EVA = (\text{Operating Profit-Taxes})$$
$$- (\text{Debt Capital Rate} \times \frac{D}{D+E} + \text{Equity Capital Cost Rate} \times \frac{E}{D+E})$$

   (D = Debt, E = Equity).

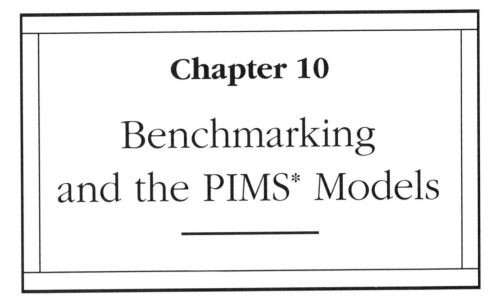

Chapter 10

Benchmarking and the PIMS* Models

INTRODUCTION

In developing a marketing strategy, benchmarking can help provide answers to the questions: are marketing resources being exploited as well as they can; and what possible advantage (when will the advantage be in place and how much of an advantage will it be) can competitors obtain? We discuss two approaches to try to find answers to these questions.

The first approach is to develop a model that illustrates the relationships between various strategies and their outcomes. For example, a model designed to reveal the effects of customer relations on return on investment (ROI). As is done in the PIMS studies, these models may be developed using historical data. With this database, the outcomes of various alternatives can be simulated. Keep in mind, however, that these data are derived from various industries, are historical, and do not give information on processes.

The fact that these data are from various industries is beneficial because they negate an industry's "tunnel vision" and provide a broader understanding of the correlations between variables and outcomes. That the data are historical may be restrictive because current or experimental practices might be excluded. The third element—that of providing information regarding processes—may be limiting, that is, the processes used may very well allow introducing strategic initiatives or at least allow maximum use of existing resources.

Our second approach, benchmarking, is used to identify the best practice for each step in the process used to satisfy customers profitably. This best practice may be one from a totally different industry. Although the practice may not be the ideal, it might provide a necessary change in direction.

*Profit Impact of Market Strategy

These approaches become necessary since the ideal solution may not be easily identifiable; or the ideal may be a "moving target" and the best way to track it may be by tracking the current best.

These approaches are useful in choosing a strategy and its processes. Their use in understanding competitive behavior comes from the assumption of rational expectations. That is, the assumption that our competitors are as smart as we. If a company can use PIMS or benchmarking, it should assume that its competitors can as well. This expectation should become part of a company's strategy.

We first discuss benchmarking, and then PIMS.

Benchmarking

According to Rob Walker, Director, Business Management Systems and Quality at Rank Xerox (UK) Ltd.,

> The 1960s to mid-1970s were Xerox's golden years. The 914 launched Xerox into an era of feverish growth and success. Not only had we created a product, we had created, and thought we owned, an industry. Competition was virtually non-existent due to patent protection, and we were the fastest company to reach $1 bn in revenues.

> We developed a kind of internal arrogance that kept us from focusing on what our customers really wanted. This short-sighted attitude opened a window of opportunity for competition, and in 1976 the Japanese entered the low end of the market. Our golden years were over—profits plummeted from $1.149 bn in 1980 to $600 mi in 1981. After 20 years of market domination, competition was a totally new experience for Xerox. Our survival as a company was at stake. We had to do something. That "something" was to begin a total change in the culture of the company!

> . . . The first action we took was to institute a process we call "competitive benchmarking."[1]

Similar reasons made other companies undertake benchmarking.

As was the case at Xerox, market externals often force management to "rediscover" the secrets of winning. Fundamental to this "rediscovery" process as well as to a discovery process is the ability to ferret out the causes for success. If a model can be developed that faithfully captures the complexities of competition and organizational processes then, perhaps it can be used to plot the best course of action. However, such is not the case. In the most complex situations, the best available guide is to study other companies and their practices to understand (a) what needs to be modeled and (b) what relative information can be obtained to help instruct and calibrate simpler models.

Benchmarking has recently emerged, primarily through the work of Robert Camp[2] at Xerox. It is one of the major methods to gain, regain, or maintain success. It involves understanding the best practices of a few select companies. It has not yet been studied rigorously by academia.

---

[1]Walker, R. "Rank Xerox–Management Revolution," *Long Range Planning,* Vol. 25, 1992, p. 8–21.

[2]Camp, R. C., *Benchmarking: The Search for Industry Best Practices That Lead to Superior Performance,* Milwaukee, WI, American Society for Quality Control, Quality Press, 1989.

Extent of Practice

A survey conducted by the consulting firm of Towers Perrin in conjunction with the American Productivity and Quality Center, found that 60% of the companies surveyed practiced benchmarking. Another 10% reported that they would begin formal benchmarking within three years.[3] In the United States, benchmarking is also a criterion to demonstrate world-class competitiveness for the Malcolm Baldridge National Quality Award.

Types of Benchmarking

Benchmarking is action oriented and seeks to make change through understanding examples of better practice. Three types of benchmarking are generally used: (a) strategic, (b) customer, and (c) cost.[4] Exhibit 10–1 is from the consulting firm of Towers Perrin that summarizes the objectives of each type. Strategic benchmarking focuses on the gap between possible shareholder value creation (attainable because a

---

EXHIBIT 10–1   Major Types of Benchmarking Methods

Strategic

Establish the premier level of shareholder value creation.

Measure the shareholder value gap to be overcome and the impact of possible gap-closing actions.

Cost

Operational Components

Focus on productivity and direct costs.

Compare productivity and cost buildup at discrete points on the value chain.

Organizational Components

Clarify the sources of organizational capability and staffing efficiency.

Compare indirect costs, both attributable and allocated, for each employee.

Process Components

Define best practices for certain processes, both within the industry and across other industries.

Set clear objectives for redesigning efforts and assist in mapping out required changes.

Customer

Determine positions of products or services related to alternatives.

Differentiate value-adding activities from low-value activities.

From Schmidt, J. A., "The Link Between Benchmarking and Customer Value," *Journal of Business Strategy*, Vol. 13, 1991, p. 8. Reprinted by permission of Warren Gorman & Lamont.

---

[3]This result is cited in J. A. Schmidt, "A Tool to Be Best-in-Class," *Directors & Boards*, Spring, 1992, pp. 29–35.

[4]See J. A. Schmidt, "The Link Between Benchmarking Marking and Shareholder Value," *Journal of Business Strategy*, 1991, pp. 7–13; and K. Jennings and F. Westfall, "Benchmarking for Strategic Action," *Journal of Business Strategy*, 1991, pp. 22–25, for consulting-based descriptions.

best-of-the-best firm has done it) and present shareholder value provision.   In 1990, for example, American Home Products, General Electric, Philip Morris, Raytheon, and nine others had an average ROI of 20.7% as compared to 12.7% for all the Fortune 200 companies.   Identifying reasons for differences between a company's current performance and what is possible is the next step toward positive change. Cost benchmarking focuses on possible cost improvements.   Customer benchmarking focuses on achieving greater customer satisfaction.

Five Phases

The benchmarking process involves the five phases of Planning, Analysis, Integration, Action, and Maturity.   The steps in each phase are shown in Exhibit 10–2.   The last stage, maturity, is attained when the entire organization is steeped in a new culture focused on excelling through customer satisfaction and shareholder value.

Benchmarking Focus

Benchmarking is divided into two parts.   The first is identifying the best *practices*. This follows identification of the processes to be benchmarked.   The exemplary company may be in an entirely different industry.   For example, Xerox benchmarked L.L. Bean's (a mail order firm specializing in outdoor products) warehousing and distribution system.   The key is to identify the best example of the process (distribution, etc.) and not to look at the process as applied to the same product or service (e.g., distribu-

EXHIBIT 10–2   The Benchmarking Process

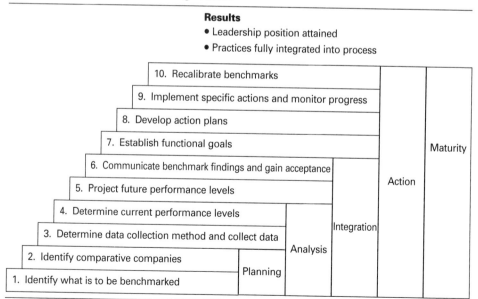

From Camp, R. C., "Learning from the Bestleads to Superior Performance," *Journal of Business Strategy,* Vol. 13, No. 3, 1991, p. 4. Reprinted by permission of Warren, Gorham & Lamont.

tion of photocopiers).   The second part is developing and using appropriate *measures* to quantify the impact of the process changes on performance.

Major Issues for Practices

The major issues that require careful attention for the first part are (a) what to bench-mark and (b) whom to benchmark against.

For the first issue, because we are discussing marketing strategy, processes that relate to customer requirements and relationships are items to benchmark.   Current processes must be mapped and priorities set before external information is sought. To benchmark these, marketing research is a natural place to start—first using focus groups and then surveys to establish current satisfaction levels and customer expecta-tions for the leading company as well as for its key competitors.

For the second issue, "cutting-edge" practices are sought.   One approach is to look at competitors as prospective benchmarks, and then to gradually expand the con-sideration set to determine the "best-of-the-best."

Camp[5] provides the following examples of companies benchmarked by Xerox:

Company	Process
American Express	billing and collection
American Hospital Supply	automated inventory control
Ford Motor	manufacturing floor layout
General Electric	robotics
L.L. Bean	warehousing
Hershey Foods Corp.	and distribution
Mary Kay Cosmetics	
Westinghouse Electric	national quality award process, warehouse controls, bar coding
Florida Power and Light	quality process

L.L. Bean benchmarked fresh flower distributors to learn how they turned around products quickly.   Flower distributors handle highly perishable commodities from around the world and turn them around quickly.   Therefore, they were deter-mined to be at the cutting edge of inventory management, quick turnaround, and assortment management.

Major Issues to be Measured

The measures chosen should, of course, be valid and reliable.   A valid mea-sure, in this context, is one that captures the salient features of the process and can also be linked to the outcome.   For example, suppose the process to be benchmarked is managing returns from customers for a catalog marketer.   The underlying processes are (a) ensuring that the order is correctly filled in the first place, (b) the

[5]Camp, R. C., "Learning from the Best Leads to Superior Performance," *Journal of Business Strategy*, 1991, pp. 3–6.

correct product is shipped, (c) the return is properly inspected, and (d) the return is properly credited.

For (a), the key part may be to help customers make the most appropriate choice. Measures which may be useful are (1) a reason(s) why customers return merchandise, (2) customer satisfaction with the descriptions of merchandise given in the catalog or by salespersons over the phone, and so forth.   An Ishikawa cause-effect diagram can provide a framework for mapping out measures for a process.[6]

Such measures will not only make it easier to justify changes, but also to monitor and make adjustments as required later.   Because the benchmarking process might involve study of a different industry, special care should be taken to develop valid measures.   This is because the context (including organizational ethos), production or service, cycle times, and so forth, of the benchmarked industry or company may be different.   Validity of a measurement needs to be carefully established before its use.

Although benchmarking is growing in popularity, it is not easy to implement. One problem is that the company (or companies) to be studied must agree to the intrusion.   A second problem is the potential for antitrust action if competitors are benchmarked.   The PIMS models to be discussed avoid the second problem and lessen the potential impact of the first.

THE PIMS MODELS

We previously examined two types of models used to evaluate strategic opportunities—financial planning models (Chapter 8) and portfolio matrix models (Chapter 9).   In each of these, variables related to long-term profitability of a product-market are identified, for example, cash flow, relative market share, and business attractiveness.   The potential investment opportunities with respect to these variables are then evaluated.   These models show the relative amount of resources that should be directed toward each product-market considered, as well as evaluate the attractiveness of strategic investment opportunities.

This chapter discusses another set of models developed in the PIMS project (which grew out of work at GE).   These models incorporate the historical experiences of a large number of businesses.   Rather than use a theoretical framework to identify key factors related to long-term profitability, variables are included in the PIMS models because they have a significant empirical relationship with the performance of business.

HISTORY OF THE PIMS MODELS

In the early 1960s, management at General Electric recognized that some divisions were doing well, while other divisions were doing poorly.   The planners had difficulty in explaining these performance differences.   To improve their understanding of divisional

---

[6]For details of the Ishikawa diagram please see K. Ishikawa, *A Guide to Quality Control,* White Plains, NY, Quality Resources, 1969.

performance, the planning group undertook a project called PROM. It was subsequently renamed and became independent of G. E. Profit Impact of Market Strategy (PIMS).[*]

The principal objectives of the PIMS project were, and still are, (1) to discover empirical generalities concerning factors related to business performance and (2) to assist managers in evaluating the performance of their business units and in developing plans for the units. As a first step, GE's planning staff gathered data on each division's performance, financial structure, marketing and manufacturing activities, market characteristics, and competition. This database was then used to identify the factors related to business unit performance.

Following its inception at General Electric, the PIMS project has evolved into a nonprofit corporation, The Strategic Planning Institute (SPI), with over 100 participating firms. Each company contributes data from some or all of its business units and pays a small annual fee. In exchange, the firms use the database and models to analyze businesses and are provided customized reports and research findings.

The PIMS project was established to overcome some limitations concerning financial planning models and the market attractiveness–competitive position matrix. Although these models are conceptually appealing, they do not provide insight into factors that make opportunities attractive—factors which result in long-term performance. The PIMS project attempts to identify the factors related to long-term performance.

THE PIMS DATABASE

Sample of Businesses

In 1989, the PIMS database contained information on over 3000 businesses. The typical business in the database is profitable and operates in a mature sector of the economy. Over 20% of Fortune 500 corporations are participating members; however, these corporations usually submit information about businesses that they wish to have analyzed. Although most of the businesses are based in the United States, a growing number are based in Europe and some in South America.

Defining the Unit of Analysis

As discussed in Chapter 4, a critical step in developing a marketing strategy is to identify the product-market opportunities—the specific alternatives to be analyzed. The first step in collecting marketing strategy data is to define the unit of analysis. How should a large company be divided into individual businesses (often referred to as Strategic Business Units or SBUs)?

SPI suggests the following rules of thumb to define strategic business units:

1. *Joint Costs.* Businesses should be defined so that less than 60% of each unit's expenses are the result of arbitrary allocations of joint costs—combined. When two organization units share a manufacturing facility that

*Thanks are due to Julie Takahashi of SPI for her input on a draft of the material on PIMS.

accounts for most of the costs associated with the products sold by the two units, the units together should be considered as one business unit. Similarly, high combined costs can arise when units share a common sales force or promote products with a common family brand name.

2. *Vertical Integration.* Businesses should be defined so that less that 60% of the revenues of a business are sales to a "downstream" business in the company. When substantial sales are made to a "downstream" business or substantial purchases are made from an "upstream" business, these businesses represent vertical integration in the company and should be combined into one strategic business unit.

3. *Homogeneity of Served Market.* Frequently a business sells its products to several markets using different product lines and distribution channels. SPI suggests that such businesses be subdivided into separate strategic units when two of the following statements are true:

   a. Each market contains markedly different competitors.

   b. Each market has markedly different growth rates.

   c. The business has markedly different market shares in each market.

4. *Company Organization.* Typically, the organization of a company is consistent with the first three suggestions. Divisions or product groups are relatively independent from other divisions. They do not have shared costs or downstream sales because such synergies would make it difficult to evaluate the unique performance of each organizational unit. Thus, from a strategy and control perspective, the present organization structure of a company is often a good place to start when defining strategic business units.

The combined cost and vertical integration criteria are needed to isolate business units from each other. If these criteria are not included, any strategic analysis including the PIMS analysis could be misleading. For example, a PIMS analysis might indicate that one SBU is in an unattractive position and should be divested, while another unit, sharing a common manufacturing facility, merits substantial investment. However, divesting the one SBU would result in excess capacity and reduce the attractiveness of the second SBU.

The previous rules of thumb can be considered suggestions for defining the "product" aspect of a product-market alternative. They are suggestions for dividing the company's production and marketing capabilities into separate units. SPI also provides guidelines for defining the market in which a business participates.

"Market" is defined as a set of customers with similar requirements for products and services. SPI also uses a concept called "served market," the portion of the market toward which a business directs its marketing efforts. For example, a business may focus its efforts only on:

Customers located in a geographic region, such as eastern Europe or the western United States.

Customers who purchase over one million dollars annually.

Customers who want quality rather than low price.

Customers who require no after sales support or service.

Customers who only use a specific size, such as TV sets with screens under 12".

The served market is then used to determine market share and other variables that describe the business' operation and environment. The "served market" is smaller than the total market.

The "homogeneity of served markets" criterion is directed toward disaggregating opportunities that face completely different strategic environments—different competitors, different competitive advantages that can be brought to bear on the markets, and different levels of attractiveness for the opportunities.

However, there is some danger in arbitrarily defining a served market. As stated earlier, the relevant market should be defined in terms of where mobility barriers exist or can be erected. These barriers arise when there are significant discontinuities in the patterns of cost, capital requirements, channel structures, or customer loyalty. We define products-markets in terms of these barriers because companies competing within such barriers are relatively isolated from those outside the barriers. In addition, all companies within the barrier can easily enter and compete in any sub-markets within the barrier.

The PIMS market definition criteria do not explicitly recognize the importance of uncovering potential barriers and using them to define markets. For example, PIMS suggests that a company may define its served market as TV sets with screen sizes less than 12". However, if the costs and activities for developing, manufacturing, and marketing small and large screen TVs are the same, the relevant market for a small screen manufacturer is the entire TV market, not just the small screen market. From a strategy standpoint, given similar cost structures, a dominant large screen manufacturer can easily enter the small screen market and use its shared experience to dominate that market. By narrowly defining its served market and by not considering the fact of barriers between small screen and large screen TV manufacturers, the small screen manufacturer is ignoring a significant competitive threat.

Variables* That Describe Each Business Unit

Each business unit provides more than 100 pieces of data concerning the business, its operating results, market and competitive environment, and general industry characteristics. A standardized questionnaire is used to collect these data. Much of the collected data is based on objective accounting measures. However, some of the data represents subjective managerial estimates. Exhibit 10–3 shows a sample page from a Core Data Form and flow charts depicting data collection on some items.

Subjective Measures.   One problem in using subjective measures is that the judgment of executives completing the forms may be influenced by the unit's performance. An executive in a high-performing unit may reason that the product quality

---

*SPI updates its variables frequently. Thus SPI should be contacted for the most current information.

EXHIBIT 10–3   Standardized PIMS Questionnaire—Sample Page [From Core Data Form]

19__	19__	19__	19__	19__

238:   INDEX OF SELLING PRICES

For each year, express your business's average selling prices as a percentage of base year unit selling prices. This index should include inflation and changes in relative price. This index is meant to measure changes in **selling prices only;** do not include the effect of changes in the product mix.

100%	%	%	%	%

239:   INDEX OF BASIC MATERIALS COSTS

For each year, estimate the unit prices your business paid for its basic materials (Line 208, page 5). Express as a percentage of your business's base year unit purchase prices. This index is meant to measure changes in **materials costs only;** do not include the effect of changes in the product mix.

100%	%	%	%	%

241:   INDEX OF AVERAGE HOURLY WAGE RATES

For each year, estimate the average hourly wage rate paid by your business. Include the costs of fringe benefits and pension plans. Express as a percentage of your business's base year hourly wage rates.

100%	%	%	%	%

428:   RELATIVE SELLING PRICES

For each year, estimate your competitor's selling prices, relative to the average selling prices of your business.

428.0   Your Business

100%	100%	100%	100%	100%

428.1   Competitor A's

%	%	%	%	%

428.2   Competitor B's

%	%	%	%	%

428.3   Competitor C's

%	%	%	%	%

must be high. If it were not, the unit would not be performing as well as it is. Thus, the unit's performance may have a halo effect on the manager's perception of product quality, relative marketing expenditures, and so forth. Consequently, the empirical relationship between product quality and performance may be because of performance causing quality rather than quality causing performance.

EXHIBIT 10–3   (Continued)

Steps to Develop Relative Quality Ratings

1. Consider A
Purchase Criterion.

2. Rate the Relative Importance
of this criterion.

3. Rate your business
on this criterion on
a quantitative scale.

4. Rate each of your
three major competitors
on the same scale
as in step 3.

5. Repeat steps 1 through 4
for each of the provided
purchase criteria.

6. Based on the ratings above,
overall relative Quality
Ratings are determined.

EXHIBIT 10-3   (Continued)

Steps to Develop Relative Cost Indices

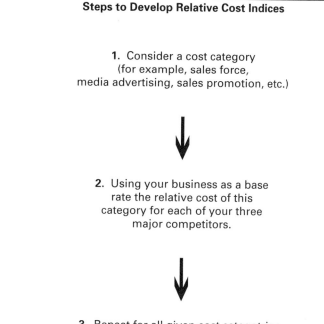

1. Consider a cost category
(for example, sales force,
media advertising, sales promotion, etc.)

2. Using your business as a base
rate the relative cost of this
category for each of your three
major competitors.

3. Repeat for all given cost categotries.

From the PIMS Program Core Data Forms. Reprinted with the permission of The Strategic Planning Institute.

Recognizing these problems, SPI recommends using consumer judgment to assess factors such as product quality. For example, a multi-attribute model can be used to measure quality as perceived by customers. First, attributes of the product are identified, then a rating scale is developed for each attribute that indicates the importance the customer places on the attribute in selecting from among competing products, and finally the customer indicates the relative quality of the product based on each attribute. A quality index is derived by multiplying the importance weight of each attribute by the relative quality rating on the attribute and totaling across attributes. Using this procedure, for example, a brand of tires would have a higher overall quality rating if it performs well on important attributes such as durability and riding comfort, even though it performs poorly on relatively unimportant attributes such as road noise and mounting ease.

Performance Measures.   The two most commonly used measures of performance in PIMS analysis, ROI and cash flow, are based on accounting data. In the PIMS database, ROI is defined as earnings before interest and taxes divided by working capital plus fixed assets at book value. Interest and taxes are not included because these expenses reflect decisions concerning the capital structure of the firm which are not under the control of the operating manager.

Accounting measures of ROI have been criticized because they do not strongly correlate with the value of the firm as reflected in its stock prices.[7] However, market value is not available for business units within a publicly traded corporation and accounting measures of ROI continued to be widely used as surrogates for financial performance.[8] SPI has developed PIMS models using other measures such as cash flow divided by investment and discounted cash flow.

Definitions of other variables used in the PIMS models are shown in the Appendix.

Quality of the Data and Benchmarking Potential

While there are problems with the PIMS data, the PIMS database continues to be the most reliable and accurate source of data relevant to strategy formulation currently available. PIMS data is useful, because they are collected at the business unit level whereas most data on business activity and performance are only available at the company level. Data at the company level are not useful because a company may contain as many as 100 units with different performances, facing different environments, and using different strategies.

Additionally, the PIMS database contains data that are not normally available in published information about a company, such as relative product quality, prices, or even market share.

These measures represent important information for managers, giving them "normal" ranges and mean values. In addition, measures such as information on size of market, number of competitors, geographic extent of served market, percentage of sales to foreign markets, extent of import competition, percentage of sales from largest selling product, frequency of product changes, delivery time, number of customers, importance of immediate customers, frequency with which customers make purchases, average purchase amount per transaction, customer costs of switching vendors, use of different distribution channels, percentage of internal sales, relative sales force, and media and promotion expenses are all available. These can provide valuable benchmarks for norms and normal ranges which can be used for planning. If the best of these is chosen, then PIMS can also provide useful benchmarking data as discussed earlier in this chapter. However, these data focus on outcomes and resource use as opposed to detailing processes.

FACTORS RELATED TO PROFITABILITY

Analysis of the PIMS database indicates that profitability and cash flow are related to nine strategic factors which account for almost 80% of business success or failure determination.[9] They are in approximate order of importance:

[7]See B. A. Kirchoff, "Organizational Effectiveness Measurement and Policy Research," *Academy of Management Review,* Vol. 2, July, 1977, pp. 347–355. Also see Robert Jacobson and David Aaker, "Is Market Share All It's Cracked Up to Be?," *Journal of Marketing,* Vol. 49, Fall, 1985, pp. 11–22.

[8]Reece, James and William Cook, "Measuring Investment Center Performance," *Harvard Business Review,* May–June, 1978, pp. 28–30.

[9]Schoeffler, Sidney "Nine Basic Findings on Business Strategies," PIMS Letter No. 1, *The Strategic Planning Institute,* 1977.

1. *Investment intensity.* Technology and the business method chosen govern how much fixed capital and working capital are required to produce a dollar-of-sales or a dollar-of-value added in the business. Investment intensity generally produces a negative impact on percentage measures of profitability and net cash flow; that is, businesses that are mechanized or automated or inventory–intensive generally show lower returns on investment and sales than businesses that are not.

2. *Productivity.* Businesses producing high value-added per employee are more profitable than those with low value-added per employee. ("Value added" is the amount by which the business increases the market value of the raw materials and components it buys.)

3. *Market position.* A business's share of its served market (both absolute and relative to its three largest competitors) has a positive impact on its profit and net cash flow.

4. *Growth of the served market.* Growth is generally favorable to dollar measures of profit, indifferent to percentage measures of profit, and negative to all measures of net cash flow.

5. *Quality of the products or services offered.* Quality, defined as the customers' evaluation of the business's product or service package as compared to that of competitors, has a generally favorable impact on all measures of financial performance.

6. *Innovation-differentiation.* Extensive action taken by a business in new product introduction, R&D, marketing effort, and so on, generally produce a positive effect on its performance if the company has strong market position to begin with. If a company's market position is weak, such actions usually do not produce a positive effect.

7. *Vertical integration.* For businesses located in mature and stable markets, vertical integration (that is, make rather than buy) generally has a favorable effect on performance. In markets that are rapidly growing, declining, or otherwise changing, the opposite is true.

8. *Cost push.* The rates of increase of wages, salaries, and raw material prices and the presence of a labor union have complex impacts on profit and cash flow—depending on how the business is positioned to pass along the increase to its customers or to absorb the higher costs internally.

9. *Current strategic effort.* The current direction of change in any of the above factors has effects on profit and cash flow frequently opposite to that of the factor itself. For example, having strong market share tends to increase net cash flow, but acquiring market share drains cash while the business is making that effort.

In addition to these nine general factors, PIMS researchers also recognized the importance of management capability (although it is difficult to measure its reliability independently in the data itself). There are such things as "good" or "poor" operators. A good operator can improve the profitability of a strong strategic position or minimize the damage of a weak one; a poor operator does the opposite. A management team that is a good operator is a favorable element in a business; it produces a better financial result than one would expect from the strategic position of the business alone.[10]

PAR MODELS

The PAR models are used to analyze the performance of a business. These models indicate expected performance, on average (that is, the average is used as a benchmark or a comparison), from a business with a specific financial structure, marketing and manufacturing activities, and confronting specific market conditions. The models also identify factors which result in a business's actual performance to differ from the performance expected.

The PAR ROI and cash flow models are developed using multiple regression with ROI and cash flow-investment as the dependent variables and other data as independent variables. Researchers examine the data to determine what variables were related to ROI and cash flow-investment. Coefficients are then estimated to weigh these variables in an equation to predict performance measures.

To illustrate, suppose an examination of the PIMS database found that ROI was *only* related to three variables: relative market share, relative product quality, and investment intensity. A linear equation for predicting ROI is:

$$ROI = B_0 + B_1 \text{ (market share)} + B_2 \text{ (product quality)} \qquad (1)$$
$$+ B_3 \text{ (investment intensity)}$$
$$\text{where } B_0, B_1, B_2 \text{ and } B_3 \text{ are constants}$$

Using multiple regression, B_0, B_1, B_2 and B_3 can be estimated. Suppose that the estimated coefficients are:

$$ROI = 16.0 + 0.3 \text{ (market share)} + 0.2 \text{ (product quality)} \qquad (2)$$
$$- 0.1 \text{ (investment intensity)}$$

Note that the signs of the estimated coefficients are consistent with the findings reported earlier. These findings show that market share and product quality are positively related to ROI. The greater the market share and the relative product quality, the higher the ROI. However, investment intensity is negatively related to ROI. Higher investment intensity results in lower ROI. Therefore, the estimated coefficient for investment intensity is negative.

Assume that a business unit has a 25% market share, a −10% relative product

---

[10]Schoeffler, Sidney, "Niseli Basic Findings on Business Strategies," PIMS letter No. 1, The Strategic Planning Institute, 1977.

quality, and a 70% level of investment intensity. The expected ROI of this business would be 14.5% using equation (2).

$$14.5\% \ = \ 16.0 + \ 0.3(25\%) + \ 0.2(-10\%) - 0.1(70\%)$$

This expected ROI is the PAR ROI. It is the ROI that a unit would typically have given that market share, product quality, and investment intensity.

PAR ROI Report

The actual PAR ROI contains 37 independent variables. Some of the independent variables are transformed to improve the predictive power of the model. A sample of a PAR ROI report for Business Number 12345 is shown in Exhibit 10–4.[11]

EXHIBIT 10–4   PAR ROI Report—Business Number 12345

PAR Return on investment (1973–1976) 32%
PAR ROI is an estimate of the pretax Return On Investment that was normal for similar businesses with respect to their:

> Market and industry environment
> Competitive position
> Capital and productive position structures
> Differentiation from competitors

Actual Return on Investment (1973–1976) 39%
Actual ROI performance has two components, PAR ROI and the deviation from PAR. The deviation between PAR ROI and actual ROI can often be explained by data errors, errors in business definition, or other factors outside the model.

If, however, such factors are not present, PAR may be used as a benchmark for profit performance. The deviation from PAR can then be interpreted as a measure of operating effectiveness in managing this strategic position.

Deviation from PAR = Actual ROI – PAR ROI
7%   =   39%   –   32%

Trend of actual ROI relative to PAR (1973–1976)

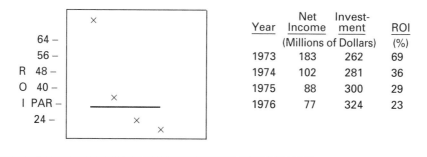

Year	Net Income	Invest- ment	ROI (%)
	(Millions of Dollars)		
1973	183	262	69
1974	102	281	36
1975	88	300	29
1976	77	324	23

(1)

[11]From "The PAR ROI Report: Explanation and Sample," *The Strategic Planning Institute,* 1977.

EXHIBIT 10–4 (continued)

PAR ROI Report

Key Strategic Factors

The key strategic factors are those descriptors of a business's strategic position which have exhibited a consistent and strong relationship with Return On Investment over a wide range of business samples and times. For this business, the impacts of these factors on PAR ROI are:

Key Factor	PIMS Mean	Business 12345	Impact on PAR ROI
	(%)	(%)	(%)
Investment Intensity Index			
Investment-Sales	x	33.0	
Investment-Value Added		65.6	
Value Added per Employee ($000)		23.8	
Capacity Utilization		76.3	
Fixed Capital Intensity		42.4	
Vertical Integration		51.9	
Market Position			
Market Share	y	15.0	
Relative Market Share		34.8	
Industry Concentration Ratio		51.0	
Marketing Expense-Sales		7.7	
Relative Product Quality		34.3	
Purchase Amount-Immediate Costs		4.0	

The equation used to calculate PAR ROI contains two classes of ROI-influencing factors:

1. The key strategic factors listed above, and
2. Support factors, which have been shown to have statistically significant impact for the period over which the model was developed.

The PAR ROI is built from the aggregate impacts of these factors:

	(%)
PIMS mean ROI	22.1
+ Impact of key strategic factors	5.9
"Strategic Par" (Expected ROI based on Key Factors)	28.0
+ Impact of support factors	4.0
PAR ROI	32.0% **(2)**

Overall Performance.   Page 1 of the report shows the PAR ROI for this business and the actual performance of the business from 1983 to 1986. The average PAR ROI for the business over the four-year period was 32%, whereas the actual ROI business average was 39%. On average, the business had a 7% greater ROI than would be expected from a business in similar conditions. However, the ROI trend is

EXHIBIT 10-4 (continued)

PAR ROI Report
ROI-Influencing Factors

IMPACT OF ROI-INFLUENCING FACTORS:
A DIAGNOSIS OF STRATEGIC STRENGTHS AND WEAKNESSES

	PIMS Mean	Business 12345	Impact	Sensitivity A Change of (%)	Sensitivity Changes Impact by (%)
ATTRACTIVENESS OF ENVIRONMENT					
1. Purchase Amount–Immediate Costs		4.0			
2. Real Market Growth, Short Run		−4.1			
3. Industry (SIC) Growth, Long Run		6.8			
4. Selling Price Growth Rate		0.5			
COMPETITIVE POSITION					
5. Market Position					
Market Share	x	15.0			
Relative Market Share		34.8			
6. Industry Concentration Ratio		51.0			
7. Employees Unionized		0.0			
8. Immediate Customer Fragmentation		25.0			
9. Market Share Growth Rate		8.1			
10. Market Share Instability		1.2			
DIFFERENTIATION FROM COMPETITORS					
11. Relative Product Quality		34.3			
12. Price Relative to Competition		100.3			
13. Standard Products-Services?		Yes			
14. Relative Compensation		102.0			
15. New Product Sales-Total Sales		0.0			
EFFECTIVENESS OF INVESTMENT USE					
16. Investment Intensity Index			z		
Investment-Sales	y	33.0			
Investment-Value Added		65.6			
17. Value Added per Employee ($000)		23.8	−1.7		
18. Vertical Integration		51.9	−0.8		
19. Relative Integration Backward		Less	−0.9		
20. Relative Integration Forward		Same	−0.3		
21. Fixed Capital Intensity		42.4	0.5		
22. Capacity Utilization		76.3	−0.4		
23. Investment Per Employee ($000)		15.6	0.4		
24. Inventory-Sales		10.7	1.0		
25. FIFO Valuation?		No	0.0		
26. Newness of P&E (NBV/GBV)		52.0	0.0		
DISCRETIONARY BUDGET EXPENDITURES			1.4		
27. Marketing Expense-Sales		7.7	1.5		
28. R&D Expense-Sales		2.5	−0.1		

(3)

From the PAR Report: Explanation and sample, 1977. Reprinted with the permission of The Strategic Planning Institute.

disturbing.   ROI has been steadily declining from 69% in 1983 to 23% in 1986, with the 1986 ROI being 9% below PAR ROI.

Factors Influencing Performance.   Page 2 of Exhibit 10–4 summarizes the key factors accounting for the difference between the business's actual performance and its PAR ROI.   The left column lists the ten key factors accounting for the performance of a business unit.   The first five measure the effectiveness of the business's use of investments.   The next two reflect competitive position and the final three indicate aspects of the business's strategic position.   These same factors are used to account for the performance of all businesses.

The mean value for all businesses in the PIMS database for each factor is given in Column 1.   For example, the mean market share is x% and mean investment as a percentage of sales is y%.   Column 2 contains the values for Business 12345 for these factors.   The market share for this business is 15% and the investment as a percent of sales is 33%.

Column 3 shows the expected impact on performance that results from the business's position as shown in Column 2.   The Impact on ROI is the expected amount by which the ROI of Business 12345 is helped by a favorable position or hurt by an unfavorable position relative to the average business in the database.   The sign of the impact for a factor depends on (1) if the business is above or below the average for all businesses and (2) if the factor has a positive impact on ROI.   The investment intensity of Business 12345 is below average.   Since investment intensity is negatively related to ROI, a low investment intensity contributes positively to ROI.   With Business 12345, the PAR ROI is increased by z% because of the lower than average investment intensity.

The magnitude of the impact on PAR ROI depends on (1) the strength of the factors' relationship to ROI and (2) the degree to which the business is above or below the average of all businesses in the database.   Note that an impact close to zero, such as −0.1 for a particular ratio, does not mean that the factor is unimportant.   It merely means, for example, that the industry concentration facing Business 12345 is close to average; therefore, industry concentration ratio suggests that the expected or PAR ROI will be about average.

Some predictor variables correlate highly with one another.   This multicolinearity makes it difficult to determine the contribution of specific factors to ROI.   For example market share and relative market share correlate strongly.   The report shows the *combined* impact of these two factors, rather than indicating the impact of each factor.

In addition to the ten key strategic factors shown on page 2, the PAR ROI model also contains 18 support factors (page 3 of Exhibit 10–4).   This summary would indicate that Business 12345 is in a slightly more attractive environment than the typical PIMS business if it has a lower than average amount of sales made to immediate customers on a single transaction.   However, it could be that the advantages due to having lower than average growth rates reduce the attractiveness of its environment.

If Business 12345 is in an average competitive position, it could be that the advantage due to a factor (say market share) is compensated for by another (say labor unionization).   The disadvantages of a factor (say market share) are compensated for by another (say another low unionization).

The business unit may be better than average in differentiating itself from competition. Its product quality may be higher than average. The lack of new products would improve its ROI. However, the lack of new product development may improve ROI in the short run, but decrease long-term ROI. The inverse relationship between ROI and percentage of new products illustrates a potential problem of the PAR model. The model is static and does not consider the dynamics of making investments for future benefits.

The largest contributor to PAR ROI comes from effective use of investments, particularly the low investment intensity.

The first three columns on page 3 of the report compare to the columns on page 2. Columns 4 and 5 used to focus on the sensitivity of PAR ROI to a change in an individual profit factor. Column 4 shows the magnitude of change in the factor from its present position. Column 5 indicates the direction and amount of change in PAR ROI which would occur if that one factor were changed by the amount indicated in Column 4. Most of these sensitivities differ from business to business because the impact of a factor on ROI often depends on the level of another factor. For example, the sensitivity of profitability to market position depends on the degree of unionization and other factors. Pages 5 and 6 (not shown) of the PAR ROI report show how pairs of factors jointly impact ROI.

The sensitivity columns indicated the sensitivity of PAR ROI to the accuracy of input data and the direction and amount of change in PAR ROI that would occur if input data for an individual factor were changed. These columns are no longer used by SPI.

As shown at the bottom of page 2, PAR ROI is calculated by adding the net ROI impact of *all* the ROI-influencing factors (both key factors and support factors) to the PIMS mean ROI. The PAR ROI is equal to the average ROI plus the combined profit consequences of being above or below average in each of 28 profit-influencing factors. PAR ROI is a baseline for appraising actual profitability in the recent past.

The PAR ROI for Business 12345 is 32% –9.9% greater than the 22.1% average ROI of all business in the PIMS database. A favorable position on the ten key strategic factors accounts for 5.9% of the expected ROI above average, while support factors contribute 4.0%.

Understanding Deviations from PAR ROI.

Understanding Deviations from PAR ROI. The PAR ROI for Business 12345 is 32%; however, the actual ROI in 1976 was only 23%. This difference warns management that the business unit should be closely examined. Some reasons for such large differences are:

1. *Definition of served market.* Management may be defining served market too narrowly. Its market share is 15% in a very narrowly defined market but much less in the broader market in which it actually competes. When the market is defined more broadly, its share is only 5% and the PAR ROI drops to 8.5%. By changing the definition of the market, the business is now performing to expectations for similar businesses, but may still be performing below corporate goals.

Incorrectly defining the served market also affects measurement of other variables. For example, the relative product quality in a narrowly defined "premium quality" market might be less than (−10%), but in a more broadly defined market, the *relative* product quality may be higher.

2. *Definition of the business unit.* Synergies or horizontal scale economies might have inflated the actual performance of a business relative to the PAR ROI. For example, businesses that share manufacturing facilities and use family brand names may realize economies of scale that are not reflected in the PAR ROI.

3. *Unusual short-term effects.* The PAR ROI of a business can be erroneous because the present position of the business may not reflect conditions that the business will be facing in the long-term. For example, transitory events such as strikes, economic cycles, and unusual weather may result in an unusually adverse, or favorable environment—an environment that the business does not anticipate encountering in the future.

Some of these short-term effects arise because of the lag time in investment decisions. For example, a business might invest in substantial advertising in launching a new product. Although the business expects returns from this advertising investment over the next years, the investment is treated as an expense during the current year. Therefore, the business will have lower profits and ROI in the current year and perhaps a higher PAR ROI because of the unusual advertising expenditures. Because of the disparity between investment and return, the accounting measure of ROI in the future may actually overstate the performance of the firm.

4. *Poor management.* A fourth explanation is management's inability to take advantage of the opportunities inherent in the strategic position of the business unit. SPI emphasizes this causal relationship when discrepancies arise.

5. *The business unit is unique.* A final explanation for the difference between actual and PAR ROI is that the business unit is different from other units in the PIMS database. Most people, when first introduced to PIMS, feel that each business is unique and that one model cannot be developed to explain the performance of a variety of business units. This suggests that there needs to be a unique set of independent variables for each type of business. A more extreme position holds that there needs to be a unique equation for each individual SBU.

These businesses are indeed unique; however, one can gain insight by focusing on common elements in each business. As an analogy, each individual is unique, but a physician focuses on a common set of variables (blood pressure, temperature, pulse rate) to diagnose an individual patient. Similarly, PIMS uses a common set of variables to diagnose SBUs. The variables are the same, but their values differ among businesses. In support of this position, SPI says the PIMS model fits the data well. It is a data based perspective to aid strategic thinking. We will return later to the defense of the PIMS model.

The position that each business is unique means that no generalizations to guide strategic planners can be developed. We are searching for some level of aggregation at which generalizations can be made. Perhaps all businesses cannot be described by one set of rules, but we should at least strive to make some generalization.

Using the PAR ROI Model.   There are two principal uses of the PAR ROI model—evaluating alternatives and determining the impact of proposed changes. In evaluation, a manager of many business units can use the PAR ROI model to calculate the PAR ROI of each unit. Units with high PAR ROIs are in a favorable strategic position and may warrant additional investments, whereas units with low PAR ROIs are in an unfavorable strategic position and should not receive investment funds.

A manager can also determine the impact that change in strategic position will have on ROI using the PAR ROI model. For example, the manager might have a plan that will improve product by 20% and improve market share by 10%. By substituting this new position into the PAR ROI equation, the manager can estimate the unit's ROI if these changes are implemented.

OTHER SPI MODELS

PAR Cash Flow

In addition to the PAR ROI model, SPI has developed a PAR cash flow model. In the cash flow model the dependent variable is cash flow as a percentage of investment and the independent variables are changes in the independent variable considered in the PAR ROI. Thus, the cash flow model indicates how much investment funds are required to achieve changes in the unit's strategic position. The development and interpretation of the PAR cash flow model are similar to that of the PAR ROI model. This model has now been retired.

Look-Alike Reports

Another approach in determining what performance can be reasonably expected from a business is to compare it to other businesses in the same competitive position. Look-Alike reports are developed by identifying businesses that are similar in major characteristics and then comparing the performance of these "look-alike" businesses with the target business. Note that the choice of "look alikes" is to develop a comparison to similar businesses. This approach is in sharp contrast to choosing best practices to be compared to and emulated in the "benchmarking" approach described earlier in the chapter.

Management chooses the bases on which the look alike companies are defined. For example, management of Business 12345 might use the following criteria (only a partial list is shown here) for selecting look alikes:[12]

	Performance Level to be Matched (%)	Importance Weight
Market Share	25.7	6
Relative Market Share	65	6
Investment Intensity (I/AVA)	121	6
Investment-Intensity (I/REV)	72.7	6
Vertical Integration	60	2

Weights with higher values are more important in selecting look alikes. In this case, management wants to compare itself to companies with relatively low market share and which are experiencing modest growth in sales.

Using these criteria, 24 look alike businesses were identified in the database. These look alikes were then divided into businesses with lower actual ROI (losers) and those with high actual ROIs (winners). Exhibit 10–5 summarizes the information based on the look alike analysis. The actual and PAR ROIs of the winners are substantially greater than those of the losers. Based on the variables shown in Exhibit 10–5, it appears that the winners have a significantly higher cash flow, less marketing expense, and introduced relatively fewer new products. It appears, based on this information, that Business 12345 could improve its performance by not attempting to introduce a large number of new products and by reducing its marketing expense.

LIM (Limited Information Model)

The Limited Information Model (LIM) is an abbreviated version of the PAR ROI model.[12] It contains only 18 variables which can be assessed with only limited information about the business being analyzed. This model is used by businesses to develop a better understanding of their competitors. Another use is to evaluate potential acquisitions.

EXHIBIT 10–5   Look-Alike Report

	This Business (%)	Losers (%)	Winners (%)
Actual ROI	18	5.9	26.2
Cash Flow/Investment	−3	−1.3	4.7
Total R&D/Sales	6.2	4.8	2.8
Total Marketing/Sales	1.2	9.1	11.4
Relative % New Products		3.7	−2.6
Fixed-capital intensity	44	57.0	33.1

For look alike reports, see for example, Alan Cleland, "PIMS Planning Guide: Acquisition Analysis, Cambridge, MA; The Strategic Planning Institute, 1979.

[12]See Bradley Cole and Donald Swire, "The Limited Information Report," Cambridge, MA, *The Strategic Planning Institute,* 1980.

Strategic Analysis Report

The Strategic Analysis Report (SAR) evaluated the effects of strategic decisions on business performance. To use this model, management provided information about the current position of the business, assumptions about the future business environment, and planning information concerning investments to be made in the business and capacity use. Using this information a simulator determined the consequences of these activities by extrapolating the results from businesses that have undertaken similar plans in similar situations. The analysis was useful in determining if plans are feasible. This report has also been retired.

USING THE PAR MODELS FOR STRATEGIC DECISION-MAKING (AN ILLUSTRATION)

The Central Air Conditioner (CAC) Division of Scott-Air Corporation was acquired in 1969 by a Fortune 500 company interested in building up its consumer durable business. The Scott-CAC division directed its efforts for 1 1/2 to 10 ton air conditioning unit market. In 1971 the company invested $85 million to double CAC capacity, bringing it to $128 million (factory sales value, two shifts). With this new capacity, their break even was $56 million. However, the corporation expected each division to return at least 22% on invested capital.

Production problems in the expanded plant resulted in missed delivery dates, causing a loss of customer goodwill, low morale among distributors, dealers, and the division's sales force. The division's sales in 1970 were $52 million (89,000 units); however, market share in 1971 declined to 4% on sales of $38 million (69,000 units). The division manager, Ben Millar, needed to develop a marketing strategy to guide Scott-CAC into the future.

CAC Industry[13]

Central air conditioners were introduced in the 1930s. Sales grew slowly at first but, since 1953, have been increasing steadily.

The CAC unit market grew at 30% to 50% per year during the 60s and was expected to grow at 15% to 25% annually through the 70s. In 1971, the market penetration of central air conditioning units was 11% of the estimated 63 million U.S. homes (compared to 40% for room air conditioner). Further, growth for central air units was *double* the growth for room air units.

Seventy-one companies manufactured central air conditioners in the United States. Most of these companies sold to ultimate consumers through wholesalers. Some of the companies sold to mass merchandisers such as Sears. A few companies did not market directly, but sold their output to other manufacturers who wanted to carry a full product line.

Some industry observers predicted a "shake out" similar to the one that had

[13]Adapted from Scott-Air (B), ICCH 3 – 578–607 by Ralph Biggadike, Colgate Darden Graduate School of Business Administration, University of Virginia, 1978.

occurred in the auto industry. Others claimed that the high cost of shipping favored regional manufacturers and the industry would remain fragmented. Some argued that the need for extensive installation also favored a fragmented structure.

In 1971, the major competitors in the CAC business and their market shares were:

Manufacturer	Market Share (%)
Carrier	20
GE	8
Lennox	8
Westinghouse	6
Sears	6
Fedders	6
American Standard	5
Scott	4
Chrysler	3
Air Temp	2
York	2
Williamson	2
Trane	2
Regional Manufacturers	26

The marketing strategies of these companies varied widely. Carrier used national advertising heavily, competed in room, central, and industrial air conditioning markets, and had sales divided among the different end-users as follows:

	(%)
new home and apartments	20
existing homes and apartments	18
commercial	27
industrial	20
institutional	8
defense, space, and transportation	7

Carrier had interests in industrial machinery and heaters but air conditioning accounted for 80% of its sales. Carrier used both factory branches and independent distributors to sell to its dealers. Carrier's total sales in 1970 were $594 million, with after tax net income of $24.1 million. Assets were $430 million, their debt to equity ratio was 34% and their earnings retention about 60% per year.

Fedders was the leader in room air conditioners. In 1971 it made a determined and successful effort to penetrate all segments of the central air conditioning market. The company's major tactics were low price, aggressive distribution and generous dealer incentives, such as luxury trips to the Amazon and Tahiti. Fedders sold to 2,500 dealers through 70 independent distributors. Fedders total sales in 1970 were

$296 million, with after tax net income of $15.6 million. Assets were $202 million, their debt to equity ratio was 47% and their earnings retention about 75%.

General Electric concentrated heavily on the building contractor business because it offered the potential for high volume and repeat business. GE showed little interest in the modernization business. GE advertised heavily in national and local media, and distribution was through factory branches to 3,000 dealers.

Sears concentrated on the modernization business and bought all its units from other manufacturers. The Sears marketing strategy was to advertise heavily in local media and capitalize on their "walk-in" traffic. They offered fast installation, after-sale service, and convenient financing.

The 1 1/2 to 10 ton CAC market was divided into (1) new residential (new home construction), (2) modernization (home improvement), (3) replacement (renewing units), and (4) light commercial. New residential accounted for 55% of the total market unit sales, modernization 18%, replacement (renewing units) 20%, and light commercial 7%. The new construction market had been growing faster than the modernization and replacements markets.

The *new residential market* was price sensitive and technical enough to require close consultation with builders and heating and cooling contractors regarding specifications. It was a "messy" market since builders "come and go." However, this market provided entry into the modernization market, because during declines in new construction builders became modernization contractors. Builders were primarily interested in low price, availability, and good financial terms.

The *modernization market* had higher margins than the new construction market. The dealer was particularly important in this market. Because the average installation cost was $1500 to $2000, installing central air conditioning represented a major investment for a consumer. Consumers were not knowledgeable and needed product and installation advice plus reassurance on reliability, maintenance, and quality.

The *replacement market* had the same high margins as the modernization market. The typical life of a CAC was seven years. Little was known about the buying behavior in this segment.

The light commercial market was sales to organizations such as McDonald's, churches, and schools. Selling to these accounts was quite specialized and often specialized units were required.

Scott's Strength and Weaknesses

Scott felt it was viewed by consumers as superior to its competition in product reliability; inferior on price, availability, and innovation; and equal on style and appearance. These perceptions also held true for dealers and distributors except that dealers and distributors serving the new construction market added that Scott's CAC products were inferior on completeness of line.

Scott's CAC unit variable costs in 1971 were about $350. Their accumulated production was 500,000 units and the slope of their experience curve was 89%.

Carrier's unit variable costs were estimated at $296 with 2,400,000 accumulated production units and an 86% experience curve.

The Scott Air Group had 73 distributors for room air conditioners; approximately three-quarters of whom also distributed central air conditioners. The distributors sold to 1,212 dealers, with two-thirds of dealers handling central air. The dealer network was somewhat smaller than Scott's competition. They were generally local business and were somewhat underfinanced.

PIMS Analysis

Using an abbreviated PIMS PAR ROI model, called the LIM model, Millar, the CAC Division Manager, examined the impact of tripling sales to $100 million per year. Then, he simulated an aggressive share building strategy using other PIMS models.

Even with $100 million in sales in 1973, Scott CAC market share was forecast to be only 8.3%. Even though capacity utilization is now about average for a business unit in the PIMS database, the poor market position severely depresses the PAR ROI. This analysis suggested that tripling sales would not result in the financial performance the corporation was expecting.

Rather than focusing on the entire CAC market, Scott should consider focusing on a market segment or niche. The potential strategic alternatives are: (1) new construction, (2) modernization, (3) replacement, (4) light industry, (5) private branding to mass merchandisers such as Sears or Montgomery Ward. The private brand and new construction markets are price sensitive. It would be difficult for a high-cost manufacturer like Scott CAC to attain a sustainable competitive advantage in these markets against low-cost manufacturers like GE and Carrier. Even though the new construction market was growing faster and was substantially larger than the other markets, the needs of this market did not fit well with Scott's capabilities.

The light industrial market was probably less price sensitive with emphasis on performance, low operating cost, and reliability. However, this segment required directing the sales force toward a new market with different needs. In addition, Scott CAC would have to develop a staff to perform the special designs needed by the market.

Since the modernization and replacement markets had similar product and marketing needs we might consider them as one market. This market differed from new construction in that it required dealer support. In addition more emphasis is placed on reliability and performance, two of Scott's strengths, and less emphasis is placed on price, Scott's weakness.

To use the PIMS models to evaluate a strategy directed toward the modernization-replacement market rather than the entire CAC market, the definition of the served market changes. The CAC market was $950 million in 1971 (Scott's sales of $38 million divided by Scott's market share of 4%). In 1971, the size of the modernization-replacement market was $361 million (38% of $950 million). If Scott CAC could realize $100 million in the modernization-replacement market, its share would be 27.7%, not 8.3%. In addition to changing the estimated share, the mean analysis would have to reexamine Scott's prices and product quality relative to the modernization-replacement market rather than the entire CAC market.

EVALUATING THE PIMS MODELS

To this point, we have emphasized how the PIMS models can be used. These models seem to provide some useful information for evaluating strategic alternatives such as Scott's alternative of focusing on the entire CAC market rather than the modernization-replacement segment. However, an important issue remaining is how good are the PIMS models?

SPI answers by emphasizing that the PIMS PAR ROI model has an R^2 of .80. In other words, the independent variables in the model explain 80% of the variations in the dependent variable, ROI. This suggests that only 20% of variation in ROI remains to be explained by management decisions, luck, and variables not in the model.[14]

Bias in Model Fit

However, this high R^2 may be caused by the construction of the model rather than "true" causal impact. Consider the relationship between ROI and investment intensity.

$$ROI = \frac{profits}{investments} \times \frac{investments}{sales} = investment\ intensity$$

Does the negative correlation between ROI and investment intensity suggest that increasing investment intensity will decrease ROI or does it reflect the fact that there is a positive correlation between sales and profits because profits are equal to sales minus costs?

Since the components of ROI, the dependent variable in the PAR ROI model, also appear as independent variables, the R^2 is biased toward 1.0. In fact, if we use accounting rules to develop a linear combination of a portion of the 37 independent variables to calculate ROI, the R^2 would be 1.0. Thus, the high R^2 of the PAR ROI model is partially the result of having the same variables as both independent and dependent variables. If the model construction problems were removed, the R^2 would be much lower.[15]

Omitted Variables

Theory suggests that some important variables are not considered in the model such as synergy, the nature of the industry, and the interaction between a unit's environment and its intended strategy. A critical aspect when evaluating a strategic opportunity is to look at the match between the factors needed to be successful in that opportunity

[14]Anderson, Carl and Frank Paine, "PIMS: A Reexamination," *Academy of Management Review,* July, 1978, pp. 602–612, and Robin Wensley, "PIMS and BCG: New Horizon of False Dawn," *Strategic Management Journal,* Vol. 3, 1982, pp. 1217–1258.

[15]See Robert Jacobson and David Aaker, "Is Market Share All It's Cracked Up to Be?," *Journal of Marketing,* Vol. 49, Fall, 1985, pp. 11–22.

and the capabilities of the business. For example, when evaluating alternatives facing Scott CAC, we looked at the degree to which the opportunities exploited Scott's strengths—reliability and performance—and avoided Scott's weaknesses—high cost. We looked at the degree to which opportunities were synergistic with Scott's present way of doing business. The modernization-replacement market was the most synergistic and, in fact, this is the market in which most of Scott's present sales are being made.

In addition, efforts directed toward the modernization-replacement market would benefit Scott's room air conditioner (RAC) business unit. A strong entry in CAC would result in strong dealer support for Scott's RAC which are sold through the same dealers. However, Scott CAC efforts directed toward the new construction market would have no impact on the RAC business unit. Abandoning the CAC modernization-replacement market entirely would have a negative impact on RAC because dealer loyalty and emphasis on Scott's products would diminish. In fact, dealers might drop Scott's RAC in favor of a competitor that had both a CAC and RAC product line.

In general, the outcome of a strategic decision is a function of the interaction between the strategy (and tactics) selected and the circumstances (or uncontrollable factors) facing the business unit. The PAR ROI model does not include variables representing these interactions.

Causality

There is an implication in the PAR ROI model (though causality has never been claimed by SPI) that changes in the independent variables result in predictable changes in the dependent variable, ROI. For example, the relationship between market share and ROI suggests that increasing market share result in higher ROI. Thus, business units should attempt to increase their ROIs.

However, any cross-section model such as the PAR ROI model only indicates factors related to the dependent variable. It does not indicate what should be done to improve the situation or even if anything can be done to improve the situation. The costs of gaining market share by far outweigh the benefit that results from higher market share.

Scholars feel that market share and ROI are both outcome measurers and are causally related. An event may occur such as a scientist in the R&D laboratory who discovers a drug that cures the common cold. This drug is patentable and the firm has a sustainable competitive advantage in the cold remedy marketplace. Sales and profits soar. The firm has a high ROI and large market share among other firms that provide cold remedies. The increased market share did not result in the improved ROI, it only indicates, like the ROI, the extent to which the company secured a sustainable competitive advantage. ROI and market share are correlated but not causally related.

The PIMS models do not show the benefit or cost associated with deliberate attempts to alter strategic position.

Applicability to Other Countries

Japanese managers also perceive the PIMS strategy principles (based on studies of U.S. businesses) to be true in Japan also.[16] They believe that a firm's market position has a critical influence on its performance.

CONCLUSION

In this chapter we have described and discussed two approaches to an important question, "What do others do?" This question becomes critically important in the complex managerial environments in which future events are difficult to predict. Further, in such environments, relationships among marketing (and management in general) processes, measurable decision variables, and outcomes are not immutable but could themselves be changed by managerial or regulatory action. Under such circumstances attempting to understand what others do is itself an important part of developing a marketing strategy.

Benchmarking and PIMS differ both as regards which businesses are chosen for comparison and what elements of these businesses are compared. Benchmarking focuses on choosing the best business (even if it is a totally different type of business, e.g., Xerox's benchmarking of L.L. Bean), and in understanding the process that is used. PIMS focuses on comparing a cross-section of businesses, or a look-alike business and on obtaining norms[17] on variables such as investment intensity, advertising expenditures, wages, and so forth. Although the chapter discusses the advantages and disadvantages of both methods, their joint use gives perhaps a more powerful approach to understanding what to expect from others (and oneself).

Another method provides a more thorough understanding of the competitive process. This is the use of a phantom competitor. In order to simulate where a competitive attack may appear, one or more teams may be created to role-play competitors. Their charge is to find the best (including radically new) ways in which competition might occur. This, in effect, is another kind of benchmarking—that may be possible.

Together these three approaches provide information that could benefit both strategic thinking and planning.

Concept Questions

1. (a.) What is benchmarking?
    (b.) What differentiates the different types of benchmarking?
    (c.) Describe the benchmarking process.
    (d.) What are the critical factors in performing a successful benchmarking exercise?

---

[16]See Masaaki Kotabe and Dale F. Duhan with David K. Smith, Jr. and R. Dale Wilson, "The Perceived Veracity of PIMS Strategy Principles in Japan: An Empirical Inquiry," *Journal of Marketing,* January, Vol. 55, 1991, pp. 26–41.

[17]See F. B. Ennis, *Marketing Norms for Product Managers,* New York, Association of National Advertisers, 1985, for an example of a book which provides rules-of-thumb, benchmarks, and other norms for product managers.

2.   (a.) How is a unit of analysis defined in PIMS database?

    (b.) What are the different measures available in the PIMS database?

    (c.) Describe the PAR models.

    (d.) What does deviance from PAR ROI of a given business unit's actual performance mean?

    (e.) How are the look-alike reports different from the PAR reports?

    (f.) How can look-alike reports be used?

Discussion Questions

1.   Prepare a report to the senior Vice President of International Marketing for carrying out a benchmarking study for the division.

2.   Compare the merits of a phantom competitor approach to Benchmarking and PIMS analysis.

3.   Suppose that other firms are using your division as an exemplar for their benchmarking activities, what should you do to enhance your competitiveness?

4.   Based on your understanding of benchmarking, how would you change the process you would use to find the job that best fits you?

5.   If PAR reports and look-alike reports give contradictory results for your division's situation, what should you do?

6.   Identify differences that exist between how business units are defined for PIMS and product-market definitions from Châpter 4. Discuss the consequence (if any) of these differences for use by marketing strategists.

APPENDIX

ROI = NET INCOME ÷ INVESTMENT

Pretax net income, *including* special nonrecurring costs, minus corporate overhead costs, as a percent of average investment including fixed and working capital at book value, but *excluding* corporate investment not particular to this business.

Sample Definitions of Some of the Factors that Influence ROI

    Capacity Utilization.   The average percent of standard capacity used during the year. Standard capacity is the *sales value* of the maximum output a business can sustain with (a) facilities normally in operation, and (b) current constraints (e.g., technology, work rules, labor practices, etc.). For most manufacturing businesses, this consists of 2 shifts, 5 days per week. For process businesses, a 3-shift, 6-day week is typical.

    Employees Unionized (%).   The percent of total employees of a business who are unionized.

Accounting Method.   Is the accounting method used for inventory valuation FIFO, or another method (e.g., LIFO [Last In, First Out])?

Fixed Capital Intensity.   Gross book value of plant and equipment expressed as a percent of sales. Gross book value includes original value of buildings, real estate, manufacturing equipment, and transportation equipment.

Immediate Customer Fragmentation.   The proportion of the total number of immediate customers accounting for 50% of total sales, expressed as a percent. For example, if five of a business's 100 immediate customers represent 50% of the business's sales, immediate customer fragmentation is 5%.

Served Market Concentration Ratio.   The amount of industry shipments accounted for by the four largest firms in the same industry expressed as a percent.

Industry (SIC) Growth, Long Run.   The annual long-term (10-year) growth rate of the SIC industry in which a business is located, expressed as a percent.

Inventory-Sales.   The sum of raw materials, work-in-process inventory, and finished goods inventory (each net of reserve for losses) as a percent of sales.

Investment Intensity Index.   A factor combining

a. Investment-Sales: Investment expressed as a percent of sales. Investment may be measured in any of the following ways:
   – net book value of plant and equipment plus working capital
   – equity plus long-term debt
   – total assets employed minus current liabilities attributed to the business

b. Investment-Value Added.   Investment expressed as a percent of value added. Value added is adjusted for profits, so that only *average* profit (PIMS mean ROI times Investment) is included.

Value added is net sales, including lease revenues, minus total purchases (which include the cost of raw materials, energy, components, assemblies, supplies or services purchased or consumed).

Investment Per Employee ($000).   Average investment, expressed in thousands of dollars, per employee.

Market Position.   A factor that combines

a. *Market Share.* The share of the served market for a business, expressed as a percent.

b. *Relative Market Share.* The market share of a business relative to the combined market share of its three leading competitors, expressed as a percent. For example, if a business has 30% of the market and its three largest competitors have 20%, 10%, and 10%: 30 divided by (20 + 10 + 10) = 75%.

Market Share Growth Rate. The annual growth rate of market share, expressed as a percent.

Market Share Instability. The instability of the market share of a business, measured as the average percentage difference from the exponential market-share trend.

Marketing Expense-Sales. The sum of sales force, advertising and sales promotion, and other marketing expenses, expressed as a percent of sales. Does not include physical distribution. Sales are the net sales billed, including lease revenues, of a business.

New Product Sales-Total Sales. Percent of sales accounted for by new products. New products are those introduced during the three preceding years.

Newness of P&E (NBV/GBV). Newness of plant and equipment, measured as the ratio of net book value to gross book value.

Price Relative to Competition. The average level of selling prices of products and services, relative to the average level of leading competitors. The average price of competitors is 100%; if your average prices are 5% higher, your price relative to competition is 105%.

Purchase Amount of Immediate Customers. The typical amount of products or services bought by an immediate customer in a single transaction. A contract covering a period of time is regarded as a single transaction.

Real Market Growth, Short-Run. The annual growth rate of the size of served market, reduced by the selling price index, expressed as a percent.

Relative Compensation. The average of hourly wage rates relative to leading competitors and salary levels relative to competitors. Competitors' wage rates and salary levels are 100%; if your wage rates and salary levels are 5% higher, your relative hourly wage rates are 105%, relative salaries are 105%, and your average relative compensation is 105%.

Relative Product Quality. The percent of sales from products and services that the customer judges "superior" to those available from leading competitors *minus* the percent of sales from those judged "inferior". For example, if 60% of the sales of a business are from products considered superior and 10% are from those considered inferior, relative product quality is

$$60\% - 20\% = 40\%$$

Note that the mean of relative product quality is about 22%, indicating that the typical PIMS business has product quality judged higher than that of its competitors.

Relative Integration Backward. The degree of *backward* vertical integration (i.e., toward suppliers) of a business *relative* to its leading competitors (less than, the same as, more than).

Relative Integration Forward.   The degree of *forward* vertical integration (i.e., toward customers) of a business *relative* to its leading competitors (less than, the same as, more than).

R&D Expenses-Sales.   The sum of product or service R&D expenses plus process R&D expenses, expressed as a percent of sales. Product or service R&D expenses include all expenses incurred to secure innovations or advances in the products or services of a business, including improvements in packaging as well as in product design, features, and functions. Process R&D expenses include all expenses for process improvements for the purpose of reducing the cost of manufacturing, processing, or physical handling of goods by a business.

Selling Price Growth Rate.   The annual growth rate of selling prices charged by a business, expressed as a percent.

Standard Products-Services.   Are the products or services of a business standardized for all customers, or are they designed or produced to order for individual customers?

Value Added Per Employee ($000).   Value added, expressed in thousands of dollars, per employee. Value added is adjusted for profits.

Vertical Integration.   Value added as a percent of sales. Both value added and sales are adjusted for profits, so that only *average* profit (PIMS mean ROI times Investment) is included.

Part 4

ALTERNATIVES AND IMPLEMENTATION

Chapter 11

Timing

Observe due measure, for right timing is in all things the most important factor.

Hesiod: *Works and Days*, 1, 11

Ib 1 694

Consider the following headlines from recently published articles:[1]

Right Time, Right Place, Right Price: How Fleet and KKR Bested the Competition for Bank of New England   *(Business Week)*.

Time Warner Says Now Is Right Moment for Australian Editions of 2 Magazines   *(The Wall Street Journal)*.

Philips Electronics to Delay Introduction of Its Digital Compact Cassette System *(The Wall Street Journal)*.

A Problem That Cadillac Likes: Buyers Must Wait For 2 Hot Models *(The New York Times)*.

[1]Smith, G., L. Nathans, and J. O'C. Hamilton, "Right Time, Right Place, Right Price," *Business Week,* May 6, 1991, pp. 28–29.

Witcher, S. K., "Time Warner Says Now Is Right Moment For Australian Editions of 2 Magazines," *The Wall Street Journal,* July 31, 1992, C9.

"Philips Electronics to Delay Introduction of Its Digital Compact Cassette System," *The Wall Street Journal,* July 31, 1992, B3.

Bryant, A., "A Problem That Cadillac Likes," *The New York Times,* November 19, 1991, C1, C18.

Shapiro, E., "Conagra May Be Moving Healthy Choice Too Fast," *The New York Times,* July 13, 1992, C1, C4.

"Isuzu Delays Plans on Car, Denies It May Exit Market," *The Wall Street Journal,* July 31, 1992, A4.

Conagra May Be Moving Healthy Choice Too Fast *(The New York Times).*

Isuzu Delays Plans on Car, Denies It May Exit Market *(The Wall Street Journal).*

These headlines underscore the importance of timing in aiding or denying competitive advantage. Timing implies both static and dynamic issues. The static question is choosing "a right time." For example, that of new market entry (Time Warner) and new product or service entry (Philips Electronics), or market exit (Isuzu). The dynamic question is choosing a trajectory. For example, the speed of expanding a product line (Conagra), capacity expansion and delivery (Cadillac), and the price path of a product or service.

Although the importance of timing has been known since the time of our earliest ancestors (note the quotation from Hesiod dating to 700 BC), its study in marketing strategy is quite recent. (Of course, marketing strategy is itself an infant compared to Hesiod!) Specifically, whereas the questions of advertising timing and the choice of a skimming-on-penetration pricing policy have been studied for some time, those of first-mover or market pioneer advantage, preemptive defense, and of signalling or announcements and bluffing are just beginning to attract attention. In this chapter we discuss order-of-entry, signalling, and time-dependent defensive considerations, all of which are essential to achieve competitive advantage.

Order-of-Entry

In a regulated market (like many cable television suppliers in the United States) being first-in is imperative. There is simply no room for being a second or a third, unless regulatory changes are made. In most other instances, markets have room for several brands. It is for such markets that the order-of-entry decision is pertinent. Two issues dominate the decision to enter. The first is whether to enter at all and, assuming the answer is yes, then the second is when. The answer to the whether-at-all question depends on if this opportunity (on a shareholder value basis) represents the best use of resources. The when question is really one of optimal entry time; when these resources will be best leveraged in this market. Also, like most strategic decisions, these issues often cannot be separated. The "whether-at-all" issue may depend on the "when." The two are intertwined when entry timing relates to the resources allocated to the project. For example, increased R&D staffing and changes in procedure could accelerate the development of a new product as in the case of Honda.[2] (To bring out their 1994 Accord in Ohio for the U.S. market, Honda moved 56 of its engineers and their families from its Marysville, Ohio plant to Japan for about three years.) Further, the two issues (whether and when) would be intertwined if the resulting outcomes also depend on the timing of entry. For example, consider a firm with a policy of entering a market only if it can sustain the market share leadership position. If this firm wishes to introduce a cola to compete against Coke, then this target is perhaps not attainable. (Coke has maintained its Number 1 position in the market since

[2]Details are to be found in Miller, K. M. and L. Armstrong, "How Honda Hammered Out Its New Accord," *Business Week,* Dec. 21, 1992, p. 86.

1923!)[3]   Being a market pioneer in the personal computer market did not assure MITS[4] of market share leadership in that market.   In fact, how many of us know that MITS was the market pioneer in that market?

So, the critical aspect is the relationship between order-of-entry and market consequences.   This relationship is examined next.

Expected Link Between Order-of-Entry and Performance

Having come this far in our study, some obvious reasons about the pros and cons of becoming an early or late entrant into the market should come to mind.   As stated in Chapter 1, outcomes depend on competitive advantage, which depends on enacting the strategic choice set of ROTR {relationship $\times$ offering $\times$ timing $\times$ resource allocation} and the context in which the enacting occurs.   Given a timing-of-strategy enactment, outcome depends on the rest of the strategy and the context.   Again, given the enactment timing, the best outcome depends on the choice of the best relationship $\times$ offering $\times$ resource allocation set in the context.   With changes in timing, the context may be less well or better known or knowable; further, the opportunity available may change.   Knowledge and opportunity directly impact the possible outcome both in sales and market share as well as in resource utilization efficiency measures of profit and profitability.

In this context, knowledge has two components.   The first is uncertainty.   Early entrants (or actors) are uncertain about what customers and channel members want, how future competitors will act and react, how technology will evolve, and so forth. Raytheon pioneered microwave ovens in 1946.   Imagine the uncertainty for Raytheon on the following questions: How would the product be used?   What form should it take?   What price should be charged?   What services, credit, and so forth, would be necessary to make this product succeed?   Which channels should or would carry this product?   Should the product be offered to hotels or cafeterias, or directly to the end user?   Who else might compete in this market?   How would they enter?   For later entrants, for example GE and Samsung (who entered in 1979), many of these questions had already been answered.   Often, the answers are provided by the efforts of the pioneers.   Although uncertainty is higher for early entrants, it is balanced by the knowledge or experience gained.   Organizational learning in matching and shaping customer and channel tastes, and learning that leads to efficient and cheaper manufacturing and delivery (e.g., use of the experience curve concept) may lead to efficiencies and a competitive edge.   Knowledge gained through uncertainty makes early entry less favorable, but knowledge gained through experience makes early entry more favorable.

Early entrance may create relationships which block new entrants.   For example, entry into the soft drink market in the United States is difficult, given the relationship

---

[3]*Advertising Age,* "Study: Majority of 25 Leaders in 1923 Still On Top," September 19, 1983, p. 32.

[4]Described in Freiberger, P., and M. Swaine, *Fire in the Valley: The Making of the Personal Computer,* Berkeley, CA, Osborne/McGraw-Hill, 1984.

between major bottlers and soft drink manufacturers. For example, in Great Britain[5] Cadbury-Schweppes owns 51% of the bottler Coca-Cola & Schweppes Beverages, which in turn holds about 35% of the 8 billion liter, £5.5 billion British soft drink market. Similarly, Pepsi's early relationship with the former Soviet Union precluded Coke's entry there.

Early entrants may flood the market with an assortment of products that effectively leaves little or no opportunity for further market entry. The ready-to-eat cereal industry in the United States is an example. By building sufficient capacity to supply the world's bulk vitamin C supply, Hoffman-LaRoche has virtually choked off further entry in this market.[6] The scale of operations of an early entrant may lower cost and thus may lower the opportunity for a later entrant either by increasing the resources necessary to compete effectively or by lowering the market price and thus lowering the later entrant's profits. Existing relationships or scale of operations (and thus its commitments) may create an inertia that thwarts an early player from adapting to changes in context. For example, as reported in *Business Week*,

> "Yet something has gone terribly awry. Seven years later, IBM operations have not topped the record profit. And IBM shares, so long the market bellwether, today trade at $105, a 1983 level that's 40% below the 1987 peak. Just how did IBM and its blue-suited legions plunge into, as Akers puts it, 'Crisis?'
>
> Put most plainly, IBM remains stuck in the past. With a corporate culture that cherishes former glories and a dependence on slow-growing sales of mainframe computers, costs remain too high. And key new products—laptop computers are but one example—find their way to market far too slowly.
>
> None of that is startling news. But why can't Akers, six disappointing years after he took the helm, turn IBM's ship around? The technological current just may be too swift. Every advance in microprocessors—the silicon chips that are any computer's brain—rewrites the economics of the computer biz. So the price of computing power has plummeted, computer hardware has become a commodity item, like so many cast iron skillets. That has allowed scads of new, nimbler rivals—Compaq Computer, Sun Microsystems, MIPS Computer Systems, and Dell Computer among them—to nibble away at IBM's market share."[7]

[5]For more information see Davis, T., "Swan's Song," *Beverage World,* July, 1992, pp. 24–35 and Davis, T. (1992), "Corner-Store Merchandising Gets A World-Class Kick-Start," *Beverage World,* September, 1992, pp. 50–60.

[6]Schmalansee, R., "Entry Deterrence in the Ready to Eat Breakfast Cereal Industry," *Bell Journal of Economics,* Vol. 9, Autumn, 1978, pp. 305–327. For the Hoffman-LaRouche example, see James, B. G., *Business Wargames,* Harnodsworth, UK, Penguin Books, 1984.

[7]Byrne, J. A., S. A. Depke, J. W. Verity, R. Neff, J. B. Levine, and S. A. Forest, "IBM: As Markets and Technology Change, Can Big Blue Remake Its Culture?" *Business Week,* June 17, 1991, pp. 25–32.

Similarly, Ghemawat uses technological inertia to explain his following observation: "On the one hand, industry experts asserted that a large installed base was a tremendous advantage in marketing PBXs. On the other hand, ever since the U.S. PBX industry had been opened up to competition, it had attracted a steady stream of entrants that had carved out profitable niches on the basis of innovative products; incumbents, in contrast, had tended to lag in both product innovation and imitation. Why hadn't the incumbents tried harder to leverage their marketing advantages into technological leadership, or at least parity?" Ghemawat, P., "Market Incumbency and Technological Inertia," *Marketing Science*, Vol. 10, No. 2, Spring, 1991, pp. 161–171. The interested reader may also see the discussion of "excess inertia" in Farrell J., and G. Saloner "Installed Base and Compatibility: Innovation, Product Preannouncement and Predation." The American Economic Review, December, 1986, pp. 940–955.

Thus, the available opportunity is affected by existing relationships and the scale of operations in the market. Existing relationships may constrict the opportunity or raise its cost for new entrants. Or, it may be an inertial flywheel that prevents adaptation to new contexts. Similarly, scale of operations could have either a positive or a negative effect, either by inflexible commitments forcing the pathway or by providing economies of scale.

Knowledge and opportunity vary with timing, but it is unlikely that any generalizations can be made about the direction of the relationship between order-of-entry and outcomes. This ambivalence is seen in the research results that are presented next. It must be emphasized that although the claim cannot be made that it is always best to be first, it is appropriate to say that between two possible entry times one is better than another. Determining the better time can only be done by thoroughly examining the knowledge and opportunity conditions as well as the context of the entry being considered. This fits with the notion of "strategic windows" advanced by Abell in 1978: "The term 'strategic window' is used here to focus attention on the fact that there are only limited periods during which the 'fit' between the key requirements of a market and the particular competencies of a firm competing in the market is at an optimum."[8] The determination of such a fit may be done using the extended SWOT analysis described in Chapter 7.

Order-of-Entry and Performance

Professors Kerin, Varadarajan and Peterson[9] provide a synthesis of the literature on this relationship in Exhibit 11–1. We reproduce their summary of the various studies conducted examining the order-of-entry to performance relationship. Many of these studies claim to have established a positive relationship between pioneering and performance. Some show how market positioning, and advertising expenditures (Urban, Canter, Gaskin and Mucha[10]), and product quality (Robinson[11]) were found to differentiate performance leaders from trailers, and almost all show that leadership depends on context. Performance leadership in these studies depends on the right strategy set for the context, as opposed to being a pioneer or an early entrant (Exhibit 11–2). Note that these studies do not incorporate any time and risk discounted performance measures. The results might be quite different if such were done.

[8]This quotation is found on page 21 of Abell, D. F., "Strategic Windows," Journal of Marketing, July, 1978, pp. 21–26.

[9]Kerin, R. A., P. R. Varadarajan, R. A. Peterson, "First-Mover Advantage: A Synthesis, Conceptual Framework, and Research Propositions," *Journal of Marketing*, October, Vol. 56, 1992, pp. 33–52.

Lambkin, Mary, "Order of Entry and Performance in New Markets," *Strategic Management Journal*, Vol. 9, 1988, pp. 127–140.

[10]Urban, G. L., T. Canter, S. Gaskin, and Z. Mucha, "Market Share Rewards to Pioneering Brands: An Empirical Analysis and Strategic Implications," *Management Science*, Vol. 32, June, 1986, pp. 645–659.

Sullivan, M., "Brand Extension and Order of Entry," Report No. 91–105, Cambridge, MA, *Marketing Science Institute*, 1991.

[11]Robinson, W-T., "Sources of Market Pioneer Advantages: The Case of Industrial Goods Industries," *Journal of Marketing Research*, Vol. 25, February, 1988, pp. 87–94.

EXHIBIT 11–1 Pioneer's Market Share Advantage in the PIMS Data

PIMS Database Studies		Sample Survey and Archival Studies	
Study	Principal Finding(s)/Conclusion(s)	Study	Principal Finding(s)/Conclusion(s)
Robinson and Fornell (1985) Analyzed 371 mature consumer goods businesses	First-movers were found to have higher market shares than later entrants. On average, first-movers had a market share of 20%, versus 17% for early followers and 13% for late entrants. Significant degrees of lateness effects were found. Early followers had significantly higher market shares than late followers; however, the difference between first-movers and early followers was much smaller than the difference between first-movers and early followers.	Bond and Lean (1977) Examined introduction dates and subsequent market shares of 11 innovations in two categories of prescription drugs (oral diuretics and antianginals).	The first firm to offer and promote a new type of product was found to receive a substantial and enduring sales advantage. Later entrants were in a position to overtake the pioneers by offering new benefits.
		Whitten (1979) Examined the introduction of 7 cigarette types.	For six of the seven cigarette types studied, the first firm to offer, promote, and widely distribute a brand for which there was a favorable market trend was found to receive a substantial and often enduring sales advantage.
Robinson (1988) Studied 1209 mature industrial goods businesses	First-movers were found to have higher market shares than later entrants. On average, first-movers had a market share of 29%, versus 21% for early followers and 15% for late entrants. Order of entry alone explained 8.9% of the variation in market share. First-movers also tended to have higher product quality, broader product lines, and broader served markets.	Spital (1983) Tracked 22 product innovations in the metal oxide semiconductor (MOS) industry.	In 17 of 22 innovations studied, the first manufacturer to produce a design was found to hold the largest market share in that design from the date of first production until the time of the study. This result was explained by the lengthy period required to qualify vendors and the practice of "designing-in" technology. No lateness effect was observed.
Lambkin (1988) Examined 129 start-up and 187 adolescent businesses	Order of market entry was found to have significant effect on market share for both startup businesses and adolescent businesses. Among startup businesses on average, market pioneers had a market share of 24%, versus 10% for early followers as well as late entrants. Among adolescent businesses, on average, first-movers had a market share of 33%, versus 19% for early followers and 25% for late entrants.	Flaherty (1983) Studied 10 types of semiconductor components, equipment, and materials. Urban et al. (1986) Analyzed 129 consumer brands across 34 product categories.	A small negative simple correlation was found between order of market entry and market share of lead technology, but product quality and skills in application engineering moderated the relationship. Of the four independent variables investigated (market positioning, advertising expenditures, order of entry, and time lag between entries into the market), the first two variables were found to be more important explanators of market share than order of entry. No lateness effect was observed.

EXHIBIT 11–1 (Continued)

PIMS Database Studies

Study	Principal Finding(s)/Conclusion(s)
Srinivasan (1988) Analyzed order of entry effects, marketing and R&D expenses, product quality, market share, and return on investment.	Early followers have lower marketing and R&D expenses than first-movers.
Miller, Gartner, and Wilson (1989) Studied 119 new corporate ventures in the consumer and industrial sectors	Early followers have marginally lower product quality and market shares than first-movers, but followers in product-markets in the initial stage of their life cycle have higher product quality and larger market shares. Early followers in the initial phase of a product-market life cycle are more profitable than first-movers because of higher market shares and lower marketing and R&D expenses. A significant inverse relationship was found between order of entry and market share. First-movers had higher quality, better service, and more differentiated products than later entrants. No lateness effect on share was observed.
Parry and Bass (1990) Studied 593 consumer goods businesses and 1287 industrial goods businesses	Pioneers were observed to have higher market shares than followers. The extent to which pioneers have a share advantage depends on industry type (concentrated, nonconcentrated) and end-user purchase amounts.

Sample Survey and Archival Studies

Study	Principal Finding(s)/Conclusion(s)
Lilian and Yoon (1990) Analyzed 112 industrial products in 7 French industry sectors	The third through fifth entrants were more successful than first and second entrants; successful products, irrespective of timing, benefited from entry early in the product life cycle; delay of entry accompanied production and marketing expertise of followers.
Mitchell (1991) Studied 314 entrants into five technical subfields of the diagnostic imaging industry.	Entry order effects on market share and survival depend on whether the first-mover is an industry incumbent or newcomer. Newcomers benefit from early entry and incumbents perform better with later entry. A significant "survivor bias" observed in relationship between entry order and market share.

Considerations in Interpreting and Generalizing Results

PIMS-Based Studies	All Empirical Studies	Sample Survey Studies
1. Operational definition of a pioneer or first-mover 2. Unit of analysis 3. Sample of heterogeneity and representativeness	1. Censored sample bias 2. Focus on averages	1. Idiosyncratic samples 2. Timing of market share measurement

From Kerin, R. A., P. R. Varadarajan, and R. A. Peterson, "First-Mover Advantage: A Synthesis, Conceptual Framework, and Research Propositions," *Journal of Marketing*, October 1992, Vol. 56, 1992, pp. 33–52 (Table 1). Reprinted with permission from the American Marketing Association.

EXHIBIT 11–2 Pioneer's Market Share Advantage in the PIMS Data

| | Market Share (%) | | | |
Study	Pioneer	Early Follower	Late Entrant	Advantage Pioneer-Late Entrant
Robinson and Fornell, 1985 consumer goods (n=371)	29	17	12	17
Robinson, 1988 industrial goods (n=1209)	29	21	15	14
Parry and Bass, 1990 concentrated industry consumer goods (n=437)	34	24	17	17
industrial goods (n=994)	33	26	20	13
Nonconcentrated consumer goods (n=156)	12	7	6	6
industrial goods (n=293)	14	10	8	6
Lambkin, 1988 start-up firms (n=129)	24	10	10	14
adolescent firms (n=187)	33	19	13	20

n = sample size.
From Golder, P. N. and G. J. Tellis, Do Pioneers Really Have Long Term Advantages? A Historical Analysis, *Marketing Science Institute, Working Paper, Report,* 1992, p. 5. Reprinted with permission by the Marketing Science Institute.

Beside the problems of performance measurement, there is the serious issue of identification of pioneers in the PIMS database and ASSESSOR[12] database studies.

An original study conducted by Golder and Tellis[13] avoids many of the problems of definitions found in other studies. It focuses however, only on market share as a measure of performance. The major results of this study are discussed next. Golder and Tellis distinguish between inventor, product pioneer, and market pioneer.

[12]The ASSESSOR database is now the property of Information Resources Inc. of Chicago, IL. It is based on the ASSESSOR methodology for pretest market measurement developed by Urban. See the reference in footnote 8 for more details.

[13]Golder, P. N. and G. J. Tellis, "Do Pioneers Really Have Long-Term Advantages? A Historical Analysis." Working Paper, Boston, Marketing Science Institute, 1992, pp. 92–124. (A later version of this paper appears as "Pioneer Advantage: Marketing Logic or Marketing Legend?" *Journal of Marketing Research,* Vol. 57, May, 1993, pp. 158–170.

Golder and Tellis, op. cit., p. 20, report that Bell had to pay 20% of its revenues to Western Union for 17 years as a settlement for patent infringement. Coca-Cola may have had its initial leadership because of its additive ingredients. According to a report in *Business Week,* Thomson Consumer Electronics of France, which acquired General Electric's GE and RCA brands for $800 million and then spent $300 million in its U.S. plants, "eked out a tiny operating profit last year on $1.5 billion in sales" in the U.S. TV business. For details see Therrien, L. and J. B. Levine, "Thomson Needs a Hit and It's Up to Nipper to Go Fetch," *Business Week,* July 6, 1992, p. 80.

Inventor: The firm(s) that develop(s) or patent(s) important technologies in a new product category.

Product pioneer: The first firm to develop a working model or sample in a new product category.

Market pioneer: The first firm to sell in a new product category.

They provide an example to demonstrate the difference between a product pioneer and a market pioneer in the mainframe computer industry. The University of Pennsylvania's ENIAC system is identified as the product pioneer. The market pioneer is identified as Remington-Rand. The Census Bureau purchased Remington-Rand's first UNIVAC in 1951.

Market Share of Pioneers

Golder and Tellis studied 50 product categories using the historical method. They studied an enormous amount of published material to track down the market pioneers in these categories. The PIMS database studies, however, used self-reported "pioneer" classification in the PIMS database as the starting point. The four PIMS based studies show the difference between the pioneer's market share and that of a late entrant to vary between 6% and 20%. Urban, Canter, Gaskin and Mucha found the average pioneer share to be 30% (Exhibit 11–3). In comparison, Golder and Tellis found an average pioneer share of only 10%. Further, they found that in only 11% of 36 categories were pioneers also leaders. In the PIMS studies[14] almost half of the pioneers are also leaders. The Golder and Tellis study also reveals that the modal and median time over which the pioneer was a leader (by definition, pioneers are leaders at entry) was only five years—which years were also the years of product category development, and therefore of lower overall sales volume.

The Leading Pioneers

Only four of the 50 product categories studied by Golder and Tellis had a sustained leading pioneer. Their complete tabulation of product pioneer, market pioneer, and the current leader in the various product categories makes very compelling reading (Exhibit 11–4). The four leading pioneers are Crisco shortening (Procter & Gamble), Coca-Cola, RCA color televisions, and Bell telephones.

EXHIBIT 11–3   Market Share of Pioneers (1990)

Class	Mean Market Share (%)	No. of Cases
Total	10	36
Pre-WWII	13	20
Post-WWII	7	16
Durable goods	7	18
Nondurable goods	13	18

Adapted from Golder, P. N. and G. J. Tellis, Do Pioneers Really Have Long Term Advantages? A Historical Analysis, *Marketing Science Institute Working Paper, Report,* 1992, p. 19. Reprinted with permission from the Marketing Science Institute.

[14]Buzzell, R. D. and B. T. Gale, "The PIMS Principles: Linking Strategy to Performance," New York, The Free Press, 1987.

EXHIBIT 11–4   Who is What in 50 Product Categories*

	Category	Product Pioneer	Market Pioneer	Current Leader
1.	Video recorders	Ampex (1956)	Ampex (1963)	RCA/Matsushita (1977)
2.	Microwave ovens	Raytheon (1946)	Amana (1966)	GE/Samsung (1979)
3.	Dishwasher	Crescent Washing Machine Co. (1900)	Crescent Washing Machine Co. (1900)	GE (1935)
4.	Laundry dryers	Canton Clothes Dryer (1925)	Canton Clothes Dryer (1925)	Whirlpool (1950)
5.	Facsimile machines	Xerox (1964)	Xerox (1964)	Sharp (1982)
6.	Personal computer	MITS (1975)	MITS (1975)	IBM (1981)
7.	Camcorder	Sony, JVC (1982)	Kodak/ Matsushita (1984)	RCA/Matsushita (1985)
8.	Color TV	Bell Labs (1929)	RCA (1954)	RCA/Thomson (1954)
9.	Wine cooler	California Cooler (1979)	California Cooler (1981)	Seagram, Bartles & Jaymes (1984)
10.	Laundry detergent	Reychler (1913)	Dreft (1933)	Tide (1946)
11.	Disposable diapers	Chux (1950)	Chux (1950)	P&G/Pampers and Luvs (1961)
12.	Frozen dinners	Swanson (1946)	Swanson (1946)	Stouffer (1956)
13.	Liquid dishwashing detergent	Liquid Lux (1948)	Liquid Lux (1948)	Ivory Liquid (1957)
14.	Light beer	Trommer's Red Letter (1961)	Trommer's Red Letter (1961)	Miller Lite (1975)
15.	Diet cola	Kirsch's No-cal cola (1952)	Kirsch's No-cal cola (1952)	Diet Coke (1982)
16.	Liquid laundry detergent	Wisk (1956)	Wisk (1956)	Liquid Tide (1984)
17.	Dandruff shampoo	Fitch's (1919)	Fitch's (1919)	Head & Shoulders (1961)

*Date of firm's market entry in parentheses.

18.	Cereal	Granula (1863)	Granula (1863)	Kellogg (1906)
19.	Camera	Daguerrotype (1839)	Daguerrotype (1839)	Kodak (1888)
20.	Canned fruit	Libby, McNeill, Libby (1868)	Libby, McNeill, Libby (1868)	Del Monte (1891)
21.	Chocolate	Whitman's (1842)	Whitman's (1842)	Hershey (1903)
22.	Vegetable shortening	Crisco (1911)	Crisco (1911)	Crisco (1911)
23.	Canned milk	Borden (1856)	Borden (1860)	Carnation (1899)
24.	Chewing gum	Black Jack/ American Chicle (1871)	Black Jack/ American Chicle (1871)	Wrigley (1982)
25.	Flashlight battery	Bright Star (1909)	Bright Star (1909)	Eveready (1920)
26.	Safety razor	Star (1876)	Star (1876)	Gillette (1903)
27.	Sewing machine	Elias Howe (1842)	Four firms (1849)	Singer (1851)
28.	Soft drinks	Vernors (1866)	Vernors (1866)	Coca-Cola (1886)
29.	Tires rubber works	Hartford Rubber Works (1895)	Hartford Rubber Works (1895)	Goodyear (1898)
30.	Copy machines	3M Thermofax (1950)	3M Thermofax (1950)	Xerox (1959)
31.	Telephone	Ries (1865) Gray (1876) Bell (1876)	Bell (1877)	AT&T (Bell) (1877)
32.	Instant photography	Archer (1853)	Dubroni (1864)	Polaroid (1947)
33.	Cola	Coca-Cola (1886)	Coca-Cola (1886)	Coca-Cola (1886)
34.	Video games	Magnavox Odyssey (1973)	Magnovox Odyssey (1973)	Nintendo (1985)
35.	Rubber	Goodrich (1869)	Goodrich (1869)	Goodyear (1898)
36.	Personal stereo	Panasonic (1970)	Panasonic (1970)	Sony (1979)

*Date of firm's market entry in parentheses.

EXHIBIT 11-4 (Continued)

	Category	Long-Lived Market Leader	Pioneer/Predecessor
37.	Bacon	Swift (1887)	Largest hog packers; sold from Cincinnati prior to Civil War; Armour largest in Chicago in 1870s
38.	Crackers	Nabisco (1890s)	Cracker bakery in Massachusetts in 1792; first brand to become No. 1 for Nabisco was Uneeda; Ritz later became No. 1
39.	Flour	Gold Medal (1880)	Largest flour mills in New York City and Chesapeake Bay area in 1700s
40.	Mint candy	Life Savers (1913)	Large-scale U.S. production from mid 1800s
41.	Paint	Sherwin Williams (1870)	Paints have been sold for hundreds of years
42.	Paper	Hammermill (1898)	Rittenhouse Mill in Philadelphia in 1690
43.	Pipe tobacco	Prince Albert (1907)	Bull Durham, Lone Jack, and Killickinnick brands since 1860s
44.	Shirts	Manhattan (1857)	Ready-made clothing in U.S. since late 1700s
45.	Soup	Campbell (1897)	Soup dates back hundreds of years; Campbell dominated market with condensed soups
46.	Soap	Ivory	Soap dates back hundreds of years; Pears since 1789; Colgate Cashmere Bouquet since 1872
47.	Tea	Lipton (1893)	Sold in Boston by two dealers in 1690; forerunner of Great Atlantic and Pacific Tea Co. (A&P) formed in 1859
48.	Toothpaste	Crest (1955)	Colgate dominated market before P&G entered with Gleem (1952) and Crest
49.	Beer	Anheuser-Busch (1952)	Brewery in North America in 1637
50.	Toilet tissue	Scott (1890)	First sold by Joseph Gayetty in 1857; Charmin (1957) is current leader

*Date of firm's market entry in parentheses.

From Golder, P. N. and G. J. Tellis, Do Pioneers Really Have Long Term Advantages? A Historical Analysis, *Marketing Science Institute Working Paper, Report,* 1992, pp. 13–17. Reprinted with permission by the Marketing Science Institute.

Failure Rate of Pioneers

Although pioneers may generally not be leaders, are they better survivors? In 1982 in the most famous of the new-product survival studies Booz, Allen, and Hamilton Company found that 33% to 35% of new products failed. The Golder and Tellis study showed that 47% of market pioneers failed, with the rate of failure 67% for pioneering durable goods and 28% for pioneering nondurable goods (Exhibit 11–5).

To be successful it is not necessary to be a pioneer. A pioneering position might provide a monopoly profit stream for a time before competitors come in. The timing of entry, however, does seem to indicate that flexibility and adaptability are more likely required in early rather than later entrants, because for them both knowledge and opportunity are less in supply and more in demand.

Signaling and Entry Timing

When should a new product be announced and when should it be introduced? There is considerable anecdotal evidence that introducing a product "too early" can irreparably damage its chances to succeed. For example, Peters and Waterman, in their extremely popular book, quote a computer peripherals executive, "We rushed to the market with a new product because it was clearly a superior technical device. We wanted to grab market share quickly. But reliability was awful. Our share peaked at 14% and is now down below 8%, while we should have had 30% or 35% of the market. A six month delay in introduction to iron out the bugs would have done it."[15] Similarly, as reported in the *Wall Street Journal*,[16] Intel Corporation delayed the introduction of its microprocessor P-5. Intel was "badly stung" in 1990 when, after introduction, its 486 chip was found to have "bugs." Several personal computer makers had to delay new product introductions. Vin Dahm, general manager of Intel's microprocessor division, is quoted as saying, "Having lived through it once, I didn't want to live through it one more time."

Announcements

Should a new product be announced far in advance? To answer this question the marketing strategist must consider the objective of this announcement, its effects on customers, channel members, competitors, investors, and the regulatory agencies.

EXHIBIT 11–5   A Comparison of Failure Rates

Study	Failure Rate (%)
Booz, Allen, Hamilton*	33-35
Page[†]	45
Golder and Tellis (1992) Overall (Footnote 13)	47
Golder and Tellis (1992) Durables (Footnote 13)	67
Golder and Tellis (1992) Nondurables (Footnote 13)	28

*New Products Management for the 1980s. New York, Booz, Allen, Hamilton, 1982.

[†]Page, A. L., "Assessing New Product Development Practices and Performance: Establishing Crucial Norms," *Journal of Product Innovation Management,* Vol. 10, 1993, pp. 273–279.

[15]Peters, T. J. and R. H. Waterman, Jr., *In Search of Excellence*, New York, Harper & Row, 1982, p. 179.

[16]Yoder, S. K., "Intel Delays Debut of P-5 Chip to Refine Production Process and Eliminate Bugs," *The Wall Street Journal,* July 23, 1992, B5.

Susceptibility to Change

The effect of announcements on customers and channel members are generally of two types: an individual's susceptibility to change; and a group-level effect on susceptibility to change.[17]   Announcements are signals either preparing for or seeking change on the part of consumers or channel members.   As preannouncements, or signals of impending new product introductions or other action, their purpose is to increase the susceptibility of potential customers or channel partners to change their behavior to include the new product in their action set when the new product is introduced.

For the individual customer or channel partner to acquire the new product requires considerable preparation that involves planning or evaluation or other actions, as well as possibly social acceptability of the change.   In fact, these do occur in practice.   For example, the introduction of frozen food (not available to most of the world's population) required the availability of freezers at all channels as well as at the point of end use.   Announcing the capability to produce and distribute frozen food may encourage the capital budgeting for freezers along the channels.   Absent the capability and intent to develop frozen food, the channels may not be ready.   The change in habit required of end users is also considerable.   Would they be susceptible to such a change?   Individuals, in changing their food consumption habits (or cafeterias using frozen food in their kitchens), besides acquiring large enough freezers, would also need assurance that such behavior would be valuable to them and be socially acceptable.   For a strategist the first question is does the market need preannouncements so that it

---

[17]In choosing entry timing, the expected rate of diffusion of the new product needs to be understood (modeled).   In her dissertation, Chang has developed a new diffusion model that incorporates consumer resistance to innovation as a key component of a new product diffusion model.   In the simulation comparison conducted, her model performed as well as, if not better than, other models in the literature.   Her dissertation contains a bibliography of existing models as well as a description of each.

Chang, Ai-Hwa, "Incorporating Consumer Resistance to Innovation in a New Product Diffusion Model: A New Model and a Simulation Comparison with Existing Models," unpublished doctoral dissertation, University of Illinois at Urbana–Champaign, April, 1992.

Kalish and Lilien in 1986 reported on a model they developed to help the U.S. Department of Energy to decide when to approve a demonstration project.   This project involved construction of 100 homes outfitted with photovoltaic systems used to generate electricity.   Over time, the quality of such systems was expected to improve and the price drop.   Improved quality and lower price were both modeled to have a positive impact on sales.   Poor quality would lead to negative response and slow down acceptance, whereas acceptable quality would lead to positive response and could accelerate the sales of such systems.   Setting parameters for their model for the U.S. Department of Energy and by conducting simulations, they were able to predict the impact on cumulative sales depending on the timing of entry.   Such efforts are not difficult and should be carried out for major new products.   This is exactly in keeping with the strategic thinking regarding simulation that has been suggested in their book.   For details see Kalish, S. and G. L. Lilien, "A Market Entry Timing Model for New Technologies," *Management Science*, Vol. 32, No. 2, February, 1986, pp. 194–205.   For another comprehensive review of diffusion models see Mahajan, V., E. Muller, and F. M. Bass, "New Product Diffusion Models in Marketing: A Review and Directions for Research," *Journal of Marketing*, Vol. 54, January, 1990, pp. 1–26.

will be at the right level of susceptibility to change when the new product is introduced?

Research suggests that such a "priming" of susceptibility is beneficial if the new product requires considerable learning or a high switching cost on the part of customers. Significant learning typically for what are called by Robertson, discontinued innovations (for example, switching to microwave ovens). Preannouncements are also necessary when significant outside network factors are involved—as in the frozen food example already discussed.[18] In other words, when a product's adoption and use are not independent. Raising social desirability and acceptability is exemplified by the intensity with which new fashions are announced and presented. Absent the "social acceptance" of midis, maxis, or miniskirts, who will buy enough of them to make them successful?

Shaping Competition

The question here is "What will (and can) competitors do with the information?" If competitors can cause harm, then do the benefits of susceptibility to change outweigh competitors' actions? Competitors may speed their own new product development activity. This might have a positive effect (for example, the synergy in the sales efforts of Eli Lilly, Pfizer, and Smith Kline Beecham in the serotonin drug market) or a negative effect.[19] Competitors may leapfrog and accelerate development time and make the new product obsolete sooner. Although this is a possibility, given the extent of information informally available, such risks from preannouncements may be much less than expected.[20]

Preannouncements

Preannouncements can affect customers, competitors, and channel members. Preannouncement behavior is quite common. For example, a study conducted by Eliashberg and Robertson found that 51% of the executives participating in a series of executive education programs reported that their companies had preannounced the introduction of their last new product or service.[21]

---

[18]A rigorous treatment of this area is found in Farrell, J. and G. Saloner (1986), "Installed Base and Compatibility: Innovation, Product Preannouncements, and Predation," *The American Economic Review,* December, 1986, Vol. 76, No. 5, pp. 940–955.

[19]A recent *Wall Street Journal* article is an example of the positive effects of competitive entry. According to this article, the entry of Pfizer and Smith Kline Beecham into the $2 billion-a-year worldwide antidepressant market in which Eli Lilly already had a product—Prozac—is expected to be mutually beneficial to all three in the selling of their new medicines. For details see Burton, T. M., "Lilly's Controversial Prozac May Benefit From Marketing of Two New Competitors," *The Wall Street Journal,* July 17, 1992, B1B2.

[20]This point is also made in Chaney, P. K., T. M. Devinney, and R. S. Winer, "The Impact of New Product Introductions on the Market Value of Firms," *Journal of Business,* Vol. 64, No. 4, 1991, pp. 573–610. Also see Brian, D., "Corporate Spies Snoop to Conquer," *Fortune,* November 7, 1988.

[21]Eliashberg, J. and T. S. Robertson, "New Product Preannouncing Behavior: A Market Signaling Study," *Journal of Marketing Research,* August, 1988, pp. 282–292.

Preannouncements may cause customers to postpone buying competitive products in anticipation of the availability of the new product. On the negative side, this postponement can reduce the sales of a company's own products as customers stop or reduce their purchasing of existing products—this is, in a sense, cannibalization.[22]

Weiss and John analyzed customers' decisions of whether to buy at all, buy an existing product, or wait for a preannounced new product.[23] Their study finds that when the current generation has been recently introduced, preannouncement of the next generation would be sufficient to make some customers decide to "leapfrog," or wait until this new generation is introduced. For others, knowing details of the new technology when it would be available might make them decide in favor of the existing generation. The decision, based on sales, would then depend on the trade-off between the number of "leapfroggers" who would have bought if not for the pre-announcement, and the number of "fence sitters" who would have waited for the new generation, if not for the preannouncement. This balance, closer to the introduction of the new generation, however, is always in favor of those postponing purchases.

Competitive encroachment on a large incumbent's customer base may also be thwarted by preannouncement. By announcing an improvement the incentive for current customers to change their "partners" is lowered. IBM protected its client base by preannouncing its 360/91 series of mainframe computers to prevent its clients from being lured away by Control Data's 6600 model, which was superior to IBM's existing machines. IBM entered into a multimillion dollar settlement with CDC to settle CDC's lawsuit.

Preannouncement may preempt certain product positions, because competitors may find it unattractive to introduce similar products. They may lead competitors to prevent or delay the formation of relationships with channel members by loading them with excess inventory or using special deals.

Litigation may be triggered by preannouncements as in the case of IBM.[24] The risk of litigation varies from country to country and perhaps from one product category to another (at least across countries), and must be carefully evaluated.

---

[22]A well-known example of this is the Osbourne Computer Company. Its computer's sales dried up because of new product preannouncements. Lack of sales prevented development of the new product, which in turn lead to the company's collapse. Osbourne is now a major computer columnist.

[23]Weiss, A. M. and G. John, "Technological Expectations and Leapfrogging Behavior: Theory and Evidence," Working Paper, Carlson School of Management, University of Minnesota, April, 1991.

[24]Fisher, F. M., J. McGowan, and J. Greenwood, *Folded, Spindled and Mutilated: Economic Analysis and US vs IBM*, Cambridge, MIT Press, 1983. "In general, there is no reason to inhibit the time when a firm announces or brings products to the marketplace. Customers will be the final arbiter of the product's quality and the firm's reputation. . . . Advance announcements of truthful information about products cannot be anticompetitive. Indeed, such announcement is procompetitive; competition thrives when information is good (p. 289).

In their stylized economic analysis, Farrell and Saloner *op. cit.,* 1986, prove a proposition (No. 3, p. 949) that says, "The preannouncement may reduce welfare, even though the conditions of Proposition 3 hold."

In deciding whether to preannounce or not, the need to improve the introduction climate by working on customer and channel susceptibility to change and the impact of competitors' changed behavior need to be carefully evaluated (Exhibit 11–6).[25]

Defensive Strategies

Any offering (product) is always potentially threatened by possible competitive entries. The defensive strategies to be used depend on the stage of the threat. The choice of defensive strategy depends on its timing. The relevant calendar for identifying the time is that set by the new product entry process of potential competitors. The appropriate defensive strategies for different stages of a potential entry process are now discussed.[26]

Stages in the Entry Investment Process

In 1985, Michael Porter identified a sequenced process for new product entry.[27] The four stages that comprise this sequenced process are pre-entry, introduction, sequencing, and

EXHIBIT 11–6   Factors to be Considered in Preannouncement Decisions

Susceptibility	Competitive Shaping
Individual: Preparedness	New product speed-up
Group: Acceptability	Preemption of positions
Channel: Preparedness, Level	Cannibalization entry blocking through relationships
Network externalities: Ancillary products	Litigation

[25]In this section we did not discuss bluffing, that is, the announcement of fake or phantom products. Bluffing behavior has been studied in new product announcement by Eliashberg, Robertson, and Rymon. Although their survey results are exploratory, their major hypotheses are:

   1 Bluffs are likely to be designed as unclear signals.

   2 Bluffs are likely to be designed as reversible signals.

   3 Bluff signals are likely to be sent by firms possessing information.

   4 Bluff signals are likely to be sent by firms with high product category strength.

   5 Bluff signals are likely to be sent by firms perceiving a moderate tendency to bluff in their industry.

   6 Bluff signals are likely to be sent by firms perceiving low entry barriers in their industry.

   7 Bluff signals are likely to be sent via private, informal, and industry-specific communication channels.

     For details see Eliashberg, J., T. S. Robertson, and T. Rymon, "Market Signaling and Competitive Bluffing," Working Paper, June, 1992, The Wharton School, The University of Pennsylvania.

   [26]This section is based largely on Gruca, T. S., D. Sudharshan, and K. R. Kumar, "A Sequential Investment Framework for Marketing Defense Against Potential and Actual Competitors," Working Paper, University of Illinois at Urbana–Champaign, 1992.

   [27]Porter, M. E., *Competitive Advantage: Creating and Sustaining Superior Performance*, New York, Free Press, 1985.

post-entry (Exhibit 11–7). In the pre-entry stage, the potential entrant evaluates alternative markets, conducts product feasibility studies, and begins pilot production.

In the introduction stage, test marketing, exploration of distribution and supplier relationships, and initial product roll-out are started.

The sequencing stage involves the growth and expansion of the entrant via market penetration, broadening of the product line and expanded relationships.

The post-entry stage is one of maintaining and defending industry position.

An incumbent in the threatened market can choose when to employ defensive strategies. For each stage of the entry process, the defensive strategy and tactics are different. The decision of which defensive process to adopt requires careful consideration of the associated risks and rewards, to maximize shareholder value.

Exhibit 11–8 provides an overview of the risk and reward factors associated with defense at various entry sequence stages. Prevention can occur only if entry is prevented. After entry, at best, any damage should be minimized.

Prevention of entry can be carried out, if at all, through the pre-entry stage. Potential firms will not enter, if and only if they know their goals cannot be met by entering this market. They know of the competition they face in this market and it is such that this "opportunity" does not match their goals. Defense calls for (1) ensuring that mobility barriers are, or can be, put in place, and (2) ensuring that potential entrants know about the expected competition in this market. Defense can be based on relationships, or offering, or resource allocation.

Relationships-Based Defense

Formal or informal relationships may be developed to prevent entry. These relationships make the switching costs prohibitive for channel members, customers, and other important publics to switch to the entrant. For example, forward vertical integration leading to the control of the availability of products is one possibility. Locating retail outlets in prime locations, thus pre-empting competition is another. Obtaining patents or lobbying for favorable regulation are other such examples.

Providing specialized training, locking in customers through incompatible technology (e.g., the operating system in personal computers, or technical standards unique to a country, thus making foreign entry more difficult), wiring into the customer's operating procedures as, for example, American Hospital Supply Corporation was able to do in hospitals—their terminals were available to order hospital supplies. These terminals acted as order entry devices for American Hospital Supply as well as

EXHIBIT 11–7   Stages of Sequential New Product Entry Process

Stages	Activities
Pre-entry	Evaluation of feasibility and potential
Introduction	Test marketing, exploratory stage of relationships
Sequencing	Market penetration, establishment of relationships
Post-entry	Maintenance and fortification

EXHIBIT 11-8   Defensive Marketing Process

Stage	Risk Factors	Reward Factors
Block Entry? (Pre-entry)	Probability of success Problems if failure Legal challenges	Costs Kinds of costs Benefits of success Standing after failure
Retaliate? (Introduction)	Entrant information Entrant commitment Entrant resources Legal challenges	Costs Benefits of success
Adapt to New Entrant (Sequencing)	Probability of further Investment Future reputation	Costs of changing marketing mix Impact of entrant on sales and profits
Post-entry		

From Gruca, T. S., D. Sudharshan, and K. R. Kumar (Footnote 26).

inventory management tools for the hospitals. Switching costs involving either changes in operating procedures or in capital requirements may be possible.

Reciprocal arrangements may be illegal; if not, they may also be considered.

Offerings-Based Defense

Price-Based.   Penetration pricing, limit pricing, and experience curve-based pricing are the three price-based defenses to prevent market entry. All are predicated on the price being too low for it to be profitable for the entrant, while being high enough for the incumbent.

In penetration pricing, low price is used. The price is so attractive that not enough customers remain to buy any new products. The residual demand is insufficient to cover entry costs. In markets in which customers make multiple purchases over time (nondurable and services) and in which variety seeking behavior is relevant, penetration pricing is unlikely to prevent entry.

Limit pricing signals the potential entrant that the profitability possible in this market is low. This contrasts with penetration pricing which signals that demand, but not the profit margin, is low. For limit pricing to work, potential entrants should be aware of costs. Without such information, prevailing price information (be it limit or otherwise) would not signal certain profit. If potential entrants, using technological innovation or synergistic relationships have lower costs than incumbents, limit pricing would not deter entry. Superior new products may also command higher prices than those charged by incumbents. Therefore, although the expected profit margin for potential entrants may be lower because of the "limit price" adopted by the incumbent, it may still be high enough to be attractive—given the entrant's alternative uses of resources.

Experience curve pricing calls for determining the rate at which unit costs will decline with experience (measured as cumulative production volume). Then, the price set is determined not on the basis of contemporaneous cost, but on anticipated costs (which are lower). This has a dual effect. By using a lower price, penetration may be accelerated and the cost may become lower much earlier (in real time) than otherwise, and lower prices may discourage competition. There are two problems with this approach. First, it might work only if the potential entrant is likely to enter long after the incumbent using the same technology, otherwise it is questionable as an entry deterrent. Second, it might create inertia to change on the incumbent's part (e.g., Ford[28] with Model T) preventing it from spending resources on innovation and instead eking out marginal benefits.

When customers are not particularly swayed by price (or the market exhibits a low price elasticity of demand), or when customers seek variety, price-based entry deterrence is not likely to be effective.

Offering Scope-Based.   Product or brand proliferation along both the function dimensions (e.g., AM-FM radios with built-in cassette recorders, portable console, etc.) may be considered. (As an example for services, travel agencies may choose to serve different functions, full-service, or just ticketing. The form they choose could be via remote terminal access or videophone or face-to-face.) Coca-Cola and Campbell Soup Co.[29] in soft drinks and soups, respectively, have used brand proliferation to acquire and

---

[28]Sloan, Jr., A. P., *My Years With General Motors,* New York, Doubleday, 1964.

[29]White, A. P., *The Dominant Firm,* Ann Arbor, MI, UMI Research Press, 1983.

There are many analytical models that provide methods to determine the product positions that would jointly satisfy all customer demand and would make entry unprofitable. For details see Hay, D. A., "Sequential Entry and Entry-Deterring Strategies in Spatial Competition," *Oxford Economic Papers,* Vol. 28, No. 2, July, 1976, pp. 240–257.

Prescott, E. C. and M. Visscher, "Sequential Location Among Firms With Foresight," *The Bell Journal of Economics,* Vol. 8, No. 2, Autumn, 1977, pp. 378–393.

Gruca, T. S., K. R. Kumar, and D. Sudharshan, "Product Positioning Strategies for Segment Pre-emption," *Proceedings, AMA Summer Educators' Conference,* Chicago, American Marketing Association, 1988.

Sudharshan, D. and K. R. Kumar, "Pre-emptive Product Positioning Under Market Share Restrictions," *Managerial and Decision Economics,* Vol. 9, 1988, pp. 93–99.

Schmalansee, R., "Entry Deterrence in the Ready-to-Eat Breakfast Cereal Market," Bell Journal of Economics, Vol. 9, Spring, 1978, pp. 305–327.

maintain dominant market position.   The basic premise is that there is a certain variety in customer requirements.   For each product in the market there is a certain demand based on the features of the product and the preferences of customers.   If the products in the market are such that a new product would not be able to reduce demand (share) from the others (based on customer preference), then entry would be deterred.   This strategy may require an incumbent to introduce several "me-too" products —because the demand for those features may be sufficient to support several products.

Other Offering Components-Based.   Advertising by building good will and brand loyalty makes it difficult for new product entry.   Advertising through relationships creates an entry barrier.   An incumbent's advertising activities might give it a cost advantage over an entrant.   This may lead to a price advantage, allowing it to use a penetration or a limit pricing strategy which acts as an entry deterrent.

After-sales training and service, credit availability, spare parts availability, and raising social desirability of a product, may all also serve to insulate customers and potential customers from external threats.

Reserve Allocation-Based.   All of the other strategies discussed require commitment and use of resources.   Pre-emptive capacity building, advertising and other marketing mix activities, and managing experience curve all take resources.

The Clorox Company[30] used an aggressive price and product promotion for Formula 409 to remove a large number of consumers from the market for up to six months by encouraging them to load up on their product.   This was when Procter & Gamble was beginning roll-out of its competitive entry, Cinch.   Clorox dramatically dropped its price for Formula 409 when Cinch was being test marketed.   The disappointing sales of Cinch dissuaded P&G from launching this product.   The timing of resource deployment by Clorox in this case was effective.   However, knowledge of such possibilities makes this strategy's success less likely in the future.

Although several deterrent measures have been discussed here and in the literature, new product activity is the "growth hormone" for almost all companies. Prevention, as evidenced by practice, rarely occurs.   Entry has occurred even in markets such as that of copper and metal containers, identified by analysts as having substantial entry barriers.[31]

Even so, over half of the responding marketing managers surveyed by Smiley[32] reported that their companies had used some type of entry-preventing strategy.   The most used methods were patents, intensive advertising, brand proliferation, and consolidation of profits in public reports (so entrants would not know the high profits in mature markets).

---

[30]For details see Solman, P. and T. Freidman, *Life and Death on the Corporate Battlefield,* New York, Simon and Schuster, 1982.

[31]See Bain, J. S., *Barriers to New Competition,* Cambridge, Harvard University Press, 1956. The documentation of entry into these markets is to be found in Osbourne, D. K. "The Role of Entry in Oligopoly Theory," *Journal of Political Economics,* Vol. 72, August, 1964, pp. 396–402.

[32]Smiley, R. (1988), "Empirical Evidence on Strategic Entry Deterrence," International Journal of Organization, Vol. 6, 1088, pp. 167–180.

The next most used methods were limit pricing, experience curve pricing, and building a reputation for toughness. The least used method was holding of excess capacity.

Defense After Entry

In the broad category of post-entry marketing responses, there are also two distinct types of strategies. Often, the immediate reaction to new competitors is a counterattack. The goal is to discourage the entrant from further investment in the market.

After a certain period, the entrant leaves or becomes established beyond the point at which it is impossible to be driven out. Adaptation to the new competitor follows. Adaptation strategies are intended to minimize the impact of the new competitor, or perhaps to leverage its presence.

In the early stages of product entry, because it has little information, an entrant is generally sensitive to success or failure. Strong defensive action at this stage first serves to reduce the impact of the new entrant, and second, it signals the entrant that the incumbent will protect itself.

In the UK potato chip (or crisp, as it is called there) market the leading firm—Smith's, by not acting—ceded considerable share and power to the new entrant.[33] By the time Smith reacted, the entrant was well-established. The entrant's weaknesses are primarily the formative stage of its relationships and also the low state of its knowledge about the market.

Information refers to the entrant's knowledge about the desirability of its offering: Will it be accepted by channel members and customers? Is it optimal? Test marketing, product testing, and sampling may reduce but not eliminate doubts on these issues. By manipulating early performance results, the entrant's actions may be turned to the incumbent's advantage. Clancy tells of an incumbent which increased its advertising and promotion expenditures by 630% as compared with an expected increase of 80%! Imagine the surprise and the importance of the signal being sent. Of course, such aggressive behavior is not sustainable. An observation by the late Bruce Henderson is worth noting: being irrational might be the rational strategy when trying to influence new rivals.[34]

Escalating commitment is a powerful signal. This is exemplified by the vigorous response from General Foods (Maxwell House brand) that greeted Procter & Gamble when it introduced Folger's into the U.S. retail coffee market. This rivalry has now lasted over 20 years.

Product-based retaliation strategies take the form of introducing a "fighting brand" or "leapfrogging." An example of a fighting brand is lemon-lime Sprite from Coca-Cola which minimized erosion of the beverage market share of Coke because of the entry of 7-Up—a citrus drink promoted as the "uncola." Other examples are San Miguel Brewing's Gold Eagle Pilsner Beer which launched Beer Hansen (a pilsner) from Asia Brewery to protect its 92-year dominance in the Philippines. Instead of a

---

[33]Bevan, A., "The U.K. Potato Crisp Industry, 1960–72: A Study of New Entry Competition," *Journal of Industrial Economics,* Vol. 22, No. 4, 1974, pp. 281–297.

[34]Clancy, K. J. and B. Henderson, "The Coming Revolution in Advertising," Journal of Advertising Research, Vol. 47, No. 5, 1990.

fighting product, a fighting product line may be used, for example, Seiko uses the Alba, Lorus, and Pulsar brands to compete with low-priced brands.[35]

There are two types of leapfrog strategy. For product categories in which consumers seek variety and in which there is considerable variety in consumer taste (e.g., soap, soup, etc.), retaliating by offering a broader array of products has two positive aspects. First, it locks up shelf space (which is always scarce) and second, it gives consumers a broader choice even within the incumbent's line. For an entrant who, because of limited information or resources, cannot enter with an entire line, this leapfrog strategy acts to limit exposure of the incumbent's line to share erosion by the entrant.

In the case of evolving products such as software, the leapfrog strategy involves continuous product upgrades. This limits the damage from even low-priced clones. An example of this strategy is the continuous upgrading of Lotus 1-2-3.[36]

Adaptation and Adjustment

Once an entrant is "here to stay," then a "new market order" is sought. The incumbent moves from a retaliation strategy to one of adaptation and adjustment. The question at this stage is one of choosing the best marketing mix.

Early study in this area was done by Hauser and Shugan in 1983.[37] Since then, general studies have begun to accumulate. The key studies available are for pricing, advertising and distribution expenditures, and product repositioning.

The best pricing[38] response to entry is that price should be lowered in adjusting to entry.[39] The one exception[40] is when a competitive entry is so close to certain segments of the market that it is not reasonable to price to attract any share of that segment by the incumbent. Given the position of the incumbent's product, price changes by the entrant would not meaningfully take away share from the incumbent's primary

---

[35]James, *op. cit.,* 1984.

[36]Theoretical support for this upgrading notion is found in Farrell and Saloner, *op. cit.,* 1985.

[37]The key papers in this area are:

Hauser, J. R. and S. M. Shugan, "Defensive Marketing Strategies," *Marketing Science,* Vol. 2, No. 4, Fall, 1983, pp. 319–360.

Kumar, K. R. and D. Sudharshan, "Defensive Marketing Strategies: An Equilibrium Analysis Based on Decoupled Response Function Models," *Management Science,* Vol. 34, July, 1988, pp. 805–815.

Robinson, W. T., "Marketing Mix Reactions by Incumbents to Entry," Marketing Science, Vol. 7, Fall, 1988, pp. 368–385.

Hauser, J. R., "Competitive Price and Positioning Strategies," *Marketing Science,* Vol. 7, Winter, 1988, pp. 76–91.

Gruca, T. S., K. R. Kumar and D. Sudharshan, "An Equilibrium Analysis of Defensive Response to Entry Using A Coupled Response Function," *Marketing Science,* Vol. 11, No. 4, Fall, 1992, pp. 348–358.

[38]The results provided here are directional only. The "exact" best decision needs to be calculated based on market parameters. The papers referred to in Footnote 35 provide references for such calculations.

[39]This result is common to Hauser and Shugan, *op. cit.,*1983, Kumar and Sudharshan, *op. cit.,* 1987 and Gruca, Kumar and Sudharshan, *op. cit.,* 1992.

[40]This exception was shown by Hauser and Shugan, *op. cit.,* 1983.

segment. The incumbent can then increase its price, lose some relative market share, but minimize its loss of profit because of the increase in its margin. Such an increase may be considered in markets in which customer preferences are lumpy.

The results for advertising and distribution expenditures are similar, because they are modeled using similar functional forms. If the primary demand for the product category is increased because of entry, then these expenditures should be increased.[41] The only other case[42] for increasing advertising and distribution expenditures is for a dominant brand that has more than 50% market share before and after new product entry. In all other cases, these expenditures should be lowered.

Products should be repositioned toward their strengths.[43] Product improvements and making sure consumers are aware of such improvements should further strengthen their advantage.

A multi-industry study using data in the PIMS start-up database by Robinson[44] found that almost half the new product entrants elicited no response. Response, if it occurred, rarely occurred in the first year following entry. When it did occur in the first year it was usually limited to price reductions and, in some cases, increases in advertising and promotion expenditures. Product repositioning (via quality improvements) were noticed only in the second year, if at all. Further, quite surprisingly, fast-growing markets were protected more often than mature markets. Inertia again seems to be in evidence![45]

Defensive strategies must be tied into the stages of new product activity by potential competitors. Exhibit 11–9 lists possible defensive strategies. For each stage the appropriate strategy is different, ranging from deterrence to retaliation to adjustment and accommodation. A full range of defensive strategies seems to work best and should be carefully considered. The nature of the competition should be kept in mind when designing defensive strategies. The key factors are their knowledge, reputation for innovation and toughness, and their entry strategies.[46] New organizational forms, for example, the alliance formed by IBM, Siemens, and Toshiba[47] to design, as *Business Week* puts it, "a 21st century chip on whose tiny silicon surface will be etched what amounts to a street map of the entire world. Those

---

[41]This result is from Kumar and Sudharshan, *op. cit.,* 1988.

[42]This result is from Gruca, Kumar, and Sudharshan, *op. cit.,* 1992.

[43]This result is from Hauser and Shugan, *op. cit.,* 1983.

[44]Robinson, W. T., *op. cit.,* 1988.

[45]McMillan, I., M. L. McCaffery, and G. van Wijk, "Competitors' Responses to Easily Imitated New Products—Exploring Commercial Banking Product Introductions," *Strategic Management Journal,* Vol. 6, No. 1, 1988, pp. 75–86, is an example of a study showing that organizational inertia slowed response to new product introductions.

[46]These sources provide evidence of the differences among entry strategies of Japanese companies and those of the United States and Britain.

Kotler, P., Fahey, L., and Jatusripitak, S. *The New Competition,* Englewood Cliffs, NJ, Prentice-Hall, 1985.

Doyle, P., J. Saunders and L. Wright, "A Comparative Study of British, U.S. and Japanese Marketing Strategies in the British Market," *International Journal of Research in Marketing,* Vol. 5, 1988, pp. 171–184.

EXHIBIT 11–9   Defense Strategies.

Intent	Possibilities

Entry Prevention	Relationships Based:
	– Vertical integration
	– Retail outlet location
	– Specialized training
	– Technology standards
	– System compatibility
	– Reciprocity
	
	Offering-based:
	– Pricing
	    • Penetration
	    • Limit
	    • Experience curve
	
	– After sales training
	– Credit availability
	– Social desirability
	
	– Offering scope-based
	    • Brand proliferation
	    • "Me-too" brands
	    • Advertising scale
	
	– Resource-based
	    • Pre-emptive capacity
	    • Advertising intensity
	    • Other marketing mix activities
	    • Managing experience curve

Retaliation	– Information denial
	    • Test market disruption
	    • Shelf space locking out
	    • Consumer locking out
	
	– Signaling commitment
	    • Increased expenditures
	    • Fighting brand
	    • Leapfrogging

Adaptation	Optimization of Marketing Mix – Product repositioning – Pricing – Advertising intensity – Distribution intensity

electronic streets—lines just 0.25 micron wide, 400 times thinner than a human hair—will link some 600 million transistors. When the chips become available around 1998, each will store 256 million bits of data, or about two copies of everything that Shakespeare wrote." Such a task is so daunting even to such powerful firms as IBM, Siemens, and Toshiba that they need to form an alliance.

SUMMARY

This chapter discusses if there is an advantage to being a market pioneer. Based on historical evidence, the answer seems to be no. However, early leaders do have an advantage and so early, but not necessarily pioneering, entry seems to be suggested. Also discussed is if products should be preannounced. Customer and channel susceptibility to change and the need to shape competitive behavior are relevant to this decision. Specific considerations in such an evaluation are presented. Finally, defensive strategies to new product entry are discussed. These strategies are linked to the state of the competitor's new product entry process. These states—pre-entry, introduction, sequencing and post-entry—are linked to deterrent, retaliatory, and adjustment defensive strategies. Specific actions based on relationships, offerings, and resource allocations pertinent to each of these stages are discussed.

Concept Questions

1. (a.) Summarize the theoretical link between order-of-entry and performance.
   (b.) Summarize the observed link between order-of-entry and performance.
2. (a.) What factors influence the preannouncement decision?
   (b.) Under what conditions should preannouncement be carried out? When not?
3. (a.) What is the sequential investment process?
   (b.) What is the relationship between defensive timing and entry sequence?
   (c.) Describe possible defensive strategies based on: (1) relationships, (2) offerings, and (3) resources.
   (d.) What is the best way to defend a product-market *after* competitive entry?

Discussion Questions

1. (a.) Why is there a discrepancy between theory and observation in the first-mover share-advantage linkage relationship?
   (b.) Based on your answers in (a), when would you recommend that a firm be a first-mover? When not?

[47]For details see Port, D., R. Brandt, N. Gross, and J. B. Levine, "Talk About Your Dream Team," *Business Week,* July 27, 1992, pp. 59–60. Also note that IBM is the world's biggest chip maker, Siemens is number 3 in Europe, and Toshiba is number 2 in Japan.

2. (a.) How can the discussion of signaling be applied to other marketing issues? (Hint: You might wish to relate it to the discussion on sequential games in Chapter 2).

   (b.) Prepare and defend a flow chart to aid in the decision of whether or not to preannounce a new service.

3. (a.) Prepare and justify a flow chart to choose an appropriate defensive strategy.

   (b.) Suppose that Coca-Cola is attacked by a new cola brand in its Western European market. Should its defensive strategy include actions in Eastern and Central Europe, Asia, and U.S.A.? Justify your answers.

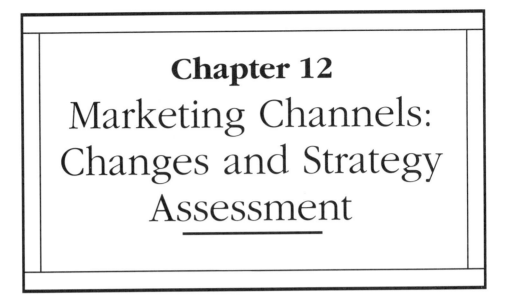

Chapter 12
Marketing Channels: Changes and Strategy Assessment

INTRODUCTION

A student of marketing strategy must have a clear understanding of the changes that occur in the needs and relationship formations in channels of distribution. The first part of this chapter attempts to help the student do so. These changes are presented as natural outcomes of the thrust of change in organizational customer requirements. Even if the specific changes themselves are transient, their direction may last, and so the discussion will have a long-lasting value. The second part describes and discusses methods for evaluating and choosing specific channels to achieve the desired objectives.

Motivating Examples

In mid-June, 1992 the New York Stock Exchange suspended trading in Gitano Group stock. In 1989 Gitano earned 28% on sales of brands like Gloria Vanderbilt, Gitano, and Regatta Sport to customers who wanted affordable, fashionable wear. Their sales outlets were department stores and other full-price retailers. Gitano also built a relationship with Wal-Mart and other merchandisers. Sales increased, but the gross profit margin fell to 18.5% in 1991.

> . . . the biggest flaw in Gitano's downmarket strategy was its baneful effect on the company's core business. Smallish, regional, full-price retailers are abandoning Gitano, since they know the goods are stacked high in every Wal-Mart, Kmart and outlet mall. Small-store owners, looking for a way to differentiate themselves from mass retailers, have turned to less overexposed brands.[1]

[1]This example and the quote are from Morgenson, G., "Greener Pastures?", *Forbes,* July 6, 1992, p. 48.

Eastman Kodak bought Sterling Drug for $5 billion in 1988. But, without adequate new drugs, Kodak formed an alliance with Sanofi (a subsidiary of Elf Aquitane of France) in 1991. The alliance created United States and French based companies with $2.3 billion in combined sales and a $500 million annual budget for development. Sterling gained access to Sanofi's new hypertension and heart drugs and Sanofi, gained access to United States and European sales outlets through Sterling.[2]

Saturn, GM's answer to Japanese automobile manufacturing dominance, was the only nonluxury model ranked in the top five, based on J. D. Powers and Associates' Satisfaction Survey of car owners in July 1992. The others were Lexus (No. 1), Infiniti (No. 2), Cadillac (No. 3) and Lincoln (No. 5). Mercedes-Benz was pushed to No. 6.[3] Alan R. Gruce, Saturn's manager of indirect materials, said of their purchasing philosophy:

> We think the old system of having purchasing agents go out to bid to drive the price down is wasteful and inefficient. Our idea is to dedicate one company to an entire commodity area, then together, work to drive costs down. You don't have to take us out to lunch, spend money in sporting events, or give us fancy Christmas presents. Just be good partners.[4]

Christine Forbes, Associate Editor of *Industrial Distribution,*[5] discusses her article by asking:

> "Partnering, quality and total cost take center stage as the distributor base diminishes. In selling to purchasing, the shift calls for a whole new approach. Are you ready for the challenge?"

These examples provide good reason for a careful strategic assessment of channel systems which are undergoing considerable change and which remain critical in fostering exchange between the parties. Recent changes in industrial distribution and purchasing are discussed next to provide a "feel" for the milieu in which distribution strategies need to be assessed. These changes address the demands being placed on these channels by industrial customers. Therefore we also discuss what industrial customers are seeking.

---

[2]"Sterling Drug Will Get a Booster Shot," *Business Week,* January 21, 1991, p. 40.

  Kodak, attempting to concentrate on its core businesses, sold Sterling to Sanofi. Sanofi in turn, sold Sterling's medical imaging business to Hofslund Nycomed of Oslo, Norway, for $450 million. This purchase also gives Hofslund Sterling's North American sales organization as well as entry into marketing channels in South America, New Zealand, and Australia. (Sanofi is a unit of Elf Aquitane, S.A. of France. In 1993 it had sales of $4.2 billion, largely from branded fragrances such as Nina Ricci, Perry Ellis, and Oscar de la Renta and other pharmaceutical and beauty products.) For more details see Ringer, R., "Sanofi Set to Sell Part of Sterling," *The New York Times,* Thursday, June 30, 1994; and Freindenheim, M., "Sanofi to get Part of Kodak Drug Unit," *The New York Times,* June 24, 1994, C1, C6.

[3]"Lexus Tops Owner-Satisfaction Survey," *The Champaign-Urbana News-Gazette,* Wednesday, July 29, 1992, B-8.

[4]Zurier, S., "Saturn Rings In a New Era," *Industrial Distribution,* October, 1991, p. 20.

[5]Forbes, C., "Buyers & Distributors: It's Time for Teamwork," *Industrial Distribution,* August, 1991, pp. 20–24.

Industrial Distribution Channel Systems—An Overview

One of the pioneers of marketing, Wroe Alderson pointed out that:

> The word customer comes from the same root as the word "customary." Both derive from "custom," meaning habit or established practice. The word "routine" is readily traced to "route," which means a customary course or way. A related word is "channel," a variation on the word *canal* in Old French. Thus channel means a fixed and clearly marked route. In marketing practice there could be no channels without routines.[6]

Routine, along with the utility of possession, time, and place are central in Alderson's thoughts on the value and functions of channels in marketing. Place utility is a channel's ability to deliver products where needed as opposed to where produced. Time utility refers to delivery when needed as opposed to when produced. Possession utility refers to reduction in effort or cost of making a transfer of goods from producer to user. Possession utility includes the four "sorting" functions of a channel.

(1) sorting out, or the breaking up of heterogeneous goods into smaller homogeneous stocks,

(2) accumulation, or the bringing together of similar stocks to make up a larger homogeneous supply,

(3) allocation, or breaking bulk, and

(4) assorting, or the bringing together of a variety of goods.

These utilities continue, in varying degrees, to be what distribution channels contribute to the utility of buyers today. The major exception is the function of value addition carried out by some channel members, for example, OEM (original equipment manufacturer) suppliers and Value Added Resellers (VARs). For Thompson Industrial Products Co.,[7] in Owings, MD, its "secret weapon" against competition is value-added service. Thompson, ranked first among the top 25 small distributors, provides application assistance and technical engineering, product testing, as well as custom crimping, coupling, and cutting. Value-added service accounts for 50% of its business.

Making transactions routine creates an efficient network of transfer of exchange entities in both directions, thereby minimizing transaction costs. A major explanation given by Alderson why certain channel structures evolve and persist in a product-market is that they minimize the transaction costs involved.

A channel's function is to provide customers goods in the assortment and vol-

[6]Alderson, W., "Factors Governing the Development of Marketing Channels," *In* R. M. Clewett (ed.), *Marketing Channels for Manufactured Products,* Homewood, IL, Irwin, 1954. Reprinted in *The Marketing Channel: A Conceptual Viewpoint,* B. E. Mallen (ed.), New York, John Wiley, 1967, pp. 35–40.

[7]"Meet #1," *Industrial Distribution,* January 15, 1992, p. 32.

ume they want, where they want, when they want and in a way that makes the transaction efficient. These functions continue to be the basis of marketing channel strategy. What are changing, however, are customer wants and needs and the nature and source of transaction costs. Manufacturing and design process systems and communications technology have rapidly changed the setting of distribution channels. These changes are discussed along with their impact on what customers look for from their suppliers.

Manufacturing and Design Systems

As firms seek competitive advantage, major innovations in managing manufacturing and service delivery and product-service design are occurring. These innovations are changing purchasing activities and have a ripple effect on the distribution channel. These innovations, aimed at quality improvements (offering), time-based improvements (timing), and cost improvements (with corresponding impact on resource allocation), are also radically changing relationships between channel members. These innovations are:

INVENTORY-ORIENTED INNOVATIONS	DESIGN AND MANUFACTURING-ORIENTED INNOVATIONS
JIT (Just-in-Time)	CAD (Computer Aided Design)
TQM (Total Quality Management)	CAM (Computer Aided Manufacturing)
MRPI (Material Requirement Planning I)	CIM (Computer Integrated Manufacturing)
MRPII (Material Requirement Planning II)	QFD (Quality Function Development)
OPT (Optimal Production Technique)	KAI (Continuous Product Improvements)
DRP (Distribution Requirements Planning)	
LRP (Logistics Requirement Planning)	

Most modern manufacturing or logistics texts provide details; however, we consider their impact by discussing two of them. JIT or MAN (material-as-needed) and ZIPS (zero inventory production system) are systems that embody the elimination of waste. This process was first popularized in Japan by Toyota. JIT systems force coordination across all functions responsible for the movement of supplies as they are converted to end-products or sub-assemblies.

A 1988 survey[8] revealed that senior logistics managers in the United States forecast that by 1995 approximately 45% of in-bound supplies would arrive under JIT conditions (compared to 18% in 1988). Cooper, Browne and Peters[9] report that European firms are also implementing JIT techniques. However, note that for it to be

[8]LaLonde, B. J., and J. M. Masters, "Logistics: Perspectives for the 1990s," *International Journal of Logistics Management,* Vol. 1, No. 1, 1990.

[9]Cooper, J., M. Browne, and M. Peters, *European Logistics: Markets, Management and Strategy,* Oxford, United Kingdom, Blackwell, 1991, p. 60.

successfully implemented, JIT should be viewed as a change in orientation/philosophy/culture/social process and not just as a technique driven "quick-fix."

The earliest major proponent and user of QFD (Quality Function Development)[10] was said to be the Kobe shipyard of Mitsubishi. Other noted users of this process are Toyota, Fuji–Xerox, Ford, Cummins Engine, Digital Equipment Corporation, General Motors, Hewlett-Packard, Procter & Gamble, and Polaroid. QFD is reputed to have improved substantially the end-quality as well as slashed development time for new products. QFD is a carefully designed product development process that converts the usual sequential- and vertical-communication-based approach to one that quickly and effectively allows the voice-of-the-customer to be communicated vertically and with understanding to all key product development players.

All these innovations principally target waste of resources and time. They treat the design-manufacturing process as a system that includes suppliers and that focuses on reducing the waste of time and resources throughout the process. Improvements in quality are stressed system-wide. Ties between suppliers and customers are strengthened, but with this closeness comes the potential for dependence and conflict.

What Customers Seek from Their Suppliers

By studying what customers want several lists of customer requirements have been proposed. These lists are provided first and then are discussed in the sorting and routine functions mentioned earlier.

Lists of Requirements

From a supplier view, the major changes[11] called for by these innovations are:

1. Supplies are to be packaged in smaller quantities than before and in the exact amount ordered.
2. Quality control is to be shifted to the supplier and eliminated or minimized at the customer through mutual effort.
3. Increased frequency of delivery.

---

[10]The interested reader is referred to the following for further readings on QFD:

Kogure, M., and Y. Aako (1983), "Quality Function Deployment and CWQC," *Quality Progress,* Vol. 16, No. 10, October, 1983, pp. 25–29.

For a recent study of QFD's implementation in nine projects in the United States see

Hauser, J. R., and D. Clausing, "The House of Quality," *Harvard Business Review,* May–June, 1988, pp. 63–73.

Griffin, A., "Evaluating QFD's Use in U.S. Firms as a Process for Developing Products," Working Paper, Graduate School of Business, University of Chicago, April, 1992.

Randlett, R. C., "The Future Belongs to the Marketers," *Industrial Distribution,* August, 29, 1991. Randlett was formerly the Vice President, Marketing, of Milwaukee Electric Company.

[11]These factors have been compiled from various sources including Cooper, Browne and Peters, *op. cit.,* 1991, p. 60; Chhajed, D. and R. Traub, "JIT: An Introduction," Working Paper, University of Illinois, Champaign, Illinois, 1992, pp. 18–19; and McDaniel, S., J. G. Ormsby, and A. B. Gresham, "The Effect of JIT on Distributors," *Industrial Marketing Management,* Vol. 21, 1992, pp. 145–149.

4. Fewer suppliers in long-term relationships.
5. Supplier also incorporates JIT/QFD.
6. Better scheduling and control of inbound freight.
7. Proximity of location.
8. Supplier works to performance specifications not to detailed design specifications.
9. Closer relationship between suppliers and manufacturers, including joint parts and manufacturing system design.
10. Information flows freely among supplier, manufacturer, and carrier.

Increased worldwide competition aided by changes in technology, communication, manufacturing, and education is giving customers the world over choices they never had before. These choices are forcing manufacturers to assemble manufacturing and design systems (including purchasing) to improve the form (given function) and price of the exchange entities. Service has become the competitive edge necessary to cement and sustain relationships. For example, a *Business Week*[12] cover story, "Smart Selling," quotes Richard A. Smith, General Manager for North American Operations of Learning International: "These days, the product has to be great just to be in the game." The story adds that customer and sales service are points of differentiation among competitors.

Stern and Sturdivant,[13] leading authorities on marketing channels, point out that required supplier services fall into five categories:

> Lot size
>
> Market decentralization, or distance of exchange
>
> Waiting time
>
> Product variety
>
> After-sales-service backup.

According to an interesting article by Kumar and Sharman[14] of the consulting firm of McKinsey and Co., on how to improve on-time-delivery, Hewlett- Packard has used these five service criteria to rate suppliers since 1985:

> Technology
>
> Quality
>
> Responsiveness
>
> Delivery
>
> Cost

[12]Power, C., L. Driscoll and E. Bohn, "Smart Selling," *Business Week,* August 3, 1992, pp. 46–48.

[13]Stern, L. W., and F. D. Sturdivant, "Customer-Driven Distribution Systems," *Harvard Business Review,* July–August, 1987, pp. 34–41.

[14]Kumar, A., and G. Sharman, "We Love Your Product, but Where Is It?", *The McKinsey Quarterly,* No. 1, 1992, pp. 24–44.

They also point out that because delivery and cost are the easiest to measure, they are also the most visible in these evaluations. They also report that a survey of companies in 11 industries found timing and reliability to be more important than brand, service (after-sale) and price.

One thousand purchasing agents who responded in a study,[15] listed these 10 criteria for rating their distributors:

> Quality
> Service
> Total cost
> Delivery
> Availability
> Price
> Technical assistance
> Ease of doing business
> Quality of product lines
> Electronic data interchange

Thrusts of Change

From a channel perspective (assuming the appropriateness of a product's technology) the fundamentals to be managed are the sorting and routine functions of Alderson mentioned earlier. This linkage is shown in Exhibit 12–1. For a supplier, at any point in time (static view), this implies carefully managed logistics, variety of products carried, and number of manufacturers represented, and from a dynamic or routine view, the changes occurring are in information exchange systems (e.g., use of EDI [electronic data interchange] and bar coding) and improved relationship management. The static and dynamic elements are interrelated.

Logistics

As Europe moves toward a single market and agreement on value-added tax and customs, and as other intercountry differences occur, a European-wide logistics approach has to be developed. Similarly, the North American Free Trade Zone also calls for a review of logistics strategy.

Where a product is sourced will be less important than how quickly it can be delivered, how reliable the delivery will be and how responsive the supplier is to changes brought about by end-market demand changes. For example, in Europe, Cooper, Browne, and Peters[16] have forecast that better providers of logistics will

[15]Cited in Forbes, C., *op. cit.,* 1991, p. 24.
[16]Cooper, Browne and Peters, *op. cit.,* 1991, p. 67.

EXHIBIT 12–1   Customer Requirements–Supplier Impact

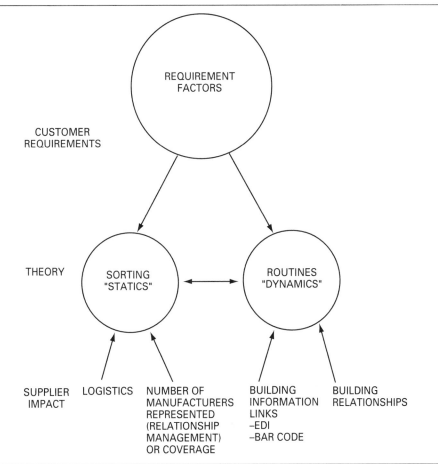

dominate.   They will provide predelivery inspection, inventory management, installation, transport and storage—"intelligent logistics."   Management must begin to carefully study location and prepare to interface with these "intelligent logistics" providers.

Coverage or Number of Manufacturers Represented

Customers wish to interact with fewer suppliers; therefore, suppliers are going to have to carry more lines, but perhaps in specialized areas.   Bob Haffty, procurement manager for Raytheon Missile Systems Laboratory, says, "We are contracting our supplier base now by identifying the 'best and the brightest' and focusing our businesses on these few distributors."[17]   In the same article, a *Purchasing* magazine survey showed

[17]Forbes, C., *op. cit.,* 1991, p. 21.

that only 19.5% of suppliers were rated excellent, 75.5%, good and 4.9%, fair. Other changes cited are:

> Plumbing Products Division of Masco Corporation (Delta Faucet Company) cut its "distributor base" by 1/3.
>
> GTE cut its distributor base from 28,000 to 3,000.
>
> NCR made a 64% reduction in its distribution base from 1985 to 1991.
>
> GE, AMOCO, and Motorola have also made major reductions in their distributor bases.

Responding to customer requests for complete networking packages, for example, the need in the grocery business to connect wholesale activities with retail stores, IBM has merged its Retail Store Systems and Wholesale Distribution groups.[18]

The Saturn[19] example, mentioned earlier, highlights these changes. Metalcutting Tool Management (MTM) of Spring Hill, Tennessee, a department of Kennametal was appointed a primary supplier to Saturn in 1988. Saturn insists that MTM supply the best tool possible, whether or not MTM carries that tool manufacturer's line. This requires MTM to supply Saturn with a Sandvik or Valentine tool if it is superior to a Kennametal tool. As J. P. Smith, MTM's senior program manager puts it, "Tools are sold at the spindle. A typical distributor salesperson will give you the best tool in his bag, but it may not be the best tool to fit the application. This system ensures that the user is going to get the best tool possible." Clearly this leads to a dilemma: the relationships between MTM and its traditional suppliers as well as the relationship between Sandrik and its distributors, for example are changing in not-so-subtle ways. Kennametal's Metalworking Systems Division[20] plans to become the country's leading direct marketer of metalcutting tooling, equipment and related supplies—a market in which its 1991 sales topped $350 million. Its plans call for it to market product lines from 30 to 35 suppliers of GIS Supply, which was absorbed into Kennametal.

Frank Lynn, a Chicago-based industry consultant, summarizes this dilemma succinctly:

> As distributors continue to align themselves with end users, the distributor becomes a buying agent for the end user. You cannot have a situation where the distributor simultaneously acts as a buying agent for the end user and represents the manufacturer on a selective or exclusive basis as well.

Building Relationships

Looking for competitive advantage by minimizing transaction costs is changing the structure of channels. For example,[21] T. Ignacio Lopez de Aeriortna who was brought in from General Motors' European operation to overhaul GM's North

---

[18]"IBM Consolidates Marketing Efforts," *Industrial Distribution,* October, 1991, p. 15.

[19]Zurier, S., *op. cit.,* 1991, p. 21.

[20]"Kennametal Revises Market Strategy," *Industrial Distribution,* May, 10, 1992, pp. 14–15.

[21]As reported in Templin, N., "GM Offers Its Outside Parts Suppliers the Use of Idle Factories and Workers," *The Wall Street Journal,* July 29, 1992, A4.

American and worldwide purchasing operation "has ripped up all of GM's contracts with suppliers and put them out to bid again." This put GM in a winning position by a thorough system-wide approach to minimizing its total costs. As part of the new approach:

(a) GM's internal parts-making operations which supplied approximately 70% of the parts for GM vehicles, are to be treated as equals with outside suppliers for all purchases,

(b) GM purchasing agents are required to obtain 10 bids for each contract, including one from Mexico or other countries,

(c) European contractors were invited to bid for GM contracts, and

(d) European and North American suppliers were offered the use of GM's idle factories and workers to be used in parts manufacture.

This is a radical approach to tackling major problems by reestablishing relationships based on competitiveness.

Structural Changes

Some of the structural changes in relationships are in the number of partners sought, emergence of buying groups, partnering and focus on relationship building via trust, commitment and communication.

Number of Partners

Wal-Mart[22] conducts business only with suppliers who sell through factory salespeople. In 1991, Wal-Mart was the largest, most profitable discounter in the United States with sales of $44 billion and net profit margin of 3.6%. Its net profit margin was half again as much as Kmart, its nearest competitor. The president of the National Association of Industrial Agents, Joe Kramer, is quoted as saying, "What's to prevent one of the large industrial distribution chains from doing the same thing?"[23] A petition filed by the Manufacturer's Agents National Association (MANA) is being studied by the Federal Trade Commission. "MANA alleges that the move by Wal-Mart violates Federal antitrust laws which prohibit manufacturers from offering discounts in lieu of commissions or broker fees." Such actions by powerful "customers" like Wal-Mart to of "cut-out-the-middleman" could change the way in which distribution channels are chosen—at least for serving such customers. Although Wal-Mart, with its ability to manage all the sorting functions, can insist on its suppliers fitting-in to provide it with flexible routines, other customers still need different channels. Thus segmentation of customers on the basis of their "system needs" is necessary.

[22]Grover, M. B., "Tornado Watch," *Forbes,* June 22, 1992, pp. 66–74.

[23]This example is based on "Retail Giant Clouds Rep's Horizon," *Industrial Distribution,* May, 1992, pp. 10–11.

Buying Groups

The following example[24] captures the essence of the formation of distributor groups. Heidelberg Harris (HH) is served by a consortium (Innovative Distribution Group [IDG]) of six noncompeting distributorships representing almost the entire gamut of the industrial distributor's products. In its first year in the partnership HH is expected to save $407,000. The savings come from reductions in paperwork and inventory. IDG was created because the purchasing department at HH sought to reduce its distributor base from 45 to 1. However, it could not find a single distributor with the expertise needed. The group was formed based on the work of three distributors (out of five) who were first contacted by HH to submit proposals to be the "single source supplier." Strong support is also provided by IDG's suppliers. For example, two of the suppliers installed a CAD/CAM system to design socket wrenches on site. As Neil Lasky, the Regional Sales Manager in New England for one of the consortium members—Parker Hannifin—puts it, "As a sole supplier, the advantage to the manufacturer is that he can lock his product into a plant for several years. The system is a win for everybody. The industrial distributor and manufacturer secure increased business, and the customer reduces his indirect overhead."

Other examples cited are:

> The nine-company distributor group ("Vendor City") from Lake Charles, Louisiana which serves PPG Industries.
>
> The Timken Company's (a leading ball-bearing manufacturer) "Supplier City," partnering program.
>
> Bethlehem Steel's Burn Harbor plant in Indiana.

Although there has been some success, the 45th Annual Survey of Distributor Operations[25] found that 86.6% of the respondents did not belong to a buying group; for 72.2% of them buying groups had little or no impact and for 50% there was no impact at all.

This also indicates a need for a segmented approach. Partnering may be important to serve mid-sized companies. For large or small companies, individual routines (at either end) may be more beneficial than having it done at the intermediary level.

Relationship Building

Emphasis on quality forces closer relationships is nicely captured in the words of Liston Coggins,[26] purchasing manager for Decatur, Alabama-based Mathews Industries, "In order to sell quality to our customers, we have to stress quality with our vendors. After all, you can't take junk and make quality out of it!" Both Pepsico[27] and Coca-Cola signed long-term contracts with the Nutra Sweet, a unit of Monsanto, for the purchase of

---

[24]This example and quotes are from Zurier, S., "Distributors Join Forces to Help Heidelberg Harris," *Industrial Distribution*, March, 1992, pp. 20–24.

[25]Zurier, S., "To Survive, Put Value In Your Value Added," *Industrial Distribution*, July, 1991, pp. 20–21.

[26]Quoted in Forbes, C., *op. cit.,* 1991, p. 23.

[27]McCarthy, M. J., "Pepsi, Coke Say They're Loyal to Nutra Sweet," *The Wall Street Journal,* April 22, 1992, B1, B5.

aspartame, even though with the ending of the patent on Nutra Sweet (the brand name for Nutra Sweet's aspartame) they were free to choose other suppliers. This avoids any possible dissatisfaction that their end consumers might feel if the distinctive swirl symbolizing Nutra Sweet were missing. This mirrors the reaction Coke faced when it announced the change in Coke's formula. Tampering with a known bond becomes dangerous.

Relationships across distribution channels are moving to new levels. In the industry view, as Fodor[28] puts it "Little or no acrimony, just communication, trust and commitment"—distribution in the '90s. In a more scholarly view, Morgan and Hunt[29] conducted a study relating trust and commitment to various channel performance measures. Their study was conducted in a survey of members of the National Tire Dealers and Retreaders Association. The survey was analyzed using a highly sophisticated "causal modeling." Their results seem to complement Fodor's summary. Trust and commitment were found to be critical to success. They are not interchangeable but are complementary. Other major findings of this study are:

1. Opportunism is the "killer" of trust and commitment.

2. Shared values seem to aid in building or maintaining commitment.

3. Trust helps in building commitment, moreso in the early rather than later stages of a relationship.

4. A relationship's intrinsic importance as well as economic considerations determine whether a buyer will accept a seller's new policy.

5. Potential business partner turnover is strongly related to relative satisfaction and relationship commitment.

With the growing importance of end point competition, sellers should bear in mind that intermediaries seek to improve their competitiveness and performance margins by adding value,[30] and by adhering to and being certified by ISO 9000 (International Standards Organization) standards.[31] Competing in the United States against global competitors or competing globally requires increased attention to partnering and adherence to quality standards.

Information Links

Two links currently growing in importance in creating exchange routines are Electronic Data Interchange (EDI) and bar coding. These are briefly discussed. It is important for a marketing strategist to be aware of such changes in system requirements as exemplified by these techniques and to build a strategy that considers them.

---

[28]Fodor, G. M., "How to Gauge the Market's Race,", *Industrial Distribution,* July, 1991, pp. 33–35.

[29]Morgan, R. M., and S. D. Hunt, "Relationship Commitment and Trust in Channels of Distribution." Paper presented at a special conference on relationships held at Emory University, May, 1992.

[30]Although value-addition is a well-known concept, what is less well-known is the fact that many intermediaries do not know what to charge for this. A fundamental flaw lies in their costing system. For more details please see Zurier, S., "Do You Charge for Value Added?", *Industrial Distribution,* May, 1992, pp. 30–32.

[31]Zurier, S., "To Survive, Put Value In Your Value Added," *Industrial Distribution,* July, 1991, pp. 20–21.

EDI

Common business communication becomes less costly and more efficient when conducted electronically. Examples of such communications are purchase orders, acknowledgments, order status queries, invoices, and even payments. EDI leads to[32]

> Accuracy
> Faster and better service
> Cost effectiveness
> Freeing up of inside salespeople
> Freeing up of other communication devices
> Improvements in ROI by lowering transaction costs and inventory
> Reducing vendor lead time

Many buyers are insisting on EDI or are seeking to impose financial penalties in lieu of EDI. A survey of 350 telephone interviews of 150 general houses, 150 specialty firms, and 50 combination houses, the 45th Annual Survey of Distributor Operations[33] found that more than 64% of firms with sales over $5 million are using EDI.

EDI is deemed to be so important that 14 trade groups sponsored by the Industrial Distribution Association and the American Supply and Manufacturing Association have agreed to pool programs and form an ongoing meeting group (for more details see reference in footnote 31). Technology is forcing a meeting of the minds!

Although in 1991 only 5% of United States EDI traffic was international, this percentage is expected to grow rapidly.[34] Complex freight documentation, customs documentation, financial data for electronic fund transfers, and language translators are impediments to the international growth of EDI. However, efforts are underway to speed up the process.[35]

Bar Coding

The other information link is bar codes which are used for:

Order picking	Merchandise ticketing
Invoice pricing	Trade deal promotion tracking
Order billing	Security
Receiving	Employee tracking
Shipping	Internal movement of
Point of sale transactions	warehouse products

[32]"EDI: No Longer an Option," *Industrial Distribution,* August, 1991, pp. 5–15.

[33]"Over Three in Five Larger Houses Use EDI", *Industrial Distribution,* December, 1991, p. 16.

Thompson, P. M., Letter to the Editor, *Industrial Distribution,* December, 1991, p. 16.

[34]Clifton, R. G., "Using EDI in the New World Market," *Industrial Distribution,* November, 1991, p. 112.

[35]As noted in footnote 33, the standard in the United States for business messages in ANSI X 12. In Europe it is EDIFACT (EDI for Administration, Commerce and Transportation), Japan has various proprietary formats.

According to the Direct Research Education Foundation, by 1990 only 15% of all distributors had installed bar code equipment. However, by the end of this decade, 81% of all distributors are forecast to have such systems in place.

Consider the example of Cameron & Barkely Co. They found that 1% to 2% of the lines of billing contained errors. On two-million lines of billing per year, and at a $40 per error cost of correction to customer, this translates into $1,600,000 of extra cost to their customers. Compare this to the less than $50,000 cost of a complete "turnkey" system including hardware and software for a multi-branch distributor—advantage bar code!

Note that only two important changes in technological links that affect the creation of routines have been discussed. The point being made, however, is that a marketing strategist should be aware of any changes that provide opportunities to achieve marketing goals. Having reviewed the basic strategy of distribution channels, the requirements of customers and their impact via sorting and the creation of routines (statics and dynamics) on supplier operations, we will now discuss design and assessment of channels.

ASSESSMENT AND DESIGN OF DISTRIBUTION CHANNELS

Two fundamental questions need to be asked in assessing an existing distribution channel: Does it serve the objectives of the products it carries? Is the channel being used adequately? For example,[36] in 1986, John Shagoury of Lotus Development Corporation detected changes in offering requirements (the prices, service levels, and information needs) of some of their large customers. Their buying center members had different levels of technical knowledge, were at different and higher levels in their corporations, and so forth. John therefore had to determine if their current channel structure was adequate or needed to be modified. The first question determines if the channel adequately leverages the value of the product, the second,[37] whether the channel relationship is being leveraged adequately. For example,[38] the salesforce of the Gillette Company's Safety Razor Division had 10% "spare capacity" to use to sell a new product. If the answer to either or both questions posed is No, then corrective action needs to be taken.

When a new product is to be introduced, the issue is to design the appropriate channel to do it. For example,[39] in 1985 Ingersoll-Rand had developed a new centrifugal compressor, the Centac-200 and had to decide on the distribution channel to take it to market.[40]

[36]This example is presented in detail in Rangan, V. K., and D. R. Scott, "Lotus Development Corporation," *Harvard Business School,* Case Number 9-587-078, 1986.

[37]Richard Hill, a colleague at the University of Illinois, provided the example of a Division of Westinghouse, in which Westinghouse carefully designed products to be offered through an existing channel (personal communication).

[38]Gillette Safety Razor Division case, in Corey, E. R., C. H. Lovelock and S. Ward, *Problems in Marketing,* 6th ed., New York, McGraw-Hill, 1981.

[39]This example is taken from Rangan, K. K., and E. R. Corey, "Ingersoll-Rand," *Harvard Business School,* Case Number 9-587-045, 1986. Both the Lotus and the Ingersoll-Rand cases are part of the collection of cases in Corey, E. R., F. V. Cespedes, and V. K. Rangan, *Going to Market: Cases in Industrial Distribution,* Cambridge, MA, Harvard Business School, 1989.

[40]Our discussion takes the view of a manufacturer like Ingersoll-Rand or IBM. However, a similar analysis may also be conducted by an intermediary like Kennametal's Metalworking Systems Division. The basic issue for an intermediary is whether their upstream (i.e., with manufacturers) relationships and their downstream (with customers) relationships are being adequately leveraged.

We now consider the issues of whether an existing channel is adequate and that of designing a channel for a new entry.   How best to use existing channel relationships is part of strategic planning and should be used to discover possible avenues to more adequately leverage these relationships via new offerings.

Assessment and Design Process

Strategically, the intent is to determine the type of intermediary (or whom) to include (distributors, wholesalers, manufacturers' representatives, direct sales force), the number of intermediaries (which reflects the resources allocated), and the offerings (service level, discount policy, delivery) to be provided to channel members.   Like much in strategic planning, this is a complex issue.   Over the years, improvements have been proposed in ways to look at this problem and its solution.   The approaches recently proposed blend both "hard" numbers and managerial judgment to aid decision making.

First, we present a summary of some of the approaches to this important analysis and then a discussion of contemporary thinking on this matter.

A Summary of Previous Approaches

Much of the literature discusses the decision of whether to vertically integrate (i.e., use a direct or owned channel) or to use intermediaries.   Exhibit 12–2, from Rangan, Menezes and Maier,[41] is a summary of the literature since 1962.   This exhibit is self-explanatory and gives the recommendations of each author, by factor (they do not consider combinations of factors) for when a direct sales force or a distributor is recommended.   The explanation of the "intuitive truths" of Aspinwall and Miracle is provided by Bucklin,[42] using the famous transaction cost minimization condition of Alderson described earlier.   We discussed the transaction cost theory of Williamson[43] in

[41]This table is reproduced from Rangan, V. K., M. A. J. Menezes, and E. P. Maier, "Channel Selection for New Industrial Products: A Framework, Method, and Application," *Journal of Marketing,* Vol. 56, July, 1992, pp. 69–82. References for the papers referred to in this table are:

Anderson, E. and D. C. Schmittlein, "Integration of the Sales Force: An Empirical Examination," *Rand Journal of Economics,* Vol. 15, No. 3, 1984, pp. 385–395.

Aspinwall, L. V., "The Characteristics of Goods Theory," In *Managerial Marketing: Perspectives and Viewpoints,* W. Lazer and E. J. Kelley (eds.), Homewood, IL, Irwin, 1962, pp. 633–643.

Bucklin, L. P., "A Theory of Distribution," *Channel Structure,* Berkeley, CA, IBER Special Publications, 1966.

John, G. and B. A. Weitz, "Forward Integration Into Distribution: An Empirical Test of Transaction Cost Analysis," *Journal of Law, Economics, and Organization,* Vol. 42, No. 3, 1988, pp. 337–354.

Klein, S., G. L. Frazier, and V. T. Roth, "A Transaction Cost Analysis in International Markets," *Journal of Marketing Research,* Vol. 27, May, 1990, pp. 196–208.

Lilien, G. L., "ADVISOR 2: Modeling the Marketing Mix Decisions for Industrial Products," *Management Science,* Vol. 25, February, 1979, pp. 191–204.

Miracle, G. E., "Product Characteristics and Marketing Strategy," *Journal of Marketing,* Vol. 29, January, 1965, pp. 18–24.

[42]Bucklin, L. P., *op. cit.,* 1966.

[43]For example see Williamson, O. E., *Markets and Hierarchies: Analysis and Antitrust Implications,* New York, The Free Press, 1975.

EXHIBIT 12–2   Factors Determining Channel Choices

	Salesforce If	Distributor If
Aspinwall (1962)		
1. Replacement rate	Low	High
2. Gross margin	High	Low
3. Adjustment	High	Low
4. Time of consumption	High	Low
5. Searching time	High	Low
Miracle (1965)		
6. Unit value	High	Low
7. Significance of purchase	High	Low
8. Purchasing effort	High	Low
9. Rate of technological change	High	Low
10. Technical complexity	High	Low
11. Need for service	High	Low
12. Frequency of purchase	Low	High
13. Rapidity of consumption	Low	High
14. Extent of usage	Low	High
Bucklin (1966)		
15. Market decentralization	Low	High
16. Lot size	Large	Small
17. Assortment	Narrow	Wide
18. Waiting time	High	Low
Lilien (1979)		
15. Order size	Large	Small
16. Product complexity	High	Low
17. Product life-cycle stage	Introduction	Maturity
18. Frequency of usage	Low	High
Transaction Cost Theory Constructs Used in Marketing Channel Studies (Anderson and Schmittlein 1984; John and Weitz 1988; Klein, Frazier, and Roth 1990)		
19. Product customization requirements	High	Low
20. Need for special equipment or services	High	Low
21. Complexity of customer buying and decision-making process	High	Low
22. Complexity of product information to be exchanged	High	Low
23. Transaction size	Large	Small
24. Rate of technological change	High	Low
25. Volatility of demand	High	Low

From Rangan, V. K., M. A. J. Menezes and E. P. Maier, "Channel Selection for New Industrial Products, *Journal of Marketing,* Vol. 56, 1992, p. 71. Reprinted with permission from the American Marketing Association.

detail in Chapter 5. For long-lasting channel relationships, Williamson's theory predicates the choice of direct vs. indirect channel choice on whether assets unique to this relationship are deployed and on the extent of uncertainty in the environment.

Although most of the writing (reviewed briefly here) discusses the question of whether a direct or indirect channel should be used, many examples of mixed or hybrid channels are found in practice. For example, the 3M Company's Audio-Visual Division distributes its overhead projectors through five distinct channels:

> Direct
>
> Full-line dealers
>
> Special-line dealers
>
> Scotch Brand dealers
>
> OEM dealers

Exhibit 12–3, from Hutt and Speh,[44] provides a summary of what differentiates these channels. Further, the efforts referred to consider the impact of only one customer requirement at a time in the direct vs. indirect decision. Customers need a "bundle" of requirements. We shall discuss in more detail two approaches to designing a channel.[45]

The Stern and Sturdivant Approach[46]

The fundamental thrust of their approach is "You design products for specific customer groups. Here's how to distribute them the same way" (p. 34).

Arguing that many American firms attempt to reach markets using "outmoded" ways, they propose an eight-step *process*. The essence of the process is to design a system to serve customers best. Their approach is to examine critically what customers need, design the "ideal" channel to deliver what they seek, and modify the

[44]Hutt, M. D. and T. W. Speh, *Business Marketing Management,* The Dryden Press, 1992, p. 363.

[45]Many other excellent papers and books are available to the ardent scholar. Although they provide "fodder" for theoretical analysis and training, their direct impact on decision-making and thinking in the nineties is less obvious.

Baligh, H. H., and L. E. Richartz, *Vertical Market Structures,* Boston: Allyn and Bacon, 1967.

The works of F. E. Balderston, F. E. Balderston and Hoggatt, and H. H. Baligh reproduced in:

Mallen, B. E., *The Marketing Channel: A Conceptual Viewpoint,* New York, John Wiley, 1967.

More recent work, principally by Corstjens and Doyle (1979), provides the seminar work by which Rangan and his colleagues provided more detailed management science models. For these see Corstjens, M. and, Doyle, "Channel Optimization in Complex Marketing Systems," *Management Science,* Vol. 25, No. 10, 1979, pp. 1014–1025.

Rangan, K. V., "The Channel Design Decision: A Model and an Application," *Marketing Science,* Vol. 6, No. 2, Spring, 1987, pp. 156–181.

Rangan, K. V. and R. Jaikumar, "Integrating Distribution Strategy and Tactics: A Model and an Application," *Management Science,* Vol. 37, No. 11, 1991, pp. 1377–1389.

[46]This section is based on Stern, L. W. and F. D. Sturdivant, "Customer-Driven Distribution Systems," *Harvard Business Review,* July–August, 1987, pp. 34–41. All quotes are from this paper. Numbers in parentheses are the page number(s) on which they appear.

EXHIBIT 12–3   Inside Business Marketing

It Takes Five Roads to Reach This Market

One would surmise that overhead projectors and transparency film would be easy to market—they are not sophisticated, they are easy to use, and they don't have a big impact on the buyer's bottom line. The Audio-Visual division at 3M thinks differently. To market 3M projectors effectively, this division has created an elaborate distribution system composed of five distinct marketing channels:

1. *Direct.* Utilizing its own sales force, 3M markets projectors through stores in New York, Chicago, and Los Angeles. These 3M stores (a) provide a performance benchmark against which other dealers are evaluated, (b) provide a testing ground for new products, and (c) allow 3M to maintain contact with end users.

2. *Full-line Dealers.* These dealers are the exclusive distributors of top 3M products. They employ high-level sales forces and receive unlimited support from 3M. The full-line dealers market new products; 25% of their product line is new every five years. These dealers focus their effort on large, important customers and sell to high-level decision makers.

3. *Special-line Dealers.* These channel members do not carry the full 3M line. Their efforts are restricted to products that are well along in the product life cycle, and their focus is on bid business—usually schools and institutions

that buy on a price basis. In an effort to control expenses, their efforts are monitored by 3M through telephone as opposed to personal contact. Expenses are further controlled by drop-shipping product directly to end users and avoiding warehousing at the dealer.

4. *Scotch Brand Dealers.* "Commodity" status products are sold through 9,000 of these dealers, who are general-line office supply distributors. These dealers carry many 3M products that support the use of overhead projectors, such as film and supplies. The focus of the Scotch brand dealer is low-volume buyers, too expensive for full-line dealers or the direct sales force to call on. Scotch brand dealers provide broad distribution at low margins and sell projectors that are nearing the end of their product life cycle.

5. *OEM Dealers.* Transparency film is sold to manufacturers of equipment used to make visual slide transparencies (e.g. Hewlett-Packard). The goal is to generate new customers for 3M in the future because the OEM includes the 3M film along with the equipment that is sold to the end user.

The wide array of channels used by 3M reflects the diversity of the industrial marketplace and the importance of channels in establishing a competitive advantage. Each channel is designed on the basis of the buyer's needs, the buyer's purchasing behavior, and the nature of the buying process.

Figure from BUSINESS MARKETING MANAGEMENT: A STRATEGIC VIEW OF INDUSTRIAL AND ORGANIZATIONAL MARKETS, Fourth Edition by Michael D. Hutt and Thomas W. Speh copyright © 1992 by the Dryden Press, reproduced by permission of the publisher.

"ideal" in view of practical constraints in order to arrive at the optimal system. This approach is shown diagrammatically in Exhibit 12–4. This process is similar in philosophy to the 4A + 3I and the Extended SWOT analysis that were presented earlier. It seeks to "push-the-envelope (stretch existing boundaries)" in examining creative ways to leverage products via "physical reach" channels. It avoids inertial responses, such as endless fine-tuning of existing systems if major changes are required. It also calls for creative thinking when new products are to be entered into the market.

EXHIBIT 12–4 Analytic Approach for Designing Customer-Driven Distribution Systems

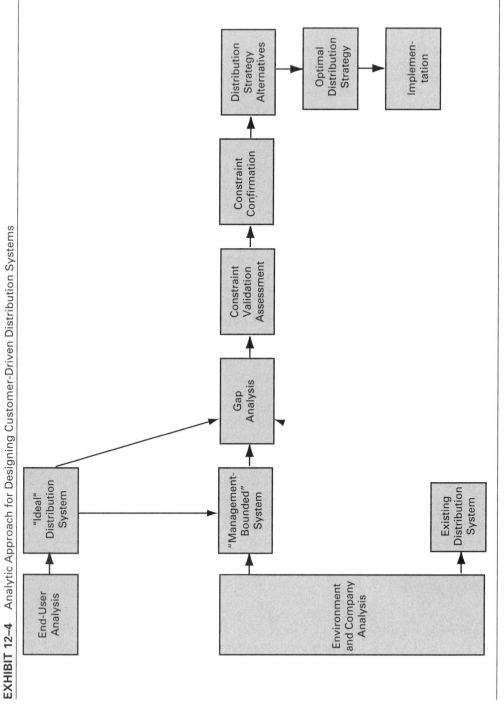

From The MAC Group, Inc., a Gemini Consulting Company, and Louis W. Stern.
Courtesy: Louis W. Stern
Reprinted from: L. W. Stern, and Adel I. El-Ansary, Marketing Channels, 4 ed, Englewood-Cliffs, NJ: Prentice Hall, 1992, p. 238.

Examples of Creative Thinking in Channel Design and Choice

When TIMEX watches were first introduced, watches were traditionally sold through jewelry stores. TIMEX management chose a novel approach to distribute their watches after they were denied access to traditional channels because of the type of watch they were offering. They were sold through drug stores with refreshingly creative communication and point-of-purchase displays.

7-Eleven and Family Mart[47] stores in Japan dramatically changed distribution systems for obtaining food deliveries to their stores. Both receive food deliveries three times a day in the heart of congested Tokyo. Family Mart's stores are clustered so that each store is no more than two hours from its distribution depot. 7-Eleven first had to convince three competing dairies to combine their deliveries. In 1984, having done so successfully, 7-Eleven combined deliveries of all refrigerated foods. Cooked rice was delivered three times a day to its stores starting in 1987. Consider,

> 7-Eleven is the exclusive customer of six food companies. It is the nation's top seller of boxed lunches and rice balls, oden (pieces of fish, vegetables, or soybean cakes which have simmered in broth), canned coffee, pastries, ramen noodles, and magazines.

Jose Collazo, CEO of El Segundo, California-based Infonet[48] is quoted as saying,

> About five or six years ago, we became entrenched in providing international datacom services. As we were growing into that marketplace we noticed that some very large corporations like AT&T and IBM were entering the very niches we were operating in. We also realized that the [European] PTTs, as they became deregulated, would want to enter that marketplace to satisfy the needs of their customers. So we looked at what was the best way for us to compete against the AT&Ts and IBMs of this world, and the PTTs, and some of these big companies. We decided that the best way for us [to compete] was to join forces with some of these people.

The Eight-Step Process

The eight steps of the Stern and Sturdivant process are:

1. Customer Requirements Determination
2. Identification of Possible Channels
3. Estimation of Costs Involved for Each Alternative
4. Specification of Management Policies and Constraints
5. Evaluation of Alternatives
6. Evaluation of Assumptions
7. Comparison of "Ideal" Solution to Existing Channel
8. Preparation to Implementation

[47]Sun, M., "Not All Shops are Behind the Times: Open-and-Shut Case," *Far Eastern Economic Review,* 17 January, 1991, p. 48.

[48]Greenstein, I., "Infonet's CEO Relies on Diplomacy to Advance Value-Added Network Services," *Networking Management,* October, 1990, p. 21

Customer requirements can be viewed as sorting and routinization needs as discussed earlier. Further, the exchange entities required as well as the mode of relationship desired were covered in Chapters 5 and 6.

Identifying alternative channels requires creative thinking. Recently, the Mobile Tronics Company was started in Champaign, Illinois. It stresses the convenience of exchange in its operation. Exhibit 12–5 is a reproduction of a door card distributed by the company to select residents in Champaign. Until Mobile Tronics appeared on the scene, the only way to get a VCR serviced was to take it to a service center between 9:00 a.m. to 5:00 p.m., Monday through Friday. Capitalizing on the need to provide this service at a time and place convenient to the customer, Mobile Tronics performs "regular cleanings" at the customer's homes, when convenient to the customer!

EXHIBIT 12–5   Bringing The Customer Back into Customer Service

Do you put rented tapes into your VCR?

Have you had your VCR for over a year and never had it cleaned?

If your VCR gets dusty and dirty on the outside, imagine what it's like on the inside!

Regular Cleanings will improve the picture quality and increase the life of your VCR.

MOBILETRONICS saves you the hassle of disconnecting your VCR, taking it to get cleaned and leaving it there for up to a week.

**WE COME TO YOU . . . AT YOUR
CONVENIENCE, NOT OURS!!**

**INTRODUCTORY OFFER
$5.00 OFF REGULAR PRICE**

**COMPLETE VCR CLEANING
$24.95**

CALL 352–9303 to set up an appointment

Regular Price $29.95

Printed on Recycled Paper

In today's environment, when PCs are virtual commodities, many individuals buy them through the mail. Corporations have also started purchasing them through the same channel. In strategic planning the question, "Which comes first the chicken or the egg?" seems almost irrelevant, because with sufficient care and incubation the fertilized egg will lead to a chicken. And, with care, the chicken will lay an egg!

Other examples (pointed out by Stern and Sturdivant) are "financial supermarkets," "discount brokerages," and so forth, created by firms like GE Credit, Merrill Lynch, and Bank One. Often, adapting channel structure ideas from other industries provides a novel and appropriate alternative. This step requires creative thinking.

The third step, assessing costs, involves assessing what needs to be offered to channel intermediaries to serve customers best. Such offerings come at a cost. Therefore understanding what each channel needs is critical to assess the associated costs. For example, does an EDI need to be installed? What type? At what cost? What is the returns policy and cost? In 1989, in Japan,[49] 39.5% of all women's fashion garments shipped to department stores were unsold and returned to wholesalers. Sales to "roadside chains" like Aoki International (122 branches specializing in suits), and Idol (300 children's clothing stores) are made on a no-return basis. Also, sales through department stores like Mitsukoshi require the approval of sales personnel. For example, 66% of the counter staff in Mitsukoshi's clothing departments are former wholesaler employees.

Leapfrog Technologies,[50] started in 1990, has Gardena Industrial Supply & Hardware Co. of Gardena, California as a distributor. Leapfrog regards its marketing program as "leveraging their feet on the street" support for its distributors. It provides both financial and informational support as well as promotional assistance. Bob Duncan, national sales manager for Leapfrog, says,

> When we began working with Gardena to develop a marketing strategy, they asked for a commitment of one week per month for joint sales calls. Although it seemed like a lot of time at first—we obliged. And jointly we sold 30% of the initial order in one week (p. 38).

This relationship has been successful for both parties. It does come at a cost, however, which must be estimated at the design stage to make a better decision.

For the next steps, Stern and Sturdivant describe the example of IBM's channel decision to market its PCs to small users. Its analysis revealed that the ideal channel is a service-intensive, decentralized network of specialty dealers carrying assorted microcomputer brands as well as other office equipment (for one-stop buying). [This brings to mind the recent self-definition and promotion of Xerox as "The Document Company—Xerox."] The existing system consisted primarily of IBM's direct sales force. However, some IBM management "assumed" that if "outsiders" distributed IBM's product, adequate service quality could not be maintained.

---

[49]The Japanese examples and statistics here are from Smith, C., "Clothing Stores which Avoid the Middleman: Wholesale Killers," *Far Eastern Economic Review,* January 17, 1991, pp. 45–46.

[50]Forbes, C., "Marketing . . . by Leaps and Bounds," *Industrial Distribution,* July, 1991, pp. 37–38.

This faulty assumption (at least partly) led IBM to open retail outlets to sell only IBM equipment. Customers, however, wished not only to obtain service but also to comparison shop. Thus the "quest" was lost at this stage of store-choice and not because of product per se. IBM's product center network was sold subsequently to NYNEX.

It is also important to point out that the existing channel may be adequate. An example, again from Stern and Sturdivant,

> . . . a specialty grocery products manufacturer discovered that it was getting its products onto supermarket shelves in ways that on the surface looked Rube Goldbergian. It was using an array of third-party players, including food brokers, grocery wholesalers, and health food distributors, some of whom carried out a remarkable range of functions between the manufacturing and the retail level of the distribution chain. When the company drew a structural diagram, it looked like a bowl of spaghetti. Nevertheless, further analysis revealed that the system met all the criteria of an ideal.

"The recommendation? Don't mess with it! Don't touch a thing!"

The Stern and Sturdivant eight-step process is important in understanding the design of distribution channels. However, details of analysis and the potential costs of switching from an existing channel arrangement to another are not considered. These are considerations addressed by Rangan, Menezes and Maier, whose work is discussed next.

The Rangan, Menezes, and Maier (RMM) Approach

The RMM approach is used for new product lines and for additions to existing product lines. However, in keeping with the Stern and Sturdivant gap-matching arguments of assessing fit with an ideal channel, this process seems suitable for other situations as well. Their approach, which they report to have successfully implemented for the 3M Company,[51] consists of three steps:

> Marketing Research
>
> Preparatory Analysis
>
> Decision Analysis

In the first step, data to set priorities for customer requirements are collected. In the second, alternative channels are developed and customer requirement priorities are quantified. In the third step, the information from step two helps choose the channel to be used. These steps are described in the authors' examples. The channel was designed for a new product which could be used for a variety of applications such as deburring metal parts, deflashing plastic and paper utensils, clean-

---

[51]E. P. Maier was the Marketing Operations Manager, Abrasives Division, 3M Company at the time this article was published.

ing golf balls, tiles, and rubber articles, gripping fabric in textile mills, and holding components for assembly. The authors used the name Scotchfiber to refer to this product.

Step 1

RMM considers eight requirements of distribution channels that customers need.

Product Information	Assortment
Product Customization	Availability
Product Quality Assurance	After-Sale Service
Lot Size	Logistics

With the help of the marketing manager, product manager, and two sales representatives, operative definitions of the eight generic requirements were provided for Scotchfiber. For example, product information was the amount of information sought on roll fiber length, fiber property, and construction density and usage properties, such as the ability to finish irregularly shaped pieces and interiors.

Ten potential customer experts (lead users[52]) and 11 company specialists provided, via interviews that lasted approximately an hour and a half, important points and evaluations for each of the customer requirements. These priorities were carried out for the first year and after three years (the expected time in which Scotchfiber would become established in the market[53]). The mean importance values and a summary of the corresponding reasoning are given in Exhibit 12–6.

Step 2

The data collected in Step 1 were analyzed and priorities were developed for use in the next step.

[52]*Lead users* was first coined by von Hippel of MIT to refer to leading-edge users who would reflect the possibilities of future uses, usage conditions, and requirements. For more details please see:

von Hippel, E., "Lead User Analyses for the Development of New Industrial Products," *Management Science,* Vol. 34, May, 1986, pp. 569–582.

[53]Lele advances propositions that link channel requirements to the stages of a product's life cycle. At the introductory stage he recommends changes that add a high degree of value. For the growth stage, a channel's capacity to handle volume, rather than its value addition, is said to be critical. At the maturity stage again, value addition is said to be of little importance, because consumer choice is primarily based on price. Finally, at the stage of decline, the focus shifts even more to price. Keep in mind that generally such propositions have general truthfulness. However, strategic victories are gained by creating *new* reasons to win.

Interested readers are referred to:

Lele, M., "Matching Your Channels to Your Product's Life Cycle," *Business Marketing,* December, 1986, pp. 61–69.

EXHIBIT 12–6 Evaluation of Distribution Functions (figures in parentheses are standard deviations)

Channel Determinants	Overall Means (Year 1)	Comments	Overall Means (Year 3)	Comments
1. Product information	.56 (.065)	Does not favor either distributor or salesforce	.44 (.066)	Does not favor either distributor or direct salesforce
2. Product customization	.81 (.067)	Viewed as highly customized, suggesting customers would probably prefer a direct sales contact	.28 (.070)	Because the customization content is low, customers would have little difficulty ordering from distributors
3. Product quality assurance	.62 (.067)	Fairly important, suggesting that a direct salesforce would be preferred		Because customers by now would probably have standardized their specifications, they would have little difficulty ordering from distributors
4. Lot size	.38 (.079)	Because lot size is not large, customers could be best served by distributors	.36 (.069)	Because lot size is not large, customers could be best served by distributors
5. Assortment	.76 (.064)	Assortment not essential; hence a distributor channel is not necessary	.50 (.071)	Does not favor either distributor or salesforce
6. Availability	.68 (.066)	Local availability (distributor) is not critical for the customer	.47 (.071)	Does not favor either distributor or salesforce
7. After-sale	.66 (.067)	Post-sale service requirements are not critical, suggesting that local availability (distributor) is not necessary	.39 (.069)	Post-sale service requirements are marginally critical, favoring distributors
8. Logistics	.07 (.063)	Simple product; a distributor could handle it as well as anyone else	.04 (.063)	Simple product; a distributor could handle it as well as anyone else

From Rangan, V. K., M. A. J. Menezes and E. P. Maier Channel Selection of New Industrial Products, *Journal of Marketing,* Vol. 56, 1992, p. 77. Reprinted with permission from the American Marketing Association.

Step 3

Based on discussions as well as information from Step 2, the preliminary planning team concluded:

> The intensity of the anticipated customer requirements for product information, product customization, and product quality assurance for the new product considerably exceeded the current capabilities of the division's general-line finishing distributors.

> The channel function profile after the product was established matched that of the division's other products currently being routed through general-line finishing distributors.

> A new class of distributors, fiber specialists, which the company did not currently use, would also be able to satisfy the functional requirement for the established product. However, they would have difficulties fulfilling the first three functional requirements for the new product, but to a lesser degree than the current distributors (76–77).

Six options were then developed for further consideration (Exhibit 12–7). Choice among these options[54] was made on attainability of sales and profit targets and of the costs.

The intensity of coverage needed for each option to attain its sales target was first estimated by management based on past experience. Then costs of achieving the required intensity of distribution for each option were estimated. Costs were estimated for seven cost elements (two of which are combined under training in Exhibit 12–8)

EXHIBIT 12–7   Feasible Channel Options

Option	Now (when product is new)	3 Years Later (when product is established)
1	Salesforce	General-line finishing distributors
2	Salesforce	Fiber specialists
3	Salesforce and general-line finishing distributors	General-line finishing distributors
4	Salesforce and fiber specialists	Fiber specialists
5	Salesforce and general-line finishing distributors	Fiber specialists
6	Salesforce and fiber specialists	General-line finishing distributors

From Rangan, V. K., M. A. J. Menezes and E. P. Maier, "Channel Selection for New Industrial Products, *Journal of Marketing,* Vol. 56, 1992, p. 78. Reprinted with permission from the American Marketing Association.

[54]Options 5 and 6 were eliminated as channel conflicts and switching costs were expected to be high.

EXHIBIT 12–8 Distribution Cost Elements

Demand Generation	:	Salesforce time, marketing, advertising
Training	:	Distributor technical training, administrative training
Sales Support	:	Inventory carrying, customer credit
Logistics	:	Order processing, transportation, warehousing
Distributor Margin	:	Actual margin
Opportunity Costs	:	Salesforce time taken away from selling existing products

Adapted from Rangan, V. K., M. A. J. Menezes, and E. P. Maier, "Channel Selection for New Industrial Products, *Journal of Marketing,* Vol. 56, 1992, pp. 69–82. Reprinted with permission from the American Marketing Association.

and are given in Exhibit 12–9. Reducing cost (given the achievement of sales target) was used as the objective for making the final choice.

A Summary of Channel Assessment and Design

First, a channel should be chosen to meet certain absolute goals, for example, sales or market share. This indicates whether a channel is effective in achieving goals. If no option is available to achieve these goals, then the goals have to be redefined.

Second, if several options are available to achieve the selected goals, then the cost of each option should be calculated. If all of them prove "too costly," the goals need to be reexamined, reestablished and the process repeated. This second step chooses a channel based on its efficiency, that is, on the costs of achieving goals.

Exhibit 12–10, is a flow chart that augments the excellent work of Stern and Sturdivant, and of Rangan, Menezes, and Maier. The key managerial considerations suggested are:

> Market Goals
>
> Strategic Horizon
>
> Current and Potential Product Set
>
> Acceptable Efficiency Levels for Achieving Market Goals (channel efficiency).

EXHIBIT 12–9 Relative Costs of Feasible Channel Options

Option	Demand Generation Costs	Distributor Training and Maintenance Costs		Support Costs	Sales Logistics Costs	Distribution Margin	Opportunity Costs	Total Cost Index
		Technical	Administrative					
1	High	Low	Low	High	Medium	Low	Medium	102
2	High	Low	High	High	Medium	Medium	High	110
3	Medium	Medium	Low	Medium	Low	High	Low	100
4	Medium	Medium	High	Medium	Medium	High	High	111

Adapted from Rangan, V. K., M. A. J. Menezes, and E. P. Maier, "Channel Selection for New Industrial Products, *Journal of Marketing,* Vol. 56, 1992, p. 79. Reprinted with permission from the American Marketing Association.

EXHIBIT 12–10   Channel Design Flowchart

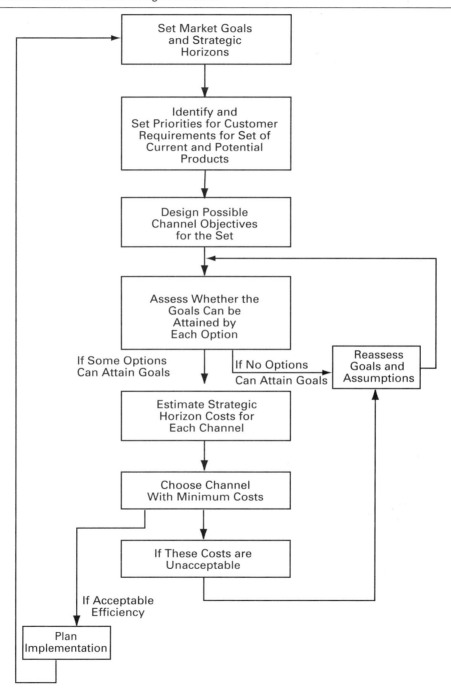

Market goals are sales targets for each product (current or potential) over the chosen strategic planning horizon. These are used to weed out channel options that would not lead to the desired market goals. Market goals also provide a uniform comparison of channel options, by forcing a comparison of only those channels that meet the required goals. This final comparison is made based on the efficiency with which each channel option leverages resources to achieve the market goals. A comparison made on efficiency alone (ignoring goal attainment) does not justify the process and would not (by definition) attain market goals.

Information for setting priorities for customer requirements is collected as suggested by Rangan, Menezes, and Maier. The menu of requirements is generated by considering static sorting and the dynamic routines requirements as shown in Exhibit 12–1.

Besides the cost elements suggested by Rangan, Menezes, and Maier (Exhibit 12–9), the costs of administering and controlling a channel must be closely considered. Further, given the strategic planning horizon used in the design process, adequate attention should be given to the switching costs and the timing of such changes,[55] if changes are part of the options under consideration.

If a channel option is effective in achieving market goals but has a low efficiency, then two possibilities should be considered:

> The channel administration may be inefficient and its routines should be thoroughly evaluated.

> The channel's sorting function may be underutilized and should be evaluated to see if other products can be added with acceptable incremental costs.

Assessment-Choice of Specific Channel Members

This section is included for the sake of completeness and is not an in-depth discussion.[56] The assessment-choice criteria are: (a) whether it meets its quota of market

---

[55]A study by Frank and Blackman showed the following switching patterns of 430 manufacturers who dropped manufacturers representatives:

Switch to	*Percentage*
Other representatives	40
Direct	30
Discontinuation of territory	12
Consolidation of several lines with one representative	8
Other changes	10

Note that 60% of the changes did not involve change of type of channel, but involved either change in intensity or change in the specific channel members used. Switching costs must consider not only the switches of type planned as part of an option over the strategic planning horizon, but also possible switches of specific members used. For details of the study see:

Frank, J. S. and D. M. Blackman, "Why Manufacturers Drop Representatives," *In* D. E. Vinson and D. Sciglimpaglia (eds.), *The Environment of Industrial Marketing,* Columbus, OH, Grid Inc., 1975.

[56]For an excellent treatment of this topic, the reader should see Chapter 11 of Stern and El-Ansary's classic textbook.

Stern, L. W. and A. I. El-Ansary, *Marketing Channels,* 4th ed., Englewood Cliffs, NJ, Prentice-Hall, 1992.

goals and (b) the efficiency with which it meets those goals. Kumar[57] developed a comprehensive method for assessing a channel member's performance. The measures suggested are:

> Sales Performance (Effectiveness)
> Financial Performance (Efficiency)
> Reseller Competence (Effectiveness-Efficiency)
> Reseller Compliance (Effectiveness-Efficiency)
> Reseller Adaptation (Efficiency)
> Reseller Growth (Effectiveness)
> Customer Satisfaction (Effectiveness)

For efficiency and that, too, based only on accounting data without incorporating costs of channel management (e.g., of ensuring compliance[58]), measures such as customer return on assets, and direct product profit (DPP) have been suggested.

SUMMARY

This chapter provides an overview of distribution channel functions and their link to customer requirements and a discussion of processes useful to the assessment-design of distribution channels.

Fundamentally, customer requirements change in their routines and sorting requirements. Driven by changes in the scope of competition, in the scope and integrity of data communication technology, and in the paradigms for design and development of new products, new balances are being struck among transaction costs, inventory costs, and the ability to respond to strategic opportunities that present in narrow slits (or slits of opportunity as opposed to windows of opportunity). These new balances are resulting in the formation of alliances, changes in the number of vendors, speed and volume of delivery and interlinked inventory, ordering and payment systems, and even in the types of channels being used to take products to market.

It is imperative to evaluate existing channels and to understand how they might best

---

[57]Kumar, N., "A Methodology for Assessing Channel Intermediary Performance from the Supplier's Perspective," Unpublished Doctoral Dissertation, Northwestern University, Evanston, IL, June, 1991.

[58]Tadashi Saito, of the Distribution Economics Institute of Japan (a Ministry of Trade and Industry sponsored Institute), in the *Far Eastern Economic Review* reported that:

> Manufacturers do not exercise financial control over retailers through equity stakes or loans, Saito says, but many companies send 'helpers' to small shops who can monitor sales policy. These helpers can discourage the proprietor from handling rival products, including imports.

This could be quite costly given the number of shops involved. Matsushita, for example, has 24,000 small retailers in its group account.

Smith, C., "Rebel Electrical-Goods Shops win Against Odds: Step Out of Line," *Far Eastern Economic Review,* Vol. 17 January, 1991, pp. 47–48.

be leveraged and if they are adequate to protect existing customer loyalties and to create new and appropriate ones. It is equally necessary to transcend conventional thinking in identifying the best channels for new products. For example, such creative thinking has resulted in the use of direct mail by Medco to sell prescription drugs (and its subsequent acquisition by Merck); the use of Federal Express by Calyx and Corolla to deliver fresh flowers; the use of telephone lines to activate on a compact disk (CD) only the tracks required and paid for by customers; and the direct order of U.S. products by customers in Japan via electronic catalogs; and the appearance of home shopping via TV.

Many more such changes are certain. With new manufacturing technology leading to smaller manufacturing lots, and rapid design and prototyping and manufacturing systems becoming even more rapid, customers will probably be even more demanding in their routines and sorting requirements—perhaps even individual customers of consumer goods. Perhaps these new technologies may lead back to a preference for dealing with many vendors, and build-up of inventory of core supplies. The latter may signal commitment in the face of slits of opportunity and preempt competition.

The first part of the chapter apprised readers of changes in customer requirements and the directions along which they are changing. The second part provided a framework for the continuous evaluation of existing channels and for the design of new ones. Together they form the basis for gaining strategic advantage using distribution channels.

Concept Questions

1. (a.) What are some of the major changes taking place in industrial channels?
   (b.) Describe a framework to view these changes parsimoniously.
2. (a.) Catalog and describe the major changes at the customer end that affect distribution channel management.
   (b.) Devise a score card to rate distribution channels.
3. (a.) What are buying groups?
   (b.) What might be the impact of buying groups?
4. Briefly describe the Stern and Sturdivant approach to channel design.
5. Briefly describe the RMM approach to channel design.

Discussion Questions

1. Compare and contrast the Stern and Sturdivant approach with the RMM approach. What are their shortcomings? Suggest an improved process.
2. What is the role of technological links between customers-channels and service originators-manufacturers in service industries?
3. Design a channel system for the distribution of your university's executive development program.
   or
   Design a channel system for an interactive computer software package you have invented. This software package also creates new games as it is being used.

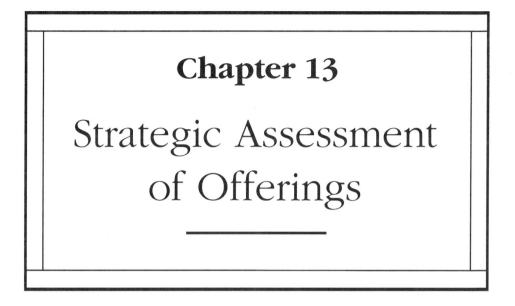

Chapter 13

Strategic Assessment of Offerings

INTRODUCTION

In Chapter 6, Relationships with Customers, the management decisions that led to customer satisfaction were given as choices of offerings and relationship modes. In this chapter we describe offerings and the key considerations in using them to obtain strategic advantage. The offering space is made up of function, form and price. Besides these, information and customer and financing service are key facilitators of exchange and therefore deserve to be considered as part of the larger offerings mix. Major considerations in the strategic use of offerings are coverage (or scope) of the offerings space, and relative positioning. These considerations are discussed at length and an overall framework using our discussion of strategic alternatives from Chapter 2 provides an overview of the major alternatives which completes this chapter.

Motivating Examples

Consider the following examples.

Apple Computer, Inc.

In its third big announcement of new products in the last six months, Apple Computer Inc. will introduce six Macintosh computers and two laser printers Tuesday at the MacWorld Expo in Tokyo. The new machines are all intended to offer higher performance at lower prices than existing Macintosh models, reflecting Apple's resolve to increase its share of the personal computer market.[1]

[1]Fisher, L. M., "Apple Computer to Roll Out Six New Macintosh Models," *New York Times,* Feb. 9, 1993, C3.

This example reinforces the function, form, and price bases for conceiving "offerings" and exchange entities as part of marketing strategy thought and action. It also sparks the need to ask: How much of the function × form × price space should be covered, or served? In the next example, American Transitional Hospitals Inc. has chosen a small part of this space. Besides the volume of space covered, this example highlights a step of intuition by the company. They questioned the conventional functions deemed necessary to be a hospital. Such questioning led them to a redefinition of hospital and an impressive opportunity in the market.

American Transitional Hospitals Inc.

There's something different about the 67-bed American Transitional Hospitals Inc. facility in suburban Dallas. Although its pastel halls are lined with rooms for patients, it has no high-tech diagnostic equipment, maternity ward or operating or emergency rooms. Even "staff" doctors are part time.[2]

The next example introduces competitive action. It focuses attention on a so-called niche product. With the metaphor of a biological niche could come a false sense of security—the niched product for the customers and the customers for the niched product only! The example highlights such dangers, and also raises the issue of the possible need for "cannibalistic" new products.

Nighttime Pain Reliever Market

"If a competitor introduces a product you don't have, you lose share," explains Hemant K. Shah of HKS & Co., an independent research company in Warren, N.J. "You'll have to launch a similar product just to remain competitive."

That was Johnson & Johnson's strategy. For nearly two decades Excedrin PM was the only pain reliever that also promised to make consumers sleepy. But Tylenol PM, propelled by an aggressive advertising and coupon program, has vaulted over its rival to become the category's best-selling brand. In the three months ended in July, its sales totaled $15.9 million, a 77% increase over the earlier period. The upstart brand now accounts for 47.9% of category sales, according to Towne-Oller. Sales of Excedrin PM, meanwhile, shrank 7%, to $11.8 million in the same period.[3]

However well-conceived the coverage of the function × form × price space is, these have to be made known to the consumer who has to be persuaded to buy for financial rewards to accrue to a company. Communication is more than simply "letting people know," it is an integral part of the offerings that customers benefit from. The following examples highlight these issues.

Coca-Cola

At a news conference yesterday in New York, the Coca-Cola Company introduced the 1992 campaign for its flagship brand, called Coca Cola Classic in America and Coca Cola in 195 other countries.

[2]"Limited-Service Hospitals Find A Market," *The Wall Street Journal,* July 23, 1992, B1.

[3]Deveny, K., "Market Scam: Stresses, Strains and Shrewd Marketing Ignite Sales of Nighttime Pain Remedies," *The Wall Street Journal,* September 24, 1992, B1.

. . . Of the campaign's initial 26 television commercials, . . 24 were developed under the auspices of The Greater Artists Agency in Beverly Hills, Calif. The remainder came from McCann-Erickson Worldwide in New York, the Coca-Cola agency since 1955, which did create the campaign's theme, "Always Coca-Cola," to replace "Can't Beat the Real Thing."

. . . the campaign (which) manages the tricky task of simultaneously achieving two seemingly contradictory purposes.

It celebrates the traditional values of Coca-Cola—its "Cokeness," as embodied by its famous contoured glass bottle, red disk logo and nostalgic memories of "Rum and Coca-Cola;" a stylized version of the logo, introduced in 1947 and modified in 1951 is omnipresent throughout.

And it also infuses the brand with a contemporary appeal more in tune with the fragmented and fractious 1990's, with production techniques borrowed from movies like fast-paced cuts, special effects and elaborate animation.

In other words, "Always Coca-Cola," presents Coca-Cola in all ways.

. . . The focus of the campaign is Coke's "ubiquity, its familiarity, its presence around the world," said Shelly Hochron, a film advertising and marketing executive . . . "There's something about the brand that appeals to everyone."[4]

"Cokeness" is a combination of function and form and communication. It is this benefit that drives the sales of Coke. Coca-Cola has achieved this through an integrated, dynamic approach to serving customers and sustaining a strong and unique relationship with them.

AST Research Inc.

"Today, AST's original add-on business is almost a memory, accounting for a scant 7% of sales. The rest is personal computers—everything from notebooks to machines that can drive huge networks. About 10% of the revenues comes from sales of PCs to other computer companies, such as Digital Equipment Corp. and Texas Instruments Inc., which put their own labels on them. . . . AST has been gaining in the stores because its prices are usually 20% to 30% lower than IBM's and Compaq's. . . . AST was one of the first PC makers to ship PCs based on Intel Corp.'s top-of-the-line 80486 chip. And AST announced a PC based on Intel's latest microprocessor, the 486SX, just one day after Intel announced the new chip.

. . . Equitable (Equitable Life Assurance Society of America), a long-time IBM buyer, recently added AST to its list of approved computer makers.

. . . That is also a sign that years of effort to create brand awareness for AST's name are finally paying off. "AST puts its advertising where the guys that use them would run across it—airports, bus shelters, taxis," says Lise J. Buyer, a Cowan & Co. analyst.[5]

[4]Elliott, S., "Coca-Cola's New Campaign Shakes Up Madison Avenue," *New York Times,* February 11, 1993, C1, C18.

[5]Armstrong, L. "This 12-Year-Old Has Come of Age," *Business Week,* May 6, 1991, pp. 122, 124.

These examples underscore the benefits a company provides its customers in the function $\times$ form $\times$ price space. They also highlight the transcendental nature of the benefits beyond this space. These all-encompassing benefits and binding ties are provided by the communication between a company and its customers.

A closer look at these examples pinpoints three essential sets of issues that are basic to understanding offering as a part of marketing strategy.

- Offering Space Coverage
- Competitive Positioning
- Facilitation of the Exchange Transaction

These three sets of issues are not mutually exclusive (just as strategy is a holistic approach to goal achievement), but by discussing each separately, their individual importance is highlighted so that sufficient consideration will be given to each of them as an overall marketing strategy is conceived and enacted. Just as beauty is said to be in the eyes of the beholder, so value is in the consumption experience of customers. The intertwining of customers and offerings-exchange entities makes customer segmentation an inherent part of any discussion of exchange entities. This is reflected in our discussion.

Coverage of the Offerings Space or Scope

How much of the offering space should be covered-served depends on the consequences of alternative approaches to covering the space and the objectives to be achieved. This decision requires an understanding of the dimensions of this space and the relationship of coverage to consequences. This relationship is provided by the link between this space and the industry context. Principally from the set of context variables, competitive and customer behavior provide the link. The following discussion describes the offering space, provides alternative approaches to covering the space, and discusses broad strategic objectives, finally tying the pieces together.

The Offering Space

The offering space is divided into: (1) The Function Subspace, (2) The Forum Subspace, and (3) The Price Subspace.

The Function Subspace

All products and services serve some function. In fact, as was discussed earlier, commonality of the function served by a set of products or services is a good first approximation of a competitive set. There is, unfortunately, no uniform specification of the dimensions of this subspace across all product categories. The functional subspace for rice, as developed by Anheuser-Bush for the Asian-American market segment, includes "stickiness."[6] For supercomputers, speed is clearly a

---

[6]Shao, M., C. Power and L. Zinn, "Suddenly, Asian-Americans Are A Marketer's Dream," *Business Week*, June 17, 1991, pp. 54–55.

functional dimension. For soap, moisturizing ability and deodorizing ability are two functional dimensions.[7]

The functional subspace dimension, as seen in Exhibit 13–1 (which shows how the functional subspaces are related to the different customer value drivers), is important in providing customers with three out of five values: functional, epistemic and conditional.

Although it is functionality that the customers sense, and essentially obtain value from when function values are sought, the delivery of functionality is fundamental because of the underlying technology and subcomponents.

In general, the functionality subspace is continuous, for example, speed, miles per gallon, strength, cleaning ability, and so forth. Improvement on any functional dimension or a combination of dimensions occurs because of technological improvements. Such technological improvements are common and require a dynamic approach in assessing space coverage. Pursuit of a technology trajectory as opposed to a single point technology strategy is the counterpart in corporate-technological thinking to marketing thinking on these issues. It is also generally true that there are physical limits to functionality improvements from technology. It requires a new technological paradigm or innovation to push the boundary further. With this paradigm shift emerges a new open continuum of possible improvements in functionality. To quote from a recent *Scientific American* article:

> For the past few decades, such visionaries as Aldons Huxley, Marshall McLuhan and Vannevar Bush have been preaching about a time when any kind of information—data, text, pictures, audio and video—would be as readily available as tap water. To that end, technology pioneers knew they needed robust communications links. But for the most part, they believed the existing telephone and computer networks offered a sturdy infrastructure for the future superhighways for data.

> Now they are facing a gigabit gridlock. "We're on the threshold of a technical discontinuity," says Richard D. Gitlin, who heads the Network Systems Research Department at

EXHIBIT 13–1 Key Relationships of the Offering Subspaces to Customer Value Drivers

		Offering Subspace		
		FUNCTION	FORM	PRICE
Customer Value Drivers	Functional	√	√	√
	Emotional		√	
	Epistemic	√	√	
	Social		√	
	Conditional	√	√	√

[7]Power, C., "Everyone is Bellying Up To This Bar," *Business Week,* January 27, 1992, p. 84.

AT&T Bell Laboratories. Arun N. Netravalli, Executive Director of Bell Labs' Communications Sciences Research Division, cites the recent spate of network failures as a symptom of the problem. "We need a new paradigm for computer network communications," he asserts.[8]

A similar theme is echoed in this quote from *Business Week,*

Packaging technology doesn't normally stoke the passions of semi-conductor engineers. The top guns in the business are the people who design circuits, not those who engineer the protective housings, or packages, for chips. But suddenly, packaging is winning the rapt attention of top scientists at Boeing, Digital Equipment, IBM, and Motorola, among others. *For without big improvements in this obscure art, the perpetual increases in semiconductor performance that spur electronics industry growth will slow drastically.* (Emphasis added.) "That's why packaging is going to be a hot topic in 1990s," says George H. Heilmeier, Chief Technical Officer at Texas Instruments Inc.

. . . The secret to computing speed is size.

. . . The leading solution . . . is multichip modules (MCMs).

These examples illustrate the nature of the functionality subspace. The laws of nature (in electronics today, physics particularly plays this role) theoretically limit functionality gains within a particular technology. These gains can often be estimated quite accurately. (This discussion is pertinent to all products and services and is not limited to computers and related products.) For example, in soap, the amount of deodorant that can be packed into a particular sized bar without compromising its other functions, can be estimated quite closely. Dramatic changes would require a new deodorizing technology. Similarly, the efficiency of processing insurance claims has a limit, given the technology (information processing) that is being used. Improvements beyond this occur through innovation. For example, changing from human data operations to expert system-based estimations might lead to a dramatic speed up of the process. Direct electronic damage entry using hand held, special purpose computers which can "read" handwriting might also lead to dramatic improvement.

The functional subspace is of major importance in choices based on functional, epistemic, and conditional values. Functional subspace dimensions are peculiar to a specific industry. Mapping competitors and potential competitors in this subspace is critical when customer choice is driven by functional, epistemic, or conditional values.

Form Subspace

Although the functional subspace is related to three of the key value drivers of customer choice, the form subspace is related to all five of the value drivers. This subspace ensures the delivery of value to customers and the cementing of relationships with them. Without form, a product or service is like the universe—it has no seeming end or beginning and thus includes everything. (Imagine marketing something that is everything to customers!) Form provides the tangible units of exchange.

---

[8]Corcoran, E., "Racing Light," *Scientific American,* December, 1992, pp. 32, 36. "All-optical networks" is a possibility that is being investigated as the new paradigm.

Exhibit 13–2 provides a view of the dimensions of form. The form subspace captures physical space in two ways. First, at a micro level it comprises the physical three-dimensional space occupied by a product or the accoutrements of a service (a bank card, checkbook, etc.). For example, big screen TVs account for less than 5% of Thomson Consumer Electronics unit sales of TVs, but make up 22% of retail sales in dollars. The gross margin for big screen TVs are approximately 35%, as compared with 20% for 20-inch sets. To gain additional share at the high end, Thomson revamped its TV sets under the GE and RCA brands by offering competitive prices and stressing style. Rounded edges replaced sharp corners, and blacks and grays the faux-wood look.[9] This 3-D emphasis is reflected in the shape and size of products. Although the function of a computer keyboard is essentially the same, shape and size differentiate one from another (Exhibit 13–3).

In the instance of "software" products that need to be displayed, or analyzed, or experienced only in their interaction with hardware and humans (intelligentware?!), a special aspect of physical form comes into play. The physical medium used to transfer possession of the software is also a critical element of the design of the product. And the coverage issue is how many different media should be used to carry a piece of software. For example, should a particular piece of music be sold on compact disks, and audio cassettes, and plastic records, or only on one, or two media? Should it also be available telephonically, over cable TV, and so forth? CNN's news is also available on America Hotline—an electronic mail (or bulletin board) service media. Second, at the macro level it comprises the larger physical space or geographic space occupied. For example, the success of McDonald's fast food restaurants, besides the size and ambiance of each restaurant and the functionality of its individual products, is based on its choice locations across the United States and now in major cities across the world. The key measure of geographic distance is closeness and convenience to customers. Or, as a specific technical formulation, the average distance to customers may be considered as a measure of geographic form.

In these days of crashing physical and psychological distances, coverage of geographic space across the globe can make or break a company. Since 1991, Campbell has affixed the name Campbell to much of its line of frozen foods in the United Kingdom. Also, by the year 2000, David W. Johnson, the CEO of Campbell Soup, seeks to have 50% of its revenues earned outside the United States. To put it in perspective, consider that in fiscal 1992 its revenues were approximately $6.3 billion, and less than 26% of its revenues came from outside the United States. Its main competitors, CPC International and H. J. Heinz in 1993 already possessed hefty shares overseas. Sixty percent of CPC's $6.6 billion sales in 1992 originated outside the United States. Also, in Argentina, CPC controls 80% of the market.[10] Occupation of geographic space is an important component of offering design.

---

[9]Brandt, R., "The Next Great Leap In Computing Speed," *Business Week,* March 4, 1991, p. 76. According to this article, it is estimated that by the year 2000 A.D., a third of all semiconductors will be housed in multichip modules (MCMs).

[10]For details see J. Weber, "Campbell is Bubbling, But for How Long?," *Business Week,* June 17, 1991, pp. 58–57; J. Weber, G. Schares, S. Hutcheson, and I. Katz, "Campbell: Now It's M-M-Global," *Business Week,* March 15, 1993, pp. 52–54.

EXHIBIT 13–2   The Dimensions of Form

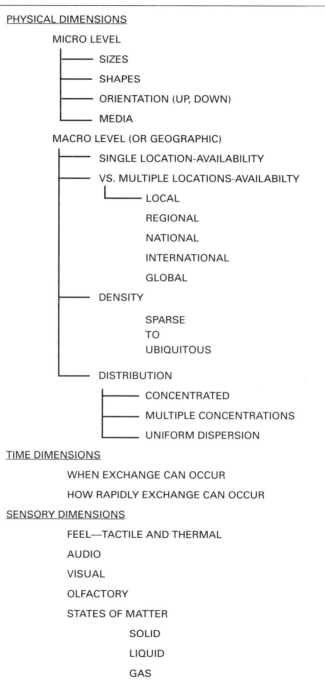

PHYSICAL DIMENSIONS

    MICRO LEVEL

        SIZES
        SHAPES
        ORIENTATION (UP, DOWN)
        MEDIA

    MACRO LEVEL (OR GEOGRAPHIC)

        SINGLE LOCATION-AVAILABILITY
        VS. MULTIPLE LOCATIONS-AVAILABILTY
            LOCAL
            REGIONAL
            NATIONAL
            INTERNATIONAL
            GLOBAL
        DENSITY
            SPARSE
            TO
            UBIQUITOUS
        DISTRIBUTION
            CONCENTRATED
            MULTIPLE CONCENTRATIONS
            UNIFORM DISPERSION

TIME DIMENSIONS

        WHEN EXCHANGE CAN OCCUR
        HOW RAPIDLY EXCHANGE CAN OCCUR

SENSORY DIMENSIONS

        FEEL—TACTILE AND THERMAL
        AUDIO
        VISUAL
        OLFACTORY
        STATES OF MATTER
                SOLID
                LIQUID
                GAS

EXHIBIT 13–3

Courtesy: Microsoft Corporation.

Although the availability of the product is important, equally as important is its density and distribution. The options are shown in Exhibit 13–2.

Beyond the physical space which defines the form of an offering is the key dimension of time. With the focus on building customer relationships as an integral part of marketing strategy, exchange continuity over time becomes critical to business success. Beside this dynamic notion of relationship maintenance is the push toward speed as a dimension of offerings. Time can really be thought of as two underlying dimensions. The first dimension is the instant nature of exchange readiness or consummation. The second is the rate at which an exchange can be satisfied. Examples of this difference are that of Dominos Pizza in the United States and of Kiwi Airlines.

A guarantee that pizza would be delivered within 30 minutes after placing an order illustrates Dominos Pizza's use of the second dimension of time. (This guarantee has since been withdrawn, because of litigation arising because their drivers violated traffic safety in trying to keep the commitment to meeting this guarantee.) It defines the speed (or rate) at which customers' requests would be satisfied. Kiwi International Airlines, to quote *Business Week*:

> . . . targets 'the small-business or leisure-traveler eager to save money, but without the flexibility to book in advance.' The airline will peg its fares to the lowest prevailing rates in a given market and offer them on an unrestricted basis. So while Delta Airlines Inc. might advertise Newark to Atlanta for $130, but free up only a dozen seats at that fare and require a 14-day advance purchase, Kiwi would sell all 150 seats on its 727 at that price.

From the Dominos Pizza example it is seen that the form dimension can be traded off. For example, by competing on time using delivery, Dominos attempted to nullify, or at least mitigate the dispersed locations of its competitors, such as Pizza Hut, for competitive advantage. Since the entry of Dominos, Pizza Hut also started home delivery. A recent invention may allow french fries to be sold through vending machines, thus making them more available. Adelaide Robotic Technologies introduced a robot-inspired machine that dispenses 33 hot, golden fries for $1.[11]

In organizational markets, as discussed in Chapter 12, the Just In Time (JIT) and Electronic Data Interchange (EDI) systems exemplifies the importance of time as a competitive dimension.

Beside the physical and time dimensions of form are its sensory dimensions: feeling, sound, visual appeal, smell, and taste, as well as the state of matter of the product—solid, liquid, or gas. Because these are more intuitive, they will not be discussed. However, ignoring the sensory dimensions of form could be catastrophic. We provide some examples.

Consuming antacid products without flavoring would be like eating paint off a wall. Merck Consumer Pharmaceuticals' Mylanta products first came in liquid form with a "regular" taste. Then came tablets, again with the same "regular" taste. Both liquid and tablet form were available in standard and double (or extra) strength (functional strength dimensions) formulations. The next step was the introduction of a variety of tastes of the tablet form (Exhibit 13–4). The colors of the various tablets are, of course, different. This example demonstrates the coverage of the sensory dimensions of taste, state of matter, and visual appeal, as well as some functional dimensions.

According to a report in The Wall Street Journal,[12]

> Japan's Lion Corp. is introducing Check-Up, a blue liquid toothpaste it hopes will supplant tubes and pumps and give it a piece of the $1.3 billion U.S. market.
>
> The syrup-like, fluoridated liquid—introduced last year in Japan—comes in a small, squeezable plastic bottle that easily fits in a medicine cabinet.
>
> The company is hoping to do for toothpaste what liquid soap has done for the soap category. Consumers do not like mess—and liquid soap sales now comprise about one-third of the $1.6 billion soap market.

The Japanese[13] seem to have taken design to new heights—especially in consumer electronics, where,

> Lack of western paths to follow has thrown Japanese designers back on their own traditions. As it happens, the essential characteristics of Japanese art are compactness and simplicity. Both accord well with contemporary trends in technology.

Also consider the following: The grand old man of Japanese design, Kenji Eknan, founder of GK, Japan's first and today its largest design consulting firm, sees

[11]"French Fries In A Machine," *The New York Times,* February, 12, 1991, C4.

[12]Reitman, V., "Lion is Hoping Liquid Toothpaste Rivals Tube, Pump," *The Wall Street Journal,* June 18, 1991, B5.

[13]These examples and quotations are taken from articles by B. Johnstone, "Sold on the Books," "High Priests of Design," and "Bye-Bye Bauhans," that appeared in the *Far Eastern Economic Review,* February 22, 1990, pp. 34–36.

EXHIBIT 13–4   Taste, Color, and State of Matter

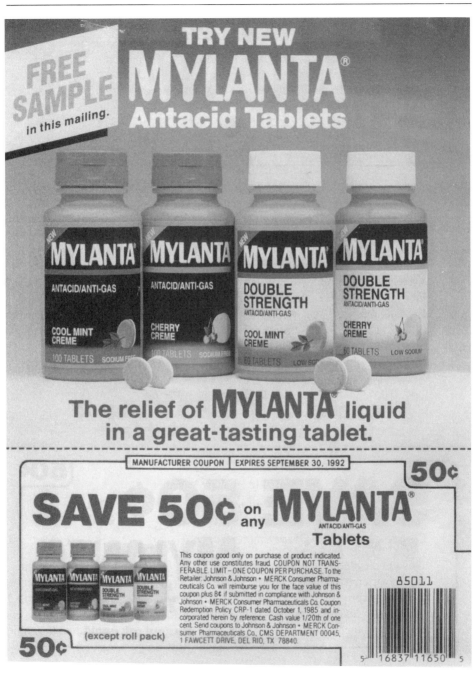

designers as "priests of the material world." Eknan, himself a sometimes Buddhist priest, believes that "designers can become responsible for good relationships between people and things." Should marketers become priests first? Of course not! But imagine how much nicer and easier the world would be with more art in technology, more form in products, and more touch in service! There needs to be selectivity in combining coverage of the sensory subspace for different parts of the geographic space. For example,[14] Campbell Soup introduced eight different varieties of soup (zupa) to Poland. *Flaki,* a local Polish, peppery tripe soup, is a variety targeted only for Poland. *Chile Poblano* soup serves the Mexican market. The Swanson brand of watercress and duck-gizzard soup, radish-and-carrot soup, and pork, fig, and date soup cover China.

Changes in the function and form dimensions often take considerable time to develop and implement. Coverage of the third subspace, price, requires decisions on the other two subspaces also. For example, the decision to stay below a particular price line may impose constraints on the possible function and form (beside those on transaction facilitators) that may be offered. Of course, coverage of various price lines may substantially change the nature of relationships. An example of change in relationships is the negotiations in 1992 by IBM[15] to buy Northgate Computer Systems. Developing this relationship with Northgate would permit IBM to sell inexpensive clones in the United States. This component of its strategy was tested by IBM in Southeast Asia by selling clones there. (This example also illustrates that the price and form dimensions should be considered in their possibly interactive effects on marketing success.) This subspace is discussed next.

Price Subspace

The strategic dimensions of the price subspace (Exhibit 13–5) are:

- Degree of Price Discrimination
- Price Lines
- Relative Price
- Short-Term Price Variance
- Speed of Entry

Degree of Price Discrimination

This dimension is anchored on one side by uniform pricing and on the other by case-by-case pricing. In other words, for a given set of offering elements other than price, a strategic choice could be made on whether all customers (this term includes inter-mediaries—since it is at this level that control typically exists—the price charged by the retailers themselves is much less controllable) should be offered the same price or

[14]Weber, J., et al., *op. cit.,* Footnote 10.

[15]Carroll, P. B., "IBM Is Said To Be in Talks for Northgate," *The Wall Street Journal,* April 27, 1992, B1, B5.

EXHIBIT 13–5   Price Subspace

Dimensions	Anchors/Possible Levels		Decision Consideration Issues
1. Degree of price discrimination	Uniform Pricing (Anchors)	Case-by-Case Pricing	Legality Gray Markets
2. Price lines	Various normative lines in industry		Quality inference Customer affordability based segmentation
3. Relative price	Premium, Par, Discount		Quality signal to customers Cost-competitiveness signal to industry
4. Short-term price variance	No Variance (Anchors)	Extremely Variant	Brand loyalty erosion Control of transaction timing Inventory management Loss of margin
5. Speed of entry	Skimming (Anchors)	Penetration	Potential to considerably accelerate Customer purchases through lower prices Importance of market share to profits Risk propensity

at the other extreme, the pricing decision would be made on a case-by-case basis. The reasons for not offering a single price for all customers (for a given offering, except price) could be many. These include the possible need to give quantity discounts, the fact that customers may have different reservation prices,[16] differences in costs of transactions across customers, variances in when customers place orders, and so forth. Although the choice of a position to occupy on this dimension may be restricted because of country regulations, there is yet another reason to pay attention to a position choice along this dimension. Choosing a less than uniform price position may lead to formation of gray markets. According to Cespedes, Corey, and Rangan,[17] approximately $7 billion to $10 billion worth of products are sold in gray markets. Gray markets transactions occur outside of manufacturers' authorized distribution channels. By one estimate,[18] approximately 20% of Sharp Electronics' United States copier sales may be through unauthorized channels. Howell, Britney, Kuzdrall, and Wilcox, in fact, call for a revision of current quantity-discount pricing

[16]Reservation price is defined as the upper threshold limit used by economists to describe the price just low enough to overcome a consumer's reluctance to purchase. Scherer, F., *Industrial Market Structure and Economic Performance,* 2nd ed., Skokie, IL, Rand McNally, 1980. In other words, a price above a customer's reservation price would result in the sale not going through.

[17]Cespedes, F. V., E. R. Corey, and V. K. Rangan, "Gray Markets: Causes and Cures," *Harvard Business Review,* July–August, 1988, pp. 75–82.

[18]This estimate is from "Gray Market Blues Hit Copier Dealers," *Business Week,* February 14, 1985, 112D–112F.

practices to control gray markets.[19]   A brief illustration of the opportunity for a gray market is provided in Footnote 20.

An example of a company chain adjusting its position on this dimension is the Sheraton Hotels chain of ITT Sheraton Corporation.   In 1992, they announced a new rate structure.   As reported in the *New York Times*:[20]

> The Sheraton Hotel chain has joined the chorus of airlines and rental car companies pitching lower—and simpler—prices to customers.
>
> . . . Sheraton's new rate structure, called "Sure Savers," reduces the number of potential discounts for roughly half of its customers to three: a weekday rate, a weekend rate and a rate for customers who book rooms 14 days in advance.   The Boston-based hotel chain will continue offering negotiated deeper discounts to large corporate customers, convention-goers and high-volume travel agencies.
>
> . . . Sheraton predicts that its own program will raise occupancy rate to 74% for the year, up from the current rate of 65.5%.   Most hotels need to fill more than two-thirds of their rooms to operate profitably.

Price Lines

The phenomenon of price lining is ubiquitous.   For a product category such as men's shirts, various competitive units may be found in a store only in a fixed number of price bands, say $89–$95, $119–$129, and $149–$160.   The strategic question is how many and which brands should be covered by a manufacturer.   Price signals quality and is a sacrifice that a customer makes in foregoing the value derived from either retaining the buying power of this magnitude or from expending it on other purchases.[21]   Often corporations, when offering products for different price lines or bands, use different brand names.   For example, General Motors Corporation's Chevrolet, Oldsmobile, Pontiac, Buick, and Cadillac brands occupy different price lines.   In GM's case, these brands are designed to serve different affordability-based consumer segments.   And, as a member of a segment with lower affordability climbed life's economic ladder, he or she could still remain within the GM family by trading up.

[19]Howell, R. D., R. R. Britney, P. J. Kuzdrall, and J. B. Wilcox, "Unauthorized Channels of Distribution: Gray Markets," *Industrial Marketing Management,* Vol. 15, 1986, pp. 257–263.   In this article, they provide an example using a typical quantity-discount pricing schedule which is illuminating.   In their example, purchasing 1 to 19 units of the product would have to be done at a list price (no discount) of $5,795.   Ordering 20 to 49 units would carry a discount of 12% off list.   A customer needing 18 units would pay $104,310 if only 18 units were ordered.   On the other hand, if 20 units were ordered, the cost would be only $101,980!   Thus, ordering 20 units would allow this customer not only to save $2,300, but also to be able to resell the two units (assuming that they are not needed).   This is the unintended consequence of such pricing, leading to gray market opportunities!

[20]Bryant, A., "Sheraton Hotels Offer Lower, Simpler Rates," *The New York Times,* April 28, 1992, C1, C15.

[21]Dodds, W. and K. Monroe, "The Effect of Brand and Price Information on Subjective Product Evaluations," *In* Hirschman, E. and M. Holbrook, (eds.), *Advances in Consumer Research,* Vol. 12, 1985, pp. 85–90, Provo, Utah, Association for Consumer Research.

Honda Motor Company,[22] in 1992, began offering a reduced-price "value" version of its popular Accord. Also, according to *The Wall Street Journal* (Thomas Elliott was the head of Honda's U.S. sales operations):

> Mr. Elliott said that the automaker would like to offer a car that is cheaper than the Civic. However, he said the auto maker isn't able to produce a new entry-level car because of financial restraints.

The decisions on this dimension are predicated on the possibility of confounding quality signals to customers versus that of serving a wider range of customers (based on ability to pay).

Relative Price

This dimension has three essential possibilities: an offering can be priced either at a premium over competitors' prices, at par with them, or at a discount with respect to them. The choice of one of these positions for an offering signals quality to customers and cost or competitiveness to competitors. A company may choose to have an offering to occupy each of the three possibilities on this dimension. While this might be cannibalization, it might also prevent the erosion of its aggregate share. It should also be pointed out that a premium price could set a price umbrella in the product category and stem (or prevent) price erosion in that category.

Degree of Short-Term Price Variance

The extremes of this dimension are none and severe. This dimension captures the essence of promotions. The strategic decision is whether price promotions should be carried out, and if so, to what degree?[23] Everyday Low Price, or Periodic Sales, are examples of alternative locations on this dimension. Sears, Roebuck and Co. switched a few years ago from having periodic sales at well-known times of the year to an Everyday Low Price strategy to compete with discount stores like Kmart and Wal-Mart in the United States. One key decision issue is whether the timing of purchases by customers may be controlled—thus leading to better management of inventory turns, or whether nonusers may be induced to try the product, store, or service. Another key issue is whether sales during promotions come exclusively from brand-loyal customers—thus actually lowering margins, in return for which the timing of the transaction is better controlled. Finally, do selective promotions increase store traffic, or does brand loyalty get replaced by savings loyalty?

Research seems to indicate that if customers form expectations of price changes and timing, then it might be better to commit to a pricing strategy rather than to vary price over time.[24]

[22]Miller, K., "Honda to Offer Cheaper, 'Value' Version of Accord," *The Wall Street Journal,* September 23, 1992, B7.

[23]While research on promotions is growing, much is still unknown. For more details please see Blattberg, R. C. and S. A. Neslin, *Sales Promotion: Concepts, Methods, and Strategies,* Englewood Cliffs, NJ, Prentice-Hall, 1990.

[24]For details, please see Lilien, G. L., P. Kotler, and K. S. Moorthy, *Marketing Models,* Englewood Cliffs, NJ, Prentice-Hall, 1992, Chapter 4, p. 188.

Speed of Entry

As its name suggests, this dimension is relevant for new product entry. The anchors of this dimension are skimming (slow entry) on one end and penetration (or rapid entry) on the other. Between the two is a continuum of entry rates.

This dimension is predicated on the existence of a relationship between price and the number of customers who can both afford and are willing to buy the product at that price. Assuming that a higher price leads to lower total demand, skimming strategy calls for an initially high price to "skim the cream," of the market—"cream" refers to those who can afford higher prices. As time passes, and as less cream remains, this strategy calls for lowering of price to keep sales growing. The penetration strategy calls for entry with a lower price to induce a higher volume of sales immediately.

The following example illustrates the difference between a standard short-term oriented American way to price and a long-term oriented Japanese way to price. Note that not all American or Japanese firms price like the example. The Japanese generally follow a penetration strategy to gain share-volume rapidly. In the example, penetration pricing is the Japanese strategy, and skimming, the American strategy.

American versus Japanese Pricing.
Consider a hypothetical product category, in which unit costs change with cumulative historical volume (or experience) (Exhibit 13–6). This captures the halving in unit price with doubling of the experience effect found in industries like semiconductors, electronics products, chemicals, and so forth. According to this table until 10,000 units are sold, the unit cost is $30. Further, a historical cost approach would apportion cost to be that at the end of the last period (an average cost calculation can also be made). If the Japanese penetration price is $20 during a six-month introductory period, at the end of this period they would have a cumulative profit of $150,000 with cumulative sales of 55,000 units. The American skimming strategy price of $35 during the same six-month introductory period would result in a cumulative profit of $75,000 and cumulative sales of 15,000 units. Assuming the products are equal, it is easy to see the accelerator effect of positive word-of-mouth advertising for the Japanese product. This would result in a further widening of the gap between the market shares of the two products, even after the American product's price is dropped following the introductory period.

This example combines the experience curve effect with demand acceleration caused by pricing. Even if no experience effect exists, but if the difference in the two strategies rests in the margins set—a higher margin for the skimming strategy and a lower one for the penetration strategy could easily lead to both a higher market share and a higher cumulative profit (even discounted over time) for the penetration strategy. The key differences in the choice between the two seems to be (1) whether customer purchases can be accelerated through lower prices, and whether an immediately higher margin with lower volume is, on a discounted time basis, superior to a lower immediate margin but higher volume; (2) whether market share is important to discounted cash flow-profit (experience effects and positive word-of-mouth effects could make this factor more relevant); and (3) the risk propensity of the decision maker. Of course, the price of the product relative to customer income and the "value" of this

EXHIBIT 13–6   Penetration vs. Skimming Pricing Example

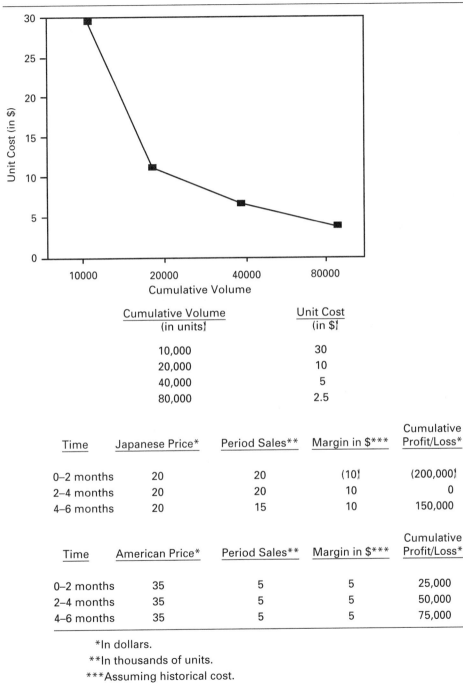

Cumulative Volume (in units)	Unit Cost (in $)
10,000	30
20,000	10
40,000	5
80,000	2.5

Time	Japanese Price*	Period Sales**	Margin in $***	Cumulative Profit/Loss*
0–2 months	20	20	(10)	(200,000)
2–4 months	20	20	10	0
4–6 months	20	15	10	150,000

Time	American Price*	Period Sales**	Margin in $***	Cumulative Profit/Loss*
0–2 months	35	5	5	25,000
2–4 months	35	5	5	50,000
4–6 months	35	5	5	75,000

*In dollars.
**In thousands of units.
***Assuming historical cost.

product are also important in defining its demand. The third key factor, risk propensity, relates to whether managers are willing to bet on the outcome. Are they willing to accept lower initial margins or even losses to create powerful forces of positive word-of-mouth communication and experience cost effects to provide a higher discounted net cash flow? The risk factor must be considered in choosing between the two extreme strategies or in adopting a middle-of-the-road position.[25]

Function, form, and price are generally not sufficient to start and maintain a relationship with customers. Transactions with customers need to be facilitated. This is discussed next.

Transaction Facilitators

All of us live in a world of bewildering consumption choices (which itself is part of a larger set of choices). The number of choices available in any consumption decision among directly comparable alternatives, for example, among ready-to-eat cereals, is formidable. Added to this decision is one of choosing between not-so-directly comparable alternatives, for example, between bacon and eggs versus pancakes and syrup for breakfast. These choices are much wider for people living in wealthy and capitalist societies. In many countries there is only one bank which consumers can use. Further, there is only one type of check they can use—and it is issued by their bank. In the United States, a consumer has a myriad of banks to choose from, a myriad of checkbook and checkleaf styles to choose from, and (though more limited) a choice of sources for obtaining the checks.

Regardless of the society or country in which they live, consumers make consumption choices. The number of choices is ever increasing. For example, in 1990, 13,244 new food and drug products were introduced in the United States alone.[26] Such choices are constrained by cognitive and financial capacity.[27] Consumption is further constrained by time. These limits and the division of labor that societies experience also lead to an expertise constraint. Increasingly complex products and services are consumed by individuals in societies. To obtain value and satisfaction from consumption itself requires the juxtaposition of appropriate needs and expertise. The expertise necessary depends on the stage of the consumption process. The expertise required at the choice stage differs from that required at the purchase stage and that at the consumption (after purchase) stage. The class structure also slowly changes mutates in organizing to serve changing needs. It is not surprising that the service sector has grown because of technological advances.[28] In the relatively short

[25]Standard books on price that may be referred to for further details are Monroe, K. B., *Pricing: Making Profitable Decisions,* 2nd ed., New York, McGraw-Hill, 1990; Simon, H., *Price Management,* New York: North Holland, 1989.

[26]Miller, C., "Marketing Briefs: New Products," *Marketing News,* April 15, 1991, p. 26.

[27]For readers who wish to use mathematical programming metaphors, the first part of "offerings" operates on the direct value or utility value that consumers may be thought of as optimizing. Facilitators, on the other hand, make the constraints nonbinding.

[28]Durkheim, E., *The Division of Labor in Society,* New York, The Free Press, 1956, is the standard reference on the topic. One has to wonder if because of the growth of silicon or gallium arscemide (or other) information storage and processing capabilities and robotics whether this growth of services will continue.

period which characterizes most consumption choices, cognitive and financial capacity and expertise do not generally expand. The primary role of facilitators is to help consumers transcend their cognitive and financial capacity and expertise constraints to obtain full value from their consumption activities. Cognitive and financial capacity and expertise are constrained, not only by the sheer magnitude of information and price, but also because of the risky nature of decisions.[29] The three types of facilitators that are part of marketing strategy are information, service, and financing.[30]

The importance and role of each of these facilitators vary with the stage of the relationship and the stage of the consumption process. Each of these facilitators is now briefly discussed.

Information

For consumer products, the major information carriers are brand name[31] and communication. In communication, the key strategy decisions are target market definition, unique selling benefit position or positioning choice, additional selling points, method of presentation,[32] and media mix.

Brand Name

The strategic decisions are whether to use an existing brand name or to create a new one. Reasons for using an existing brand name are many.

1. *Cognitive Capacity.* Leading scholars,[33] having studied human decision making, have inferred that humans have a limited capacity for information processing. They develop rules-of-thumb or heuristics to deal with decision making. Such heuristics minimize the cognitive capacity required. The notion of consideration sets (also discussed earlier) becomes important, because consumers tend to restrict their serious alternatives to a small set. Limited processing capacity also implies that consumers seek information of high value as opposed to irrelevant information. Therefore, to be useful, a brand name should be of high value.

[29]The interested student should read the wonderfully rich discussion of growing environmental complexity and the dynamics of cognitive complexity in Lane, R. L., *The Market Experience,* Cambridge, United Kingdom, Cambridge University Press, 1991, Chapter 8. In fact, the whole book is worthwhile reading.

[30]This could also include help in explaining financing options to customers.

[31]Some authors classify brand name as an attribute of the product. Here, since we use a broader definition of offering, brand name could fit either under form or under communication. To give it the special attention it deserves and the role it often plays in positioning and communication, it has been placed under communications. It is also discussed extensively in Chapter 6.

[32]These components are abstracted from Schultz, D. E., *Essentials of Advertising Strategy,* Chicago, Crain Books, 1981.

[33]Some references Simon, H., *The Sciences of the Artificial,* Cambridge, MA, MIT Press, 1969; Norman, D. A. and D. G. Bobrow, "On Data-Limited and Resource-Limited Processes," *Cognitive Psychology,* Vol. 7, January, 1975, pp. 44–64; A good summary may be found in Bettman, J. R., *An Information Processing Theory of Consumer Choice,* Reading, MA, Addison-Wesley, 1979.

2. *Uncertainty.* Often the mapping from the sensory information space to the value or satisfaction space is uncertain.[34] For example, on the back of a plastic jug of Purex® laundry detergent (from the Dial Corp.) the contents are described as:

> An aqueous solution to remove soil from clothes (anionic and nonionic surfactants), builders, stabilizing agent, viscosity control agent, perfume, fabric whitener, preservative, chelating agents, colorant.

On the front it says:

> All Temperature Purex®, Laundry Detergent; cleans, whitens, and brightens in all temperatures.

Based on this information, how does a consumer know it will have the "needed" effect on laundry? (Remember, the consumer's gratification occurs only after the clothes are washed, whereas the retailer has immediate gratification.)

A known brand name often allays the uncertainty in assessing whether a product will deliver what is promised. Branding commodities like fruits (for example, Sunkist oranges, Sunmaid raisins, etc.) speaks to this issue as well.

3. *Risk.* There is an old saying (given how young IBM is, it can't really be that old!) that "No one gets fired for buying IBM." Then there is the classic teaching case from Harvard called Optical Distortion Inc., in which an entrepreneur wished to sell contact lenses for chickens to chicken farmers. (to improve productivity). Students inevitably raise the issue of how foolish a farmer might appear at a Farm Bureau meeting were it announced that the chickens now wear contact lenses. But, if the lenses were from a well-known veterinary product company, perhaps the response would be different. The use of known names is likely to diminish the perceived risk of making a purchase.

4. *Efficiency.* A study by Smith and Park[35] found that the advertising cost to sales ratio was significantly lower for brand extensions than it was for new brands.

Countering these positive reasons for using an existing brand name and building on its strengths is the argument that an extension might dilute the original name.

---

[34]The use of uncertainty here is similar to that in Cunningham, S. M., "The Major Dimensions of Perceived Risk," *In* Cox, D. F. (Ed.), *Risk Taking and Information Handling in Consumer Behavior,* Cambridge, MA, Harvard Business School, 1967, pp. 82–108. Also see Bettman, *op. cit.,* p. 94.

[35]Smith, D. C. and C. W. Park, "The Effects of Brand Extensions On Market Share and Advertising Efficiency," *Journal of Marketing Research,* Vol XXIX, August, 1992. The reader is also referred to Aaker, D. A., "Managing Brand Equity," New York, The Free Press, 1991, for an extensive treatment of brand equity management.

Another study, by Aaker and Keller,[35a] based on experimental studies, comes to the following conclusions:

- Whether an existing extension was very similar or only somewhat similar and did not effect proposed extension evaluations.
- Multiple extensions in the market have a different effect than single extensions.
- The effect of the failure of a few of a set of multiple extensions had the same effect as the failure of a single extension.
- For high-quality and average-quality core brands—with a successful earlier extension, the evaluation of new extension was higher.
- A prior unsuccessful extension lowered the evaluation of a new extension.

But,

- while an unsuccessful extension did not lower the evaluation of a high-quality core brand,
- a successful extension did improve the evaluation of an average-quality extension.

These results seem to imply that leveraging existing brand names is beneficial.

Market evidence also seems to support the same judgment.   For example, to quote a *Business Week* report

Of the 6,125 new products placed on the shelves in the first five months of 1991, just 5% bore new brand names, according to Gorman's New Product News.   The rest are variations on existing brands: Tropicana Twister Light fruit juices, Huggies baby wipes, and the like.

Of course, for a new company, the ability to use an existing brand name does not exist (unless it was obtained through acquisition).   A name-developing industry has come into existence for the express purpose of, developing new brand names.   For example, Name Lab Inc. devised the name Sentra for Nissan Manufacturing Corporation.[36]

The right brand name (for example, Healthy Choice for Conagra Inc. line of frozen dinners to health-conscious shoppers, Kellogg's RTE cereals that describe the product—Corn Flakes, Fruit Loops, Muselix, sports car names with numbers) communicated adequately, can be used to help consumers make the "right" product choice, by taking advantage of their limited cognitive capability and the amount of risk they wish to take.   Federal Express, the company that revolutionized overnight

---

[35a]Aaker, D. A. and K. L. Keller, "Consumer Evaluations of Brand Extensions," *Journal of Marketing,* Vol. 54, No. 1, January, 1990, pp. 27–41.

[36]For more details on Name Lab see Dolan, C., "Concocting Zingy New Names Starts Turning Into A Business," *The Wall Street Journal,* August 5, 1981, B1.

delivery, has changed its name to FedEx. Its logo has also been redesigned with the E and X spaced to form an arrow symbolizing its speed and efficiency. Brand name is most important at the choice and purchase stages of the consumption process.

Marketing Communications

In marketing communications, care must be taken to ensure that a thorough assessment of the various publics or relationship partners is carried out in building relationships with them. An example of such a process is that recommended by the international firm of Burson-Marsteller (Exhibit 13–7). This process highlights the importance of analysis *before* action.[37]

EXHIBIT 13–7   The Burson-Marsteller Communications Strategy Process

How is Corporate Positioning Developed?

The process of developing a corporate positioning is as important as the end product because of what the corporation learns about itself, how it is changed and the degree of commitment generated through the process. The process consists of four basic elements:

Analysis:	Internal and external research.	Communications:	Implementation of the positioning through internal programs aimed at management development and employee commitment and involvement and external relations programs that convey the positioning to key audiences through both actions and words.
Synthesis:	A comprehensive account of the organization's current position.		
Development:	A facilitated process wherein senior management develops and achieves commitment to the positioning.		

While no single positioning process is appropriate for every organization, these four elements are common to every successful positioning effort.

From *Insights*, Burson-Marsteller Corporate Communications Update, Vol. 4, Issue 1, August 1990, p. 5.

[37]This is reminiscent of an ancient folktale in which a king bought wisdom from a Brahman boy in the bazaar. He had the piece of wisdom inscribed on his drinking cup. One day (as always, in such tales) one of his queens and his minister conspired to poison him. They brought him a poisoned drink in this cup. The unsuspecting king chanced to look at the inscription and began to think about it. The minister succumbed to conscience and confessed. The guilty were punished, the Brahman boy rewarded. Chalk up one more victory for thinking! This story is excerpted from "The Boy Who Sold Wisdom," *In* Ramanujan, A. K., "Folktales from India," New York, Pantheon Books, 1991, pp. 240–243.

The fundamental strategic questions to be asked when assessing and promulgating marketing communications are derived from an understanding of how customers process information. Although the detailed understanding of such processes is still being researched and is in flux, the major themes have been available for quite some time.

First, any communication to be acted on has to be received. The strategic question is: Will the communication reach the desired information processors?

Second, any communication received will be acted upon—except in purposeful ignorance (or given the Garbage-In Garbage-Out GIGO treatment). The strategic question is: Will the communication attract the attention of the desired information processors?

Third, is the process of evaluating and integrating the information with prior knowledge-information to enhance stored information or make a decision? The decision may be either one of evaluation, considering both emotional and cognitive inputs, or it may be an action decision. (Which one depends on the stage of the consumption process and its context.) The general question is: Will the marketing communication move the relationship with the appropriate information processors in the desired direction?

Exhibit 13–8 provides a breakdown of target information processors. Each of these categories can be further defined for corporate, product category, or brand level communications.

The underlying, more specific, questions are:

- Does it reinforce or project the communicator's strengths?
- Does it project or reinforce the desired uniqueness?
- Does it aid the evaluation-action decision process?
- Does it reinforce a prior positive decision?

In the above:

- Does it help in minimizing risk?
- Does it require the appropriate level of cognitive capacity?

EXHIBIT 13–8   Categories of Target Information Processors

Target Information Processors

1. Negative new contracts
2. Unaware new contracts
3. Positive new contracts
4. Exclusive relationship seekers
5. Limited-Multiple relationship seekers
6. Experimental relationship triers with relationships with competitors/others
7. Experimental relationship triers with existing relationships with communicator
8. Routinized switchers among other competitors
9. Routinized switchers among a set including communicator
10. Favorable other-competitor loyals
11. Neutral other-competitor loyals
12. Unfavorable other-competitor loyals
13. Influencers
14. Gatekeepers

Adapted from Rossiter J. R. and L. I. Percy, *Advertising and Promotion Management*, New York, McGraw-Hill, 1987, Table 4–1.

An interesting example of getting consumers ready is described.[38]

When in the summer of '91, the Star TV network began to beam its way into the Indian household it had a viewship of 4,000. Not many could have predicted that these figures would touch approximately 2 million only a year later.

... Indian manufacturers with their eyes on a wider Asian market are naturally the keenest to avail of the newer network. For those looking at Hong Kong and the Middle East, it is ideal.

... "It works both ways," comments Siddharth Ray. "For example, Evita Soaps plans to market itself in Asian markets and it is creating a brand exposure for itself prior to its launch. And Coca Cola, which is looking for an entry into this country, is also advertising out of Singapore and preparing a brand consciousness here."[39]

Customer Service

In many instances, the full value of a purchase cannot be attained without additional assistance or service support. For example, a new automobile needs to be "serviced" at regular intervals. In other instances, even a purchase does not occur without the help of "expert" help. For example, acquisition of companies, purchasing insurance, choice of college, and so forth. Expertise may be needed at the choice or purchase or consumption stages.

The strategic questions are:

- What services are necessary?
- Who in the distribution channel should provide the service?
- Who should pay for the service?
- How automated can and should the service be?

Examples abound about the key role of customer service in the success of products and firms. A few are provided.[40]

Word Star (from Micro Pro) vs. WordPerfect
As late as 1987 Micro Pro was deservedly known as being indifferent to customers, who would call with problems and not be able to get through. The firm had the industry nickname, "Micropro-please-hold."

[38]"Star TV ads make inroads into Doordarshan: Clients Happy," 1993, Chicago, *India Tribune,* March 6, 1993.

[39]Another issue to keep in mind in conceptualizing marketing communications strategy is that the decision to choose a particular set of target information processors, by definition, identifies those chosen not to get the communication. Given imperfections in message targeting, some who should get the message may not, and some who shouldn't, may. This latter may be especially important in the context of social message.

[40]For a well-thought-out, readable, and practical source on designing customer service, please see Carr, C., *Frontline Customer Service: 15 Keys to Customer Satisfaction,* New York, John Wiley, 1990.

. . . By contrast, WordPerfect developed an unlimited access, toll-free, phone-in advisory service which became an important point of distinction in part because of the Micro Pro legacy. One writer noted that the WordPerfect systems provided a no-questions-asked, all-questions-answered technical help with a style and class that others lacked, and sarcastically concluded: "Paying customers like the idea of a software vendor that answers the phone when they call."[41]

Don Beyer Volvo

The typical member of the "Auto Age 500," the sales-based ranking of America's five hundred largest dealership compiled by Auto Age, generates 12 percent of its annual revenue from after-sale service. At Beyer Volvo, the figure is closer to 30%, and Beyer has convincing evidence that satisfied service customers will keep traffic moving for new cars, too—more than 80% of 1987 sales were to people who were either previous customers of the dealership or had heard about Beyer Volvo from another satisfied customer.

It shouldn't be surprising, then, to learn that since Volvo initiated its Dealer of Excellence Awards in 1981, Beyer Volvo, a second-generation family business that Don and his brother, Mike, bought from their parents a few years back, has been named among the Scandinavian manufacturer's U.S. elite not once, but every year.[42]

Colgate-Palmolive in Poland

Wojtek Krol is used to ornery characters. As Colgate-Palmolive Co.'s top salesman in Poland, Krol, 30, wrangles daily with hostile ex-communists and grouchy sales clerks, all to sell Colgate toothpaste and Ajax cleanser in a land adapting pell-mell to Capitalism. At a dingy, state-owned grocery store, or skelp, in Warsaw, a saleswoman glowers on Krol when he walks in. "I have a problem with this lady," he tells a companion. Then, he grins and asks her how the toothpaste is selling. Krol has been working since May on getting better shelf space, but he rubbed this clerk the wrong way on an earlier visit. Now, he is pouring on the charm to get her to move a large spider plant that's blocking the Ajax, languishing on the bottom shelf.

This skelp will take several more weeks' work, Krol figures. But across the town, in the Warsaw suburb of Wola, his efforts have already paid off. In a bustling private department store called Centrum, several smartly dressed saleswomen greet him warmly. The Polish-born Krol, a consummate schmoozer who once sold furniture in the U.S., asks after their families. Among the well-stocked shelves in the personal-care section, Ajax, Colgate toothpaste, and Palmolive soap and shampoo clearly have the best placement.

Financing

"Diamonds Are Forever" goes the deBeers ad, but do most consumers pay cash for their wedding rings? Or, for their homes? Or, for their cars? Or, for college tuition?

---

[41]This example is from p. 36 of D. A. Aaker's book on Brand Equity (*op. cit.*). The quotation in the example is from Seymour, J., "Leave A Wake-Up Call for December 1990," *PC Magazine,* January 16, 1990, p. 15.

[42]This example is from Zemke, R. and D. Schaaf, *The Service Edge,* New York, NAL Books, 1989, p. 252.

The issue of buying versus leasing has quite an established tradition in the finance literature. Consumer financing, on the other hand, has received little or no attention in the marketing literature. It is undoubtedly often an important part of the purchasing decision and deserves attention. A brief discussion is provided.

The biggest strategic question for a firm, in which financing has been determined through prior research and analysis to be necessary, is: Should it be provided by this firm?

If financing is not to be provided, then the channel of distribution to be used may be different. Obviously, some member of the channel should either provide the financing or be able to broker it. If it is to be provided, then the specification of particular package(s) to be put together becomes important.

Exhibit 13–9 provides a summary of the Second Annual Survey of Retail Credit Trends conducted by Arthur Anderson. Credit card sales are expected to grow, credit authorization should be "on-line," and billings provide an additional opportunity for communication.

In many export marketing situations, for example, capital goods to developing nations, arranging for financing is an essential part of the transaction. In the sale of military hardware, airplanes, power plants, computer equipment, and so forth, financing through ExIm (or export-import banks) and the government becomes critical.

EXHIBIT 13–9   Summary of Arthur Anderson's Second Annual Survey of Retail Credit Trends

	Type of Store		
	Convenience Stores	Home Furnishing Retailers	Specialty Apparel Retailers
Percentage offering credit cards	55	50	25
Percentage accepting third party cards	90	100	100
Percentage predicting increase in credit card sales	46	NA	63
Credit card sales as a percent of total sales	16	33	35
Loss of credit card operations as a percent of sales	0.5	0.5	1.8
Cost of credit card operations as percent of credit sales	1	0.4	2.2
Percent using billing stuffers	50	85	NA
Percentage performing credit authorization at point-of-sale	77	90	89

From *Chain Store Age Executive* (Section 3), Vol. 68 Issue 1, January 1992.

Getting into the financing business is not without danger.   Consider the following from a *Business Week* article:

> Sears. ITT. Xerox. Westinghouse. All proud names of Corporate America that rushed eagerly into the promised land of financing services in the 1980s.
>
> . . . Now, battered by severe losses, those adventurers are retreating, anxious to limit exposures and get back to their basic businesses.
>
> Except for General Electric Co. The maker of jet engines, light bulbs, and home appliances is enjoying incredible benefits from its finance arm.
>
> . . . An example of its quick action philosophy: When Eastern Air Lines Inc. collapsed, GE Capital's Polaris Aircraft Leasing operation got stuck with a handful of Boeing 757s. Polaris executives discovered that USAir Inc. wanted some of the widebody planes but had McDonnel Douglas MD-80s leased from Polaris that it no longer needed. So GE released the 757s to USAir, taking the MD-80s back and leasing them in a new deal to a Chinese Carrier.[43]

Although this example is about a whole division set up for the purpose of financing, its message is more general.   Financing is dangerous, but if done right it can provide a growth opportunity in and of itself.   But, without it there might be no sale!

Another example is illustrated in the ad of Smart Jewelers (Exhibit 13–10).   By breaking the payment for a Rolex watch into 24 monthly installments, Smart Jewelers makes it possible for a new segment of consumers to buy a Rolex.   Of course, it also does not require a down payment or payment of interest.[44]

As part of a marketing strategy design or analysis review, it must be determined if financing is an impediment to success.   If so, then this fact must be considered in any plan of action.

The space of offerings has been discussed.   The dimensions of the subspaces and the anchor points or alternative positions on each dimension have also been explained. In the next section, attention is focused on the thinking behind coverage of this space. Coverage of this space implies the positions in this space which are to be occupied.   This next section discusses competitive positioning in the offerings space.

Competitive Positioning in the Offerings Space

The two fundamental issues in competitive positioning are scope or extent of coverage of the cpace, and positioning relative to competition.

[43]Smart, T., "GE's Money Machine," *Business Week,* March 8, 1993, pp. 62–67.

[44]As an aside, it is a personal observation that the availability of consumer credit really spurs a consumer driven economic expansion—evidence of this may easily be seen both in the United States and India.   In fact, financing (or really, the lack of it) can break a small business's back. *Business Week,* March 22, 1993, p. 42, reports that "While President Clinton wrangles with Congress over his economic stimulus plan, the White House is pushing ahead with another effort to jump-start the economy on the cheap.   On March 10, the White House unveiled a package of changes in banking regulations it hopes will generate more lending, particularly to small businesses."

EXHIBIT 13–10   Financing A Rolex

To illustrate, consider Exhibit 13–11 (also used in Chapter 7). This exhibit is a map of consumers perceptions of various cars. Assuming that this is the appropriate space of offerings, for a firm, the coverage issue is one of how many cars to have in this space (or market). The relative positioning issue is whether to position either exactly on top of or close to competitors' cars. These two issues are discussed next. Exhibit 13–12 provides a graphic summary of this section.

Extent of Coverage

Hofer and Schendel, in their book *Strategy Formulation,* refer to an organization's scope as being a key component of its strategy. In their words:

> To us an organization's scope (domain) defines the range of its interactions with its environment in the ways most pertinent to that organization. Thus, for many firms, scope would be defined in terms of product/market segments. Some companies, however, might more appropriately define their scope in terms of geography or technology or distribution channels.[44a]

EXHIBIT 13-11   Example of Offering Space

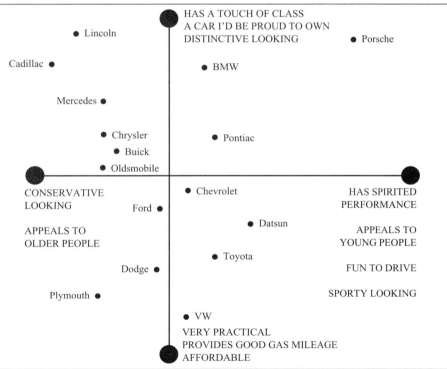

[44a]Hofer, C. W. and D. Schendel, *Strategy Formulation: Analytical Concepts,* St. Paul, MN, West Publishing, 1978.

EXHIBIT 13-12 Competitive Positioning

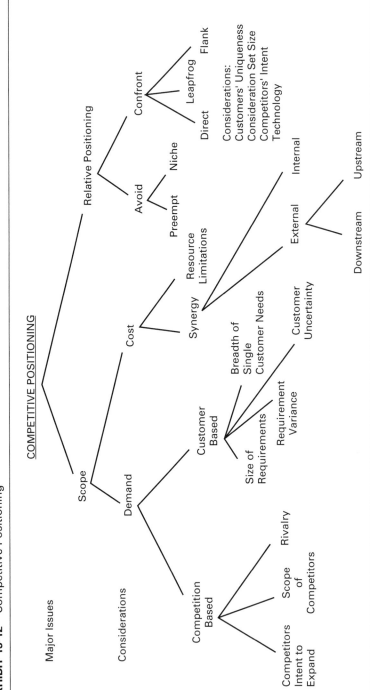

In marketing strategy, scope means the extent of coverage of the offerings space. In thinking of the coverage of this space, both the demand side and the cost side should be considered.

Demand Considerations in Scope Decisions

Demand is based on the options available to customers as well as on the information available to customers.

The options available to customers are the competitive offerings they would consider to fill their needs. These options are offered by competitors. Scope decisions would be influenced by competitor's scope, competitor's intent to expand, and rivalry.

In an offerings space with competitor(s) covering large parts of this space, market share and sales objectives may require wider scope—unless there is a large unattended customer group or segment available to the firm. Profitability goals may, on the other hand, suggest a narrower scope.

If competitors intend to expand their scope and threaten a firm's offerings (or if a new entry occurs), and it does not expand its scope, assuming a fixed total market size, it is necessarily going to lose market share. This has been well established in marketing literature by the use of spatial competition models.[45] Preservation of share and a need to minimize losses necessitates an expansion of scope.

The rivalry that a firm's expansion of scope plans faces could limit its scope. Consider the following excerpt from *Business Week*:

> While the major carriers continue to suffer, once lowly commuters, which operate as partners to big airlines, are flourishing. . . . And regionals still are held hostage by the majors, who can horn in on more lucrative routes or leave their smaller partners stranded if they pull out of major hubs. . . . There's also the dicey possibility that a commuter will develop a good market only to have its major-airline partner take it back. That happened to Air Wisconsin Inc. five years ago, when United pushed into the Chicago-Madison and Chicago-Milwaukee routes, crowding Air Wisconsin out.[46]

When the scope of a firm exceeds a certain threshold, it might "draw attention to itself" and thus be vulnerable. This vulnerability may lead to lowered profitability, and perhaps loss of even the original market share. Growth must be supported by strength—either customer relationships or deep pockets.

[45]For more details see Hauser, J. R. and S. M. Shugan, "Defensive Marketing Strategies," *Marketing Science,* Vol. 2, No. 4, 1983, pp. 319–360; Kumar, K. R. and D. Sudharshan, "Defensive Marketing Strategies: An Equilibrium Analysis Based on Decoupled Response Function Models," *Management Science,* Vol. 23, No. 7, 1988, pp. 405–413; and Gruca, T. S., K. R. Kumar, and D. Sudharshan, "An Equilibrium Analysis of Defensive Responses to Entry Using A Coupled Response Function Model," *Marketing Science,* Vol. 11, 1992, No. 4, pp. 348–358.

[46]Schine, E. and A. Rothman, "The Big Time Beckons the Small Birds," *Business Week,* March 24, 1993, pp. 57–58.

Customer requirements, of course, impact scope decisions by their direct influence on demand.   The main customer requirements that influence demand are:

- Size of Requirements
- Variance in Requirements
- Requirement Uncertainty
- Breadth of Single Customer Needs

The larger the size of a market, the higher the number of offerings that it can support. Assume that each offering needs a certain revenue base to support it.   The ratio of market size to the minimum revenue required to support a single offering provides a quick approximation of the number of offerings that can be supported by this market.[47]   Thus, the size of a market naturally limits the scope of offerings of all competitors, and therefore of any single competitor as well.

Although size of experience places a natural limit on scope, variance in such requirements (or variety in customer tastes, preferences, needs) may call for expanded scope (assuming that such offerings are profitable or viable).   By not being "close" to some customers, an opportunity is created for competitive entry or expansion. Variance of requirement within a customer (for example, because variety-seeking) also permits an opportunity for expanded scope.

If customers are uncertain about their exact needs and choose based on comparisons of available offerings, perhaps at the point of purchase—consider purchasing a TV set—what set of functions really constitute exactly what a customer wants?   Does a customer know this exactly?   Or, does the customer choose based on a comparison of available options?   If such uncertainty exists, then a wider scope increases the probability of serving more customers, and leads to possibly higher market share.

In several instances, again perhaps because of the choice and consumption constraints of cognitive capacity, financing capacity, time, or expertise, customers may choose to restrict their buying to one or just a few suppliers.   In other words, they may seek "full-service" or "single-stop" shopping.   In such cases also a wider scope of offerings is mandatory.   When customers have a breadth of needs and they seek to minimize their suppliers, wider scope is a strategic necessity.

Cost Considerations in Scope Decisions

There are essentially two different ways in which cost influences the scope decisions.

The first is from the extent of synergy that may be possible in the offerings set. Such synergy may arise from either externally-based cost interactions or internal cost interactions.   External cost interactions leading to "economies of scale or scope"

[47]For more details, please see Prescott, E. C. and M. Visscher, "Sequential Location Among Firms with Foresight," *The Bell Journal of Economics,* Vol. 8, No. 2, Autumn, 1977, pp. 378–393; Eaton, B. C. and R. G. Lipsey, "The Theory of Market Preemption: The Persistence of Excess Capacity and Monopoly in Growing Spatial Markets," *Economica,* Vol. 46, May, 1979, pp. 149–158; and Gruca, T. S., K. R. Kumar, and D. Sudharshan, "Product Positioning Strategies for Segment Pre-emption," *Proceedings of the American Marketing Association Summer Educators' Conference,* San Francisco, 1988.

could either be on the downstream (toward customers) or on the upstream (toward raw materials). On the downstream side, the common use of distribution facilities, logistics, brand name, advertising, salesforce, and so forth might lead to greater profitability with expanded scope than without. On the upstream side, purchasing efficiencies and even purchasing possibilities (when a certain minimum volume of business may be necessary to establish a relationship with suppliers) may dictate greater scope than otherwise. Internal synergies are those caused by economies in production and internal organizational activities. Wider scope, in the presence of experience curve effects, even in the absence of economies of scope perse, might lead to quicker lowering of costs, if the learning is of the shared variety. (That is, if learning is based on the entire set of offerings.[48]) Lack of synergy allows efficiency in operation with lower scope. The presence of synergy necessitates wider scope, especially if competition has wider scope.

The second way in which cost impacts the scope decision is directly through resource requirements. The resources required compared to resource availability place a limit on the possible scope. If resource availability is not a constraint, then this factor does not influence the scope decisions.

Relative Positioning

There are two fundamental approaches to positioning relative to competition: avoidance and confrontation. In the offerings space in Exhibit 13–11, relative positioning is, for example, how close to introduce a new car after a competitor's. (So, relative positioning in such spaces is not strictly an avoid or confront issue, it is how close or how distant the new car's position should be from an existing one.) If, however, customers were to be seen using the classification shown in Exhibit 13–13, the avoid-confront dichotomy is more obvious. Trying to serve competitors' customers is confrontation. Trying to serve new customers is avoidance.

The choice of whether to avoid, or to confront, and that of choosing specifically from the various alternatives within these two broad approaches, depends on how unique customers (or segments) are, the consideration set size of customers, the intent of competitors, and technological capability. If customers' needs are unique, then an offering serving one of them would not impact on sales from the others. Serving a customer would not impact on the sales of a customer who serves another customer. (This uniqueness may be because of the geographic separation, for example, in international markets.) This might permit avoidance approaches. If customers' needs are not unique, then avoidance approaches would be inadvisable.

If customers seek variety, for example, in breakfast foods, then some amount of stealing of share may occur, again minimizing the opportunities for avoidance approaches. If competitors intend to pursue confrontation, then avoidance approaches are, by definition, ruled out. Finally, technological capability is neces-

---

[48]For an analytical treatment and some formulations of synergy function, please see Sudharshan, D. and K. R. Kumar, "Multiple Brand Synergy and Market Structure," *Proceedings of the American Marketing Association Summer Educators' Conference,* Toronto, 1987, pp. 145–150.

EXHIBIT 13–13   Visualizing Customers Relative Positioning

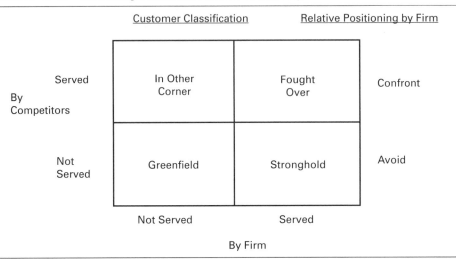

sary to improve the offerings (or their cost) compared with competition. The absence of such a capability rules out the use of some approaches.

There are two possible approaches to avoidance. The first is to pre-empt competition, that is, to provide offerings to customers, such that there is no opportunity (at least in a profitable way) for competitors to attempt to compete for these customers.

The second approach is market niching. In this approach an attempt is made to find a set of customers who could be exclusively served by the firm and which would then be no longer attractive to other competitors. This approach is often recommended for small firms. The difficulty is that such a set of customers may provide a profitable, stable base, but may not grow. In such a circumstance, this approach leads to stagnation.

Stealing share from competitors is confrontation. There are three relative positioning approaches to confrontation. The first is direct attack; often called the "me-too"[49] approach. To be successful, this approach requires a technological advance that permits profits to be made with fairly low volume or market share (assuming the incumbent will keep most of its share), or an existing relationship with customers. This approach includes distribution channel members, which allows an imitative late entrant to garnish sufficient share.

The second approach, leapfrogging, is the introduction of a vastly superior offering, which (often) subsumes the function(s) being served by the competitor's offerings. It also implies that the lead time for competitors to react is significant. This approach implies having the requisite technological capability.

The third approach is flanking, or introducing offerings slightly different from those available. To succeed, this approach requires either customers who seek variety, or customers who value fine differences in offerings.

[49]Levitt, T. C., "Innovative Imitation," *Harvard Business Review,* September–October, 1966, pp. 66–70.

SUMMARY

This chapter deals with the offerings with which a firm would serve customers and uses a space metaphor to discuss these offerings. The first part describes this space, and the second part describes how to cover this space given competition. The dimensions of the function, form, and price subspaces are defined and described. In doing this, the possible positioning on these dimensions is identified. Customers, while they seek to gain value from function, form, and price, do so under constraints of cognitive capacity, financial capacity, and limited time and expertise. Thus transaction facilitators of information, customer support, service, and financing are also described.

The space coverage issues are discussed under competitive positioning. The key issues discussed are those of scope of coverage and relative positioning. Demand and cost considerations for scope decisions are also discussed. Finally, the relative positioning approaches are discussed using avoidance and confrontation approaches. The conditions under which specific avoidance and confrontation approaches were appropriate concludes this chapter.

Concept Questions

1. (a.) What are the subspaces of the offerings space?
   (b.) What are the dimensions of each of these subspaces?
   (c.) What is the relationship between the offerings subspaces and (a) customer values, and (b) channel relationships?
2. (a.) What are transaction facilitators?
   (b.) Why is there a need for using transaction facilitators?
   (c.) What are the key issues involved in choosing and designing the appropriate transaction facilitators?
3. (a.) Describe the various scope choices in competitive positioning.
   (b.) Describe the various relative location choices in competitive positioning.
   (c.) Discuss the various considerations leading to specific scope and relative location choices.

Discussion Questions

1. Discuss the Apple Computer, American Transitional Hospitals, Inc., Nighttime Pain Reliever, Coca-Cola and AST Research, Inc. examples in terms of the concepts introduced in this chapter.
2. Discuss the role of transaction facilitators in internal marketing. Are additional facilitators needed in international marketing? Justify your answer.
3. Critique the relative positioning recommendations made in Exhibit 13–13. Provide recommendations with adequate justification.
4. Evaluate a program-marketing unit of your choice on its offerings strategy.

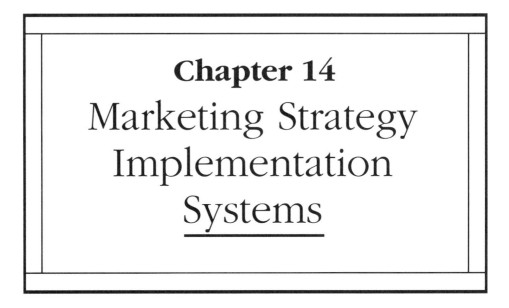

Chapter 14
Marketing Strategy Implementation Systems

INTRODUCTION

What makes the ROTRs spin? Can a ROTR set be designed or chosen without answering this question? This chapter tries to answer these questions.

Peter Walker, of the consulting firm McKinsey & Company, says in a Foreword to an article written by two of his colleagues:

> For years, the primary focus of management was on strategic issues. This was a natural consequence of the external forces—the energy crisis, double digit interest and inflation rates, rapid technology advances, and deregulation—that triggered fundamental changes in industry structure and led many companies to rethink both their market positions and their sources of competitive advantage. Today, however, we believe that a new management focus is emerging which, in many industries, is already playing a greater role than the creativity of strategies in driving corporate performance—the superior execution of the core skills of the business.[1]

An article in *The Economist* starts this way:

> It sounds like a parody of a management fad—no mean feat considering that many people view management fads themselves as parodies of rational thought. Instead of learning from past mistakes and triumphs, say the proponents of "business process re-engineering," managers should forget everything they know about how their companies operate, and reinvent their businesses from scratch. The reward? Leaps in productivity and competitiveness.

[1]Walker, P., in Foreword to Irwin, R. A., and E. G. Michaels II, "Core Skills: Doing the Right Things Right," *The McKinsey Quarterly,* Summer 1989, p. 4.

Despite its ugly terminology and grandiose claims, re-engineering has been embraced publicly by scores of companies, including AT&T, Texas Instruments, Ford, Citicorp, Aetna Life and IBM. Many firms began "re-engineering" parts of their businesses before the term was first popularized by Michael Hammer, an American management consultant, in 1990. Hundreds more are now planning to do the same.

To anyone not running a company, the fuss among businessmen about re-engineering—or "process redesign" as it is also called—seems puzzling. Its two basic ideas sound obvious, and neither is new. The first is to start with a clean sheet of paper and design all or parts of the operations of a company in the best way possible. The second is to look on companies as performing a small number of continuing processes, rather than as collections of people performing hundreds of distinct, though related, functions.[2]

The cover story of a *Business Week* article is titled "The Horizontal Corporation." Its byline reads, "Forget the pyramid. Smash the hierarchy, break the company into its key processes and create teams from different departments to run them."[3] The seven key elements of such a horizontal corporation identified in the article are:

1. Organize around process, not task.
2. Flatten hierarchy.
3. Use teams to manage everything.
4. Let customers drive performance.
5. Reward team performance.
6. Maximize supplier and customer contact.
7. Inform and train all employees.

Gordon C. Brunton, President of International Thomson Organization, said:

It is absolutely fundamental that any planning system take into account what might be termed the culture of a company, rather than try to impose a style to which managers have to conform. I have a strong belief that planning is a line function. Planning is a little like religion. It's a way of life, not something to turn to now and again when the mood takes you. Planning is not something that line managers can leave to "professionals." All International Thomson senior managers now understand that unless they demonstrate their ability to think strategically, their future career potential will be limited accordingly.

Their commitment to think strategically must come from the top. I review the company's objectives and broad strategy personally and communicate them directly to senior management. I regard this as an essential part of every chief executive's job.[4]

[2]"Take a Clean Sheet of Paper," *The Economist,* May 1, 1993, pp. 67–68.

[3]Byrne, J. A., "The Horizontal Corporation," *Business Week,* December 20, 1993, pp. 76–81.

[4]Brunton, Gordon C., "Implementing Corporate Strategy: The Story of International Thomson," *The Journal of Business Strategy,* Vol. 5, No. 2, pp. 6–14.

Strategy and its implementation are like two strands of a DNA molecule. Interwoven and matched they make a good DNA molecule and in the right environment they carry the seeds of their future. If they are not in phase, or drifting apart they are mere chemicals, and could end up disfiguring, disabling, and ending years of careful progress.

The preceding chapters discussed and described in detail the ROTRs (relationships, offerings, timing, and resource allocation) that make up a marketing strategy set. Imagine these ROTRs in a force field (Exhibit 14–1). The components of this force field synchronized with each other and with the right rotor lead to the desired output—barring chance events. The components of this force field are three internal subsystems through which implementation occurs in an organization: social, technology, and human resources.

According to the famous scholar of management history, Professor Chandler,[5] these three subsystems constitute organizational structure.[6]

EXHIBIT 14–1.   ROTR in an Implementation Force Field

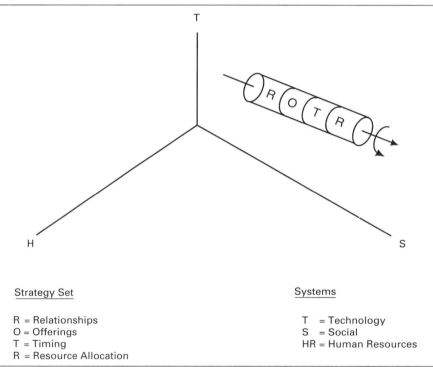

Strategy Set	Systems
R = Relationships	T = Technology
O = Offerings	S = Social
T = Timing	HR = Human Resources
R = Resource Allocation	

[5]Chandler, Jr., A. D., *Strategy and Structure: Chapters in the History of the American Industrial Enterprise*, Cambridge, MA, MIT Press, 1962.

[6]In the academic literature time has been spent discussing which came first. There is also debate about whether strategies are designed or emerge. For example, see Goold, M. "Research Notes and Communication Design, Learning, and Planning: A Further Observation on the Design School Debate," *Strategic Management Journal*, 1992, Vol. 13, pp. 169–170.

Embedded in this structure is the organizational "heart": policies, systems, programs, and action.[7]   These deliver the "realized" strategy to the outside world.   We shall discuss the three subsystems (social, technology, human resources) and the policies, systems, programs, and action embedded in them.

OVERVIEW

We begin with an introduction to the different types of strategic management systems and their evolution. This discussion provides a brief overview of such systems and highlights the key implementation requirements necessary to manage in complex environments.

We next discuss Bonoma's work on implementation which provides a framework to get the job done.   The various elements and structure of this framework are described and examples provided.

Finally, putting in place any strategy requires the appropriate S, T and H subsystems.   Alternatively, a given S, T, and HR narrows down the permissible focus.   Our discussion on the S, T, and HR subsystems focuses on: the different social systems that are transforming organizations, for example, horizontal organizations, alliances, transnational organizations; the special needs in developing control systems for strategic projects; examples of technology subsystems; and exploring the differences between strategists and implementers, and the special requirements for decision-making in complex and fast-moving environments.

STRATEGIC MANAGEMENT SYSTEMS

The essence of strategy is managing change: regulating change, causing it, or preventing it. Or, as said before, making the probable, possible. Controlling growth, gaining market share, increasing value, or simply preventing erosion of market share, all constitute managing change.   When does such management require a strategy?   When should a strategy be explicitly planned and executed?   When should it occur as unplanned, intuitive responses?   In our book, the 4A + 3I process that combines the analytical, or formal thinking processes, with those of intuition to create a template for strategic planning in marketing is proposed.[8]

---

[7]The terms actions, programs, systems and policies were coined by Tom Bonoma. He uses them to define a set of structural levels that together constitute the four structural levels of marketing practice. For more details see Bonoma, T. V., *The Marketing Edge, Making Strategies Work,* New York, The Free Press, 1985.

[8]Another approach is found in a new field of study called Artificial Life. A wonderful and highly readable book in this area is Levy, S., *Artificial Life: The Quest for a New Creation,* New York, Pantheon Books, 1985.

On page 105, Levy describes Chris Langton's work in the study and simulation of ants. Langton is one of the pioneers of this field. In his studies he is said to have been "particularly struck" by this quotation from a book called *The Sciences of the Artificial,* by Herbert Simon:

(Continued on p. 405)

EXHIBIT 14–2   Evolution of Management Systems

		Change-ability	1900	1930	1950	1970	1990
Unpredict-ability of the future			Familiarity of events ←Familiar →*←Extrapolable →*←Familiar discontinuity →*←Novel discontinuity →				
Recurring		• Systems and procedures manuals • Financial control		**Management by control**			

Forecastable by extrapolation		• Operations budgeting
		   • Capital budgeting
		      • Management by objectives
		         • Long range planning
				Management by extrapolation			

Predictable threats and opportunities		**Management by anticipation of change**	• Periodic strategic planning • Strategic posture management			

Partially predictable opportunities
 	
Unpredictable surprises
		Management by flexible, rapid response	• Contingency planning
			   • Strategic issue management
			      • Weak signal issue management
			         • Surprise management			

Turbulence level		1 Stable	2 Reactive	3 Anticipating	4 Exploring	5 Creative

From Ansoff, H. I. and E. J. McDonnell, *Implanting Strategic Management,* 2nd ed., Englewood Cliffs, NJ, Prentice Hall, 1990, p. 13.

Ansoff and McDonnell[9] provide a concise view of management systems (Exhibit 14–2). The sequence of development of these systems is: management by control, management by extrapolation, management by anticipation of change, and management by flexible, rapid response. This development parallels the "turbulence" level or volatility in the business environment. The differences between the newer systems are summarized:

1. Long range planning (LRP) and strategic planning (SP) have different views of the future. LRP assumes that the future can be foreseen as an extrapolation of the past. SP assumes that the future may neither be better than the best already seen nor extrapolated from the past. It calls for SWOT analysis, competitive analysis, portfolio analysis, and risk management through diversification.

2. Strategic posture management adds general management capability planning to SP. It also brings in a systematic consideration of implementation.

3. With environmental changes occurring more quickly than the length of the strategic planning cycle, contingency planning, strategic issue management (SIM), weak signal issue (WSI) management, and surprise management (SM) have slowly come into use.

---

[8](Continued) An ant, viewed as a behaving system, is quite simple. The apparent complexity of its behavior over time is largely a reflection of the complexity of the environment in which it finds itself.

Steven Levy goes on to say that:

While Langton found this true for solitary ants, he considered it a massive understatement when applied to cooperating colonies of ants. He saw this in his vants*; though absurdly simple, they seemed to display genuinely cooperative behavior.

*(virtual ants)

The conflict between Simon's observations of a single ant and what he observed in his colony of vants was to him resolved by his reading the following writing of the great Harvard entomologist E. O. Wilson:

Certain termites give every appearance of accomplishing their astonishing feat by means of what computer scientists call dynamic programming. As each step of the operation is completed, its result is assessed, and the precise program for the next step (out of several of many available) is chosen and activated. Thus no termite need serve as overseer with blueprint in hand.

Langton thought of this as a "bottom up" approach.

To Langton, this was nature's way of taking advantage of complicated phenomena that occurred when several variables combined to form a complex system. From billions of trials and errors—evolutionary process—out of the interaction would come something useful. It not only seems that those little nonconscious pieces of matter are cooperating; Langton contends they are cooperating. Quite literally.

This bottom-up behavior results in emergent behavior of a system. "Something had to happen that was not specifically programmed in." This emergent behavior has also been observed in business organizations. Relying purely on the emergence of strategy cannot be acceptable, for then, it will not be strategy anymore. Neither does this purely emergent behavior specify how those initial rules came into being. These rules are the pathways that we refer to as marketing strategy. Put together with the right structure, "emergent behavior" leads to success.

[9]Ansoff, H. I. and E. J. McDonnell, *Implanting Strategic Management,* 2nd ed., Englewood Cliffs, NJ, Prentice Hall, 1990.

Strategic Issue Management (SIM)

A schematic of SIM is given in Exhibit 14–3. Issues identified by surveillance systems are classified as important and unimportant. The important ones are further classified according to the urgency with which they need attention. This system fits into an existing strategic planning system and provides the strategic planner with important issues that have longer impact and action horizons and directs urgent attention where necessary. It is also called a real-time system.

Weak Signal Issue (WSI)

Issues that the surveillance system picks up need to have at least a certain signal strength. However, some important issues might be present at low intensity, but, may

EXHIBIT 14–3   Strategic Issue Management

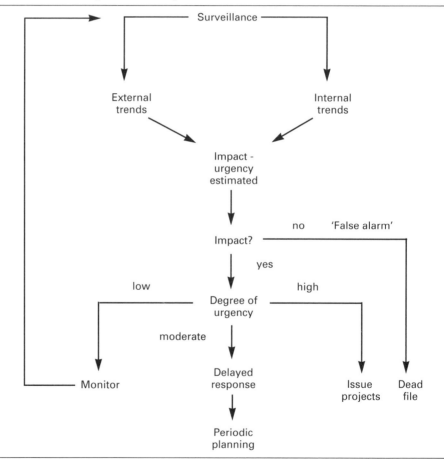

From Ansoff, H. I. and E. J. McDonnell, *Implanting Strategic Management,* 2nd Englewood Cliffs, NJ, Prentice Hall, 1990, p. 19.

rapidly build up and threaten an unprepared corporation. This situation requires special amplifier systems to pick up these weak signals and bring them to appropriate attention. These amplifier systems need to be watched closely. A system for capturing, amplifying, and monitoring weak signals is called a weak-signal management system. The response to such signals may be graduated and flexible, because along with their low intensity, are signal distortion and noise. Resources need to be committed carefully until signal and noise can be reasonably identified and separated. This is all part of the weak-signal management system.

Surprise Management (SM)

Surprises that might "tunnel through" surveillance systems need to be planned for. What processes need to be brought into play and what roles need to be assumed? The Tylenol tragedy and Union Carbide's experience with an explosion at its pesticide plant in Bhopal, India are examples of surprises. The key first steps suggested for managing such surprises constitute a surprise management system.[10]

1. Provide the public with enough information to protect the corporation.
2. Identify all parties affected by the crisis.
3. Set priorities in making decisions.
4. CEO should assume primary responsibility.
5. Form an interdisciplinary task force.
6. Seek or take help from external agencies.
7. Be guided by a humane attitude.

In particular, for communication:

1. Establish communications professionals as the company's spokespersons.
2. Provide as much written information as possible.
3. Do not use incomplete information about the crisis as an excuse for stonewalling the media.
4. Communicate the most critical information to the public.

Complexity

In a simulation study of information movement in complex dynamic systems, Langton[11] found a parametric region for which information movement ceased. Another region produced "boring, intransigent patterns." A third where the most "engaging events" arose, "those that would support the kind of complexity that was the mark of living systems." The last region was where information moved about too

---

[10]These steps are summarized from Shrivastava, P., *Strategic Management: Concepts and Practices,* SouthWestern Publishing, Cincinnati, Ohio 1994, pp. 205–209.

[11]Same reference as in Footnote 8. Diagram is from page 110.

freely and chaos reigned. These regions are shown in Exhibit 14–4 and are labeled Fixed, Periodic, Complex, and Chaotic. Although they are metaphorical to our purposes, the metaphor is powerful. The most interesting, enduring, and prevalent marketing situations are likely to be those corresponding to the complex region system of Langton. Many people, many organizations, many publics, vast numbers of planned and unplanned interactions (information transfers) within and among these many bodies can only be sustained in this complex setting. Other regions cannot sustain such interactions. Although it has always been true that complexity is the milieu in which management and marketing endure, a change has occurred over the years. The magnitude of complexity has changed, as information flow and the number of persons engaged in and forming key components of the business world have grown exponentially. The speed with which some of this information flows and the rate with which it needs to be managed has become faster. With information-action systems, each of which has its own cycle, a multiplicity of management systems is needed; each system

EXHIBIT 14–4   Artificial Life

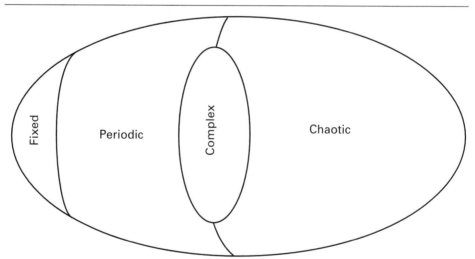

"Langton's view of information movement in complex dynamical systems such as CAs. At the left is the regime where information is frozen; nothing can live there. To the right of that is a somewhat more flexible regime where behavior such as crystal growth can be seen; still, the limited movement of information cannot support life. To the far right, information moves so freely that its structure cannot be maintained; the regime is too chaotic to support life. Only in the center 'sweet spot' can information be stable enough to support a message structure and loose enough to transmit messages. Life lives there"

tuned to a different periodicity. That which keeps these systems synchronous is senior management's "vision" and the increased sophistication of management systems.

These systems are put into play using execution and implementation skills. We next review a framework for looking at marketing strategy implementation.

Strategic Planning at Unilever

An article in *Long Range Planning,* written by the Chairman of Unilever, a $30 billion global company, is titled "Strategic Planning and Intuition in Unilever."[12]   He provides a fascinating glimpse at his views and his company's practice of strategic planning. In summary:

He argues that strategy and implementation are interdependent. Strategy formulation at a global company like Unilever requires a balance between a top-down approach to accommodate overriding corporate goals and a bottom-up approach to build on the strategies at lower levels. At Unilever an equilibrium between the two is arrived at by decentralization enmeshed in a common corporate culture and linked by common services.

Among his specific observations are:

"Decisions are made quickly, based on experience and intuition as well as thorough analysis."

Time.   Unilever uses a 3 to 5 year horizon. Although this fits a consumer goods company, a company such as Shell might need a longer (20 to 25 year) horizon.

Intuition.

As part of the Agribusiness operations, research had been done into certain animal vaccines. During the early 1980s it was suggested that the expertise that had developed in monoclonal antibodies might also be applicable to humans. There was great uncertainty about the commercial and technical problems which the application of research in a new environment would bring. However, the consensus within Unilever was that the idea felt right. Resources were invested, commitments made. As a result a revolutionary home pregnancy test was launched in Britain that brought the test time down from 2 hours to 30 minutes; at the same time the technology made the product available in a form that was much more convenient for the user.

Strategic Fashions.   "A firm's strategy is successful only as long as it is not being copied by the competition."

Regarding implementation, he emphasizes the need to manage "managerial resistance" and to "communicate the strategy" effectively. These have to fit the corporate culture.

A framework proposed to manage implementation was developed at the Harvard Business School by Bonoma. This is described next.

---

[12]Maljers, F. A., "Strategic Planning and Intuition in Unilever," *Long Range Planning,* Vol. 23, No. 2, 1990, pp. 63–68.

Bonoma's Marketing Implementation Framework[13]

Consider the following examples:

Kramer Pharmaceuticals had a "lean and mean" sales force management staff.

Each DM had responsibility for 14 sales representatives, to each of whom were assigned some 200 active accounts. Assuming a 'standard' five calls per day from each representative, the DM was receiving some 350 call reports per week, 1,400 a month, and was supervising 16,800 calls per year!

. . . Further, it was Kramer policy that the district manager make 10 to 15 percent field visits per representative supervised per year. Assuming 12 such visits, a simple calculation shows that the district manager spent over 80 percent of his/her time on the road!

The vice president of a high-technology start-up business was concerned that

(1) its four agents were not following up on leads sent to them (one agent had 70 percent of its leads outstanding); (2) when leads were followed up, closed sales were not achieved as frequently as desired (the agents were closing approximately one out of every 10 leads approached); and (3) when a sale was closed, multiple units weren't being sold.

. . . When the manager of agent distributors was questioned, the following information was learned. Management's actions to date vis-à-vis distributors consisted of the following: (1) The agents received a quota. While there was some discussion of the quota level, it essentially was set by vendor management. (2) The agents received a book of selling practices and procedures recommended by the vendor. (3) Vendor management traveled around to distributorships to assure themselves that agent salespeople had indeed read the book.

What had been done with agents was to (1) make a demand, (2) give a document, and (3) give an examination on the document!

Management at Binney & Smith determined that its greatest asset was its Crayola name. To leverage this asset they decided to distribute their many crayon and art-related products in an integrated "Crayola Fun Center"—a stand-alone display rack in chain and discount stores.

The Fun Centers worked beyond management's wildest dreams. Fifteen hundred units had been placed in a year, mostly to large chains like K-Mart. The units were selling as fast as they could be produced. Indeed, conservative projections indicated that the Fun Center line could add some $10 million to corporate sales in the fiscal year. With burgeoning sales, however, came a problem management had anticipated but couldn't devise a good way to deal with. Large retail chains do not service their own shelves and are particularly averse to paying anyone else to do this job for them.

[13]Same reference as in Footnote 7. This section is based on Bonoma's book. These examples are from pp. 44–52.

To diagnose such problems and to ensure a fit between strategy and implementation, Bonoma devised the model of marketing execution shown in Exhibit 14–5.

According to this model, marketing execution takes place at four structural levels: actions, programs, systems, and policies. These are executed using the skills of Interacting, Allocating, Monitoring, and Organizing.

Actions. Some of the detail work that needs to be accomplished to get the marketing job done is: pricing, distributor management, new product development, post-sale service, and advertising. Common mistakes that need to be avoided are:

1. *Management by assumption.* Do not assume that the detail work will get done somewhere by someone. Part of a manager's job is to know this detail. Questions to be asked: Who will do it? Is it feasible?
2. *Structural contradiction.* As in the case of Crayola Fun-Center. The organizational structure is set up for one set of activities and is required to perform another. Question to be asked: Does the lower-level structure support the strategic decision?

EXHIBIT 14–5   A Model of Marketing Implementation

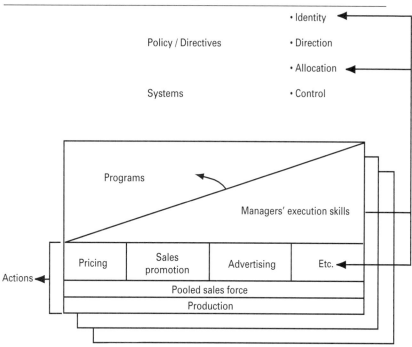

3. *Global mediocrity.* When attention and budgets are aimed at being good at everything, and everyone being at least somewhat happy. This leads to a lack of distinctive competence for the marketing area. Questions to be asked: What are the priorities? Can excellence be attained where desired?

Routines move incrementally from their original set-up. Soon they can be unrecognizable, falling to the just-noticeable-difference phenomena—each change just enough not to be noticed. But cumulatively, they result in metamorphosis. Yet, assumptions might reflect the starting point. The result is obvious! The solution to management is—manage by walking around. (This may be just a cliché but should be more than that.)

Programs.   Marketing programs are often equated to a tactical playbook. The key is to pick the right program—one which fits and integrates the actions-structure and for which management can provide a theme and direction and then support it with appropriate resources. An example is Frito-Lay's introduction of single-serving cookies and snack bars under the Grand Ma's label. The larger chain stores and supermarkets resisted allocating shelf space to single-serving cookies. Therefore, the program was not right.

Systems.   "These are the formal or semiformal devices management has available to inform, control, or facilitate its marketing decision making."

Policies.   They "are the broad rules of conduct that affect marketing practices. Policies are unlike systems in that they are not techniques and often have a more general scope than systems." Policies are prescriptions and systems are descriptions. At Frito-Lay, for example, they believe that as John Granor, vice president of marketing is quoted as saying (p. 97).

> "We have two seconds to reach the average shopper with our display of Frito-Lay high-quality snack foods. That means consistent displays in all areas of the country, and attention not only to the big supermarket customer but to the little delicatessen owner as well . . . both the trade and the end user know that Frito-Lay means quality goods."

These structures of Bonoma are to be set-up and operated using the four key execution skills of Interacting, Allocating, Monitoring, and Organizing. We shall discuss them later under human substructure.

These discussions of management systems and an implementation framework, lead to the conclusion that planning strategy and implementation occur simultaneously and their evaluation and modification is constant. Crises, surprises, and long-term developments require strategy to be changed at different times and paces. The social, technology, and human substructure issues germane to implementation, especially in the contemporary complex global and interconnected commercial environment are discussed next. The S, T, and HR systems in this context must be flexible, customer-oriented, forward thinking, coherent with the strategic pathways, and set up to adapt, innovate, and thrive.

Social System

In GE's 1990 annual report, CEO Jack Welch wrote:

> Our dream for the 1990s is a boundaryless company . . . where we knock down the walls that separate us from each other on the inside and our key constituencies on the outside.

Kenichi Ohmae begins one of his articles saying:

> Companies are just beginning to learn what nations have always known: in a complex, uncertain world filled with dangerous components, it is best not to go it alone.[14]

An article in *Fortune* reported:

> A recent survey of 5 major U.S. companies by Kaiser Associates, a Vienna, Virginia, consulting firm found that practically all put time-based strategy, as the new approach is called, at the top of their priority lists. Why? Because speed kills the competition.[15]

The social-organizational system which develops and implements marketing strategy, as indicated by the above quotations, is changing with the demands of the environment. Lawrence and Lorsch,[16] famous organizational theorists, suggest that organizational structure and management style depend on environmental demands. Simple demands fit well with an integrated structure; complex demands with a differentiated one. For an integrated structure to work in a complex environment, there must be a strong leader who is the focus of the organization. To match the demands of complex environments, several organizational forms are being put in place. In this section we briefly discuss four basic themes that seem to be prevalent: Alliances, Transnational Organizations, Horizontal Organizations, and Inquiry Centers.

Alliances

Intra-country and inter-country alliances are emerging daily to provide value to customers and to add value to companies. The General Electric Company (GEC) of Britain has all its main businesses involved in inter-country alliances. Some have failed. Some of the alliances:

- A telecommunications joint venture (GPT) with Siemens (Germany)
- A 50-50 partnership with GE in 100%-owned Hotpoint domestic appliances industry

[14]Ohmae, K., "The Global Logic of Strategic Alliances," *Harvard Business Review,* March–April, 1989, pp. 143–154.

[15]Dumaine, B., "How Managers Can Succeed Through Speed," *Fortune,* February 13, 1989, pp. 54–59.

[16]Lawrence, P. R. and Lorsch, J. W., *Organization and Environment,* Homewood, IL, Richard D. Irwin, 1969.

- A partnership with GE in its medical systems and electrical distribution businesses in Europe
- A merger with Alsthom (France) in power generation

A failed alliance was a joint venture with Hitachi to manufacture television sets in South Wales in the United Kingdom.

The obvious questions are: Why should alliances be formed?   How can they be made to succeed?

The major reasons why alliances are formed are:[17]

- To gain access to customers—primarily in specialty areas requiring intimate customer contacts for development or support.
- To gain access to technology—primarily in new or rapidly evolving technologies.
- To understand and respond to different local requirements.
- To meet (or avoid) regulatory, financial or political protectionist requirements.
- To recruit foreign talent, particularly application skills, and top talent in short supply at home (p. 15).
- To pool financial (capital) resources.

A common theme is the need to pool resources and skills in order to minimize learning time and time to market.

A summary of the considerations in building successful alliances is provided by Devlin and Bleackley.[18]   These guidelines are divided into two parts.   The first deals with the choice of a partner, the second with managing the alliance.

Choice of Partner

Questions to be asked are:

- What will the partner's strategic position be as a result of the alliance, both now and in the next few years?
- Why should the partner wish to enter into such an alliance?
- What weaknesses of the partner are likely to be strengthened by this alliance?

These questions and similar ones directed at the company need to be answered to ensure that there is a valid reason for an alliance and that it does have enduring value for both parties.

---

[17]The GEC example is from "GEC's Joint Ventures," *The Economist,* May 26, 1990, pp. 74, 79.

[18]For more details see Devlin, G. and M. Bleackley, "Strategic Alliances—Guidelines for Success," *Long Range Planning,* 1988, Vol. 21, No. 5, pp. 18–23.

To increase the probability of success of an alliance the following are suggested:

- Commitment of top management and assigning high priority to the alliance.
- Alliance monitoring.
- Establish clear lines of accountability and responsibility.
- Establish conflict resolution procedures.
- Establish information channels to shorten feedback learning.
- Allocate sufficient resources.
- Assign the best employees and those with positive attitudes.
- Recognize limits of outcomes and common purpose.

These require careful and detailed analysis of the alliance's purpose. The more time taken upfront, the greater the chances of success later.

Transnational Organizations

This term was coined by Bartlett and Ghoshal[19] and was used to describe organizations that managed across country boundaries. The major lessons from their study are three:

1. Based on trying to understand how Matsushita was successful worldwide with consumer electronics products from its center in Japan, they propose the following success factors.
   Making Central Management Flexible
   This is done by
   - gaining the input of subsidiaries into its management processes;
   - ensuring that development efforts were linked to market needs; and
   - managing responsibility transfers from development to manufacturing to marketing (p. 57).

2. Based on their studies at Philips of Holland they postulate that their second set of success factors is:
   Making Local Management Effective
   This requires
   - a Cadre of entreprenurial expatriates.
   - an organization that forces tight integration within a subsidiary; and
   - a dispersion of responsibilities along with the decentralized assets (p. 62).

3. Their study of L. M. Ericsson led to the following success factor:
   Building Transnational Capabilities

[19]Bartlett, C. A. and S. Ghoshal, *Managing Across Borders: The Transnational Solution,* Boston, MA, Harvard Business School Press, 1989. A summary of this book may be found in "Organizing for Worldwide Effectiveness: The Transnational Solution," *California Management Review,* Fall, 1988, pp. 54–74. The quotations are from this source.

This means building

- an interdependence of resources and responsibilities among organizational units;
- a set of cross-unit integrating devices; and
- a strong corporate identification and a well-developed worldwide management perspective (p. 66).

Their "battle cry" is:

a gradual approach that, rather than undermining a company's administrative heritage, both protects and builds on it. Having built flexible central and local management capabilities, the next challenge is to link them in an organization that allows the company to do what it must to survive in today's international environment—think globally and act locally (p. 74).

The key contribution of studies such as this is the insight they provide into the detailed thinking required to make strategies work.

A fascinating story of the building of a transnational organization is provided by Christopher Lorenz, the Management Editor of London's *Financial Times*.[20] The company he writes about is Electrolux of Sweden. Electrolux, with major businesses in chain saws, garden appliances, vacuum cleaners, refrigerators, washers, dryers, car seat belts, aluminum smelting, laundry services, farm machinery, industrial shelving, and artificial flowers, has set about building a transnational organization largely through acquisition. Its goal is to be number one, two or three worldwide in most of its businesses. The focus of its structural change has been to build from "hundreds of independent villages" a set of "interdependent" but flexible "networks"—with product development, manufacturing, and supply all spanning international borders (p. 74).

(An organizational chart for its white goods product line is shown in Exhibit 14–6.)

Four types of tension created by this structure were

- — between product divisions and marketing companies;
- — between these two and country managers;
- — between country managers and international product area managers; and
- — between country managers and the international marketing coordinators.

[20]Lorenz, C., "The Birth of a 'Transnational'," *The McKinsey Quarterly,* Autumn, 1989, pp. 72–93. Some of Electrolux's acquisitions are Zanussi (Italy), Thorn, EMI's Tricity and Bendix interests, Corbero and Domar (Spain), Zanker (Germany). The ICI example is from "Reshaping ICI," *The Economist,* April 28, 1990, pp. 21–23. A question that arises is what these marketing strategy groups will center on—relationships or offerings?

EXHIBIT 14–6   The Multi-Dimensional Structure of the Electrolux White Goods Product Line

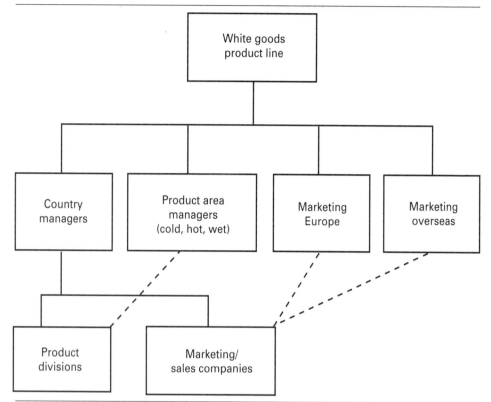

Reprinted with permission by McKinsey & Co. Lorenz C., The Birth of a Transnational, The McKinsey Quarterly, Autumn, 1989, p. 79.

These tensions need to be anticipated and managers walked through the conflict resolution procedures and processes to ensure success. In the case of Electrolux, its open top management style has lessened the "Machiavellian" intrigues that could have arisen in a less open system. The key in such a system is to build in synergy and yet respond locally.

Another example of a company building in synergy is ICI. For example, they have set up eight science-strategy groups to promote the flow of scientific information across national and territorial boundaries. Electrolux's present organization seems to favor creating "marketing strategy groups" to do the same.

One of the specific mechanisms that marketing managers in multidivisional or transnational organizations has to use to manage effectively is transfer pricing. If managed carefully transfer pricing should provide "valuable debate about . . . real business issues, marketing strategy, competitors, and so on," says Leif Johansson of Electrolux. The process has within it the seeds of change for the strategy itself. This leads to our discussion of studying organizations.

EXHIBIT 14–7   How To Create A Horizontal Corporation

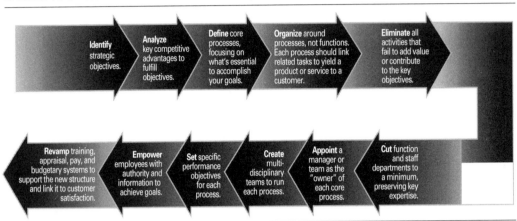

Reprinted from December 20, 1994 issue of Business Week by special permission. Copyright © 1994 by McGraw-Hill, Inc.

Horizontal Organizations[21]

Frank Osteroff and Douglas Smith of McKinsey & Co. are credited with having coined this term. Some of the companies identified as moving toward this type of organization are: AT&T, Eastman Kodak, General Electric, Lexmark International, Motorola, and Xerox.

The key steps in the process of moving to a horizontal structure are shown in Exhibit 14–7.

Strategic Flexibility

A marketing activity is viewed as part of a larger process. More teamwork activities would result, and, in fact, crossfunctional teams would become the norm rather than the exception. A theme common to both horizontal and alliance movements is strategic flexibility. Based on a study of 50 interviews in 20 companies, Aaker and Mascarenhas developed a framework to represent strategic flexibility (Exhibit 14–8).

[21]The examples and quotations used in this subsection are from the *Business Week* article cited in Footnote 3. See also Hirschhorn, L. and T. Gilmore, "The New Boundaries of the 'Boundaryless' Company," *Harvard Business Review,* May–June 1992, pp. 104–115; and also Aaker, D. A. and B. Mascarenhas, "The Need for Strategic Flexibility," *The Journal of Business Strategy,* Fall, 1984, pp. 74–82. J. Ernie Riddle, senior vice-president for marketing at Ryder System. See also Semler, R., "Managing Without Managers," *Harvard Business Review,* September–October, 1989, pp. 76–84, for an exciting example from Brazil. Some techniques to facilitate communication of pertinent information in cross functional teams are being used and developed. One such is QFD (Quality Function Deployment). This was originally developed at General Motors Institute in Detroit. It was first commercially used, however, at the Kobe Shipyard of Mitsubishi in Japan. It has since been used by major Japanese and American corporations. Further information on this process may be found in Hauser, J. R. and D. Clausing, "The House of Quality," *Harvard Business Review,* May–June, 1988, pp. 63–73. King, R., *Better Designs in Half the Time: Implementing QFD in America,* Metheun, MA, GOAL/QPC, 1987.

EXHIBIT 14–8 Illustrative Method of Increasing Flexibility

Functional Area	Diversification Strengths	Investment in Underused Resources	Reducing Commitment of Resources to a Specialized Use
Research and Development	Have several technologies underlie firm's position. Employ multiproduct programs.	Maintain R&D capability that can be used when needed.	Use a policy of being a technological follower.
Finance	Maintain transferability of funds among SBUs.	Have liquidity of assets. Have emergency borrowing and stock-issuing power.	Use the sale and leaseback of assets. Use financing instruments that permit options in the applicable interest rate.
Operations	Produce from multiple plants in different locations.	Use general-purpose manufacturing facilities and equipment. Use inventories as a buffering mechanism.	Avoid vertical integration. Subcontract work. Maintain an assembly operation. Use small machines. Use multiple suppliers. Use temporary workers.
Marketing	Participate in multiple product markets. Develop capability of using multiple distributing channels.	Develop "excess" customer loyalty to buffer competitive actions.	Avoid reliance on few customers. Follow product leaders. Do not build an umbrella name.
International	Maintain a presence in several countries.	Maintain duplicate production facilities for international sourcing.	Use exporting or licensing to enter foreign markets rather than local production.
Managerial/Structural	Decentralize decision-making. Give subunits greater discretionary authority.	Maintain "organizational slack." Design operating procedures to be able to handle environmental changes.	Maintain conflicting perspectives in organization. Do not rely on few channels of communication with the external environment. Use a policy of role overlapping.

From Aaker, D. A. and B. Mascarenhas, "The Need for Strategic Flexibility," *The Journal of Business Strategy*, Fall, 1984, p. 75. Reprinted with permission from Warren, Gorham & Lamont.

Three fundamental methods of building strategic flexibility are to diversify strengths, build slack, and restrict commitment to specialized use-driven resources.

Some examples are:

GE's $3 billion lighting business scrapped a more traditional structure for its global technology organization in favor of one in which a senior team of 9 to 12 people oversees nearly 100 processes or programs worldwide, from new-product design to improving the yield on production machinery. In virtually all the cases, a multidisciplinary team works together to achieve the goals of the process.

At Ryder System,

To purchase a vehicle for leasing, for instance, required some 14 to 17 handoffs as the documents wended their way from one functional department to another at a local, and then a national, level. We passed the baton so many times that the chances of dropping it were great,

says Ernie Riddle of Ryder. By viewing this paperwork flow as a single process from purchasing the vehicle to providing it to a customer, Ryder has reduced the handoffs to two from five. By redesigning the work, weeding out unnecessary approvals, and pushing more authority down the organization, the company cut its purchasing cycle by a third, to four months.

Some startups have opted to structure themselves as horizontal companies from the get-go. One such company is Astra/Merck Group, a new stand-alone company formed to market antiulcer and high-blood pressure drugs licensed from Sweden's Astra. Instead of organizing around functional areas, Astra/Merck is structured around a half-dozen 'market-driven business processes,' from drug development to product sourcing and distribution.[22]

A question yet unanswered is how big can an organization get before it becomes either multiple organizations or it starts developing a different form of hierarchy? Perhaps some of the work in the area of Artificial Life might help here. If it could be determined using those simulations what perpetuates cooperation and cohesiveness among the local "cooperative elements" that are formed "naturally" as opposed to what leads to the emergence of a "leader" or a break up into non-cohesive and perhaps non-competitive organizational entities, then such answers could aid in the recognition of the limits to horizontal extensions.

The Inquiry Center[23]

The horizontal and alliance movements are new ways being adopted to reconfigure corporations. In contrast, the Inquiry Center is proposed as a special unit within a

---

[22]As reported in Jabbonsky, L., "Things are Looking Up at Pepsi," *Beverage World,* October, 1992, pp. 42–54. Pepsi Cola Company eliminated its geographic divisions, created 16 business units out of its 24 operating areas and created 107 market units with the mission of providing all front-line sales, marketing, and local customer activity. They call it the newly inverted company employing a three step process: (1) Start with the customer; (2) Understand ourselves and plan improvements; (3) Do it.

[23]Barabba, V. P. and G. Zaltman, *Hearing the Voice of the Market: Competitive Advantage Through Creative Use of Market Information,* Boston, MA, Harvard Business School Press, 1991. For a summary see Barabba. V. P. and G. Zaltman, "The Inquiry Center," *Planning Review,* March–April, 1991, Vol. 19, No. 2, pp. 4–9, 47, 48.

corporation.   Its purpose is to provide a nucleus to conduct market-based inquiry. Exhibit 14–9 provides a graphic example of such market-based inquiry.   The concept of the Inquiry Center was introduced by Vincent P. Barabba of General Motors and Gerald Zaltman of Harvard University.

In order for an inquiry center to be successful, these tenets must be followed:

— it must harness the energy and foster collaboration of decision makers, implementers, and the affected publics (e.g., customers and distributors);

— it should kindle, ignite, and be illuminated by the imagination of decision makers, implementers, and the affected publics.

In the words of Barabba and Zaltman, the basic reason for this type of an organizational unit as opposed to a standard market research department is,

In today's complex world it is no longer of value for a manager just to seek information in order to make the "right" decision.   Rather, the greatest value is in managing the decision-making process in a way that increases the chances of choosing the best decision among the available alternatives—given all the circumstances at that time—and in having the decision effectively implemented (p. 5).

This concept does not mean eliminating the marketing research unit; rather, it calls for integrating this unit into the various cross-functional process and action teams that are the hallmark of today's successful corporation.

EXHIBIT 14–9   Market-based inquiry.

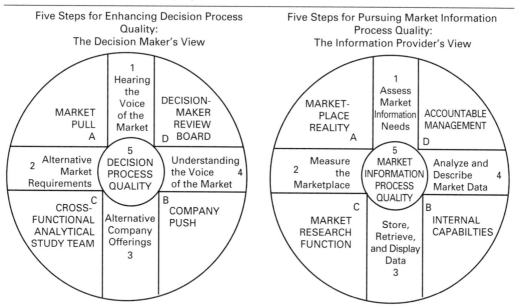

From Barabba, V. P. and G. Zaltman, *Hearing the Voice of the Market: Competitive Advantage Through Creative Use of Market Information,* 1991. Reprinted with permission from Harvard Business School Press.

A marketing strategy can be bolder and its implementation easier because of the speed of decision making and the focus on implementation inherent in the newer organizational social systems.

To monitor and ensure that the implementation process is moving toward strategic goals requires strategic control systems. These are briefly discussed next.

Strategic Control Systems

Consider the following example from Unilever:[24]

> Unilever discovered that when faced with creating a 5-year plan, managers liked to propose significant capital expenditures in the early years (Exhibit 14–10A). This was justified by planning ambitious results for the last couple of years of the period. The combination of certain early investment and uncertain late return could have dire consequences on the corporate cash-flow (Exhibit 14–10B).
> Within the company this phenomenon was popularly known as the "hockey-stick" effect. Although it was actively discouraged it took a long time to disappear. To avoid its recurrence Unilever now emphasizes the importance of the third year in all discussions for company 5-year plans (p. 66).

Strategic control has to be inherently different from normal control. This is illustrated by Ansoff in his discussion of strategic control. Exhibit 14–11 shows a hypothetical cash flow-time relationship. The solid curve represents the forecast cash flow used to approve the project. The dotted curves indicate "true" values. Given the uncertainties involved at the initial preapproval stages, the solid and dotted curves are not likely to be congruent. At what is designated the control point, the variance between plan and forecast were almost 100%. If a traditional variance-based control system were in use, the project would be scuttled at this juncture. However, the critical point is not what has happened, but what is likely to happen—the future. The question is what is likely to be the trajectory from that point on. This requires careful forecasting and a look-ahead model of control as opposed to the traditional variance-from-plan based control system. A control system framework that seems to incorporate the observations at Unilever and the look-ahead suggestions of Ansoff is the STEMCOM model of Sharma and Achabal.[25] A diagram of this steering control model is shown in Exhibit 14–12. The essence of this model is the monitoring of the impact of the current situation on the future cost-benefit scenario. This feature is actually what makes it a strategic control system. In keeping with our earlier discussions on strategic intent and on option values of strategic decisions, the cost-benefit analysis should include the strategic intent objectives as well as an analysis of options and opportunities created by the strategic action.

The social subsystem aims at organizing humans and technology into providing enduring rewards for the organization and its shareholders. Technology enables the

[24]This example is from Maljer's article referred to in Footnote 12.

[25]Sharma, S. and D. D. Achabal, "STEMCOM: An Analytical Model for Marketing Control," *Journal of Marketing*, Vol. 46, Spring, 1982, pp. 104–113.

EXHIBIT 14–10

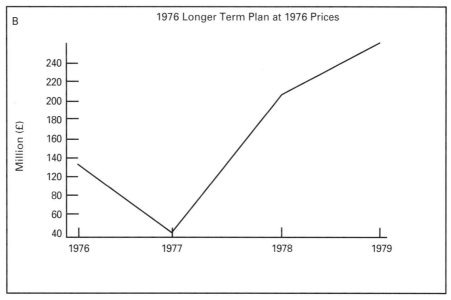

Unilever Capital Investment 1976–1979

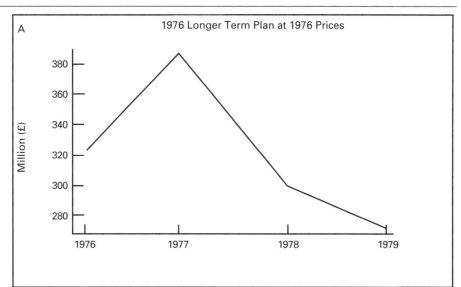

Unilever Operational Cash Flow 1976–1979

Reprinted from Long-Range Planning, Vol. 23, No. 2, Maljers F. A., Strategic Planning and Institution at Unilever, pp. 63–68, Copyright © 1990, with kind permission from Elsevier Science Ltd., The Boulevard, Langford Lane, Kidlington 0V5 1GB, UK.

EXHIBIT 14–11   Control of Strategic Projects

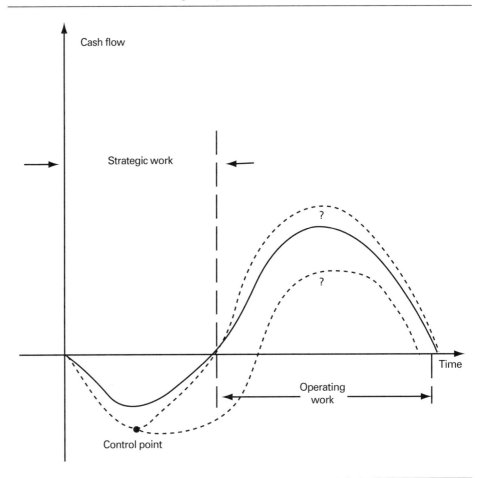

From: Ansoff, H. I. and E. J. McDonnell, *Implanting Strategic Management,* 2nd Englewood Cliffs, NJ, Prentice Hall, 1990, p. 353.

use of better communication and reward systems that ultimately provide the strategic control for a company. Consider the following example.

> Employees of Chemical Banking Corporation had been shaken by work-force cuts, reorganizations and a pending merger. Rumors often raced through the ranks, sapping productivity and morale.
>
>   But Bruce Hasenyager found a way to squelch the gossip in the bank's corporate-systems division: The senior vice president let employees post anonymous questions on an electronic bulletin board, accessible to anyone who was on the office computer network. Then he responded to the questions on-line.

"It became a powerful tool for building trust," Mr. Hasenyager says. "We could kill off the crazy rumors. When it was whispered around the water cooler that part of our group's work might be contracted out to IBM, I had a way to tell everyone at once that it was baloney." . . . When Mr. Hasenyager resigned last year, following the completion of Chemical's merger with Manufacturers Hanover Trust, his successor became uncomfortable with this unruly forum. After barbed criticism of management began appearing on the system, the new executive pulled the plug.[26]

This leads us to a discussion of the technology subsystem.

EXHIBIT 14–12   STEMCOM: Steering Marketing Control Model

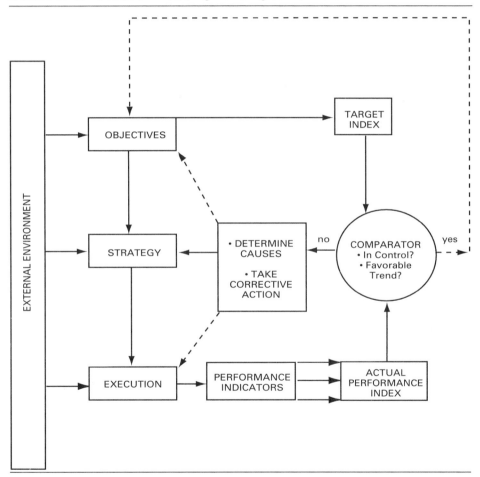

From Sharma S. and D. D. Achabal, "STEMCOM: An Analytical Model for Marketing Control," *Journal of Marketing,* Vol. 46, Spring 1982, pp. 104–113. Reprinted with permission of the American Marketing Association.

[26]Wilke, J. R., "Computer Links Erode Hierarchical Nature of Workplace Culture," *The Wall Street Journal,* December 9, 1993.

Technology Subsystem

Although any of the three subsystems, Social, Technology, and Human Resources could each take several books to elucidate, this subsystem would perhaps take not only several books but also would need to be "written" on a medium which could be updated rapidly and constantly. In our discussion we focus on some examples of technology presently in use that have considerable impact on the development and implementation of marketing strategy.

In marketing strategy, technology affects all the elements of the ROTR set. New technology is changing relationships with customers as well as with channel members; it is changing the possibilities for offerings beyond the wildest imagination; timing, of course, has been impacted and so has investment of resources in technology to leverage the rest of an organization's capabilities.

A large part of the technology revolution is driven by changes in information technology. As in the example of Chemical Banking Corporation, communication within a company has been or is capable of being tremendously changed. Some examples of the impact of technology on marketing follow.

Technology in Relationships and Timing

Clark[27] reports the example of a Japanese high-precision die maker who receives a sketch for a new part from Hitachi by fax. This is converted, in a few hours, using computer-aided-design (CAD) systems, to generate specifications for a new die for this part. A database maintains information about various suppliers: their skills, capacity, and work-in-progress, and the details of the die design are used to decide whether to subcontract and if so, to whom.

This process has changed the marketing relationship between Hitachi, this die-maker, and between the die-maker and its suppliers. What now is the role of bidding and quoting systems? There is no time for protracted negotiations.

Technology for In-Store Service

> When every man, woman and child enters the K-Mart store in Oak Park, they are scanned by one of 14 infrared beams.
>
>   . . . The Troy-based retailer's strategy is simple—improve customer service or risk losing business.
>
>   Every time we record someone coming in our doors, that information is fed into a computer, which calculates how many checkout lanes should be staffed in 20 minutes,

said David Carlson, senior vice president of corporate information services for K-Mart.

K-Mart is not the only retailer to invest in computers. Both Wal-Mart and

[27]Clark, K. B., "What Strategy Can Do for Technology," *Harvard Business Review,* November–December, 1989, pp. 94–98.

Sears, K-Mart's two largest competitors, have also experimented or incorporated customer counting, just-in-time delivery schedules, and electronic scanning into their store operations.[28]

Technology for Offerings and Timing

In mass-market retailing, what distinguishes one store from its competitors is the ability to put the latest product, whether it's a new fall fashion or the trendiest bottled mineral water on its shelves before consumers can buy it anywhere—and everywhere—else. Timing, therefore is everything when purchasing new merchandise from suppliers, keeping shelves stocked, coordinating distribution and delivery systems, and beating your competitors to the punch (p. 48).[29]

Given this requirement, Marks & Spencer has been using information technology for engineering its retailing. It includes scanning, computerized warehouses, EDI networks, and stock reordering terminals.

An interesting example that changed the offerings of Canon Company is seen in the following example.

Visitors to a Canon Inc. technology exposition in New York recently saw printers, copiers, cameras—and heaps of vividly colored neck-ties. No, Canon isn't going into haberdashery. It was showing off a new technique for textile printing that comes straight from the world of office machines. Canon's computer-driven Bubble-Jet printers have arrays of micronozzles that spit droplets of yellow, cyan, magenta, and black ink. The version for textiles works the same way, except that it's a two-ton machine.

Since printing plates don't have to be prepared, Canon says its Bubble-Jet system requires far less ink, labor, and setup time. It also produces small lots more cheaply, in finer detail, and with a wider range of colors than current technology does, Canon says. Textile maker Kaneko Ltd., Canon's development partner, has exclusive rights in Japan for three years. Canon expects to sell its first two systems abroad in June.

Technology for Frontline Systems

Alone among the world's banks, including the formidable Japanese institutions, Citicorp is attempting to build a consumer-banking empire across the Asia-Pacific region.

. . . It is also laborious to locate small customers without a large number of offices dotted throughout a territory.

Citicorp is attempting to get around the branching constraints in several ways. To build deposits, the bank has entered into agreements with—and sometimes offered its advanced technology to—local financial institutions with large automatic-teller machine networks.[30]

[28]King, R. J., "Retailer Keeping Track of Patrons to Boost Service," *Daily Tribune,* Friday, November 26, 1993. K-Mart Retail News Update, December, 1993.

[29]Ogilvie, H., "Electronic Ties That Bind: Marks & Spencer's Pan-European JIT Inventory System," *The Journal of European Business,* September–October, 1991, pp. 48–50. The Canon example is from "Canon Color Copiers Make a Splash in Textiles," *Business Week,* April 5, 1993, p. 83.

[30]Friedland, J., "Streetwise Strategy," *Far Eastern Economic Review,* March 8, 1990, p. 38.

The tools that form part of marketing and sales information systems are primarily of three types:[31]

> Direct mail and fulfillment
> Telemarketing
> Sales and marketing management

These systems impact directly on improved service to customers and therefore company value. They also help streamline operations and reduce operating costs. This dual impact on customers and operations is what leaves a company without such technology totally vulnerable to competitors who actively build and strengthen advantage using technology.

A retail chain, Virginia Specialty Stores of Newport News (VSS) operates 108 large-size women's specialty apparel stores in 19 states under the names The Answer and Added Dimensions. It uses a target marketing system from STS systems.

All information about a customer can be obtained by simply entering the telephone number. This query provides an opportunity to enter a new customer's particulars onto the database. According to Wayne Hutnik, COO of VSS, this system led to savings of $1.2 million, money that would have been otherwise spent on unnecessary promotional mailers in 1992. Some other benefits of this system according to Hutnik are: better service for customer returns (accurate purchase records minimize conflicts and provide better service); increased accuracy of records (as compared to paper based first-entry later systems); "seamless merger" with its merger partner (which also had an STS system); and tracking of shopper relationship programs (frequent shoppers can be tracked and programs set in place to reward them).[32]

Technology for Customer Information Systems[33]

A major supermarket chain, The Great Atlantic & Pacific Tea Company (A&P), targets both individual customers and centralizes buying. It also runs a frequent-shopper program.

The fourth largest U.S. mailorder company, Fingerhut, succeeds in selling merchandise on credit to households earning less than $25,00 a year.

Philip Morris and R. J. Reynolds, cigarette companies, have some of the most advanced database marketing programs.

R. R. Donnelly prints up to 8,000 different editions of *Farm Journal* every month.

As a survey article in *The Economist* began, "Information technology is no

---

[31]Moriarty, R. J. and G. S. Swartz, "Automation to Boost Sales and Marketing," *Harvard Business Review,* January–February, 1989, pp. 100–108.

[32]This example is from "For VSS, Program is the Answer," *Chain Store Age Executive,* January, 1993, pp. 144–153.

[33]Examples here are based on Bessen, J., "Riding the Marketing Information Wave," *Harvard Business Review,* September–October, 1993, pp. 150–160.

longer a business resource; it is the business environment."[34]   The meshing of the social and technology subsystems have to be managed carefully and they have to be carefully built into both strategy formulation and implementation.   Implementation planning needs to take into consideration the opportunities and constraints that the technology subsystem places on it.

Social and technology subsystems are lifeless without the human resources subsystem.   The three together constitute an organization that either makes a strategy possible or hampers its implementation.

The Human Resources Subsystem

The key issues (summarized here) are (1) is there a difference between strategists and implementers? and (2) how should or is decision-making carried out given sketchy information scenarios.   Since it is expected that the user of this book has already been exposed to organizational science, only a specifically pertinent discussion is provided.

Strategists and Implementers[35]

The stereotype of implementers prior to Bonoma's research was:

> They are primarily goal-oriented.
> They are highly internally controlled.
> They are highly intolerant of noncompliance.
> They are "Type A" individuals.

Bonoma, in a two-year study of 101 marketing directors, vice presidents, and general managers summarized his findings comparing strategists and implementers (Exhibit 14–13).   He reports that his most surprising findings were:

> . . . good strategists tended to *emphasize* corporate culture in both defining the main case problem and suggesting fixes for it, while good implementers tended to *ignore or minimize* corporate culture aspects in both problem definition and recommendations (p. 173).

As seen in Exhibit 14–13, there were other differences as well.   The implementers were more positive and the strategists gave more reasons why it could not happen. Strategists did more analysis and used fewer action alternatives.   The implementers, on the other hand, suggested many action alternatives.   The implementers made contingency plans, the strategists were more "absolutists."   Finally, the implementers were older than the strategists.

This suggests that there is considerable potential for conflict between "strategists" and "implementers" especially when they come from different functional areas.   A solution is careful training to make individuals aware of their biases as they work together.

---

[34]Browning, J., "Information Technology," *The Economist*, June 16, 1990.

[35]This section is based on Bonoma's work cited in Footnote 7.

EXHIBIT 14–13
Results from Study I: Strategists Versus Implementers

GOOD STRATEGISTS	GOOD IMPLEMENTERS
Emphasized culture in their problem definitions	Ignored culture in problem definitions
Emphasized culture in their action plans	Ignored culture in action plans
Did not give an exact price for the pipe	Gave an exact price for the pipe
Suggested fewer action alternatives	Suggested many action alternatives
Were highly inhibited (many "nots")	Showed low inhibition
Were younger and less experienced	Were older and more experienced
Were not as contingency-oriented	Were highly contingency-oriented

Results from Study II: Strategists Versus Implementers

GOOD STRATEGISTS	GOOD IMPLEMENTERS
Emphasized doing more research on the problem	Emphasized incentives and other specifics
Emphasized the "big picture"	Emphasized increased product knowledge on the sales force's part
Suggested few action alternatives	Suggested many action alternatives
Were younger and less experienced managers	Were older and more experienced managers

Reprinted with permission of The Free Press, a Division of Simon & Schuster from THE MARKETING EDGE: Making Strategies Work by Thomas V. Bonoma. Copyright © 1985 by The Free Press.

Decision Making in Turbulent Environments

Kathy Eisenhardt[36] presents the example of a company, Zap Computers, at which top management makes decisions in two or three months, which in other companies might take a year or longer. The results of her study of 12 microcomputer firms are summarized in Exhibit 14–14.

The three strategies suggested by conventional wisdom she reports, regarding strategic decisions which need to be made quickly and with sketchy information are: skimp on analysis; limit conflict; and accelerate choices. Her results, however, reveal that these are myths—following them would lead to poor choices. What does seem to happen is: fast decision makers use real time operating information; perform fast, comparative analysis of multiple alternatives to speed cognitive processing; resolve conflicts quickly, yet maintain group cohesion; use advice and integrate decisions and choices. All this heightens their self-confidence and allows fast decision making. They also use measures which can be acted on directly in their analysis as opposed to more abstract or refined ones. Combining the work of Bonoma and Eisenhardt, it appears that fast decision makers combine the attributes of both strategists and implementers. In another study reported by Kathy and Jay

[36]Eisenhardt, K. M., "Speed and Strategic Choice: How Managers Accelerate Decision Making," *California Management Review*, Spring, 1990. Also see Bourgeois III, L. J. and K. M. Eisenhardt, "Strategic Decision Processes in High Velocity Environments: Four Cases in the Microcomputer Industry," *Management Science*, Vol. 34, No. 7, July 1988, pp. 816–835.

EXHIBIT 14–14   Fast versus Slow Strategic Decision Making

Fast

- Track real time information on firm operations and the competitive environment
- Build multiple, simultaneous alternatives
- Seek the advice of experienced counselors
- Use "consensus with qualification" to resolve conflicts
- Integrate the decision with other decisions and tactics

Implications

- Acts as a warning system to spot problems and opportunities early on
- Builds a deep, intuitive grasp of the business
- Permits quick, comparative analysis
- Bolsters confidence that the best alternatives have been considered
- Adds a fallback position
- Emphasizes advice from the most useful managers
- Provides a safe forum to experiment with ideas and options
- Boosts confidence in the choice
- Offers proactive conflict resolution which recognizes its inevitability in many situations
- Is a popular approach which balances managers' desires to be heard with the need to make a choice

- Signals possible mismatches with other decisions and tactics in the future

Slow

- Focus on planning and futuristic information, keeping a loose grip on current operations and environment
- Develop a single alternative, while moving to a second only if the first fails
- Solicit advice haphazardly or from less experienced counselors
- Use of consensus or deadlines to resolve conflicts
- Consider the decision as a single choice in isolation from other choices

Implications

- Can be time-consuming to develop
- Quickly obsolete in fast changing situations
- Obscures real preferences
- Limits confidence that the best alternatives have been considered
- Eliminates a fallback position
- Fails to take best advantage of the experienced executives
- Consensus is often wishful thinking in complex business decisions
- Deadlines may not exist and so decisions can be postponed indefinitely
- Increases stress by keeping the decision in the abstract
- Risks the chance that the decision will conflict with other choices

Bourgeois, they summarize their overall findings as what they term a set of paradoxes. These are: careful and analytical planning, but bold and quick moves; decisive but delegative style, quick choice and articulation of strategy but implementation only as necessary, and finally high standards for decision quality, speed, and implementation are all sought, rather than trading one off against the other.[37]

[37]These notions of obtaining advice and incremental implementation of strategy are also present in what Etzioni calls "humble decision making." Etzioni, A., "Humble Decision Making," *Harvard Business Review,* July–August, 1989, pp. 122–126.

Although complexity in the environment calls for flexibility and direction, how can these be achieved? An interesting approach to this dilemma is to be found in a study conducted by Daniel Isenberg.[38] He quotes an executive he studied as saying,

> Sometimes I feel like a rhinoceros who doesn't see well and whose power of concentration is terrible; he charges at something that's a long way off, then forgets where he's going and stops to eat grass.

Based on his investigation, Isenberg proposes an action plan that he calls "strategic opportunism." The essential elements are:

* Habits of thinking
      collecting ideas
      creating a vision
      summarizing
* Ways of acting
      planless by design
      binding to goals
      piecing the puzzle

Habits of thinking refers to developing a way of approaching management, looking for ideas anywhere and jotting them down. For example,[39] Ran-Hong Yan of Bell Labs was inspired by watching falling snowflakes to think of a new way of doping silicon in microchips to radically alter the speed of silicon chips. Collecting such ideas, having a broad idea of what is being sought and periodically forcing a summary of ideas and observations to discern an overall pattern are all important in combining opportunism with strategy.

This calls for a certain way of acting—particularly leaving opportunities to "ad lib," and perhaps for a "dynamic programming" approach—as briefly introduced in our description of Langton's virtual ants. To ensure that important goals are striven toward, the use of tickler files and time schedules has been found to be effective. Piecing the puzzle is the act of seeking out information and using summarized data with managerial knowledge, intuition, and experience to obtain a holistic picture that would not be obtainable otherwise.

All these activities and ways of thinking lead to what Isenberg calls "sinning bravely." In his words,

> Thinking both strategically and opportunistically is clearly not easy. It requires a tolerance for ambiguity, intellectual intensity, mental hustle, and a vigilant eye for new ideas.

[38]Isenberg, D. J., "The Tactics of Strategic Opportunism," *Harvard Business Review,* March–April 1987, pp. 92–97. For a more formal treatment, please see by the same author, "Thinking and Managing: A Verbal Protocol Analysis of Managerial Problem Solving," *Academy of Management Journal,* December, 1986, pp. 775–788.

[39]Reported in Port, O., "A New Lease on Life for Old-Fashioned Chips," *Business Week,* December 20, 1993, pp. 100–101.

It requires, in other words, a tough-minded approach to an inherently messy process, the ability to take action in the midst of uncertainty, to "sin bravely."

Strategic opportunism, paradoxically, thus calls for greater discipline than strategic or opportunistic behavior in isolation. In complex environments, a melding of the two is imperative.

Successful strategy formulation and implementation require a careful analysis and use of the three subsystems: social, technology resources and human resources in concert.

CONCLUSION

Exhibit 14–15 summarizes the cross-impact of the implementation subsystems on the strategic set variables. The social, technology, and human resources subsystems all have to work in concert for success. The first two are beginning to overlap, with one forcing a redefinition of the other. In companies like Chemical Banking Corporation,[40] use of e-mail and a Notes set up can create unintended problems. Asking for constant posting of information negates this relationship and may not work. It also quickly highlights if someone is not meeting a commitment, for example, failing to meet a deadline.

Groupware can often be beneficial. Lotus Development Corporation's President Jim Manzi is reported to have said that his company's Notes software (for

EXHIBIT 14–15   Summary of the Impact of the Implementation Subsystem on ROTR

Implementation Subsystems	Relationships	Offerings	Timing	Resource Allocation
Social	The Inquiry Center International Markets Closeness to Customers	QFD Cross functional New Product Teams	Speeding up through trimming bureaucracy Horizontal organizations	Conflict Resolution Transfer Pricing Strategic Control
Technology	New vendor-supplier relationships (Hitachi's die maker)	Novel products and services (Canon textile printer)	New product cycle time reduction Response to Competition (K-Mart)	Options and opportunity analysis
Human Resources	Within Cross-functional teams: Strategists vs. Implementers	Innovation New Ideas (Silicon Doping)	Rapid Decision Making Blending Strategic vs. Opportunistic Behavior	Flexibility Reversible Incremental-Commitment

[40]This example is also from the Wilke report cited in Footnote 26.

networks) "creates electronic kereitsu" or high-tech versions of integrated Japanese business groups. In 1993, sales of Notes doubled over the previous year, to $100 million. But, they can also lead to problems of information overload. Managers are overloaded with information, so much so that "bozo filters" have to be installed. In other words, the system has to attenuate noise and amplify the important, though weak signals to reach a manageable signal-to-noise ratio.

At MTV Network (a unit of Viacom Inc.) a groupware network is reported to have helped them compete against Turner Broadcasting System's Cartoon Channel. Its salesforce was having a hard time getting cable operators to carry its new Comedy Central channel instead of the Cartoon Channel. They did not quite know why. That is, until a Chicago saleswoman learned that a two-year, rock-bottom price was being offered by Cartoon Channel. When entered into the Company's salesforce tracking groupware system it provided the reason that the others were searching for. A Florida salesman quickly confirmed that he had heard about "a new aggressive deal." This intelligence, quickly verified, led to rapid action that saved other deals that were still pending. Therefore, this ability to respond quickly and lead from strategy to desirable goals needs careful nourishment of human skills.

The five secrets of skill building that are key to implementation as developed at McKinsey & Co.[41] are:

1. Forge a clear link between strategy and skills. You must be able to deliver to customers what is promised.
2. Be specific—and selective—about core skills. What really are the key skills and exactly how.
3. Clarify the implication for pivotal jobs. This leads to proper hiring and training necessary and feasibility assessment.
4. Provide leadership from the top.
5. Empower the organization to learn. Learning means creativity and risk taking. Both need to be encouraged and rewarded.

A marketing strategist now has to demonstrate nimbleness of mind, thoroughness of thinking, creativity, and a "can do" spirit more than ever. As cross-functional teams put together marketers in close contact with players from other disciplines which traditionally have been associated with more rigor, their own confidence and analysis will have to live up to the challenge. That of course is what marketers thrive on—challenge.

Concept Questions

1. What are some of the major organizational changes taking place today?
2. Trace the evolution of management systems during the 1900s.

---

[41]This is to be found in detail in the article cited in Footnote 1.

3. (a.) What is the Strategic Issue Management system?

   (b.) What is a Weak Signal Issue management system?

   (c.) What is a Surprise Management system?

4. Describe Bonoma's Marketing Implementation Framework.

5. (a.) Why are marketing alliances formed?

   (b.) How should alliances be managed?

6. How should transnational organizations be managed to satisfy both customers and managers?

7. (a.) What is strategic flexibility?

   (b.) Why is it necessary?

   (c.) How can it be developed and deployed?

8. What are the key characteristics of horizontal organizations?

9. (a.) What is an Inquiry Center?

   (b.) What are the advantages of an Inquiry Center?

10. Describe a strategic control system.

11. What role does technology play in marketing strategy implementation?

12. (a.) What are the similarities and differences between strategists and implementers?

    (b.) Can an individual be both a strategist and an implementer?

13. What are the differences between fast and slow strategic decision making?

14. What is strategic opportunism?

Discussion Questions

1. Assume that a company has decided to change from its current vertical organizational structure to a horizontal one. Discuss the impact of this change on (a) the marketing strategy of a division of this company, (b) the organization of marketing activities.

2. (a.) Identify the different technological systems that support (a) marketing strategy decisions, and (b) marketing activities.

   (b.) Describe the relationship between the technology choices of a company and its (a) marketing strategy, and (b) marketing activities. (Note: This answer may require the use of library resources.)

3. How would you go about setting up an Inquiry Center for your MBA program office?

4. *Self-assessment*

   (a.) Are you a strategist or an implementer?

   (b.) Devise a scorecard to determine if a manager is likely to be a good strategist.

INDEX

Note: Page numbers followd by E indicate exhibited material.